ABSENCE OF NATIONAL FEELING

Davis W. Houck, Series Editor

ABSENCE OF NATIONAL FEELING

EDUCATION DEBATES IN THE RECONSTRUCTION CONGRESS

MICHAEL J. STEUDEMAN

University Press of Mississippi / Jackson

The University Press of Mississippi is the scholarly publishing agency of
the Mississippi Institutions of Higher Learning: Alcorn State University,
Delta State University, Jackson State University, Mississippi State University,
Mississippi University for Women, Mississippi Valley State University,
University of Mississippi, and University of Southern Mississippi.

www.upress.state.ms.us

The University Press of Mississippi is a member
of the Association of University Presses.

Copyright © 2025 by University Press of Mississippi
All rights reserved
Manufactured in the United States of America

∞

Publisher: University Press of Mississippi, Jackson, USA
Authorised GPSR Safety Representative: Easy Access System Europe –
Mustamäe tee 50, 10621 Tallinn, Estonia, gpsr.requests@easproject.com

Library of Congress Cataloging-in-Publication Data

Names: Steudeman, Michael J., author.
Title: Absence of national feeling : education debates in the
   Reconstruction Congress / Michael J. Steudeman.
Other titles: Race, rhetoric, and media series.
Description: Jackson : University Press of Mississippi, [2025] |
   Series: Race, rhetoric, & media series |
   Includes bibliographical references and index.
Identifiers: LCCN 2025013892 (print) | LCCN 2025013893 (ebook) |
   ISBN 9781496858467 (hardback) | ISBN 9781496858511 (trade paperback) |
   ISBN 9781496858481 (epub) | ISBN 9781496858474 (epub) |
   ISBN 9781496858504 (pdf) | ISBN 9781496858498 (pdf)
Subjects: LCSH: Education—Political aspects—United States—History—
19th century. | Education and state—United States—History—19th century. |
   Education and state—Social aspects—United States. |
   Democracy and education—Social aspects—United States. |
   Public schools—Political aspects—United States. | Public schools—
United States—History—19th century. | Reconstruction (U.S. history, 1865-1877)
   Classification: LCC LC89 .S6687 2025 (print) | LCC LC89 (ebook) |
   DDC 379.7309/034—dc23/eng/20250423
   LC record available at https://lccn.loc.gov/2025013892
   LC ebook record available at https://lccn.loc.gov/2025013893

British Library Cataloging-in-Publication Data available

publication supported by a grant from
The Community Foundation for Greater New Haven
as part of the Urban Haven Project

For Celeste

CONTENTS

Preface xi
Acknowledgments xv

Introduction: Education and Estrangement:
The Postbellum Crisis of Public Feeling 3

Chapter One: Federalism and Feeling:
Enforcing Education in the South, 1865–1871 29

Chapter Two: A System of Shame:
Founding the Bureau of Education, 1865–1872 57

Chapter Three: An Atmosphere of Altruism:
Renewing the Freedmen's Bureau, 1866–1870 83

Chapter Four: The Method of Mingling:
The Civil Rights Act and Educational Reunion, 1872–1876 113

Conclusion: Schooling and Sentiment:
Reconciliation and the Limits of Good Feelings 147

Notes 161
Index 203

PREFACE

In 2010, I joined Teach for America (TFA), a nonprofit program claiming to be a "movement to end educational inequity" in the United States.[1] At the time, I yearned for some greater sense of connection to my nation. I felt alienated by the intense pro-war nationalism that characterized the decade after the 9/11 attacks. I identified with President Barack Obama's appeals to a more expansive vision of patriotism, one that implored Americans to "serve our fellow citizens with . . . selflessness and optimism."[2] More than just an entry point to a profession I had long considered, TFA presented itself as a form of national service—a way to close the chasm between ideals of equal opportunity and lived realities of vast racial and class inequalities.

In retrospect, my first impression of TFA proved to be deeply naive. The organization's five-week institute in Atlanta did little to prepare me for the day-to-day challenges of teaching.[3] Above all, my TFA training failed to anticipate the unique culture, racial dynamics, or material challenges facing the students I taught that autumn in Plaquemines Parish, Louisiana. Spanning the banks of the Mississippi River southeast of New Orleans, the Plaquemines community had been devastated by Hurricane Katrina. Six-meter storm surges subsumed the towns of Boothville, Venice, Buras, and Port Sulphur, destroying the area's three high schools. After the storm, the schools were merged in a single campus housed in temporary trailers. Each morning, students traveled as far as twenty-five miles to attend school, passing the ruins of their former homes and schools along the way. This situation persisted five years later when I arrived.

As a white, middle-class Midwesterner with no background in K–12 education, I was out of my depth. Plaquemines students had endured a shared trauma I could not comprehend. Many students lived transient lives, splitting time between family members in Plaquemines and others displaced by the storm. Most families struggled with a depth of financial precarity I had never experienced—circumstances intensified by the Deepwater Horizon oil spill that summer. Thrown together by a cataclysm, students had deep communal tensions and racial differences that I had no idea how to navigate. More than that, the school lacked the resources needed to cope with students' overwhelming challenges. Students needed more wraparound services, counselors, and special education professionals. They needed teachers with roots in the community and substantial training. Instead, they had me.

I went to Plaquemines hoping to feel some stronger connection to my nation by helping students reeling from a disaster. But for all my efforts to learn about the community, my students and I remained strangers to each other. After two years, I became one of the many teachers who abandoned them.

My experience in Louisiana left me with many questions that I have since explored through my scholarship. What does it mean to feel like part of the United States, and what is education's role in producing that feeling? Why does education resonate as a transcendent national issue even as local educational conditions remain so fragmented and disjointed? Why do Americans craft policies that leave schools so underfunded and unequal even as those same people sing paeans to education's ameliorative potential? As a scholar of rhetoric and public address, I sought the answers to these questions as they emerged in political debates at specific historical moments. My questions led me to the Reconstruction era, a moment when public schools became intertwined with questions of race, reunion, and the fate of the republic.

In the aftermath of the Civil War, many Republicans believed that schools could ameliorate the unruly passions and sectional hostilities that had just torn the nation apart. By analyzing the debates their educational views ignited in Congress, *Absence of National Feeling* illuminates the central role education played in the idealistic visions and tragic compromises of the Reconstruction era. The book examines clashes over local control, educational statistics, freedpeople's education, and desegregation, tracing how educational arguments evolved during the most tumultuous twelve years of US history. By the end of Reconstruction, Congress abandoned bold visions of educational change that sought to confront prejudices at their root in childhood, instead accepting a conception of schooling that promoted shallow feelings of abstract loyalty even as it reified deep racial and economic inequalities.

As a work of rhetorical scholarship, *Absence of National Feeling* explores postwar education debates through a careful reading of thousands of pages of legislative transcripts. The result is a valuable addition to recent rhetorical work on the relationships among feeling, race, and national belonging. Legislators imagined education as an intervention in prejudices and sympathies at a societal scale. The idea of national education allowed policymakers to envision Reconstruction as not just a legal transformation of the South but also an emotional one. Congressional advocacy for education as a uniform panacea for problematic feelings relied on racialized understandings of emotion. Members of Congress viewed freedpeople, Native Americans, Chinese immigrants, and other groups as possessing different capacities to receive, interpret, and regulate feelings. Likewise, many legislators circumscribed certain white feelings—such as Southern whites' visceral disgust regarding integrated schooling—as untouchable through social intervention. Attending to the racialized dynamics of congressional argument, *Absence of National Feeling* answers recent calls for rhetorical scholars to trace the historical development of racist rhetorics.[4]

Beyond rhetorical studies, *Absence of National Feeling* also contributes to several areas of historical inquiry. First, the book provides historians of education in the United States a nuanced look at early clashes over perennial questions of local control, statistics, federal aid, and desegregation. Second, for historians of emotion, *Absence of National Feeling* examines how legislators' divergent understandings of emotion informed competing appeals to public education and its institutional function. Third, for scholars of American political development, this book explores the specific role educational thinking played in the post–Civil War struggle over American federalism and the evolving priorities of the Republican and Democratic Parties. Finally, this book adds to Reconstruction historiography by tracing educational themes across multiple postwar debates that have often been studied as discrete episodes. Any meaningful reckoning with the nation's abandonment of Black civil rights during the 1870s must recognize how Congress compromised in its approach to education.

Above all, this book is for anyone who cares about public education in the United States. As I write this preface, public schools are under siege from extremist actors who aim to privatize learning, ostracize queer students and teachers, silence the grievances of students of color, and censor earnest discussions of the nation's past injustices. Against this backdrop, postwar educational arguments provide a vital cautionary tale. The tragedy of Reconstruction-era education policy was that it half succeeded: Republicans in Congress established schools as a national priority but left inegalitarian actors to decide what, when, how, and with whom students would learn. To avoid allegations of promoting "divisive" partisan educational ends, legislators abandoned freedpeople's learning. Under the presumption that integrated schools would stir a white backlash, they discarded school desegregation. Accepting education as an inherent good—a boon to public feeling, no matter its pedagogy or content—they left schools in the hands of state governments. Their choice allowed schools to become an active evil, reifying the sources of alienation they were meant to resolve.

Present-day policymakers continue to reiterate the tragic choices that guided legislators during Reconstruction. Too often, the promise of generating "good feelings" in the present becomes a pretense to stifle acknowledgment of students' divergent experiences or reasons for alienation. Too often, policies aim to preserve illusory beliefs about educational merit rather than to actualize education's promises. Too often, the allure of national education myths leads to decisions that elide the material needs of marginalized communities. Too often, policymakers ask schools alone to confront complex social problems, only to abandon those policies the instant they spark political resistance. Despite everything I have experienced, I still believe that schooling can help to make society more just. But that can only happen with sober reflection on the ways we talk about education, the constraints that schools face, and the historical failures that led us to this moment. Perhaps naively, I still feel hope.

ACKNOWLEDGMENTS

I began the research that eventually became *Absence of National Feeling* more than a decade ago. During that time, I experienced many life-changing events, both terrible (a global pandemic) and transcendent (the birth of my child). Navigating these challenges and completing this project depended on the support of countless people. It would be impossible to name everyone who honed my arguments, offered feedback on my writing, shared resources, or otherwise aided me through the difficulties of writing this book. I apologize to anyone I failed to remember here.

At the University Press of Mississippi, Amy Atwood, Emily Bandy, Joey Brown, Craig Gill, Pete Halverson, Laura Strong, Rae Switzer, Katie Tucker, and Steve Yates provided exceptional guidance as I worked through the publication process. Cassie Winship designed the book's powerful cover. Race, Rhetoric, and Media series editor Davis Houck offered thoughtful appraisals of my project and astute advice as I revised my manuscript. Two anonymous reviewers shared constructive notes that significantly strengthened the final version. Kristin Kirkpatrick generated the book's index. Finally, copyeditor Ellen Goldlust helped to enhance the quality and accessibility of my prose throughout the book.

An earlier version of chapter two appeared as "From Civic Imperative to Bird's-Eye View: Renegotiating the Idioms of Education Governance During the Reconstruction Era," *History of Education Quarterly* 58, no. 2 (2018): 199–228. I thank Nancy Beadie and two anonymous reviewers for their detailed feedback on that article.

I am thankful to the archivists and librarians who helped me navigate the labyrinths of memory. These include Elaine Heavy at the Massachusetts Historical Society, Amber Paranick at the Library of Congress, and Rodney A. Ross at the National Archives and Records Administration's Center for Legislative Archives. The Colored Conventions Project digital archive was an invaluable resource.

This book benefited from countless conversations with fellow rhetorical scholars. A nonexhaustive list includes Ira Allen, Robert Asen, William Aungst, Timothy Barney, Maegan Parker Brooks, Daniel Brouwer, Leah Ceccarelli, Carolyn D. Commer, Lisa Corrigan, Emerson Cram, Nathan Crick, Candace Epps-Robertson, David Gold, Matthew Houdek, José G. Izaguirre III, Sharon Jarvis, Robin Jensen, Jeremy David Johnson, Lisa Keränen, Abraham Khan, Caroline Koons, Jessica Kurr, Charles Morris III, Roxanne Mountford, John Murphy, Jeff Nagel, Kelly Williams Nagel, Nikki Orth, Patricia Roberts-Miller, Ryan Skinnell, Belinda Stillion Southard, Bjørn Stillion Southard, Amy Wan, Craig Weathers, and David Zarefsky. I am especially grateful for my friend, mentor, and fellow education rhetoric scholar Mark Hlavacik, whose shared enthusiasm helped sustain my motivation to finish this book.

This project originated during my time at the University of Maryland. Trevor Parry-Giles provided me with detailed feedback, productive conversations, and moral support throughout the earliest version of this project. In honing my argument, I received valuable guidance from Jessica Enoch, Ethan Hutt, James Klumpp, Kristy Maddux, Shawn Parry-Giles, Tirza Wilbon, and Michelle Murray Yang. I am grateful for the insights I gained writing alongside peers including Rebecca Alt, Will Howell, Jessica Lu, Thomas McCloskey, Cobalt Nichols, Jade Olson, Devin Scott, Yvonne Slosarski, Janna Soeder, and Meredith Styer.

At the University of Memphis, I revised and expanded this project with the help of many fellow faculty members, including Tony de Velasco and Andre Johnson. In addition to being a phenomenal colleague and collaborator at Memphis, Amanda Nell Edgar provided me with professional support as a writing coach during the final stretch of this project. After the tough transition out of COVID, she helped me regain my confidence as a writer.

Finally, at Penn State, I am surrounded by thoughtful scholars whose input shaped the final form of this book. I am grateful to Joshua Trey Barnett, Johan Bodaski, Stephen Browne, Rosa Eberly, Jeremy Engels, Lisa Flores, Ekaterina Haskins, Debbie Hawhee, Andrew High, Mary High, Michele Kennerly, Marcy Milhomme, Jessica O'Hara, Brad Serber, Mary Stuckey, Kelly Sweeney, Pamela VanHaitsma, Bradford Vivian, and Dara Walker. As heads of my department, Denise Solomon and Kirt Wilson provided unwavering support for my research and for my well-being. As my research assistant, Brandon Johnson provided careful reviews of this manuscript and identified countless ways to strengthen it.

Throughout this process, I dealt with mental health challenges related to depression, anxiety, and ADHD. I have been forthright about these challenges in hopes of helping to destigmatize them. I would have never completed this book if not for the great many people who showed me patience, grace, and compassion along the way. The counsel of Joyce Harrison and Claudia Hutchinson helped me through the toughest times.

I have learned a great deal from people working in journalism, policy, and education contexts. Thoughtful conversations with Sarah Baraba, Chana Joffe-Walt, Richard Kahlenberg, Chris Kardish, Halley Potter, and Kent Strader helped me think through the relevance of this project for contemporary debates about education.

Completing this manuscript would not have been possible without a village of people providing child-care support. I am *eternally* grateful to Yasemin Beykont, Maggie Courts, Jessy Defenderfer, Robin Duffee, Sydney Forde, Faith Hampton, Kelly Williams Nagel, Cecilia Salomone, and Alyson Zdenek for showing such love to Celeste while I drafted the final chapters.

Stephanie Madden, your compassion, your community-building, your patience, your academic brilliance, and your strength make you the most wonderful person I know. I could not have finished this book without you. I cannot express how thankful I am to have you as a partner. Every page here I owe to your boundless love.

And Celeste! You are a perpetual source of joy. Watching you learn and grow has transformed everything I thought I knew about myself and my values—for the better. Hearing you sing to yourself in your crib every morning inspires me to face the day. Reading books to you before bed soothes my soul every night. I worry a lot about the world you were born into, but I know it will be a better place for having you in it.

ABSENCE OF NATIONAL FEELING

Introduction

EDUCATION AND ESTRANGEMENT

The Postbellum Crisis of Public Feeling

In the summer of 1865, just months after the formal end of the Civil War, President Andrew Johnson enlisted General Carl Schurz to prepare a report on conditions throughout the war-torn South. As a German immigrant who had long grappled with what it meant to be a "conscious American," Schurz set out to evaluate white Southerners' feelings of pride for the United States. Throughout his tour, he listened for words and deeds that exhibited an affinity for the Union and the "symptoms of 'returning loyalty.'" He was disappointed by what he found. Seldom did he hear "an expression of hearty attachment to the great republic, or an appeal to the impulses of patriotism." Instead, Schurz found former rebels reluctant to abandon their allegiance to the fallen Confederacy. He found white men who lamented the overturned plantation system and were consumed by "hostile feeling against the negro" and a "general spirit of violence." The scene in Southern common schools gave Schurz the most alarm. There, he found white schoolchildren still learning "hate and malignity toward the Union," singing "rebel songs," and reading history books with *US* scratched out and *CS* written in its place. National reunion could hardly succeed if the children of rebels inherited the same resentments as their parents. In a report that caused a stir among members of Congress, Schurz concluded: "There is, as yet, among the southern people an *utter absence of national feeling*."[1]

When the Republican-led Congress surveyed the ruins of a nation just at war, many members shared Schurz's fixation on feeling.[2] Southerners had shown no contrition for igniting the conflict. An unrepentant rebel assassinated President Abraham Lincoln. Southern legislatures passed Black Codes to resubordinate people freed by the Thirteenth Amendment. Southern voters even attempted to send notorious secessionists back to Congress mere months after the war's end. During its first postwar session in December 1865, Congress assembled a joint committee to study ongoing social upheaval in the South. During hearings at which freedpeople, generals, judges, preachers, and politicians testified, legislators' questions evinced their apprehensions about how Southerners *felt*. Across more than eight hundred pages of transcripts, the word *feeling* appears 941 times, and the word *sentiment* appears 378 times.[3] Members of Congress asked interviewees about the "state of feeling among the rebel people" toward Unionists, freedpeople, and the federal government. Respondents echoed Schurz's anxieties, describing former rebels as full of "contempt," "defiance," and "disdain." As Virginia Unionist Joseph Stiles reported, "The rebels say, 'We know that we are whipped; we are overpowered; but we hate you, and we will teach our children's children to hate you!'" The committee concluded that Southerners' "bitter hostility" illustrated "the necessity of providing adequate safeguards for the future, before restoring the insurrectionary States."[4] An absence of fellow feeling warranted the Reconstruction of the South.

As policymakers contemplated the scene of postbellum disunion, their gaze was not limited to white rebels in the South. They also wondered about how and whether four million freedpeople could become part of a postwar union of fellow feeling. Before the war, leading white educators, philanthropists, and Republican politicians believed that neither Black people's "degraded" status nor white people's "deep-rooted" prejudices could be overcome to create a shared political community.[5] Instead, many promoted the complete relocation of Black people to a colony outside the United States.[6] These attitudes persisted among many Republican politicians throughout the Civil War. As late as July 1865, prominent Ohio Republican and gubernatorial candidate Jacob D. Cox touted the creation of a free Black colony along the South Carolina and Georgia coast as the only answer to the "irreconcilable hostility" of white and Black Southerners. "Their permanent fusion in one political community" was, he argued, "an absolute impossibility."[7] However, the haphazard course of wartime emancipation caused congressional Republicans to abandon the idea of colonization. At war's end, the fate of the Republican Party's electoral strategy, economic ideology, and political vision for the South would all depend on the formation of a multiracial political coalition. After decades of doubting that enslaved people had the emotional capacity to participate in public life, Republicans now sought ways to discipline freedpeople's feelings to instill self-restraint and sympathy.[8]

Beyond the South, members of Congress also understood the challenge of forging fellow feeling as part of the nation's wider vision of westward expansion. Over the course of Reconstruction, Republicans projected hopeful visions of national reconciliation onto the West, imagining the region as a blank slate for white settlement untainted by the hostile feelings of the Civil War.[9] Of course, the vast territories west of Nebraska were not blank slates but populated lands acquired through military campaigns and colonial coercion. The region was inhabited by Native American nations, American citizens of Mexican descent in the Southwest, Mormons who had fled religious persecution to Utah, Chinese immigrants, Catholic immigrants from Europe, and other groups at the margins of American culture.[10] For myriad reasons—language differences, imputed "barbarism," religious "heathenism," or assumed racial inferiority—all were groups that the white Protestant constituencies of the Republican Party viewed as threats to the formation of peaceful sentiments. When postwar legislators tried to confer political and civil rights on Black Southerners, those lawmakers' attempts to speak in a language of natural or universal rights were routinely vexed by the demographic complexity of the West. Party members diverged over who belonged in the polity, on what grounds, and by what mechanisms they should be included.[11] Republicans sought consistent language with which to speak about divergent groups without collapsing the racial hierarchies that structured life in the territories. They sought a unified means to adjudicate who belonged in a community of fellow feeling.

Members of Congress believed that the postwar republic faced a crisis of feeling. To rebuild the Union on stronger emotional foundations, many legislators turned to the institution Schurz found so disconcerting during his tour of the South: public education.

Speaking in a nineteenth-century idiom of feeling, Republican legislators embraced the idea that common schools could strengthen loyalties to the nation, discipline unruly passions, and build affection across race and region. For some policymakers, promoting the mere existence of common schools seemed a sufficient means to provide US denizens with a shared, familiar cultural experience and inculcate a love for the Union. The boldest Radical Republicans went further, claiming that education had the potential to uproot prejudices and resentments in childhood and lay the groundwork for multiracial democracy in the South. Driven by this faith in schools, members of Congress took up public education as a sustained subject of debate for the first time in the nation's history.[12] Advocacy on behalf of educational interventions recurred throughout the twelve years of Reconstruction. Legislators debated whether to mandate that Southern states include schools in their new constitutions. Congress created the Bureau of Education to shape state-level education policies. Through the Bureau of Refugees, Freedmen, and Abandoned Lands (known as the Freedmen's Bureau), officials supported missionary teachers' efforts to educate formerly enslaved people. Legislators considered a bill for a national system of education and contemplated a national school fund, a ban on taxpayer funds for parochial schools, and school desegregation. Across these and other educational debates, leaders returned again and again to the question of how best to guarantee fellow feeling across the polity.

On the floor of the House of Representatives and Senate, Radicals' ambitious vision of public schools faced intense disagreement. Many moderate Republicans agreed in theory that schools could be a salve for strained passions but imagined only a constrained role for the federal government in promoting those ends. Others, usually Democrats, rejected outright the idea that schools should promote national feeling, arguing instead that schools should merely reflect the sentiments of parents and local communities. As policymakers debated these positions, their shifting perceptions of the nation's emotional atmosphere influenced the policies they supported. By the early 1870s, many Republicans began to blame the party's own policies—including its education reforms—for sustaining racial antagonisms and sectional hostilities. Convinced that white Northerners were fatigued and disgruntled with the program of Reconstruction, both parties' positions on education shifted. Many Democrats once hostile to taxpayer-financed education began to embrace common schools, recognizing constituents' emotional attachments to newly created schools as a potent way to galvanize resistance to desegregation. Most Republicans, in kind, abandoned Radicals' vision of schools as a way to transform the hierarchical feelings that undergirded Southern aristocracy. They instead acquiesced to the idea of schools as a means to promote a superficial sense of national loyalty, even if those schools would reify unjust hierarchies and deepen racial prejudices.

In the end, the Republican retreat from a robust vision of education played a crucial part in the tragic failure of Reconstruction. More than perhaps anyone else in Congress, proponents of an educational intervention in the South recognized the depth of social change required for the project of reconstructing the region to succeed. Representative George Frisbie Hoar (R-MA) warned in June 1870 that the laws and amendments enacted after the Civil War would be as "impotent as bands of tow against the fires of treason and hate . . . unless they are followed by ample provision for the education of the people."[13] The tragedy of Reconstruction-era education policy is that it only halfway fulfilled the goals of postwar radicals. Although

Republicans cemented schooling as a national interest, ensuring that states adopted taxpayer-financed school systems required that they acquiesce to a concept of education that permitted disparate, racialized tracks of learning. They likewise left inegalitarian state governments to decide how, what, and with whom children would learn. Decades later, the schools Hoar imagined undoing Southern hatreds instead became segregated spaces where pupils learned mythic Lost Cause narratives that upheld the Jim Crow system.

Absence of National Feeling examines how postwar legislators talked about feeling. It is primarily a work of rhetorical public address scholarship, analyzing the ways that members of Congress adapted their language in an era of political and emotional tumult. The book focuses on the voluminous transcripts of congressional debates, hearings, and speeches between 1865 and 1877. Each of the four chapters centers on a specific postwar controversy in which education played a prominent role: the readmission of Southern states; the formation of the Bureau of Education; the renewal of the Freedmen's Bureau; and the passage of the Civil Rights Act of 1875. By examining how arguments developed across these episodes, this volume foregrounds the often-overlooked role that public schools played in congressional visions of the postwar republic.[14] Members of Congress reached for education as an intervention in public feeling. Schools promised a way to reunite North and South, to assimilate freedpeople into a free labor economy, and to bring cohesion to an empire inhabited by peoples estranged by race, class, religion, and birthplace. By tracing debates over those efforts and their consequences, this book captures how ideas about education, feeling, and civic belonging were reforged in the crucible of postbellum debate.

"ITS ADVANTAGES WE KNOW, WE FEEL": STUDYING PUBLIC ADDRESS AND RHETORICS OF FEELING

On March 30, 1870, the Freedmen's Bureau neared its expiration date. The agency would soon be disbanded and with it the federal government's most serious foray into supporting education for formerly enslaved people. Seeking to defend the institution, Representative Oliver H. Dockery (R-NC) was at a loss for words. Growing up, he had attended public schools in North Carolina—a rare opportunity for children in the South.[15] But he had trouble articulating why he so valued that experience or why preserving it for freedpeople mattered: "Education is in itself, I admit, a trite theme, and in the abstract scarcely admissible of argument or illustration. Its advantages we know, we feel."[16] Dockery's speechlessness underscores the complexity of writing about educational arguments in the post–Civil War Congress. While policymakers often did present the case for education policies in the familiar modes of reasoned debate, they just as often alluded to something ethereal, tacit, and beyond the scope of language. Over the course of *Absence of National Feeling*, I draw on and expand the tradition of public address scholarship to illuminate how appeals to feeling imbued education with unique, felt significance.

As a scholar of public address, I do work that analyzes visual, spoken, and written discourses to make sense of how historical actors negotiated the "idioms of public life" at discrete moments and over time.[17] The primary discourses under consideration here are the "archives of living speech" contained in the *Congressional Globe* and *Congressional Record*.[18] Following the development of advanced stenographic methods during the 1840s and 1850s, the *Globe* and *Record* provided a reliable—though imperfect—word-for-word transcription of what was said on the floor of the House and Senate.[19] In engaging these texts, I remain attuned to how the existence of transcripts implicated how people in Congress argued. The *Globe* and *Record* allowed legislators to craft lengthier speeches and engage each other's words in asynchronous ways. Likewise, these texts enabled members of Congress to tailor speeches to wider audiences who encountered these words in newspapers, pamphlets, and federal reports. As Zornitsa Keremidchieva writes, the transcripts had a "constitutive political function," influencing "the agents and agency of congressional power as well as the substance and character of political issues."[20] The *Globe* and *Record* actively intervened in the history they purported to represent, becoming the context of subsequent debates as soon as the Government Printing Office put ink to paper. I consequently strive to avoid treating these transcripts as static snapshots of history.

When examining discrete moments of rhetoric—such as a floor debate over passing a bill—I follow an analytical approach James Jasinski describes as "abductive": a "back and forth tacking movement" between contexts, texts, and theoretical concepts.[21] I strategically reconstruct the political, ideological, racial, educational, and emotional contexts of discourse to identify argumentative resources available to rhetors.[22] Through examinations of multiple types of evidence—including government reports, archived letters, pedagogical tracts, newspapers, biographies, and histories—I account for the linguistic resources, political constraints, and ideological frameworks on which members of Congress relied to craft their arguments. Informed by these reconstructions of context, I engage closely with the texts in the *Globe* and *Record*, attending to the modes of reasoning, rhetorical tropes, and narrative forms deployed by speakers as they negotiated the myriad contexts in which they spoke. To deepen my engagement with these rhetorical choices, I also turn to various conceptual frameworks (e.g., humanistic perspectives on collective feelings) to facilitate further critical (re)evaluations of discourses. As I navigate among context, text, and theory, my argument develops in a spiral, with each tack illuminating new points of connection, curiosity, or complexity.

I also consider these discrete episodes of debate in chronological sequence to trace the development of discourses over time. Tracking subtle changes in language helps me map the changing ideas, coalitions, and policy goals of various members of Congress. Likewise, as Robert Asen observes, in public policy discourses "what may constitute text at one historical moment changes into context at another."[23] Tracing legislative discourse illustrates how decisions made over the course of debates circumscribed or expanded possibilities for future action. Moreover, considering the sequential development of education policy debates reveals what Jasinski describes as "the refractions and modifications of political concepts and ideas . . . as they unfold in textual practice."[24] In their contingent moments, legislators adapted their language of education for countless reasons—to convince one another, to appeal to constituents, to make policies more palatable, to define their coalitions, to name adversaries, to rationalize shifts in position, to discipline populations deemed deviant, and to reckon with an ever-shifting scene of postwar tumult. Stepping back to consider quotidian choices over a wider span of time enables the identification of patterns, continuities, and ruptures in discourse. In this way, methods of public address help to explain how antebellum ideas about education were solidified, modified, dissolved, and contorted in the discursive cauldron of debate.

Weaving through the contexts and texts of postbellum argument, my analysis draws on the "affective turn" in the humanities and theories of feelings as collective phenomena.[25] Among scholars of rhetoric and public address, the affective turn has led researchers to move beyond traditional concerns with parsing and critiquing textual messages to consider the sensed, felt dimensions of rhetorical activity.[26] By attending to emotion, Jenny Edbauer Rice argues, scholars can better understand "how rhetorics cohere in(to) publics" through the circulation and accumulation of feelings.[27] Scholarship on collective feeling illuminates postwar legislators' efforts to devise educational interventions that could alter ecologies of feeling, (re)constitute the public, and (re)articulate conceptions of national identity. In taking up this area of scholarship, my primary concern is not affect, which I understand to refer to bodily intensities, forces, and energies that precede and resist capture by language.[28] Instead, like Lisa Corrigan's work on rhetorics of feeling in the Black Power movement, my inquiry centers on "language about feeling" and the political consequences of that language.²⁹ By chronicling overt discussions of feeling among members of Congress, I gain insight into how they conceptualized the circulation of emotions through the polity and into the role education could play in shaping that ecology.³⁰

Legislators' disagreements about education often reflected their competing norms and expectations about feeling. When members of Congress arrived in Washington, DC, they brought with them assumptions about how emotions work. Throughout their lives, they had moved among what historian Barbara Rosenwein calls "emotional communities": collectives that cohere through "the evaluations they make about others' emotions; the nature of the affective bonds between people that they recognize; and the modes of emotional expression that they expect, encourage, tolerate, and deplore."³¹ The *Globe*, *Record*, and other texts contain traces of these communities' assumptions, which are revealed in the ways policymakers evoked feelings as both individual and communal phenomena.³² These communities' assumptions collided in the emotional arena of Congress, where education policy debates served as proxies for wider efforts to shape the contours of national feeling.³³ When legislators debated education, their assertions emanated from distinct suppositions about how feelings work, where they originate, and under what circumstances they can be reshaped. Policymakers with backgrounds promoting common schools in New England, supervising schools in rural Pennsylvania, or teaching free Black children in postwar South Carolina all conceptualized the relationship of schooling and sentiment in divergent ways.

By engaging legislators' rhetorics of feeling, *Absence of National Feeling* explores the felt dimensions of how disparate strangers learn to imagine themselves as part of a nation.³⁴ For rhetorical scholars, the formation of national belonging is viewed as a constitutive process of identification and division.³⁵ In Kenneth Burke's influential account, identification entails aligning people's ways of thinking, speaking, and acting to forge a common identity while also aligning them against out-groups thought to lack these shared traits.³⁶ Ersula J. Ore argues that in the nineteenth-century United States, rhetorical constructions of the nation established "an 'us' that figured 'the people' as a racially homogeneous group and 'them' as a collection of subhuman nonwhite others."³⁷ I am concerned with how identification and division not only occur through language and belief but are also felt.³⁸ Nations cohere not solely through acts of speech and exertions of belief but also through feelings people associate with their fellow citizens or maligned outsiders. As Danielle S. Allen observes, the formation of a sense of "wholeness" in the United States has routinely been vexed by corrosive feelings of distrust, a byproduct of the uneven sacrifices borne by a citizenry.³⁹ In the postwar Congress, many legislators invoked education because it promised to alleviate these distrustful feelings.

By foregrounding the function of feelings in identification, *Absence of National Feeling* considers the ways that processes of racialization implicated post–Civil War education debates. Following Sara Ahmed, I view feelings not as inhering in people's minds but rather as relations circulating among and between objects, bodies, and institutions. Feelings are sticky—as they move, the repetition of their associations with objects orients people to respond to them in particular ways.[40] As Ahmed writes, over time, felt linkages "work to align individuals with collectives," reifying social belonging and otherness through "the very intensity of their attachments." In this way, collectives form around racialized identities, organizing social and physical space to avoid bodies felt as threatening, disgusting, or upsetting.[41] For Radical Republicans in Congress, white policymakers' association of Black bodies with such feelings posed a recurring obstacle in efforts to promote multiracial democracy. Many legislators tried to work around those feelings, distinguishing between the "civil equality" promoted by their policies (concerned with access to public spaces and services) and more intimate forms of "social equality" more likely to incite white backlash (concerned with the formation of friendships, marriages, or sexual relationships).[42] Yet, as Kirt Wilson observes, these distinctions collapsed as debates over civil rights wore on: "Every instance of integration within a public setting became a point of intrusion on the private lives of white citizens."[43] The white polity had organized itself in antithesis to the feelings of disgust, contempt, pity, fear, and hate attached to Black bodies. Any policy that produced proximity, that brought the threat nearer, prompted white resistance. Education offered the possibility of short-circuiting those feelings before they could ever take shape.

To promote and adjudicate civic belonging, Reconstruction-era rhetoric situated education as a policy intervention designed to alter public feeling. This argument builds on Asen's assertion that "public policy [is] a mediation of rhetorical and material forces."[44] Crafted by and through language, policies solidify rhetorical meanings to shape institutional structures, allocations of resources, and social arrangements. To add to Asen's formulation, I argue that feeling suffuses this entire process. Devised to respond to circulations of feeling, policies rely on and cement interpretations of public moods. Their existence (or lack thereof) can instill hope or despair, altering the public's sense of whether perceived problems are intractable or solvable. Reorganizing social space, policies can make bodies more or less proximate to one another, moving people into new arrangements that implicate bodily responses and formulations. Emotions circulate in and through policies, implicating how people respond to the institutions that enact those policies over time. In this way, people become aligned for or against certain policy arrangements: in Ahmed's words, "Subjects become *invested* in particular structures," forming different degrees of attachment to them.⁴⁵ Policymakers envisioned schools as ways to alter feelings at a societal scale, creating a point of interface with the idealized nation and orchestrating pupils' feelings through embodied interactions.⁴⁶ Moreover, members of Congress sought to shape feelings about education as well: to promote pride and shame about state systems, to sustain the hope associated with missionary teachers, or to preserve emotional investments in schools amid calls to dismantle them.

As members of Congress sought to shape feeling, they tailored their policies to wider interpretations of public moods. To put it mildly, the 1860s and 1870s were decades of intense feeling in the United States. Historians of emotion have explored at length the myriad ways that fear, trauma, depression, homesickness, jealousy, hostility, and resentment circulated through postbellum life and inflected political experience.⁴⁷ Passion had, as Lincoln noted, "strained . . . our bonds of affection."⁴⁸ Members of Congress played an active role in interpreting those emotional strains. In debates, these legislators clashed over which feelings to take seriously as a basis for policy and which to dismiss as inauthentic. They fought over which feelings harmed the nation and which would help. They interrogated which populations' feelings mattered and who to blame when hostile feelings prevailed. They corroborated reports of some feelings and contested accounts of others. They portrayed some feelings, like Southerners' resentment of taxpayer-funded schools, as remediable through policy. Other feelings—like the disgust white parents felt about school integration—were deemed too visceral for federal policies to influence.⁴⁹

During Reconstruction, policymakers' ever-shifting contests over the state of public feeling informed their appeals for education policy. When Radical Republicans reached their peak of influence in 1867, they attributed ongoing sectional tensions to Southerners' lack of guilt over the war or lack of love for the nation. By 1872, a breakaway faction of Liberal Republicans argued that policies of Reconstruction had intensified white Northerners' fatigue and deepened racial animus in the South. Schurz, the former Union General who had decried the South's absence of national feeling and now a Republican senator from Missouri, discarded his original assessment of the nation's ongoing sectional tensions and instead blamed the "feverish atmosphere" generated by his own party.⁵⁰ Rather than transform hostility by altering its material causes or interfering with the circulation of prejudicial feelings, this position sought to extend mercy and charity to former rebels, end military protections for Black people, and put the war in the past.[51] This shifting interpretation of postwar feeling implicated how Congress debated issues of public education. Rather than a serious intervention into the feelings responsible for war, schools became a way to symbolize a commitment to reconciliation. As with the Democratic South's acquiescence to the Reconstruction amendments after 1870, a symbolic acceptance of schools did not entail any effort to implement schools in their intended spirit. In this way, reinterpretations of public feeling underpinned legislators' tragic abandonment of Radicals' educational vision.

"OBLITERATE FACTITIOUS DISTINCTIONS": THE ANTEBELLUM RHETORIC OF EDUCATION AS INTERVENTION IN FEELING, 1830-1861

The Civil War and its aftermath expanded federal power in innumerable ways, transforming the fabric of citizenship, social policy, and federalism in the process. But even in an era marked by revolutionary constitutional amendments and nationalist passions, legislators seldom talked about any issue with the quixotic enthusiasm they reserved for education. Voicing his support for the Bureau of Education, Representative Nathaniel P. Banks (R-MA) said that Congress had the responsibility to generate "that amity and comity of feeling which must exist between the people of the different States and the General Government." Advocating a national school system, Representative William F. Prosser (R-TN) traced rebellious sentiment in the South to the learning underway in white Southern classrooms. Holding up a copy of a popular textbook used in Southern schools, he condemned nascent school systems in Democratic-led Southern states for promoting "false and treasonable statements . . . intended to inculcate sentiments hostile to the United States Government." In a more optimistic key, Representative William T. Clark (R-TX) touted schooling as a way to avert future racial and sectional strife. By supervising schools, he argued, the federal government could facilitate "crowds of happy children singing on their way to the free fountains of learning . . . all bitterness and prejudice absorbed in a proud emulation to work together for the common good—a people contented and united once more in heart as well as in name."[52] Schooling was, in the view of these policymakers, an intervention in feeling.

These bold claims about education policy did not spring into legislators' minds after the Civil War ended. As Asen writes, "Since no policy arises ex nihilo, policymaking does not inaugurate unprecedented meanings as much as it intervenes in an ongoing symbolic field."[53] Appreciating the development of congressional argument requires understanding the policy landscape as it existed at the onset of the Civil War and the rhetorical resources it provided.

In connecting emotion and education, postbellum speakers drew on the rhetorical inventions of the common school movement that swept westward across Northern states from Maine to Minnesota between the 1830s and 1850s. Responding to social schisms and denominational diversity, leaders of this movement argued that schools could promote social cohesion, behavioral discipline, and fellow feeling. Reformers contended that by bringing together students from various socioeconomic strata or from different Christian religious sects, the classroom could forge common sentiment between people with distinct upbringings and identities.[54] As famed school reformer Horace Mann put it, "The spread of education, by enlarging the cultivated class or caste, will open a wider area over which the social feelings will expand; and . . . do more than all things else to obliterate factitious distinctions in society."[55] Devised to address questions of feeling and cohesion at the state level, this rhetoric by 1860 had been cultivated, deployed, and revised across numerous state-level debates. Facilitating the creation of school systems from Connecticut to Minnesota, the tropes, themes, and ideas expressed in these discourses were familiar to Reconstruction-era members of Congress. The development of common school rhetoric thus provided a repertoire of policy arguments from which legislators drew after the Civil War.

The Rhetoric of Education for Fellow Feeling

In appealing to fellow feeling, education proponents invoked a concept common in nineteenth-century efforts to manage diversity and distance across empires.[56] The concept of "fellow feeling" had complex origins, deriving from Puritan religious beliefs, Masonic ideals of brotherhood, and Scottish commonsense philosophy.[57] In Adam Smith's influential account, fellow feeling was produced through the sympathetic process of imagining the emotional states of others. Limited not just to a sense of pity or shame at others' situations, fellow feeling, in Smith's view, was inseparable from (white) human capacities for tolerance, conversation, and social harmony.[58] From the onset, the concept of fellow feeling propounded by Smith and other philosophical elites excluded racialized others deemed incapable of sympathy. As Xine Yao writes, the "specter of the unfeeling subject acts as the antisocial corollary to sympathy as the 'fellow-feeling' basis of civilized society."[59] Presumptions about sympathetic capacity provided a basis for adjudicating who belonged in an enlightened political community and who was instead steeped in uncivilized barbarism. By the mid-nineteenth century, the common usage of *feeling* in the United States incorporated much of Smith's philosophical definition, referring to the use of the senses, to being "easily affected or moved" by others, or to sharing in aesthetic experience.[60] The common school movement drew on this logic to position educational institutions as generators and arbiters of fellow feeling.

The linkage of education and sympathy had deep roots in New England culture. The Puritan founders of Massachusetts's earliest schools shared a "theology of fellow-feeling," preaching the necessity of shared sympathy for heavenly salvation.[61] Insistent on biblical literacy and preserving the sentimental bonds of community, those Puritans enacted the American colonies' first compulsory school laws.[62] After the American Revolution, political leaders adapted the covenantal concern for shared feeling into a rhetoric of national cohesion.[63] Recognizing the complexity of maintaining political allegiances across a federal republic, they cultivated what Michael E. Woods calls an "affective theory of the Union," a vision of the United States as "a polity cemented by feeling."[64] That rhetoric was soon embraced in the schoolroom, where early school reader collections and textbooks invited children to display what Courtney A. Weikle-Mills terms "affectionate citizenship"—a performance of love for the nation and its laws.[65] As common schooling grew more ubiquitous, the associations among education, feeling, and national identity grew more pronounced.

By the onset of the Civil War, the term *education* had a presumed emotional connotation. Distinguishing the term from *teaching* and *instruction*, the 1865 edition of *Webster's Dictionary* explained, "Education . . . implies not so much the communication of knowledge as the discipline of the intellect, the establishment of the principles, and the regulation of the heart."[66] Common school reformers drew particular inspiration from Swiss pedagogue Johann Pestalozzi, who insisted that teachers should aim to "cultivate confidence, gratitude, love and hope, without a destructive conflict with opposing feelings."[67] Pestalozzi's views resonated with dominant educational ideas articulated by influential political philosophers such as John Locke and Jean-Jacques Rousseau. As Sara Ahmed summarizes, these intellectual traditions viewed education as an "orientation device" for feeling, a way to direct people's attention toward certain ends as objects of happiness.[68] In a racialized ecology of emotion, that view of education presumed that different groups had different capacities to be oriented toward the ends of Enlightenment reason, market capitalism, or the settler state. In a variety of ways, Reconstruction-era legislators drew on these influences, translating state-level approaches into a federal vision.

The rhetoric of common schooling as a project of shaping fellow feeling relied heavily on gendered notions of emotional influence. During the first half of the nineteenth century, a confluence of factors—including a rapidly changing economy, shifting ideas of domesticity, growing access to schools, and women's pursuit of professional autonomy—led to a dramatic shift in the gender composition of the teaching force. Between 1800 and 1860, women went from a minority to the majority of common school educators in most of the North and Midwest.[69] In some parts of New England, women represented more than 80 percent of the profession.[70] These demographic shifts in the teacher labor force aligned with changing attitudes about common schools' role in the acculturation of children and the preservation of national cohesion.

In the gendered domestic ideology of the nineteenth century, the preeminence of women teachers implicated how influential writers talked about public feeling. As popular author and reformer Catharine Beecher explained, Americans' "deficiency in the free expression of kindly feelings and sympathetic emotions" could "never be efficiently remedied, except in the domestic circle, and during early life."[71] Agreeing with Beecher, reformers hired women teachers to serve as conduits between the private and public spheres, enlisting women to inculcate children with the proper sentiments for civic engagement.[72] As Jessica Enoch argues, concurrent with this shift, reformers reimagined the schoolhouse itself as a domestic space in which carefully cultivated experiences could shape children's emotional dispositions.[73] Reformers believed that teachers could subtly determine where, when, and how students directed their attention and could then reorient those feelings.[74] Acting as surrogate mothers within the sanctuary space of the schoolroom, teachers could instill familial relationships among children and prevent the formation of hatred and resentment across lines of class and religion.[75] As postbellum policymakers grappled with how to alleviate sectional disdain and teach freedpeople the dispositions demanded of a free labor economy, they embraced these idealized understandings of pedagogical labor and space.

Pedagogies of Proximity

Beyond producing spaces of domesticity, schooling also promised to cultivate fellow feeling through the embodied interaction of pupils themselves. As Rita Koganzon explains, early proponents of national education such as Benjamin Rush and Samuel Knox believed that "the very foundation of their project rested on educating children together" to develop feelings of mutuality and counteract the antirepublican tendencies of an accelerating market economy.[76] In many states, promoting common schools meant contesting two-tiered systems in which the poor attended charity or state-financed "pauper" schools while the wealthy attended private schools. To that end, advocates emphasized that children educated in the same space should learn to "imbibe the republican spirit, and be animated by a feeling of perfect equality."[77] By framing equality as not merely a matter of legal access but a sensate relationship, supporters developed an affirmative case for school systems open to pupils across economic strata. Through embodied interactions, schools could foster investments in meritocracy and bonds of sympathy that would persist even when children later entered a stratified market economy.[78]

In a culture shaped by a diversity of Protestant religious denominations, common school proponents of the 1830s and 1840s appealed to the virtues of "mingling" to overcome religious resistance. By meeting as equals to sing in harmony, learn together, and read directly from the King James Bible, these reformers argued, children would cultivate a sense of common religious fellowship across sects.[79] In the words of Congregationalist reverend W. S. Dutton, common schooling "brings the children of all sects together . . . and by the commingling, acquaintance, and fellowship which it involves, in the early, unprejudiced, and impressible periods of life, assimilates and unites them."[80] As many Catholic immigrants of the era recognized, the rhetoric of mingling tended to obfuscate the assimilationist aims of common schools.[81] Nativist policymakers found power in fusing common school ideas with white Protestant nationalism, reframing Catholic resistance to common schools as an un-American aversion to religious pluralism itself.[82] To refuse to mingle was, in this framework, to willfully exclude oneself from a community of fellow feeling with other Americans.

By the 1840s, the benefits of economic, denominational, and other forms of "mingling" had become core to the idea of common schooling. In Mann's words, schools could not be considered truly republican unless peers learned "together, under the same roof, on the same seats, with the same encouragements, rewards, punishments, and to the exclusion of adventitious and artificial distinctions."[83] By grounding the abstract ideal of schools as a uniting force in the concrete image of children interacting with each other, appeals to pedagogical proximity provided a potent way to frame schools' intervention in public feeling. At the same time, evoking the intimate association of children also risked prompting visceral reactions of disgust and hate, especially when reformers extended the logic of mingling to race. During Reconstruction, a subset of Radical Republicans embraced the potential of mingling as key to schools' potential transformation of hostile sentiments and racial prejudices. The common school thus became a central flashpoint in debates over civil rights, desegregation, and the possibility of interracial fellow feeling in the postwar republic.[84]

Intuiting Education

As schooling became a more ubiquitous feature of childhood in the North, intuitions about education provided a proxy for evaluating others' connection to public feeling. Based on how others spoke, where they were from, how they worked, and what beliefs they espoused, Americans in the years before the Civil War routinely rendered judgments about whether others had received formal education. With those inferences came conclusions about whether the person truly deserved "sympathy"—whether they should be imagined as part of a shared emotional community.[85] Seen as evidence of national loyalty, fellow feeling, and an ability to regulate emotions, intuitions about education stood in for an array of aspects of national belonging. In Abraham Lincoln's "free labor" arguments, education made the difference between "thorough work" and drudgery, determining whether a farmer merely plowed a field as a menial act or plowed thoughtfully and inventively in "the hopeful pursuit of . . . discovery."[86] Increasingly throughout the nineteenth century, to ask whether people were educated was to ask whether they felt their way through life in certain ways, responded predictably to public events, possessed a devotion to their labor, loved the same nation, or exercised control over their ugliest passions. It was to ask, in Ahmed's words, whether someone had learned "to be affected in the right way by the right things" or whether they remained an "affect alien" detached from the community of fellow feeling.[87] Connected with qualities including loyalty, literacy, religiosity, self-discipline, efficiency, and ingenuity, educational evaluations provided enormous latitude to interpreters. As postbellum reformers reckoned with the shifting emotional demands of national belonging, education offered a malleable way to make legible others' investments in public feeling.

As a way to determine one's status in an emotional community, the practice of intuiting educational capacities for fellow feeling was inextricable from logics of race. As Kyla Schuller argues, nineteenth-century reformers understood race through logics of emotional "impressibility," or a population's capacity to receive and internalize sensory impressions from their social circumstances. The idea of impressibility allowed reformers to distinguish between "civilized" populations capable of emotional discipline and "savage" populations too degraded over multiple generations to experience sympathy.[88] In turn, discourses of impressibility informed understandings of which populations could be educated and in what ways. For instance, perceiving Native Americans to be generations behind in progress toward "civilization," antebellum missionaries adopted assimilationist educational projects to tame unruly passions, instill emotional investments in European modes of agriculture, and promote filiations based on white Protestant ideas of family.[89] Perceptions of a group's progress from a status of "barbarism" or "savagery" implicated whether the educational experiences of that group constituted a project akin to the common schooling of white children or something perceived to be more rudimentary and tailored for noncitizens.

Educational Exclusion and Inclusion

Throughout Northern cities, the logics of impressibility and common schooling provided complementary rationales for civic exclusion that allowed local leaders to elide acknowledgment of blatant racial ascriptions. As Hilary J. Moss recounts, the antebellum common school movement in New England forged a "symbolic and symbiotic relationship between political inclusion and public schools."[90] White school leaders emphasized pupils' embodied interaction in a shared classroom space as a vital prerequisite to participation in civic life. At the same time, these leaders excluded Black students from those spaces, citing their inability to receive the same impressions as white children.[91] Having relegated Black pupils to separate and unequal schools, white leaders then cited a lack of proper civic education and preparation as a rationale for denying Black adults from wider participation in public life.

Learning from exclusionary precedents, postwar legislators cited intuitions of ignorance as a basis for unequal distributions of rights, often without explicitly naming the notions of race, religion, or origin that informed those intuitions.[92] Owing in part to its malleability as a form of exclusion, education assumed a dual character as a policy. On one hand, educational rhetoric presented schooling as a single, unified policy solution capable of promoting common national loyalties. Invoking the ideal of education and supporting the creation of common schools facilitated talk of aligning all denizens of the United States into a united whole. On the other hand, white political actors also tacitly understood education through a racialized framework that situated pupils along distinct curricular tracks depending on their capacity to access and regulate their feelings.[93] The purported universality of education tended to obfuscate how legislators believed schools would actually engage the feelings of distinct groups of people. When members of the postwar Congress promoted white settlement in the West, they could thus invoke schools as a way to promote sympathetic feeling without disrupting racial hierarchies.

While antebellum school rhetorics legitimated logics of inclusion and exclusion in the present, they also delimited who could join in a future polity united in feeling by public schools. As Christopher Castiglia notes, nineteenth-century reformers' dream of institutions "carry[ing] current social interests unhindered into the future" implicitly "made a democratic *now* nearly impossible to conceive."[94] Education offered a meaningful promise only to uncorrupted children, "infantile citizens" who lacked meaningful agency in the present and thus could be conceived as ideal future Americans.[95] Reformers believed that if children were ushered into sanctuaries walled off from the vicissitudes of the postwar world and allowed to interact as equals with other unprejudiced youth, they could—to varying degrees depending on race, religion, class, and gender—be honed by teachers into citizens with proper dispositions.

Policymakers' emphasis on children tacitly assumed that adult generations had been mostly lost to the wiles of disloyalty, bigotry, or degradation. As Pennsylvania school reformer James Pyle Wickersham remarked at the close of the Civil War, a proportion of white Southerners "would scornfully reject all proffers of education at our hands.... We must treat them as Western farmers do the stumps in their clearings: work around them, and let them rot out."[96] Many educational advocates extended the same logics to populations deemed too "uncivilized" to be assimilable, including Chinese immigrants, most Native Americans, and Catholics who resisted sending their children to public schools. At the start of Reconstruction, a subset of reformers held out more hope for adult freedpeople, who were regarded as resembling children and thus as educable—but only to a point of self-sufficiency and seldom any further.[97] The allure of education was its ability to conjure a future beyond scornful rebels and degraded freedpeople, promising a new emotional community that assimilated a willful portion of these people's descendants. The turn to schooling often reflected a certain hopelessness about the present.

Uneven Regional Developments and Calls for Intervention

Though the rhetoric of common school reform swayed many people in the antebellum United States, the development of public education proceeded unevenly across states and regions. At the state level, the adoption of common school systems proceeded through a fitful process routinely set back by economic crises and opposition from defenders of local, parochial, or private schools.[98] Usually championed by Whig Party politicians, common school reforms often hinged on the party's success in local and state elections.[99] The reception of education likewise depended on state and regional political cultures. In much of New England, developing common systems meant systematizing long-established schools in disparate communities. In the Old Northwestern states of Ohio, Indiana, Illinois, and Minnesota, creating systems entailed starting from the ground up by shaping local enthusiasm for the concept of common schooling itself. And in much of the South, promoting schools meant overcoming a deeply entrenched resistance to taxpayer-funded education. Owing to these disparate developments, children in the North, South, and West had wildly different educational experiences. By 1850, more than 70 percent of the nation's public school pupils and teachers lived in the rural North.[100] At the onset of the Civil War, the proportion of Northern children enrolled in school was between 20 and 30 percent higher than the proportion of Southern children.[101] At the extremes, more than 80 percent of white children in Maine, New Hampshire, and Massachusetts were enrolled in school, compared to just over 30 percent in Arkansas and Florida.[102]

For those Northerners invested in the linkage of schooling, citizenship, and fellow feeling, divergent sectional commitments to education had long generated a sense of anxiety. In his 1835 sermon "A Plea for the West," Lyman Beecher declared regional disparities in schooling a threat to the nation's future. Regarding the South as a cautionary tale, he argued that the only way to form "homogenous public sentiment" in the diffuse western United States was through common schools.[103] Speaking in the late 1850s, Massachusetts secretary of education (and future US senator) George S. Boutwell expressed similar anxieties about the accelerating pace of national expansion without a commensurate growth in education systems. Portraying education as crucial to US imperial projects, he argued, "If . . . by conquest, annexation and absorption, we acquire new territories, and strange races of men, and yet neglect education, every step will but increase our burdens and perils, and hasten our decay."[104] After the emotional collision of the Civil War, policymakers already had access to a vocabulary that linked sectional discord to disparate educational commitments and readily did so, suggesting that schooling had dictated whether a person embraced the Union itself. As Wickersham intoned in an 1865 speech, "In the late rebellion, the line of free schools marked the line of loyalty to the Government. We must push that line to the Gulf."[105] Members of Congress encountered such arguments and adapted them to the legislative situation they faced.

For those Reconstruction-era legislators steeped in the emotion-laden language of common school reform, education offered both a diagnosis and a cure for sectional tumult. For example, before arriving in Congress, Representative Ignatius Donnelly (R-MN) attended a Philadelphia high school dubbed the "School of the Republic" for its zealous public school philosophy.[106] On the floor of the House, he exemplified that zeal, declaring that the "permanent safety" of the republic was at stake unless Congress acted to "enforce education."[107] Figures such as Donnelly were not the first to declare education the panacea for America's social ills and certainly would not be the last.[108] Nonetheless, their educational advocacy broke from a tradition of treating schooling as a local issue, carrying the rhetoric of common school reform onto the federal stage with a new boldness. Before the Civil War, few people would have asserted as boldly as Representative James A. Garfield (R-OH) that federal policy "will prove a disastrous failure unless [Congress] makes the schoolmaster its ally, and aids him in preparing the children of the United States to perfect the work now begun."[109] Few had contended, as Representative George Frisbie Hoar (R-MA) did in late 1869, "that Congress had the constitutional right to establish a system of National Education and to tax the people to pay for it."[110] Breaking through decades of resistance to education as a national issue, these policymakers introduced discourses of reform to a new emotional arena of debate.

Emulating the state reformers of the first decades of the nineteenth century, vocal members of the postwar Congress sought to expand, promote, or systematize the educational efforts underway across the nation. They interwove the rhetoric of common schooling into a wide range of policy initiatives, responding to the moods they felt endangered a fragile union. These figures' bold assertions echoed and altered the feeling-centered language of their common school movement predecessors.[111] For these reformers, education had a transcendent quality, drawing on a range of religious pieties. Connected to assumptions about maternal domesticity, schooling had a presumed capacity to calm and discipline unruly emotions. It offered a way to arrange human interaction to cultivate fellow feeling across lines of religion, class, and (for some) race. It provided an emotional sanctuary purified of prejudice or hatred. Many people took a lack of appreciation for the inherent goodness of schooling as a self-evident reason to feel shame. Attending to these assumptions about emotion and education, *Absence of National Feeling* offers a novel account of how and why legislators advocated a diverse array of education policies during Reconstruction and traces how this language transformed as it clashed with competing assumptions about education and feeling on the floor of the House and Senate.

"HEARTS DEVOTED TO THE UNION"

In the hours before Congress's first postwar assembly, the challenges of suturing the Union were already clear. Representatives from Southern states, many of them leaders who had mobilized the rebellion, arrived seeking their seats in the House. Northern Republicans, reticent about persistent loyalties to the Confederacy, refused to seat them. When Speaker of the House Schuyler Colfax (R-IN) gaveled in the Thirty-Ninth Congress, he acknowledged "the vacant and once abandoned seats around us." He assured his colleagues that those seats would be filled soon enough—with "hearts devoted to the Union for which they are to legislate, jealous of its honor, proud of its glory, watchful of its rights, and hostile to its enemies."[112] In subsequent years, many in Congress turned to education to generate the feelings Colfax described. By attending to the emotional contours of those policymakers' rhetoric, *Absence of National Feeling* advances an account of how and why members of Congress advocated schooling as an intervention in public feeling. Connecting educational appeals to the wider racial, cultural, and political struggles of Reconstruction, I explore the fitful process through which this rhetoric of schooling changed across time.

Each chapter of *Absence of National Feeling* centers on a debate over a specific policy approach pursued in Congress. The chapters move through overlapping time periods, highlighting concurrent developments in debates that often unfolded at the same time. Taken as a whole, the chapters exhibit how policymakers' attitudes toward schooling and rhetoric of education shifted by Reconstruction's end. By 1877, the educational vision that began as a Radical Republican approach to transforming a nation had been whittled into a form that even once-resistant Southern Democrats accepted as a basic responsibility of state governments. The rest of the book traces this rhetorical and political shift and considers its consequences for the late nineteenth century United States.

Chapter one, "Federalism and Feeling: Enforcing Education in the South, 1865–1871," begins with the first session of the Thirty-Ninth Congress as Radical Republicans asserted control over Reconstruction and sought to reshape Southern culture. As part of their sweeping vision of change in the South, Radical Republicans embraced education to reimagine the relationship of federalism and feeling. With deep roots in the New England common school movement, Radical figures like Senator Charles Sumner (R-MA) and Representative George Frisbie Hoar (R-MA) contended that antebellum federalism had failed in its efforts to manage the nation's emotions. They believed that public schooling—directly supervised and enforced by federal authority—offered an alternative way to instill the fellow feeling necessary to avert another war and alleviate racial prejudice. Though grounded in a vision of multiracial democracy in the South, this vision also aligned with imperialistic projects of assimilation in the West, underscoring the double-edged implications of common school ideology when it came to questions of race.

Throughout this chapter, I examine how policies proposed by Sumner and Hoar triggered disputes over the proper locus of federal authority to develop schools and shape the emotional lives of the citizenry. The chapter first explores how the common school movement influenced Sumner's arguments to mandate public education as a part of rewritten Southern state constitutions. From there, the chapter turns to Hoar's more assertive proposals to create federally administered schools in any states that failed to establish education systems. Inspired by European models, Hoar and his allies envisioned a national system capable of uniting the disparate corners of an American empire and managing its diverse populations. Yet they faced fierce opposition predicated on a rival, Democratic-led view of education as grounded in local sentiment. Key Radical Republicans envisioned education as a cornerstone of a reconstructed South and an empire in the West, while a counterrhetoric of educational localism undermined this vision and set the stage for less direct approaches to promoting a national school system.

While New Englanders tried to enforce education, policymakers from Ohio to Minnesota sought to encourage it through indirect means. Drawing on efforts to promote common schools in their states, these policymakers sought to instill feelings about education as a matter of state pride or shame. Chapter two, "A System of Shame: Founding the Bureau of Education, 1865–1872" begins by tracing how regional approaches to school promotion among diffuse populations of the Northwest Territory relied on a logic of seeing educational status at a remove through the collection and publication of school journals and official reports. Approaches toward seeing and shaming informed the actions of Representative James A. Garfield (R-OH), who in 1866 advocated a federal Bureau of Education as a way to indirectly motivate states to adopt public schools. By laying states' disparate educational commitments and attainments side by side, he insisted, the bureau could "shame out of their delinquency all the delinquent states of the country."[113] Moreover, by contrasting rates of literacy among Black and white pupils, policymakers hoped that the bureau could ignite feelings of dishonor among Southern whites and spur their support for school reforms.

By tracing seven years of debates over the bureau and its shame-centric methods, chapter two illustrates how policymakers gradually came to accept a diffuse, indirect model of federal influence over schools. For its first several years, legislators questioned the bureau's logic of indirect influence and called for its abolishment. Yet over time, legislators began to enact rhetorics of shame precisely as Garfield and other Western leaders anticipated. During the debate over an 1872 bill introduced by Representative Legrand Perce (R-MS) to create a bureau-managed national school fund, Republicans wielded statistics to inflame Southern whites' racial anxieties. Southern Democrats, in turn, defended their states' honor by turning educational embarrassments on immigrants in New England. These regional and racial logics of shame presented policymakers with an alluring possibility—a way to promote a national system of education without any form of direct federal intervention. In the process, however, they displaced the New England reformers' insistence on federal oversight of schools. The adoption of specific education policies would depend in part on whether state leaders accepted the logics of pride and shame that underpinned official reports.

As Republicans clashed over how to systemize public education, they also wrestled over the future of the military-operated Freedmen's Bureau. Beginning its operations weeks before the Confederate surrender at Appomattox, the bureau was initially imagined as a temporary response to freedpeople's hunger, displacement, and lack of education. By the time Congress reconvened in December 1865, the bureau had become closely imbricated with missionary efforts to support freedpeople's schools. Chapter three, "An Atmosphere of Altruism: Renewing the Freedmen's Bureau, 1866–1870," traces how Congress invoked representations of teachers' influence on the impressible feelings of freedpeople to advocate both for and against renewing the agency. Republicans invoked the popular image of white women teachers creating hopeful, domestic spaces conducive to freedpeople's emotional development. To elide fears of freedpeople's economic radicalization, these proponents framed the bureau as a patriarchal protector that would stand outside the feminine space of the classroom.

Though a focus on protection secured the bureau's renewal, the agency's leaders struggled to maintain a clear line between bureau protection and missionary teachers' labors. The bureau and organizations such as the American Missionary Association were far too intertwined—in finances, administration, leadership, objectives, and on-the-ground activities—to disentangle their efforts, either practically or rhetorically. The close relationship between government and philanthropy quickly became the bureau's peril. Opponents seized even the smallest hint of bureau influence over teachers' labor as evidence of a federal (Republican-led) conspiracy to indoctrinate freedpeople into partisan sentiments. In 1868 and 1870, opponents took aim at the agency's blurry relationship to philanthropy to allege that the government had violated the sacred space of the classroom and corrupted benevolent teachers. Stoking white anxieties about Black men's newly conferred voting rights, bureau critics claimed that the agency had inculcated pupils with corrosive partisan loyalties and hatred for their white former masters. Republicans gave up on renewing the agency after the passage of the Fifteenth Amendment. They defended the bureau's legacy but did so in ways that portrayed the classroom as a fragile domestic space easily corrupted by federal influence. These policy and rhetorical choices foreclosed future possibilities for meaningful federal intervention on Black citizens' behalf.

By the waning years of Reconstruction, a growing number of legislators assented to the idea of public education as an ameliorative force that would aid in reconciling North and South. Yet they disagreed on a premise vital to the common school vision of New Englanders: the mingling of pupils from different backgrounds in the classroom. Long accepted as key to schools' capacity to cultivate pupils' sympathy, this concept proved most incendiary when applied to questions of race. In chapter four, "The Method of Mingling: The Civil Rights Act and Educational Reunion, 1872–1876," I argue that congressional debates over school desegregation reinforced education's centrality to sectional reconciliation while rejecting any need for pupils to experience contact across lines of identity. The chapter begins by exploring how antebellum school reformers developed the idea of mingling as central to schools' efforts to alleviate social tensions of religion, class, and national origin. Among Black activists and their allies, this idea became a powerful tool in efforts to pursue access to public education throughout the 1850s and after the Civil War. In the postbellum Congress, Sumner and other Republicans invoked this rhetoric of mingling as part of the rationale for what became the Civil Rights Act of 1875. In their view, requiring integration in nascent public schools in the South was vital to pupils' formation of sympathetic fellow feeling.

Critics of racial integration in schools interrogated the logic of mingling itself and above all its applicability to race. Citing a visceral rhetoric of racial prejudice and disgust, Democrats and disaffected Republicans claimed that schools would be powerless to alleviate the depths of instinctual hatred felt by white pupils.[114] At the same time, they also stoked anxieties that schools would alleviate prejudices too well—fostering friendships, romances, and sexual relationships that would erode white racial purity. Vacillating between these positions, Democratic opponents to the Civil Rights Act claimed the mantle of advocating and protecting common schools from their Radical Republican colleagues. In this reframed appeal, Democrats were the ones seeking to defend the sacred space of schools from the inevitable racial animus that Republican visions of mingling would produce. Between 1872 and 1875, members of

Congress gradually abandoned the idea of racial integration in schools as too controversial, gutting educational provisions from the final Civil Rights Act. In the process, the legislation's supporters dissociated the idealistic rhetoric of education from the concrete policy question of which children would sit together in classrooms. This process set the stage for a system of education that superficially sustained myths about national fellow feeling while developing along separate and unequal lines that inculcated interracial distrust.

Between 1865 and 1877, members of Congress from a wide range of regional, political, and racial backgrounds came to accept a basic relationship between public schooling and national feeling. This acceptance formed the foundation of a post-Reconstruction rhetoric of educational reconciliation: a set of underlying premises, ideals, and appeals that policymakers continued to invoke and adapt in the decades that followed. The volume's conclusion, "Schooling and Sentiment: Education, Reconciliation, and the Limits of Good Feelings," explores how Congress's rhetorical and policy choices circumscribed later educational efforts, including bills for national education funding introduced by Senator William Henry Blair (R-NH) during the 1880s. I examine how postwar legislators' bipartisan acceptance of education as a national—but not federal—project facilitated sectional reconciliation while laying the groundwork for Jim Crow. And I consider how the postwar Congress's assumptions about gender, religion, race, and literacy provided a rhetorical framework that reified hierarchical views of citizenship. Identifying future avenues for research, I contemplate the historical inheritances of this early era in federal education policy, contending that linking education with the superficial formation of good feelings stifled education's potential as an institution.

"THAT OBSTINATE, HOSTILE SPIRIT": A PRELUDE

As I read twelve years of congressional debates and speeches by hundreds of legislators, one figure stood out to me as representing the magnitude of postwar social change and the lost possibilities of the Reconstruction era. Born into slavery in antebellum South Carolina, Joseph H. Rainey gained his freedom around the age of ten. Living in a state that barred Black children, free or enslaved, from receiving public education, he worked as a barber to sustain himself and fund his own learning. At the onset of the Civil War, he fled to Bermuda to avoid being forced to labor for the Confederate military. After the conflict, he gained sufficient clout in Charleston's free Black community to build a political career, becoming the first of several Black men to serve in the US House of Representatives.[115]

The trajectory of Rainey's life—from enslavement to freedom, from refugee to representative—epitomized the revolutionary possibilities enabled by Reconstruction. Yet Rainey also encountered the violence that would rapidly destroy the era's potential. White Southerners reacted viscerally to Rainey's presence in the halls of Congress. After his first speech to the House of Representatives, he opened a letter to find a message emblazoned in red ink: "Prepare to meet your God."[116] He grew used to such death threats. As one observer of Congress noted, Rainey appeared ready to seize a weapon in self-defense at a moment's notice.[117] Emblematic of the era's hope, Rainey nonetheless moved through ecologies of hate.

Despite his well-warranted fears, Rainey remained steadfast in his defense of Black civil rights, military protection, and educational opportunities. On February 3, 1872, he passionately defended the need for a national common school fund to benefit white and Black children alike. He believed that schools could foster a felt connection to the nation—they could "impart a better understanding of our institutions, and thus cultivate a loyal disposition and lofty appreciation for them." More than that, schools could reorient how people felt about each other. If common schools had been a national priority before the Civil War, he believed, "there would have been a better understanding and more fraternal feeling between the North and the South, which would have annihilated that obstinate, hostile spirit which engendered the late 'unpleasantness.'"[118] Schools could, in Rainey's view, secure a loyal republic, quell efforts to revive slavery, alleviate interracial hostility, and avert war. Schools could unite a public in feeling, not just on paper.

It is easy, 150 years later, to dismiss Rainey and other Radicals as naive in their educational faith. But as I navigate the twists and turns of postwar education debates, it often seems that these Radicals alone recognized the depth of social change needed to reconstitute the nation. More than anyone else in Congress, Rainey knew the stakes of Reconstruction. He knew the oppression free Black people endured in the South and what it would take to change white feelings. He knew the benefits of the education he fought tooth and nail to acquire. Despite so many reasons to be a cold-sober realist, Rainey still found in educational rhetoric a way to open a horizon of possibility. Through the idea of an education system, he imagined a nation in which people like him belonged—not just in law, but in feeling.

Chapter One

FEDERALISM AND FEELING
Enforcing Education in the South, 1865-1871

Well before the common school movement developed during the 1830s and 1840s, many towns and villages in the northeastern United States had established schools for children.[1] Built to fulfill local economic, religious, and civic prerogatives, schools became sites of both financial and emotional investment for the people who helped build them. As Campbell F. Scribner writes, local governance of schools took on mythic significance, "evok[ing] such deep-seated values as egalitarianism, self-determination, and civic participation."[2] Yet by the 1830s, reformers in New England found the piecemeal development of community schools inadequate to the needs of a diversifying nation. For early secretaries of education such as Horace Mann of Massachusetts and Henry Barnard of Connecticut, threats to political fellow feeling seemed to encroach from every direction. These leaders were anxious about an influx of Catholic immigrants from Europe, the deepening class divides of an industrial economy, and the contentious political style ushered in by Jacksonian democracy.[3] Beyond their own state boundaries, these reformers were aghast as the sectional crisis between North and South intensified. They believed that these social tensions could be traced back to fundamental differences in how people acculturated their children. To rectify tensions both local and national, reformers contended that schools everywhere needed to train teachers in common ways and to align pupils toward common sentiments.

The common school movement influenced how many New England politicians interpreted the tumultuous events of subsequent decades. After the Civil War, many of those leaders served in Congress, where they reinvigorated the movement's antebellum rhetoric to confront issues of a national scope. Leading the effort were Senator Charles Sumner (R-MA) and Representative George Frisbie Hoar (R-MA), who invoked education as a way to reconcile regions that had just been at war, to ameliorate the disloyalty and prejudice of recalcitrant rebels, and to manage the demographic diversity of an envisioned American empire in the West. Between 1866 and 1870, Sumner and Hoar made assertive calls for Congress to mandate common schools in the South. In the Senate, Sumner drew on his experience supporting Mann's common school reforms, regarding education as the centerpiece of Reconstruction.[4] Throughout debates over whether, when, and how to readmit Southern states to the Union, Sumner insisted that Congress deny entry to any state that failed to provide for education in its constitution.[5] In the House of Representatives, Hoar carried Sumner's educational appeals a step further. Believing mass education to be "a necessity of self-preservation for the state," Hoar proposed a "national education bill" that would grant the federal government the authority to mandate public schools, establish standards for evaluating them, and create school systems in any state that failed to meet those standards.[6] Together, these two figures' arguments brought the ideas of New England common school reform to Congress.

Though New Englanders saw their common school ideals as common sense, their policies represented a dramatic rethinking of federalism. Since the founding of the republic, most policy leaders viewed federalism strictly as a legal construct. For nearly a century, the federalist idea allowed policymakers to sidestep passion-inducing topics such as slavery by deferring to constitutional procedures of jurisdiction.[7] In 1861, it became painfully clear that state and federal conflicts reflected deeper—often festering—tensions among people's felt affinities. As Malcolm M. Feeley and Edward Rubin contend, legal theories of federalism tend to elide the "tragic aspect of politics" that federalist systems represent. Emerging "as a compromise between unity and dissociation," federalism takes hold in nations where people cannot fully reconcile conflicting identities and attachments.[8] For Radical Republicans in the postwar Congress, the tragic dimension of federalism moved from the background to the foreground of debate. In their view, the legal frameworks that failed to avert a Civil War could not adequately manage the racial, religious, and regional heterogeneity of a growing nation that just fought a cataclysmic war. Drawing on the rhetoric of the New England common school movement and models of centralized education in Europe, they advocated a substantive intervention into public feeling: a guarantee of taxpayer-funded education in every state.

Both Sumner and Hoar rejected antebellum ideas about limited federal influence over education, arguing that the Constitution both empowered and obligated Congress to enforce the creation of state school systems. Moreover, both men's proposals cited schooling as a solution to the discordant feelings that had divided the body politic. The classroom would serve, in Lauren Berlant's phrase, as a "crucial interface between the state and the person as affectively invested and experienced"—a space within which the abstract idea of the United States could become something sensed, felt, and loved.[9] In this way, common school ideology presented an alternative conception of federalism. Rather than devise a system to anticipate and sort out tensions over jurisdiction, these school reformers aspired to align groups' feelings so that tensions over jurisdiction would seldom arise. Put simply: if everyone shared a baseline of common sentiments, there would be no divergences severe enough to require a layered system of divided sovereignty to adjudicate them. Sovereignty would not be divided. In the most radical formulation advanced by Sumner, schooling could upend the aristocratic order of the Southern plantation class that had triggered the Civil War. In place of the feelings of superiority associated with slavery, schools would inculcate sympathy between Black and white Southerners and lay a foundation for future multiracial government in the region.

Beyond the immediate aim of incorporating Black Southerners into a community of fellow feeling, advocates of the Hoar Bill linked their education policy to the Republican Party's wider imperialist vision. In a series of lengthy speeches, Representative William F. Prosser (R-TN) portrayed a national common school system as a way to assimilate the myriad populations subsumed by westward expansion. Illustrating education's allure as a unified policy response to demographic diversity, Prosser posited that Native Americans, Mormons, Mexican Americans, Catholic immigrants, and other populations could be taught to feel a deeper connection to the nation and to one another. Yet the seeming uniformity of Prosser's proposal also belied the divergent, racialized ways in which he imagined disparate groups' emotional capacities and thus their ability to be educated. In tethering Sumner and Hoar's vision to Republicans' imperial ambitions, Prosser demonstrated education's dual character as a policy intervention: as a single policy, it promised to bind all US denizens in feeling, yet it would do so by disciplining groups' emotions in stratified, unequal ways.[10] Linking New Englanders' school vision with the imperial project of "civilizing" Native Americans in the territories, Prosser's argument revealed the implied interplay of identification and division in the Hoar Bill: to forge common feeling through education meant to align "American" identity against those deemed uneducable.

Like the common school reformers of the 1840s, New Englanders' proposed postwar educational interventions faced intense local resistance. Many in Congress remained committed to the principle of divided state and federal authority, objecting to laws that would permanently entrench federal influence over states.[11] Many also had deep personal stakes in perpetuating a vision of schools as local, community-controlled institutions. Figures including Representatives Michael C. Kerr (D-IN) and Thompson McNeely (D-IL) argued for education as an exertion of parental, religious, and communal will, a means of perpetuating local emotional attachments across generations. Localists objected to New Englanders' claims that federal interventions could resolve tensions over state and federal authority. Rather, localists believed that national education policies would exacerbate those conflicts, generating communities' fears about external influence on their children's formation of feelings. For a national system of schools to fulfill the promise of fellow feeling, proponents of this view argued, that system would have to emerge organically from local and state leaders attuned to their communities' sentiments. In the emotional arena of Congress, the clash between reform and localist views of feeling revealed competing beliefs about where feelings originate, how they circulate, and who they can influence. The assertiveness of localist backlash led most Republicans to reject the Hoar Bill and adopt a more constrained approach to federal education policy.

The debate over Sumner and Hoar's proposals tested the outer limits of common school rhetoric as an intervention into public feeling. Schisms over feeling divided Radical Republican reformers from their localist Democratic opponents. Both the relative success of Sumner's advocacy and the failure of the Hoar Bill played significant roles in the tragic story of Reconstruction-era education reform. Sumner's insistence on education as a condition for Southern readmission reflected a sober recognition that building new forms of collectivity required shaping not just laws and institutions but the feelings of the Southern people. While the Senate balked at his proposals, the Black delegates empowered under the Reconstruction Acts to participate in Southern constitutional conventions shared Sumner's educational convictions. Recognizing schools as vital to Black people's full acceptance in both law and feeling, delegates codified education into their states' new founding documents. These efforts thus cemented a place for taxpayer-funded schooling in postbellum Southern life. Building on this success, the Hoar Bill set out to ensure that the South's new school systems would be implemented and supported as intended even if Southern Democrats regained control of state governments. To be sure, there was nothing tragic about the demise of Prosser's imperialist interpretation of the bill. But the legislation's failure still had a tragic dimension: it foreclosed serious debate about federal oversight of Southern education. In the decades ahead, the schools Sumner and Black Republicans fought to build would not promote the forms of multiracial fellow feeling they had imagined.

"A GENERAL INTERCOURSE OF SENTIMENTS": EDUCATION, FEDERALISM, AND THE FOUNDERS, 1787-1860

Long before Reconstruction reformers took up public education as a federal issue, members of the founding generation tried—and largely failed—to enact ambitious programs of public education. Anxious about the precarious unity of the nascent republic, key signers of the Declaration of Independence and delegates to the Constitutional Convention viewed some form of public education as a way to prevent factional discontent.[12] Informed by Montesquieu's assertion that republics require an education in "love of the laws and the homeland" to survive, the Founders sought ways to instill a properly republican character across a vast nation.[13] As George Washington stressed, "The assimilation of the principles, opinions, and manners of our country-men by the common education of a portion of our youth from every quarter" would be essential to "our prospect of permanent union."[14] Despite this common conviction, the Constitution itself said nothing about the topic of public schools, and most of the Founders' cherished proposals never became policy. Interred in the graveyard of rejected ideas were Benjamin Rush's outlines of a republican school system, Washington's call for a national university, and Thomas Jefferson's bill for common schools in Virginia.[15] Federal leaders quietly sustained missionary education projects in the territories but adopted a hands-off approach to promoting schools in the states. Through the onset of the Civil War, federal policymakers widely adhered to James Madison's assumptions about the management of national feeling.

Many early attempts to involve the federal government in schools faced an uphill battle against the Antifederalist defenders of local sentiment. For Rush, Washington, and Jefferson, the appeal of a national university or centralized school system lay in its potential to forge a national character aligned with Enlightenment values.[16] For most Antifederalists, this concept of a citizenry made homogenous from the top down threatened to disrupt the natural development of local religious and communal sentiments. As James Jasinski explains, the Antifederalist conception of civic judgment was predicated on empathy, honest affection, and fellow feeling—emotional capacities they believed to be fostered through citizens' direct participation in churches and local affairs.[17] As a result, Antifederalists were generally suspicious of the Federalists' secular, nationalist education proposals.[18] Antifederalist legislators during Washington's administration rejected calls for a national university, fearing that it would draw young adults away from the intimate influences of community and church.[19] For this significant subset of leaders in the early republic, attempting to cultivate a national sentiment appeared counterproductive: the circulation of common feeling first depended on the cultivation of emotional bonds within local communities.

For Madison, resistance to federal involvement in education did not represent a significant hurdle to the orchestration of feeling throughout the republic. As Jasinski argues, Madisonians imagined that the Constitution itself could counteract "heated passions, the sudden breezes of opinion, and distorting prejudices with a vision of cool and impartial deliberation."[20] In Madison's view, because the federal and state governments were "designed for different purposes" and focused on their own spheres, there was minimal risk that the two layers of government might find themselves in passionate conflict.[21] Conflicting affinities were inevitable in a diffuse republic but could be managed through the dispassionate application of reason.[22] Yet Madison was not naive about how competing affections for state and nation could disrupt constitutional designs. As Rogan Kersh observes, Madison contended that "affective connections among the people were required to secure political bonds between the states."[23] On these grounds, Madison supported a national university and state school systems, but he also doubted their ameliorative force.[24] He believed that stronger and more lasting emotional ties would emerge through cultural and economic trends outside the realm of federal or educational influence: "a general intercourse of sentiments" could be fostered by "good roads, domestic commerce, a free press, and particularly *a circulation of newspapers through the entire body of the people*."[25] To the extent that schooling would help forge common sentiment, he trusted that the states, through "salutary emulation" of one another's policies, would gradually develop school systems without federal involvement.[26] The virtues of schooling for public sentiment would thus be too self-evident for states to ignore.

There is an important exception to the limited federal role in education before 1860. Even as federal leaders avoided shaping schools in the states, they did not hesitate to exert federal influence over Native American education in the territories. To gradually bring Native Americans "within the pale of civilization," federally financed religious groups sought to indoctrinate their pupils into Christian religious faiths, cultivate European agricultural skills, and instill positive feelings toward white settlers.[27] By promoting economic and imperial visions through the "benevolent" labors of Quakers and other religious groups, officials indelibly shaped the development of federal territories while maintaining an illusion of limited government involvement.[28] These educational projects formed the entering wedge for a process that culminated in Native American dispossession, white settlement, and the incorporation of new states into the US empire.[29] In the antebellum United States, education thus proceeded along two parallel tracks: federal projects to "civilize" Native Americans, and local or state-run common schools to foster fellow feeling among white pupils. Though separate, these two tracks served a unified end of aligning white settlers in sympathetic identification while displacing those deemed uneducable.

Over the first eighty years of the republic, intensifying sectional conflicts tested both Madison's idea of a dispassionate system of divided sovereignty and public faith in the natural blossoming of fellow feeling throughout the states. Even during ratification debates, the Constitution's carefully crafted delineation of state and federal jurisdictions proved difficult to disentangle in practice.[30] As the nation expanded its imperial territories and granted them statehood, the Constitution strained under the challenge of negotiating different regions' claims to autonomy. Tensions intensified over banking, tariffs, and slavery, generating protracted dilemmas over federal decision-making authority. Meanwhile, states pursued distinct educational paths that reified a sense of sectional estrangement. Northerners blamed the South's absence of school systems for the region's aristocratic hierarchies; Southerners, in turn, claimed that Northerners' school systems fostered social disorder and destabilized traditions. "The education of the New England common school . . . bears no better fruits than presumption, disrespect to superiors, a vain passion for reform, infidelity, and the agitations of revolution," newspaper editor (and later popularizer of Lost Cause mythology) Edward Pollard wrote.[31] Educational distinctions became part of a wider narrative of deteriorating feeling.

The compromises that sustained American political identity grew more unstable as the emotional dissonances of the population grew more pronounced.[32] As Michael E. Woods writes, by the onset of the Civil War, Southerners justified secession by inverting Madison's claim that emotional bonds needed to be cultivated to preserve the Union. Secessionists proclaimed that the absence of emotional bonds meant that the Union no longer meaningfully existed: "those bonds had already been dissolved."[33] In the aftermath of the Civil War, policymakers sought more assertive ways to promote the fellow feeling that Madison had thought would emerge without government involvement. Rather than rely on states to adopt common schools of their own volition, reformers advocated a stronger federal hand in education. In making their case, they found a powerful model in the rhetoric of the 1830s common school movement.

"NO NORTH NOR SOUTH": HORACE MANN'S EDUCATIONAL NATIONALISM, 1839-1860

Throughout the 1830s and 1840s, cultural elites in Massachusetts grappled with ways to alleviate the dissonant feelings of their state's polity.[34] Amid the economic inequalities created by industrialization and a rise in Irish Catholic immigration to the state, reformers feared that the bonds of social sympathy would give way to class resentments and religious factions. Among reformers who took up the banner of education reform, the corrosive dangers wrought by partisanship, pauperism, commerce, immorality, and alcoholism shared a common root: the emotional susceptibilities of the population.[35] At the zenith of these anxieties about the Bay State's emotional harmony, Mann became the state's first secretary of education. Fretful about religious riots and proslavery violence, Mann feared "a public opinion of almost uncontrollable power" at work in antebellum America.[36] To redress this crisis, he propounded what David Hogan calls a pedagogy of "affective individualism" that aimed to shape children's internal conscience through the development of emotional ties.[37] Though this approach, Mann hoped that schools could become the "balance wheel of the social machinery," supplanting the divisive sentiments of class, sect, and nativity with a culture of merit and mutual sympathy.[38]

For a nation approaching civil war, Mann's rhetoric of school reform had significant implications for federalism. Placing matters of shared political identity at the heart of education's social mission, he drew direct inspiration from centralized school systems in Europe. He returned to Boston from a trip across the Atlantic in the early 1840s enamored by the centralized schools he observed in Prussia.[39] In the first decade of the nineteenth century, Prussia had instituted a set of pedagogical reforms designed to cultivate a sense of national consciousness among culturally and religiously disparate territories. International observers regarded such Prussian reforms as teacher seminaries, curricular supervision, and student evaluations as a blueprint for cultural cohesion.[40] According to Mann, Prussian leaders had wisely "act[ed] from a set of ideas or a frame of mind which embraces the whole people" rather than allowing education to develop discordantly as locales saw fit.[41] In short, he believed the discourses of Prussian education could be grafted onto the fragmentation of the United States in the mid-1800s, shoring up feelings of common national identity.

As the city of Boston's 1842 Fourth of July orator, Mann applied his reasoning about the virtues of Prussia's centralized system to the United States as a whole. With so many Americans swept up by differences in class, region, and ideology, he warned, civil conflicts would continue to intensify. This potential turmoil, he said, stemmed from the states' disparate commitments to schooling. By rejecting schools, many states had doomed their populations to an inability to feel loyalty to the nation or sympathy for their fellow citizens. Decrying the absence of schools in the South, he intoned, "Let us suppose that we were now overtaken by some great crisis in our national affairs . . . in the issue of some presidential contest, for instance. War impends."[42] In delivering this warning, Mann provided an education-centric explanation for the nation's deepening disunion. Two years later, school reformers in Congress would hearken back to the speech as a portent, extolling Mann's prescience as a reason to embrace common schools as a national cause.

Mann's vision of a polity united in fellow feeling by education had its limits. For all his talk of schooling as a means of leveling social distinctions and uniting children of disparate backgrounds, he refrained from comment in debates over school desegregation and allowed unequal schools for Black pupils to persist throughout his time as secretary.[43] That silence allowed a tiered system of schools to develop, reifying inequalities in a society that viewed education as a proxy for civic worth. Moreover, Mann's efforts to mitigate the nation's divided sentiments faced resistance from local religious and community leaders. In Boston, his report on Prussian education inspired a localist retort from thirty-one of the city's seasoned schoolmasters, who noted that the faraway politician lacked practical classroom experience and "has not, for several years, visited their schools."[44] They opposed Mann's call to eliminate corporal punishment, which they viewed as essential to the preservation of localized authority.[45] Outside the elite pedagogic circles of Boston, communities viewed reformers' proposals with even greater suspicion. In some cases, pupils would display local resistance by barricading schoolhouse doors against outsider teachers.[46] The resistance to Mann's reforms underscored communities' emotional investments in their extant schools. Grounded in conceptions of schooling as a reproduction of communal sentiment, the backlash in Massachusetts anticipated key points of contention that emerged when postwar policymakers brought Mann's philosophy to the Capitol. Despite scattered efforts to defend local authority, Mann and other elite reformers nonetheless fostered a bureaucratic revolution that took hold in much of the Northeast.

The crusade to transform the Massachusetts school system left an indelible impression on the state and its rising politicians. From the emotional community of the common school movement emerged a generation of reformers who embraced education as a vehicle through which the state could alleviate feelings of dissonance among the people. After the Civil War, leaders turned to Mann's language as a means of interpreting the conflict. A few months after the South's surrender at Appomattox, officials in Boston unveiled a statue of Mann and applied his ideas to the immediate challenge of reunion. As one of the city's school leaders argued, Mann's ideas could help forge a "newly regenerate nation" with "no North, nor South, no East nor West."[47] Sharing that sentiment, Boston school reformer Charles Brooks presented a petition to Congress calling for sweeping national education policies. Viewing schools as "a promoter of fraternal and political union," Brooks implored legislators to centralize the nation's schools, establish a cabinet-level secretary of public instruction, and deny marriage rights to anyone born after 1880 who failed to attain literacy.[48] When Congress convened in December 1865, Representative Nathaniel P. Banks (R-MA)—a former school promoter for the Massachusetts Board of Education—read his constituent's petition on the floor of Congress.[49] Though neither Brooks nor Banks would be central voices in subsequent policy debates, the introduction of such a provocative proposal signaled a significant break from antebellum debates over schools. Two other Bay State politicians—Sumner and Hoar—would soon mount a significant attack on the principle of federal noninvolvement in public schools.

"A CORNER-STONE OF RECONSTRUCTION": SUMNER AND THE RECONSTRUCTION ACTS, 1865-1870

After reading Horace Mann's 1842 Fourth of July address, thirty-one-year-old Charles Sumner declared Mann the "apostle" of education and his speech, "the noblest production ever called forth" at the city's annual holiday celebration.[50] Galvanized by the speech's warning, Sumner added education to the long list of reform causes he championed. He published editorials echoing Mann's praise of the Prussian school system and in 1844 ran for the Boston School Committee to champion Mann's school reforms.[51] Sumner lost that election but continued to pursue social reforms through the education system. Going further than Mann in defending the principle of education as an ameliorator of social distinctions, Sumner represented a Black pupil seeking to desegregate city schools in *Roberts v. City of Boston* (1850).[52] He went on to become a prolific figure in antebellum movements for abolitionism, desegregation, and the founding of the Republican Party. The survivor of a violent attack by a proslavery representative on the Senate floor, he carried the air of martyrdom among many of his fellow Radical Republicans. He also frustrated moderate Republicans with his firm insistence that a "moral principle cannot be compromised."[53]

Sumner believed that the Founders had compromised their principles—among them, the principle of public education—to placate proslavery Constitutional Convention delegates. By reviving their original republican intentions, he argued, post–Civil War leaders could produce a shared sense of common feeling throughout the polity: "Local jealousies and geographical distinctions will be lost in the attractions of a common country."[54] To that end, Sumner revitalized the common school rhetoric of his early career as a centerpiece of his Reconstruction proposals for the postwar South. Between 1865 and 1870, he advocated schooling as the primary means by which to lay an emotional foundation for the stable reunion of the states and to ensure the long-term success of multiracial democracy in the South.

Sumner's Educational Advocacy During the First and Second Reconstruction Act Debates, 1865–1867

Sumner's insistence on education in the South developed alongside his disquiet with President Andrew Johnson's policy of "restoration" in the region.[55] Throughout the summer and fall of 1865, Johnson sought to resume political business as usual by pardoning former rebels, returning confiscated lands to plantation elites, and resisting protections for freedpeople. As the restoration policy unfolded, Northern newspapers circulated stories of growing violence in the South and deepening resistance to Union authority.[56] Reading such accounts, Sumner feared that Johnson had ignited "a political volcano, spouting with smoke and red-hot lava, in an extended region whose first necessity is peace."[57] Sumner feared that hasty attempts at sectional conciliation would embolden the "lawless vindictiveness" of rebels.[58]

Against Johnson's policy, Sumner contended that the Southern states could not be "restored" because their governments had committed acts of "state suicide."[59] For Sumner, this term referred not solely to legal status but also to the deeper bonds of political society. Classically trained in rhetoric, Sumner regarded healthy communities as sharing a sensus communis, a shared substratum of felt attachments sustained across time through common myths, values, and institutions.[60] By dissolving the sources of all feeling, the Southern states had become "senseless communities who have sacrificed that corporate existence which makes them living, component members of our Union of States."[61] In depicting the South as an explosive region that lacked bonds of feeling, Sumner was building his case for an assertive federal policy in the South—one with education at its center.

Sumner sought an approach to Southern Reconstruction that provided the requisite time for cultural transformation. He found a rationale for long-term change in the "sleeping giant" of the Constitution, the "guarantee to every state in this union a republican form of government."[62] Sumner believed the Guarantee Clause to be more than just a promise to protect states from insurrection: it gave Congress a duty to foster the conditions of republican community.[63] The formation of educational institutions that would cultivate, safeguard, and perpetuate republican ideals and feelings was inherent in that duty. To that end, in a September 1865 speech in Worcester, Massachusetts, Sumner advocated the creation of a New England–style school system in the South. Asserting that "character is not changed in a day," he braced his audience for the antithesis to Johnson's calls for rapid restoration. Where others in Congress imagined Reconstruction timelines of months or at most a few years, Sumner had a more extensive vision. He wondered aloud, "Who can say that a generation must not elapse before these rebel communities have been so far changed as to become safe associates in a common government?"[64] Sumner thus signaled a view of federalism that went far beyond crafting new amendments to strengthen federal authority. He sought to target the tensions of feeling that had made federalism necessary.

In early 1867, as Congress debated its program of military oversight and political transformation in the South, Sumner argued that the legislature should explicitly mandate common school requirements in newly rewritten state constitutions. Most senators viewed Sumner's requirement as unnecessary, preferring to evaluate the constitutions on a state-by-state basis. When the first Reconstruction Act passed in the final days of the Thirty-Ninth Congress, Sumner's proposed educational language was omitted.[65] Undeterred, Sumner redoubled his efforts to make education a "corner-stone of reconstruction" when the Fortieth Congress began in March 1867.[66] Galvanized by a stronger Radical Republican presence in both the House and Senate, he again urged Congress to mandate taxpayer-financed education in Southern constitutions. During debates over the second Reconstruction Act, Sumner insisted that such requirements were vital to mitigate the South's emotional aimlessness. In his view, the more education a population received over multiple generations, the greater a member of that community's capacity to feel proper affinities toward fellow citizens.[67]

Sumner believed that the South lagged centuries behind in the development of sympathetic capacities. Massachusetts had established its system of community-funded schools as early as 1671, teaching generations of its children the meaning of sharing in a political community. In Virginia, by contrast, colonial governor Sir William Berkeley had been openly hostile to public education, infamously declaring, "I thank God *there are no free schools*." Even at that early date, Sumner argued, the South was emotionally unmoored. Unable to resist the impulses of rebellion and slavery, the "political monsters" of the South became "like the creature of imagination, a human being without a soul, living and moving blindly, with no just sense of the present or future." Without an emotional orientation provided by education, white Southerners could not foresee the moral consequences of slavery and rebellion. They responded only to the impulses of their local jealousies, which were inflamed by the demagogic manipulations of the plantation class. Without federal intervention to ensure that Southerners established school systems, Sumner warned, the "rebel spirit" would continue to be passed on in the "nurseries of rebellion." To Sumner's chagrin, fellow legislators remained unmoved by his argument. Most senators preferred to evaluate new constitutions as they were submitted to Congress rather than to dictate their language in advance. The Senate rejected Sumner's proposal in a tie vote, then declared him "out of order" when he tried again to raise the issue.[68]

Educational Provisions in Southern State Constitutions, 1868-1869

At least at first, Sumner's fears about new Southern constitutions were not borne out in practice. The Reconstruction Acts barred most antebellum officeholders and leading rebels from participating in state constitutional conventions, locking out many staunch opponents of taxpayer-financed education. More important, that legislation required that those conventions include delegates regardless of race, thus allowing Black men to participate. The multiracial Republican coalitions at the conventions proved strongly supportive of public schools. Since the end of the Civil War, Black activists from both North and South had met at conventions to insist on their rights and policy preferences. Education consistently topped their priorities.[69] As the participants in South Carolina's Colored People's Convention explained in 1865, "The sad recollection of our *forced* ignorance and degradation in the past, and ... bright and inspiring hopes of the future" motivated their desire "to see that schools are at once established in every neighborhood."[70] When Black leaders gathered with white allies in Charleston and across the South to craft constitutions, the multiracial Republican Party gave these educational demands the force of law, guaranteeing public schools to Black and white children alike. These appeals sought to rebuild the South's political community by invoking the same Massachusetts and Prussian models as Sumner.[71]

In adopting school provisions, Black convention leaders in the South shared Sumner's interpretation of the Guarantee Clause and his aims of fostering fellow feeling between North and South. As the South Carolina convention delegate and future US representative Robert B. Elliott claimed, "It is republicanism to educate the people, without discrimination. That has made New England great, and made her citizens, poor as well as rich, low as well as high, black as well as white, educated and intelligent." Like Sumner and other Radicals in Congress, Elliott suggested that education would be crucial to averting sectional hostility and hostile feelings in the future: "If [children] are compelled to be educated, there will be no danger to the Union, or a second secession of South Carolina from the Union."[72] Embracing Congress's insistence on republican constitutions, conventions in nine former Confederate states incorporated language requiring statewide, taxpayer-funded school systems. In each rewritten constitution, delegates' language echoed the specific phrasing Sumner had used in his proposed addition to the Reconstruction Acts: to guarantee "a system of public schools open to all."[73] Largely through the efforts of Black delegates, Sumner's initial concerns were assuaged.

Sumner's Call to Enforce Education in Virginia, 1869-1870

Although most of the South ratified constitutions that reflected Sumner's educational priorities, events in 1869 vindicated his anxieties about white resistance to schools. That year, schisms over the question of Black suffrage and the continued disenfranchisement of disloyal white rebels began to fragment Republican coalitions in the Upper South and border states. In Tennessee, pressure over the issue led interim governor DeWitt Senter to restore voting rights for former secessionists.[74] This decision allowed Democrats to regain significant political power. As Tennessee rejoined the Union prior to the passage of the Reconstruction Acts, the state lacked a constitution with substantial educational safeguards. Unencumbered by such legal constraints, Democrats seized their opportunity to dismantle state school laws and reverse nascent efforts to support Black education.[75]

In Virginia, a protracted struggle over the question of rebel amnesty delayed ratification of the state's Radical-drafted constitution and its school provisions. After months of compromises, the state's white majority acquiesced to ratification on July 6, 1869, as a necessary step to end military rule and rejoin the Union. Yet as they approved the constitution, they also signaled their discontent by voting to restore political rights to recalcitrant rebels and electing a conservative coalition to control the state government.[76] Uniting disaffected Republicans with Democrats, conservative gubernatorial candidate Gilbert C. Walker and his allies campaigned on a pledge to eliminate "objectionable provisions" from the constitution. By permitting "speedy amendments," he noted, the constitution had "furnishe[d] a sword to lop off its own head."[77] The only provision Walker explicitly pledged to repeal involved the constitution's method of organizing counties. Nonetheless, his sweeping vagueness—his vow to "by future amendments, . . . so improve [the constitution] as finally to make it what it should be"—raised questions about how much of the document the conservatives hoped to transform.[78] With the example of Tennessee fresh in their minds, Radicals in the federal Congress grew alarmed about whether Walker would attempt to eliminate guarantees of public schools.

Taking Tennessee as a warning and Virginia as a catalyst, Sumner again pressed for education in the remaining unadmitted states in January 1870. Objecting to a proposal to restore Virginia to the Union, Sumner defended the federal government's authority to evaluate states' commitments to education.[79] In his view, the conduct of Virginia's leadership represented a flagrant disregard of republican principles. Gesturing toward a copy of a Democratic newspaper, Sumner read aloud quotes from Governor Walker, including a vow to oppose "that foul refuse which the North has, as it were, vomited over our country."[80] Sumner interpreted "foul refuse" to refer primarily to provisions for common schools. By suppressing Black votes and appealing to unrepentant rebels, Sumner argued, Virginia's conservatives had made clear their intention that the state's "constitution should be nullified and the common school system trampled out." For Sumner, Walker's flagrant opposition and inflammatory speech revealed white Virginia elites' ongoing resistance to educating a loyal population with control over its partisan passions. Walker was aware that "knowledge is dangerous to tyranny," "to slavery," and "to wrong and injustice" and thus was naturally "afraid to see a system of public schools established in Virginia."[81] For Sumner, education and loyalty were so deeply intertwined that one was a metonym for the other. To love the Union was to love education. And to reject education, as he believed Walker would, was to oppose a reunited nation.

After five years of foiled efforts, Sumner's attacks on Walker helped convince legislators to impose educational requirements on a Southern state. As the Senate finalized its bill to restore Virginia to the Union, Sumner's Massachusetts colleague Henry Wilson proposed an amendment forbidding the state from changing its constitution "to deprive any citizen or class of citizens of the United States of the school rights and privileges secured by the constitution of said State."[82] The amendment passed, affirming Sumner's interpretation of the Guarantee Clause.

For the first time, Congress directly asserted an authority, however narrow, to mandate the implementation of a state's school system.[83] Yet the victory did not come easily, as Sumner's efforts revealed schisms over how members of Congress understood the task of emotional reunion. In one furious critique of Sumner, Senator Lyman Trumbull (R-IL) inquired whether maligning Virginians as ignorant and untrustworthy was truly "the way to bring about reconciliation and good feeling." For moderates like Trumbull, the primary obstacle to emotional reunion was his Radical colleagues' self-fulfilling prophecies about irreparable tears in the nation's emotional fabric. Such disagreements over how best to promote public feeling only intensified that year when the first-term representative George Frisbie Hoar (R-MA) began his educational efforts in the House. Echoing Sumner, Hoar contended that "education is the strongest bond of a union which is to depend for its endurance on the attachment of the people."[84] But where Sumner pursued educational enforcement through contingent Reconstruction measures, Hoar had a bolder ambition. Less than a week after the fight over Virginia, Hoar expressed his desire in a resolution proposed as chair of the House Committee on Education and Labor: "That it is expedient that this Committee prepare and propose to the House of Representatives a National System of Education."[85] That resolution paved the way for the most assertive educational legislation yet to be brought before Congress.

"COMPOSITE NATIONALITY": EMOTIONAL UNION, LOCALISM, AND THE HOAR BILL, 1870-1871

By February 1870, Hoar and his Republican allies believed that the trajectory of postwar education policy trended toward federal intervention. Galvanized by Sumner's Senate arguments, the creation of a Bureau of Education, and the accomplishments of the Freedmen's Bureau, Hoar crafted an audacious proposal to intervene in state-level education. Under the bill, states would be required to meet a standard of educational support set by the federal commissioner of education. Should a state fail to meet that standard, the federal government would be empowered to build schoolhouses, train teachers, superintend districts, and select curricular materials. The bill proposed a total annual expenditure of $2.2 million for national school supervision, dwarfing the $14,500 annual allocation to the recently established Bureau of Education. Supporters routinely cited passages from Mann's portentous 1842 Fourth of July speech, insisting that schools built under the law could get beneath the conflicting affinities of Americans and forge a coherent national identity.[86] Proponents of the Hoar Bill also stressed that it went beyond suturing North and South and had implications for wider projects of US imperialism. Representative William F. Prosser (R-TN) touted the Hoar Bill as a way to mitigate a lack of federal feeling across the nation's vast territorial empire.[87] Drawing analogies between various populations deemed threatening by white Protestant policymakers, Prosser articulated education's dual character as a uniform policy predicated on divergent notions of feeling.[88]

In 1871 the Hoar Bill received sustained debate in the House and met with vocal opposition. Emboldened by schisms in the Republican Party coalition, Democratic localists offered a competing view of schools' role in shaping national feeling. Agreeing with the premise that schooling should play a role in rebuilding the Union, these localists nonetheless argued that a federal interventionist approach would serve only to inflame local animosities. They contended that education needed to emanate from existing communal sentiments, not from a faraway bureaucracy. Dismissing Republicans' sense of urgency, proponents of this view asserted that this process of locally driven reform was already underway: states already understood the necessity of education and had begun to pursue it.

Interlocutors in the debate over the Hoar Bill made explicit an often-implicit set of understandings about the relationship between schooling and sentiment. The clash between these perspectives and the bill's decisive failure illustrated both the alluring and the illusory qualities of education as a solution to postbellum problems. Once placed on the defensive, Hoar Bill supporters discovered that education did not dissolve tensions over local, state, and federal authority. Rather, it simply channeled conflicts over public feeling into a new policy context: the classroom. As the outcome of the Hoar Bill debate foreclosed a direct role for the federal government in shaping schools, then, it also underscored the stakes of schooling as a space in which future struggles over the sources of sentiment would be fought. Establishing a perception of need but failing to enact a policy to address it, the debate paved the way for more moderate Republican reformers to champion indirect forms of educational influence.

William F. Prosser's Imperial Case for the Hoar Bill, January 1870

By the start of the 1870s, many Republican political leaders viewed Reconstruction as a process that encompassed not only reforming the South but also bringing greater social stability to the North and fostering settlement of the West.[89] Despite commitments to white settler expansion, policymakers fretted about the nation's institutional capacities to preserve fellow feeling across such a wide territory and especially among its many groups marked as religiously or racially deviant. These anxieties were amplified by the 1870 ratification of the Fifteenth Amendment, which secured voting rights not only for Black voters in the South but also for a range of populations across the West. Throughout Reconstruction, legislators' concerns about demographic complexity in the West motivated an array of policies targeting Mormons, Catholics, Chinese immigrants, and Native Americans. Most notably, such imperial anxieties underpinned President Ulysses S. Grant's "Peace Policy," a program that restricted Native American movement to reservations while financing missionary campaigns to "civilize" them.[90] Extending the congressional debates that informed these policies, Prosser recognized the Hoar Bill as an opportunity to reframe the diverse forms of difference in both the South and the West as a single political question requiring a unified institutional solution.

Having lived in both California and Tennessee, Prosser brought a national perspective to a bill with national ambitions; for this reason, he introduced the first significant arguments on the bill's behalf. Years before the Civil War, Prosser had been a schoolteacher in Pennsylvania, working under local administrators who sought a "necessary fusion" among the "heterogeneous" European immigrant populations settling in the state.[91] Echoing this theme years later, Prosser's January 1870 speech to Congress argued that the Hoar Bill would widen the sphere of educated fellow feeling across the divergent groups under the aegis of American power. At the same time, he implicitly maintained that those groups' pedagogical experiences would reflect extant racial ideologies, affirming a scale from "barbarism" to "civilization."

Prosser's speech emphasized the dual character of schooling as a means to foster common feeling while preserving racialized difference. From the onset, Prosser deployed the idea of illiteracy to combine disparate groups into a single demographic category and a single problem. Across the nation, he posited, discordant feelings could be attributed to a "vast army of illiterates" easily swayed by passionate whims and visceral prejudices. This single problem could, he implied, be redressed with a single solution: education. As Prosser elaborated on his argument, however, he provided a whirlwind tour of differentiated threats to public feeling across both the states and the federal territories. Among Southern whites, he argued, estranged feeling manifested as a "strong sentiment of hostility" against Northern people, institutions, and common schools. In Utah Territory, the threat to public feeling stemmed from Mormon polygamy, a practice that Prosser and other Republicans analogized to slavery as a "peculiar institution" that threatened the nation's emotional fabric. If the fifteen thousand untaught children there could be provided common (and implicitly nondenominational Protestant) schools, the "chronic troubles" of the territory could be resolved. Turning to New Mexico, Prosser blamed an absence of national sentiment on a failure to promote English among the region's Mexican American population. What "might to-day have been a flourishing State in this Union," Prosser lamented, instead languished as a territory in which "two generations of school children... yet speak a foreign language." And throughout the West, the costly and deadly wars between Native Americans and white settlers could be attributed to a national failure to educate Native Americans "out of their state of barbarism and ignorance."[92] By using categories of illiteracy and ignorance to link social groups, Prosser claimed that a diverse array of social ailments—poverty, polygamy, immorality, imputed barbarism, or demagogic susceptibility—could be addressed with a single, sweeping cure.

For Prosser, a centralized school system provided a vehicle to extend national feeling to spaces distant from the nation's capital. Drawing on the gender ideology of the common school movement, Prosser attributed this power to the nation's teachers, "more than two thirds of whom are of that class whose delicacy of organization forbids their bearing arms in battle." Through the efforts of "women teachers," a national system of schools would be a "silent force" from which positive feelings "flow to the whole Union and to each particular part of it." Their labors would "exert a more mighty influence upon the destinies of humanity than all the soldiers ever marshalled... upon the battle-fields of Europe." Because the nation's problems stemmed from unruly internal emotions, the creation of spheres of domesticity through the classroom provided a means of taming and properly directing those emotions. Not coincidentally, Prosser cited the Freedmen's Bureau—an institution widely associated with women teachers' benevolence—as a blueprint for how a national system could be administered.[93] Through a women-led army of feeling, policymakers thus sought to promote a widespread project of emotional influence across every state and territory.

Through the spread of domestic spaces and common behaviors, reformers asserted that schools established under the Hoar Bill would carry a sense of federal feeling to the farthest reaches of the republic. Prosser's speech provided the starkest illustration of this point in his remarks on Native American education in the Nebraska Territory. In 1863, the Ho Chunk (Winnebago) nation had been forcibly displaced from its ancestral lands, ultimately resettling on the northern part of the Omaha Reservation. Since then, the Ho Chunk people had grown increasingly estranged from federal leadership, a point Prosser made by reading an 1864 letter supposedly penned by tribal officials that began, "Father, we cannot see you. You are far away from us. We cannot speak to you." To alleviate those feelings of distance, the letter requested schools like those "in operation among your Omaha children." Prosser was incensed that the letter had gone unacknowledged for six years. In his view, the "supreme indifference of the 'Great Father' toward the education of his red children" had left a sense of disconnection that gradually evolved into resentment and violence among other Western tribes. The allusion to the better educational opportunities among the Omaha—an adjacent tribe often lauded by federal officials and religious missionaries for its "loyalty and cooperative spirit"—reinforced Prosser's underlying point about the connection between schooling and love for the nation.[94] To be schooled, even under a colonial curriculum, was nonetheless a path to feeling closer to federal authority.

Prosser's remarks about Native Americans illustrated the dual character of the Hoar Bill's imperialistic vision of public education. Throughout the speech, Prosser referred to "universal education" and "general education" as his theme and the goal of the Hoar Bill. Yet when he spoke about the Ho Chunk and the Pueblo people, he introduced another word: *civilization*. Prosser noted that under Spanish and Mexican rule, the Pueblo had been "instructed in the various arts of civilization, in the Spanish language, in religion, and the elements of a common-school education," only to backslide "to barbarism instead of improving" under US rule. Prosser's rhetoric conjured what he called a "scale of civilization"—a linear trajectory leading from barbarism through civilizing education—to common schools of the sort in which he had taught white Pennsylvanians. Prosser did not use the language of barbarism or civilization in reference to any of the other groups in his speech, referring instead in those cases to "ignorance," "illiteracy," or "impoverishment." Beneath these distinct terminologies were divergent conceptions of who would be included in a "school population, those preparing by education for the important duties of citizenship." These terms implied a limit to who had the capacity for sympathetic association in the body politic. With the imminent ratification of the Fifteenth Amendment, Prosser opted to speak of freedpeople's "elementary instruction" rather than their "civilization," a phrasing that implied that Black men had the capacity to be incorporated into the community of fellow feeling mediated by common schools.[95]

In "universal education," then, Prosser imagined a policy designed to produce fellow feeling even as it implied distinct pedagogical tracks based on racialized differences. In line with antebellum US policies toward colonized Indigenous peoples, education would aim—under a benevolent guise—to discipline Native American sentiments while forging loyalty to the republic. Education thus represented a way not only to negate the tragic compromises of federalism but also to bring a sense of coherence to the Republican Party's inconsistent (and unequal) treatment of marginalized populations throughout a growing empire.

George Frisbie Hoar's Advocacy for His Bill, June 1870

In June 1870, Hoar spoke to promote his own legislation. Whereas Prosser's address emphasized the management of distant feelings across a diverse empire, Hoar stressed the more immediate issues of protecting Black civil rights and strengthening sympathy between North and South. Echoing Sumner's contentions throughout the Reconstruction Act debates, Hoar insisted on the inadequacy of restoring the Union without intervening in the hierarchical culture of the South. In the rush to put the war in the past, he argued, Congress had failed to enact durable measures to protect Black civil rights or avert hostile relations between the sections. "You have busied yourselves to devise barriers of paper, parchment, wax—impotent as bands of tow against the fires of treason and hate," he warned. "I say that all these [legislative activities] are a snare and a delusion unless they are followed by ample provision for the education of the people."[96] Hoar implicitly recognized a view of federalism as a tragedy of divided affinities rather than a matter of defining rights and jurisdictional boundaries.

Following Sumner's lead, Hoar imagined the legislation as an emotional intervention that would place Southern states on a more egalitarian and republican foundation. In part, doing so meant ensuring that newly enfranchised Black citizens gained "defenses of intelligence and virtue" to protect their civil rights and republican institutions from future attempts to dismantle them. More fundamentally, reconstructing the South meant introducing an institution for Black and white Southerners alike that would instill the emotional dispositions required of stable republican rule. "Education is the strongest bond of a union which is to depend for its endurance on the attachment of the people," Hoar explained. "While the diversities of character and of opinion caused by pursuits, climate, race, interests are to have their full natural operation, let us not add to them the estrangement of feeling occasioned by ignorance."[97] Reinforcing Sumner's interpretation of the conflict between North and South, Hoar imagined his "national system" bill as a means of reorienting sentiments to better avert future resentments.

Going a step further than Sumner, Hoar made specific curricular recommendations. By engaging in common habits and behaviors, he speculated, children in different regions could develop a sympathetic connection to peers engaged in the same exercises elsewhere. Following Mann's precedent, Hoar drew inspiration from the Prussian school system. During the previous decade, Prussia had won the Austro-Prussian War and further consolidated its control over Germany, an outcome that Hoar believed demonstrated the wisdom of Prussia's policy of requiring military education within the schools: it both lessened the need for a constant standing army and, more important, forged deep national loyalties. Hoar claimed that the true reason for the Union's Civil War victory was "the soldier himself, intelligent, full of resources, educated, stimulated by that generous love of country which comes of knowledge of her history, knowledge of her institutions, [and] knowledge of her value to himself and to mankind." Calling to have "pupils drilled in military tactics," Hoar imagined a parallel curriculum across schools devised to ensure that students experienced identical routines that would, regardless of distance, help to produce common sentiments.[98]

The Republican Party's "New Departure" and Education, January 1871

In the months between Hoar's June speech and the early 1871 debate over the bill, the proposal for a national system of education emerged as a core part of the Republican Party's vision of emotional reunion. Following the passage of the Fifteenth Amendment and the readmission of most Southern states to the Union, many Northerners began to resist further assertions of federal authority predicated on the need to reconstruct the South. Once dismayed by the "absence of national feeling" in the South, Senator Carl Schurz (R-MO) insisted by late 1870 that restoring "fraternal feeling" between sections required that Northerners show "a spirit of peace and good-will" to the defeated South and bring Reconstruction to a close.[99]

Against this backdrop and in line with Prosser's appeals, Republicans reframed their support for education as not merely a sectional intervention but a policy of national scope capable of forging a multiracial, Protestant coalition across North and South.[100] Events abroad reinforced this appeal. When Prussia defeated Napoleon III's armies in the Franco-Prussian War, influential school reformers in Congress attributed the kingdom's victory to its pedagogical philosophy. According to Senator Henry Wilson (R-MA), Prussia's example provided a blueprint for a "New Departure" of the Republican Party. In a January 1871 *Atlantic Monthly* editorial, he raised the national profile of the Hoar Bill as the heart of this political program. Dismissing constitutional concerns, Wilson endorsed his Bay State colleague's bill as a way to forge a "composite nationality" from the "heterogeneous and discordant materials" of American culture.[101] Through this argument, Wilson aimed to shift educational argument from matters of legislative authority to questions of political identity and public sentiment. Without formally altering the structure of federalism outlined in the Constitution, he indicated that the Hoar Bill could dissolve conflicts of political emotion and in time make immaterial jurisdictional questions about state and federal authority. Published just a month before Hoar's final push for a national system, Wilson's editorial framed the ensuing House debate as a clash over the orchestration of national feeling.

Localist Resistance to the Hoar Bill, January-February 1871

While Republicans turned to the Hoar Bill as the cornerstone of a "New Departure," their Democratic rivals honed their defenses of local control arguments. As soon as the Hoar Bill was reintroduced during the final weeks of the Forty-First Congress, Representative John T. Bird (D-NJ) delivered a speech preempting reformers' appeals with an incisive critique of its educational logic. For a year, he had heard Hoar and Prosser frame the bill as a way to eliminate clashes over state and federal authority without altering the formal structure of the Constitution. Against this notion, Bird believed the legislation simply reframed the question of authority inherent to federalist systems by relocating the debate over decision-making to the schoolhouse.[102] Rather than avert battles over constitutional jurisdiction, Bird predicted, creating a national system of education would inaugurate ever more divisive debates over who would decide the feelings appropriate to the body politic. Bird took particular umbrage with the bill's provision that states could avoid federal intervention if they proved within one year that they had "a system of common schools which provides reasonably for all children therein." For Bird, questions of conflicting authority were unavoidable and left deceptively unclear by the bill: "How proved? By whom? By what authority? Who are the individuals to be summoned to testify as to the sufficiency of what the State proposes to do?" If these questions went unanswered, "there would be an endless controversy as to the honest execution [of the system], waxing warm and factious as party necessity might dictate or require."[103] In short, Bird argued, Hoar's proposed method to avert future battles over state and federal governance did no such thing. It only shifted those battles to a new argumentative front.

Tying the Hoar Bill to broader claims of corruption in the Republican ranks, localists framed the bill's vague ascriptions of authority as a ploy to turn the classroom into a vessel of political influence. Bird was mortified by talk of emulating the Prussian landwehr system, which he claimed had made Chancellor Otto von Bismarck "secure in the affections of the German people" and could have the same effect for President Grant.[104] Representative Michael C. Kerr (D-IN), who had previously taught in common schools, echoed Bird's anxieties, sharing concerns about reformers' overt calls to forge a national identity through the classroom.[105] Kerr implored his colleagues to consider seriously the implications of Prosser's vision of women teachers spreading sentiment across the republic. "Not content alone to invade the sacred functions of Statehood," he warned, "they seek by this bill to enter the domestic circle and to control the opening minds of infancy and youth." Alluding to Hoar's talk of tactical military training, Kerr likewise cautioned that the bill could "justify Congress in assuming supreme and minute control and regulation of the physical education and habits of the people." Rather than scoffing at the idealism of the common school proponents, Kerr's critique accepted their premises. He agreed—and feared—that schooling represented an extension of the domestic sphere and that teachers could forge sentiment through habit: "The very fountains of knowledge might be poisoned . . . to inculcate the superstitious, sectarian, or partisan opinions or fanaticism of a class, party, or denomination."[106] The policy was dangerous because it would work. Centralized schools could align the feelings of the nation toward a unitary political identity that Kerr would not accept.

Adding to Kerr's argument against centralization, localists insisted that the Hoar Bill would in reality impede reformers' goal of promoting common feeling. As a former rural school board member, Representative Thompson McNeely (D-IL) sympathized with what he called New England reformers' "zeal" for education.[107] Yet as a longtime opponent of consolidated educational authority in Illinois, he viewed Hoar's proposal with suspicion.[108] To "contribute . . . to the maintenance of free institutions," he argued, a movement for schooling had to emanate from existing local interest. An attempt to establish a national system would work against this end by interfering with communities' existing familial bonds. "Stand[ing] in the shoes of the parent," he explained, teachers were "clothed with a delicate trust" that could be fulfilled only by those familiar with community values, concerns, and investments. Violating that trust, educators under the Hoar Bill would pledge "loyalty to the Federal Administration" and thus "consult their own pleasure and peculiar notions as to their duties rather than the wishes of those among whom they are sent to act."[109]

Whereas Kerr worried that teachers would impose their will on students, McNeely argued that communities would simply turn their ire against public education itself. In the absence of meaningful ties to the community, such schoolteachers would provoke "outrage" rather than foster fellow feeling.[110] In taking this stance, McNeely offered a rival theory of education's relationship to public sentiment based on preexisting intimate relationships. Among New Englanders, the idea of in loco parentis was routinely invoked to justify the state's authority to prepare children for citizenship even when parents failed to do so at home.[111] McNeely turned that logic on its head, arguing that teachers operated best as direct representatives of parental prerogative. Attempts to promote reunion through the classroom would need to begin from localized emotional communities, not the chambers of Congress.

Republican Retreat and Democratic Revisionism, January-February 1871

As potential supporters of the bill were swayed by localist arguments, the Hoar Bill's proponents adjusted their rhetoric of federal intervention.[112] For Prosser, doing so meant confronting localists' notion that sentiment could be constrained within individual communities, a point belied by the fact of Southern rebellion. "The line of separation which divides State and national authority seems to be an imaginary one," he contended, and so "the defects, faults, and crimes of one member of the Union corrupt and demoralize those around it, and the whole body-politic suffers the consequences."[113] Based on this reasoning, a rural locale like McNeely's hometown of Petersburg, Illinois, did not reside within a silo: bad feelings cultivated there would spread throughout the republic.

As Prosser redoubled his commitment to shaping a union of feeling, Hoar pivoted away from his bold arguments from the previous June. Gone was talk of uniformity through military exercises. Gone was talk of federally mandated textbooks, which Commissioner of Education John Eaton Jr. had warned would rouse opposition.[114] Instead, Hoar made the more modest argument that his bill was in fact a "scheme for strengthening the power of the State and for preventing the consolidation of power at Washington." If each state's citizenry could make intelligent decisions, he reasoned, the odds of better-educated states dominating their rivals would dissipate. Placating concerns about federal administration of schools, he even conceded that he did "not believe, if we should pass this law, that it will ever be necessary to put it in force in any State of the Union."[115] The national system bill, then, was spun into a spur for state action. He accepted the idea that the prospect of federal involvement in schools was so odious that states would enact their own systems to avoid it.

Amid portents of Republican brainwashing, prospects of localist backlash, and Hoar's own reframing, the bill quickly lost momentum. The urgency of reformers' calls for legislation was sapped by localists' appeal for patience as the South pursued its own education policies. As Bird contended, public education was so self-evidently vital to the "peace, happiness, and prosperity" of communities that it "smacks too much of egotism" to suggest that Southerners would resist it. McNeely added that given the recent decimation of treasuries and school buildings by war, the South was "coming forward as rapidly as could be reasonably expected of them."[116] Strategically omitting the important role of congressional Radical Republicans—especially Sumner—in imposing educational requirements on the South, McNeely highlighted new state constitutions as proof of the region's commitment to schooling. The South could be trusted to administer its own schools fairly and equally; no further federal role would be needed to promote fellow feeling.

Erasing the crucial role of Black delegates in adding educational provisions to Southern state constitutions and Black legislators in enacting state school policies, McNeely further speculated that Southern whites would already have built effective systems if not "forced by Federal bayonets to stand back and submit to the rule of their late slaves." Through this completely counterfactual appeal, localists linked the Hoar Bill to broader currents of racist resentment and anticorruption sentiment brewing against the Republican Party at the start of the 1870s. Moreover, they resurrected James Madison's overly confident understanding of how a national school system would form. Unencumbered by federal oversight, state leaders would, as Bird put it, "provoke the people to emulation" of their neighbors' school systems.[117] Emotional union could thrive once again if only Republicans would step aside and let it. With that appeal, the localists helped stall the Hoar Bill's momentum. The Forty-First Congress closed without voting on the measure, leaving the next legislature at an impasse over the sources of sentiment in American classrooms.

DIVIDED LOYALTIES, RACIALIZED FEELINGS, AND THE AFTERMATH OF THE HOAR BILL DEBATE

Sumner's proposals and the Hoar Bill debate illustrate the allure of education as an intervention in public feeling. For policymakers reckoning with how to reestablish a nation on more egalitarian and less hostile foundations, the common school movement's rhetoric opened a horizon of possibility. Schooling made it possible to imagine Reconstruction as not just a legal and economic transformation of the South but also an emotional one. Common schools could get beneath the compromises over feeling that made federalism necessary, negating future tensions between state and national feelings. Part of what legal scholar Doni Gewirtzman describes as a postbellum rethinking of "the Constitution's emotion management function," portraying education as a constitutional guarantee elevated the role of feeling as a legislative consideration.[118] Amid the wider postbellum struggle over the scope of federal power, appeals to education thus widened the scope of what legislators believed they had power to change.

As part of education's intervention in public feeling, schools offered Republicans a malleable way to reimagine the formation of racialized emotions. For Sumner, education promised to produce sympathy between Black and white Southerners by aligning childhood experiences, deepening a sense of equality, and creating interracial proximity. In the face of many Northerners' deep pessimism about Black and white Southerners' capacities to coexist in peace, Sumner's educational philosophy insisted on thinking about other ways that feelings can shape collectives. Yet the logic of education also contained its own exclusionary implications. If schools aligned people in sympathy based on educational experience, it also arrayed them against those deemed unwilling or unable to be educated. In Prosser's account, appeals to universal education left intact underlying racialized assumptions about different groups' capacity to share in a community of fellow feeling. In this way, education provided a flexible basis on which to rationalize civic exclusions otherwise barred under the newly ratified Fourteenth and Fifteenth Amendments. As white settlers expanded their territorial domain further into the West, education thus provided them a means to manage the region's diversity without discarding accepted racial hierarchies.

For all the boldness of Sumner and Hoar's policies, the confrontation with localist opponents raised serious questions about the formation of national fellow feeling through schools. Neither reformers nor localists devoted much time to discussing pedagogical specifics. They all agreed that schools shaped feeling as an abstract proposition but said little about how they did so. That the Hoar Bill debate devolved into familiar contentions over "who decides" was telling. Introducing education to debates did not settle conflicts over feeling any more than did the Constitution's attempts to draw jurisdictional lines between state and federal authority. The substantive disagreements once displaced into the courts and the battlefield were now displaced to the classroom. The main difference was temporal. Rather than settle questions of feeling after they emerged through procedural authority, calls for national common schooling sought to settle emotional conflicts before they emerged. But the question remained: Whose feelings would be given priority in shaping future policy? The failure of the Hoar Bill began to answer that question in states' favor.

Localists' success in bringing the Hoar Bill to a quiet end was a major development in post–Civil War education reform. The efforts of Sumner and state constitutional convention delegates ensured that children across the South would have access to schools of some sort. But without enforcement mechanisms like those outlined in the Hoar Bill, federal officials would have no way to oversee those schools, monitor their curricula, or ensure that Black and white pupils received equitable support. Not until the 1880s debates over legislation sponsored by Senator William Henry Blair (R-NH) to provide federal education funds would another measure come close to the Hoar Bill's scope or potential implications. The result was that the schools Republicans built to instill fellow feeling in the South unfolded along uneven lines under Democratic Redeemer governments, reifying the feelings of superiority, inferiority, hate, disgust, and estrangement that Sumner had set out to dissolve.

The demise of the Hoar Bill did not spell the end of federal efforts to influence public feeling in the states through education, though it did quash the most direct attempts. Localists dismissed Hoar's efforts as a usurpation of local and state authority but remained open to some forms of federal involvement. McNeely thought that a common school policy modeled after the 1862 Morrill Act, which provided states with funding for colleges from the sale of public lands, would not interfere with the transmission of local feeling.[119] Hoar and other reformers adopted precisely that approach with their next major education bill in 1872. As they abandoned direct interventions modeled after Mann's Massachusetts reforms, these reformers embraced the emotional logics associated with policymaking in the Old Northwest and the recently founded Bureau of Education. Before schools could shape public feeling, proponents of education realized, communities had to form emotional attachments to schooling itself and associate it with national belonging. Rather than enforce education, they would first entice people to embrace schools by cultivating feelings of pride or shame in state systems.

Chapter Two

A SYSTEM OF SHAME
Founding the Bureau of Education, 1865-1872

Sixteen years after serving as the principal of a Cleveland, Ohio, common school, John Eaton Jr. returned to the city to begin a more daunting education leadership role.[1] The National Teachers' Association invited the newly appointed federal commissioner of education to speak to the group's annual convention in August 1870. There, Eaton sought to define his position to an audience of professors, principals, superintendents, and government officials, including President Ulysses S. Grant.[2] Even while New Englanders and numerous Radical Republicans in Congress fought to make Eaton the leader of a "national system of education," he defined his role in more modest, even delicate, terms. Education in the United States should be like a "flower clock," with an arrangement of plants, naturally blooming throughout the day, providing an accurate way to tell time. He imagined the Bureau of Education as the botanist spreading the seeds, water, and sunlight—that is, "scatter[ing] its publications freely among the people" to allow state systems to bloom in harmony. Aiming to assuage localist anxieties, Eaton stressed that the natural rhythms of each flower would be ruined by an overzealous gardener: his educational goals would be "defeated the moment harm is brought to the local vigor, wisdom, or results." Though this gentle metaphor departed from the interventionist logics of Massachusetts school reformers such as Representative George Frisbie Hoar and Senator Charles Sumner, Eaton advanced an argument that in a way was even more audacious. Eaton did not see a need for federally funded schools or a hierarchy of supervisors to produce a national school system. People would learn the virtue of education through exposure to bureau publications, in time coming to "regard each other's interests spontaneously by choice."[3] The bureau could bring about a cohesive, uniform school system through subtler acts of persuasion.

Eaton's approach reflected the reform philosophy of education leaders from the Old Northwest. Whereas Massachusetts and Connecticut reformers of the 1830s and 1840s primarily sought to systemize existing schools, reformers from the region spanning from the Ohio River to eastern Minnesota faced a different persuasive task. Driven by the religious concerns of the Second Great Awakening, they needed to generate initial public support for nondenominational, taxpayer-funded schools.[4] To forge national feeling through education, reformers from the Old Northwest sought first to instill emotional investments in schooling itself, taking a cue from the disciplinary practices of the common school classroom. Regularly employing dunce caps and public exhibitions, nineteenth-century educators understood that being seen by an audience of peers, community members, or the teacher could instill feelings of pride or more often shame in pupils.[5] Influenced by these feelings, pupils then internalized expectations and began to regulate their own behaviors.

Reformers in the Old Northwest adapted the emotional logics of pride- and shame-based pedagogy to state-level policy. They embraced a vision-centric approach to governance that aimed to address social problems by making them systematic, visible, and thus comprehensible.[6] Throughout the mid-1800s, the region's reformers pursued this goal by elevating government experts, distributing informational reports, and incentivizing local activity. Making such reports visible provided a mechanism to encourage local policymakers to feel pride or shame through juxtaposition with their neighboring communities. In the Reconstruction Congress, politicians including Representatives James A. Garfield (R-OH), Samuel W. Moulton (R-IL), and Mark H. Dunnell (R-MN) modified these techniques to connect seeing and shaming on a national scale. At the center of their efforts was a proposal to gather and propagate reports on the nation's schools through the federal Bureau of Education. The bureau would portray schooling as an object of state pride and shame, inspiring less-educated states to emulate their better-educated neighbors.

Though calculated to inspire less backlash than New Englanders' interventions, the bureau proved controversial in the emotional arena of Congress. Some Radical Republicans questioned whether the bureau's gaze would inspire meaningful change, preferring more direct forms of federal aid and intervention. Conversely, localists treated the Old Northwestern reform philosophy as a gateway to more insidious federal impositions on community and state control of schools. Policymakers also disagreed about the scope of the commissioner of education's position, clashing over whether the role should resemble that of a state superintendent, an association president, a journal editor, or something else altogether. After its 1867 founding, the bureau's survival remained in question. Claiming that the agency's reports diverged from the social scientific expectations of legislators, some critics questioned its capacity to truly see the status of state education. If the bureau could not see, it could not shame. On those grounds, critics tried to defund, discredit, and abolish it.[7]

Despite initial resistance to the bureau, its indirect approach to reform grew in appeal as the more overt designs of New Englanders succumbed to localist criticism and reactionary backlash. For education reformers who were reticent to concentrate federal power, the bureau promised a way to assert indirect influence through existing channels of state, local, and associational communication.[8] For this group, the benefits of national fellow feeling could be achieved without any form of federal mandate. Moreover, the shame-centric rhetoric of Old Northwestern reformers appealed to leaders worried about the South's emotional disposition. Concerned about a lack of remorse among Southern whites, many policymakers sought, in the words of Representative Samuel McKee (U-KY), "something more to humiliate" the region and "to make them obedient to the law as good citizens."[9] The bureau provided a way to inspire regret and contrition from Southerners without any need for federal bayonets—or even federal school inspectors. Instead, the agency inflamed the racist core of the South's culture of honor and stoked humiliation by statistical categorization, defining poor whites and freedpeople as equals in their ignorance.

Examining debates over the founding, renewal, and expansion of the Bureau of Education, this chapter argues that Old Northwestern reformers translated the pedagogy of pride and shame into an idiom of national reform. Whereas New Englanders critiqued regional pride as a source of disunion, the bureau's advocates reframed that pride as a resource. Igniting pride or shame in states offered a way to entice competition and emulation that would indirectly produce a common national system and with it, common feeling. Yet many policymakers doubted that the bureau could connect sight and shame, casting skepticism over the efforts of its first commissioner, Henry Barnard. In 1870, with Eaton at the helm, the agency redoubled its commitment to the sight-centric vision of the social sciences. Gradually, legislators began citing the agency's reports as its designers envisioned: to shame states into adopting education reforms. In 1872, as the bureau's place in federal debate grew more secure, Representative Legrand Perce (R-MS) proposed a bill to empower the commissioner of education to collect and administer a national common school fund to incentivize state activity. The debate over that legislation signaled an at times grudging acceptance of the bureau's role and its statistical suppositions. Even a number of Southern Democrats tacitly signaled their acceptance of a system that substituted statistical shame for direct federal intervention. As bureau proponents anticipated, Southerners defended their honor by heaping statistical scorn on Yankee states' educational failings.

The bureau's shame-centric approach to reform altered the language of educational argument in Congress. Like the New England reformers, proponents of the bureau sought to strengthen fellow feeling in pursuit of national cohesion. But they chose to do so along a paradoxical path. Rather than enforce education directly, they would instead provoke the anxieties, embarrassments, and boastfulness that animated the nation's myriad emotional communities. This policy worked as intended to a remarkable extent: many policymakers adopted the idiom of pride and shame, associating populations with "good" or "bad" feelings based on their commitments to education. In this way, the bureau and Perce Bill debates began to cement a view of education as an element of reconciliation between North and South. Part of the wider tragedy of Reconstruction-era education policy, this tenuous consensus was reached only by circumscribing the federal government's capacity to ensure equitable access to schools. Federal authority could attempt to influence how people felt about education but not education itself.

"SHALL FOREVER BE ENCOURAGED": PRIDE, SHAME, AND SIGHT IN THE OLD NORTHWEST, 1787-1866

Alongside apprehensions about disunion between Northern and Southern states, the founding generation anticipated threats to public feeling from the nation's Northwest. After the passage of the Articles of Confederation in 1781, members of the Congress of the Confederacy squabbled over how to allocate 260,000 square miles of land northwest of the Ohio River. Many legislators sought to sell and develop the land quickly to pay down war debts, stave off speculators, and preempt Indigenous peoples' potential organization against white settlement.[10] Yet others feared what would happen if the region were occupied by self-interested people susceptible to internal divisions or the influence of surrounding European powers.[11] In 1787, Virginia legislator Edward Carrington wrote that he hoped that the region would be settled by "men who will fix the Character and politics throughout the whole territory."[12] To attract and mold such a population, policy leaders turned to public education.

The founding generation made schools a cornerstone of the white settlement of the vast western territory. In 1785, Congress required that townships in the Old Northwest dedicate central sections of land to the construction of schoolhouses. Two years later, the Northwest Ordinance promoted republican institutions in the territory.[13] Anxious about the prospect of new states with unvirtuous populations entering the Union on equal footing, the drafters of the ordinance incorporated a vague but significant obligation: "Religion, morality, and knowledge, being necessary to good government and the happiness of mankind, Schools and the means of education shall forever be encouraged."[14] To meet this charge, political leaders of northwestern territories and states modified the language of the New England common school movement to meet the needs of a diffuse region with diverse religious and regional backgrounds. By the 1860s, they developed strategies of seeing that indirectly encouraged education by shaping pride and shame. The idiom of shame became central to education politics in the Old Northwest, reifying racial ideology and informing leaders' views on federal reform.

Despite the Northwest Ordinance's educational guarantees, many settlers found the expectation to maintain schools unreasonable and paternalistic.[15] Their reluctance was compounded by the denominational diversity of the region's settlers, whose religious disagreements made it difficult to forge common curricula.[16] Lamenting the slow spread of churches and schools, church leaders claimed that the region had succumbed to "infidelity, stupidity and licentiousness."[17] For Protestants in the early throes of the Second Great Awakening, this spiritual decay represented more than a threat to the future of the nation. They believed that the millennium—Jesus Christ's thousand-year rule in America—would be delayed by an intransigent and amoral public. At spiritual revivals, they sought to hasten Christ's reign through shared performances of shame and penance.[18] To diffuse sentiments of shame beyond their camp meetings, religious leaders turned to schooling as a vehicle for "awakening the social conscience of Protestant Christians."[19] By invoking shame, religious leaders urged the region's inhabitants to treat education as a subject of common concern. For Disciples of Christ founder Alexander Campbell, citizens deserved to feel "shame and guilt for those untaught thousands of adults . . . who cannot read the Saviour's name, nor one line of the gospel of eternal life!"[20] The blame for this illiteracy fell not on parents, he argued, but "the State," with culpability "distributed amongst" its citizens.[21] In this way, a rhetoric of shame and pride became the currency of school promotion in the Old Northwest.

Religious anxieties about moral erosion permeated schoolhouses as well, making shame-based pedagogy central to efforts to shape emotional communities. Even as parenting manuals, penal institutions, and New England common schools phased out many shame-based punishments by the 1830s, educators in the Northwest continued to rely on dunce caps and other strategies of humiliation.[22] Embracing the power of the communal gaze to make

GENERAL EXHIBIT FOR THE TERM ENDING ———, 186—.													
	Days in Term.	TICKETS		GRAMMAR			ARITHM'TIC		GEOGR'PHY		READING.		REMARKS.
		Good.	Bad.	Perfect.	Good.	Imperfect.	Perfect.	Good.	Imperfect.	Perfect.	Good.	Imperfect.	
John Stone...	60	60	...	44	10	6	50	10	...	45	12	3	41	11	9	....
Samuel Jones	58	56	2	...	...	...	47	11	2	46	10	...	36	18	6	.... [health.
James Smith	50	46	...	44	6	2	46	4	...	...	...	...	20	24	6	Detained by ill
Sarah Smith	60	60	...	52	8	...	44	10	6	46	10	4	38	14	8	............[first day.
Mary Pratt..	46	44	2	34	10	2	38	8	...	36	9	5	40	8	4	Did not commence
Susan Sharp	54	54	...	50	4	...	48	3	1	48	6	...	32	4	4	Good but irregular.

Figure 2.1. Table from William Slocomb, "School Government," *Ohio Educational Monthly* 18, no. 1 (1868): 5.

pupils beam or blush, inhabitants of the Old Northwest were also slower to replace public exhibitions with written examinations as a form of assessment.[23] Together, these modes of punishment and assessment inculcated in students a sense of being witnessed, a sense that was vital to what Sara Ahmed describes as shame's capacity to teach "the affective cost of not following the scripts of normative existence."[24] The curriculum of Old Northwestern common schools also reinforced shame's normalcy as an emotional structure of public life. Ohio professor William H. McGuffey's *Readers*, a series of texts ubiquitous in primary school classrooms, were designed to infuse reading instruction with a generalized Protestant morality, featuring readings that extolled the consequences of being "devoid of shame": "A young man is not far from ruin, when he can say without blushing, *I don't care what others think of me*."[25] Designed to train students to be hypervigilant about others' impressions, the pedagogy of pride and shame grew increasingly systematic by the 1860s. One issue of the *Ohio Educational Monthly* urged teachers to meticulously track student learning and behavior to display it "in a conspicuous place in the school-room on the day of the public examination" (figure 2.1).[26] Through such technologies, the religious idiom of shame became the foundation for practices of pedagogical influence.

As a language of educational promotion, the discourse of pride and shame provided a way to foster standardized public schools without a direct state intervention. People in the Old Northwest harbored a deep suspicion of centralizing authority in schools. Families with the most wealth and property wielded their disproportionate influence to avert state control, viewing schools as an investment over which they should retain autonomy.[27] Likewise, among Protestants who cooperated to form schools across disparate sects, state-directed education seemed dangerously akin to the hierarchical

Catholic schools they unequivocally opposed.[28] An effective approach to education reform needed to assuage these landowning and religious constituencies. So, whereas New Englanders such as Horace Mann promoted European structures of direct school supervision and control, reformers in the Old Northwest sought to empower states to engage in public persuasion. Following a trip to Prussia, Ohio reformer Calvin E. Stowe expressed less enthusiasm for that European model than his Massachusetts counterpart: "Among us, more must be left to popular action—to the free choice of the community—and less attempted in the way of positive legislative enactment."[29] To that end, the Old Northwest's reformers worked through such indirect persuasive channels as teachers' institutes and school journals.[30]

When reformers secured state educational leadership roles, they sought to be influencers rather than enforcers. Downplaying his own authority, Ohio's first superintendent, Samuel Lewis, insisted to the public that he was "powerless, except as your organ . . . laying before your legislature your several thousand voices."[31] For Lewis as for other Northwestern reformers, the goal was to amplify local pride and shame through vessels of statewide influence. As successful school districts came into existence, they were extolled as objects of pride for their more shameful neighbors to emulate. Pride and shame thus proved mutually complementary in the quest to shame more locales into embracing education.

To shape public feeling, reformers developed a vision-oriented rhetoric of governance through which educational progress could be "abstracted, ordered, [and] rendered legible."[32] Since the era of the Northwest Ordinance, settlers in the Old Northwest had purchased and settled land in a grid formation that encouraged systematic ways of seeing and developing the territory.[33] Especially in agriculture, the grid formation encouraged side-by-side comparative statistics for evaluating crop yields and other measures of farm productivity.[34] Education reformers devised a vision of educational promotion inspired by the model of agricultural associations and reports.[35] Drawing on the region's long-developing idiom, reformers like Lewis recognized that statistics could widen the pride or shame of locales to encompass whole states. Though Ohioans had no reason to "blush at a comparison of the Common Schools of [their] own State with those of any other land," he explained, statistics were necessary for "avoiding the imputation, that we neglect to educate our youth."[36] Heeding Lewis's call, school journals drew on statistics to link immoral behavior to unschooled ignorance.[37]

From the superintendent to the schoolroom, logics of seeing and shaming converged in a regionally distinct language of education reform that spread further west in parallel with agricultural settlement.[38] As state systems expanded, the region's reformers grew more convinced that their system of shame had worked as they envisioned. By midcentury, white citizens of Ohio, Indiana, and Illinois could report rising enrollments, more formally trained teachers, and greater taxpayer commitments to schooling than existed in many far older states.[39] The technologies that generated shame thus also provided a basis for pride among state leaders. As a group of Ohio University trustees put it in 1861, their state "is justly proud of her noble system of common schools. She occupies a prominent and most honorable position among her sister States in the cause of popular education."[40]

As the idiom of pedagogic pride and shame advanced across the frontier, it strengthened the role of schooling in legitimizing racial hierarchy. A reliance on shame produced an acute double bind for the state's Indigenous and free Black populations. The dominant racial ideology presumed that nonwhite peoples were incapable of feeling shame with meaningful depth yet also demanded ever-more assertive performances of shame as an unending path to assimilation.[41] Under the federal Civilization Fund Act of 1819, Protestant missions throughout the territory sought to induce Native American populations to accept a linkage between illiteracy, idleness, and shame.[42] At one mission for the Wyandot people of northern Ohio, students were warned that expulsion for misbehavior signaled "that they were too bad to live in society."[43] Yet white leaders cited a refusal or inability to be schooled as a rationale for expulsion even among populations that embraced white notions of education, conduct, and literacy.[44] These practices in turn warranted white settlement of territories occupied by those unwilling to be "civilized."

White citizens denied Black communities' demands for equal educational access before finally making some meager concessions in the late 1840s.[45] Recognizing the social status conferred on formal schooling, Black civic leaders were forced to accept the idiom of shame in their requests to white policymakers. As a resolution from the 1851 State Convention of the Colored Citizens of Ohio put it, the denial of schooling "degrade[s] us . . . we can never be good citizens without being educated."[46] As white Ohioans found themselves caught in the crosscurrents of national debates over slavery and racism, this tacit link between ignorance and degradation offered a compelling way to elide a language of biological inferiority.[47] When Ohio legislators finally opened schools to Black children in 1849, they did so on a largely segregated and unequal basis, thereby allowing whites to claim their privileges as deserved by education, not inherited based on race.[48]

Beneficiaries of the school system's inherent whiteness, the Old Northwesterners elected to the postbellum Congress treated their public schools as a point of pride. The spread of public education sustained regional myths about how enterprising (white) individuals had hewed an enlightened public out of a wilderness.[49] Buoyed by the establishment of new universities with funds provided by the Morrill Act of 1862, many policymakers from the region arrived to the postbellum Congress with the same zeal for public education as their colleagues from New England.[50] But the Old Northwesterners also brought a different understanding of what approaches to school reform would best serve the future of the republic. As a preacher for the Disciples of Christ, James A. Garfield echoed Alexander Campbell's shame-centric rhetoric of school promotion. During Garfield's time as president of the Ohio's Western Reserve Eclectic Institute, he lectured at teaching institutes and promoted school journals as part of the broader movement to systematize the state's schools.[51] He viewed educational influence as a matter of sustaining local efforts through information gathered and disseminated at the state level. In Minnesota, Superintendent of Public Instruction Mark H. Dunnell similarly promoted school reforms by waging a campaign to first shift public sentiment on behalf of common schools. As one critic put it, Dunnell's approach to reform entailed "circulars upon all conceivable sorts of subjects . . . fallen thick and fast over the state."[52] Elected to Congress, Garfield, Dunnell, and others shared a conviction that the mass dissemination of information about schools could and would shame the public into creating a unified national system after the Civil War. In pursuit of common feeling, these men focused on creating and strengthening a national Bureau of Education to hold states' educational failures up to the light of public critique.

"SHAME OUT OF THEIR DELINQUENCY": THE BUREAU OF EDUCATION STRATEGY, 1866-1867

Agitation for the creation of a Bureau of Education began almost as soon as the Civil War ended. Speaking to the National Teachers' Association in August 1865, Cleveland superintendent of schools Andrew Jackson Rickoff delivered an impassioned plea for a federal education agency as a Reconstruction priority on par with protecting the civil rights of freedpeople.[53] Four months later, Representative Ignatius Donnelly (R-MN) echoed Rickoff's argument in proposing a bureau "to enforce education, without regard to race or color, upon the population of all such States as shall fall below a standard to be established by Congress."[54] Like New Englanders' later proposal for a "national system of education," Donnelly's resolution represented a federal intervention that was too rapid for many members of Congress to accept. Adapting the rhetoric of indirect influence that shaped school reform in Ohio,

Indiana, and Illinois, Garfield developed a bill better attuned to the emergent but still reluctant state-building impulses of the Reconstruction Congress. Synthesizing familiar paeans to education with a nascent discourse of social science, Garfield and his supporters sought to convince Congress that merely seeing statistical reports would sufficiently shame state-level policymakers into reforming their school systems. This legislation was explicitly presented as a Reconstruction policy tailored for Southern whites' culture of honor and heightened susceptibility to racist shame in the wake of abolition.

Garfield's approach to bureau legislation borrowed from the vision-centric idiom of reform in the Old Northwest. Three months after Donnelly's failed resolution, the National Association of School Superintendents descended on Washington, DC, for its annual convention. To an audience that included several members of Congress, Ohio school commissioner Emerson E. White deferred to his state's tradition of seeing and shaming. Rather than enforcing education, his envisioned bureau would "induce each state to maintain an efficient school system" by issuing government-sanctioned reports.[55] After hearing the speech, Garfield invited White to his home, where they drafted a bill to create a "national department of education," basing the measure section by section on the legislation that had recently founded the Department of Agriculture.[56] A way to promise national influence without federal coercion, statistics formed the linchpin of Garfield's proposal. Enamored of treatises on political science, Garfield believed that a revolution was underway in theories of human government. As a Disciple, Garfield believed that God's word could be revealed without interpretation through an individual's direct engagement with the words of the Bible. Garfield viewed statistics as an extension of God's word—an objective and irrefutable expression of truth. As he asserted in a speech to the American Social Science Association, "We can control terrestrial forces only by obeying . . . those great laws of social life revealed by statistics."[57]

Samuel W. Moulton and Ignatius Donnelly's Theories of Influence, February–June 1866

When Garfield's bill reached the floor of Congress in June 1866, Moulton explicated its shame- and pride-driven approach to education reform. As a former teacher and an advocate in the Illinois legislature for a statewide school system, he drew on a nuanced knowledge of educational bureaucracy. Using his state as an example, he clarified the process of social scientific administration. Thirteen years earlier, the Illinois system had been "in chaos. We really had no educational system at all. . . . Everything was in confusion." The problem, as in the postbellum United States, was that "there was no common center; no one to advise, direct, and suggest." The introduction of a state superintendent charged with gathering and producing evidence provided that guidance. After instituting those mechanisms, Illinois now had "twelve thousand school districts established, with magnificent school-houses dotted all over the prairies, and every Monday morning when the clock strikes nine o'clock half a million of bright-eyed girls and boys are within the walls of the common schools."[58] The science of statistics had brought about a system in which student life imitated the superintendent's orderly charts and tables.[59] Moulton argued that the same process would unfold nationally under the aegis of a federal bureau that would "shed light in the dark places by disseminating facts and statistics, vitalizing and influencing by persuasion rather than by authority."[60] Even after a Civil War that had unequivocally demonstrated the limits of political persuasion, Moulton presumed that shame could exert persuasive force over behavior at both the individual and institutional levels. Just as public wall charts of student conduct and performances brought uniformity to frontier classrooms, simple exposure could bring schools themselves into alignment.

Whereas Moulton left the role of shame latent in his argument, Donnelly made it blatant: shame could drive reform by aggravating the ideas of honor central to the South's emotional community.[61] Northern policymakers knew well that white Southern men had long sustained their sense of honor through the subjugation and humiliation of enslaved Black people.[62] These leaders also knew that Southern honor demanded that acts of public shaming be met with performative rebukes to defend regional pride, reputation, and masculinity.[63] For Donnelly, the racial dynamics of Southern honor became a tool to influence the region's education policy. In February 1866, he advocated an amendment to the Freedmen's Bureau bill that would directly fund freedpeople's education. Citing census statistics to connect white illiteracy with support for secession, Donnelly claimed that his amendment could "strike out at one blow a large proportion of the ignorance of the South; we shame the whites into an effort to educate themselves, and we prepare thus both classes for the proper exercise of the right of suffrage." Key to Donnelly's argument was the connection of honor and white supremacy; he assumed that Black educational attainment would humiliate whites into building school systems. Speaking in support of Garfield's Bureau of Education bill in June, Donnelly drew on the same comparative statistical logic to compare white Southerners to their neighbors in Mexico. In a stream of slurs against poor whites and Mexicans, he mused, "How many degrees are the 'corn-crackers,' the 'sand-hillers,' and the 'clay-eaters' above the 'greasers' and 'guerrillas' of Mexico?" The bureau's reports would properly place "the dirty, unkempt hordes of ignorant men" who had fought for the Confederacy in the same inferior category as uneducated freedpeople and Mexicans, thus embarrassing white Southerners into making necessary reforms.[64]

In their implicit and explicit descriptions of the bureau's shame-centric mission, Moulton and Donnelly articulated a tension over the extent of the agency's influence. Critics' reactions drew attention to this tension. Responding to Moulton, skeptics pondered how disseminating statistics could concretely shape school systems. In 1866, policymakers still doubted that education could be "scientifically" influenced in the same way as agriculture—the analogy at the heart of the proposal. Representative Frederick Pike (R-MN) criticized the unclear and limited "machinery" of the bill, asking whether the bureau would "collect new facts" as the Census Bureau did, "send[ing] out its agents to gather them up and embody them," or would simply "take the returns of the different States and analyze them." Regardless of how it gathered its information, legislators questioned the domino-effect logic by which Garfield claimed the bureau would influence policy. Representative Samuel J. Randall (D-PA) lambasted the envisioned bureau's detachment from the lived realities of classrooms: the bill "does not propose to teach a single child, white, black or colored, male or female, its a b c's."[65]

While Moulton's critics argued that the bill would have no influence, those reacting to Donnelly's speech focused on his ambitious claims on the bureau's behalf and what those claims might portend. For Representative Andrew J. Rogers (D-NJ), Donnelly's attempt to shame poor whites signaled the encroachment of elitists "with their sheep-skin rolls and high sounding degrees" who would treat others as "groveling in low ignorance." Invoking the localist critiques that would soon derail proposals for a national system of education, he worried that the bureau would form the basis for future educational interventions and constitute a "warrant . . . to control and regulate the educational system for the whole country."[66] Together, the localists paradoxically cast the bill as both an impotent expenditure and an audacious consolidation of federal authority. Their vacillating critiques represented two poles of argument between which bureau proponents had to navigate with their novel appeal to social scientific influence.

James A. Garfield Threads the Needle of Influence, June 1866

At the close of the debate, Garfield sought to prove that a small bureau in Washington could shape faraway education policies and at the same time to dispel charges of federal overreach. He stressed that the federal government "does not allow us to establish a compulsory system of education, as is done in some of the countries of Europe." But such a mandate was not necessary to bring about a nationwide school system. In every state, reformers like Moulton were toiling to promote school systems with access to only superficial Census Bureau statistics and inconsistent state reports. The Bureau of Education would come to their aid by making visible the realities of educational disparity. By providing accurate and uniform data, the new bureau would enable "that power, so effective in this country, the power of letting in light on subjects and holding them up to the verdict of public opinion."[67]

For Garfield, "public opinion" entailed more than just support for or opposition to certain policies. It also encompassed a community's sense of pride or shame in managing problems of shared concern. By appealing to that pride or shame, Garfield noted, a single commissioner and a few clerks could indeed assert nationwide influence. If data for states without robust school systems could "be placed beside the records of such States as Massachusetts, New York, Pennsylvania, Ohio, and other States that have a common-school system," Garfield argued, "the very light shining upon them would rouse up their energies and compel them to educate their children." To illustrate his point, he rattled off a series of statistics demonstrating the financial commitment to common school education "in my own State of which I am most proud." If such information were revealed to other states' citizens, they would long to share in Ohio's pride and feel embarrassed about their own systems' shortcomings. "The very light" of bureau reports "would shame out of their delinquency all the delinquent States of this country."[68]

Garfield also directly exhibited rhetorical strategies of seeing and shaming. By invoking educational statistics, he constructed categories of intelligence and ignorance in ways that recast hierarchies of race, class, and nativity. Garfield drew on census data to portray 800,000 illiterate "American-born citizens" as part of the same category as immigrants and freedpeople, warning that "we must make them intelligent, industrious, patriotic citizens or they will drag us and our children down to their level."[69] Garfield relied on the bureau's vision-centric logic in two ways. First, he naturalized an implied "us"—white, self-made, Protestant, native-born Northerners—that was superior to an ignorant "them" by virtue of educational attainment rather than religion, race, or birthright. Showcasing the rhetorical force of education as a way to redraw categories of citizenship, Garfield's appeal posited the fate of his House colleagues' social standing—and thus their sense of dignity and pride—as contingent on the continued education of those lower in the hierarchy.

Second, Garfield's appeal constructed a category of "ignorance" that cut across racial lines. He placed the bill's implied legislative targets—poor white people in the "delinquent States" in the South—in the same category as uneducated formerly enslaved people. Garfield's deployment of interracial shaming was subtler than Donnelly's but relied on a similar assumption: the prospect of being grouped with Black people based on education would inspire white people to invest in schools. In short, then, both Garfield's bureau proposal and his wider advocacy assumed a theory of emotional influence based on stoking shame through visibility and comparison. Whether contrasting states or demographic categories, the evidence collected by the bureau would produce an emotional ecology that would motivate states to invest both financially and emotionally in their schools.

Through policies of seeing and shaming, Garfield sought a route to shaping fellow feeling that was more circuitous than were the direct interventions proposed by his Massachusetts colleagues. For Garfield, transforming public feeling through schools demanded that policymakers first alter how communities felt about schools. He believed the surest way to do so was to channel communities' feelings of hostility, jealousy, and resentment toward each other in more productive ways. By linking education to the pride and shame felt by residents of various states or members of demographic groups, Garfield believed, people would be convinced to place resources in education. Once school systems existed, they would dissolve the regional, racial, and religious prejudices that had made schooling necessary. In the end, Garfield believed that his proposed bureau would obtain the same results as his colleagues' more assertive legislation. A small investment in a bureau of education in earlier decades "would have saved us the blood and treasure of the late war," he argued, and would "save our children from a still greater calamity" in the future.[70] Garfield's shame-centric bill made greater headway than other education legislation proposed in the Reconstruction Congress, but it too went down to a narrow 61–59 defeat in a House vote taken after his June 8, 1866, speech. Unfazed, Garfield proposed the bill again on June 19. This time, thanks to behind-the-scenes lobbying, the bill passed by a margin of 80 to 44. The bill swept through the Senate.[71] But despite the measure's passage, promoting the idea of shame-based influence had been difficult. Continuously demonstrating the efficacy of that idea to a contentious and skeptical Congress would prove even more challenging. Legislators from different regions and emotional communities had competing ideas of what a "scientific" education report should look like and how it might circulate shame. Appointed commissioner of education, Henry Barnard soon became acutely aware of these tensions as he struggled to adapt his experiences as an education professional to the vexing demands of federal administration. Over the next three years, congressional critiques shaped bureau research to better reflect Garfield's initial concept of a system of shame.

"LET THEM BLUSH": REFINING THE BUREAU'S VISION, 1868-1871

The bureau's advocates and agents immediately felt the pressures of Reconstruction-era politics. President Andrew Johnson had considered vetoing the bill prior to its enactment until he received assurances that it would merely expand on the work of the Census Bureau.[72] In February 1868, less than a year after the Bureau of Education began operating, members of the House Committee on Appropriations attempted to quietly deny its funding. Incensed, Garfield compared eliminating the agency to tearing down a valuable lighthouse and proudly declared, "I am not one of those who seek to pluck out the eyes of the nation." Echoing Garfield, Donnelly defended the bureau as "an eye watching the condition of that whole country, in an educational point of view." But opponents remained doubtful regarding the bureau's purported vision. One of many Republicans who challenged the new agency, Theodore M. Pomeroy of New York, retorted that the agency was "but a glass eye; it has no sight in it; it has no power; it cannot inspect the system of education anywhere in the United States."[73] These visual metaphors revealed a lack of clarity about what the state should see in education and an underlying confusion about the role of social scientific shaming as an approach to federal policy. Over the three years of Barnard's tenure at the helm, this confusion resulted in attacks on the bureau's supervisory ability, scope of research, and professional domain. Once Eaton took over, the bureau made overtures toward a more statistics-centered approach to research, which led to a more prominent role in Congress's deliberations. In debates over censoring Eaton's work, policymakers invoked the bureau's publications as Garfield had intended, with legislators imputing feelings of shame in reaction to its findings.

Critiquing the Bureau's Vision under Henry Barnard, 1868-1870

Continuing critiques first made during the June 1866 bureau debates, many in Congress still doubted that aggregating data about literacy rates, school funding, and student attendance would have any meaningful influence on state systems. Surprisingly, many of these skeptics were Radical Republicans who otherwise endorsed federal intervention, including in education. For Garfield, the most shocking opposition came from Representative Thaddeus Stevens (R-PA). Three decades earlier as a state legislator, Stevens had established a firm reputation as an advocate of public schools.[74] In his 1866 speech advocating the bureau's creation, Garfield had lavished praise on the elder statesman's "earnest and brave eloquence," which had given "a noble system of common schools to Pennsylvania."[75] Stevens was not flattered. He blindsided Garfield, voting against the bureau and in 1868 calling for its abolition.[76] How did Garfield so miscalculate Stevens's position? In part, his error stemmed from the regional and generational differences that shaped how the two figures became educational advocates. In 1835, Stevens was fighting for the principle of public schools against legislators who sought to maintain a stratified system of pauper and private schooling. By contrast, Garfield's university leadership began four years after the passage of Ohio's 1853 statewide law requiring local tax-funded common schools.[77] Where Stevens had been an evangelist for public education as a fundamental need, Garfield's priorities had been closer to the systemizing efforts of superintendents in the Northwest. For Stevens, common school advocacy did not entail "the gathering up of these facts by" Barnard, whom Stevens described as a "worn-out man."[78] Instead, Stevens saw a more immediate need to directly demonstrate education's merits to a reluctant public. To that end, he thought that the funds devoted to the bureau would be better spent on a model school system in Washington, DC.

Other Radical Republican adversaries of the bureau represented districts with competing educational priorities, maligning the bureau as too far removed from material human need. Representative John F. Farnsworth (R-IL), for instance, questioned how Barnard—"a gentleman stuck up here in the third or fourth story of some building in Washington"—could somehow influence a student's learning by disseminating "learned statistics" to other men "who never were inside a school-house." The bureau's approach, Farnsworth inveighed, privileged "a book for the learned" over resources for those in need: "If this was an appropriation to purchase school-books, spelling books, and primers, to be distributed among the poor for the country, "I would vote for it." Farnsworth objected to the analogy between the Department of Agriculture and the bureau on which Garfield relied to pitch the bureau, arguing, "You cannot send out education as the Commissioner of Agriculture does seeds, done up in parcels." He believed that Garfield had "gone mad on the subject of statistics."[79] Beyond just stoking anti-intellectual resentments, Farnsworth was speaking on behalf of a constituency with an acute need for concrete educational aid. His Illinois district included Chicago, which was experiencing explosive population growth.[80] Schools there had struggled to keep pace with rising demand: between 1865 and 1867 alone, the city acquired more than $680,000 in loans and state-issued bonds to erect new schoolhouses.[81] Against that backdrop, Farnsworth had reason to malign the bureau's approach to reform as obtuse. His city did not need to be shamed into founding schools: it needed the resources to do so.

In their critiques of the bureau, many members of Congress questioned the supervisory capacities of the commissioner of education. For someone who was supposed to be the eyes of the nation, Barnard proved notoriously difficult to find. Legislators lamented his tendency to spend most of his time in Connecticut and cracked jokes about the whereabouts of his office, which was frequently relocated to inconvenient corners of Washington. While in the nation's capital, Representative Thomas Jenckes (R-RI) ran into a Southern school commissioner searching for information about other states' public schools who was surprised to learn of the existence of the bureau and its commissioner. Representative John F. Benjamin (R-MO) bluntly asserted that no one in Congress "could tell where the office was located, or what it had been doing, or what had been the result of its labors." To feel shame requires a sense of being watched, an internalized if not an actual gaze.[82] If the commissioner could not be seen, who would notice him watching?

Somewhat paradoxically, congressional critics also disparaged the agency for trying to see too much, attacking the composition of Barnard's unruly nine-hundred-page annual report.[83] Though none of the content was unusual for educational research at the time, members of Congress were baffled by what Senator Thomas A. Hendricks (D-IN) dubbed "a collection of floating matter." He could not fathom how this "gathering together of old things" would provide more helpful information to teachers than the more up-to-date, synthetic, and concise annual report of Indiana's superintendent. Even the bureau's supporters conceded that the reports strayed from Garfield's synoptic ideal. Following Barnard's resignation in May 1870, Senator Philetus Sawyer (R-WI) described what he saw as the only viable future for the bureau—publishing narrowly tailored reports featuring state-by-state statistical comparisons.[84]

Focusing the Bureau's Vision and Applying Shame, 1870-1871

When Eaton became commissioner of education in 1870, he reoriented the bureau toward Garfield's original vision. He found that Barnard had left the office "so crowded with books, pamphlets, and desks as to be wholly unfit for successful clerical work."[85] Eaton envisioned his task as bringing visible structure to his predecessor's untidy efforts. His résumé suited him to the challenge of organizing chaos: he had organized support camps for people fleeing slavery during the Civil War, restructured the Freedmen's Bureau to partner with aid agencies, and served as superintendent of public instruction in Tennessee during a period of postwar tumult.[86] In the first three years of his term, Eaton revised the commissioner's role to address congressional critiques. His first report differed markedly from Barnard's in both form and

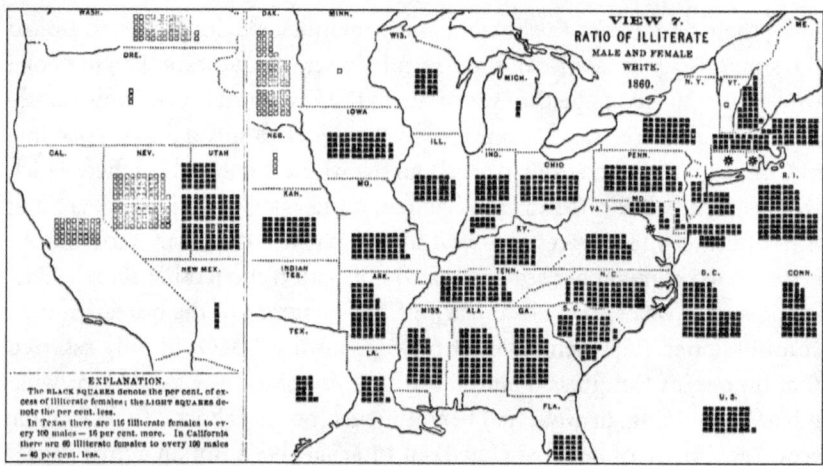

Figure 2.2. "Ratio of Illiterate, Male and Female, White, 1860," in *Report of the Commissioner of Education Made to the Secretary of the Interior for the Year 1870* (Washington, DC: Government Printing Office, 1870), 492.

content: one of its features was identically formatted comparisons of various state systems.[87] Even with a large appendix full of miscellaneous topics, the report more closely resembled a Department of Agriculture or Census Bureau report than anything Barnard had published. In perhaps the closest attempt to capture Garfield's original proposal, Eaton incorporated a section of "Bird's Eye Views" of illiteracy rates by state. Innovatively for American government reports at the time, these consolidations of Census Bureau data purported to provide "'pictures of numbers'" as they would appear "to the eye of a person passing over in a balloon" in each state (figure 2.2).[88] Directly relating demographics of race, birthplace, and gender, the charts invited comparisons of the sort Donnelly and Garfield propounded four years earlier.

As Eaton shifted the bureau's focus, its logic of showing and shaming began to influence congressional debate. On February 11, 1871, Senator Thomas Bayard (D-DE) objected to printing and distributing Eaton's report unless the section on his state was "expunged." Unable to obtain any official information about Delaware, Eaton had begun that section of the report with a terse statement: "There appears to be an absence of any school supervision." Lacking a state report or meaningful data, he instead included quotations from anonymous educators criticizing state schools. Bayard was particularly offended by the claim that "boys did not stand in a straight line when they stood up to spell, and that they spat tobacco juice." The ensuing argument centered on the question of what could be considered scientific evidence, what the synoptic state should see, and at what level of abstraction it should describe educational conditions.[89]

Bayard ultimately persuaded the Senate to strike the page from Eaton's report to rebuke him for using unverifiable commentary.[90] At the same time, many senators interpreted Bayard's protest as proof of the agency's efficacy as an instrument of shame. If Delaware was frustrated by the lack of statistics, Senator Frederick A. Sawyer (R-SC) mused, that was a spur for the state to develop much-needed structures of leadership: "Let the people of Delaware... take care that in the next report they are fairly represented." Senator William M. Stewart (R-NV) agreed: "Let them blush, not the Senate.... When States appear to disadvantage a few times in this report, they will furnish the necessary information."[91] Inferring shame from Bayard's words, Stewart's remark employed the bureau's report as Garfield had envisioned, connecting feelings of embarrassment to the need for state-level change. The bureau had facilitated a discourse of shaming as an indirect alternative to federal intervention.

"HUMILIATING TO OUR NATIONAL PRIDE": THE PERCE BILL AND SOUTHERN HONOR, 1872

As the bureau cemented its role in congressional debate, it offered a compelling model for Republican policymakers. With the demise of Hoar's proposal for a "national system of education," reformers retreated from their calls for direct federal intervention.[92] During Congress's December 1871 holiday recess, Hoar and other Republican members of the Committee on Education and Labor regrouped to discuss "the relation of the National Government to education" and the "adoption of one general measure on that subject."[93] Disconnecting the bill from Hoar's name, the committee enlisted Representative Legrand Perce (R-MS) to serve as its sponsor. They also relied on Dunnell, now a representative from Minnesota, to draft parts of the bill, incorporating reform strategies he had developed as superintendent of the state's common schools.[94]

With Perce and Dunnell's leadership, the final bill combined the Morrill Act's land grant model with the statistical ideology of the Bureau of Education. The Perce Bill called for a perpetual common school fund generated through land sales and apportioned based on population. Debates over the legislation evinced a growing acceptance of showing and shaming as both a rhetorical tactic and a mode of policy influence. As Perce Bill advocates heaped statistical and racialized shame on Southern states, embarrassed targets defended their honor in ways that met their rivals on common rhetorical ground. By the time the House voted on the legislation, a growing number of policymakers—including some outspoken opponents of the Perce

Bill—adopted the idiom of pedagogic shame. Above all, they embraced the Old Northwest's core reform premise: educational attainment, measured by literacy or other means, was a matter of state pride or humiliation.

Building on the Bureau of Education's Shame-Centric Approach, January-February 1872

Extending Garfield's vision for the bureau, Dunnell advocated the Perce Bill as a way to assist local reformers struggling to persuade state legislatures. Given financial assistance, he argued, "educational people in those States may gather about this sum, and persevere in the work of organization, and it may widen and spread." As the bill sought to indirectly incentivize state activity, it also proposed strengthening the bureau's ability to see state-level education actions. Citing abuses of Morrill Act funds, Perce explained that the bill would grant funds only to states that prepared thorough reports on school finance, enrollment, and other statistical measures.[95] Cleverly, the bill's advocates framed this data-collection as voluntary. If states wanted federal funding, they needed to show how they spent their money; if they opposed federal involvement, they could choose to forgo the funds. Acceptance of those terms would furnish the Bureau of Education with more materials from which to develop reports, enhancing its sight and capacity to foster pride and shame.

An enthusiastic supporter, Garfield praised the Perce Bill's roots in the reform tradition pioneered by Ohio. Rather than emulating New Englanders' Prussian-inspired approach of imposing reforms from above, the Perce Bill eschewed "any control over the educational system of the States" and instead merely "require[d] reports of what they do with our bounty; and those reports brought here and published for the information of the people will spread abroad the light, and awaken the enthusiasm and emulation of our people."[96] Tailored to reconcile reformers' concerns for national feeling with localists' anxieties about federal control, the Perce Bill would promote nationwide reform through emotional channels.

Perce Bill advocates centered their arguments on Southern states' refusal to finance, support, and mandate education, which failed to instill proper moral character among citizens. Delaware—a former slave state that lacked compulsory schooling—again became a target of criticism. Representative Washington Townsend (R-PA) feigned incredulity at the state's illiteracy rates, given the "highly prized and benign educational institutions" its leaders favored: "the whipping-post and the pillory." Townsend's quip implied that Delaware needed the punitive discipline of public forms of shaming to remediate the character of adults who failed to internalize proper character in school.[97]

Hoar similarly combined moralistic rhetoric with the idiom of pedagogic shame to single out states with high illiteracy rates. In Arkansas and Florida, widespread illiteracy weakened the "general brainpower," limiting new inventions and patents. In Tennessee, where "the Ku Klux Klan ... burn the school-house and murder or whip the teacher," "county after county" had no one enrolled in schools. In Kentucky, a border state where "Democratic rule has been uninterrupted for years," nearly three-fourths of the "native white population" remained illiterate. Hoar added that the numbers were probably worse than they appeared, since "the pride of the ignorant person" likely caused them to mislead census takers.[98] In linking illiteracy rates to state failures and prejudices, Hoar thus aimed to decouple ignorance from feelings of pride. That dissociation was the linchpin of advocacy for the bureau and the Perce Bill: only if people accepted ignorance as shameful would the agency's efforts at statistical persuasion have their intended effects.

As they condemned uneducated states, the Perce Bill's advocates invoked education as a way to redistribute shame across racial lines. This was explicit in Perce's opening argument for the bill, in which he described "free-born American citizens, white men, who in all the debasement of ignorance are upon a level with the lowest of our Indian tribes."[99] The most incisive version of this appeal was advanced by Representative Joseph Rainey (R-SC), a formerly enslaved person. His mere presence in the House offended white supremacist notions about his place in society.[100] Keenly aware of these racial dynamics, Rainey began his argument by addressing Southern claims that the Perce Bill could desegregate schools. To embarrass the members of the South's plantation class, he confronted their hypocrisy about racial intimacy: "Why this fear of the negro since he has been a freedman, when in the past he was almost a household god, gamboling and playing with the children of his old master? And occasionally it was plain to be seen that there was a strong family resemblance between them."[101] In insinuating that enslavers raped and fathered children with their slaves, Rainey echoed an antebellum Northern appeal that, as Susan Zaeske says, "stabbed brutally at the heart of Southern honor," in large part "because it was true."[102] After rebuking Southern whites' alleged concerns about racial "mixing," Rainey speculated that the "appalling array of illiterate" people exposed in Bureau of Education reports meant that Southerners resisted the Perce Bill because they feared "competition with a negro" on terms of equality. "In the southern States it was a pride in the past to exult in the extraordinary ability of a few representative men, while the poorer classes were kept illiterate and in gross ignorance," he explained.[103] Free, compulsory schools—especially integrated ones—thus directly threatened the undeserved privilege of the South's white elite, casting doubt on the region's conception of honor.

Defending Southern Honor from Pedagogic Shame, January-February 1872

The shaming strategies used by figures such as Townsend, Hoar, and Rainey were no longer directed at empty seats in the House. Every seceded state had rejoined the Union, and several were represented by Democratic politicians. These men responded predictably to provocations of their honor, issuing indignant defenses of their states' reputations. Representative John Critcher (D-VA) explicitly replicated the procedure of a duel, "ventur[ing] to offer a challenge to" Hoar: a debate over who could provide a better "illustration of intellectual superiority and moral excellence" in his state's history. Less predictably, many Southern Democrats acceded to the basic premise of reformers' argument, accepting that state pride could and should be gauged by commitments to public schooling. Representative John M. Bright (D-TN) rose to challenge Hoar for making "a statement which scandalizes the educational reputation of Tennessee." While "county after county" lacked publicly funded common schools, the state had an "independent system of education" that taught more children. He conceded that "Tennessee, in its educational statistics, may not compare favorably with the ancient Commonwealth" represented by Hoar but protested that Tennessee had had less time to develop an education system and a more diffuse population to teach. Similarly, Representative Archibald T. MacIntyre (D-GA) accepted Townsend's allegation that "every other one in [Georgia] is illiterate" but insisted that the numbers had been inflated by the high illiteracy rate among formerly enslaved people. Still, according to MacIntyre, his party and state favored "the education, not only of the whites, but of the blacks" and had in the prior month appropriated funds to that end. In conceding their states' illiteracy, Bright and MacIntyre accepted the logic of shaming implicit in the Perce Bill, objecting mainly to its application to their states and to its failure to differentiate illiterate populations by race.[104]

For many of the South's defenders, embracing alternative educational measures allowed them to redirect feelings of shame back toward their critics. Drawing on his background as a rural county school official, Representative John B. Storm (D-PA) offered immorality as an avenue to counter-shame New Englanders.[105] In his view, the Perce Bill faltered in its narrow "mathematical" assumption "that education is simply the training of a man's intellectual faculties." The problem was the presumption "that a man who is educated is worth about twenty-five per cent more than a man who is not." Citing the decline in Massachusetts's native-born population, Storm warned that this view of schooling could erode the "moral and physical" health of a society, a problem truly "humiliating to our national pride." As Storm redefined the basis of pedagogic shame to encompass population data, Representative Benjamin Biggs (D-DE) impugned Massachusetts schools for failing to avert criminality. "You would suppose that they were all saints up there with their great learning," he scoffed, yet statistics revealed a high rate of embarrassing crimes, among them "horse-stealing," "polygamy," and "selling obscene prints." Confronted by laughter from the galleries, Hoar tried to save face for his state by attributing such crimes to "persons of foreign birth, every one of whom votes the Democratic ticket!" Yet the idiom of pedagogic shame cut across the categories of native and foreign-born: no matter the criminals' place of birth, Biggs argued, "the State of Massachusetts must father them."[106] These arguments demonstrated how the ambiguity of "education" and "ignorance" made pedagogic shame a flexible language of policy influence. More important, in co-opting reformers' idiom to attack Massachusetts, they helped solidify the relationship between a state's honor and its educational commitments.

The Outcome of the Perce Bill Debate, February 1872

Even as Southerners and New Englanders performed the idiom of pedagogic shame, the underlying logic of the Perce Bill persuaded policymakers from both regions. Though critics identified the legislation as a "cunningly-devised measure" to create a national system "by indirection," the bill passed the House on the strength of its interregional and bipartisan support. Five Southern Democrats backed the bill, as did such staunch localist Northern critics of the Hoar Bill as Storm and Representative Michael C. Kerr (D-IN).[107] In doing so, these Democrats signaled a growing willingness to support education as an element of national reconciliation—but only if Republicans made numerous compromises. First, fretful about Sumner's concurrent arguments for racial integration in the Senate, Democrats refused to support the Perce Bill until an amendment guaranteed that its funds could not be denied to states with racially segregated schools. Second, Southerners hesitated to support the bill until an amendment promised to allocate funds based on the "ratio of illiteracy" in every state.[108] This shift ensured that the vast majority of the funds distributed under the bill would support education in the South, an appealing proposition in a region deep in debt. This change also affirmed literacy and illiteracy as measurable demographic categories that could form the basis of targeted policymaking. The bill thus won an unusual coalition in the House.

However, the Perce Bill died in the Senate Committee on Education and Labor, where it was repeatedly deferred until the end of the second session of the Forty-Second Congress. Senator Justin Smith Morrill (R-VT)—the architect of the 1862 education bill that bore his name—quietly killed the bill, a choice that Hoar later attributed to Morrill's pride in his legislation.[109] Nevertheless, the Perce Bill debate represented a key moment in Reconstruction-era education discourse. That a major national education bill had passed in the House with bipartisan support signaled that the Old Northwest's approach to reform had more persuasive traction than the heirs to Mann's common school movement. The ubiquitous use of shaming in the debate by both the bill's supporters and its opponents illustrated that the orchestration of emotion could exert indirect influence on policy decisions. In the end, invoking pedagogic pride and shame allowed policymakers to make judgments about states' commitments to education and with it, their dedication to emotional reunion.

SHAME, PRIDE, AND FEDERAL INFLUENCE IN EDUCATION

Over six years, the Bureau of Education went from rejected legislation to an established government office. By 1871, even Farnsworth, the bureau's most persistent critic in the House, admitted that it would be "impossible to get rid of, however useless it may be."[110]

In preferring the Old Northwest's vision of educational change over New England's, Congress pursued an alternative understanding of schooling's relationship to federalism. During debates over the Reconstruction Acts and the Hoar Bill, Massachusetts policymakers had posited schooling as a way to alter the emotional foundations of states to instill republican feeling and sympathy toward fellow citizens. In the words of Representative Henry L. Dawes (R-MA), state boundaries were "imaginary lines" that schooling would gradually blend into a common national sentiment.[111] In contrast, policymakers from the Old Northwest accepted the perpetuity of divided sovereignty even as they sought to minimize the divided loyalties it produced. Rather than reject James Madison's hope that states would emulate each other's systems, the Bureau of Education and Perce Bill sought to nudge forward processes of emulation. The result was a paradoxical approach to altering public feeling: fostering national loyalty by stoking state pride. Competition would beget sympathy and cohesion.

Many members of Congress found this approach compelling because it adapted federal policy to the forces they tacitly understood as already and invisibly driving educational change. For much of the nineteenth century, the federal government exerted significant influence over public policy but did so at a remove. Federal policymakers collaborated with state, local, economic, and associational actors to promote policy change, acting through what Brian Balogh describes as the "braided nature of public authority."[112] For this reason, Williamjames Hull Hoffer argues, most postbellum Republicans willing to expand federal power gravitated toward policies of "sponsorship, supervision, and standardization" that left the labor of policy implementation to actors outside the federal government.[113] They consequently found comfort in Garfield's contention that "a great American system of education" already existed, driven by a combination of local, voluntary, and individual efforts. For federal inducements to work, he argued, they had to be made "through the channels of this, our American system."[114] The bureau and Perce Bill debates thus reified a federal preference for modes of policymaking based on government reports and inducements, suggesting a rhetorical path for future policymakers while constraining the possibilities for direct federal action.

By beginning to build a consensus around a weaker form of federal educational influence, the bureau and Perce debates were key episodes in Reconstruction-era education reform. That several Democratic policymakers vociferously opposed the Hoar Bill but pivoted to vote for the Perce Bill captured an emerging cross-regional and bipartisan acceptance of education as a national concern. At the same time, Democratic acceptance depended on Republicans' willingness to compromise regarding many fundamental New England ideals, removing most federal authority over states' school spending and allowing racial segregation. The rest of Reconstruction would follow a similar course. As moderate Republicans began to call for an end to Reconstruction and a rapid reconciliation with the South, they became more willing to discard policy interventions championed by the antebellum common school movement. These leaders became less concerned with the specific form education would take as long as it took some form. For Democrats, especially in the South, state-run, taxpayer-financed education became akin to the Reconstruction Amendments: an outcome of the war they would accept as a condition of reunion but only on their terms. The Perce Bill debate thus captured shifting partisan assumptions about schooling that reverberated well into the 1880s.[115]

As the Bureau of Education and Perce Bill debates reshaped the partisan politics of federal education policy, they also helped to reinforce literacy as a proxy for evaluating populations' capacity for fellow feeling. The pressure on the Bureau of Education to produce uncontroversial modes of comparison led its supporters to foreground literacy as a key measure of educational attainment. Literacy appealed to policymakers as a way to collapse various civic categories, combining the populations many Republicans deemed threatening to public feeling—uneducated freedpeople, white rebels, and immigrants—into a single population of "illiterates." At the same time, literacy also allowed these populations to be placed side by side to accentuate their progress relative to each other, facilitating the circulation of pedagogical pride and shame. During a time of shifting legal boundaries of citizenship, literacy's illusory objectivity made it a powerful way to warrant the exclusion and inclusion of groups deemed incapable of sharing in a community of fellow feeling. Though presented as objective, literacy was still complicated to measure; it could be used to legitimate an array of civic exclusions. Several members of Congress raised this concern during the debate over the Fifteenth Amendment, attempting in vain to bar states from restricting voting rights based on education.[116] By making literacy a centerpiece of educational persuasion and a basis for policy, both the bureau and the Perce Bill helped reify the idea that literacy could warrant denying a population's full inclusion in civic life.

Even as Congress debated the scope of federal educational influence, federal military agents on the ground in the South were actively working to support freedpeople's education. Collaborating with Northern missionary agencies, the Freedmen's Bureau at its peak supported the education of nearly 250,000 students.[117] Amid the patriotic fervor of war and its immediate aftermath, policymakers invoked the altruistic sacrifices of white women teachers to marshal feelings of optimism in support of the Freedmen's Bureau. Capitalizing on its status as a military agency, legislators framed its labors as a means of protecting the work of missionary agencies and their educators. Yet as Black people gained civil and voting rights, critics of the Freedmen's Bureau raised the specter of government indoctrination. They proclaimed that partnership with the federal government had corrupted the influence of teachers and instilled partisan sentiments among emotionally impressible freedpeople. In the end, even Republicans who supported the agency defined its legacy in ways that downplayed direct government support for education. More broadly, they posited the classroom as a fragile, domestic space easily corrupted by federal influence, leaving a void that would be filled by voluntary associations and philanthropies. As with the Bureau of Education and the Perce Bill, the fate of the Freedmen's Bureau signaled Congress's gradual distancing from New Englanders' bold visions of educational intervention in the South.

Chapter Three

AN ATMOSPHERE OF ALTRUISM
Renewing the Freedmen's Bureau, 1866-1870

Though C. Anna Harwood trained at a normal school before the Civil War, her classes did not prepare her for the decision she faced in May 1866.[1] Just months after arriving in Grenada, Mississippi, to teach with the American Missionary Association (AMA), she found herself without the guidance of her two closest mentors. The first, her AMA supervisor and school superintendent, the Reverend J. P. Bardwell, had fled Grenada after being violently assaulted. Shortly thereafter, assassins killed her Freedmen's Bureau liaison, Lieutenant J. B. Blanding. Feeling "weary and tempest tossed," Harwood did not know where to turn for guidance. She wrote to Bardwell, "I see but one or two things to be done; either to give up the schools and abandon the place, or let [her life partner] Carrie Segur come, and she and I will live in that little old cabin by ourselves and try to get along some way." In the absence of a clear directive, she said, she would continue to answer God's call to teach former slaves: "I shall go quietly forward until I hear from you."[2] Harwood remained in Grenada where she and Segur maintained the AMA school.[3] In the subsequent weeks, an account of Harwood's selflessness circulated widely in the North, evincing the sacrificial spirit that motivated freedpeople's teachers.[4] For Freedmen's Bureau inspector John W. Alvord, the story helped make the case for renewing the embattled federal agency in 1866. In his biennial report to Congress, Alvord wrote of how "two young ladies ... with courage greater than that of a soldier, remain[ed] at their post" even as violence unfolded around them. Now subsumed into a wider narrative of altruistic white women, Harwood and Segur needed "reliable guarantees of protection" as they directed the "vitality and hope" of freedpeople toward productive ends.[5]

Narratives of white women teachers like Harwood played an outsized role in postbellum debates about federal support for freedpeople. These teachers embodied what Melinda Lawson calls the "mystical aura" of wartime Protestant nationalism, extending that aura into spaces marred by battlefield horrors and sectional resentments.[6] Commenting on the founding of a freedpeople's school on the site of Georgia's infamous Andersonville Prison, one author rejoiced that war-torn sites would be "cleansed and sanctified ... by the purity, the presence, the labor and the love of woman."[7] These hopes of purification reinforced schooling's emerging reputation as an extension of the home: a domestic space capable of reorienting pupils' feelings.[8]

For Northern policymakers fearful of what a surge of Black civic and economic participation could portend for fellow feeling in a reunited nation, these narratives of educational altruism proved appealing. Racist ideas of the period regarded slavery as a degrading influence that lingered after emancipation, leaving freedpeople in a state of emotional impulsivity. Yet many Northern reformers believed that Black feelings could be molded, especially by the maternal care of teachers like Harwood.[9] In the "prepolitical" space of the classroom, Black students could learn the emotional control necessary for involvement in a market economy and, perhaps in time, politics.[10] As one religious newsletter proclaimed, "We have only to multiply the corps of such teachers to complete the work of elevating and redeeming this emancipated race."[11] Stories of self-sacrificing teachers thus enticed members of Congress as they considered renewing the Freedmen's Bureau.

When it founded the bureau in 1865, Congress did not intend to have the agency focus on education. Rather, the bureau was created to temporarily provide humanitarian aid, adjudicate legal disputes, manage confiscated Southern land, and facilitate freedpeople's transition to an economy predicated on wage- and contract-based free labor.[12] Influenced by the Methodist faith of bureau commissioner Oliver Otis Howard and close cooperation with groups such as the AMA, the bureau soon shifted its energies to aiding missionary teachers in freedpeople's schools. An array of legislators welcomed the bureau's decision to prioritize education, citing that reorientation as a basis for renewing the agency in early 1866. Proponents such as Senator Lyman Trumbull (R-IL) and Representative Thomas D. Eliot (R-MA) believed that bureau-sponsored education could reshape the emotional lives of freedpeople, producing economic harmony in the South and mitigating future interracial discord.

Yet many in Congress fretted that federal involvement in freedpeople's education could hinder rather than help the cause of promoting fellow feeling among Black and white Southerners. To assuage these opponents and overcome President Andrew Johnson's veto, Republican leaders drew a dividing line between the labor of the military bureau and the voluntary efforts of missionary teachers. Borrowing from the gender ideology of the common school movement and Northern missionary groups, bureau supporters touted the agency as a patriarchal force that would protect but not directly influence teachers' voluntary, self-sacrificing work. With the schoolroom inscribed as a domestic space, the school's capacity to shape public feeling would depend on its isolation from military, partisan, and political forces outside its walls. By separating patriarchal protection from feminine teaching, bureau proponents reassured enough Republicans to secure the agency's renewal.

Although the bureau survived, Congress left unresolved a vexing issue: whether federal support infringed on the classroom's character as an apolitical, domestic space capable of instilling fellow feeling. This controversy only intensified over the agency's short lifetime. Practically and rhetorically, the dividing line between the bureau and its missionary partners proved challenging to maintain. At the administrative level, the bureau was deeply intertwined with philanthropy. Bureau agents worked closely with missionary officials and teachers, playing an active role in coordinating aid agencies, procuring textbooks, funding schoolhouses, and supplementing teachers' salaries.[13] In turn, policymakers had difficulty determining where military support ended and educational labor began. Likewise, at the level of individual classrooms, teachers had to balance the idealized, apolitical conception of their labor against the inherently controversial goal of shaping Black students' agency.[14] These tensions inflected how members of Congress debated the bureau's renewal. With each renewal attempt, legislators wrangled over how and under what conditions missionary teachers would be best positioned to orient the emotional dispositions of their pupils.[15] Indexed to deepening Northern anxieties about Black impressibility, controversies over bureau teachers' partisan influences intensified with the expanded political rights granted to Black men by the first Reconstruction Act and the Fifteenth Amendment. As Congress clashed over the best ways to promote common national feeling, the emotional influence of bureau-affiliated teachers became a source of contestation. Critics charged that rather than sustaining the atmosphere of altruism generated by missionary teachers, the bureau corrupted educators and poisoned the Southern atmosphere with hostile sentiments.

Within five years, opponents reframed a federal agency designed to assuage concerns about Black feeling as a cause of racial and sectional resentment in the South. In 1866, legislators who supported the bureau portrayed teachers as preparing freedpeople for a hopeful but indeterminate future of civic participation. Channeling currents of postwar feeling, Republicans argued that the bureau would sustain and protect the optimistic energies generated through teachers' interactions with freedpeople. Two years later, shifts in Black political participation transformed the terms of the next renewal debate. After the 1867 Reconstruction Acts conferred voting rights on Black men in the South, legislators' future-tense hopes about Black civic activity were displaced by present-tense anxieties about their actual political involvement. As a result, the entanglements of bureau and missionary teachers faced greater scrutiny. In this altered political environment, opponents attacked the bureau as a corrupt confluence of federal agents and missionaries. Critics depicted the bureau's far-reaching involvement in Southern life and especially in education as an attempt to sow interracial hostility and indoctrinate impressionable Black voters. By 1870, opponents initiated formal corruption hearings against the bureau, accusing it of fostering "animosities and hatreds in the heart of the poor colored man against white men amongst whom he lives."[16] Claims that a politicized bureau was encroaching on missionary classrooms underpinned calls to dissolve the agency.

The Freedmen's Bureau renewal debates trace the emergence of an educational idiom predicated on gendered and racialized understandings of emotion. Members of Congress both for and against the bureau's continuation reinforced an ideal of classrooms as fragile, domestic spaces easily corrupted by influences deemed political. This ideal helped to position schools as a domain of maternal influence uniquely capable of supporting freedpeople's rapid emotional assimilation. Yet this conception of the classroom also positioned any federal influence as inherently corrupting, dooming efforts to make the bureau permanent. Moreover, the renewal debates helped cement a linkage between formal education and freedpeople's capacity to join a community of fellow feeling. Concepts of freedpeople's impressibility were invoked to both eliminate the bureau and warrant limits on Black political rights, illustrating the malleability of education as a tool for civic exclusion under the guise of protecting democracy. These debates both diminished freedpeople's access to education and cast suspicion on their emotional fitness for electoral participation.

"THE CHILDREN OF THE GOVERNMENT": THE BUREAU'S EDUCATIONAL TURN, 1862-1865

Throughout the Civil War, members of Congress wrangled over how and whether to address the humanitarian needs and uncertain futures of nearly five hundred thousand freedpeople crowded into military camps.[17] At first, Congress left the question to religious and private charities. By 1863, however, leaders of aid agencies insisted that the challenges of emancipation were proving "too large for anything short of Government authority, Government resources, and Government ubiquity to deal with."[18] As formal emancipation grew more likely, most members of Congress agreed that a federal intervention on behalf of freedpeople was necessary. Yet the nature, extent, and duration of that intervention remained contested. Passed in 1864 and enacted in March 1865, the original legislation for the Freedmen's Bureau reflected the ambiguities and competing visions of Congress and the wider public. As designed, the bureau would be a catch-all response to the conditions facing freedpeople and loyal white refugees alike, including a system of courts, a land distribution program, and several forms of material assistance.[19] Underfunded and overextended, the military officials directing the bureau decided to pick their battles. They developed close partnerships with missionary groups such as the AMA and Western Freedmen's Aid Commission, adapting wartime military bureaucracy to coordinate disparate agencies' efforts. The bureau emulated Northern missionary groups' emphasis on schooling as a mode of emotional intervention in freedpeople's lives. By aligning the bureau with the existing raced and gendered assumptions that animated the freedpeople's aid movement, agency leaders molded it into a different form than Congress had intended—a form amenable to the circumstances legislators faced when Congress reconvened in December 1865.

Early in the Civil War, Northern missionary associations had taken up the cause of education to promote Protestant faith, free labor principles, and emotional self-control among former slaves. These religious, economic, and emotional goals were intimately connected. Republican policymakers had argued since the 1850s that a free labor system imparted self-restraint over impulsive feelings. By orienting workers' emotions toward objects of material acquisition, self-improvement, and social mobility, free labor could transform unruly feelings of discontent into a forward-looking hopefulness. Concurrently, this ideology believed that slavery denied the domestic conditions necessary to orient children's emotions early in life. In place of incentives for internal self-control, the slave labor system imposed a system of external coercion.[20] Now that this coercive system had been lifted, white Republicans feared that the newly freed would be subject to the whims of untrained passions. Howard dramatized this anxiety, recounting how freedpeople in a military camp responded to news of emancipation with "wild, noisy, uncouth demonstrations . . . singing, dancing, leaping and screaming for hours together . . . to give vent to their emotion of indescribable joy."[21] Treating such displays as evidence of emotional impulsivity, Howard and other policy leaders fretted that freedpeople would capitulate to excess, idleness, or political manipulation.[22] Above all, reformers feared that freedpeople might be seduced by a postwar wave of labor agitation, joining strikes or outright rejecting the logic of contract labor.[23] As Saidiya Hartman argues, white reformers thus intervened in Black emotion to impart a "love of gain" and a "dispassionate acquisitiveness."[24] Reformers insisted that by learning the constrained hopes of free labor and Protestantism, freedpeople could peacefully coexist with whites in the South.

To impart their ideal of hope, policymakers and philanthropists imagined freedpeople as particularly amenable to white teachers' emotional influence. Kyla Schuller writes that mid-nineteenth-century philanthropic leaders believed that over countless generations, nonwhite populations had accrued "savage propensities" that left them unable to control their emotions. Yet reformers also viewed racialized bodies as "impressible" by outside influences and thus "subject to the objects, people, and forces pressing on it for its own self-constitution."[25] This view regarded Black pupils as natural imitators who could learn more rapidly than white pupils but with less capacity for original thought.[26] While this perspective underpinned anxieties about Black susceptibility to demagogues and labor agitators, it also sustained a belief that education—imparted through the "sympathetic affect" of the benevolent white teacher—could rapidly mold freedpeople's dispositions.[27] When the first group of Northern reformers arrived in Port Royal, South Carolina, to work with freedpeople in 1862, they sought to prove the impressibility of their pupils. Edward L. Pierce, the director of the Port Royal effort, dubbed it an "experiment" to discern the best ways to impart a "religious zeal for faithful labor" among those who had been enslaved. To that end, he requested that the Northern public support the project by sending "missionaries . . . to address the religious element of a race so emotional in nature."[28] Responding to requests like Pierce's, a wave of mostly white missionaries traveled to contraband camps to prove the malleability of freedpeople. Eliding formerly enslaved people's reasons for pursuing literacy and teaching, reformers touted freedpeople's eagerness to learn as evidence of white missionaries' capacity to rapidly assimilate them into a free labor system.[29]

To impart free labor ideas, leaders of the freedpeople's aid movement drew on the gender ideology of antebellum common school reform. During the 1830s and 1840s, Horace Mann, Henry Barnard, Catharine Beecher, and others reimagined the schoolroom as a domestic space headed by idealized white women.[30] Laboring within an extension of the home, women teachers enacted self-sacrificial motherhood to instill appropriate "affective dispositions" among future male citizens.[31] Postbellum reformers extended this ideal, enlisting white women teachers to generate the domestic spaces freedwomen were believed unable to provide for their children.[32] The AMA and other aid agencies supported wider diversity among teachers—including Southerners, men, and Black educators—but issued promotional literature and reports that downplayed those stories.[33] Instead, they amplified white women's accounts and nurtured assumptions about classrooms' intrinsic domesticity.[34] A focus on white women teachers allowed philanthropists to elevate imagery that soothed white Northerners' concerns about public feeling. As Susan M. Ryan argues, popular portrayals of "pseudomaternal" relationships between white women teachers and Black pupils evoked the prospect of "a harmoniously interracial United States." At the same time, such imagery also reassured audiences that racial hierarchy—embodied in the pedagogical relation of student and teacher—would remain intact.[35] Written and visual portrayals of this dynamic circulated widely through missionary newsletters, Northern magazines, and teachers' letters, inviting the Northern public to share in the glow of teachers' benevolent feelings.[36] For leaders of the Freedmen's Bureau and their allies in Congress, the prospect of marshaling and sustaining those hopeful feelings offered an alluring response to the challenges posed by emancipation.

In centering the experiences of white women teachers, philanthropists had to manage public perceptions about women's involvement in public life. As one of the few mid-nineteenth-century professions that granted women a degree of personal and financial autonomy, teaching tended to attract women involved in wider social causes.[37] Regarding such extracurricular political activity as antithetical to the production of an apolitical, domestic space in the classroom, antebellum common school reformers tamped down women teachers' activism. They enjoined teachers to confine their curricular visions, abstain from political life, and accept the emotional wage of self-sacrifice as compensation for their labor.[38] During the wartime and postbellum freedpeople's aid movement, male leadership faced similar tensions over women's activity—and responded in similar ways. As Caroline Faulkner argues, many women drawn to aid former slaves had backgrounds in social reform movements. Contrary to male leaders' emphasis on rapidly promoting former slaves' self-sufficiency, these women sought more holistic forms of aid as a matter of "justice rather than charity."[39] Fearful that such efforts would alienate public opinion, agencies like the AMA narrowed the scope of women's decision-making and drew a boundary between masculine administration and feminine teaching, only rarely allowing women to serve as officers or school leaders.[40] Agencies also adopted what Louise Michele Newman calls a stance of "patriarchal protection" that granted white women political agency only if they acquiesced to the supervision, financial support, and physical protection of male philanthropic bureaucrats.[41] Despite these efforts to contain women's activity, tensions over preserving the domesticity of the classroom persisted through Reconstruction and animated congressional debates over the future of the Freedmen's Bureau.

"TO DISSIPATE OUR PREJUDICES": THE BUREAU'S APPEAL FOR CONGRESS, 1864-1866

By the close of the Civil War, the confluence of education, philanthropy, and gendered ideals of teaching appealed to Freedmen's Bureau administrators as they sought to define the agency's mission. Initially, the bureau's support for education was more latent than blatant. Although Eliot, the bill's sponsor, described the bureau as a way to "help into active, educated, and useful life" the "children of the government," the measure Abraham Lincoln signed in 1864 did not say a word about education.[42] When the bureau began operating in March 1865, administrators focused on managing lands confiscated from Southern rebels in hopes of both raising revenue and providing an economic toehold for freedpeople. Within just two months, President Andrew Johnson began to undermine that effort by issuing amnesty and pardons to former rebels, thereby ensuring that land would be returned to its antebellum owners.[43] Absent its central mission and revenue source, bureau officers found themselves reliant on close relationships with philanthropic missionary efforts already underway throughout the South. As Ronald E. Butchart contends, the bureau and Northern aid agencies developed an "interlocking" relationship characterized by a mutual exchange of leaders, finances, and ideas.[44] As it cultivated these relationships, the bureau adopted aid agencies' focus on education and with it the gendered ideology of Northern school reformers in Congress.

In converting the bureau into an educational agency, administrators aligned themselves with the concerns of Republicans in Congress. For legislators worried that material aid would, in Eric Foner's words, "deaden the very spirit of enterprise and ambition" among freedpeople, education offered a compelling alternative approach to addressing humanitarian needs.[45] As Alvord insisted in his January 1866 report to Congress, freedpeople's uniquely "emotional, imitative, and affectionate" dispositions made them especially amenable to the impressions of missionary teachers. Moreover, as voluntary missionaries, teachers could shape Black feeling at minimal federal expense. Alvord's report assured legislators that neither the "self-sacrifice and fidelity" of teachers nor the financial backing of Northern philanthropists would abate. "Popular donations are rapidly increasing," he explained, "and you may rely upon the continuance of sympathy and the increase of this important aid."[46] By marshaling the emotional energies for education already generated by Northern missionaries, Congress had a means of sidestepping controversies over aid.

The bureau also appeared to offer Congress a path toward confronting their anxieties about hostile feelings between Black workers and white employers, a key concern in facilitating a transition to contract-based labor in the South. As Howard explained to members of the Maine Freedmen's Relief Society in late 1865, the bureau's efforts disproved the notion that "white and black races cannot permanently live together in this country." Rebuking proponents of Black colonization, Howard argued that educating freedpeople into the free labor system could transform the sentiments of their former owners. As an employer, he said, he could hire Black laborers "and live with them, not only without hating them, but I could love each and every one of them. . . . Our intercourse, which we must hold with them as our employés, will serve to dissipate our prejudices."[47] By appealing to Republican faith in free labor ideology, Howard's argument provided a compelling account of how the bureau could assuage apprehensions about an absence of national feeling in the South.

Even as this educational rhetoric appealed to Republicans in Congress, the agency's leaders struggled to reconcile its limited institutional scope with the benefits they claimed to have gained. As the concurrent debate over the Bureau of Education underscored, Congress remained reticent to fund public schools out of the federal treasury. Bureau leadership vacillated between claiming tremendous results for the bureau's efforts and downplaying its direct involvement in classrooms. At the same time that he attributed missionaries' successes to the bureau's presence, Alvord requested only that Congress provide funds for work tangential to teaching itself: acquiring schoolhouses, organizing agencies, and protecting schools from racist hostility. In the language of patriarchal protection, he positioned the bureau as a military barrier around the intimate space of the classroom: "Protecting power is called for to give that sense of quiet and consciousness of security which the calm duties of both teacher and pupil always require."[48] As members of Congress contemplated the bureau's renewal, they inherited this tension in officials' discourse. Legislators who took up the issue in 1866 faced the challenge of justifying the bureau as crucial to the South's educational transformation without acknowledging the work undertaken in schools. They struck that balance by emphasizing the bureau's status as a military agency enlisted to protect the domestic space of the classroom from white Southerners' violence.

"THE TRUE CHRISTIAN CENTAUR":
PRESERVING AND PROTECTING BENEVOLENT FEELINGS, 1865-1866

A few weeks after the Thirty-Ninth Congress convened in December 1865, throngs of people braved a winter storm to observe proceedings from the gallery of the House of Representatives. They were there not to hear legislators but to witness testimony from Congregationalist preacher, common school advocate, and social reformer Henry Ward Beecher, who was speaking on behalf of the Freedmen's Aid Commission. Rev. Beecher's presence signified the confluence of government, education reform, and Protestant philanthropy embodied in the Freedmen's Bureau. Beecher offered his interpretation of the newly ratified Thirteenth Amendment and advice on how best to support former slaves. "Without education," he instructed his audience, a person is "man and animal, with the animal on top. It was education that placed the two parts of his nature in their proper relation, making the true Christian centaur."[49] Implicitly depicting freedpeople as animalistic and impulsive until educated, Beecher's remarks framed the ensuing debate on the fate of the Freedmen's Bureau.

At the time Beecher spoke, the trajectory of federal responsibility toward formerly enslaved persons remained uncertain. For some in Congress, the Thirteenth Amendment represented the end of congressional duty; with abolition enacted in law, freedpeople would be on their own. At the opposite extreme, some saw a need for a continued humanitarian intervention as justice for those, in the words of Senator Henry Wilson (R-MA), "now thrown upon their own resources, into a hostile community."[50] After considering various options, legislators gradually embraced Beecher's position: prioritizing the production of "Christian centaurs" capable of regulating their emotions. Against a backdrop of Southern recalcitrance, racist violence, and presidential obstruction during the first half of 1866, Republicans converged on an argument for bureau renewal. They resolved to protect the fragile domesticity of missionary classrooms to enable teachers to generate hopeful feelings among freedpeople and throughout the South.

The First Renewal Attempt, January-February 1866

As the renewal debate began in early 1866, the Freedmen's Bureau's emphasis on education responded to Republican anxieties about Black feelings. Trumbull, a leading moderate Republican and the sponsor of the renewal bill in the Senate, framed the bill as a vital corrective to the "system of legislation" enacted under slavery. That system, he asserted, had designs "of keeping the negro in ignorance, of blotting out from his very soul the light of reason . . . that he might not think, but know only, like the ox, to labor." As in Beecher's centaur analogy, Trumbull's ox allusion reflected a common view that, absent the strict disciplinary regime of slavery, freedpeople would be unable to regulate their animalistic feelings. Policies to "educate, improve, enlighten, and Christianize the negro" were therefore necessary. For bureau proponents, cultivating the capacity to reason—to exercise calm, dispassionate judgment—would reorient freedpeople's emotions. Responding to Democrats' denial of the Black capacity for learning, Senator Waitman T. Willey (R-WV) argued that slavery, not nature, had suppressed freedpeople's desire to strive for themselves. Given "a hope of improvement in their condition," he argued, "that idleness, to some extent at least, will pass away." Building on Willey, Wilson claimed that the bureau had proven instrumental in instilling such hope. By imparting the economic desires associated with a free labor economy, he explained, the bureau had already begun to dissolve the basis of racial animosity in the South. Where the bureau had sufficient support, he claimed, it had "harmonized the old masters and the new freedmen."[51] At minimal expense, then, the bureau offered a response to the perceived crisis posed by Black feeling and a way to secure the Republican free labor vision for the South.

The bureau's congressional champions linked the agency to the optimistic feelings associated with teachers, especially white women, who worked with freedpeople. Informed by his roots in Boston reform culture, Representative Eliot praised the bureau for "avail[ing] itself of the experience gained before its organization by the benevolent associations." To illustrate the bureau's relationship to missionary hopes, Eliot read a lengthy letter from an "earnest, intelligent, and cultivated" woman teacher who had traveled from New England to teach former slaves on Edisto Island, South Carolina. For years, the teacher's pupils had cultivated land abandoned by plantation owners who fled Union forces during the war. President Johnson's decision to pardon prominent Confederates returned those lands to their former owners, demolishing former slaves' prospects of acquiring it from the government. Even on the day when the Edisto Island freedpeople learned this devastating news, a group of all ages still gathered with her to learn to read from the Bible: "It was interesting to hear the old men apply the situation of the Israelites, after they were freed from their bondage in Egypt, to their own present situation; and my reading was often interrupted by questions or exclamations. How thankful I was that I was with them, and could in some slight degree assist them—leading them in the first steps of knowledge."[52]

The teacher's letter centered the white woman as crucial to freedpeople's capacity to regulate their emotions. With their hopes of owning their homesteads dashed, freedpeople would justly have felt outrage or hopelessness. Yet in this account, the teacher channeled those emotional energies toward a biblical interpretation that restored hope and a willingness to labor. The implication of the account was clear: by sustaining "real, earnest workers, working with heart and hand for these needy people," Congress could adequately shape Black feeling in the South.[53]

While foregrounding the selfless sacrifices of white women teachers, renewal proponents also stressed the need for military force to protect those teachers from violence. Senator Charles Sumner (R-MA) read a letter from New Orleans concerning "a Mrs. ——— in this place who teaches the colored children." White residents, "not liking [Black children] having the advantages of education, expressed their disapproval by shooting at the teacher. At one time she was nursing a sick baby when a shot passed over her shoulder." In this account, the teacher was portrayed as under siege from bullets that interrupted acts of maternal intimacy, short-circuiting the generation of feeling in intimate space. As a "poor widow" living in a town where "all in office . . . are rebels," the teacher had few options for masculine protection. She "became so much alarmed for her safety that she petitioned the officers to allow the troops to remain, which they did for a few days."[54] Only the presence of military officials allowed the classroom to fulfill its function as a maternal space for orienting Black feelings.

Throughout the debate over renewal, legislators in both chambers of Congress emphasized the same theme as Sumner's letter. Wilson read a letter from a general stationed in Georgia insisting that "in almost every case . . . the withdrawal of troops has been followed by outrages on the freed people; their school-houses have been burned, their teachers driven off or threatened with death." In a similar appeal, Representative Fernando Beaman (R-MI) read a report in which Tennessee's governor claimed that if "restraints of the General Government are removed from Tennessee, . . . in two cases out of every three, the school houses would be burned and the teachers rode upon a rail."[55] In all of these cases, a protective military force was cited as vital to securing the domesticity of educational space. In that way, the bureau and missionary teachers formed a symbiotic relation essential to shaping freedpeople's emotional orientation.

Whereas advocates portrayed the bureau as a force to protect benevolent feelings, opponents framed bureau-backed teachers' potential influence in more ominous terms. Representative John W. Chanler (D-NY) read aloud a letter from a Confederate general discounting the need for further Northern intervention. "If let alone, by the end of the year there will no longer exist any general distrust between the races, but mutual confidence and kind feeling arising from a sense of mutual dependence." The letter expressed "apprehension" about the "teachers among us who are entirely ignorant of the real feelings and the true character of both races." "Bitterly hostile to the whites, and weakly sentimental on the negro," those teachers would exacerbate conditions of strife and disrupt the formation of a free labor economy. Echoing the same theme, Representative George S. Shanklin (D-AR) reasoned that schoolhouses built under the renewal bill would be filled by "those political preachers who have covered the land during the war." There, those partisans would teach freedpeople "to hate those who had been their masters, and with whom they had lived" and "to vote the whole Abolition or Republican ticket."[56] As these arguments suggest, bureau advocates faced a challenge in connecting the agency to the activities of missionary teachers. If teachers became too associated with Republican political projects in Congress, the educators' apolitical, self-sacrificing innocence fell into question. Moreover, positions like Chanler's and Shanklin's underscored the double-edged nature of arguments about Black impressibility. If freedpeople could rapidly be assimilated into free labor ideology, they would also more readily emulate expressions of partisan hostility. Though these opponents had diminished influence in 1866, their appeals limited the scope of the bureau bill and foreshadowed critiques that intensified after Black men received voting rights.

Despite their meager power in Congress, critics of the bureau had an ally in the White House. After the renewal bill passed both the House and Senate in February, President Johnson blindsided legislators with a vitriolic veto message. Taking aim at the provisions for material aid and courts to protect Black legal rights, Johnson claimed that the bureau would render freedpeople dependent on the "overseers" of the federal government. He maligned the bureau's support for education as an overexertion of federal power that would be of little use. And contrary to Republican designs, he predicted that the agency would deepen Southern whites' "feeling and sentiment against the government" by prolonging the federal presence in the South and providing undue power to Black Southerners.[57] Alongside Johnson's veto of the Civil Rights Bill the next month, the bureau veto signaled the president's all-out refusal to cooperate with Congress on matters of Reconstruction.[58] An immediate attempt to override the veto in February failed, leaving Republican legislators with no choice but to either abandon or considerably revise the bill. Mustering the two-thirds majorities necessary to overcome Johnson's veto would thus require further concessions and an even greater emphasis on the bureau's role in protecting the domesticity of classrooms. The events of that spring strengthened their case.

Surging Violence and the Veto Override, April-July 1866

Over the next three months, surging violence in the South drew renewed attention to missionary sacrifices in schools and revived the salience of arguments for bureau protection. Few of these "outrages" stoked more national attention than the May 1866 Memphis Massacre.[59] At least forty-six Black men, women, and children died in racist violence across the city. As was the case throughout Reconstruction, white supremacists directly targeted freedpeople's schools as a symbol of Black political agency and federal influence in the region.[60] Northern commentators were aghast at white Memphians' disregard for the recently passed Civil Rights Act, ongoing refusal to accept the outcome of the war, and violence toward missionary teachers and their schoolhouses. The May 26, 1866, issue of *Harper's Weekly* featured a graphic depiction of a burning school surrounded by white men wielding weapons (figure 3.1). A letter printed in the *Iowa State Daily Register* contrasted the "murderous ferocity" of the mob with the "Christian heroism" of the teachers, all of whom were "young ladies from the North."[61] Reinforcing the public perception of a maternal space under siege, violent episodes targeting freedpeople's schools shaped the rhetorical strategies of bureau proponents. Less than a week after the massacre, Howard delivered a speech to the American Missionary Association in which he cited the events in Memphis as a reason for the bureau's continuation.[62] Echoing Howard's appeal for protection, legislators began revising the bill to overcome Johnson's veto.

After the Memphis Massacre, the House of Representatives undertook a detailed investigation of the event that emphasized the need for schoolhouse protection. Based on days of interviews with witnesses both Black and white, the official report reiterated postwar anxieties about the South's absence of national feeling. As Representative Elihu B. Washburne (R-IL) wrote in his conclusion to the report, Southerners seemed to still harbor "envenomed feeling" toward "Union men and colored people." While the report described acts of horrific violence directed against freedpeople throughout its nearly four hundred pages of interviews, it dedicated special attention to attacks on teachers and schoolhouses. Waving aside accusations that bureau agents or educators had radicalized freedpeople, the report stressed that "many of the teachers of the schools were young ladies from the northern States" with "unblemished characters" who had dedicated themselves solely to "elevating a down-trodden and oppressed race." The women, "engaged in a work of benevolence and Christianity, were themselves obliged to flee from the city for personal safety; and as they left, they were guided in their pathway by the light reflected from their burning school-houses."[63] Through such

EXCHANGING ARMS: GLAUCUS AND DIOMEDES

αὐτὰρ ὃ μειλιχίοισι προσηύδα ποιμένα λαῶν
ἦ ῥά νύ μοι ξεῖνος πατρώϊός ἐσσι παλαιός
Οἰνεὺς γάρ ποτε δῖος ἀμύμονα Βελλεροφόντην
ξείνισ' ἐνὶ μεγάροισιν ἐείκοσιν ἤματ' ἐρύξας
οἳ δὲ καὶ ἀλλήλοισι πόρον ξεινήϊα καλά
Οἰνεὺς μὲν ζωστῆρα δίδου φοίνικι φαεινόν,
Βελλεροφόντης δὲ χρύσεον δέπας ἀμφικύπελλον
καί μιν ἐγὼ κατέλειπον ἰὼν ἐν δώμασ' ἐμοῖσι. [...]
τὼ νῦν σοὶ μὲν ἐγὼ ξεῖνος φίλος Ἄργεϊ μέσσῳ
εἰμί, σὺ δ' ἐν Λυκίῃ ὅτε κεν τῶν δῆμον ἵκωμαι.
ἔγχεα δ' ἀλλήλων ἀλεώμεθα καὶ δι' ὁμίλου [...]
τεύχεα δ' ἀλλήλοις ἐπαμείψομεν, ὄφρα καὶ οἵδε
γνῶσιν ὅτι ξεῖνοι πατρώϊοι εὐχόμεθ' εἶναι.
ὣς ἄρα φωνήσαντε καθ' ἵππων ἀΐξαντε
χεῖράς τ' ἀλλήλων λαβέτην καὶ πιστώσαντο
ἔνθ' αὖτε Γλαύκῳ Κρονίδης φρένας ἐξέλετο Ζεύς,
ὃς πρὸς Τυδεΐδην Διομήδεα τεύχε' ἄμειβε
χρύσεα χαλκείων, ἑκατόμβοι' ἐννεαβοίων.

And so he [Diomedes] spoke gently to the shepherd of people [Glaucus]: 'Truly, you are a guest-friend of my father's from the old days (*xeinos patrōios* [...] *palaios*)! For godly Oineus once entertained the blameless Bellerophon in his halls, and kept him there for twenty days. And they gave each other beautiful guest-gifts (*xeinēia kala*): Oineus gave a shining crimson belt, and Bellerophon a golden double cup, which I left behind in my palace when I came here. [...] So now I am your dear guest-friend in the heart of Argos, and you mine in Lycia, if I ever travel there. Let us avoid each other's spears, even in a crowd! [...] Let us exchange arms with each other (*teuchea d'allēlois epameipsomen*), so that these men may know that we are guest-friends since our fathers' time.' When they had talked in this way, they both leapt down from their chariots and clasped each other's hands and pledged their faith (*pisteusanto*). And Zeus, the son of Cronos, took away Glaucus's wit (*phrēn*), when he changed arms (*teuchea ameibe*) with Diomedes, son of Tydeus, giving gold for bronze (*chrysea chalkeiōn*), the value of a hundred oxen for that of nine (*Il.* 6.214-21; 224-26; 230-36).

The final statement, in which the unequal nature of the exchange is pointed out, was duly noted by Finley: 'The poet's editorial comment, so rare for him, reflects the magnitude of Glaucus's mistake in judgement'.[61] But the statement did not have any influence on Finley's view of the character of gift-exchange as a kind of exchange without profit. In the meantime, the question of value has received much more attention. So the anthropologist Thomas O. Beidelman sees it as a clear indication of the originally agonistic character of gift-giving in the Greek world.[62] Ancient historians argue in a similar vein, as when William M. Calder III, following Marcel Mauss, interprets the unequal exchange of arms as a vague memory of the custom of an 'Indo-European *potlatch*', still practised in Mycenaean times but no longer intelligible to the poet and thus giving rise to the comment about Glaucus's unwise conduct.[63] Mauss himself had argued similarly in his essay on Thracian *potlatch*: 'So the Greeks of the Homeric period observed the customs and considered them insane.'[64] Starting with the assumption that gift-exchange is always competitive in character, Chester G. Starr even arrives at the conclusion that the poem contains no reference to the practice of gift-exchange apart from the arms-exchange between Diomedes and Glaucus.[65]

Both models of interpretation are beset with internal contradictions. To my mind, the arms-exchange is not adequately characterised either as an expression of the binding powers of guest-friendship, or as an evocation of an obsolete form of *potlatch*. Rather, the exchange of unequal arms enacts a contradiction between status and achievement which is also emphasised in Diomedes's *aristeia*. On the one hand this demonstrates the close link between person and object that is often pointed to in scholarship on gift-exchange: the value of a person can be demonstrated through objects. On the other hand, however, the arms-exchange as it is depicted has no causal link with the guest-friendship, which is portayed as hereditary, and it does not prove the binding force of guest-presents. In the poem, compacts are not formed by giving arms but by swearing oaths. Gifts of arms appear in the poem to act as substitutes for personal armed service, tending more to

---

61. Finley 1967: 63. See also Herman 1987: 61.
62. Beidelman 1989: 236–42 referring to the conflict between Agamemnon and Achilles. See also Hiltbrunner 1972: 1981.
63. Calder 1984: 31–35. Similar Redfield 1983: 243.
64. Mauss 1921: 391.
65. Starr 1986: 32. Recently the unequal exchange is again interpreted as an example of asymmetrical reciprocity. See Bertelli 2014 and Domingo Gygax 2016: 35.

resemble tributes. To expand on this view, it is important first to discuss the competitive character of gift-giving and then to turn to the problem of guest-friendship as a binding force by analysing further examples of arms-gifts.

To insist on the idea that the inequality of the arms indicates the competitive character of gift-giving is to contradict the explicit statement which points to the lack of consideration (*phrēn*) shown by Glaucus when he exchanges the more valuable arms for the less valuable ones. This contrast gave rise to irritation even in antiquity and has led to various interpretations. So Plato makes use of the turn of phrase *chrysea chalkeiōn* as a metaphor for cheating or doing someone down in the Symposium.[66] In contrast, Aristotle argues in the Nicomachean Ethics that Glaucus did not suffer injustice because of the inequality in value because it was in his power to give the gift, voluntarily.[67] Alexandrian commentators thought that Diomedes faked the ritual of guest-friendship in order to cheat Glaucus.[68]

In present scholarship there are two lines of debate. According to Calder, Diomedes, as the one who gives less, recognises Glaucus's superiority.[69] Donlan's opinion is that the scene expresses the opposite state of affairs: The superior partner, in this case Diomedes, receives more, and Glaucus's gift is to be seen as a gesture of subordination.[70] Donlan identifies a similar imbalance in the gift-exchange between Oeneus and Bellerophon. Bellerophon is at a disadvantage here as he receives, with the purple belt, a lesser gift than the one he gives, while the gift of gold given to Oeneus indicates his higher status.[71] With this interpretation Donlan rejects the categorisation of the arms-exchange as part of the tradition, assumed by Calder, of an Indo-European *potlatch*. Donlan does not absolutely reject such a 'true *potlatch*', but for him the representation of such a practice is not a mere relic but a reflection of the circumstances of the Geometric period.[72] However, Donlan's view is that competitive giving applies only to

---

66. Plat. *Symp.* 219 a.
67. Arist. *Eth. Nic.* 1136 b.
68. The sources are collected by Maftei 1976 and Fornaro 1992. On the Roman reception of the scene, see Behrends 2002.
69. Calder 1994: 34: 'Diomedes, after hearing the glorious lineage and noble attainments of Glaucus, whom momentarily he had thought a god (*Il.* 6.128-9), admits by his offer of the unequal exchange Glaucus's superiority.'
70. Donlan 1989: 11–12.
71. Donlan 1989: 12.
72. The competitive character is also stressed by Qviller 1981: 124–27; even Finley 1967: 125 hints at this: 'Gift-giving too was part of the network of competitive honorific activity. And in both directions: it was as honorable to give as to receive'.

bridal gifts and prizes handed out at funeral games, and he exempts the arms-exchange from this pattern. He interprets most gifts handed out in the poem, including the gifts of arms, as 'gifts of submission', with which the more generous giver intends to secure the good will of the recipient. The poet's final remarks on Glaucus's behaviour do not, according to Donlan, signal a lack of knowledge of the practice of gift-exchange but instead demonstrate bias: Homer intends to show his audience that the Achaeans are superior to the Trojans and their allies not only in strength (*biē*) but in cunning (*mētis*) too.[73]

In essence, Donlan's argument is based on the inequality of the exchanged objects from which he draws conclusions regarding the status of the giver and the receiver. It is more persuasive than Calder's in so far as it assumes the coherence of the poetic world, while Calder needs to draw on the notion that the gift ritual is a relic from a different time. This idea goes against the conclusions drawn by research into oral poetry, which make it highly improbable that the epic contains a layer of tradition from Mycenaean times, as Calder suggests.[74] More recent research into the distribution of gift-exchange rituals also casts doubt over the suggestion of exchange as a relic.[75] Apart from all this, the notion of competitive giving is amongst the most dubious aspects of gift-exchange theory, especially in view of Mauss's discussions of the North American *potlatch*, as I have shown in chapter 1.[76] I will therefore, with some essential modifications, follow Donlan's argument.

When he infers a difference in status between Oineus and Bellerophon from the difference in value between the gold cup and the purple belt, Donlan overlooks the significance of purple for the visual demonstration of status in antiquity. In the poem the colour purple is associated with high status, with leaders in battle and in the assembly, such as

---

73. Donlan 1989: 2 and 6. See also Scott 1982: 1–19, who interprets the generous giving of Glaucus as loss of honour. According to Sitta von Reden (1995: 26) the gift was transformed into booty.
74. Calder 1984 follows Nilsson 1933. The Swedish scholar stressed the connection of the epos with Mycenaean times. Actually, the link with the rise of the *polis* (eighth century BCE) is widely accepted (see Patzek 1990 and 1992: 136; Latacz 1988; Raaflaub 1991; 1998; Anderson and Dickie 1995). For discussion see now Crielaard 2002; Osborne 2004; Ulf 2011.
75. Cf. e.g. Herman 1987; von Reden 1995; Domingo Gygax 2016.
76. The *potlatch* developed its agonistic character in the context of competition between different lineages of the Kwakiutl to increase their influence on the sea-otter skin trade near Fort Rupert in the nineteenth century. Cf. Wolf 1982: 182–92. For further references see ch. 1.2, n. 130.

Agamemnon and Nestor.[77] Obtaining the purple dye from sea snails was a time-consuming process and hardly less difficult than mining for gold.[78] In Athenaeus's discussions on luxuries, purple and gold are at the top of the hierarchy of status symbols (Ath. 12.526 c). In Attic tragedy purple fetches its weight in silver.[79] In the visual arts, when the sheen of gold cannot be represented, it is marked by the colour purple.[80] There is no reason to suggest that the purple belt is any less valuable than the gold goblet. Any inequality in value becomes explicit only in the exchange of the arms, and even then its function is narrative. It is my thesis that the question of unequal values is intended to highlight a contradiction between status and achievement, which serves to emphasise Diomedes's *aristeia*, as Donlan rightly notices.

Both the context of the scene and the character of the objects suggest this interpretation. The arms-exchange in Book 6 is preceded by a series of duels in Book 5, from each of which Diomedes emerges as victor. Despite the reminder of inherited guest-friendship, Diomedes's actions in the arms-exchange scene, which is depicted from an Achaean point of view, point to victory over the opponent here too. The opponent's arms form one visible sign of this victory. They are collected with zeal and industry by the heroes. They are fought over even after the opponent's death because they carry the message of the warrior's glory or *kudos*.[81] When Hector obtains the beautiful and famous arms of Patroclus, he wants the Trojans to take them safely into the city, so he can gain great glory (μέγα κλέος ἔμμεναι αὐτῷ, *Il.* 17.131). He is prevented from doing this by Glaucus (the very man who exchanged weapons with Diomedes), who demands that Hector fight for the weapons and the body of Patroclus in order to be able to exchange them for the body of Sarpedon, which is in the hands of the Achaeans. At this, Hector decides to exchange (*ameibō*, the same word as that used for the exchange between Diomedes and Glaucus) Patroclus's arms for his own

---

77. Stulz 1990: 96–120. See ch. 3.2.
78. Stulz 1990: 103; Reinhold 1970: 17; Blum 1998.
79. Jenkins 1985: 124; Flintoff 1987: 126; Wagner-Hasel 2007: 325.
80. Stulz 1990: 88.
81. See for example *Il.* 11.110 and 247 (Agamemnon); 11.432 (Odysseus); 11.334 (Diomedes); 16.664–65 (Patroclus); 13.181 (Teucer); 17.125 (Hector); 17.536–37 (Automedon); 17.60 (Menelaus); 21.183 (Achilles). The aim to visualise military success by the trophy is stressed by Finley 1967: 128: 'there could be no honour without public proclamation, and there could be no publicity without the evidence of a trophy'. See also Willenbrock 1969: 59: 'Der Waffenraub am Schluß des Kampfes besiegelt die Schmach des Unterlegenen, so wie in unserer Zeit der Verlust der Fahne als größte Schmach gilt'.

and to have the latter taken to Troy (*Il.* 17.192-94). Similar to the arms of Glaucus compared with those of Diomedes, these enemy arms too have a higher value. They are not made of gold but of bronze (*Il.* 16.130) and they have divine provenance. For this is the 'immortal armour' (ἄμβροτα τεύχεα) that the gods once gave to Achilles's father on the occasion of his marriage to Thetis, and which Achilles has now furnished Patroclus with (*Il.* 17.194-97). In this armour, taken from his enemy, Hector now shows himself gleaming (λαμπόμενος) to his comrades (*epikouroi*, *Il.* 17.213-14).

Looking back to earlier work, Barbara Patzek has drawn attention to the high significance of the sheen attributed to heroes' armour in the poem. Gold or bronze do not represent the actual materials of the objects but are to be understood as metaphors of differences in status.[82] Gold armour has the highest sheen and thus the highest status, reserved almost exclusively for gods. When the sheen of Achilles's or Hector's armour is referred to then this is an expression of their success in battle and of their newly acquired status, just as it is for the characterisation of Diomedes's and Glaucus's arms as, respectively, made of gold and bronze.

Success in battle and social status tend to coincide in the poem and are visually represented by the sheen of armour. It is assumed in recent scholarship that individual achievement in battle justifies social status.[83] But looking closely at the battle scenes it instead becomes clear that success is frequently justified by genealogical proximity to the gods.[84] So, when fighting Polydorus, the son of Priam and Laothoë (*Il.* 21.85), Achilles throws his descent from a divine mother into the balance (*Il.* 21.109). Before his victory over Asteropaius, whose family line goes back to the river god Axius (*Il.* 21.140-43; 157), Achilles boasts about his paternal lineage, which goes back to Zeus via Peleus and Aiacus (*Il.* 21.185-90). Duelling with Aeneas, whom Achilles must recognise as a darling (*philos*) of the gods (*Il.* 20.347), both maternal and paternal lineages are drawn on. The Trojan's closeness to the gods stems from the maternal side, as he is the son of Aphrodite and the shepherd Anchises. He boasts about this to Achilles, while also mentioning the latter's descent from the goddess Thetis, making sure to point out her inferior rank (*Il.* 20.206-9). On the paternal side Aeneas, like Achilles, claims descent from Zeus (*Il.* 20.214-41). The heroes are potentially of equal status, and a victory thus is impossible

---

82. Patzek 1992: 188-93. She follows Willenbrock 1969: 19.
83. See Ulf 1990: 110-13 who denies any correlation between status and birth.
84. See Svenbro 1976: 124-27 and 135-38.

EXCHANGING ARMS: GLAUCUS AND DIOMEDES

for either of them.[85] When Achilles is hit by Aeneas's spear, the new gold armour provided by Thetis protects him (*Il.* 20.268). But this does not equate to success in battle. At the moment when Achilles's arms become a danger to Aeneas, the gods intervene directly to remove him from battle, as they do with Paris in the duel with Menelaus (*Il.* 20.309–12).

The principle of genealogical proximity to the divine and support in battle is knowingly used by the gods. In cases of conflict, Hera makes the decision in consultation with the other gods. When Zeus wishes to save Sarpedon, to him the 'dearest among men' (φίλτατον ἀνδρῶν, *Il.* 16.433), Hera stops this but allows the body to be saved by Apollo in order to give it the proper honour of burial (*Il.* 16.431–61). Similarly, Hera agrees to Poseidon's removing Aeneas from battle (*Il.* 20.309–12). When it comes to removing Hector's abused body, Hera is keen to deny this because of the Trojan hero's lowly descent from a mortal mother (*Il.* 24.55–63). On this occasion the solution is arrived at through Zeus, who concedes the inequality in familial status between Hector and Achilles but nonetheless achieves the release of the body through Thetis's mediation (*Il.* 24.55–76). In the theomachy Hera usually either personally defeats other gods like Artemis (*Il.* 21.512–13) or achieves victory with Athena's help over Ares and Aphrodite, and Hephaestus (*Il.* 21.391 and 330). Knowledge about genealogical status and its consequences lies with Hera as the highest-ranking goddess; both maternal and paternal lineage may play a role in decisions over victory or defeat.[86]

Against this background the unequal exchange between Diomedes and Glaucus makes much more sense. In terms of lineage, Glaucus initially appears the likely victor, as he is Bellerophon's grandson and can trace his line back to Aeolus. Glaucus's genealogy takes up a whole sixty-six verses (*Il.* 6.145–211). Diomedes on the other hand claims not to know much about his father, Tydeus, whose father, Oineus, exchanged gifts with Bellerophon (*Il.* 6.222). This status difference is also underlined through the sheen of the heroes' armour. Glaucus's proximity to the divine is demonstrated

---

85. When a duel ends in stalemate, it is clear that both parties are equally close to the gods. So, Ajax and Hector whose duel ends without a winner, are both loved by Zeus.
86. For the correspondence between status and success in the battle of the gods, compare Svenbro 1976: 136. He stresses the closeness to Zeus as decisive. But this close relationship to Zeus is important only for the decision whether a fight should take place. Apollo refuses to fight with Poseidon because he is a brother of his father (*Il.* 21.469). Hermes accepts Leto as victor without fighting because of her status as his divine father's *alochos* (*Il.* 21.497–501). But the decision of the victory lies in Hera's hands.

through his gold armour, while Diomedes's bronze armour, appropriate for a mortal, shows his inferior status. The arms-exchange inverts the principles of status and achievement, and the final comment on its inequality shows that this inversion is established knowingly by the poet. The genealogically inferior man, who is thus also subordinate in terms of the unity between status and success in battle, receives the gold armour. The genealogically superior man, who is also the stronger in battle, makes do with the bronze armour. With this inversion Diomedes's *aristeia*, the theme of the previous book, is given greater prominence. Unlike Hector, who exchanges his armour for that of the defeated enemy, Diomedes receives his opponent's armour without a fight. The gleam of the armour distinguishes him as the real victor.[87]

The comparison of value undertaken by the poet at the end of the depiction of the arms-exchange cannot then be put down to forgetfulness. Nor does it point to any essential superiority or inferiority on the part of the recipient of gifts. Instead, it highlights what is unusual about the situation: the inversion of status and achievement. It is possible that this also points to a difference between Greek and Trojan practice. Arguments against this are as follows: (1) in the theomachy the principle of unity of genealogical superiority and superior fighting skills applies; (2) the genealogical principle is applied in order to establish decisions in conflict situations.[88] It is more likely that there are a number of different criteria for establishing rank and that the poet chooses from case to case which one to emphasise. Without a thorough examination of the principles of familial relationships represented in the epic, any conclusions can only be preliminary.[89]

If we can firmly establish that the arms-exchange scene is not evidence for competitive giving, we can further discuss whether it provides evidence for the binding function of guest-friendship. The context within which the unequal exchange is described argues against this.

As Diomedes underlines, the effects of guest-friendship are felt at each guest-friend's home: in Argos and in Lycia (*Il.* 6.224–25). It is not unusual in antiquity to find that such guest-friendships bear consequences in battle-situations. Even Pausanias, centuries later, in observations on

---

87. The connection between the gleam of the armour and strength in battle is underlined by the semantic meaning of the term for success, *kudos*, which lies according to Greindl (1938: 30–51) in the shine emanating from things.
88. Cf. ch. 4.2.6.
89. After the revision of the idea of a tribal stage in early Greece (see Finley 1985 and Bourriot 1976) kinship was no longer a central focus of research. See ch. 1.4, n. 223.

EXCHANGING ARMS: GLAUCUS AND DIOMEDES

the wall-painting by Polygnotus in the Cnidian treasury at Delphi, can be found speculating that Laodice was spared slavery after the fall of Troy because her father-in-law, Antenor, had been a guest-friend of Menelaus and Odysseus (Paus. 10.26.8). Pericles's offer at the start of the Peloponnesian War, of his own land as public property (*dēmosia*), if his Spartan guest-friend Archidamos spared his *agros* when the Spartans invaded Attica, shows how common the convention of sparing guest-friends was. It should be noted, however, that in Pericles's case there is a conflict between two loyalties: the obligation to the *dēmos*, and the connection with the guest-friend (Thuc. 2.13).[90]

Gabriel Herman's study of ritualised friendship in Greece shows that guest-friendships played an essential role in military conflicts in Greek *poleis* of the fifth and fourth centuries.[91] According to Thucydides, one such guest-friendship between the Spartan Agis and the Argives Thrasyllus and Alkiphron even led to the cessation of war between Sparta and Argos in 419 BCE. This did, however, result in the confiscation of Thrasyllus's property as a consequence (Thuc. 5.59–60). Such grave consequences of guest-friendship are unknown, however, in epic. The arms-exchange between Glaucus and Diomedes does not exclude the continuation of battle and in no way cancels out the obligation each warrior has to his respective leader.[92] The *Odyssey* gives us only one instance of guest-friends who do not fight one another, and this is not in battle but in a competition: it is Odysseus's refusal to fight the son of his host Alcinous, since he is a *xeinos* to him: 'He is my guest-friend. Who would fight against one who has been welcoming?' (ξεῖνος γάρ μοι ὅδ' ἐστί τίς ἄν φιλέοντι μάχοιτο, *Od.* 8.208).[93]

An existing guest-friendship may, however, result in support in the case of war, as is demonstrated a number of times in the poem. Agamemnon spurns Diomedes on to fight in *Iliad* 4 by evoking the shining example of Tydeus, who had once come to Mycenae with Polyneices as *xeinos*, in order to win allies (*epikouroi*) for the battle against Thebes

---

90. For further examples see Herman 1987: 3–4 and 142–61. See now Domingo Gygax 2016.
91. Herman 1987: 155–56 does not see any relevant difference between Homeric and classical practices of ritual friendship.
92. See Scheid-Tissinier 1994: 160: 'Ce pacte ainsi renouvelé devra cependant coexister avec les alliances qu'ils ont l'un et l'autre conclues avec Priam et Agamemnon et qui ne sauraient être remises en cause'.
93. Compare the translation of Benveniste 1969: I, 342: 'qui pourrait lutter contre son hospiteur'. For the meaning of *phileō* see ch. 2.3.

(*Il.* 4.376-79).⁹⁴ Nestor and Odysseus had enlisted followers, *laoi*, for the expedition to Troy in Phthia and had won over Achilles (*Il.* 11.765-70). On the Trojan side we see Paris wishing to avenge the death of Harpalion, who had once been his *xeinos* (*Il.* 13.660-1). Phainos, the son of Asios of Abydos, is 'the dearest of all guest-friends' (ξείνων φίλτατος) to Hector, for whom he fights, and from whom he receives rich gifts (*dōra*) in return (*Il.* 17.584). We hear in Book 18 of the many goods already spent on the allies by once-wealthy Troy (*Il.* 18.287-92).

Charis, the word for this form of military support, and also for the thanks given for it in the form of goods and gifts, will be the subject of chapter 3. Here, it is important to discuss further the role played by *xein(ē)ion* as a gift of arms. When *xeinion* is given in the form of arms, it is in most cases a substitute for personal military support or service. So, the armour, a *thōrax*, handed as a favour to Agamemnon by Kinyras is described as a *xeinion* (*Il.* 11.20-23).⁹⁵ The boar's tusk helmet worn by Odysseus at Troy had been given by Amphidamas to Melos's father as a *xeinion* (*Il.* 10.260-71). Both objects are described in detail, and both have a history which lends them a particular quality. Kinyras's *thōrax*, with which Agamemnon arms himself for battle, is described using images of battle captured in a rainbow simile: 'Truly, there were ten bands of dark blue enamel, and twelve of gold, and twenty of tin. Blue serpents writhed up towards the neck, three on each side, like rainbows that Zeus placed among the clouds, a sign to mortal men' (*Il.* 11.24-28).⁹⁶ The boar's tusk helmet given to Odysseus by Meriones was 'made of leather and made stiff inside with many tight-stretched thongs. Outside the bright teeth of a white-tusked boar were set close all around it, well and cunningly, and inside it was lined with wool. Autolycus stole this out of Eleon when he broke into the well-built house of Amyntor the Ormenid. And he gave it to Amphidamas of Cythera to take to Scandeia, and Amphidamas gave it to Melos as a gift of hospitality (δῶκε ξεινήιον εἶναι), Melos in turn gave it to Meriones his son to wear. And now, placed around it, it covered the head of Odysseus (*Il.* 10.262-70).⁹⁷ The genealogy of the object described here takes

---

94. For the recruitment of *epikouroi* see Ulf 1990: 157-64; van Wees 1992.
95. For the role of Cyprus in the epics see Giuffrida 1985: 15-39. In *Iliad* 15.529-33 a *thōrax* is called a gift (*dōron*) of a *xeinos*. Cf. the horse of Echepolos, which functions as gift of compensation for personal service. Menelaus uses it for his chariot (*Il.* 23.296-97). See Ulf 1990: 161.
96. The rainbow functions as a sign of battle. See *Il.* 17.547.
97. Grave finds indicate that helmets were part of standard Mycenaean warriors' equipment and were still in use during the eighth century BCE by the Greeks' northern and eastern neighbours. Cf. Patzek 1992: 193-94, who interprets the description as acknowledgement of the handicraft.

it from plunder to guest-gift, from guest-gift to heirloom, and finally to a gift of arms given as support to a battle ally. This underlines the connection between guest-friendship and battle alliance, but it does not lend the gift itself any bonding function.

There is only one example in the poem of an object that does function as a bond: this is the sword Odysseus gives to Iphitos as the start of a close guest-friendship (ἀρχὴν ξεινοσύνης προσκηδέος), after the latter had given him the bow of his father, Eurytos (*Od.* 21.31–35). This is the only occasion outside of battle situations that we hear of an exchange of arms as gifts (*xeinia*). Unlike the arms gifts discussed earlier, which are always given only by one party for the purpose of immediate support in battle, the bow is given as a 'memento of a guest-friend' (μνῆμα ξείνοιο φίλοιο) and is kept along with other treasures inside the home (*Od.* 21.40).

Besides this example there are only two instances of reciprocal arms-exchange, both as interruptions of battle action in the *Iliad*. We have already discussed the first of these exchanges; the second exchange takes place between Hector and Ajax and is no less anachronistic than that between Glaucus and Diomedes.[98] When nightfall necessitates the cessation of fighting, Hector suggests to Ajax that they should exchange 'gifts full of glory' (δῶρα [...] περικλυτὰ) in order to demonstrate to all that they part 'in friendship' (ἐν φιλότητι). Hector gives a silver sword, Ajax a purple belt (*Il.* 7.299–305). Despite this friendly conclusion to the fighting, Ajax is characterised as the victor (*Il.* 7.312). The explicit pointer to the victorious party suggests irony, similar to that we have already seen in the exchange between Diomedes and Glaucus.

While in the case of Glaucus and Diomedes the unequal exchange is made against the background of inherited guest-friendship, Hector's purpose in visualising a bond of friendship is to evoke the earlier bond made between Achaeans and Trojans in Book 3. In both cases the bond is described as φιλότης (*philotēs*). In Book 3, the establishment of *philotēs* was intended to restore the state of play as it was before Paris had wronged his host, *xeinodokos*, Menelaus, who had extended *philotēs* in the form of hospitality (*Il.* 3.345). The term *philotēs* combines hospitality and friendship (or better: closeness or kinship). Yet, while the bond of guest-friendship is constant, the establishment of *philotēs* amongst warriors tends only to have a temporary effect. This type of bond is not secured through the exchange of gifts but through oaths, libations, handshakes, and through

---

98. This is also stressed by Donlan 1989: 10.

sacrifices to Gaia, Helios, and Zeus. Such gestures oblige warriors to a leader (*Il.* 2.339-41), and they perform the ritual of peace-treaties between groups such as the Achaeans and Trojans (*Il.* 3.94-105).[99] Such obligation lasts no longer than Hector's promise of *philotēs*. In both cases, fighting continues. Hector announces the resumption of battle on the following day; the Achaeans and Trojans resume hostilities after the treaty is broken by a Trojan and Menelaus is hit by an arrow. Agamemnon puts it to his wounded brother that the Trojans have 'trodden on the trusted oaths' (ὅρκια πιστά) and threatens:

οὐ μέν πως ἅλιον πέλει ὅρκιον αἷμά τε ἀρνῶν
σπονδαί τ' ἄκρητοι καὶ δεξιαὶ ᾗς ἐπέπιθμεν.
εἴ περ γάρ τε καὶ αὐτίκ' Ὀλύμπιος οὐκ ἐτέλεσσεν,
ἔκ τε καὶ ὀψὲ τελεῖ, σύν τε μεγάλῳ ἀπέτισαν
σὺν σφῇσιν κεφαλῇσι γυναιξί τε καὶ τεκέεσσιν.

The oath once made is never in vain, and the blood of the lambs, and the offerings of unmixed wine, and the hand-shakes in which we put our trust. For even if the Olympian does not fulfil it straightaway, he will do so, even after a long time, and they will pay a big price, with their own heads, and their wives and children' (*Il.* 4.158-62).

We see, when Agamemnon first swears the oath, that cursing the potential oath-breaker is an essential part of it: 'Zeus, Father, who reigns on Ida, noblest and greatest, and Helios, you who see everything and hear everything! And rivers, and earth, and you underneath who punish those who swear falsely. Be witnesses and keep watch over the trusted oaths (φυλάσσετε δ' ὅρκια πιστά) we swear' (*Il.* 3.276-80).

This form of agreement through a sworn oath is ultimately also in play between Glaucus and Diomedes, who not only exchange arms but also clasp each other's hands and place their faith in one another (χεῖράς τ' ἀλλήλων λαβέτην καὶ πιστώσαντο, *Il.* 6.233). The epithet *pista* characterises the *horkia* sworn by the Achaians and the Trojans—or indeed the sacrifices made, as is suggested by the verb *tamnein* (to cut) taken with *horkia* (*Il.*

---

99. For the difference between *horkia* and *philotēs* see Karavites 1992: 48-73; Cohen 1980: 49-68; Taillardat 1982. On the narrative aspects of oath-making rituals see Kitts 2005.

3.94).¹⁰⁰ In the context of hospitality we do not find such a ritual except for the pouring of libations to the gods.¹⁰¹ When individuals commit to one another through oaths, this is done with the intention of preventing harm and keeping a promised favour, without the need for establishing guest-friendship.¹⁰² So Eumaeus's Sidonian wet-nurse demands that the Phoenician sailors who are to take her home should swear an oath (ὅρκῳ πιστωθῆναι, *Od.* 15.436). Odysseus, too, has Circe promise to 'swear a great oath' (μέγαν ὅρκον ὀμόσσαι, *Od.* 10.343) in order to avoid harm caused by her sorcery.

I am inclined therefore to doubt the idea that the arms-exchange between Glaucus and Diomedes has a causal connection with the inherited guest-friendship and thus proves that guest-friendship forms the basis of political ties and treaties.¹⁰³ It is clear from my observations above that the arms-exchange is not based on guest-friendship but is a form of *horkia*, a bond made specifically between combatants, and which is demonstrated

---

100. For the meaning of *horkia* as oaths ('Eidschwüre') and sacrifices ('Eidopfer'), see Cohen 1980: 55, who interprets *horkia tamnein* as 'cutting of the hairs' of the sacrificed animals 'as well as of the cutting of their throats at the end of the ceremony. Further, the hairs are distributed to all Greeks and Trojan leaders [...]'. The ritual will bind the people to the pact (56). On the meaning of oaths as contract in ancient Greece see also Hirzel 1902: 65–75. For evidence in classical Greece see Sommerstein and Torrance 2014.
101. Cf. ch. 2.3.
102. The term is ὅρκον ὀμόσσαι. See *Od.* 5.178 (Calypso); *Od.* 12.298 (Eurylochus); *Il.* 20.313: (Hera and Athena). Only individuals swear oaths, *horkoi*, whereas oaths connected with sacrifices, *horkia*, are sworn by collectives. This is the case even in Ithaca where the families of the killed suitors finished the battle by *horkia* (*Od.* 24.546). Cf. Cohen 1980: 49–52. For a different view see Herman 1987: 49–54. According to him clasping each other's hands (*dexiai*) and pledging faith (*pisteuesthai*) were typical elements of the ritual of friendship between individuals. This is true in classical times but does not correspond with epic evidence. Taillardat 1982: 1–14 interprets *dexiai* and oaths as elements of the ritual of guest-friendship with contractual value. But in the epics, handshakes (*dexiai*) are only used when individuals are received by collectives. Cf. the invitation of Telemachus by the Pylians to their sacrificial meal (*Od.* 3.35). Normally guests were taken by the right hand. Cf. e.g. the reception of Odysseus and Nestor by Achilles (*Il.* 11.778) of Thetis by Charis (*Il.* 18.385), of Mentor by Telemachus (*Od.* 1.121) and of Odysseus by Alcinous (*Od.* 7.168). This can be read as a gesture of protection. It is not a sign of a contract.
103. According to Widzisz 2012: 166–67 the simultaneous character of the exchange makes it impossible to create a gift-exchange relationship between Glaucus and Diomedes. Cf. also van Wees 1992: 228.

in all its fragility and ambivalence on a number of occasions. Even when *horkia* are not broken, as in the cases I have discussed, they are often intended to be only of limited duration. This is the case when agreements are entered into for the purpose of burying the dead, or when obligations are entered into for the duration of a particular campaign of battle.[104] I do not mean to support the notion that oaths such as those sworn between Greeks and Trojans should be interpreted as treaties between nations, or as an early form of 'international law', as some have done in the past.[105] Instead, I wish to go beyond this and to argue that such agreements by oath between warriors merge together with guest-friendship to form one institution only after the point at which those who assume the political character of guest-friendship see it as having been replaced by institutionalised forms of treaty-making.[106] Even alliances of the classical period that are made in writing still represent bonds of friendship. Described as *xenia*, *philia*, or *symmachia*, the treaties of the classical period still share the constitutional elements of oath and sacrifice with the Homeric *horkia*.[107] The need for written contracts in the classical period can be explained, as has been done for the medieval period, through the increasing complexity of the agreements made.[108] This does not result in a new character of 'international law' for this form of bond. All we have is a blending of the individual and collective forms of bond, which in their Homeric form are still differentiated.

Such continuity, to be expected at the level of collective alliances, is mirrored in observations made by Gabriel Herman on the subject of personal

---

104. *Il.* 7.69; 411; 2.110. Cf. the reintegration of Achilles into the army of the Achaeans, which was sealed by *horkia* (*Il.* 19.190–91). Cohen (1980: 52–53) therefore differentiates between temporary and permanent existing contracts, called *horkia*. This is correct, insofar as in some cases permanence is aimed for. In these cases, the term *philotēs* is used additionally to denote this permanence. See further below.
105. For a discussion see Phillipson 1911: I, 46–66 who stresses the principles of juridical equality and reciprocity of nations as main features of international law (60). For evidence in the epics see Köstler 1950: 18–19; Wéry 1967: 169–205 against Audinet 1914: 29–63. Gschnitzer 1991: 182–204 interprets the oath as an institution of law and stately order. For a middling position see Karavites 1992: 8–9 who stresses the informal and personal character 'of international law'. A system of reciprocal obligations is assumed by Cohen 1980: 52. See now Elmer 2013 who underlines the reciprocal aspects in situations of collective decision-making in the *Iliad*.
106. Donlan 1982: 149.
107. See Baltrusch 1994: 5–15, 66–68, 144.
108. Althoff 1990: 88.

friendships in the classical period.[109] His results prove a close connection between individual guest-friendships between leaders and the forming of military alliances between collectives. I will conclude with an example from Xenophon's *Hellenica* (4.1.29–40) in which a meeting is arranged by Apollophanes of Kyzikos between the Persian Pharnabazus and the Spartan king Agesilaus. Apollophanes, a guest-friend (*xenos*) of both the Persian and the Spartan, suggests to Agesilaus that he should establish a bond of friendship (*philia*) with Pharnabazus, against whom he is currently engaged in warfare. Agesilaus grasps the opportunity of a truce, which is sealed with a handshake (*dexia*), and he is led to meet Pharnabazus. The latter reminds Agesilaus that he had been a friend (*philos*) and ally (*symmachos*) of the Lacedaemonians when they had been at war with Athens, and that he now expects a favour in return (*charis*) from Agesilaus. The Spartan king counters by explaining that in the Greek states guest-friends (*xenoi*) still have to fight one another when their *poleis* are at war. Nonetheless, he suggests that they should become *philoi* and *symmachoi*. Pharnabazus, in turn, has to reject this out of loyalty to the Persian king, as he is his general. Despite this, Agesilaus is able to promise to spare Pharnabazus's possessions, and to enter into guest-friendship with the Persian's son, sealed with an exchange of gifts: Agesilaus gives his horse's headgear and Pharnabazus's son gives his javelin.

The example demonstrates clearly the personal character of military alliance, here described as *philia*; it also shows the decisive role played by existing guest-friendships in the establishment of such alliances in the fourth century.[110] The fact that a military consensus between Pharnabazus and Agesilaus is not realised is attributed to the existence of alternative, civic ties and obligations that affect both leaders. Significantly, however, the Greek's loyalty to his *polis* is not seen as preventing him from forming an alliance with the Persian satrap; rather it is Pharnabazus who brings the superiority of his obligation to the Persian king to bear on the situation.[111] The satrap's loyalty to his king may prevent the two leaders from becoming allies (*symmachoi* and *philoi*). This does not stop them from establishing guest-friendship on a personal level and sealing it, in the same manner as the bond of friendship between Iphitos and Odysseus, with an exchange

---

109. Herman 1987.
110. For evidence of *philia* as term for 'Bundesgenossenschaft' see Dirlmeier 1931: 34. According to him *philia* is not used in political contexts before Herodotus. He considers earlier references in poetry to be 'Attizismus'.
111. For another view see Herman 1987: 2. He stresses ties with the *polis*. But such ties are not relevant in this episode.

of arms. The guest-friendship established between Agesilaus and the son of Pharnabazus becomes effective when the latter loses his throne to his uncle and is able to count on the hospitality and support of his Spartan guest-friend, Agesilaus (Xen. *Hell.* 4.1.40).[112]

In the classical period the term used to describe such personal guest-friendships that often occur in military situations is *xenia*, which is frequently used by Herodotus in particular. So Herodotus tells of Xerxes forming a bond of *xeinia* (ξεινίην τέ σφι συνθέμενος, Hdt. 8.120) with the people of Abdera on the Hellespont and making them gifts of a golden sword and a gilt headdress. Herodotus also claims that Amilcas was induced to act as commander for Terillus because of guest-friendship (7.165). According to Herodotus, guest-friendship can lead to alliance, which can then result in obligation to provide military assistance (Hdt. 7.27–39). As Gabriel Herman has convincingly argued, classical *xenia* is not just guest-friendship but a kind of 'ritualised friendship'.[113] In Homeric epic there is, however, no specific word for guest-friendship apart from *xeinosynē*. The noun *xenia* is used only in the final book of the *Odyssey* to describe proven hospitality (*Od.* 24.286 and 314). This would suggest that guest-friendship that specifically includes military and political alliance comes into being only in the classical period. Such a formalisation of guest-friendship in terms of military alliance is merely suggested when the term *xeinosynē* is used to describe the relationship between Iphitos and Odysseus in Book 21. As in classical *xenia*, this relationship is sealed with an exchange of arms. When such relationships between guest-friends are formed elsewhere in the epics, gifts (for instance golden vessels or textiles) are given as pledges, such as those exchanged by the ancestors of Glaucus and Diomedes. I will be examining the function of such gifts in what follows, before returning to the various forms of relationships and bonds formed in the epics.

2.3. Goblets and textiles: Xeinion as keimēlion and the ritual of guest-friendship

'There are no whole oxen here, no gold (ὄυτε χρυσός), no bright red carpets (ὄθτε πορφύρεοι τάπητες), but there is a gracious spirit, the pleasant

---

112. Cf. the description of guest-friendships by Herodotus, which existed between the Alcmaeonids of Athens and the Lydian king Croesus. The Alcmaeonids received gifts of gold and supported the embassy of Croesus on their way to Delphi in return (Hdt. 6.125).
113. Herman 1987: 7.

GOBLETS AND TEXTILES: THE RITUAL OF GUEST-FRIENDSHIP

Muse and sweet wine in Boeotian cups.' This is Bacchylides's promise to the Dioscuri, Helen's brothers, in a fragmentary lyric (Bacch. *fr.* 21 = Ath. 11.500 a). The contrast between the display of items associated with Homeric hospitality—the sacrificial feast, golden apparel, and purple cloth— and the less ostentatious values represented by spirit, song, and the simple Boeotian cups clearly implies the superiority of the latter. This is especially clear when Bacchylides is read against the background of fifth-century ideas of equality, which go hand in hand with the negative valuation of conspicuously luxurious dress.[114] By contrast, heroic epic never questions differences in status and their display. When it does thematise a contrast similar to that just seen in Bacchylides, between inner value and outward appearance, it never represents the former as superior to the latter. Rather, such contrast will always take the form of a critique of the insufficiency of the display with a view to the demands made by social status. In Homeric epic the appearance of a hero or heroine, and of the objects they surround themselves with, are visible markers of their social status. This indicative function is seen especially clearly in the gifts handed to guests as mementoes of existing guest-friendships. Such guest-gifts bear symbolic significance and are distinguished from other gifts described as *xeinia* and which belong (along with natural *xeinia* and with the gift of arms as *xeinion*) in the context of relationships of service. The word used for symbolic mementoes or guest-gifts is therefore not *xeinion* but *dōron*. I will now first discuss these differences and will then pursue the function of different gifts in the ritual of friendship, along with the terms used to evoke this ritual.

2.3.1. Mementoes and tributes: Tripods, goblets, mixing bowls, and cloth

There are only three instances in the *Odyssey* of *xeinia* that are neither natural goods nor weapons. These are the textile and metal goods Odysseus receives from the Phaeacians, and the gifts reportedly given to Odysseus by an alleged guest-friend. Let us begin with the Phaeacians. After Odysseus has proven himself to the hospitable Phaeacians as both a delightful speaker and a good fighter in contest (*Od.* 8.186–236), Alcinous requests that each of his twelve chieftains (*basilēes*) grant a *xeinion* to their guest:

---

114. For this interpretation see Stulz 1990: 148. For the discussion on luxury in the fifth century BCE see Geddes 1987: 307–31. On aristocratic cloth luxury of the sixth century BCE see Stein-Hölkeskamp 1989: 104–10; Bernhardt 2003; Wagner-Hasel 2007; Lupi 2019.

ὁ ξεῖνος μάλα μοι δοκέει πεπνυμένος εἶναι.
ἀλλ' ἄγε οἱ δῶμεν ξεινήϊον, ὡς ἐπιεικές. [...]
τῶν οἱ ἕκαστος φᾶρος ἐϋπλυνὲς ἠδὲ χιτῶνα
καὶ χρυσοῖο τάλαντον ἐνείκατε τιμήεντος.

The guest (*xeinos*) seems to me to be a man of understanding. So, come on, let us give him a guest-gift (*xeinēion*) as is fitting. [...] Let each give him a well-washed cloak (*pharos*), and a tunic (*chitōn*), and a talent of precious gold (*Od.* 8.388-89 and 392-93, tr. E. Theodorakoulos).

The queen, Arete, places these golden and textile *xeinia*—later also described as *klyta* and *kallima dōra*, glorious and very beautiful gifts (*Od.* 8.417 and 439)—in a trunk, which she locks (8.438-39).[115] She herself has added, at her husband's request, a particularly beautiful cloak or cloth (*pharos kalon*, 8.425) and a *chitōn* (8.441). While the gold is specified by weight, the textile goods are differentiated according to types into *pharea* and *chitōnes*. A *chitōn* is an item of male clothing, while the *pharos* is a large rectangular piece of cloth used as a cloak for both sexes and also as a coverlet at night or as shroud or pall. Both can be made from linen,[116] the weaving of which Phaeacian women appear to specialise in (this is indicated by their looms dripping with oil, which was used as a form of finish in linen production).[117] These types of textile gifts are also described

---

115. Such chests are placed in the *thalamos*, the only room which could be locked with a key and used for storing textiles as we see in the *Odyssey* (15.104-5; 2.345) and in the *Iliad* (6.286-95; 24.228).
116. Adjectives such as σιγαλόεις (*sigaloeis*), 'glossy, glittering', and ἀργύφεος (*argypheos*), 'silver-shining', may be read to suggest the gleam of linen. See the argumentation of Studnizka 1886: 13; Abrahams: 1964: 19-27; Evans 1964: 5; Bieber 1977: 16; 1967: 23. For another position see Marinatos 1967: 8, who does not deny the use of linen but argues in this case that the men's *chitōn* was made of wool. His argumentation is based on his translation of τερμιόεις (*termioeis*), literally: at the border—τέρμα, as 'am Ende elastisch gestrickt'. More convincingly Bieber 1967: 23. She argues that this type of *chitōn* had a patterned or coloured border as seen on vases. This is now proved by Ellen Harlizius-Klück 2016. See my argumentation in ch. 5.3.
117. Blümner 1912: 196. Cf. the description of the *chitōnes* of the young men on the shield of Hephaestus, glistening with oil (χιτῶνας [...] στίλβοντας, *Il.* 18.595-96). Fragments of linen were found in the graves of Lefkandi (tenth century BCE) and in Gordion (seventh century BCE). Cf. Blome 1984: 12; Lemos 2007; de Vries 1980: 35; Burke 2010. For more detail see ch. 5.3.

with the collective terms for cloth and garments, ἐσθῆτες (*esthētes*) and εἵματα (*heimata*).¹¹⁸

Another gift-giving scene occurs during Odysseus's tale in Book 11, when Arete, reminding the Phaeacian lords of the many riches (*ktēmata*) they have stored in their halls (πολλὰ γὰρ ὑμῖν | κτήματ' ἐνὶ μεγάροισι θεῶν ἰότητι κέονται, *Od.* 11.340-41), asks them once again to give gifts (this time called *dōra*) to their guest (τῷ μὴ ἐπειγόμενοι ἀποπέμπετε μηδὲ τὰ δῶρα | οὕτω χρηΐζοντι κολούετε, 11.339-41).¹¹⁹ The assembled Phaeacian lords and Alcinous himself agree to give these gifts, which are characterised as mobile goods through the use of the term *ktēmata*.¹²⁰ Alcinous uses the word *dōtinē*, which we have met already in the context of natural goods given as *xeinia*. Here again the word is ambiguous and could be taken to mean the gifts as a whole or the escort (*pompē*) promised by Alcinous:

τοῦτο μὲν οὕτω δὴ ἔσται ἔπος, αἴ κεν ἐγώ γε
ζωὸς Φαιήκεσσι φιληρέτμοισιν ἀνάσσω
ξεῖνος δὲ τλήτω, μάλα περ νόστοιο χατίζων,
ἔμπης οὖν ἐπιμεῖναι ἐς αὔριον, εἰς ὅ κε πᾶσαν
δωτίνην τελέσω. πομπὴ δ' ἄνδρεσσι μελήσει
πᾶσι, μάλιστα δ' ἐμοί τοῦ γὰρ κράτος ἔστ' ἐνὶ δήμῳ.

Let this word of hers hold true, while I live and rule over the oarloving Phaeacians. But let the *xeinos* for all his craving for home, stay put until tomorrow, until I shall have completed the entire *dōtinē*. His passage (*pompē*) shall be the men's responsibility, all of them, but most of all mine, for the power in the *dēmos* is mine (*Od.* 11.348-53).

In his reply to this offer, Odysseus refers to the *pompē* as well as to the promised goods, now characterised as shining gifts, *aglaa dōra* (ἀγλαὰ δῶρα, *Od.* 11.357). It is not until Book 13, after Odysseus has completed his story, that we find out the exact nature of these gifts, with talk of a tripod (τρίπους) and a cauldron (λέβης), the cost of which will be collected from the people, and the already promised cloths (*heimata*) and gold (13.10-15).

---

118. *Od.* 8.440; 13.137; 13.218.
119. For interpretation of the question of Arete see ch. 4.1.
120. The term *ktēmata* denotes mobile goods which are deposited inside houses (*Od.* 7.150; 15.11; 17.532). It is Penelope who takes care of them (*Od.* 23.354-60). Cf. ch 5.

Arete repeats that she will contribute a well-washed *pharos* and a *chitōn*, and also at this point bread and wine for the journey (13.66–69). Both the *pompē* and the tripod and cauldron are afforded by the collective, the *dēmos* of the Phaeacians, while the individual chieftains, the *basilēes*, and the hosts themselves, Arete and Alcinous, contribute the textiles. When the packing of the goods is described, the gifts are listed in terms of materials as bronze, gold, and woven cloth (χαλκόν τε χρυσόν τε ἅλις ἐσθῆτά θ' ὑφαντήν, 13.136). When he returns to Ithaca, Odysseus counts (ἠρίθμει) the goods, this time listing them in terms of their use as tripods (τρίποδας), cauldrons (λέβητας), and woven garments (ὑφαντά τε εἵματα, 13.217–18). It is noted that there is more than Odysseus could have obtained at Troy in spoils (13.137). In receiving these gifts, Odysseus achieves a godlike position, as Zeus had prophesied (5.36–38): 'They will honour him like a god (θεὸν ὣς τιμήσουσιν)' and 'give him bronze and gold and garments (χαλκόν τε χρυσόν τε ἅλις ἐσθῆτά τε δόντες)'. With this turn of phrase, principally used for *basilēes*, Odysseus is characterised as not just a guest but as a *basileus* similar to Alcinous himself. He too holds a godlike position; the *dēmos* listen to him as to a god.[121] As in the Polyphemus episode, Odysseus plays a double role as a stranger, *xeinos*, and as *basileus*, receiving tributes from the *dēmos* (with Polyphemus his other role had been that of the master, *anax*, over his shepherds). This is also supported by the listing of the goods in terms of their materials—this represents a form of abstraction which must indicate that it is not the individual gift and its significance that counts but the quantity of goods and the wealth that they represent.

Odysseus receives two separate types of gifts: one is the *xeinion*, consisting of cloth (*chitōnes* and *pharea*) and gold, and it comes from the *basilēes*' homes; the other type are gifts described as *dōra*, which consist of bronze articles (tripods and cauldrons), and which are given by the people. Added to this is the escort, that is, the granting of a ship and rowers. The overall term for these gifts from the people is *dōtinē*, although we cannot say for certain whether this means just the escort or also includes the other gifts made by the people.

A gift from Alcinous, a *dōron*, is distinct from those just listed. This is a gold goblet, handed over with an appeal to be remembered: 'I will give him this very beautiful gold cup of mine (ἄλεισον ἐμὸν περικαλλὲς ὀπάσσω | χρύσεον), so that he may remember me (ἐμέθεν μεμνημένος) forever when he pours libations in his palace to Zeus and to the other gods'

---

121. See ch. 4.1.

(Od. 8.430-32). Elsewhere Odysseus promised to remain a *xeinos* after his departure and when he lives in a home far away (ὑμῖν ἔω καὶ ἀπόπροθι δώματα ναίων, Od. 9.18). The clothing Nausicaa gives to the shipwrecked Odysseus functions similarly as a memento, if indirectly: when Odysseus has been handed the clothing, and has bathed and dressed, Nausicaa asks him to remember her in the future, as it is to her first that he owes his life (μνήσῃ ἐμεῦ, ὅτι μοι πρώτῃ ζωάγρι' ὀφέλλεις, Od. 8.462). Odysseus promises to appeal to her every day as to a goddess, since she saved his life (Od. 8.467-68).

Telemachus, too, receives gifts as mementoes when he renews the former guest-friendship between Odysseus and Menelaus during his expedition in search of his father. Although the term *xeinion* is not used here, Menelaus offers Telemachus 'gleaming gifts', *aglaa dōra*, in the form of three horses and a chariot, and a beautiful cup (Od. 4.589-91). Once Telemachus's identity has been established and the banquet finished, Menelaus announces the gifts, along with the same injunction to remember the giver that we have just observed with Alcinous's cup, given to Odysseus. 'I will give you a beautiful cup so that you may pour libations to the immortal gods and remember me in forever (δώσω καλὸν ἄλεισον, ἵνα σπένδῃσθα θεοῖσιν | ἀθανάτοις ἐμέθεν μεμνημένος ἤματα πάντα, Od. 4.590-92). Telemachus finds himself unable to accept the horses, since Ithaca lacks the necessary conditions to keep them, so that Menelaus promises him instead the most beautiful and valuable piece from his treasures (*keimēlia*): a finely wrought mixing bowl, a *kratēr*, made of silver and gold (δώσω τοι κρητῆρα τετυγμένον· ἀργύρεος δὲ | ἔστιν ἅπας, χρυσῷ δ' χείλεα κεκράανται, Od. 4.615-16 = 15.115-16). The vessel had been given to Menelaus by Phaedimus, the king of the Sidonians, when Menelaus had been a guest in his house (Od. 4.617-19 = 15.117-19). When Telemachus is ready to depart, Menelaus and Helen go down to the *thalamos* in which the *keimēlia* are kept, where Menelaus gets the promised objects, the double-handled cup and the silver mixing bowl (Od. 15.99-104). Helen adds a textile *dōron* of her own, a πέπλος (*peplos*), said to be her best and largest, patterned (*poikilos*), and shining like a star (ὃς κάλλιστος ἔην ποικίλμασιν ἠδὲ μέγιστος, ἀστὴρ δ' ὣς ἀπέλαμπεν, Od. 15.107-8). This gift also is given with a request for remembrance, as Helen addresses Telemachus with the robe in her hands: 'I give you this, a remembrance of Helen's hands for your bride to wear on the day of your longed-for marriage' (τοῦτο δίδωμι | μνῆμ' Ἑλένης χειρῶν, πολυηράτου ἐς γάμου ὥρην σῇ ἀλόχῳ φορέειν, Od.

15.125-27). This request is confirmed as a norm, just before the handing over of gifts of remembrance, in the advice given to Telemachus by his companion Peisistratus, who reminds him that a *xeinos* will always remember the host (*anēr xeinodokos*) who shows him *philotēs* (ξεῖνος μιμνήσκεται ἤματα πάντα | ἀνδρὸς ξεινοδόκου, ὅς κεν φιλότητα παράσχῃ, *Od*. 15.54-55). While it is possible that *philotēs* in this case means just hospitality, it is clearly endowed with the more concrete sense of the giving of gifts, since Peisistratus is also asking his friend not to leave without the promised gifts (ἀλλὰ μέν' εἰς ὅ κε δῶρα φέρων ἐπιδίφρια θήῃ [...] Μενέλαος, *Od*. 15.51-52).

Besides the gifts of remembrance, other possible gifts are mentioned at Sparta, similar to those given to Odysseus by the Phaeacian *dēmos*: bronze tripods and gold (here given in the shape of cups) as well as mules (omitted by the seafaring Phaeacians). When Telemachus announces his intention to return to Ithaca, Menelaus suggests a tour of Hellas and Argos, promising to escort the younger man himself and to lead him to all the cities: 'Nor will anyone send us away empty-handed, but they will give us something to take away with us, a tripod made of good bronze, or a cauldron, or a pair of mules, or a golden cup' (*Od*. 15.82-85). Telemachus turns this offer down and returns home to Ithaca bearing only the textile and golden gifts of remembrance. These are described similarly to Odysseus's own *xeinia*, according to their material value as garments and gold (ἐσθῆτα χρυσόν τε, *Od*. 15.206-7).

Both episodes of memory-related gift-giving appear to display a gender-specific pattern in which metal memorial items are given by men while textile mementoes are given by women.[122] The latter are also mentioned as intended recipients, as when Helen's *peplos* is intended for Telemachus's future wife and is to be kept in storage by his mother until it is needed (*Od*. 15.127-28).[123] Thus the relationships formed when gifts of remembrance are given involve not only the individuals who are present themselves but also their absent and their future relations. Helen is named as a direct

---

122. See Pedrick 1988. The commemorative function is now stressed by Mueller 2010, Karanika 2014: 39, and Canevaro 2018: 51. According to Canevaro, Helen's behaviour is unusual 'within their society'. Karanika, however, observes the association of weaving with memory and authoritative female speech and argues: 'The product of one woman's work becomes the locus of memory making'. Mueller (2010: 11) stresses the female character of the network created by textile gifts.
123. Papadopoulou-Belmehdi (1994: 123) interprets the gift of cloth by Helen as a hint at the reconstruction of the bond between Odysseus and Penelope. According to her, both Sparta and Pylos were characterised as places where the ritual language, which was disturbed at Ithaca, is still known.

MEMENTOES AND TRIBUTES

recipient of *kallima dōra*, the golden distaff and the silver wheeled basket that Alkandre, the wife of Polybus, a guest-friend of Menelaus from Egyptian Thebes, had given her (*Od.* 4.130-32). Polybus himself gave Menelaus two silver baths, two tripods, and ten talents of gold (4.127-28). Later texts also mention feminine objects associated with spinning as gifts given to women. So Herodotus has golden spindles and distaffs as gifts from Euëlthon of Salamis in Cyprus to Pheretime of Cyrene (Hdt. 4.162).[124] Theocritus has a spindle given as a memento to the wife of the Athenian Nicias (*Id.* 28.1-25). In Xenophon's *Anabasis* we find garments given as gifts to Thracian women with the intention of forming a bond of *philia* (Xen. *An.* 7.3.17 and 27).[125]

All these types of metal and textile gifts—be they golden cups, bronze tripods and cauldrons, silver mixing bowls, woven *chitōnes*, *pharea*, or *peploi*—are mentioned as *xeinia* in Odysseus's lying tales when he impersonates the Cretan Aëthon upon his return to Ithaca. He lists an especially long list of gifts when speaking to his father: 'I gave him fitting gifts of friendship (δῶρα πόρον ξεινήϊα). I gave him seven talents of gold, a mixing bowl made of silver and decorated with flowers, and twelve single-fold cloaks (χλαίνας), as many coverlets (τάπητας) and beautiful mantles (φάρεα) and as many tunics (χιτῶνας), along with this he could select for himself four beautiful women skilled in excellent handiwork' (*Od.* 24.273-79).[126] The differentiation between the specific types of garment would usually occur only when ransom payments are described, while the giving of skilled women usually occurs when prizes or war-booty are distributed; it is thus fair to assume that the wealth of *xeinia* listed here are not intended to evoke only guest-gifts but also goods obtained as booty.[127] The *xeinia* Odysseus enumerates to his father are predominantly material objects. Speaking to Penelope in the guise of the Cretan, Odysseus also mentions natural *xeinia*, such as grain, wine, and cattle, which he claims were collected from the people for Odysseus (ξείνια δῶκα, *Od.* 19.185, and δημόθεν ἄλφιτα δῶκα καὶ αἴθοπα οἶνον ἀγείρας | καὶ βοῦς ἱρεύσασθαι, *Od.* 19.197-98). He also mentions specific objects, such as a bronze sword, a

---

124. An ironic reference to the system of gender roles in the epics cannot be excluded here: Pheretime had asked for an army and received a golden spindle like Helen's in the *Odyssey*.
125. Barber 1991: 299 interprets spindles of gold and ivory, found in bronze-age graves, as gifts between women.
126. For the different types of clothes see Bieber 1977: 23; Marinatos 1967: 6-15.
127. See ch. 4.

beautiful purple cloak, a double *diplax* such as shepherds and warriors wear, and a bordered *chitōn* (καί οἱ ἐγὼ χάλκειον ἄορ καὶ δίπλακα δῶκα | καλὴν πορφυρέην καὶ τερμιόεντα χιτῶνα, *Od.* 19.240–41).[128] The decorative epithets point to similar memorial functions as those attributed to Alcinous's golden cup and Helen's *peplos*.

In Odysseus's house, guest-gifts are spoken of but never described with the term *xeinēion* or *xeinion*. So Penelope promises many gifts, *polla dōra*, to her husband's supposed guest-friend in the event of Odysseus's return (*Od.* 19.130). These include a sword, clothing, and an escort pledged to Odysseus disguised as the beggar, should he win the bow contest (*Od.* 21.339–42). Telemachus promises the same—using the same words—when he meets the beggar at Eumaeus's hut (*Od.* 16.79–81). It is striking that none of the gifts announced by Penelope or Telemachus actually materialise: not a *chitōn*, nor a *chlaina*, nor any of the promised garments is handed over, and no promised sword reaches its recipient. The gift, the *dōron*, offered to Athena in her guise as Mentes by Telemachus is also not actually handed over. Mentes refuses to accept it and promises instead to take a *dōron* with him on the way back which 'will bring its worth in return' (δ' ἄξιον ἔσται ἀμοιβῆς, *Od.* 1.318). The allusion to a potential return gift or reciprocation, entailed in the word *amoibē*, reminds us that guest-gifts, whether natural goods or material objects, are not part of a one-way flow.[129] However, just as the exchange of goods between the household and the herdsmen is disturbed at Ithaca, so the normal exchange between guest-friends is also in disarray in Odysseus's household because the suitors are not abiding by the rules of reciprocity, and they do not, as Telemachus asks them to 'change from house to house' (ἀμειβόμενοι κατὰ οἴκους, *Od.* 1.375). Similarly, the supposed guest-friend of Odysseus may not count on gifts of reciprocation (δώροισιν ἀμειψάμενος) in the hero's absence, as Laërtes makes sure to tell him (*Od.* 24.285).

Just like the scenes of granting natural *xeinia*, scenes of hospitality involving the giving of material goods and gifts of remembrance seem to complement each other. The hospitality of the Phaeacians, unlike the

---

128. Such a *diplax* is also worn by Athena at her meeting with Odysseus after his return to Ithaca. *Od.* 13.222–24. According to Marinatos (1967: 10) and Bieber (1977: 24) a δίπλαξ was a double (διπλῆ) folded χλαῖνα. See now Harlizius-Klück 2016 and 2019 who has proven by experimental weaving that the *diplax* must have been a double-faced woven cloth.
129. For the meaning of *amoibē* as counter-gift see Laum 1924: 31 and Scheid-Tissinier 1994: 37–40.

Polyphemus episode, acts as a kind of positive antithesis to the disturbed hospitality in Odysseus's own home.[130] A long time ago, John A. Scott asked why the many and generous gifts of the Phaeacians play no role after the return to Ithaca, even though the hero himself had anticipated that they would bring him much honour when he came home (*Od.* 11.360). 'Did Homer forget', Scott asked, 'or did he leave all this to the imagination of the hearers?'[131] The answer has to be: neither.

The bond of guest-friendship with the Phaeacians is not real because they, like Calypso and Polyphemus, belong to mythical landscapes. Therefore, neither Alcinous's cup nor Nausicaa's garments, though handed over as gifts of remembrance, can play any further role as the epic narrative progresses. Through them, and through the *xeinia* and *dōtinē* given by the Phaeacian *dēmos*, Odysseus regains his identity after the shipwreck and his stay in the in-between world of Calypso. The golden cup returns to him his identity as a member of the banqueting community of the kings, or of an aristocratic symposium;[132] the fresh clothing returns him to his identity as a member of a domestic community; the ability to attract tributes of *xeinia* and *dōtinē* confirm his identity as *basileus*.[133] The gifts and the godlike honours bestowed on him anticipate the developments in Books 23 and 24: Penelope recognises her husband from the precise description of garments she made herself and of their joint bed and its coverings (*Od.* 19.215–35 and 23.206).[134] To his father, Odysseus gives an unmistakable sign of his identity through the memory of the fruit and fig trees, and the vines that he had once given him (*Od.* 24.336–46). Both times, it is said that the sign is recognised (σήματ' ἀναγνούσῃ, *Od.* 23.206; σήματ' ἀναγνόντος, *Od.* 24.346). In Book 24, Odysseus is reinstated as *basileus* on Ithaca, and with this regains his position amongst the local leaders and with regard to the *dēmos*. Zeus orders the swearing of solemn oaths, which restore the peace between the embattled families of Ithaca and the

---

130. See the argumentation of Vidal-Naquet 1983: 60–68. According to him Scheria represents an ideal society. Cf. also Scheid-Tissinier 1994: 171. Doherty (1992: 170) hints at the complementarity in the description of the couples in Scheria and Ithaca. The harmony between Alcinous and Arete can be seen as a prediction of the relationship between Odysseus and Penelope.
131. Scott 1938/39: 103.
132. Following Gras (1986: 353) Scheid-Tissinier (1994: 115) stresses the connection with the aristocratic symposium.
133. For another view see Scheid-Tissinier 1994: 173. According to her, the *xeinia* of the Phaeacians were symbols of the warlords' wealth.
134. Wagner-Hasel 1988: 72.

nearby islands, and orders that Odysseus shall rule for the rest of his life: *basileue* (*Od.* 24.483). This is the reason why only Odysseus brings home gifts collected for him by a *dēmos*, while Telemachus, who had such gifts offered to him, brings only gifts of remembrance by means of which he has reestablished his father's guest-friendships. Only the *basileus* has a right to collect gifts from the people.[135]

Just like the fictitious gifts enumerated in the Cretan's tale, the gifts of the Phaeacians never need to be presented at Ithaca because once the hero's position as king and his relationships with Laërtes and Penelope have been reestablished, the domestic community is completely restored. And with this restoration the availability of domestically produced goods, and of tributes paid by the people, is secured.

2.3.2. The ritual of guest-friendship: Bathing, libation, and dressing

Almost all those material gifts that hold symbolic significance through their function as mementoes also have specific utilitarian functions within the ritual of guest-friendship. Textiles (*chlainai*, *pharea*, *rhēgea*, and *tapētes*) are used to prepare beds for guests. *Chlainai* and *pharea* are used as cloaks as well as coverlets, and *chitōnes* serve to dress guests in fresh clothes. Linen *peploi* decorate the chairs used for guests at the Phaeacians' banquet. Golden cups (*depas*, *kypella*) such as those given as mementoes to guests are used for drinking wine at the banquet, while a mixing bowl (*kratēr*) such as that given to Menelaus by Phaidimus, is used to mix the wine. Baths (*asaminthoi*), tripods, and cauldrons (*lebētes*), such as those given to both Odysseus and Menelaus, are used for the rituals of bathing and handwashing before the meal. Horses and mules, as promised by Menelaus, are used for the guest's escort or conduct, for the *pompē* (*Od.* 15.81 and 17.116–17).

Amongst the paraphernalia of guest-friendship textiles are especially distinguished by qualifying epithets similar to those used for the textile mementoes and *xeinia*, such as 'purple-coloured', 'finely-wrought', or 'made from wool'. Indeed, ownership of such items is a prerequisite for guest-friendship, as is made clear when Nestor reminds his guest, Telemachus, that it is not possible to host a guest in an appropriate fashion if you have no clothing (*aneimōnos*), cloaks, and coverlets (*chlainai*, *rhēgea*). These are Nestor's words on the subject, delivered after the shared banquet at Pylos:

---

135. See ch. 4.1.

Ζεὺς τό γ' ἀλεξήσειε καὶ ἀθάνατοι θεοὶ ἄλλοι,
ὡς ὑμεῖς παρ' ἐμεῖο θοὴν ἐπὶ νῆα κίοιτε
ὥς τέ τευ ἢ παρὰ πάμπαν ἀνείμονος ἠὲ πενιχροῦ,
ᾧ οὔ τι χλαῖναι καὶ ῥήγεα πόλλ' ἐνὶ οἴκῳ,
οὔτ' αὐτῷ μαλακῶς οὔτε ξείνοισιν ἐνεύδειν.
αὐτὰρ ἐμοὶ πάρα μὲν χλαῖναι καὶ ῥήγεα καλά.
οὔ θην δὴ τοῦδ' ἀνδρὸς Ὀδυσσῆος φίλος υἱὸς
νηὸς ἐπ' ἰκριόφιν καταλέξεται, ὄφρ' ἂν ἐγώ γε
ζώω, ἔπειτα δὲ παῖδες ἐνὶ μεγάροισι λίπωνται
ξείνους ξεινίζειν, ὅς τίς κ' ἐμὰ δώμαθ' ἵκηται.

May Zeus forbid this, and the other immortal gods, that you should go from me to your swift ship as from one completely without clothing (*aneimōnos*), and poor, who does not have plenty of cloaks (*chlainai*) and coverlets (*rhēgea*) in his house (*oikos*), on which he and his guests may sleep softly. But in my house, there are cloaks and beautiful coverlets. Surely the dear son of Odysseus shall never lie down upon the deck of a ship, while I live and while there are children of mine still in the palace to welcome guests (*xeinous xeinizein*), whosoever may come to my house (*Od.* 3.346-55).

Eumaeus's shepherds suffer from just such a lack of textile wealth, as they have no *chlainai* or *chitōnes* to spare to make up a bed for Odysseus (οὐ γὰρ πολλαὶ χλαῖναι ἐπημοιβοί τε χιτῶνες | ἐνθάδε ἕννυσθαι, μία δ' οἴη φωτὶ ἑκάστῳ, *Od.* 14.513-14). Only Eumaeus himself is in possession of one spare *chlaina*, which he is able to give to Odysseus as a blanket for the night (14.420). The generous and hospitable Phaeacians have garments to spare (εἵματά τ'ἐξημοιβὰ), and they love warm baths, banquets, music, and dance, of which the bath especially plays an important role in the ritual of hospitality.[136] There are two elements to the hospitality ritual in a house such as Nestor's. To begin with, the guest is bathed and dressed, after which there is the communal feast. Both genders are involved, as the bath is the business of either the daughters of the house, or of servant women, variously called *dmōiai*, *dmōiai gynaikes*, or *amphipoloi*. For Telemachus, the ritual is performed by the youngest daughter:

---

136. See Edwards 1975: 51-72.

τόφρα δὲ Τηλέμαχον λοῦσεν καλὴ Πολυκάστη,
Νέστορος ὁπλοτάτη θυγάτηρ Νηληϊάδαο.
αὐτὰρ ἐπεὶ λοῦσέν τε καὶ ἔχρισεν λίπ' ἐλαίῳ,
ἀμφὶ δέ μιν φᾶρος καλὸν βάλεν ἠδὲ χιτῶνα,
ἔκ ῥ' ἀσαμίνθου βῆ δέμας ἀθανάτοισιν ὁμοῖος·
πὰρ δ' ὅ γε Νέστορ' ἰὼν κατ' ἄρ' ἕζετο, ποιμένα λαῶν.

Meanwhile beautiful Polycaste bathed Telemachus, the youngest daughter of Nestor, son of Neleus. Once she had bathed him and anointed him with rich oil and put a beautiful *pharos* around him and a *chitōn*, he emerged from the bath looking like the immortals, and he went and sat down by Nestor the shepherd of the people (*Od.* 3.464-69).

The bath is followed by a feast attended only by men (*Od.* 3.470-72), with meat roasted on spits and shared out, and wine served in golden cups (ἐνὶ χρυσέοις δεπάεσσιν).

In Sparta the ritual is enacted in a similar manner. Bathing and dressing are dealt with by the *dmōiai* and *amphipoloi*, servants whose status is not clear. Telemachus and his companion Peisistratus climb into well-polished baths; the serving women wash them and oil them, and then clothe them with woollen *chlainai* and *chitōnes* (*Od.* 4.48-50). During the subsequent feast, water is provided over silver basins (ἀργυρέοιο λέβητος) for hand-washing, and once again golden cups (χρύσεια κύπελλα) are used for drinking wine. The carver places platters of meat before the guests, while the *tamiē*, who is in charge of provisions, provides bread and other items (*Od.* 4.51-55).[137] Finally (*Od.* 4.297-99) the women make up bedsteads with beautiful purple blankets (ῥήγεα καλὰ | πορφύρε'), such as those mentioned by Nestor, along with rugs (*tapētes*) and woollen cloaks or coverlets (*chlainai*).

Hospitality rituals at the homes of Circe and Arete follow a similar pattern. In these mythological landscapes, the serving women tend to be called *amphipoloi*, a term found as early as the Linear B tablets from Mycenaean Greece.[138] At Circe's house four *amphipoloi* are responsible for the ritual, each of them in charge of a separate object. Drinking vessels are mentioned, as are textiles, used not only for clothing but also as home decoration, and tripods such as those mentioned as tributes

---

137. Wickert-Micknat 1982: 53, 77-79 and di Fidio 1979: 204.
138. Hiller 1987: 230-55.

THE RITUAL OF GUEST-FRIENDSHIP   125

from the people. As in Scheria, so here too these are used for heating the bathwater for the guest:

> ἀμφίπολοι δ' ἄρα τεῖος ἐνὶ μεγάροισι πένοντο
> τέσσαρες, αἵ οἱ δῶμα κάτα δρήστειραι ἔασι. [...]
> τάων ἡ μὲν ἔβαλλε θρόνοισ' ἔνι ῥήγεα καλὰ
> πορφύρεα καθύπερθ', ὑπένερθε δὲ λῖθ' ὑπέβαλλεν
> ἡ δ' ἑτέρη προπάροιθε θρόνων ἐτίταινε τραπέζας
> ἀργυρέας, ἐπὶ δέ σφι τίθει χρύσεια κάνεια
> ἡ δὲ τρίτη κρητῆρι μελίφρονα οἶνον ἐκίρνα
> ἡδὺν ἐν ἀργυρέῳ, νέμε δὲ χρύσεια κύπελλα
> ἡ δὲ τετάρτη ὕδωρ ἐφόρει καὶ πῦρ ἀνέκαιε
> πολλὸν ὑπὸ τρίποδι μεγάλῳ· ἰαίνετο δ' ὕδωρ.

In the meantime her handmaids toiled in the halls, four of them who were her working women in the house. [...] one of them threw beautiful purple rugs (*rhēgea kala porphyrea*) over the top of the chairs, and placed linen cloth (*lita*) beneath them. Another placed silver tables in front of the chairs, and put golden baskets on them. The third mixed pleasant, honey-sweet wine in a silver mixing bowl and poured it into golden cups. The fourth brought water and lit a fire under a great tripod to heat up the water. (*Od.* 10.348–59).

The purple *rhēgea*, which had been used for Telemachus's bedstead, as seen above, now serve to decorate the hall in which Odysseus will take his meal. Before this, he is bathed by one of the *amphipoloi* who heats up his bathwater in the tripod. She places the guest in a bath and then pours the water over his head and shoulders, relieving his weariness (10.361–63). She also dresses him, as Odysseus tells the Phaeacians (*Od.* 10.364–65): 'When she had bathed me and anointed me with rich oil, she placed a beautiful cloak (*chlaina*) around me, and a tunic (*chitōn*)'. His companions, whom Circe has initially turned into swine, will also, in due course, be dressed and receive woollen *chlainai* and *chitōnes* (*Od.* 10.451). Water for hand-washing is brought in a silver basin here, just as in Sparta (ἀργυρέοιο λέβητος, *Od.* 10.369). The *tamiē* responsible for food brings bread and other items (10.371–72). Bread, meat, and wine are served at the farewell meal (*Od.* 12.18–19). Calypso, too, grants her guest Odysseus a bath, a meal, and fragrant garments (εἵματά [...] θυώδεα) such as those worn by the gods (*Od*. 5.264; cf. 5.167 and 7.259-60).

Both Nausicaa and Arete give Odysseus clothing (εἵματα), a *pharos*, and a *chlaina* and *chitōn*, respectively, when he arrives on the island of the Phaeacians. On first meeting Nausicaa on the beach, Odysseus considers whether she might give him clothes (εἵματα δοίη, *Od*. 6.144) and then asks for only a rag (ῥάκος, *Od*. 6.178) such as beggars wore. Nausicaa promises clothing (*esthētes*) if he will come to the city (6.192) but gives him initially, as a small gift (*dosis*, *Od*. 6.208), a *pharos* and *chitōn* (*Od*. 6.214), items which Arete will later recognise as garments made by herself and her *amphipoloi* (*Od*. 7.234-35). Nausicaa asks her *amphipoloi* to bathe Odysseus and to give him food and drink (*Od*. 6.209-10); he will later tell Arete that he received bread and wine (*Od*. 7.295). Just like Telemachus, whose appearance is enhanced after Polycaste bathes and dresses him, so Odysseus also appears taller and more beautiful after bathing (unassisted) in the river (*Od*. 6.227-28). The ritual of bathing and dressing is repeated in Alcinous's palace, where Arete's *dmōiai* bathe and oil him and clothe him in a beautiful *chlaina* and *chitōn* (*Od*. 8.454-55). As at Circe's, the handmaidens, on Arete's orders, place a tripod over a fire in order to heat the bathwater (*Od*. 8.433-36). After he is washed, Odysseus rises from the bath (*asaminthos*) and joins the men drinking wine (*Od*. 8.456-57). The guests' chairs are draped with linen cloths (πέπλοι λεπτοί, *Od*. 7.96-97). Finally, Arete has Odysseus's bed made up with beautiful purple coverlets and rugs (ῥήγεα καλὰ | πορφύρε'[...] τάπητας) and woollen blankets (χλαίνας οὔλας, *Od*. 7.335-38).

At Odysseus's house, the suitors take advantage of the rituals of hospitality as they are bathed and provided with *chlainai* and *chitōnes* by Penelope's *dmōiai* (*Od*. 17.89). But their presence denies the ritual of hospitality to guest-friends of Odysseus, just as it makes impossible the handing over of gifts. Mentes is promised a bath by Telemachus, an offer he rejects just as he rejects a gift from the treasures kept in the house (*Od*. 1.311-12). Similarly, the supposed guest-friend of Odysseus to whom Penelope wishes to offer a bath and shining coverlets (ῥήγεα σιγαλόεντα, *Od*. 19.318) must refuse this ritual and make do with a footbath, a bedstead of sheepskins, and a *chlaina* (*Od*. 19.335-48; 20.3-4 and 141-43).[139] Only once he has revealed his identity can the ritual of bathing and dressing be performed in his own home. He emerges from the bath, fitted out

---

139. A similar bedstead is prepared for Phoenix in the tent of Achilles: *Il*. 9.661.

with a beautiful *pharos* and *chitōn*, to be tested one last time by Penelope (*Od.* 23.154-63). After Odysseus's return, his father also allows himself to be bathed and newly clothed, as he, like his son, had been wearing a filthy old tunic (*Od.* 24.227-28). His Sicilian maid bathes and oils him, and clothes him in a beautiful *chlaina*. When he emerges from the bath, Laërtes is also transformed in appearance, and, like Odysseus, he regains his old identity (*Od.* 24.366-70).

The hospitality rituals described here involve more than merely supplying strangers with appropriate care in providing water and nourishment and a bed for the night. Bathing and dressing are an act of transformation, which effects the acceptance and (re)integration of the stranger into a domestic community. Scholarship has frequently pointed out the transforming effect of the bathing and clothing scene. Wolfgang Schadewaldt and Hans Schwabl and, more recently, Elizabeth Block note the way in which the giving of clothes, especially in the Phaeacian episode, is connected to reestablishing dignity and identity.[140] In his examination of ancient hospitality, Cristiano Grottanelli discusses the role of the bath as 'ritual of purification and incorporation' comparable to Christian baptism.[141] Gabriel Herman also describes the hospitality ritual as a '*rite de passage*' in his study on ritualised friendship.[142] But it is not only a matter of the creation of individual identities. What matters is that individual identity is realised through the forging of bonds that emerge through belonging to a household. In keeping with the structure of the Homeric household, both its male and its female members take part in the act of welcoming the new member. But it is through the women's action especially that the transformative effect takes place. The particular bonding function that is ascribed to textiles in the world of Homeric epic goes some way towards explaining this. This is demonstrated through the material content of the word for friendship or belonging, *philotēs*, and through the terminology used to describe hospitality.

2.3.3. *The terms of hospitality: Xeinizein, komizein, phileein*

The ritual of hospitality is described in terms of ξεινίζειν (*xeinizein*), κομίζειν (*komizein*), and φιλέειν (*phileein*). The terms are not especially

---

140. Schadewaldt 1959: 13-26; Schwabl 1982: 13-33; Block 1985: 1-11.
141. Grottanelli 1976-77: 191.
142. Herman 1987: 69.
143. The evidence was collected by Landfester 1966: 108-9.

sharply differentiated from one another, with *xeinizein* and *phileein* being treated as identical by ancient lexicographers[143] and most modern authors.[144] On closer inspection, however, a tendency towards gender-specific differentiation emerges in these terms, much as it did in the giving of memorial gifts and in the performance of the hospitality ritual. So *xeinizein* never refers to female actions but only and specifically describes the male act of sharing out meat at the sacrificial banquet, while *komizein* mostly refers to women's provision of goods from the home, such as food, bathwater, and garments or other textiles. Both terms are linked to *phileein*, which has a more abstract significance and can describe both the ritual as a whole and its result, the formation of a bond of belonging. Used in connection with *xeinizein*, *phileein* can also take on the meaning of the supply of the very items that enable the transformation of the stranger and his integration into a household member, namely the bath and garments.

A striking aspect of the use of *xeinizein* is that it is often linked to location: mostly this will be the main hall, the *megaron*, where guests are looked after, but it can also be the *oikos*, the house itself, or the land or estate. So Penelope questions the Cretan Aëthon, her husband's supposed guest-friend, on the veracity of his claims, and asks if he really 'entertained my husband in the *megaron* (ξείνισας ἐν μεγάροισιν ἐμὸν πόσιν), as you say' (*Od.* 19.217).[145] Oineus also entertained Bellerophon in the *megaron* (ξείνισ᾽ ἐνὶ μεγάροισιν, *Il.* 6.217), and kept him there for twenty days, as Diomedes reminds Glaucus in the arms-exchange scene discussed earlier. The specification of time is here linked to a specification of the quantity of oxen sacrificed: 'he entertained him for nine days, and sacrificed nine oxen' (ἐννῆμαρ ξείνισσε καὶ ἐννέα βοῦς ἱέρευσεν, *Il.* 6.174). We find *xeinizein*, which I translate here as 'entertain', linked explicitly with the formal meal and sacrifice, when Alcinous encourages the Phaeacian leaders to offer hospitality to Odysseus: 'we will entertain the stranger in the *megaron* and sacrifice to the gods' (ξεῖνον ἐνὶ μεγάροις ξεινίσσομεν ἠδὲ θεοῖσιν | ῥέξομεν ἱερὰ καλά, *Od.* 7.190–91). When Nestor speaks of the ability to entertain guests, *xeinous xenizein*, he links this to the fact that he has sons precisely in the *megaron*, the place where men feast together (*Od.* 3.354–55).

When Helen recalls hospitality at Sparta in *Iliad* 3, it is not the *megaron* she mentions but the *oikos*. Whilst watching the battle from the top of the

---

144. Scheid-Tissinier 1994: 129–35.
145. Cf. *Od.* 24.288–89. Laërtes asks the stranger how long it was when he entertained (ξείνισσας) Odysseus in his home.

city walls with Priam and Antenor, and identifying the Greek warriors for them, she says of Idomeneus that Menelaus often entertained him in their house (πολλάκι μιν ξείνισσεν [...] | οἴκῳ ἐν ἡμετέρῳ, *Il.* 3.232) whenever he would come from Crete. However, when Antenor tells of entertaining Menelaus and Odysseus when they came as ambassadors to Troy, he speaks of welcoming them (*philēsa*) in the megaron (τοὺς δ' ἐγὼ ἐξείνισσα καὶ ἐν μεγάροισι φίλησα, *Il.* 3.207).

Menelaus also uses the term *phileein* with reference to Helen's actions. Facing Paris for their duel, Menelaus appeals to Zeus for revenge, so that future men should be afraid to do harm to the host (*xeinodokos*) who granted them *philotēs* (*Il.* 3.354). After the agreement between Greeks and Trojans has been broken, and he has an enemy at his mercy, Menelaus does not spare him, recalling how the Trojans carried off his wife and much treasure, even though, or after, they had been welcomed by her (ἐπεὶ φιλέεσθε παρ' αὐτῇ, *Il.* 13.627). The gender-specific application of the terms *xeinizein* (used by Helen for the actions of Menelaus) and *phileein* (used by Menelaus for the actions of Helen) suggests that the terms refer to two different aspects of the hospitality ritual: bath and dressing, as carried out by women, and the sacrificial feast, as arranged by men. This interpretation is further confirmed by the use of *phileein* in connection with goods stored in the house, which may allude to the wealth of garments spoken of by Nestor in his welcoming of Telemachus. In his Cretan guise, we find Odysseus telling Penelope (*Od.* 19.195) how he brought her husband into this house, entertained him well (ἐὺ ἐξείνισσα), and treated him with careful welcome (ἐνδυκέως φιλέων) from the wealth of store that was in the house (πολλῶν κατὰ οἶκον ἐόντων).[146] The expression *endykeōs phileein* is used also by Telemachus with the seer Theoclymenus. To begin with, Telemachus simply asks the seer to follow him with the promise that he will be treated with kindness, such as they have (αὐτὰρ κεῖθι φιλήσεαι, οἷά κ' ἔχωμεν, *Od.* 15.281). Subsequently he asks his companion Peraeus to look after Theclymenus in his stead: 'Give him kindly welcome and show him honour (ἐνδυκέως φιλέειν καὶ τιέμεν), until I come' (15.543). In Peraeus's response (15.546) the expression *endykeōs phileein* is replaced by *komizein*: 'I will look after him (τόνδε τ' ἐγὼ κομιῶ) and he shall want for nothing that is due to guests (ξενίων).'

In the context of hospitality *komizein* is frequently used instead of *phileein*, often with the concrete meaning of bathing, dressing, and nourishment.

---

146. The same expression is used by Odysseus with his father Laërtes. *Od.* 24.271–72.

Telemachus uses both terms, each time with the adverb *endykeōs* when he tells his mother of the treatment he received at Nestor's home: 'He gave me kindly welcome (ἐνδυκέως ἐφίλει), as a father might to his son who, after a long time, has newly returned from far away. So kindly did he look after me (ἐνδυκέως ἐκόμιζε), together with his glorious sons' (*Od.* 17.11-13). In this instance it is not possible to say which aspects of hospitality are referred to specifically with the uses of *phileein* and *komizein*. There are, however, two other instances that do allow us to define *komizein* specifically as the provision of bathing and dressing for the guest. Odysseus uses the term in his report to Eumaeus about his stay with the Thesprotians, whose king took care of him (ἐκομίσσατο, *Od.* 14.316).[147] This care is subsequently specified in terms of clothing prepared, not as in Phaeacia by the daughter of the house, but by the son who is said to have provided the stranger with *chlaina*, *chitōn*, and *heimata* (14.320). The connection between *komizein* and bathing is made through the remembrance of Odysseus's stay with Calypso. When he is pleased to see the hot water made ready in Scheria for his bath, this is because 'he had not had such care (ἐπεὶ οὔ τι κομιζόμενός γε θάμιζεν) since he left the house of fair-haired Calypso, but until then he had received care (κομιδή) as constantly as a god' (*Od.* 8.451-53). In telling the Phaeacians about Calypso's hospitality, Odysseus uses both *komizein* and *phileein* (ἥ μ' ἐφίλει τ' ἐκόμει τε, *Od.* 12.450) as well as *trephein*, which is interchangeable with *komizein*, to refer specifically to nourishment (ἥ με λαβοῦσα | ἐνδυκέως ἐφίλει τε καὶ ἔτρεφεν, *Od.* 7.255-56).[148]

Both clothing and nourishment come into play when *komizein* and *phileein* are used for Eumaeus's acts of hospitality when he receives Odysseus in his hut. Odysseus announces his departure in order to test the hospitable swineherd and to see if he would still 'show him kindly care' (ἐνδυκέως φιλέοι, *Od.* 15.305). Eumaeus stops him and promises that Telemachus will bring him a new cloak and tunic when he comes (*Od.* 15.338). Once Telemachus arrives at the hut, he lets the swineherd decide whether to keep the guest there and continue to look after him (εἰ δ' ἐθέλεις, σὺ κόμισσον ἐνὶ σταθμοῖσιν ἐρύξας, *Od.* 16.82) but promises to send out clothing (*heimata*) and bread (*sitos*) so as not to put a strain on the meagre provisions available at the hut (16.83-84). But this is Penelope's business. Eumaeus has

---

147. See also *Od.* 16.322. Here the terms *phileein* and *xeinizein* are used to describe the hospitality of the Thesprotians.
148. For the meaning of *trephein* as 'nourish' see *Il.* 5.71. Here it is said that Theano kindly nourished (ἔτρεφε) the child of her husband, a *nothos*. For further meaning see LSJ s.v. τρέφω.

told the disguised Odysseus that strangers come and tell Penelope all manner of stories about Odysseus for the sake of *komidē*, 'care' or 'provision', since she 'receives [them] well and looks after [them]' (εὖ δεξαμένη φιλέει, *Od.* 14.128). The fact that clothing is involved in this case of *komidē* and *phileein* becomes clear from Eumaeus's next remark, when he suggests that Odysseus also would make up a story if he could get a *chlaina*, *chitōn*, and *heimata* for it (14.132).

While in the two preceding examples we find *phileein* in a more concrete sense as a synonym for *komizein* and with the meaning 'to provide with garments', the term mostly encompasses the entire hospitality ritual. This is especially the case when we find *phileein* on its own and connected to an indication of time, or accompanied by an allusion to the host's wealth: so Odysseus says of his stay at the home of Aeolus, where there was plenty of food and blankets (*tapētes*) for the beds that 'for a whole month he looked after me' (μῆνα δὲ πάντα φίλει μ', *Od.* 10.14). In the *Iliad* (6.14–15), Axylus of Arisbe is described as rich in goods (ἀφνειὸς βιότοιο) and as a friend (*philos*) to all men who cared for all (πάντας γὰρ φιλέεσκεν). A similarly all-encompassing use of *phileein* is found in Eteoneus's use of the word when the steward goes to ask Menelaus whether he should send the new arrivals, Telemachus and Peisistratus, to someone else who might look after them (ὅσ κε φιλήσῃ, *Od.* 4.29). Once Menelaus and Helen have welcomed Telemachus, they dress him and feed him, and give him gifts. And Menelaus assures the young man that if Odysseus himself were to come that he would look after him (φιλησέμεν, *Od.* 4.171) above all the other Argives. In this case *phileein* is not meant as temporary hospitality only. 'For I would have given him a city in Argos to live in, and built him a house, after I had brought him from Ithaca with his goods and his son and all his people' (*Od.* 5.174–76); so, Menelaus offers thanks for Odysseus's support at Troy.

Such a permanent welcome is extended in the *Iliad* to Phoenix by Peleus in Phthia, after he had fled there in fear of his father (whose lover he had become involved with on his mother's request). Phoenix tells Achilles that Peleus received him with a ready heart and was kind to him (καί μ' ἐφίλης'), as a father is kind to his child (φιλήσῃ), his only darling child, 'the heir to many possessions'. He adds to this, more concretely, that Peleus 'made me wealthy, he gave me many people, and I lived on the outer border of Phthia, ruling over the Dolopians' (*Il.* 9.481–84). In this case *phileein* expresses the formation of a close bond, compared to that with a blood-relative, from which material wealth and a high position ensue.[149]

---

149. See ch. 4.1.

Such a close relationship between guest and host is envisaged by Alcinous, when he asks Demodocus to cease his song after Odysseus has broken down in tears:

ἀλλ' ἄγ' ὁ μὲν σχεθέτω, ἵν' ὁμῶς τερπώμεθα πάντες,
ξεινοδόκοι καὶ ξεῖνος, ἐπεὶ πολὺ κάλλιον οὕτω
εἵνεκα γὰρ ξείνοιο τάδ' αἰδοίοιο τέτυκται,
πομπὴ καὶ φίλα δῶρα, τὰ οἱ δίδομεν φιλέοντες.
ἀντὶ κασιγνήτου ξεῖνός θ' ἱκέτης τε τέτυκται
ἀνέρι, ὅς τ' ὀλίγον περ ἐπιψαύῃ πραπίδεσσι.

Let the bard stop playing, so that we can all be merry, hosts (*xeinodokoi*) and guest (*xeinos*) alike. How much pleasanter this is! For it was on account of our worthy guest (*xeinos aidoios*) that all this has been arranged, this farewell (*pompē*) and these friendly gifts (*phila dōra*) that we give as welcoming hosts (*ta hoi didomen phileontes*). To any man with the slightest claim to common sense a guest (*xeinos*) and a suppliant (*hiketēs*) is as close as a brother (*kasignētos*) (*Od.* 8.542-46, tr. Rieu).

Both the suppliant (*hiketēs*), such as Phoenix for instance, and the guest (*xeinos*) are put on a par with the brother (*kasignētos*), putting the relationship with the guest, and with the suppliant, on an equal footing with blood-relationship.[150] Furthermore, in this last case, the relationship is also endowed with benefits (*phila dōra* and *pompē*). The emotional content of the process, as suggested by E. V. Rieu's translation of *phila dōra* as 'friendly gifts' is only one aspect of a complex state of affairs.[151] Both

---

150. Such a transformation of the foreigner into a temporary relative which took place among the Tallensi in Northern Ghana in 1934 is described by Meyer Fortes 1975: 229-53.
151. Cf. Scott 1982: 9, who argues against a purely emotional meaning and against any connection with altruism: '*Philein* is to bring a person within [...] a circle of co-operation whose members have a right to feel mutual reliance, and a right to whatever basic necessities are available for consumption'. Similarly, Dirlmeier (1931: 28-29): 'Bei Homer sind auffallend häufig solche Stellen, die einen Affekt ausdrücken und gleich daneben ein Verbum aufweisen, das tatkräftige Hilfeleistung, Fürsorge usw. ausdrückt. [...] Von dieser Einstellung aus, die wir also als ganz ursprünglich ansehen dürfen, ergibt sich ungezwungen die Wertschätzung des Nutzens. Der Utilitarismus bleibt in der griechischen Freundschaftsethik auch in den feinsten Verzweigungen bei Platon und Aristoteles. [...] Wo der Nutzen betont ist, muß folgerichtig auch die Gegenseitigkeit der Leistung verlangt werden'. In more recent studies the emotional aspect is stressed once again. Cf. Hooker 1987a: 55-56.

phileein and the adjective *philos* express a social relationship which leads to the giving of gifts such as are deemed fitting for the guest.[152]

To sum up, I would define *phileein* as acting within the framework of a relationship or bond that goes hand in hand with supplying goods as appropriate to the respective competencies of the man or woman initiating the bond. Furthermore, *phileein* can also express actions taken in order to form the relationship or bond.[153] The overall term for all this is *philotēs*, which we now turn to in conclusion of these reflections on hospitality.

2.4. Woven textiles, sacrifice, and the formation of bonds: Philotēs

In epic the key term for friendship is φιλότης (*philotēs*). Mary Scott summed up its meaning thus: 'There is either active warfare or *philotēs*'.[154] A. W. H. Adkins, who produced a series of examinations of Homeric friendship sees *philotēs* as an opposite of competition and views the essence of *philotēs* as cooperation.[155] Peter Karavites emphasises the transformative character of *philotēs* as a transition from negatively defined relations to positive: '*Philotēs* changed the status of the parties from a state of enmity to one of explicit and steady friendship.'[156] Émile Benveniste highlights the

---

152. Cf. Landfester 1966: 31. He translates *phila dōra* as 'Gaben an ihn'. Benveniste (1969: I, 348) interprets them as 'cadeaux d'hospitation'. The idea that *philein* is used to express the existence of a close relationship, implied by the provision of appropriate gifts, is also supported by the use of the term in other contexts. For example: Hermes is said to give property (κτῆσις) to Ilioneus, whom he loved (ἐφίλει) in *Il.* 14.491. Odysseus gives *ktēsis* to Eumaeus whom he loves with kindness (ἐνδυκέως ἐφίλει) in *Od.* 14.62. In both these cases we must assume that the gift in question is cattle. When *philein* is used in connection with gifts given by women, these will be textile gifts. So Odysseus's mother, who is also said 'to love' (φίλει) Eumaeus, gives him *chlainai* and *heimata* (*Od.* 15.368–70). Where we hear of gods loving their favourites, *philein* takes the concrete form of success in battle (*Il.* 7.204 and 280; 16.64). When Odysseus (*Il.* 10.280) and Diomedes (*Il.* 5.117) appeal to Athena with the phrase ἐμὲ φῖλαι, which can only mean a request for her support in battle. Agamemnon and Odysseus can count on gleaming gifts (*aglaa dōra*) because Hera and Athena favour them respectively (*Il.* 1.196 and 209 and 213: φιλέουσα). Phoenix allows Achilles to take part in the men's banquet because he loves him with all his heart (ἐκ θυμοῦ φιλέων, *Il.* 9.486).
153. For the basic meaning of φιλέω (*phileō*) as 'gastlich aufnehmen, bewirten, freundlich behandeln', see Landfester 1966: 109. According to Benveniste (1969: I, 344) *phileein* always goes ahead with reciprocity. For a similar argument see Scott 1982: 9.
154. Scott 1982: 15.
155. Adkins 1971: 4; 1963: 34–35; 1960.
156. Karavites 1986: 479.

reciprocal character of friendship in his examination of the term *philos*.[157] In his view, *philotēs* encompasses the household ('foyer') and hospitality ('hospitalité') within which he includes relations between warriors. A close examination of the term *philotēs* reveals, however, that its true framework is not hospitality but the integration of strangers in relationships between warriors and within household communities. It is striking that the word is not used for relationships that exist by virtue of bloodline or convention but those which are formed by means of a specific ritual: between men and women belonging to different families, between members of different communities, between strangers and enemy warriors.

In the *Iliad* the word *philotēs* is frequently used to express belonging to a warrior community. Bonds formed between enemy parties are also defined as *philotēs*. A warrior's belonging to a community is visible through external signs. So, when Patroclus, equipped with Achilles's armour, joins the ranks of the Achaeans, the troops believe that Achilles has chosen *philotēs* after all (φιλότητα δ' ἑλέσθαι, *Il.* 16.282). What is meant by this is belonging to the Greek army, from which Achilles had withdrawn after his quarrel with Agamemnon. This belonging cannot only be freely given up, it can also be taken away, as happens to Paris after Aphrodite removes him from the duel with Menelaus. No Trojan would then have hidden him from the rage of Menelaus on the grounds of *philotēs* (οὐ μὲν γὰρ φιλότητί γ' ἐκεύθανον εἴ τις ἴδοιτο, *Il.* 3.453).[158] It is *philotēs* again, as a generational bond, that motivates Ithaca's young men to follow Telemachus to Pylos (οἱ δ' ἄλλοι φιλότητι νεώτεροι ἄνδρες ἕπονται, *Od.* 3.363).

With reference to military enemies, *philotēs* is arranged by the gods. So, Greeks and Trojans together pray for *philotēs* after Hector and Paris have proposed to duel for Helen and the goods (Ἑλένην [...] καὶ κτήματα πάντα, *Il.* 3.282). In the joint prayer *philotēs* is used together with *horkia*, another significant term that points to the means by which the bond of *philotēs* is formed, namely oath and sacrifice: 'grant us friendship and oaths of faith' (ἡμῖν δ' αὖ φιλότητα καὶ ὅρκια πιστὰ γενέσθαι, *Il.* 3.323).[159] After Aphrodite's removal of Paris from the battle, the gods discuss whether to

---

157. Benveniste 1969: I, 335–53. Cf. Scheid-Tissinier 1994: 133–35. She prefers to differentiate between several social levels of *philotēs*, the relationship between equals and the ties with people of lower status.
158. Cf. Hector's failed attempt to obtain a guarantee from Achilles that he will return his body in case of a defeat. Achilles rejects the plea, arguing that there cannot be any belonging (φιλήμεναι) and *horkia* between them (*Il.* 22.265–66).
159. Cf. *Il.* 3.73; 94; 256.

establish *philotēs* among the mortals (φιλότητα μετ' ἀμφοτέροισι), or let the battle continue (*Il.* 4.14-16).¹⁶⁰

The realisation of *philotēs*, however short-lived, involves objects we are already familiar with from the hospitality ritual. The herald, Idaeus, brings a shining mixing bowl (κρητῆρα φαεινὸν) and a golden cup (χρύσεια κύπελλα) to the assembly (*Il.* 3.247-48). Wine and water are mixed in the *kratēr* and the leaders wash their hands as guests do before a meal (3.269-70). Agamemnon slaughters the sacrificial victims with his sword, just as Nestor does when he receives Telemachus at Pylos, and the others pour libations for the gods (3.292-95). The terms of the agreement are stated, and Zeus and Helios, as well as the shades of the dead, are called upon to witness the oath and to take revenge upon anyone who breaks it (3.267-91). The curse on those who break oaths is repeated during the libations by the warriors on both sides (3.295-301). The swearing and cursing distinguish the ritual performed on this occasion from a hospitality ritual. Nonetheless, there is a connection to the bond of guest-friendship.

The forming of *philotēs* between Greeks and Trojans serves to restore *philotēs* between guest-friends. This becomes clear when we see Menelaus, before the start of the duel with Paris, demand punishment for his opponent, so that in the future men should be afraid to do harm to a host who has granted them *philotēs* (ξεινοδόκον κακὰ ῥέξαι, ὅ κεν φιλότητα παράσχῃ, *Il.* 3.354). In this case, *philotēs* may allude to the concrete act of hospitality or to the bond that results from it. In the *Odyssey* we find the latter meaning in the phrase *philotēta parechō* (φιλότητα παρέχω), as used by Peisistratus in persuading Telemachus not to take off for Ithaca without allowing Menelaus to complete his hospitality:

[Τηλέμαχ', οὔ πως ἔστιν,] ἐπειγομένους περ ὁδοῖο,
νύκτα διὰ δνοφερὴν ἐλάαν· τάχα δ' ἔσσεται ἠώς.
ἀλλὰ μέν', εἰς ὅ κε δῶρα φέρων ἐπιδίφρια θήῃ
ἥρως Ἀτρεΐδης, δουρικλειτὸς Μενέλαος,
καὶ μύθοισ' ἀγανοῖσι παραυδήσας ἀποπέμψῃ.
τοῦ γάρ τε ξεῖνος μιμνῄσκεται ἤματα πάντα
ἀνδρὸς ξεινοδόκου, ὅς κεν φιλότητα παράσχῃ.

---

160. The term used by the gods for the establishment of *philotēs* is *ballein*, which is also used for the dressing of a stranger after the ritual bath. When the Greeks and Trojans worry whether the war will continue, or whether Zeus will establish *philotēs* on both sides, the term used instead is *tithēmi* (φιλότητα μετ' ἀμφοτέροισι τίθησι, *Il.* 4.83-85).

[...] However eager we may be to start, we cannot possibly drive in complete darkness. It'll soon be dawn. Wait and give the famous spearman Menelaus the chance of putting some presents (*dōra pherōn*) for us on the chariot and sending us off with a friendly farewell. All his life a guest remembers the host who had treated him kindly (*philotēta paraschē*) (*Od.* 15.49-55, tr. Rieu).[161]

The granting of *philotēs* is linked here to the memory of the host, which leads us to suspect that there is more involved than just the friendly gestures of bathing, dressing, bed, and supper: there must be a specific allusion intended here to the gifts of remembrance which we see in the same book. This would suggest that *philotēs*, within the framework of hospitality, should be understood concretely as the giving of gifts as well as in a more abstract sense as the bond formed through those gifts.

There are further passages in the *Odyssey* that show *philotēs* in its concrete sense as the giving of gifts. Both Penelope and Telemachus promise *philotēs* and many gifts (γνοίης φιλότητά τε πολλά τε δῶρα) to the seer Theoclymenus (*Od.* 15.337) and to the beggar in the event of Odysseus's homecoming (*Od.* 17.164; 19.310). In these instances, *philotēs* must be understood as emphasising, or doubling, the offer of gifts, without clearly indicating whether a lasting bond is anticipated. In another example of concrete *philotēs*, Odysseus asks Eumaeus's shepherds for the grant of a blanket, *chlaina*, for the sake of *philotēs* (δοίη κέν τις χλαῖναν [...] φιλότητι καὶ αἰδοῖ, *Od.* 14.504-5). Aeolus lets Odysseus have the bag of winds out of *philotēs* as a favour (οἱ τάδ' ἔδωκε χαριζόμενος φιλότητι, *Od.* 10.43). In the last two examples *philotēs* denotes the state of mind that leads to the handing over of gifts by the host. *Philotēs* may be understood then, within the framework of hospitality, as the concrete granting of a gift which has the effect of a bond or obligation, and also as the state of mind which leads to the granting of the gift.

As we are aware, it is impossible for strangers to receive *philotēs* at the house of Odysseus while the suitors are freely availing themselves of his goods. Just like Paris's injury of his host Menelaus, the suitors' trespass will be avenged with violence. The threatened outbreak of war after the killing of the suitors, however, is prevented by the formation of *philotēs* between Odysseus and the relatives (*philoi*) of the suitors, and

---

161. Scheid-Tissinier 1994: 133 translates: 'qui a donné l'hospitalité' instead of 'who had treated him kindly'.

their children (*paides*) and brothers (*kasignētoi*). This peace is made possible through divine intervention. Using the same words as those used by the warriors in the *Iliad*, Athena asks Zeus whether he wishes to allow the war to continue or whether he will establish *philotēs* instead: 'Will you further this evil war and the grim battlecry or will you establish *philotēs* between the two sides?' (ἢ προτέρω πόλεμόν τε κακὸν καὶ φύλοπιν αἰνὴν | τεύξεις, ἦ φιλότητα μετ' ἀμφοτέροισι τίθησθα, *Od.* 24.475–76). Zeus decides that they must be friends again (τοὶ δ' ἀλλήλους φιλεόντων, 24.485). The bond between the two sides, described through the noun *philotēs* and its verb *phileein*, is established, as in the *Iliad*, through binding oaths and sacrifice (*horkia pista*). Zeus adds the decree that Odysseus should rule for ever (ὅρκια πιστὰ ταμόντες ὁ μὲν βασιλευέτω αἰεί, *Od.* 24.483), while for the other side Zeus decides that they must forget the killing (φόνοιο | ἔκλησιν θέωμεν, *Od.* 24.484-5). Thus, within a political community, the bond is guaranteed not only by ritual but by people, and by the person of the *basileus*.

While *philotēs* between enemies is finally realised in the *Odyssey*, it is made impossible in the *Iliad* through the interference of a different bond. When Aphrodite has whisked Paris off the battlefield and into Helen's bedroom, he reminds her of the bond of love, which he calls *philotēs*, that they established on the island of Cranaë after he abducted her:

ἀλλ' ἄγε δὴ φιλότητι τραπείομεν εὐνηθέντε
οὐ γάρ πώ ποτέ μ' ὧδέ γ' ἔρως φρένας ἀμφεκάλυψεν,
οὐδ' ὅτε σε πρῶτον Λακεδαίμονος ἐξ ἐρατεινῆς
ἔπλεον ἁρπάξας ἐν ποντοπόροισι νέεσσι,
νήσῳ δ' ἐν Κραναῇ ἐμίγην φιλότητι καὶ εὐνῇ,
ὥς σεο νῦν ἔραμαι καί με γλυκὺς ἵμερος αἱρεῖ.
Ἦ ῥα, καὶ ἄρχε λέχος δὲ κιών· ἅμα δ' εἵπετ' ἄκοιτις.

Come, let us go to bed together and enjoy the pleasures of love (*philotēs*). Never has such desire overwhelmed me, not even in the beginning when I carried you off from lovely Lacedaemon in my seafaring ships and spent the night making love to you (*emigēn philotēti kai eunē*) on the isle of Cranae—never till now have I felt such desire for you, or has such sweet longing overwhelmed me (*Il.* 3.441–46; tr. Rieu).

In the main, *philotēs* is used as here to denote sexual union.¹⁶² To exercise this, there is need for a bed, εὐνή (*eunē*), and the textiles with which it is dressed. Hera's famous seduction of Zeus gives us an instance of this connection between *philotēs* and textiles, when Hera turns to Aphrodite for help, under the pretext of wishing to reunite Oceanus and Thetys, but in reality intending to seduce Zeus and keep him off the battlefield: 'Give me *philotēs* and desire' (δὸς νῦν μοι φιλότητα καὶ ἵμερον, *Il.* 14.198). *Philotēs* is materialised here in the colourful girdle (κεστὸν [...] ποικίλον), into which is worked *philotēs* as well as desire, intimacy, and persuasion (ἔνθ' ἔνι μὲν φιλότης, ἐν δ' ἵμερος, ἐν δ' ὀαριστὺς | πάρφασις, ἥ τ' ἔκλεψε νόον πύκα περ φρονεόντων. *Il.* 14.216-17)—all those things that appeal to the senses: touch, sight, and hearing. Such a girdle is also amongst the items Nausicaa is laundering in anticipation of her wedding (*Od.* 6.38). In epic poetry and in later texts 'loosening the girdle' often denotes the consummation of sexual intercourse.¹⁶³ Before being married, brides offer their girdle to the goddess Artemis. On vase-paintings depicting wedding rituals, images are occasionally found of brides handing bands, which may depict such girdles, to a man.¹⁶⁴

The bed and the joint coverlet or cloak are similarly laden with erotic symbolism. Penelope recognises her husband from his knowledge of the bed (*eunē*), which was fitted out with furs, coverlets (*chlainai*), and shimmering sheets (ῥήγεα σιγαλόεντα, *Od.* 23.180). In Athenian tragedy the bed, referred to as εὐνή (*eunē*), λέχος (*lechos*), or λέκτρον (*lektron*) is the term used for the bond of marriage (e.g. Eur. *Med.* 206, 265, 436). In red-figure vases of the same period the bridal procession leading to the wedding couch, dressed with coverlets and patterned cushions, is a

---

162. Other examples of *philotēs* as sexual union: Laomedon and the Naiad Abarbarea share a bed in *philotēs* (μίγη φιλότητι καὶ εὐνῇ, *Il.* 6.25); Thersites accuses Agamemnon of greedily wanting a woman to join with in *philotēs* (μίγεαι ἐν φιλότητι, *Il.* 2.232); the Phoenician nurse of Eumaeus joins in *philotēs* with the sailors (μίγη [...] | εὐνῇ καὶ φιλότητι, *Od.* 15.420-21); Odysseus enjoys *philotēs* with Calypso (τερπέσθην φιλότητι, *Od.* 5.227) and joins Circe in bed in *philotēs* (μιγέντε | εὐνῇ καὶ φιλότητι, *Od.* 10.334); in Demodocus's famous song, Helios sees Ares and Aphrodite joined in *philotēs* (μιγαζόμενους φιλότητι, *Od.* 8.271).
163. Cf. e.g. Hom. *Hymn Aphr.* 164; Eur. *Alc.* 177; Anth. Pal. 7.164. For further evidence see King 1983: 120-21; Speyer 1983.
164. Cf. Lissarrague 1991: 169-71, Fig. 5; Oakley and Sinos 1993: Fig. 9; Hampe and Simon 1985: 27-28; Foxhall and Stears 2000: 5 (dedication of the girdle to Artemis). Onians 1989: 368 considers the girdle as an object with magical properties. For the symbolic meaning of the girdle see now Schmitt Pantel 2019.

prominent motif.¹⁶⁵ The coverlets themselves have their own symbolism. In Apollonius's *Argonautica* a *peplos* like the one given to Telemachus for his future bride serves as the wedding bed for Ariadne and Dionysos (Ap. Rhod. *Argon.* 4.423–34). Hellenistic epigram has examples of a coverlet, a *chlaina*, that enfolds two lovers (Anth. Graec. 5.165; 169). In Theocritus's *Idyll* 18, we find Helen lying with Menelaus underneath a coverlet (ὑπὸ τὰν μίαν ἵκετο χλαῖναν, Theoc. *Id.* 18.19). A Mycenaean terracotta figure (thirteenth century BCE) depicts a couple in a bed underneath a coverlet.¹⁶⁶ In classical times, the joint coverlet is found as a motif on drinking bowls (Figure 1 a and b).¹⁶⁷ It is little wonder then that for Hesiod *philotēs* is a child of the night (Νὺξ [...] τέκε [...] φιλότητα, Hes. *Theog.* 224). The bed reveals itself as the specific locus of *philotēs* between the sexes.

We are dealing then with different relationships in epic, which are all formed through specific rituals and symbolised through different objects. Homeric friendship has a material dimension insofar as *philotēs* is thought of as materialised through objects. The practice of hospitality is only one aspect of the concrete meaning of *philotēs*. It is true that some of the objects we meet in the ritual of hospitality are also found in the formation of *philotēs*. When *philotēs* takes on a concrete meaning, however, it does not mean only guest-friendship but beyond that the bond formed by marriage, and specifically the sexual union of the couple and the symbols of the bond, the girdle, and the joint coverlet. This explains why presents are given to guest-friends when they have a memorial function (as is the case with Helen's *peplos* given to Telemachus) that consists of just such textile items which symbolise a couple's union. With these items the guest becomes integrated into the bond between the couple, whereas the golden cups, with which libations are poured by leaders and warriors, bind into the supraregional community of warriors. As a relationship, guest-friendship is subordinate to the two central forms of bonds between people: the bond between warriors and that between a couple. It follows then that epic lacks an independent term for guest-friendship, with the one exception discussed in the context of the exchange of arms.

165. Oakley and Sinos 1993, Fig. 24, 104, 109, 122. Xenophon of Ephesus 1.8.2 (ed. G. Dalmeyda, Paris 1962) describes the bed of the bride as golden *klinē* covered with purple cloth (*strōma*). The canopy (*skenē*) was a patterned Babylonian fabric with pictures of Aphrodite, Eros, and Ares.
166. Vermeule 1979: 54, Fig. 10.
167. Koch-Harnack 1989: 137, Fig. 6 and 7. Whereas Koch-Harnack stresses the erotic meaning of the common mantle (109–95), Buchholz 1987: 1–20 interprets the garment as a symbol of belonging ('Zugehörigkeit').

Figure 1a: The joint coverlet. Red-figure *kylix*. Paris. Louvre G 99. *Photo:* Egisto Sani, https://www.flickr.com/photos/69716881@N02/9195936448

Figure 1b: Couple sitting on a *klinē* and wrapped in a common mantle. Attic red-figure *kylix* of the Marlay painter, ca 430 BCE. Vienna, Kunsthistorisches Museum 131. After Koch-Harnack 1989: 137, Fig. 7.

The gods are approached via both types of bond, through gender-specific means in the forms of animal sacrifice and donation of garments. When the Greeks threaten to overwhelm Troy, the dedication to Athena of a garment or veil is called for by a prophecy, and Hector asks his 'honoured mother'(*potnia mētēr*) to donate her dearest garment (οἱ πολὺ φίλτατος αὐτῇ). Of the many patterned *peploi* brought back from Sidon by Paris, Hecuba selects one described as particularly richly coloured and shining like a star (*Il.* 6.90 = 271; 288–95).¹⁶⁸ The superlative, *philtatos*, used here of the *peplos* in question, usually refers only to relationships between people.¹⁶⁹ The nouns *philos* and *philē* are used in epic poetry to denote all members of a bond called *philotēs*: these can be participants in a bond formed between warriors via oath-swearing, or relations bound by birth or marriage, or guest-friends, or lower-status members of a household.¹⁷⁰ Used in apposition, *philos* or *philē* are frequent epithets for a guest-friend or for the married bed-fellow, referred to as ἄκοιτις (*akoitis*) or ἄλοχος (*alochos*).¹⁷¹ Especially close friends and relations are referred to with the superlative *philtatos*.¹⁷² Used in apposition, *philos* does not have just emotional meaning (as in 'dear') but expresses belonging (as 'own' in English or *suus* in Latin).¹⁷³ This is true of the passage just quoted where *philtatos* tells us

168. For the title *potnia mētēr*, see ch. 4.2.
169. Landfester 1966: 89–99.
170. The most frequent occurrence of *philos* in the epics is the vocative addressing warriors (see Landfester 1966: 31–33 and 73–74). Priam's *philoi* are his *paides* and *gambroi*, that is direct descendants and in-laws (*Il.* 24.327 and 331). After he is welcomed in Alcinous and Arete's home, Odysseus is called a *philos* of the Phaeacians (*Od.* 13.302); Nestor also calls Telemachus a *philos* (*Od.* 3.198). Penelope refers to her servant women as *philoi* (*Od.* 4.722).
171. For evidence see Landfester 1966: 21–22; Benveniste 1969: I, 345–46.
172. Dead members of a group of warriors or dead relatives connected by marriage are esteemed as *philtatoi*. Cf. e.g. the mourning of Achilles after the death of Patroclus (Il. 9.198) and Helen's mourning after the death of Hector (*Il.* 24.762).
173. There is much debate on the interpretation of *philos*, and its meaning which can vary between 'one's own' and 'dear to one' or 'loved'. Some see the reasons for this difference in historical change, suggesting either that possessive meaning (one's own) gave way to emotional meaning ('dear to one') or vice versa. Paul Kretschmer 1927: 267–71 and Eric Hamp 1982: 251–62 assume an original meaning in the sense of the Latin *suus*. Hooker 1987a: 44–45 argues the opposite, assuming that *philos* originally had emotive meaning which became attenuated over time. In this he disagrees with Adkins who argues that *philos* denotes anything used in battle to protect the *oikos*. Hooker also disagrees with Benveniste (1969: I, 341–43) according to whom *philos* plays a role wherever there are reciprocal relationships of obligation. Such contradictions dissolve if one understands *philos* as used for the purpose of denoting belonging, so that both emotional and material

that the item to be gifted to the goddess is close to the person dedicating it, that it is her own (*suus*).¹⁷⁴

With the dedication of the *peplos*, carried out by the priestess Theano, the Trojan women place themselves and the community under the protection of the goddess. They promise the sacrifice of twelve oxen in the event of a good outcome (*Il.* 6.274). Such animal sacrifices are also described as *phila dōra*. And *philos* in this case does not denote just worth: we may understand *phila dōra* as gifts that are dear to the gods as well as gifts that are their own, or belong to them.¹⁷⁵ When Zeus expresses himself in favour of an appropriate burial for Hector during the quarrel over his body, the god's reason is that Hector always provided *phila dōra* (ἐπεὶ οὔ τι φίλων ἡμάρτανε δώρων, *Il.* 24.68). Rieu translates this as 'he never failed to give me what I like', suggesting both the personal and the possessive meaning of *phila* in this context.¹⁷⁶ What is meant, however, is the portion of the sacrificial meal that forms the tribute to the gods, the *geras* (*Il.* 24.69-70).¹⁷⁷ Hector's closeness to the gods is achieved through this *geras*, as Zeus makes clear in stating that of all those who live in Troy, he is the dearest and the closest to the gods (φίλτατος ἔσκε θεοῖσι βροτῶν οἳ ἐν Ἰλίῳ εἰσίν, *Il.* 24.67). In practice this means that Zeus arranges the release of Hector's body in exchange for goods (metal and textile) from

---

or possessive connotations are relevant. Dirlmeier (1931: 7) argued this in defining *philos* as a pronominal possessive adjective that expresses a relationship of belonging, although he rather overemphasises familial blood-ties.

174. See Willenbrock 1969: 61 in the context of weaponry.

175. Gifts owed to the gods and to Odysseus the stranger are described as φίλα (*Il.* 24.68; *Od.* 13.41; 8.545). The gift (*dosis*) Odysseus receives from Nausicaa (*Od.* 6.208) and Eumaeus (*Od.* 14.58) is said to be modest but *philē*. The *geras* Achilles wishes to take home with him is also small but *philē* (*Il.* 1.167). Where the term *philos* is used adjectivally to describe objects or material goods, it mostly refers to things that are close to, or belong to, an individual—be that the home (*Od.* 18.421) or the paternal lands (*Il.* 9.414), one's bed (*Od.* 8.277) or one's own clothes (*Il.* 2.261). Used predicatively, the term *philos* also denotes fields of activity related to the bonds between warriors and guest-friends. So strife, war, and battle are as dear to Hera and Ares as they are to Achilles (*Il.* 5.891; 2.177) The hospitable Phaeacians on the other hand are fond (*philē*) of banquets, music, dance, clothes, warm baths, and beds (*Od.* 8.247-48). Speeches are dear (*philoi*) to Priam, although given the impending attack by the Greeks, this fondness cannot be indulged (*Il.* 2.796). On the phrase φίλον ἐστίν see more fully Landfester 1966: 95-98; 105-8.

176. Landfester (1966: 30) here translates *phila* as follows: 'denn er hat es nicht an Geschenken *an mich* fehlen lassen'.

177. See ch. 4.2.

Priam's household (*Il.* 24.229-35).[178] In moving the angry Achilles, through Hermes, to accept the lavish goods, Zeus is keeping his bond of *philotēs* with Thetis, who acts in support of her son. It is because of this bond that Zeus rejects the other gods' idea of removing the body in secret from the Greek camp (*Il.* 24.211).

The dedication of garments and the sacrifice of animals complement each other. Both rituals establish close relationships with the gods, based on (not always realised) reciprocity.[179] The dedication of the *peplos* is intended to establish a relationship, but the intention is not achieved, as the goddess denies her protection.[180] The sacrifice promised by the women is meant as thanks for the favour expected as a result of the relationship. In using the specific symbols associated with the two central forms of bond between humans to establish closer ties with the gods, the gods are themselves integrated into the system of *philotēs*, allowing it to gain its own transcendence. We will discover that the death ritual aims to reproduce just this structure.

---

178. These goods are called *apoina*. For the meaning of this term see ch. 5.2.
179. Benveniste (1969: I, 343-44) rightly underlines reciprocity, without excluding an emotional component. See also the following chapter.
180. In the *Odyssey* Aegisthus unsuccessfully seeks divine protection by hanging up fabric offerings (*hyphasmata*) in the temple (*Od.* 3.274).

CHAPTER 3

Structures of Reciprocity and the Production of Signs: *Charis* and the Charites

While Zeus keeps watch over the laws of hospitality, reciprocity is the business of the Graces, the Charites, who almost always appear as a group and are similar to the Muses. Aristotle tells of shrines dedicated to them in order to ensure the maintenance of *antapodosis*, or recompense (διὸ καὶ Χαρίτων ἱερὸν ἐμποδὼν ποιοῦνται, ἵν' ἀνταπόδοσις | ᾖ, Arist. *Eth. Nic.* 1133a3-4). 'For this is the special characteristic of *charis*', Aristotle says, 'since it is necessary not only to repay the person who has shown *charis*, but another time to be first in giving *charis* oneself' (τοῦτο γὰρ ἴδιον χάριτος ἀνθυπηρετῆσαι γὰρ δεῖ τῷ | χαρισαμένῳ, καὶ πάλιν αὐτὸν ἄρξαι χαριζόμενον, Arist. *Eth. Nic.* 1133a 4-5). In Aristotle the Charites embody *charis*, the action or attitude which can denote a service rendered, a favour, or a material gift, and the action or state of mind described by the verb *charizomai*. Karl Polanyi calls this 'reciprocity on the square'.[1] The Charites guarantee the flow of giving and reciprocation which for Aristotle is a matter of just balance. Stoic philosophy accordingly receives the Charites as the personification of reciprocity.[2]

In epic *charis* occurs in the context of any relationship or bond: between warriors, in marriage, and in relationships between humans and gods.[3]

---

1. Polanyi 1957b = 1968: 110. See also Vernant 1966: 131; Meier 1985: 29-30; Bodei Giglioni 1989-1990: 55-64; and MacLachlan 1993: 49-51. According to Jesper Svenbro (1976: 164), Aristotle's remark is relevant to the ethics of repayment of services by a *misthos* rather than to the concept of gift-giving. For the worship of the Charites in Athens, see Pirenne-Delforge 1996: 195-214, who discusses their role in the context of marriage and the oath of the ephebes. For the relationship of the Graces with civic festivals see Fisher 2010.
2. MacLachlan 1993: 51. For the reception of the Charites in Greek philosophy, see Deichgräber 1971: 51-59. For archaeological findings, see Schwarzenberg 1966.
3. On the connection of *charis* with *philotēs* see Scott 1983: 12: '*charis* is used of the pleasure to be found still within the relationship of *philotēs*, friendship, but outside the context of an exchange of gifts [...] the exchange of *charites* arises as a consequence of the realisation that one cannot survive alone, that one needs others'.

Charis can here denote a variety of acts: a military service rendered, and the thanks expected for it; a labour of love; divine favour.[4] The Charites themselves are connected with the more specific field of the production and giving of textile gifts whose symbolic meanings were discussed in the previous chapter. In the divine sphere the Charites see to Aphrodite's bathing and dressing, and they produce her patterned garments. In the world of epic they do not, then, represent a personification of abstract ideas but embody concrete actions, which in the human sphere are undertaken by *amphipoloi* and serving women.[5] In what follows I will investigate the three forms in which *charis* is afforded: the warrior's service, the favour of the gods, and the service rendered by *amphipoloi* and Charites. Following from this, I will turn to the role of the Charites and to the significance of their services in Greek memorial culture.

Apart from its range of meanings connected to the senses of 'favour', 'grace', 'kindness', and 'thankfulness', *charis* has a further semantic dimension as the visual effect emanating from a person or speech. This is often rendered as 'loveliness' or 'charm'. Joachim Latacz rightly characterises this aspect of *charis* as 'drawing-all-eyes'.[6] Scholarship is divided on the question of priority between the two semantic fields of *charis*. Évelyne Scheid-Tissinier assumes an original meaning connected to favour and thanks,[7] while others focus on the visual aspect of *charis* and propose an original meaning of 'shine' or 'light'.[8] Bonnie MacLachlan's interpretation of *charis* as reciprocal 'social pleasure' is an attempt to contain the range of meanings within one common idea.[9] But the contradictions can be more easily resolved through a focus on the concrete actions of the Charites, and in particular by considering the central importance of their weaving. A careful analysis of those situations in which *charis* acquires the meaning of

---

4. For evidence see Latacz 1966: 78–98 and Scheid-Tissinier 1994: 30–36.
5. See the argumentation of Deichgräber 1971: 9. Zilienski 1924: 158–63 identified them as goddesses of the dead (Totengöttinnen); their chthonic character is stressed by Scott 1983: 1–2. MacLachlan 1993: 39–54 underlines their connection with festivities, especially with marriage and the cult of the dead. Like Athena they are worshipped as patrons of the skill of weaving. See *Anth. Pal.* VII 726. In Sicily their names are found on loom-weights. See Isler 1994: 104–6.
6. Latacz 1966: 82.
7. Scheid-Tissinier 1994: 35–36, 258–61.
8. See Borgeaud and MacLachlan 1985: 5–14, who stress a connection between baltic-slavic *zir-* (luire, briller, regarder) and Greek *char* (χαίρω—je me réjouis). See also MacLachlan 1993: 4–7, 52. According to Scott (1983: 2) *charis* goes back to the verb *chairō* (I rejoice). She defines *charis* as 'source of pleasure'.
9. MacLachlan 1993: 147.

an outward shine or luminosity shows that the brightly patterned weavings produced by the Charites can be interpreted (alongside images and reliefs worked in metal) as a significant medium for the visual power of *charis*. Once *charis* is understood as the light or visual power that radiates from a woven image, especially of a red colour, it is easy to see how such visual power can also be spoken of with reference to the *charis* of a speech or song (as for instance in Homer, Pindar, or Bacchylides). As we saw in the first chapter, poets also create images, or visual effects, which are inscribed in the memories of their audiences.

To properly illustrate the material dimensions of this meaning of *charis* we must consider ancient techniques of polychrome weaving, which have acquired new cultural significance through research by Elizabeth Wayland Barber.[10] Scholarly research into cultural memory has mostly turned to the medium of writing as a form of storing such memory. It is clear from the observations made here, however, that patterned weaving provides another form of storing and commemorating knowledge. This memorial function helps to explain the prominent role played by the Charites in classical Greek festival culture. Alongside the recitation of memorial texts of social significance (as for instance the epics recited at the *Panathenaia*), the Charites were responsible for visual aspects of the festival. In charge of the proper arrangement and ritual configuration of the participants, and of the effectiveness of the poetically produced images, they contribute significantly to society's sense of its own order. Misunderstood as goddesses of death or fertility, the Charites' responsibility for the visual in fact means that they possessed an important integrative function, which is inadequately described through the notion of reciprocity.

3.1. The warrior's service and the gods' favour

In epic poetry *charis* frequently denotes a military service rendered and the thanks given for such service. The phrase χάριν φέρειν (*charin pherein*) describes the performance of a military service or favour for a person (or in the case of the gods, the granting of favour) which may ensure success in battle. The giving of thanks for military success or for divine favour is expressed with the phrase χάρις/ν εἶναι/διδόναι (*charis/n einai/didonai*).[11] In place of these phrases we also find the verb χαρίζομαι (*charizomai*),

---

10. Barber 1991.
11. Scheid-Tissinier 1994: 30-36.

rendered by Joachim Latacz as 'eine erfreuende Leistung erbringen' ('to afford a pleasing or agreeable service').[12] Used with the dative, *charizomai* denotes kindness or favour done for a person's benefit; with the accusative it frequently expresses the offering of favours or gifts in return for favours or gifts received.

Pandarus, for example, comes from Lycia to support the Trojans against the Greeks 'to do a favour to heavenly Hector' (φέρων χάριν Ἕκτορι δίῳ, *Il.* 5.211). The Trojans themselves, when they set fire to the Greek ships, are fighting 'to please Hector, stirred up by him' (χάριν Ἕκτορος ὀτρύναντος, *Il.* 15.744). Odysseus's support of Agamemnon is also described with the phrase *charin pherein*. Odysseus, in danger of shipwreck and drowning, laments his imminent fate and praises the Greeks who found honourable death at Troy as they were 'doing a favour to the sons of Atreus' (χάριν Ἀτρεΐδῃσι φέροντες, *Od.* 5.307). In another case the phrase is used of persuasive speech in the leader's favour rather than military support. When Phoenix attempts to persuade Achilles to abandon his wrath and return to arms, Achilles accuses his friend of doing Agamemnon a favour (Ἀτρεΐδῃ ἥρωϊ φέρων χάριν, *Il.* 9.613) by trying to dissuade him with his weeping and sorrow.

The verb *charizomai* is also used in the context of armed service, as in the cases of Cleitus and Hippomachus who fight against the Greeks 'doing a favour to Hector and the Trojans' (Ἕκτορι καὶ Τρώεσσι χαριζόμενος, *Il.* 15.449; 17.291). There is one single occurrence of *charizomai* describing the granting of a material gift in the context of military support. The *thōrax* worn by Agamemnon in *Iliad* 11 is a gift, *xeinēion*, from Kinyras of Cyprus, sent 'to give pleasure to the king' (χαριζόμενος βασιλῆϊ, *Il.* 11.23) when the news of the campaign against Troy had reached Cyprus. It is not clear whether Cinyras's gift is in fulfillment of obligation as a form of tribute, or a service for which he might expect to receive a return. It is possible that Cinyras's gift is in lieu of actual military service, similar to the gift of the horse Aëthe, given to Agamemnon by Echepolus of Sikyon so that he might stay at home and enjoy his wealth instead of joining the campaign to Troy (*Il.* 23.293–300).[13] We also hear, however, of the similarly wealthy Euchenor of Corinth who avoids the payment of a penalty (*thōē*/θωή) and

---

12. Latacz 1966: 104.
13. Therefore, he is characterised as 'Ahnvater der Drückeberger' ('father of all shirkers') by Andreadas 1931: 14, n. 14. Nilsson 1927: 29 deduced a feudal system of military service, which is now replaced by the idea of reciprocal relationship. See Scheid-Tissinier 1994: 256.

joins the campaign even though his death is foretold (*Il.* 13.663-72). The *thōē* is a penalty imposed by a collective—in this case it would be the Danaans—which in classical times became due when, for instance, the laws of mourning were contravened.[14] The seer Halitherses is also threatened with *thōē* by Penelope's suitors when he speaks in favour of Telemachus (*Od.* 2.192). It makes sense then to assume that there are degrees of obligation to support a military campaign, as we also see in the Odyssey. Odysseus distinguishes between giving service to others, for which *charizomai* is used, and taking part in war independently and with one's own allies, when he says that he did not wish to offer service to Idomeneus's father as an attendant (οὐχ ᾧ πατρὶ χαριζόμενος θεράπευον) but led his own men into battle against Troy (*Od.* 13.265).

Warriors are described on a number of occasions with the perfect participle form of *charizomai*, suggesting a relationship of service between war leaders and between a leader and his men. Close companions are often addressed with the phrase ἐμῷ κεχαρισμένε θυμῷ (*emō kecharismene thumō*) which carries emotional overtones suggesting intimacy and can be rendered as 'dear to my heart'.[15] Diomedes is such a *kecharismenos* to Agamemnon, as are Sthenelus and Patroclus to Achilles (*Il.* 10.234; 5.243; 11.608). The phrase is also used for bonds between humans and gods, as when Athena describes Diomedes as *kecharismenos* (*Il.* 5.826). Since the perfect tense denotes an action completed or repeatedly completed in the past, the effects of which continue in the present, a *kecharismenos* (literally: one who has provided a service or favour) must be, in a military context, one who continues to do military service.[16] The term is used in the context of other bonds, such as those between or within households, which are also characterised by continuity but which are initially formed by performance of a ritual (e.g. the bond between a father-in-law and his potential son-in-law, offering bridewealth).[17] Emotional bonds form a part of such lasting relationships of service, and a *kecharismenos* must

---

14. See Vatin 1987: 275-80, with further evidence.
15. According to Latacz (1966: 117) a κεχαρισμένος is 'a person who once and repeatedly rendered me a service which was pleasing to me, and who is therefore now himself pleasing, welcome, dear, etc'. The transition from 'one who rendered me something pleasing' to 'one who is pleasing to me' may not make strict grammatical sense, but psychologically it is immediately understandable.
16. Latacz 1966: 116-20. See also MacLachlan 1993: 29, n. 23.
17. *Od.* 2.54. See also *Il.* 19.287 where Briseis calls Patroclus πλεῖστον κεχαρισμένε because of his promise to arrange her marriage to Achilles. Patroclus would have taken the role of the father of the bride.

be considered someone whose service gives rise to positive emotion; this becomes clear in a remark made by Alcinous when Odysseus is crying during Demodocus's recital. Alcinous asks Odysseus whether a companion of his fell at Troy, a man who knew how to give service (κεχαρισμένα εἰδώς, *Od.* 8.584). In this instance it is not the warrior himself but his service that is described using the perfect participle of *charizomai*. The choice of the participle instead of the noun *charis* clarifies that the service is not rendered once but repeatedly and continuously. Odysseus's grief shows that such service given continuously is understood in terms of an emotional bond, which also fits with the fact that the life of the warrior involves not only fighting together but also communal feasting.[18] The idea of a continuous bond is also strengthened by the fact that comrades in arms can be described in terms of blood-relations, such as *kasignētos* (brother), even though kinship does not feature in the structure and organisation of the Homeric armies.[19]

In the past, scholars such as Martin P. Nilsson, Gustave Glotz, and Henri Jeanmaire interpreted Homeric armed service in terms of feudal military obligation and thus considered Agamemnon as an over-lord over the vassal-kings subordinated to him.[20] The model of military obligation, and of Agamemnon as feudal lord, seemed unlikely to scholars like Erich Bethe and Gunther Jachmann who believed that alliances were formed through missions sent abroad.[21] Moses I. Finley, whose rejection of the idea of feudal kingship was the most radical, argued in a similar way in his study *The World of Odysseus*.[22] Since then a number of studies have underlined the mostly voluntary character of Homeric military service with its emphasis on reciprocity; most recently the observations made by Hans van Wees show that it is best understood in terms of friendship (i.e. *philotēs*).[23]

As military service *charis* may then also be denied when it is not appropriately returned, for instance with a portion of booty or with a return service. So when Hector hesitates to fight over the body of Patroclus whose armour he has already appropriated, he is taunted by the Lycian

---

18. *Il.* 17.576. For further evidence see Ulf 1990: 132–33; Scheid-Tissinier 1994: 272–74. See also ch. 4.
19. Ulf 1990: 131.
20. The former positions are presented by Carlier 1984: 179–82.
21. Bethe 1931: 229–30; Jachmann 1953: 243. See also ch. 4.1.
22. Finley 1967: 109–11.
23. Van Wees 1992: 44–48. The concept of feudal kingship is rejected by Ulf 1990: 85–98, who denies that there is complete reciprocity between warrior and leader (128), whereas Scheid-Tissinier 1994: 258–59 stresses the reciprocal relationship.

chief, Glaucus, who announces that no Lycian will continue to fight since it seems that 'there is no *charis*' (ἐπεὶ οὐκ ἄρα χάρις ἦεν) for the 'great advantage' (πόλλ' ὄφελος) provided by Sarpedon (*Il.* 17.147; 152). The Lycians want Patroclus's body in order to exchange it for that of Sarpedon, which is in the hands of the Greeks. Achilles too justifies his own refusal to fight for Agamemnon after Brisëis has been taken from him by pointing out that there is no *charis* (οὐκ ἄρα τις χάρις ἦεν, *Il.* 9.319).[24] In both instances *charis* is easily rendered as 'thanks'. There are, however, two types of thanks suggested. In the Lycians' case it is a matter of returning the favour of military support in kind, by fighting for the body of Patroclus; in Achilles's case *charis* is a portion of booty due to the warrior as a gift of honour (*geras*) in the form of a woman.[25] For Pandarus, there are more material gifts in play, when the Trojans promise him thanks (χάριν) in the form of shining gifts (ἀγλαὰ δῶρα) should he succeed in mortally wounding Menelaus with an arrow (*Il.* 4.95-97).[26]

Reciprocity is especially prominent when *charis* is demanded for a previously offered service. In such cases *charis* as thanks does not take the form of a service rendered or gift given in return for military service. Instead, in a kind of inversion, *charis* can involve refraining from violent or military action. This happens on a number of different occasions when the Trojans Adrastus, Dolon, and Hippolochus ask Achilles to spare their lives, offering a ransom (*apoina*) in return. Each time, the immeasurable *apoina* of bronze, gold, and iron is the means by which the warrior's father will show his *charis* (χαρίσαιτο: *Il.* 6.49; 10.380; 11.134). The potential offer of material goods is clearly meant to be understood as based on reciprocity: it would only be realised if Achilles were to agree to spare the life in question. Another example of *charis* in the sense of sparing is seen when the suitor Leiodes asks for *charis* from Odysseus for good deeds done in the past on the grounds that he did not, like the other suitors, avail himself of the women in the house (*Od.* 22.319).[27] Odysseus rejects this plea for *charis* and kills Leiodes since he did not show similar restraint when it came to wooing Penelope (*Od.* 22.320-25). Penelope had already reproached the

---

24. See also van Wees 1992: 48.
25. See ch. 4.
26. Latacz 1966: 85 interprets *charis* here as 'Beliebtheit', 'Anziehung', 'Geltung', and 'Prestige' (popularity, charm, status, and prestige) without discussing the role of the *aglaa dōra*.
27. See also Latacz 1966: 92 who interprets the *charis* Leiodes asks for as a service in return for a past favour.

suitors for not showing thanks for the good deeds (χάρις [...] εὐεργέων) of Odysseus and committing only unseemly deeds (ἀεικέα ἔργα) themselves (*Od.* 4.694-95). These unseemly actions, with which the suitors in essence deny Odysseus the *charis* due to him for his good deeds consist of the abuse of the (sexual) services of the women in the house, and the appropriation of Odysseus's property. Not only do they consume without recompense, they also use goods that are not theirs in order to give *charis* to others (ἀλλοτρίων χαρίσασθαι, *Od.* 17.452).[28] They will be repaid in the end for their behaviour when Athena and Odysseus prepare a banquet for them that could not be more lacking in *charis* (ἀχαρίστερον, *Od.* 20.392). This use of the comparative form of the adjective *acharis* may well allude to the usual function of the feast as a return gift for military service, or to the normal reciprocity of hospitality which of course the suitors did not keep to.[29] Equally the denial of *charis* here may suggest the relationship to a king, who takes on the role of war-lord (*anax*) and political leader in the community and as such receives gifts such as those due to the gods.[30] Such divine *charis* operates in a similar framework to that shown by warriors to one another.

Reciprocal bonds of service, such as those between leaders in war and between a leader and his companions, also exist between men and gods. The help given to fighters by the gods is even described with the same phrase: *charin pherein*. *Charis* given to fighters by the gods can take the form of actual divine engagement in battle or that of favour shown to their own. It is striking that divine *charis* is given to a group rather than an individual. So Ares, wounded while fighting against the Trojans complains to Zeus: 'We gods always suffer most horribly for you [...] when showing favour to men' (χάριν ἄνδρεσσι φέροντες, *Il.* 5.873-74). Apollo is chastised by Poseidon for his support of the Trojans and reminded that the Trojan ruler Laomedon once cheated them of their shepherds' wages. For that reason Poseidon considers the Trojans undeserving of divine *charis* in the form of victory over the Greeks and demands their downfall: 'That is the man whose people you are now so anxious to oblige (τοῦ δὴ νῦν λαοῖσι φέρεις χάριν) instead of joining us and trying to ensure that these insolent

---

28. See Scheid-Tissinier 1994: 31, who translates: 'à être généreux avec le bien d'autrui'.
29. See Latacz (1966: 104), who translates ἀχαρίστερον as 'weniger erfreulich' (less pleasing). His translation is based on his interpretation of *charizomai* as 'eine erfreuende Leistung erbringen' ('to render a pleasing service'). According to him the comparative ἀχαρίς does not underline the lack of beauty but the emotional effect. On the duty to provide food and drink see Ulf 1990: 132-33.

Trojans are utterly wiped out, together with their children and their honoured wives' (*Il.* 21.458-60; tr. Rieu). Elsewhere, Zeus is also said wrongly to favour the Trojans (χαρίζεαι, *Il.* 13.633).

There is a case of *charis* as a reward assured by the gods, when Odysseus tells Eumaeus that Hermes grants *charis* and glory for their deeds to all humans (πάντων | ἀνθρώπων ἔργοισι χάριν καὶ κῦδος ὀπάζει, *Od.* 15.319-20). With Joachim Latacz this would mean that Hermes lends lustre to the deeds of men; in my view, given the context, it means that Hermes affords recompense to men for their deeds.[31] Odysseus is considering putting himself into the suitors' service for the sake of a meal, which suggests *charis* is viewed almost as a payment (*Od.* 15.315-16). Such payment, usually called *misthos*, is received in archaic and classical times by mercenaries, called *misthotes*, in return for military service to foreign rulers in Egypt, Persia, Macedonia, and even in Athens.[32] But relationships involving *misthos* are only temporary, lacking the sense of permanence implied by *charis*.[33]

The goodwill of the gods, their *charis*, is won through the offering of sacrificial gifts, which are themselves characterised as χαρίεις (*charieis*). According to Scheid-Tissinier the word indicates the joy or satisfaction the gifts evoke in their recipients.[34] The sponsors of such gifts can be individuals or collectives, or individuals representing collectives. In *Iliad* 8 Hera reproaches Poseidon for not helping the Greeks, who have already sent many and pleasing gifts (δῶρα [...] πολλά τε καὶ χαρίεντα) to Aigae and Helice. These gifts entitle the Greeks to victory in Hera's view (*Il.* 8.203-4). A similar scenario presents itself when the people of Pylos offer sacrifice to Poseidon in *Odyssey* 3, and Athena asks the god on their behalf for a 'gracious requital' (χαρίεσσαν ἀμοιβὴν, *Od.* 3.58-59). Athena also argues that the sacrifice Odysseus had offered long ago by the Argive ships to Zeus as *charis* (χαρίζετο ἱερὰ ῥέζων) should entitle him to divine favour and to a successful return home (*Od.* 1.61). Chryses is able to count

---

30. See Scheid-Tissinier 1994: 259-61. She underlines the reciprocal meaning of *charis euergeōn* in the relationship between king and *dēmos*. On the difference between *basileus* and *anax* see ch. 4.1.
31. Latacz 1966: 86-87.
32. For evidence see Herman 1987: 10 and Domingo Gygax 2016. This contrast is an interesting one in the Athenian context because it implies that wealthy citizens' relationships with the *polis* are shaped by permanence, receiving *charis* as they do (at least following Ober 1989) for their services such as liturgies, whereas ordinary citizens have only a temporary relationship with the political institutions shaped by *misthos*. I thank Claire Taylor for this comment.
33. See Scheid-Tissinier 1994: 266. For more detail see ch. 5.1.
34. Scheid-Tissinier 1994: 33.

on Apollo's support in avenging the rape of his daughter because he put a roof over the god's temple to please him (χαρίεντ' ἐπὶ νηὸν ἔρεψα, *Il.* 1.39). The plague which decimates the Achaean army until Agamemnon finally returns Chryseis is Apollo's favour to Chryses.[35] The gods' favour can also be begged by third parties on behalf of others. So Nestor, after Achilles has awarded him a prize at Patroclus's funeral games, wishes that the gods may give *charis* to Achilles (χάριν [...] δοῖεν). The context indicates that in this case *charis* is the favour of success in battle, which the gods will indeed afford Achilles. In their roles as leaders in battle in the case of Odysseus and Achilles and as intermediary to the gods in the case of Chryses, all three are examples of figures who do not act in their own interest, although they are all seen to gain advantage from divine gifts and support.

Further evidence for the reciprocal relationship between gods who grant *charis* and the men who give them pleasing sacrificial gifts can be found in the use of the middle perfect participle κεχαρισμένα (*kecharismena*) to characterise those gifts. As Latacz puts it 'when κεχαρισμένα is used of objects, these are validated as [not only] concrete signs of the personal effort and attitude of the offerer'.[36] The use of the perfect tense also draws attention to the recurring character of the offers, and to the expectation of reciprocity. So for instance, Aeneas can count on divine assistance in a dangerous situation in battle because of the gifts, described as *kecharismena*, which he is said to have repeatedly offered to the gods (κεχαρισμένα δ'αἰεὶ δῶρα θεοῖσι δίδωσι, *Il.* 20.298–99). Autolycus, Odysseus's maternal grandfather, was taught to swear and to deceive by Hermes, to whom he gave burnt offerings of legs of lambs and goats in return (τῷ γὰρ κεχαρισμένα μηρία καῖεν ἀρνῶν ἠδ' ἐρίφων, *Od.* 19.397–98). Here too one must assume that the offerings are recurring.

There are two cases of gifts owed to men and described with the adjective *charieis* and the participle *kecharismena*. Both instances involve the relationship between a high-status, godlike individual and a collective. In Phoenix's story of Meleager (told to persuade the sulking Achilles to rejoin battle), Meleager attains many and pleasing gifts (δῶρ' ἐτέλεσσαν | [...] πολλά τε καὶ χαρίεντα) from the Aetolian elders for joining battle against the Curetes (*Il.* 9.598–99; see also 9.576). The gift offered here is land (a *temenos*) for the cultivation of wine and grain (*Il.* 9.576–79). Such gifts are otherwise offered only to gods and to godlike kings. The story of Meleager

---

35. See ch. 4.1.
36. Latacz 1966: 117.

alludes to the godlike status of the gift's recipient in so far as Achilles—for whom the story is intended as encouragement to abandon his current stance—is offered the expectation of similarly godlike honours: 'No, come for the gifts (*dōra*)! The Achaeans will honour you as a god!' (*Il.* 9.602-3).

The second example relates more directly to the godlike status of the recipient. Here Telemachus on catching sight of Odysseus, whose appearance has been changed by Athena with new attire, believes him to be a god and offers to give him 'pleasing sacrifice' (κεχαρισμένα [...] ἱρά) and 'golden gifts' (χρύσεα δῶρα, *Od.* 16.184-85).[37] We know that Odysseus has already received similar gifts from the Phaeacians, albeit without the use of words such as *charieis* or *kecharismena*. Alcinous does, however, use the verb *charizomai* for the recompense which the Phaeacian leaders may count on in return for their tribute to Odysseus. The king explains that the tripods and cauldrons can be recouped through the people, for it would be burdensome for individuals to be expected to bear the price of such gifts (ἀργαλέον γὰρ ἕνα προικὸς χαρίσασθαι, *Od.* 13.15).

Reciprocal relationships between warriors and their leaders and between men and gods are part of epic's structure of reciprocity and are based on, or mediated, by rank. So reciprocal relationships between different leaders in war, or between leaders and their troops, are mirrored in the system of divine *charis*: the very services and favours given by warriors to one another may also be offered by the gods. The system of divine *charis* is not identical, however, to that which takes place between warriors, because divine *charis* is not granted to individuals but to the collective. So when high-ranking individuals are said to have been rewarded by the gods with a favour in return for their actions, it is by no means certain that this happens as part of a purely personal reciprocal relationship with the gods. This is especially true in cases where sacrificial offerings have been given, and where the sacrifices are carried out by the whole group. It can be assumed that individuals who claim a particular proximity to the gods (such as priests or those in kingly positions) act as mediators on behalf of a group of warriors or a *dēmos*. But such kingly figures, or *basileis*, whose roles I will return to in more detail, can appear as godlike and can accept offerings which are comparable to those given to gods; through this there is a tendency to transcend, by which I mean to eternalise, their function. Before we return to this idea, we must first explore the significance of

---

37. See also *Il.* 24.661, where the ceasefire agreed for Hector's funeral is seen as a favour.

3.2. Women's thanks and the weaving of amphipoloi and Charites

There is one sole instance of the use of the word *charis* in connection with a relationship of *philotēs* between men and women. In this instance, *charis* is not given but seen. In *Iliad* 11 we hear of the Thracian Iphidamas:

> ὣς ὃ μὲν αὖθι πεσὼν κοιμήσατο χάλκεον ὕπνον
> οἰκτρὸς ἀπὸ μνηστῆς ἀλόχου, ἀστοῖσιν ἀρήγων,
> κουριδίης, ἧς οὔ τι χάριν ἴδε, πολλὰ δ' ἔδωκε
> πρῶθ' ἑκατὸν βοῦς δῶκεν, ἔπειτα δὲ χίλι' ὑπέστη
> αἶγας ὁμοῦ καὶ ὄϊς, τά οἱ ἄσπετα ποιμαίνοντο.

> So there he [Iphidamas] fell, to sleep the unbreakable sleep—a pitiable end, helping his fellow Trojans, far from his wife, the new bride from whom he had seen no *charis*, though he had given so much to her. He had already handed over a hundred head of cattle and promised a thousand more sheep and goats from his countless flock (*Il.* 11.241–45; tr. adapted from Rieu).

We are dealing here with a reciprocal relationship between partners in marriage and their families; Homeric epic mostly describes only the male part of this relationship: the transfer, πορεῖν (*porein*) of 'bridewealth' by the groom to the bride's father, called ἕδνα (*hedna*) or ἐέδνα (*eedna*). The bride's transfer to the groom's household takes place as a consequence of the delivery of gifts by the groom, which is why Rudolf Koestler refers to the *hedna* as 'Heimfuehrungsgaben' ('bringing-home-gifts').[38] It is assumed that these gifts took the form of herds and flocks as seen in the cited passage on the gifts given by Iphidamas.[39] These were presumably handed over to the father of the bride, while the bride was given gifts of jewellery and clothing, described as δῶρα (*dōra*). As I have shown elsewhere, both types of gifts ensured the husband's possession of the wife's children and of her handiwork as well as of the work of her servant women: those woven works with their symbolic and practical functions in the ritual of

---

38. Köstler 1950: 48 and 60.
39. Leduc 1990: 270; Scheid-Tissinier 1994: 113.

guest-friendship.[40] In the context of marriage, *charis* can then mean both thanks and benefit, with the former made concrete by the service of love and the latter by that of weaving.[41] The wife's thanks are made visible in the woven works which are sometimes characterized by *charis* in the sense of a shine or lustre. *Charis* is also made visible in the very person of the wife, who herself, in the divine sphere, can embody *charis*.

When Hera, for instance, wants to distract Zeus from the battlefield at Troy she does not collect only Aphrodite's famous girdle with its power of *philotēs*.[42] She also turns to Hypnos to ask him to put Zeus to sleep, and in return she promises him *charis*:

ἐγὼ δέ κέ τοι ἰδέω χάριν ἤματα πάντα

and I shall show you *charis* for ever. (*Il.* 14.235)

Indeed, as it turns out, Hera will need to show Hypnos *charis*, by making her visible: he turns down the offer of a golden chair, because he is afraid to incur the wrath of Zeus, and agrees to help Hera only when she promises to give him one of the Charites as wife (*Il.* 14.265-75). In this way *charis* will really be visible to Hypnos forever—and Hera literally shows him her thanks.

The Charites are Aphrodite's divine entourage and provide service in bathing and dressing her as well as weaving for her (*Od.* 8.364-66; *Hom. Hymn Aphr.* 61). So for instance, the *peplos* worn by Aphrodite when she storms into battle to protect Aeneas is said to have been made by the Charites (*Il.* 5.338). In the *Hymn to Aphrodite*, she offers woven clothing (ἐσθῆτά θ' ὑφαντὴν) as a gift to Anchises (*Hom. Hymn Aphr.* 139-40). But this service also implies a social bond, as we hear in the *Odyssey* that Aphrodite joins in dance with the Charites (*Od.* 18.192-94).

---

40. Wagner-Hasel 1988. These brides are often characterised as objects. See e.g. Lyons 2003: 101, who argues that '(i)n marked contrast to the *Iliad* [...] the *Odyssey* represents women not merely as objects but also as participants in gift exchange'. Gifts of clothing made to brides also appear in later times, e.g. a woman complaining in a twelfth-century Byzantine epic about the lack of gifts of clothing made to her by her husband (Ptochoprodromos 1.45, ed. Eideneier 1991).
41. See Scott 1983: 5. Cf. also Latacz 1966: 95-97. In this context he understands *charis* as the pleasure of a counter-gift. Reciprocity is also emphasised by MacLachlan 1993: 27 who speaks of 'mutual benefits'. The raising of illegitimate children (described by the verb *charizomai*) is one of the benefits of marriage. See Theano raising her husband's *nothos* as her own child (*Il.* 5.71 χαριζομένη πόσεϊ).

As a divine personification we meet *charis* in the figure of Hephaestus's wife, whose name in the *Iliad* is Charis (*Il.* 18.382). In the *Theogony*, it is Aglaia, 'the shining one' (Hes. *Theog.* 945–46). She embodies the lustre of the *aglaa dōra*, the 'gleaming' gifts of metalware and textiles received by guests. In the *Odyssey* it is of course Aphrodite, the leader of the Charites, who is the wife of Hephaestus.[43]

In the mortal sphere we see this structure replicated in the domestic domain, where ἀμφίπολοι (*amphipoloi*) assist high-ranking women (and in two cases also men).[44] *Amphipoloi* provide service when it comes to bathing and clothing, and weaving.[45] Like the Charites, *amphipoloi* also appear almost always in groups. Their plurality is suggested in the word itself: *amphipoloi* are those who move or stand (πέλω, πέλομαι) on both sides (ἀμφί). Stefan Hiller has proposed a connection to the Mycenaean term *a-pi-qo-ro*, a collective term for groups of female workers, which also appears at Thebes in the context of textile work. Because of the word's association with a *potnia* on the Linear B tablets, Hiller suspects a religious origin and interprets *amphipoloi*/*a-pi-qo-ro* as the attendants of a priestess.[46] A connection with weaving is more likely, however, and is also suggested by pictorial evidence: the only extant ancient Greek depiction of weaving shows women walking up and down on both sides of the loom, although it is unclear whether the two women depicted on the sixth-century Attic Lekythos meet in the middle of the loom or walk on past one another.[47] We know from modern parallels, as well as from ancient depictions found in Egypt, that two people may work together on one piece of weaving.[48] What is striking about the image on the Lekythos is that other aspects of the work (the weighing of the wool, spinning, and the folding of the finished product) are also represented as activities undertaken by two women together. It has also been suggested that the image on our vase is

---

42. See ch. 2.3.
43. On Aphrodite and Charis see Simon 1985: 236.
44. Laërtes has two *amphipoloi* (*Od.* 1.191; 6.209; 24.366), and Hephaestus is supported by two golden *amphipoloi* (Il. 18.417–18).
45. See ch. 2.3.2.
46. Hiller 1987: 239–55.
47. New York, Metropolitan Museum 31.11.10; von Bothmer 1985: 185–86. No. 48. A similar interpretation is suggested by the use of the verb *erchomai* for Calypso's weaving in the *Odyssey* (although it is debatable whether the verb refers to the weaver's movement or to the shuttle's). See also Wace 1948: 55. For weaving pictures on vases see Ferrari 2002.
48. Barber 1991: 81 and 105.

Figure 2: Wool working at Athens. Attic black-figure *lekythos* of the Amasis painter. 540 BCE. New York, The Metropolitan Museum of Art, Fletcher Fund 1931, 31.11.10. https://www.metmuseum.org/en/art/collection/search/253348.

connected to the weaving of Athena's *peplos* for the *Panathenaia*.[49] Even if we must assume a cultic connection, we may suppose that working in pairs made sense for textile workers (Figure 2).

Another noteworthy aspect of our image is the combination of scenes of socialising with the representation of a female sphere of work: on the vase's shoulder there is a group of eight dancing girls. This combination of work and play can be observed also in our literary sources: Nausicaa and her *amphipoloi*, for instance, play a ball game when they do the laundry at the beach (*Od.* 6.100). And the girl's relationship with one of these companions, Dymas, who guards the entrance to Nausicaa's bedroom, is described

---

49. Von Bothmer 1985: 185–86; Lissarrague 1991: 229, fig. 47.

with the verb *charizomai* (κεχάριστο δὲ θυμῷ, *Od.* 6.23). Just as we saw in the case of the relationship between a warlord and his companions, the pluperfect tense (*kecharisto*) once again is used to express the lasting character of the pleasing service which the *amphipoloi* render their mistress.[50]

Not unlike the warriors, the women too receive divine support. So Nausicaa's two *amphipoloi* received their beauty from the Charites (*Od.* 6.18). And when she wishes to stir the suitors' desire for Penelope, Athena anoints the mortal woman with just that ambrosial oil used by Aphrodite when she goes to dance with the Charites (*Od.* 18.192–95).

It is not clear whether such divine support is earned through offerings and whether this divine-mortal collective is governed by the same reciprocity we assume for a warlord and his companions. We know that warlords provide their troops with meals. Nausicaa also eats together with her *amphipoloi* (*Od.* 6.97). Penelope laments her fate before her *amphipoloi*, who are also addressed as *philai* (*Od.* 4.722). The verb *philein* which, like the address by the noun *philos*, indicates a close relationship, is also used for the relationship between Helen and a wool-worker from Sparta who is very close to her (ἥ οἱ Λακεδαίμονι ναιετοώσῃ | ἤσκειν εἴρια καλά, μάλιστα δέ μιν φιλέεσκε, *Il.* 3.387–88). Helen also left behind at Sparta a group of friends she had grown up with; it is possible that this was also a team who worked together at weaving, as male *hetairoi* collaborated in battle (λιποῦσα | παῖδά τε τηλυγέτην καὶ ὁμηλικίην ἐρατεινήν, *Il.* 3.174–75). While the women who work for Arete and Nausicaa in the Phaeacian kingdom are said to be free women, Penelope's working women are not: they are said to have been acquired in battle or gained as gifts.[51] Eurycleia who, alongside Penelope, taught the servant women in the household how to go about their work, is an example of the latter (ἔργα διδάξαμεν ἐργάζεσθαι, *Od.* 22.422). Such unfree women are rarely called *amphipoloi*; more often they are described as 'δμῳαὶ γυναῖκες' (*dmōiai gunaikes* = 'serving women').[52]

The word used for the work such women do is 'ἐργάζεσθαι' (*ergazesthai*), which Raymond Descat views as indicating work carried out for others.[53] The word is also used in the context of metal-working, such

---

50. On the relationship of Nausicaa and her maidens see now Karanika 2014: 46–66, who stresses the performative character of the washing-scene and interprets Nausicaa as leader of a chorus of young girls.
51. See Wickert-Micknat 1982: 40; Uchitel 1984: 257–82; Wagner-Hasel 1988: 61; Battegazzore 1987: 30–40; de Fidio 1979: 188–217.
52. For evidence see Gschnitzer 1976: 68–73, Scheid-Tissinier 2015 (on Eurycleia).
53. Descat 1986: 48–58, suspects a Mycenaean origin.

as when the goldsmith Laërkes calls Menelaus to work (κελέσθω [...] ἐργάζετο, *Od.* 3.425), or when Hephaestus sets his bellows to work (*Il.* 18.469). This does not automatically imply unfree status. In the context of labour carried out by prisoners of war, *ergazesthai* is supplemented with ἀναγκαῖος (*anankaios*) or ἀνάγκη (*anankē*) to describe enforced labour, as when Odysseus's companions are said to have been taken prisoners in order to carry out such enforced labour (σφίσιν ἐργάζεσθαι ἀνάγκῃ, *Od.* 14.272 = 17.441). At Ithaca, only Laërtes's male labourers are described in this way (*Od.* 24.210),[54] never Penelope's *dmōiai gunaikes*, even though they are at times descended from the male *dmōes*. This is, for instance, the case for Melantho, of whom it is said that Penelope cared for her as a child, and gave her toys as gifts (*Od.* 18.322-23).[55]

In the divine sphere, the daughters of Pandareus enter the type of labour described as *ergazesthai* after they are orphaned and Aphrodite and Athena look after them. They are taught, just as we are told the maidservants of Penelope are, by Athena to undertake 'glorious work' (ἔργα [...] κλυτὰ ἐργάζεσθαι, *Od.* 20.72). Given Athena's association with weaving, this can only mean that they were taught to work as weavers.[56] The fact that this work is characterized as '*kluta*' (glorious), clarifies that the work of weaving cannot be regarded as dishonourable—unlike the work imagined by Andromache in case of the enslavement of her son Astyanax, described as 'unseemly' (ἔργα ἀεικέα ἐργάζοιο, *Il.* 24.733). Whereas the work taught to Penelope's women is not called '*kluta*', the word is used for the work Helen calls (*keleue*) her *amphipoloi* to do (ἀμφιπόλοισι περικλυτὰ ἔργα κέλευε, *Il.* 6.324).

The same term κελεύειν (*keleuein*) is used for calling warriors to battle and *amphipoloi* or serving women to work. So we hear in *Iliad* 4 that 'each leader should call his people' (κέλευε δὲ οἷσιν ἕκαστος ἡγεμόνων, *Il.* 4.428-29) when battle recommences after the truce.[57] This is exactly what women such as Helen, Arete, Andromache, or Penelope do when it is time to get *amphipoloi* to make up beds for guests or to send *dmōiai*

---

54. See also the remarks made by Eumaeus about Odysseus's *dmōes*: that they will not work unless masters enforce their power (*Od.* 17.320-21).
55. Lenz ([1790] 1976: 41) is already aware that these are hired workers. According to Beringer 1985: 47 the use of the terms *dmōes* and *dmōiai* does not suggest enslaved status.
56. Cf. *Il.* 5.735; 8.384; 9.390; 14.178; *Od.* 7.110; 2.116; 20.72; *Hom. Hymn. Aphr.* 14-15; *Hes. Op.* 63-64.
57. Cf. *Il.* 13.230 where Idomeneus asks Thoas that everyone must 'give orders' (κέλευε). Hector gives orders to his brothers (*Il.* 16.545) and Ajax to the Danaans (*Il.* 15.586).

gunaikes off to work at the loom or the spindle.[58] This symmetry between service given in battle and service given on the loom is especially pronounced in Hector's farewell to Andromache, when he designates their two separate spheres of responsibility: his is war, and hers is weaving: 'give orders to the *amphipoloi* to go about their work (ἀμφιπόλοισι κέλευε ἔργον ἐποίχεσθαι), but let the men take care of the war' (*Il.* 6.492-93).[59] The activities to which *amphipoloi*, warriors, and in one case smiths (*Od.* 3.425), are called are all specialized, skilled labour.[60] The words *ergazesthai*, *keleuein*, and *charizomai* suggest the relationships within which such skilled labour is carried out, while the effort and technical skill afforded to carry out the work is described by the word κάμνειν (*kamnein*). According to Felix Eckstein, *kamnein* represents 'careful work and detailed technique'.[61] The term is used in the context of war as well as weaving, and especially for metal-working, and frequently with reference to divine activity in the spheres of textile and metal work.[62] The *peplos* worn by Aphrodite as she hurries into battle to help Aeneas has been carefully worked by the Charites (ὅν οἱ Χάριτες κάμον αὐταί, *Il.* 5.338). Athena loses her *peplos* twice in battle: she had made it herself and crafted it carefully by hand (ὅν ῥ' αὐτή ποιήσατο καὶ κάμε χερσίν, *Il.* 6.734-35). The many *peploi* that Helen keeps in her trunk when Telemachus is visiting at Sparta are also worked carefully by herself (κάμεν αὐτή, *Od.* 15.105). Whenever *kamnein* is used, we are dealing with objects made with especially elaborate care, be they textiles or metalwork such as the armour or shields made by Hephaestus. These are qualified as exceptional by adjectives such as δαιδάλεος (*daidaleos*) or ποικίλος (*poikilos*), which allude to techniques

---

58. *Od.* 7.335 (Arete); *Od.* 4.296; *Il.* 6.324 (Helen); *Od.* 1.357 and 21.351 (Penelope); *Il.* 6.491 and 22.442 (Andromache).
59. See also *Il.* 22.442 for Andromache's orders to her *amphipoloi*. Telemachus's words to Penelope are almost a verbatim repetition of Hector's to Andromache (*Od.* 1.357-58; 21.351-52). See Hölscher 1983: 106, suggesting this is a direct reference rather than characteristic of the formulaic nature of oral poetry. For the phrase as indicative of the patriarchal nature of Homeric society see e.g. Finley 1967: 91; Wöhrle 1999: 122; Clark 2001; Gottesman 2014; Beard 2017. For critique and discussion see Wagner-Hasel 1997: 127-46; 2018.
60. This is stressed by Wickert-Micknat 1982: 38-45 who counts weaving as one of the *technai* that needs to be learnt. See also Schneider 1989: 11-31.
61. Eckstein 1974: 6. See also Schneider 1989: 17-18. Another term, used for the Phaeacian women's skilled weaving, is *technasthai* (*Od.* 7.110).
62. When it is used for metalwork, the term mostly refers to the labour of Hephaestus (*Il.* 2.201; 8.195; 18.614; 19.368). See also unnamed *chalkēes* in *Il.* 4.187 = 216, and the smith Tychios (*Il.* 7.220).

of depiction developed in the arts of metalwork and weaving. This applies to the *thōrax* made for Diomedes by Hephaestus, which is referred to as *daidaleos* (δαιδάλεον θώρηκα, τὸν Ἥφαιστος κάμε τεύχων, *Il.* 8.195), and to the shield of Achilles, also made (κάμε) by Hephaestus (*Il.* 18.614). The shield is said to be adorned with many pictures (*daidala*), and to be illustrated (*daidaleos*).[63] As Françoise Frontisi-Ducroix has shown, the term *daidaleos* is mostly used in the context of metalwork and carpentry to refer to inlaid patterns or plastic images, such as are seen in archaeological evidence from the geometric and archaic periods.[64] This kind of technique is clearly employed by Tychios who furnishes Ajax's oxhide shield with its layer of bronze (*Il.* 7.220).

We can assume that a similar technique is referred to when *kamnein* is used of woven images. *Daidala* are often also seen on textiles, such as those worked by Athena into the veil (*heanos*) worn by Hera at the seduction of Zeus (τίθει δ' ἐνὶ δαίδαλα πολλά, *Il.*14.179). In the *Odyssey* the word *daideleos* is used for the cloths which are draped over the chairs in Odysseus's and Penelope's *megaron* (αὐτὴν δ' ἐς θρόνον εἶσεν ἄγων, ὑπὸ λῖτα πετάσσας, | καλὸν δαιδάλεον, *Od.* 1.130-31). The veil given to Pandora, the first woman, by Athena in the Theogony is also called *daidaleos* (κατὰ κρῆθεν δὲ καλύπτρην | δαιδαλέην χείρεσσι κατέσχεθε, θαῦμα ἰδέσθαι, Hes. *Theog.* 574-75), while in *Works and Days* Athena is said to have taught Pandora herself to weave such richly illustrated '*erga*' (αὐτὰρ Ἀθήνην | ἔργα διδασκῆσαι, πολυδαίδαλον ἱστὸν ὑφαίνειν, Hes. *Op.* 64-65).

In the context of weaving, *daidaleos* can be replaced by *poikilos*, which indicates a colourful or patterned cloth, especially when textiles feature at special occasions such as sacrificial offerings, weddings, or when receiving guests. The adjective is used for the *peplos* dedicated to Athena by the women of Troy and for the belt worn by Hera for the seduction of Zeus (*Il.* 6.289; *Il.* 14.220). *Poikilos* features especially when *kamnein* is used to refer to textile production, such as for Athena's handmade *peplos* (πέπλον [...] ἑανὸν [...] ποικίλον, *Il.* 5.734-35). The many handmade *peploi* in Helen's storage chest, one of which she gives to Telemachus as a gift for his future bride, are also richly patterned (πέπλοι παμποίκιλοι, οὓς κάμεν αὐτή, *Od.* 15.105).

Next to the general *kamnein*, the technical term used for the production of such patterns in both these cases is πάσσειν (*passein*), which can

---

63. *Il.* 18.482 and 612; 19.13 and 19, and 380; 22.314.
64. Frontisi-Ducroix 1975: 29-59. For an opposing view see Morris 1992: 30.

be translated as laying on, or sprinkling.⁶⁵ This is used of Andromache decorating the purple mantle, a *diplax*, she is weaving for Hector with multicoloured roses, or rosettes, called *throna* (*Il.* 22.440–41).⁶⁶ Similarly we see Helen applying images of the battles between Trojans and Achaeans on a purple *diplax* she is weaving (*Il.* 3.125–27).⁶⁷ In the past, *poikilos* was erroneously thought to refer to embroidery placed on woven cloths because of the mistaken assumption that the warp-weighted loom commonly used in Greece did not allow patterned weaving.⁶⁸ Arguments against this were raised by Margarete Bieber and Alan J. B. Wace, who assumed a technique similar to that used for Kelims, where threads are worked in by hand in smaller areas.⁶⁹ This theory was revised by Elizabeth Wayland Barber in the 1990s. Experiments and observations in other cultures have shown her that patterns can be made on a warp-weighted loom by lacing the additional pattern weft into the warp—this would explain the use of the term *passein*, to lay on or sprinkle, for the production of pattern.⁷⁰ Such a technique was used in Norway until the 1950s for the production of patterned blankets on warp-weighted looms (Figure 3 and 4).⁷¹

---

65. Buschor 1912: 46 views this as a weaving term, while Marinatos 1967: 3-4 assumes that it describes the art of embroidery. For the metaphorical use of the term see Bergren 1980.
66. There is debate over the meaning of *throna*, with some ancient commentators suggesting roses, others poisonous plants. See Buschor 1912: 30-31, who suspects a palm motif that Andromache might have learnt from her Sidonian slaves. Marinatos 1967: 4 interprets it as a poisonous plant. Barber 1991: 372-73 suggests roses, as a traditional magical motif. Winkler 1990: 172-74 also makes a connection with magic. Others see a rosette-motif in keeping with geometric vase painting (Wickert-Micknat 1982: 46-50; Koch-Harnack 1989: 24-32, 168-71). Such rosettes can be seen on a fifth-century BCE carpet, traditionally thought to be of Phrygian-Anatolian origin, now viewed as Lydian (Greenewalt and Majewski 1980: 134). For an image of this carpet see Bennett 1977: 39.
67. For *passein* connected with *daidala* see Apollonius Rhodius, *Argonautica* 1.728-29. On this see Levin 1970: 17-36; Shapiro 1980: 263-86.
68. See Blümner 1912: 158.
69. Wace 1948: 51-55; Bieber 1928: 10-11; 1934: 26. Cf. Pekridou-Gorecki 1989: 41-44.
70. Barber 1991: 91-113. See also Barber 1992: 103-17. Barber describes her own experiments in her popular book, Barber 1994: 17-27. There is, however, no evidence from ancient textile finds to support her thesis. But new experimental research has proved the possibility to weave pattern even with warp-weighted looms. See now Harlizius-Klück 2016. For the new results in research on textile technology, see Anderson and Nosch 2003; Michel and Nosch 2010.
71. In addition to Barber see also Carroll 1983: 96-98. On pattern weaving with the warp-weighted loom in ancient Greece see now Spantidaki 2016: 48-70.

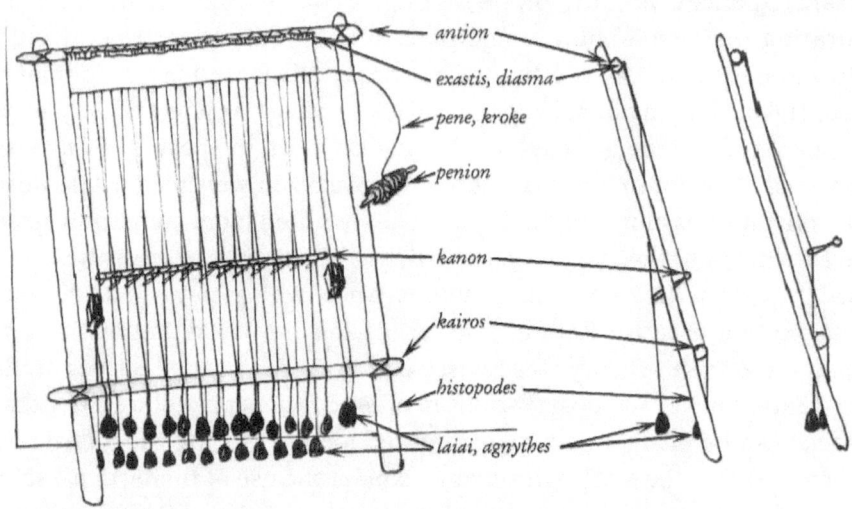

Figure 3: The warp-weighted loom. Harlizius-Klück 2004: 103, Fig. 11, cf. also Barber 1991: 270, Fig. 12.3 with modifications.

Even today, in Indonesia, such techniques of supplementary pattern weaving are used for the production of ceremonial cloths, whose patterns bear remarkable similarities with depictions in geometric vase painting.[72] Barber's research now may provide a technical explanation for the old (nineteenth-century) assumption that geometric vase painting might have its origins in the art of weaving.[73] The stylized character of geometric vase paintings comes about as a result of the imitation of the technique of adding in the pattern weft.[74] We cannot be certain that the situation here is comparable to that found in Palmyra, where a wealth of textile finds provide good evidence for a clear congruence of patterns in textiles and architecture during the early centuries of the post-Christian era.[75] The very sparse textile finds (such as the fragment of a shroud from Vergina) from ancient Greece provide evidence for the existence of pattern—but they do not allow us to draw conclusions regarding the appearance of the entire

72. Kahn Majlis 1991: 41 and 100; Hecht 1989: 36–38 (Figure 5 and 6).
73. Conze 1870: 522; Semper 1878: 12. Buschor 1912: 5–10, without wishing to exclude the independent development of geometric vase painting, also thought textile models a possibility.
74. Barber 1991: 365–75.
75. Schmidt-Colinet 1995; Schmidt-Colinet 2019.

Figure 4: Warp-weighted loom with figured weave. Ellen Harlizius-Klück 2016: 70, Fig. 5.2.

pattern.⁷⁶ Our only idea of the kinds of motifs that might have been used is to be found on depictions of garments in vase paintings. Here we do find patterns not unlike the rosettes and the battle-scenes used by Andromache

---

76. Barber 1991: 145-208. On the textile find from the Philip tomb see Andronikos 1980: 48 and Andronikos 1984: 25 and 233. Textiles are also found in Geometric graves in Attica. Andronikos 1968: 74. See now Spantidaki 2016: 5-8 with a catalogue of textiles found in graves (106-44); Gleba 2018; Gleba, Marín-Aquilera and Iacona 2018. See also Shaw and Chapin 2016 on the reconstruction of pattern in the Minoan and Mycenaean period.

Figure 5: Prothesis. Geometric Attic mixing bowl, ca 750 BCE. Paris, Louvre A 517. After Kurtz and Boardman 1971: Fig. 7.

and Helen, so that at least we can see some commonality between painted and poetic representations.[77] Since the rosettes motif is often found in wedding scenes,[78] we may suspect that, in epic poetry, specific patterns are associated with different contexts or relationships, as we know to be the case in tragedy.[79] In any case, the results of this research on the uses of supplementary pattern wefts and its parallels in inlaying techniques used in metal-working underlines the significance of textile and metal gifts discussed earlier.

Since the words *kamnein* and *passein* are used in epic mainly for the production of patterned clothing by goddesses or high-ranking women, the

77. On findings from vase painting see Carroll 1965: See now Spantidaki 2016: 71–77; Harlizius-Klück 2019.
78. On the rosette-motif see Koch-Harnack 1989: 109–85. For literary descriptions of patterned clothing see e.g. Shapiro 1980 (Jason's cloak in Apollonius's *Argonautica*); Harich-Schwarzbauer 2011 (Claudian's description of the cloak of Proserpina).
79. See Aesch. *Cho.* 231–32 where Orestes asks Electra to inspect his woven cloth (*hyphasma*) which is decorated with animal patterns. In Eur. *Ion* 224 and 1413–28, Creusa recognises Ion as her son from the detailed description of the clothes in which he was found (the head of a Gorgon had been woven into the cloth). In Eur. *IT* 814–17 Orestes's knowledge of the patterns woven by Iphigenia proves he is her brother. See now Gherchanoc 2019.

Figure 6: Indonesian ceremonial cloth. Supplementary weft weave. Sumatra, Lampung, late nineteenth century CE. After Kahn-Majlis 1991: Fig. 78.

work of weaving acquires a similarly high status to the masculine arts of warfare and metal-working. Reciprocity inheres not only in the services rendered in warfare, and is described with the words *charis* and *charizomai*; it is equally a factor in the arts and crafts for which *kamnein* is used. The careful labour described as *kamnein*, invested by Hephaestus into the production of the shield for Achilles, is to be understood as a return for previous favours rendered. This work is Hephaestus's repayment to Thetis for saving his life and welcoming him after his fall from Olympus; he has already been making many items of jewellery for her during his nine-year stay but views the shield as his way of repaying her fully (*Il.* 18.394-400).

In battle contexts, *kamnein* is often used to describe the physical efforts of the heroes who carry weapons and then relax while drinking wine.[80] The labour of grieving is also once described as *kamnein*, with the return service here being a meal: when Achilles invites the grieving Priam to share a meal, he reminds him of the example of Niobe, who also turned her mind to eating when she was weary from the shedding of tears (ἐπεὶ κάμε δάκρυ χέουσα, *Il.* 24.613).[81] The shedding of tears, for which *kamnein* is used here, is a gift for the deceased; mourners are given sustenance in return for their labour. There is explicit reference to recompense for the careful labour of an individual in the case of Eumaeus, who complains to Odysseus that 'others are consuming our *kamatos* without compensation' (ἄλλοι δ' ἡμέτερον κάματον νήποινον ἔδουσιν, *Od.* 14.417). The swineherd is referring to the suitors consuming the animals he had raised without giving anything in return, so we may assume that *kamatos* refers to the result of Eumaeus's careful labour. Normally, Eumaeus would be able to count on some return for such *kamnein*. As he tells the disguised Odysseus, a benevolent master will compensate a man who labours with care (ὅς οἱ πολλὰ κάμῃσι) with a house, some land, and a wife sought by many wooers (*Od.* 14.65). Such women are also proffered as compensation to warriors who labour for their leaders, as Achilles reminds his men during the funeral rites for Patroclus (*Il.* 18.341). And of course, Achilles's withdrawal of his own *kamnein* in the service of another is the result of the denial of just such a form of compensation for it (ἐπεί κε κάμω πολεμίζων, *Il.* 1.168).[82]

Following these observations, we can regard the relationship of the married couple which forms the basis of the domestic community as one of reciprocity, similar to that between the warlords. A warrior who renders service in battle to his leader, and thus shows *charis*, is supported by comrades-in-arms; a wife who renders *charis* to her husband in recompense for the bridewealth given is similarly supported by a group of women who help her with her work at the loom and on the spindle. We will see how this work is related to a third form of *charis*: the aura which emanates from a person. This is communicated through the woven images whose production was discussed in the present chapter. The asymmetry in the relationship

---

80. See for example *Il.* 4.230; 5.797 and 811; 13.485 and 711; 15.365; 16.106; 19.170; 21.52; *Od.* 12.332. Recovery with wine: *Il.* 6.261.
81. On Niobe, and on tears and food see Monsacré 1984: 191-96. On *geras* for the dead see in more detail ch. 4.3.
82. In detail, see ch. 4.1.

between a high-ranking woman and her female entourage is greater than that between a war leader and his men because war is, according to Homeric epic, the chief means for the recruitment of women weavers. These captured women are a benefit for the warriors whose beds they share, at least during times of war; but they also benefit the warriors' wives. In war, women are captured and subjected by male violence—but they end up in the service of other women. Hector knows this, as he refers not only to the sad fate of the captured woman who must weave for another (πρὸς ἄλλης ἱστὸν ὑφαίνοις, Il. 6.456) but also to the joy of the mother at the booty brought home by her son (φέροι δ' ἔναρα βροτόεντα | κτείνας δήϊον ἄνδρα, χαρείη δὲ φρένα μήτηρ, Il. 6.480-81). Given that the relationship between a woman and her *amphipoloi* and *dmōiai gynaikes* is mirrored in the divine sphere by Aphrodite and the Charites, we might assume that in the divine working-group some form of transcendence takes place. The relationship between Aphrodite and the Charites appears to take on a model structure, the normative significance of which can also be observed in poetry and in images of weddings in classical vase painting.[83]

3.3. Visualizing status: Charis in appearance and speech

Charis is not only a pleasing service rendered with a view to a return gift or service; it is also a visual power or effect owned by objects and people. In the *Iliad charis* mainly emanates from precious objects, while in the *Odyssey* we also find people who are radiant with *charis*, although here too it seems likely that a person's *charis* actually emanates from their clothing. Jewellery with *charis* is worn exclusively by women, while people who emanate *charis* are exclusively men. The bestower of such *charis* is always Athena, although her action in these cases is described using the terminology of metal-working rather than weaving.

Odysseus is the primary recipient of such *charis*. When he is stranded at Scheria and has bathed and dressed himself in the clothes given him by Nausicaa, Athena ensures he looks bigger and stronger, and that his hair falls on his shoulders like a Hyacinth flower:

ὡς δ' ὅτε τις χρυσὸν περιχεύεται ἀργύρῳ ἀνὴρ
ἴδρις, ὃν Ἥφαιστος δέδαεν καὶ Παλλὰς Ἀθήνη
τέχνην παντοίην, χαρίεντα δὲ ἔργα τελείει,

---

83. Oakley and Sinos 1993: 41; MacLachlan 1993: 41-55.

ὡς ἄρα τῷ κατέχευε χάριν κεφαλῇ τε καὶ ὤμοις.
ἕζετ' ἔπειτ' ἀπάνευθε κιὼν ἐπὶ θῖνα θαλάσσης,
κάλλεϊ καὶ χάρισι στίλβων

Just as a craftsman trained by Hephaestus and Pallas Athene in the secrets of his art puts a graceful finish to his work by overlaying silverware with gold, she endowed his head and shoulders with *charis*. When Odysseus retired to sit by himself on the seashore, he was radiant with *charis* and beauty (*Od*. 6.232-37; tr. adapted from Rieu).

Seeing him like this, Nausicaa is overcome with admiration and desire, and wishes to make Odysseus her husband (*Od*. 6.237 and 244).

In this example *charis* is a radiance which adheres to the body like an ennobling shine or polish, the crowning of external beauty, which gives rise to desire in observers.[84] Although attributed explicitly to the work of the goddess, *charis* is also connected in the narrative to the change in Odysseus's appearance effected practically by the processes of bathing and dressing. At Ithaca these processes are ministered for Odysseus by Eurynome, the highest-ranking of the servant women, significantly a namesake of the mother of the Charites (*Od*. 23.153-63).[85] In this case the effect of *charis* is aimed at Penelope, who is meant now to recognize her husband once he is clean and dressed appropriately. She had not recognized him previously because of the wretched clothing he wore (ἄλλοτε δ' ἀγνώσασκε κακὰ χροῒ εἵματ' ἔχοντα, *Od*. 23.95). The iterative aorist shows that she had repeatedly failed to recognise him.

While in these two cases *charis* has an effect on the other sex, there are three other examples in the *Odyssey* where it affects others of the same gender. In these cases, there is no need for bathing or anointing, but *charis* is mobilised instantly by Athena. So Athena pours divine *charis* over Odysseus's head and shoulders, and makes him look bigger and fuller, when he is to appear before the assembled Phaeacians (*Od*. 8.19-21). She does this in order to ensure that her protégé is treated by the Phaeacians as *philos* and accepted into their community.

Telemachus undergoes similar treatment when he takes up his father's place at the assembly in Ithaca:

---

84. See the definition in Latacz 1966: 84.
85. For Eurynome as the mother of the Charites see Hes. *Theog*. 907.

θεσπεσίην δ' ἄρα τῷ γε χάριν κατέχευεν Ἀθήνη
τὸν δ' ἄρα πάντες λαοὶ ἐπερχόμενον θηεῦντο.

Athena endowed him with such supernatural *charis* that all eyes turned on him in admiration as he came up (*Od.* 2.12-13; tr. Rieu).

The same phrasing is used when Telemachus appears before the suitors upon his return from Pylos and Sparta, when Athena again endows him with divine *charis* and everyone marvels at him (χάριν κατέχευθεν, *Od.* 17.63-64).

In all these cases, *charis* is a visible radiance manifested publicly: before Nausicaa and her companions, at the assembly of the Phaeacians, in front of Penelope, and at the assembly in Ithaca. Its character is exhortative: in the kingdom of the Phaeacians it effects the acceptance of Odysseus as *philos*; at Ithaca its consequence is support for Telemachus's trip to Pylos. When dealing with the opposite sex, it arouses desire, and in the case of Penelope leads to the restoration of her marriage and the bond of *philotēs*.

Even if *charis* always emanates from men, women also possess a radiance that affects the other sex and results in the giving of gifts of jewellery, which in turn radiate *charis*.[86] The medium of radiance for women is usually their clothing, and specifically a veil described with the adjective *liparos*, which suggests gleam or shine. Here too Athena's intervention is needed. The goddess alters Penelope's appearance, to make her look taller and fuller, as we have seen already, by the application of the ambrosial oil used by Aphrodite when she goes to dance with the Charites (*Od.* 18.195).[87] When Penelope later appears before the suitors, flanked by two *amphipoloi*, she is not endowed with *charis* but is wrapped in a gleaming veil (λιπαρὰ κρήδεμνα) and arouses the suitors' desire to sleep with her (*Od.* 18.210-19). Following this, one of the suitors, Eurymachus, praises Penelope: 'you surpass all women in appearance and size, and in the wisdom within you' (*Od.* 18.248-49). His praise conforms to the female ideal Agamemnon subscribes to in the *Iliad* when he refuses to return Chrysëis, as she is equal to his wife Clytemnestra in appearance, size, and wisdom or knowledge: *phrēn* (*Il.* 1.115). As in Odysseus's case, the radiant appearance of Penelope is also exhortative: she receives gifts of jewellery, including a

---

86. See MacLachlan 1993: 32.
87. For height as a sign of status see Ulf 1990: 224. For the meaning of *liparos* see ch. 4.2.2., n. 67.

pair of earrings of which it is said that they shine with much *charis* (χάρις δ' ἀπελάμπετο πολλή, *Od.* 18.298). A similar effect is achieved by the earrings worn by Hera during the seduction of Zeus: these too are intended to have an effect on the opposite sex and they shine with much *charis* (χάρις δ' ἀπελάμπετο πολλή, *Il.* 14.183).

Charis therefore has an effect on both women and men. Joachim Latacz was keen to see in *charis* an accidental effect which causes joy or desire. But our findings show that *charis* is the property of a lustrous body or object. This can of course be jewellery, whose shine is produced by the smith working with gold and silver. But the effect of *charis* is not only caused by the shine of the metals; it must also be produced by the artistry and skill discussed earlier, with which the smiths work images into the metal. The hairband given to Pandora by the Charites and Peitho in Hesiod's *Works and Days* is such a jewel (Hes. *Op.* 73-74).[88] In the *Theogony*, where Athena places the hairband on Pandora's head, it is decorated with pictures, and it is from these that charis emerges:[89]

ἀμφὶ δέ οἱ στεφάνην χρυσέην κεφαλῆφιν ἔθηκε,
τὴν αὐτὸς ποίησε περικλυτὸς Ἀμφιγυήεις
ἀσκήσας παλάμῃσι, χαριζόμενος Διὶ πατρί.
τῇ δ' ἔνι δαίδαλα πολλὰ τετεύχατο, θαῦμα ἰδέσθαι,
κνώδαλ' ὅσ' ἤπειρος δεινὰ τρέφει ἠδὲ θάλασσα·
τῶν ὅ γε πόλλ' ἐνέθηκε, χάρις δ' ἐπὶ πᾶσιν ἄητο,
θαυμάσια, ζωοῖσιν ἐοικότα φωνήεσσιν.

(a)nd about her head she placed a golden diadem, which the renowned Ambidexter made with his own hands to please (*charizomenos*) Zeus the father. On it were many designs (*daidala*) fashioned, a wonder to behold (*thauma idesthai*), all the formidable creatures that the land and sea foster: many of them he put in, charm (*charis*) breathing over them all, wonderful designs, like living creatures with a voice of their own (Hes. *Theog.* 578-84, tr. West).

---

88. According to the lexicographers, Peitho is one of the Charites. For references see Schwarzenberg 1966: 20 and Solmsen 1954: 5. The role of Peitho in marriage rituals and democratic speech is discussed by Meier 1985: 11-13 and Pirenne-Delforge 1996: 199.
89. On the connection between *daidala* and *charis* see Frontisi-Ducroix 1975: 72. She understands the gleam of *charis* here as the result of craftsmanship.

It is not just the connection with the female business of bathing, anointing, and dressing that suggests that clothing is the medium of *charis* when it is radiated by people with an effect on the opposite sex. Just as Odysseus gleams with beauty and *charis* after bathing and dressing in the house of Arete, so Paris shines in the *Iliad* (κάλλεϊ τε στίλβων καὶ εἵμασιν, *Il.* 3.392). *Charis* is only here replaced by a garment: *heima*. A glance at Pandora's outfitting allows us to see that such textile media of *charis* must be colourful and patterned garments. In *Works and Days* Pandora receives *charis* from Aphrodite, who pours it on her head just as we have seen Athena do with Odysseus (καὶ χάριν ἀμφιχέαι κεφαλῇ χρυσέην Ἀφροδίτην, Hes. *Op.* 65). More concretely, in the *Theogony*, she is given a patterned veil instead of *charis*; the gift comes from Athena, quite appropriately, who is also said in *Works and Days* (Hes. *Op.* 63-64) to have taught Pandora the art of colour weaving:

κατὰ κρῆθεν δὲ καλύπτρην
δαιδαλέην χείρεσσι κατέσχεθε, θαῦμα ἰδέσθαι.

down over her head she drew a patterned veil (*kalyptrēn daidaleēn*) with her hands, a wonder to behold (Hes. *Theog.* 574-75).

Penelope's gleaming veil is not the only example of visually effective clothing in epic poetry. The garments placed on Aphrodite by the Charites after her bath are also a 'wonder to behold' (*Od.* 8.366). The same thing is said of the purple textiles woven by the Nymphs at Ithaca (*Od.* 13.108), and of the threads on Arete's spindle (*Od.* 6.306). Athena, the goddess who endows men with *charis*, is also responsible for giving the Phaeacian women the skill to create 'most beautiful works' (ὡς δὲ γυναῖκες | ἱστὸν τεχνῆσσαι· περὶ γάρ σφισι δῶκεν Ἀθήνη | ἔργα τ' ἐπίστασθαι περικαλλέα καὶ φρένας ἐσθλάς, *Od.* 7.110-11). Such products of female artistry have a similar effect to *charis* on the opposite sex. The clothes in which Paris gleams with *charis*, like Odysseus, are intended to maximize his attractiveness to women. Aphrodite gives them to him when she removes him from the battleground and places him in the bedroom to await Helen and renew their love (*Il.* 3.374-446). In the *Hymn to Aphrodite*, Anchises is aroused not only by the beauty of Aphrodite's body but also by the gleam of her clothing (*Hom. Hymn Aphr.* 85-91). In Aristophanes's comedy

Peace (859) the groom, who is represented in patterned garments on vase paintings, is described as brightly shining: λαμπρός (lampros).[90]

In epic poetry, garments are often described with epithets that point to the shine or gleam associated with *charis*. So Odysseus leaves Ithaca in a tunic that shines brightly like the sun (λαμπρὸς δ' ἦν ἠέλιος ὥς, *Od.* 19.234). This tunic also causes women to marvel at it (ἦ μὲν πολλαί γ' αὐτὸν ἐθηήσαντο γυναῖκες, *Od.* 19.235). The patterned *peplos* dedicated to Athena by Hecuba (*Il.* 6.295), and the one given to Telemachus by Helen (*Od.* 15.108) both 'shine like a star' (ἀστὴρ δ' ὣς ἀπέλαμπεν). The veil thrown aside by Hecuba when she hears of Hector's death is described as 'gleaming', *liparos* (λιπαρὴν [...] καλύπτρην, *Il.* 22.406), just like Penelope's veil. A similar gleaming veil is also worn by Charis, Aphrodite's double, and the wife of Hephaestus, when she receives Thetis (*Il.* 18.382). Additionally, the city of the Charites, Orchomenos, is also given this attribute by Pindar (ὢ λιπαρᾶς ἀοίδιμοι βασίλειαι | Χάριτες Ἐρχομενοῦ, Pind. *Ol.* 14.3-4).

It is possible to attribute the lustre associated with garments and their effect described with λαμπρός (*lampros*), λιπαρός (*liparos*), στίλβειν (*stilbein*), and λάμπειν (*lampein*) to the fact that linens were finished with oil so as to give them a kind of water-repellent coating.[91] This is said of the tunics worn by the youths on the shield of Achilles: the tunics have a gentle sheen of oil (οἱ δὲ χιτῶνας | εἵατ' ἐϋννήτους, ἧκα στίλβοντας ἐλαίῳ, *Il.* 18.595-96). But such linen clothing is also often described as colourful, so that the lustrous effect might also refer to effects caused by the patterns, which as we have seen earlier was the business of the Charites.[92]

In ancient colour theories, which in fact represent theories of perception, colour was thought to be an emanation of light which either originates from an object or flows through it (so Aristotle), or a stream of light or fire that emanates from the eye and meets the light emanating from the perceived object, thus making it visible.[93] This would explain the lustre of garments: *lampein* and *stilbein* would then signify both the light streaming

---

90. Cf. also Waldner 2000a: 211-213 on the Attic heros Theseus as ideal groom who receives his wedding cloth from the goddess Amphitrite. For evidence in vase-painting see Oakley and Sinos 1993.
91. Thus Blümner 1912: 196 and Bieber 1967: 23. Marinatos 1967: 4 takes a different view, assuming that the garments are woollen and that their shine stems from treatment with lanolin during the dyeing process, which ensures that colours stay vibrant and lends them a metallic sheen.
92. On the evidence of linen see ch. 5.3.
93. For detail on pre-Socratic colour theory see Stulz 1990: 23-64; Hagner 1987: 22-25. On ancient colour theory and on colour and brilliance see also Gage 1993: 11-27.

from the eye and the return stream of light from the object. Greek colour adjectives never convey a clearly defined colour, such as 'white' (though *lampros* and *leukos* are often translated thus), or purple or violet as *porphyreos* is sometimes translated. Rather such terms indicate different intensities of shine or gleam.[94] The same doubleness applies to *charis*. Just like the light of colours, *charis* does not emanate only from objects, it also radiates from the eye. In the Homeric *Hymn to Demeter*, in Metaneira's address to the goddess, *charis* is a power manifested in the goddess's eye itself,[95] alongside the power of *aidōs* (ἐπί τοι πρέπει ὄμμασιν αἰδὼς | καὶ χάρις, *Hom. Hymn Dem.* 2.214-15). It is a power held by kings who watch over traditional justice, *themis* (ὡς εἴ πέρ τε θεμιστοπόλων βασιλήων, *Hom. Hymn Dem.* 2.215). Pindar refers to the Charites who reign over Orchomenos as *episkopoi*, or 'sharp-eyed', thus referring to the moral dimension of *charis* (Pind. *Ol.* 14.4).[96] For Xenophanes the eye itself, which judges the effect of *charis*, has divine qualities.[97]

All this suggests that we must see *charis*, especially as it is given to Odysseus, as the radiance that emanates not only from the gleam of gold and silver but also from colourful patterns on clothing made using the techniques described earlier. This is not just a matter of observing patterns and images in clothing and jewellery. In the sense of radiance, *charis* makes status visible through the medium of dress or jewellery; it ensures the right perception of a person in the eye of the beholder. Thus the term has both aesthetic and moral connotations.[98]

The impact of colourful clothing and jewels is evidenced in many recognition scenes as well as in situations when military decisions are taken.[99] So in the Achaean assembly the gleam of the golden sceptre and the purple colour of his clothing ensure that the decision-maker stands out and that his performance makes an impact. The effect of the colour purple is like

94. Stulz 1990: 25-28, 71; MacLachlan 1993: 65-68; Gage 1993: 12-14. See also Handschnur 1970: 74-78; Dürbeck 1967: 61-70. For a collection of groups of colours see Moonwoman 1994: 37-65. See now Grand-Clément 2011; Spantidaki 2016: 86-90.
95. See ch. 4.1.
96. See Sappho fr. 151 (Diehl), where *charis* emanates from the eye.
97. See Svenbro 1976: 99.
98. See MacLachlan 1993: 149, who stresses the ethical-aesthetic dimension of *charis* without considering the material meaning.
99. For instance, Athena transforms herself into a woman skilled in 'lustrous work' (ἀγλαὰ ἔργα) who dresses Odysseus in new garments and makes his stature appear larger (*Od.* 16.172-74). The use of *aglaa* to describe Athena's work points to the impact and attraction achieved by means of the clothing.

'the spotlight which picks out a new protagonist just before the action'.[100] Purple is worn in the *Odyssey* precisely by those who emanate *charis*: Odysseus (*Od.* 14.462; 19.225) and Telemachus (*Od.* 8.114–16; 21.118).[101] In the *Iliad*, purple is worn on the Greek side by high-ranking leaders such as Agamemnon (*Il.* 8.221) and Nestor (*Il.* 10.133–34).[102]

Special garments displaying the kinds of colour and shine seen in those worn by Odysseus and Agamemnon may also be described with the adjective *charieis*. But those who wear them are—almost without exception—of divine descent. This includes gods who have powers of transformation, such as Circe, Calypso, and Hermes. So Hebe, working for the Charites, clothes Hermes in 'shining garments' (εἵματα χαρίεντα, *Il.* 5.904). She herself is the embodiment of youth, which also carries the adjective *charieis*. Appearing as 'most shining youth' (χαριεστάτη ἥβη), Hermes warns Odysseus of Circe's magical potions (*pharmaka*) with which she has already transformed his companions into swine (*Od.* 10.279; cf. *Il.* 24.348). Circe herself wears a garment described as *charieis*, a 'delicate and shining *pharos*' (φᾶρος [...] λεπτὸν καὶ χαρίεν, *Od.* 10.543). When Hermes arrives, he finds Circe walking up and down at her loom singing, while weaving an 'immortal web, like the works of the goddesses, delicate and shining and gleaming' (Κίρκης δ' ἔνδον ἄκουον ἀειδούσης Ὀπὶ καλῇ | ἱστὸν ἐποιχομένης μέγαν ἄμβροτον, οἷα θεάων | λεπτά τε καὶ χαρίεντα καὶ ἀγλαὰ ἔργα πέλονται, *Od.* 10.221–23).[103] Calypso (the 'coverer' from *kaluptein* = to wrap up or cover) also wears such a fine and shining garment (φᾶρος [...] λεπτὸν καὶ χαρίεν, *Od.* 5.231). She too has transforming powers, in so far as she furnishes Odysseus with the sail which transports him from the world of the immortals back to the world of mortals.[104] Among garments used by mortals the description *charieis* is used only of textiles which are closely connected with the divine or with death. These would be the

---

100. Stulz 1990: 120. See Willenbrock 1969: 19; Patzek 1992: 188–93, on the dramatic use of the imagery of metallic shine.
101. The *pharos* Odysseus receives from Nausicaa is also purple (*Od.* 8.84).
102. The epithet *porphyreos* is associated with patterned garments woven by Helen and Andromache (*Il.* 3.126; 22.441).
103. On the relation between singing and weaving see now Karanika 2014: 71. She refers to Anthony Tuck (2006) who has argued that weavers 'use song as a memory aid: like a counting system, the rhythm helps them remember the pattern'. The research on rhythm and work goes back to Karl Bücher's *Arbeit & Rhythmus* (1896). See Wagner-Hasel 2011: 188–94.
104. On the relationship of Calypso with death see Vernant 1982: 147–48; Crane 1988: 20; Murnaghan 1992: 250; Papadopoulou-Belmehdi 1994: 171–80.

patterned *peplos* intended as an offering for Athena, and the garments Andromache wishes to burn after the death of Hector (*Il.* 22.511; 6.90 = 271). This suggests that such garments, similar to *charis* itself when it is poured by Athena over someone's head and shoulders, effect a transformation of status intended to recognize immortality. This is precisely what happens, as will be shown in more detail, during rituals for the dead.[105]

Death itself is described as the loss of *charis* in its sense of radiance, both in epic and in later literary sources. So Hector's once radiant head lies in the dust on the ground after his defeat by Achilles: its radiance is no longer visible (κάρη δ' ἅπαν ἐν κονίῃσι | κεῖτο πάρος χαρίεν, *Il.* 22.402-3).[106] It appears here that Hector's hair is the seat of his radiance, as we have seen how the appearance of hair is changed when Athena pours *charis* over her protégé's head (κάρη) and shoulders in the *Odyssey*. We also hear that Euphorbus's hair is decorated with gold and silver like that of the Charites (*Il.* 17.51).[107] *Karē/kara* is not necessarily only the head but can encompass the whole figure and its clothing, as can be seen in a different passage.[108] When Patroclus falls by Hector's hand we hear that Apollo removes from Patroclus's head the helmet that once protected the 'radiant head' (κάρη χαρίεν) of Achilles (*Il.* 16.798). When Achilles later pours ash over his 'radiant head' (κεφαλῆς, χαρίεν), the ash stays on his tunic and so robs not only his head but also his clothing of radiance (*Il.* 18.24-25).

When the dead lose their radiance, it is restored to them in different form through the rituals of washing, anointment, and dressing in garments described as *charieis* or *ambrotos*. These do not confer *charis*, but they do confer immortality and they heighten *kleos*, the glory of the dead. By contrast, while Hector's radiant head lies covered in dirt on the ground, Andromache laments as though the 'radiant clothing' can be a substitute for the dead:

νῦν δὲ σὲ μὲν παρὰ νηυσὶ κορωνίσι νόσφι τοκήων
αἰόλαι εὐλαὶ ἔδονται, ἐπεί κε κύνες κορέσωνται
γυμνόν· ἀτάρ τοι εἵματ' ἐνὶ μεγάροισι κέονται

---

105. Cf. ch. 4.3.
106. See also Stesichorus fr. 68 (D. L. Page, Stesichorus, The ΓΕΡΟΝΕΙΣ, in: JHS 93, 1973, 138-54); Eur. fr. 736.3-6 Nauck; Soph. *Aj.* 1266-67. For discussion see MacLachlan 1993: 75; Morris 1989: 307-10, n. 78.
107. In ancient literature the Charites are often praised for their marvellous clothing and their wonderful hair. Sappho (fr. 90 Diehl) und Pindar (*Pyth.* 5.45) call them καλλίκομοι. For further evidence see Simon 1985: 236-41; Deichgräber 1971: 402.
108. Vernant 1986: 19-46.

λεπτά τε καὶ χαρίεντα τετυγμένα χερσὶ γυναικῶν.
ἀλλ' ἤτοι τάδε πάντα καταφλέξω πυρὶ κηλέῳ
οὐδὲν σοί γ' ὄφελος, ἐπεὶ οὐκ ἐγκείσεαι αὐτοῖς,
ἀλλὰ πρὸς Τρώων καὶ Τρωϊάδων κλέος εἶναι.

And you, by the beaked ships, far from your parents, naked, will be eaten by maggots when the dogs have had their fill. Yet delicate and radiant (*lepta te kai charienta*) clothing made by women's hands is still stored at home. I am going to burn it all in the consuming fire. It is of no use to you: you will never be buried in it. But the men and women of Troy will do that for you as their last mark of honour (*kleos einai*) (*Il.* 22.508-15, tr. adapted from Rieu).

From the account of Achilles' burial in *Odyssey* 24 we learn that the dead were burnt in their clothes, described here as *ambrota heimata*, immortal clothing (*Od.* 24.59). The same phrase is used for the clothes the gods place on the dead Sarpedon when they take him off the battlefield to give him an honourable burial (*Il.* 16.670 and 680). The clothing of the dead is also distinguished by colour and shine and is described as purple or as shining brightly (*leukos*) or gleaming (*aglaos*).[109]

In Democritus's colour theory *leukos* and *lampros* are synonymous and signify a bright translucent light which turns a reddish black to purple.[110] The shroud Penelope weaves for Laërtes is also described in terms of the lustre associated with burial clothes: it shines like the sun and the moon (ἠελίῳ ἐναλίγκιον ἠὲ σελήνῃ, *Od.* 24.148). Such a pattern of light and dark may be observed on shrouds in representations of death rituals on geometric vase paintings (Figure 5).[111] The garments of the dead associated with the attribute *charieis* seem to promote a change in status, just as *charis* does when poured by Athena over the heads and shoulders of her

---

109. The shroud Penelope weaves is a shining web (ἀγλαὸν ἱστόν, *Od.* 1.109); the *pharos* used to cover the body of Patroclus is *leukon* (*Il.* 18.353). The *peploi* used to wrap Hector's remains are purple (*Il.* 24.796).
110. Stulz 1990: 38-39.
111. Marwitz 1961; Barber 1991: 358-83. Papadopoulou-Belmehdi 1994: 118 reads gender-specific symbolism into the imagery of the sun (Odysseus) and moon (Penelope). Lewis 1981: 95 stresses a fundamental connection between geometric vase-painting and social values: 'What we see in the full range of Geometric designs is nothing less than icons of spiritual meaning central to the life of the culture.' See also ch. 4.3.

protegés. The transition of the dead corpse from the world of light and life to the darkness of Hades is guided by Hermes, who himself is dressed in *charienta heimata*.[112] A substantial portion of the ritual of transition, namely the washing and dressing of the dead, is carried out by the women of the household; their divine representatives, the Charites, also form the entourage of Hermes in post Homeric literature.[113] Charon only appears in fifth-century literature.[114] Since the glory and reputation of the dead is associated with these lustrous garments, they function as emblems of immortality, they represent 'immortal garments' as a form of memorial ('Gedächtniszeichen'). It would make sense to attribute this special quality of remembrance not only to the lustre and colour of the fabrics but also, and indeed especially, to the coloured patterns and images which are produced thanks to the skill of the Charites and their human representatives.

Such an interpretation of *charis* as a visual effect emanating from coloured images worked in weaving or metalwork is linked to a further function of *charis*, that of the radiance, or charisma, associated with speech or song. This latter form of *charis* is also visualized as an object—a garland or wreath. So, Odysseus berates Euryalus because '*charis* does not garland his words' (οὔ οἱ χάρις ἀμφὶ περιστέφεται ἐπέεσσιν, *Od*. 8.175). Odysseus himself is confirmed by Alcinous as speaking 'not without *charis*' (οὐκ ἀχάριστα μεθ' ἡμῖν ταῦτ' ἀγορεύεις, *Od*. 8.236). This form of *charis* is also a divine gift, as Odysseus reminds Euryalus: 'the gods do not give lustre to every man: not in appearance, not in sense, not in speech' (οὕτως οὐ πάντεσσι θεοὶ χαρίεντα διδοῦσιν | ἀνδράσιν, οὔτε φυὴν οὔτ' ἄρ φρένας οὔτ' ἀγορητύν, *Od*. 8.167–68). As well as public speaking, the adjective *charieis* also qualifies the performance of divinely inspired song. So Agamemnon in the underworld praises Odysseus when the dead suitors report on Penelope's constancy: 'The immortals will make a lustrous song about sensible Penelope among the earth dwellers' (τεύξουσι δ' ἐπιχθονίοισιν ἀοιδὴν | ἀθάνατοι χαρίεσσαν ἐχέφρονι Πηνελοπείῃ, *Od*. 24.197–98). The location for the performance of such songs is the banquet, which too is characterized with the comparative form of *charieis*. So Odysseus comments on Demodocus's song in Phaeacia:

---

112. So say the suitors in the underworld (*Od*. 24.1–14). For life as light see Griffin 1984: 90.
113. Zilinski 1924: 159.
114. See e.g. Aesch. *Sept*. 850–60. For further evidence and discussion see Sourvinou-Inwood 1995: 303–61.

οὐ γὰρ ἐγώ γέ τί φημι τέλος χαριέστερον εἶναι
ἢ ὅτ' ἐϋφροσύνη μὲν ἔχῃ κάτα δῆμον ἅπαντα,
δαιτυμόνες δ' ἀνὰ δώματ' ἀκουάζωνται ἀοιδοῦ
ἥμενοι ἑξείης, παρὰ δὲ πλήθωσι τράπεζαι
σίτου καὶ κρειῶν, μέθυ δ' ἐκ κρητῆρος ἀφύσσων
οἰνοχόος φορέῃσι καὶ ἐγχείῃ δεπάεσσι·
τοῦτό τί μοι κάλλιστον ἐνὶ φρεσὶν εἴδεται εἶναι.

I myself feel that there is nothing more delightful (*chariesteron*) than when joy (*euphrosynē*)[115] reigns in the hearts of the entire people and banqueters listen to a singer form their seats in the hall (*dōma*), while the tables before them are laden with bread and meat, and a steward carries round the wine he has drawn from the bowl and fills their cups. This, to my way of thinking, is perfection (*Od.* 9.5-11, tr. adapted from Rieu).[116]

According to Joachim Latacz the image of the garland points to the idea that *charis* in speech or song is a quality of form rather than content: 'Attraction [i.e. *charis*] is placed on the words [...] as it is on the body [...] like a garland'.[117] This is a matter of the effect of speech or song, rather than the specific content. Content is the business of the Muses, while their

---

115. In Hesiod the name of one of the three Charites is Euphrosyne, which means 'Joy'. Joy is the goal (*telos*) of the poet's song which functions as medium to reach a higher measure of pleasure, that means: *charis* (Hes. *Theog.* 908). Here the Charites are spatially associated with the Muses (94), who inspire the bards in epic and even chant the dirge for the dead (*Od.* 24.60). Pindar (*Isth.* 7.16-19; *Pyth.* 11.55-58) and Sappho follow Hesiod in their interpretation of the Charites. See Scott 1983: 11; Deichgräber 1971: 29-36; MacLachlan 1993: 76 and 93-98. On the link between the Charites and feasting see Meier 1985: 50 and Fisher 2010.
116. In the Homeric Hymn to Hestia, which celebrates the goddess's service (*amphipoleuein*) at Delphi, *charis* is a quality of song (*Hom. Hymn Hestia* 24.5: χάριν δ' ἅμ' ὅπασσον ἀοιδῇ). Apollo himself taught the lyre all manner of enchanting *charienta* (*Hom. Hymn Hermes* 4.485). In visual representations the Charites are by Apollo's side. Compare for instance the statue of Delian Apollo with a statue group of the Graces placed on the right hand. Fehr 1979: 72.
117. Latacz 1966: 86: 'Wie χάρις dort nur eine Vervollkommnung der Form bewirkte, nicht auf das Wesen ging, so auch hier: auf den Inhalt der Reden kommt nichts an, "Lustbereitung", "Anziehung" geht von ihnen nicht ihres Inhalts willen aus, sondern auf Grund ihrer Form' (μορφὴν 170). (Just as χάρις only effected a perfection of outward form rather than essence there, so here too: it is not about the content of the speeches. Their attraction and the pleasure they provide stems from their form (μορφὴν 170) not from their content).

immediate neighbours (according to Hesiod), the Charites, take charge of the delivery and effect of that content. In a fifth-century hymn we find Bacchylides invoking the 'garland-bearing' Charites (φερεστέφανοι Χάριτες), who wreath his hymns with honour (Bacchyl. *Dith.* 19(5).6-8, ed. Maehler 1997: 26-27). Elsewhere the poet has Menelaus's winning rhetoric in a Trojan assembly attributed to the 'beautifully robed Charites' (εὐπέπλοισι κοινώσας Χάρισσιν, Bacchyl. *Dith.* 15(1).48-49, ed. Maehler 1997: 5). In Pindar, the tongue draws words of praise and memorial from the mind (*phrēn*) by favour of the Charites (Pind. *Nem.* 4.6-7).[118] Both poets make use of the terminology of pattern-weaving to refer to their own activity. So Pindar speaks of a 'Lydian crown, woven through with sound' presented for Deinias of Aegina (φέρων Λυδίαν μίτραν καταχηδὰ πεποικιλμέναν, Pind. *Nem.* 8.14-16). For the sons of Amythaon he weaves a colourful headband (ὑφαίω [...] ποικίλον ἄνδημα, Pind. *fr.* 169 Bowra). In *Nemean* 4, where he also refers to the favour of the Charites, Pindar exhorts the lyre to 'weave out' his song (ἐξύφαινε, Pind. *Nem.* 4.44-45). In Bacchylides's *Ode* 19, in praise of the Athenians, we find further weaving imagery: 'weave something new in lovely, prosperous Athens' (ὕφαινέ νυν ἐν ταῖς πολυηράτοις τι καινὸν Ὀλβίαις Ἀθάναις, Bacchyl. *Dith.* 19(5).8-10, ed. Maehler 1997: 26).[119]

Jane McIntosh Snyder views this use of weaving metaphors as evidence of a new self-awareness on the part of the poets, who see themselves as independent and skilled producers of their songs, and view poetry as a learnt *technē*, akin to the craft of weaving.[120] The key to the use of the metaphor is, however, not merely *technē* itself but more specifically the technique with which pictures are crafted. This technique then is not only the domain of skilled weavers and smiths, whose products exude *charis*, but also belongs to poets and singers. Through their crafting of visual images that are no less persuasive than the decorative images on metal objects and textiles, the poets, too, partake in the poetics of visualization that has been discussed.[121] In this context *charis* must again be interpreted as a visual power that ensures the emotional effect of the images created by poets and orators. The fact that these images produced by poets and singers are described in terms of weaving by Pindar and Bacchylides is not

---

118. See also Pind. *Isth.* 7.16-19; Pyth. 11.55-58. On the ability of *charis* to grant memory see MacLachlan 1993: 87-98.
119. See MacLachlan 1993: 63.
120. McIntosh-Snyder 1980: 196.
121. On the similarities between woven and poetic pictures, see Bergren 1980: 22. For a poetic of visualization in oral poetry see ch. 1.5.

so much due to any similarity in the effect of woven and literary images as it is connected to the emergence of the new medium of writing. Unlike Homeric bards, the poets of the fifth century create a written text which they send to their patrons (cf. Pind. *Nem.* 8.46).[122] In this sense, they produce, metaphorically, a piece of cloth, a text into which they weave, through the use of words, mental images. Both texts and woven textures are associated with memorializing. Even if the woven image may only strengthen and support the viewer's own imagination and so support memory, without being able to take the place of highly differentiated images created in poetry, both types may function as bearers of glory and memory. While the memory in Pindar's woven hymn is of the individual glory of the winners in panhellenic contests, in epic poetry the glory of the dead hero is conveyed through the patterned garments and shrouds connected to the funeral ritual alongside grave memorials and prizes.[123]

Following these observations, *charis* emerges as a central term in both social and symbolic exchange. In examining the terms for guest-gifts, we were able to gain insight into the various temporary ties and relationships forged between strangers. *Charis* shows us more of the reciprocal structure that governs these ties and relationships: reciprocity in the exchange of services and favours and gifts of gratitude in warrior communities and domestic communities as well as in relation to the gods. When a warlord renders *charis* to another warlord in the form of some service in war, there is a collective of warriors behind him; similarly, a wife who owes *charis* to her husband as thanks for his bridal gifts is backed up by a group of dependent women who perform services for her. If woven images are as much bearers of *charis* as are works of metal, then work on the loom is a part of this female *charis*—and this work in turn is responsible for *charis* in the sense of the lustre or radiance, the visual power, with which certain persons are endowed. We also find this feminine form of *charis* in the garments of the immortals, which are described as *charieis*. *Charis* then shows itself also to be connected to the production of textile and metal gifts which circulate in various ties and relationships. The reciprocal structure of a relationship is visualized doubly in that both genders present each other with the lustre and sexual attraction of *charis* in the form of jewellery and garments endowed with *charis*. This form of *charis* is, in turn, a part of *charis* in the sense of services recruited by high-ranking women and men

---

122. Scheid and Svenbro 1996: 117–22; Pöhlmann 1990: 11–30; Thomas 1992, ch. 4.
123. Ch. 4.3.

from smiths and skilled weavers, and the products of which, jewellery and clothing, they offer to one another as gifts. It is because of this hierarchical structure, to which I shall return, that this form of *charis* which adheres to the objects and images is represented as divinely mediated. Since gods appear as producers of *charis*, we see a close connection between the spheres of production and consumption, which is also evidenced in the fact that high-ranking individuals are also represented as skilled craftsmen and craftswomen.

This underlying, mutual code governing the production of *charis* is reflected in the way in which the metaphors used to evoke *charis* in woven garments, jewellery, and poetic texts are interchangeable.[124] In epic poetry, *charis* adheres to images created by words, to the songs of bards delivered at banquets, and to the speeches of men in assemblies; this creates a sense that material as well as verbal signs form the components of a basic structure which is determined by visibility. In sum, the term *charis* encompasses appearance and being, achievement and status made manifest through external appearance, aesthetically pleasing speech, and ethical content.

However, this is also problematic. Hector's reproach to Paris, that the Greeks had assumed him to be brave in battle because of his beautiful appearance (καλὸν | εἶδος) but now despise him for his cowardice in not facing Menelaus in a duel, is underscored by the assumption that moral virtue is linked to beauty (*Il.* 3.44–45). An individual whose actual achievements do not measure up to the status suggested by their physical appearance is threatened with stoning. This punishment is invoked with a striking image that underlines the link between achievement and appearance, when Hector warns that it is only the Trojans' cowardice that has saved Paris from becoming wrapped in a cloak of stones (λάινον ἕσσο χιτῶνα, *Il.* 3.57).[125] In response to this, Paris does indeed prepare to face Menelaus but not without first defending the gifts of Aphrodite to which he owes his beautiful appearance and his lovely hair (*Il.* 3.55). In Hesiod's *Theogony* (585–99) a similar criticism is levelled at Pandora, in whom outward beauty does not correspond to virtue. She is famously a beautiful evil (καλὸν κακὸν) and thus a false image (εἶδον δόλον). Her moral failure is transmitted to the whole race of women, who feed like drones off the labour of others.

---

124. Dougherty 1993: 157–63: 'Metaphor, one word colonizing another's space, helps the Greeks negotiate their place in an alien environment—both in trying to understand the new world and in staking out a place for themselves in that world.' See also Lonsdale 1990: 125, and—more generally—Haverkamp 1996.
125. On the connection between status and physical appearance see Cobet 1981: 25–26.

In both cases, Paris and Pandora, the aesthetic problem—that beautiful appearance does not correspond to virtue—suggests that *charis*, the radiance or lustre which ought to guarantee the correct perception, fails to do so. In both cases, the problem arises because of a failure in the reciprocal exchange of *charis* in the sense of services or goods between warriors or between man and woman.

The following chapter will focus on conflicts in the operation of networks of *charis*. In epic narrative such conflicts tend to centre on the breakdown of reciprocities of service rendered on the battlefield or at the loom.

CHAPTER 4

Timē and *Geras*: Gifts of Honour and Structures of Power

4.1. Homeric kingship

The flow of gifts and services we observed through the analysis of the terms *xeineia* and *charis* is not without conflict. Indeed, the *Iliad* begins with a refusal of service, when Achilles withdraws from war duty (*charis*) for Agamemnon because he feels dishonoured (*atimos*) by the loss of his share of the spoils and his gift of honour, his *geras*, in the form of Brisëis. The *Odyssey* ends with the punishment of Penelope's suitors, who had aimed to obtain Odysseus's privileged position (*geras*) by marrying his wife, and who had availed themselves of his goods without recompense (*atimos*). The restitution of Odysseus is made possible by Penelope's refusal of service at the loom, by her trick of unravelling her day's weaving at night and thus delaying the promised remarriage. Through this focus on Penelope's trick, the *Odyssey*—called by some scholars the *Penelopeia*—becomes the feminine counterpart to the *Iliad*.[1]

The key terms for understanding these conflicts are τίμη (*timē*) and γέρας (*geras*) and their cognate verbs and adjectives.[2] They all have very strong material connotations.[3] *Timē* can be rendered as either 'honour' and 'esteem' or as 'status'; *geras* may describe a concrete prize or gift awarded

---

1. See Finley Jr. 1978: 3; Murnaghan 1987: 103-15; Winkler 1990: 133, who discuss the idea of female authorship of the *Odyssey* developed by Samuel Butler in the nineteenth century. Although they do not follow this concept, new research has underlined Penelope's role for the narrative composition of the *Odyssey*. See Katz 1991; Papadopoulou-Belmehdi 1994; Clayton 2004 and Canevaro 2018.
2. For evidence see Greindl 1938: 59-82; Riedinger 1976: 244-64; Katluhn 1914: 1-63; Schmidt 1982: 133-36.
3. This is underlined by many authors. See Greindl 1938: 67-68; Katluhn 1914: 1-6 and 76, Schmidt 1982: 134-35; Steinkopf 1937: 17-23; Benveniste 1969: I, 68-69; Vleminck 1982: 151-64; Cobet 1981: 30; Ulf 1990: 4-12; Scheid-Tissinier 1994: 196-203, 234-44.

to an individual as well as the status conferred through the receipt of the gift. The status or esteem conveyed in the terms *timē* and *geras* is always measurable and quantifiable: honour and dishonour are always tied to giving and withholding, while an individual's status is always connected to the goods or services the individual receives. Hence Jean-Claude Riedinger views *timē* as a key term for the manifestation of a Homeric ethics of reciprocity.[4]

Terms of honour and esteem, such as τίμαν (*timan*), τίειν (*tiein*), and ἀτιμάζειν (*atimazein*), involve all those relationships affected by *phile(e)in*, the term that expresses the sense of belonging as discussed above: relationships between men and gods, warriors and their leaders, men and women, parents and children, women and their servants, masters and servants, and finally between guest and hosts. We may add to this another relationship which we have only touched on so far, but which is of some significance for an understanding of *timē* and *geras*: that between a high-ranking individual, such as a master, ἄναξ (*anax*), king, βασιλεύς (*basileus*), or queen, βασίλεια (*basileia*) and their people, described as a δῆμος (*dēmos*) or λαός (*laos*).[5] Such high-ranking individuals are akin to gods and appear alongside the singer of songs and elder councillors (the bard Demodocus: *Od.* 8.480, and Nestor: *Il.* 23.648) as owners of *timē*. Their *timē* can be held (ἔχειν, *Od.* 1.117; 11.302 and 495), received (λαγχάνειν, *Od.* 11.304), or shared (ἔμμορεν, *Od.* 5.335; 11.338; *Il.* 1.278; 15.18), and it is possible to rule or master it (ἀνάσσειν, *Il.* 20.181). *Timē* may be shared in halves (ἥμισυ [...] τιμῆς, *Il.* 6.193; 9.616), and it can be unequal (οὔ ποθ' ὁμοίης ἔμμορε τιμῆς, *Il.* 1.278).[6] It can be withdrawn (ἀπεέργειν, *Od.* 11.503), withheld (λανθάνειν, *Il.* 23.648), or returned (ἄγειν, *Od.* 22.57) and it can be paid back (ἀποτίνειν, ἀποτίνασθαι, *Il.* 3.286, 288, and 459) or owed (ὀφέλλειν, *Il.* 1.353 and 510). It is owed to the gods, from whom it originates

---

4. Riedinger 1976: 251-52: 'Il ne faut pas se la représenter comme un fait d'ordre psychologique, un sentiment d'honneur, mais pas d'avantage comme un objet, une sorte de capital qui comprendrait les possessions et le courage qui les défend. Τίμη est en fait conférée par les autres, elle désigne une relation. Elle reconnaît à celui qui la reçoit une valeur, et, pour l'obtenir, une qualification est nécessaire'. 263-64: 'Deux éléments apparaissent donc ici, et qui sont indissociables. D'un côté l'exploit crée une obligation, attend une réciprocité. Mais cette obligation fonctionne comme un appel à une réponse généreuse, aussi bien dans son intention que dans sa dimension [...] Réciprocité et générosité: telles sont les deux composante du lien de *timè* [...] Et dès lors on peut parler sans hésiter d'une morale de la *timè*'.
5. Riedinger 1976: 247.
6. See also *Il.* 9.319: ἰῇ τιμῇ; 9.605: οὐκέθ' ὁμῶς τιμῆς ἔσεαι; 24.57: ὁμὴν [...] τιμήν.

(εἶναι, Il. 2.197; 17.251) and who provide it (τιθήμεναι, Il. 4.410; 24.57). It is possible to need it or not to need it (οὔ τί με ταύτης χρεὼ τιμῆς, Il. 9.608), and it can be wished for (ὡς ὄφελες τιμῆς ἀπονήμενος, Od. 24.30). Battles are fought for the sake of *timē* (εἵνεκα τιμῆς, Il. 17.72; Od. 24.70 and 117), and it can be won in battle (ἀρέσθαι, Il. 1.159; 5.552; 16.84).

Because of this clustering of *timē* around high-ranking individuals and because of its divine origins, past scholarship took *timē*, like *geras*, to mean the privilege of kings,[7] and by extension such scholarship was keen to distinguish between public and private or domestic *timē*.[8] Epic, however, does not draw the modern distinction between public and private spheres. It is true that terms such as ἴδιος (*idios*), 'pertaining to oneself', and δήμιος (*dēmios*), 'communal' or 'pertaining to the *dēmos*',[9] suggest a difference between action taken on behalf of the individual and on behalf of the *dēmos*.[10] Although this distinction may correspond to the contrast between the good of the community and the pursuit of individual benefit common in later sources, it does not suggest a division into public and private spheres for Homeric society. Given that the honouring or dishonouring of an individual always takes place in the public eye, the crucial aspect of visibility connected to the public sphere[11] is a significant factor

---

7. According to Finsler 1906: 319-20, *timē* denotes the royal dignity bestowed by the *dēmos*. Fanta (1882: 49) understands *timē* as an institutional ('staatsrechtlich') term which does include not only honour but also obedience. Riedinger (1976: 246) interprets *timē* as 'dignité royale' in a nonjuridical sense (261). Cobet (1981: 82) argues that *timē* has the meaning of an office. Carlier (1984: 141) sees *geras* as the real term for the office. No institutional relevance is accepted by Ulf (1990: 4) who argues that *timē* was esteem available to everybody.
8. See Riedinger 1976: 247. He classifies the relationship between *hetairoi*, between parents and children, between couples, and between servants and masters, as private.
9. Cf. Gschnitzer 1991: 198; 1992: 158-59; Ceccarelli, Létoublon and Steinrück 1998: 47-58.
10. The juxtaposition of *dēmios* und *idios* occurs twice in the *Odyssey*: once when Telemachus explains to Nestor that he is travelling on his own 'private' business and not for affairs of the *dēmos* (Od. 3.82: πρῆξις δ' ἥδ' ἰδίη, οὐ δήμιος), and then when Menelaus draws the same distinction asking Telemachus upon the latter's arrival if his own need or that of the *dēmos* has brought him to Sparta (Od. 4.312-14: τίπτε δέ σε χρειὼ δεῦρ' ἤγαγε [...] δήμιον ἦ ἴδιον). In both cases, that which is described as *idios* is the anxiety about the missing father and the state of affairs at home. Elsewhere we find the state of affairs at home forms the subject of discussion at an assembly of the *dēmos* (Od. 2.44), while by contrast the approach of an army is seen as communal (*dēmios*) business (Od. 2.43). For more detail see ch. 5.1.
11. For the meaning of 'public' as the 'visible' see Habermas 1968: 11; Hölscher 1979: 37-39.

in estimating the *timē* accorded an individual. Both *timē* and *geras* require the gaze of others, of the community, in order to be effective. There can be no such thing as private, or hidden, *timē*.

This public effect is expressed through the term αἰδώς (*aidōs*). *Aidōs* denotes both shame and fear of public opinion and incorporates the attention paid to the perception of those who observe *timē* or *geras*. Since the *dēmos* both bestows the material goods by which *timē* and *geras* are demonstrated, and represents the public opinion by which status is measured, *timē* is clearly connected to communal action. Both *timē* and *geras* denote not only esteem but also authority ('Herrschaft'). By authority I am not here suggesting Max Weber's sense of the chance to command obedience for certain actions from specific individuals.[12] In the Homeric world the reciprocal aspects of rulership are more important than elements such as obedience and command. *Timē* and *geras* do not denote such one-sided dominance; instead they form the foundations of a reciprocal system for the provision of gifts and services we have discussed in previous chapters. We will see that this same reciprocity (even if it is not always entirely symmetrical) applies also to the relationships between the *dēmos* as a whole and the high-ranking kings and queens who rule over it.

Discussion of the terms *timē* and *geras* must involve discussion of the character of Homeric kingship, which has a long and varied history in scholarship. Interpretations of the status of the Homeric *basileus* range from 'patriarchal kingship',[13] 'oriental despotism' and 'divine kingship',[14]

---

12. Hilger 1982: 99–100; Rebenich 2012: 1113.
13. This position was widely accepted at the end of the nineteenth century. See e.g. Fanta 1882 and Bréhier 1904: 1–34. Both underline obedience as a key element of the patriarchal kingship, but they differ in their concept of the state. Fanta assumes a developed form of statehood and sees kingship as a public office. Bréhier questions the public character of kingship and views the state in Homer as a confederation of families, one of which stands out as royal (13–14). He sees kingship as legitimated by religion rather than law.
14. Finsler 1906: 412 argues that in Homer a rudimentary form of divinely sanctioned kingship ('Königtum von Zeus' Gnaden') is contrasted with oriental tyranny at Troy. In his view, however, Homeric kings are merely regents within a system of aristocratic rule. The concept of divinely sanctioned kingship ('Gottesgnadenkönigtum'), in that the role of the king is legitimated as divine, differs from the idea of sacred kingship where the king is imagined as a representative of the divine. The concept of sacred kingship goes back to James Frazer's *Golden Bough* (1912) and has been particularly influential in studies of Mycenaean rulership. See Puhvel 1958: 327–333; Mondi 1980: 203–216; Vernant 1962.

to 'feudal rule',[15] 'chiefdom' or the 'big-man' system.[16] Contradictions and inconsistencies in any given model are often attributed to the Mycenaean past,[17] or to the lack of institutionalization in Homeric kingship.[18] The argument over Achilles's *geras*, and the suitors' competition for Penelope, are key events in terms of the understanding and evaluation of Homeric kingship. Agamemnon's taking of Achilles's prize is seen by some as evidence for the existence of a form of oriental despotism; the suitors' behaviour at Ithaca is conversely read as pointing towards the fundamental instability of a king's status, and the predominance of a 'big-man' system.

I do not want to add a further model to the various current images of Homeric kingship. In what follows I am taking my lead only from what the epics tell us about themselves. This does not mean a refusal to clarify the positions suggested by terms of ranking such as *basileus*, *basileia*, and *anax*. But given that my point of departure is the content of the honours awarded to high-ranking individuals, as expressed in the terms *timē* and *geras*, there is no need to fall back on typologies of kingship, nor indeed on

---

15. Martin P. Nilsson's concept of feudal kingship (1927: 23-40) has long been controversial. Cf. e.g. Bethe 1931; Jachmann 1953. Feudal kingship was often seen as a peculiarity of Mycenaean times, with military kingship following in later eras. See Deger 1970; Thomas 1966: 387-407; 1978: 187-204; Andreev 1979: 361-84 working with this model. The latter envisages a hereditary monarchy contrasted with Mycenaean theocracy and oriental tyranny. For a critique of the concept of oriental despotism which goes back to Montesquieu see Venturi 1963 and Harbsmeier 1994. Cf. also Demand 1996 who rejects the concept as not useful to understanding ancient Cypriot kingship.
16. See e.g. Qviller 1981: 109-55; Donlan 1982: 34; 1989: 5-29; Halverson 1985: 129-45; 1986: 119; Ulf 1990: 213-31; Sancisi-Weerdenburg 2000: 5-8.
17. The differences and continuities between Homeric and Mycenaean rule have been the subject of several studies since the deciphering of the Linear B-tablets in the 1950s. Cf. e.g. Gschnitzer 1965: 99-112; Thomas 1978; Starr 1961: 129-38; Descat 1979: 229-40; Carlier 1984; Barceló 1993: 24-48. Barceló assumes that Mycenaean society is monarchical, with divinely sanctioned kingship and lacking central and territorially expansive power (27-30). For the Dark Ages he argues for a big-men model (48); for the subsequent era for aristocratic rule. He draws on Homeric evidence for this but assumes the eighth century as a reference point. See also Hildebrandt 2007 and Crielaard 2011: 87-103, who stresses the differences in rulership but the continuity of the bureaucratic system.
18. See Finley 1954, who first argued that the Homeric *basileus* was not a king but only the head of the *oikos*. For another view see also van Wees 1992: 282 who argues that the rulers at Troy, Lycia, Mycenae, and Ithaca have an institutional status. In current research the existence of monarchy is more and more denied, and the idea of collective leadership as a common feature has been seeing acceptance. See e.g. Morris 2003: 17-21. Cf. also ch. 1.4.

constitutional terms such as 'monarchy' or 'aristocracy' which arise only once Greek culture comes into contact with Persian systems during the sixth and fifth centuries.[19] Indeed, it will become clear that inconsistencies and contradictions, which are so often a mere side-effect of the scholarly application of typologies and models of kingship and constitutions, can be resolved upon close consideration of the concrete terms within the poems themselves. I am thinking of contradictions such as that between the rule of a single *basileus* and several *basilēes*, or that between a *basileus*, a *basileia*, and an *anax*. Such apparently contradictory manifestations of leadership are not to be explained by historical change from monarchy to aristocracy or from great Mycenaean kingship to lesser Homeric kingship or a 'big-men' system. In fact these inconsistencies are expressions of the functional differentiation in terms of areas of competence according to which values, gifts, and services are afforded and recruited, and according to which decisions are taken. Such decision-making is expressed in the term *basileuein*, which I want to consider as the key term concerning leadership and power. The term *anassein*, connected with the title *anax*, is more representative of the socioeconomic aspects of rulership involving the recruitment of gifts and services.[20]

Power, here, is not regarded in Weber's sense, simply as the chance of an individual to achieve their own goals even against the resistance of others.[21] What is of far more interest here are the mechanisms by which consensus is reached.[22] Especially in systems based on reciprocity, there is a need for processes by which the higher ranking of specific individuals is determined and agreed upon. This is particularly true in the epics, where there are a range of different rankings and areas of power so that we are dealing with a number of different fields of authority or power. The distribution of power in different fields demands processes for achieving consensus and balance.[23] These processes, which include ritual practices as well as institutions such as council assemblies, achieve harmony and

---

19. Drews 1983 and now Meister 2020.
20. One can argue with Pierre Bourdieu's ([1972] 1977) view on economic and social capital. Social capital can be understood as the resources an individual has access to because of belonging to a group.
21. Weber 1980: 28.
22. For a critical view on the Weberian concept of authority and power based on obedience see Hilger 1982: 100.
23. This is underlined by Lenz 1990: 47 drawing on Eleanor Leacock 1978 and 1981. Generally, Mann 1986.

sanction social ranking via communal activity and speech.[24] It is no coincidence that no one clear term for power and rule developed in Greek; instead Greek has a number of terms, alongside *timē*, to describe functional aspects of the exercise of power such as leadership (*hēgemonia*, *archē*) or the use of strength (*bia*, *kratos*).[25] What is lacking is the institutionalisation and centralisation of power, which would have given rise to the development of more abstract terminology. Hence the distinction made in Homeric scholarship between *anax* and *basileus* as, respectively, a leader generally and the leader of a community, is too generalised and requires reference to concrete spheres of power. Thus, when we discuss power in this chapter, it is not in the sense of the individual process of achieving dominance over others but in the sense of the social mechanisms by which leadership responsibilities are distributed and justified.

Beginning with the dispute over Achilles's *geras*, I will now proceed to outline the semantic field of the terms *geras* and *timē*, taking my lead from the poems' own narrative logic. This examination concludes with a consideration of the *geras* of the dead, which of course also forms the conclusion of both epics. Both poems end with funerals: the *Iliad* with Hector's funeral, the *Odyssey* with Agamemnon's account of the funeral of Achilles. The honouring of the dead is thus given an important position within the narrative. My discussion of the specifics of the gifts afforded the dead will show that the epics reflect the significance of such honours for the dead in the social system they celebrate. Here we will encounter again both key forms of relationship bonds: the warrior community and the domestic community. We will also see again, as gifts for the dead, or as prizes awarded in funeral games, all those goods we came across in our discussion of guest-gifts and services. Some of these have special symbolic significance. In his book, *The Sources of Social Power*, the American sociologist Michael Mann asks whether human societies should be understood as 'seamless webs spun of endless multicausal interactions in which there are no overall patterns' or whether there are 'keystones' which ultimately determine the shape of society.[26] To answer this question Mann uses two images which are representative of society in Homeric epic: the woven work (or shroud) and the stone monument (or grave

---

24. On the meaning of the principle of consensus in Homeric society see Flaig 1994: 13–31; Raaflaub 1997: 1–27; Schulz 2011: 60–62, 66–69.
25. This is stressed by Meier 1982: 820.
26. Mann 1986: I, 3.

monument). By considering these images we open up a view of Homeric society in time and space which is of central significance for understanding Homeric rulership, and which will lead us back to our original question regarding the place of Homeric epic within a society of hero-cults, and the development of the *polis*.

4.2. The visibility and socioeconomic value of honour: Fighting for Agamemnon's timē and the geras of Achilles

While *charis* often denotes a warrior's service, the winning of *timē* (τιμὴν ἀρέσθαι) is the phrase used for the purpose and goal of such service. Concretely, in the *Iliad*, *timē* consists of Helen and her goods, which the Greeks aim to reclaim from the Trojans. In return for his efforts in battle, a warrior can count on receiving his portion of *timē*. This includes *geras* in the form of a woman taken captive as well as an honour paid to him, τίειν (*tiein*) in the form of a special share of the sacrificed animal at the banquet. We are not dealing here with a simple reciprocal arrangement between leader and follower in battle. Rather, this is a network of relations between leaders and collectives. In this network it is collectives who are the sponsors of honour in the form of shares in the feast and in whose eyes a leader's status as lacking in *timē* (ἀτίμητος/ἄτιμος) and *geras* (ἀγέραστος) is determined. Success in battle, κῦδος (*kudos*), manifested in the quantity of weaponry taken as booty, and the (re)gaining of *timē* become impossible when relations between leaders and collectives are out of balance. At the start of the *Iliad*, we are presented with a lament for the loss of many souls that have descended to Hades after the argument between Agamemnon and Achilles over their respective prizes. Achilles withdraws from battle having first been assured of *timē* by the gods who now give the winning power (κράτος) to the Trojans (*Il.* 1.1-7 and 509-10).[27] Both Agamemnon's *timē* and the *geras* of Achilles are connected to the feminine form of *charis* in so far as both cases involve the producers of material and symbolic *charis*.

This chapter is divided into three parts: the first clarifies the material content of *timē* and of the honours connected with the words *timan* and *tiein*. The second considers the relationship between the recipients and the sponsors of honours, and in particular the relationship between a *basileus*

---

27. See Patzek (1992: 130), who interprets the epic plot as a tragic conflict between 'heldenhaftem Durchsetzungsvermögen und der Schuld des Helden gegenüber der Gemeinschaft'.

and the *dēmos*. The concluding third part deals with the returns offered by those in possession of *timē* and considers the nonmaterial significance of *timē* and *geras*.

4.2.1. The terminology of social value: τίμη (timē), τιμήεις/τιμήεσσα (timēeis/timēessa), τίμιος (timios), and ἄτιμος (atimos)

Conflict breaks out when Agamemnon refuses to return his own prize for a ransom.[28] The prize in question is Chryseïs, the daughter of Chryses, a priest of Apollo, who has come to the Greek camp to attempt to retrieve his daughter. Agamemnon is forced to return Chryseïs only once Apollo has sent a plague on the camp as punishment for the initial refusal, and the prophet Calchas, summoned by Achilles to the assembly, has made the connection between the two events. Agamemnon then seeks compensation for his loss from the prizes of Ajax, Achilles, or Odysseus. Achilles, of course, rejects his claim:

ὤ μοι ἀναιδείην ἐπιειμένε κερδαλεόφρον
πῶς τίς τοι πρόφρων ἔπεσιν πείθηται Ἀχαιῶν
ἢ ὁδὸν ἐλθέμεναι ἢ ἀνδράσιν ἶφι μάχεσθαι;
οὐ γὰρ ἐγὼ Τρώων ἕνεκ' ἤλυθον αἰχμητάων
δεῦρο μαχησόμενος, ἐπεὶ οὔ τί μοι αἴτιοί εἰσιν
οὐ γὰρ πώποτ' ἐμὰς βοῦς ἤλασαν οὐδὲ μὲν ἵππους,
οὐδέ ποτ' ἐν Φθίῃ ἐριβώλακι βωτιανείρῃ
καρπὸν ἐδηλήσαντ', ἐπεὶ ἦ μάλα πολλὰ μεταξὺ
οὔρεά τε σκιόεντα θάλασσά τε ἠχήεσσα
ἀλλὰ σοὶ ὦ μέγ' ἀναιδὲς ἅμ' ἑσπόμεθ' ὄφρα σὺ χαίρῃς,
τιμὴν ἀρνύμενοι Μενελάῳ σοί τε κυνῶπα
πρὸς Τρώων· τῶν οὔ τι μετατρέπῃ οὐδ' ἀλεγίζεις
καὶ δή μοι γέρας αὐτὸς ἀφαιρήσεσθαι ἀπειλεῖς,
ᾧ ἔπι πολλὰ μόγησα, δόσαν δέ μοι υἷες Ἀχαιῶν.
οὐ μὲν σοί ποτε ἶσον ἔχω γέρας ὁππότ' Ἀχαιοὶ
Τρώων ἐκπέρσωσ' εὖ ναιόμενον πτολίεθρον
ἀλλὰ τὸ μὲν πλεῖον πολυάϊκος πολέμοιο
χεῖρες ἐμαὶ διέπουσ'· ἀτὰρ ἤν ποτε δασμὸς ἵκηται,

---

28. *Apoina* always means goods offered for a raped or killed person. For evidence see ch. 5.2. The goods are often identical with the *xeineia* presented to guest-friends. See e.g. *Il.* 6.46 and 49; 10.380; 11.131 and 134. For further evidence see Scheid-Tissinier 1994: 184–88.

σοὶ τὸ γέρας πολὺ μεῖζον, ἐγὼ δ᾽ ὀλίγον τε φίλον τε
ἔρχομ᾽ ἔχων ἐπὶ νῆας, ἐπεί κε κάμω πολεμίζων.
νῦν δ᾽ εἶμι Φθίην δ᾽, ἐπεὶ ἦ πολὺ φέρτερόν ἐστιν
οἴκαδ᾽ ἴμεν σὺν νηυσὶ κορωνίσιν, οὐδέ σ᾽ ὀίω
ἐνθάδ᾽ ἄτιμος ἐὼν ἄφενος καὶ πλοῦτον ἀφύξειν.

You shameless, self-centred [...] ! How can you expect any of the men to comply with you willingly when you send them on a raid or into battle? It was no quarrel with Trojan warriors that brought me here to fight. They have never done me any harm. They have never lifted oxen or horses of mine, nor ravaged my crops back home in fertile Phthia, nurse of warriors. The roaring seas and many a dark range of mountains lie between us. We joined your expedition, you shameless swine, to please you, to get satisfaction (*timēn arnymenoi*) from the Trojans for Menelaus and yourself, dog-face—a fact you utterly ignore. And now comes this threat from you, of all people, to rob me of my prize (*geras*), in person, my hard-earned prize which was a tribute from the army. It's not as though I am ever given a prize (*geras*) equal to yours when the Greeks sack some prosperous Trojan town. The heat and the burden of the fighting fall on me, but when it comes to dealing out the spoils, it is you that takes the lion's share (*geras poly meizon*), leaving me to return to my ships, exhausted from battle (*kamō polemizōn*), with some pathetic portion to call my own. So, I shall now go back home to Phthia. That is the best thing I can do—to sail home with my beaked ships. I can see no point in staying here to be insulted (*atimos eōn*), while I pile up wealth (*aphenos*) and luxuries (*plouton*) for you (*Il.* 1.149-71; tr. Rieu).

Achilles's rejection of Agamemnon's claim clearly sets out the basic rules that govern the Greek warrior community. The battle at Troy is fought in order to gain *timē* for Agamemnon and Menelaus (τμὴν ἀρνύμενοι). This is not true only for Achilles but for others too. So Krethon and Orsilochus die at Troy, having come to win *timē* for the sons of Atreus, Agamemnon, and Menelaus (τιμὴν Ἀτρεΐδης [...] ἀρνυμένω, *Il.* 5.552-53). In the *Odyssey* we hear that Odysseus himself went to Troy for the sake of Agamemnon's *timē* (Ἀγαμέμνονος εἵνεκα τιμῆς, *Od.* 14.70 and 117). When Patroclus finally joins the Greeks in battle, he too fights and dies for the *timē* of Menelaus, for which Achilles had refused to work in the passage just cited. Menelaus reflects on this after Patroclus has fallen:

ὤ μοι ἐγών εἰ μέν κε λίπω κάτα τεύχεα καλὰ
Πάτροκλόν θ', ὅς κεῖται ἐμῆς ἕνεκ' ἐνθάδε τιμῆς,
μή τίς μοι Δαναῶν νεμεσήσεται ὅς κεν ἴδηται.

Ah woe is me! If I leave behind the beautiful arms, and Patroclus, as he lies there for the sake of my *timē*, I fear that some Danaan will see it and resent me for it (*Il.* 17.91–93).

Both sides are aware that efforts on the battlefield (*kamnein polemizōn*) on another's behalf must be compensated. Such compensation may consist of honourable burial, as we gather indirectly from Menelaus's words just cited, in which he worries about his own loss of face were he not to extricate the dead warrior and his arms from the battlefield. In his own speech, also cited above, Achilles points clearly to his entitlement to *geras*—to be provided not by Agamemnon or Menelaus but by the Greeks as a whole. This *geras* is a manifestation of Achilles's *timē* so that he sees himself as *atimos* if he is deprived of the prize. His speech points to both the material and the symbolic value of *timē*. That value is manifested in the female *gera*, Chryseis, whom Agamemnon must give up in order to lift the plague from the camp, and Briseis, Achilles's prize, whom Agamemnon wants to claim as compensation for himself. But the value of *timē* can also be found in the material goods suggested by the terms *aphenos* (hinting at wealth of cattle) and *ploutos* used by Achilles.[29]

With regard to an opponent, *timē* must be repaid in the form of satisfaction or retribution or ποινή (*poinē*). But unlike *poinē*, which suggests quit-money for spilt blood, *timē* aims at the return of the taken object or person.[30] *Timē* takes on the form of *poinē* only when an agreement for the restoration of *timē* is broken. A clear example of this can be seen in

---

29. After Hesychios s.v. εὔπλουτον the word πλοῦτος means originally the wealth of corn. In tragedy *ploutos* also denotes textile wealth (Aesch. *Ag.* 1383: πλοῦτον εἵματος κακόν). On cattle raiding see ch. 5.1.
30. See Vatin 1982: 276–77. It is not necessary to differentiate between two roots of τιμή (τί-τίσις and τῑ-τιμή) as Swoboda 1905: 161–62 did. See the argumentation of Greindl 1938: 60–61, who does not see any contradiction between the double meaning of *timē* as honour and compensation or fine because of the material character of honour.

Menelaus's words before the duel with Paris. Were Menelaus to win, the consequence would be the return of Helen and all her goods (Ἑλένην καὶ κτήματα πάντ' ἀποδοῦναι), and the restoration of the Argives' *timē* (τιμὴν δ' Ἀργείοις ἀποτινέμεν). He then continues as follows:

εἰ δ' ἂν ἐμοὶ τιμὴν Πρίαμος Πριάμοιό τε παῖδες
τίνειν οὐκ ἐθέλωσιν Ἀλεξάνδροιο πεσόντος,
αὐτὰρ ἐγὼ καὶ ἔπειτα μαχήσομαι εἵνεκα ποινῆς
αὖθι μένων, ἧός κε τέλος πολέμοιο κιχείω.

But if Priam and Priam's sons are not willing to compensate (*tinein*) my *timē* once Alexandros has fallen, then I will continue to fight for the sake of *poinē* and stay here until the war is finished (*Il.* 3.288-91; cf. also 3.459)

There is some scholarly dispute over the meaning of *timē* in this passage: is it only a matter of the return of the stolen goods (and the wife of Menelaus) or is additional compensation suggested?[31] Since the agreement between the Trojans and the Greeks, as initially suggested by Paris, then mediated by Hector and finally announced by the herald Idaeus, makes no mention of any additional compensation, it is possible that *timē*, here, represents the abstract value of Helen and her goods.[32] *Timē* is used in such a sense in the context of the punishment of the suitors at Ithaca, who have been consuming goods there without *poinē* (νήποινον) or *timē* (ἄτιμον).[33]

---

31. Greindl 1939: 67 speaks of compensation or reparation for the costs of war ('Kriegskostenersatz'). Benveniste 1969: II, 50-55 reads the passage to tell of a tribute which acknowledges Agamemnon's power. Vatin 1982: 276-78 argues from the evidence of the narrative itself that the duration of the war has made additional contributions necessary. Vatin suggests that both the return of goods taken and the additional contributions are referred to as *timē*, and *poinē* becomes due when there is failure to offer *timē*. He points to the additional gifts offered to Achilles when Agamemnon returns Briseis as well as to post-Homeric practice.
32. This is stressed by Vatin 1982: 275.
33. In the constant complaints about the suitors' behaviour the dominant term is *nēpoinos* (e.g. *Od.* 1.160; 2.142 and 145; 14.377 and 417; 18.280) Only Penelope states that 'you devour his home without compensation' (τοῦ νῦν οἶκον ἄτιμον ἔδεις; *Od.* 16.431). Swoboda (1905: 152) translated 'dessen Haus du ohne Ersatz aufzehrst' and saw here the original meaning of *atimos* as 'outlawed' and thus excluded from the rule of law and free to kill without punishment. Swoboda sees no contradiction between this and what he considers the later meaning of *atimos* as 'without honour' because of the material connotations of honour. (Cf. Greindl 1938: 68).

One of the suitors, Eurymachus, promises *timē* as compensation: 'We will make amends to you by a public levy for all the food and drink that has been consumed in your house. We will each bring compensation (τιμὴν ἀμφὶς ἄγοντες) to the value of twenty oxen, and repay you in bronze and gold' (*Od.* 22.55-58). In this example *timē* clearly takes the shape of compensation for the cattle and wine consumed. It is not quite clear whether *timē* is repaid in metal goods, or actually with cattle (the term *agein* suggests driving animals to slaughter).[34] After the killing of the suitors, the talk is only of the sheep Odysseus aims to obtain from the Greeks to replenish his estate (*Od.* 23.355-58).

We must consider also a third meaning of *timē*. Compensatory *timē* may substitute not only what was taken unlawfully but also such goods as were prevented from accruing to their owners because of the taking of Helen or because of the continuing consumption of the possessions of Odysseus. This would be, for instance, textiles woven by Helen and her women, or the meat and wool of the sheep, which Odysseus was not able to make use of for himself. The complaint about the suitors 'shearing' the goods of Odysseus seems to underline this interpretation: κειρέειν οἶκον (*Od.* 2.142-43; 4.686; 2.313-14; 22.36).[35]

The adjective τιμήεις (*timēeis*) also suggests a meaning of value or compensatory value for *timē*. It is used to describe gold, for instance, but also appears in connection with people, especially in the comparative form.[36] In such cases the adjective suggests the increased value of a person, which is achieved through the receipt of goods. When, for example, Athena makes Penelope show herself to the suitors in order to enhance her value in the

---

34. *Il.* 1.99 and 431: ἄγειν [...] ἑκατόμβην. See also *Od.* 4.621-22, where the companions of Menelaus bring sheep (*mēla*) and wine (*oinon*) for the wedding of his daughter and son whereas their women send corn (*siton*): οἱ δ' ἦγον μὲν μῆλα, φέρον δ' εὐήνορα οἶνον· | σῖτον δέσφ' ἄλοχοι καλλικρήδεμνοι ἔπεμπον. Besides this the verb *agein* is also used to denote the rape of human booty. For evidence see Scheid-Tissinier 1994: 27.
35. Cf. ch. 2.1.
36. In these cases, *timēeis* appears to be linked to processes of measuring or valuation, as in the following examples: valued gold and silver, used by Hephaestus for the shield of Achilles (χρυσὸν τιμῆντα καὶ ἄργυρον, *Il.* 18.475); a talent of valued gold, received by Odysseus from each of the Phaeacian *basileis* (χρυσοῖο τάλαντον ἐνείκατε τιμήεντος, *Od.* 8.393); valued gold, received by Eriphyle for her husband (χρυσὸν φίλου ἀνδρὸς ἐδέξατο τιμήεντα, *Od.* 11.326); the silver mixing jug Menelaus gives to Telemachus is described as very highly valued (τιμήστατον, *Od.* 4.614 = 15.114); the treasure kept back for Mentes by Telemachus is also qualified as τιμῆεν (*Od.* 1.312).

eyes of her husband and her son, the word used is *timēessa*: τιμήεσσα γένοιτο μᾶλλον πρὸς πόσιός τε καὶ υἱέος ἢ πάρος ἦεν (*Od*. 18.161-62). The enhancement of Penelope's worth in her husband's and son's eyes follows as a result of the gifts of jewellery and clothing offered by the suitors (*Od*. 18.291-301). The perception of Penelope as *timēessa* in the sense of 'valued' can be measured through the worth and quantity of the gifts she receives.

A similar connection with material gain is suggested in Telemachus's speech to the suitors, when the esteem afforded him as *timēeis* is connected to the position of *basileus*. I will return to this later. Telemachus says (*Od*. 1.392-93) that it would be no bad thing to be king (βασιλευέμεν) because this would see him enriched (ἀφνειὸν) and his value enhanced (τιμηέστερος). In a similar sense we find (just once in Homer) the adjective *timios*. It is used by Odysseus's men (*Od*. 10.38) to characterise their leader who has an enviable amount of treasure because so many hold him in high esteem (τίμιος).[37]

Among the gods, Poseidon's rule over the sea, received as honour (*timē*), is connected with his status as *timēeis* (*Il*. 15.189-90). When the Phaeacians help Odysseus, Poseidon complains to Zeus that he will no longer be held as *timēeis* by the gods (*Od*. 13.128-30) if mortals do not respect him (ὄυ τι τίουσι). Poseidon is entitled to revenge for the loss of status he experiences as a result of the wrongful giving of gifts by the Phaeacians, and he will take this revenge by hiding their city behind a mountain so that they may no longer offer help to seafarers (*Od*. 13.139-86).

The term for this loss of status is ἄτιμος (*atimos*), as used by Achilles in his accusation against Agamemnon cited above. Deprived of the appropriate compensation for his efforts in battle, Achilles sees himself as *atimos*. The loss of status expressed by the term is manifested in the loss of the prize and is equivalent to a form of social death. We find Achilles return to this subject in Book 9 when he complains that Agamemnon treats him as if he were some wanderer or immigrant, lacking in *timē* (ὡς εἴ τιν' ἀτίμητον μετανάστην, *Il*. 9.649 = 16.59). This condition also affects relatives so that his mother, Thetis, finds herself reduced in status to become *atimotatē* 'least respected' amongst the gods (*Il*. 1.516). There is a danger that this loss of status could be exacerbated if Patroclus were to fight in battle for his personal success instead of recovering Achilles's *timē* and *kudos*. Achilles warns him to refrain from seeking *kudos* for himself, as this would lessen Achilles's own honour (ἀτιμότερον δέ με θήσεις, *Il*. 16.83-88). Here

---

37. This is the only place where τίμιος is used. Only goods are denoted by the adjective ἐρίτιμος: *Il*. 2.447; 15.361 (the Aegis of Zeus); 9.126 and 268 (gold).

too the object of the battle for *timē* is the recovery of a woman, although she is not an embodiment of *timē*. Brisëis is a part of the *gera*, which are not themselves to be counted as *timēenta* but whose value is measured in cattle which would otherwise be given as bridewealth. Given as first prize at the funeral games, alongside a bronze tripod, a captive woman who is a skilled weaver is said to have the worth of four oxen (*Il.* 23.704-5).[38] Brisëis is part of the spoils of war, but she determines Achilles's *timē* because she is a manifestation of what he is able to gain in status and value from fighting. This should be distinguished from *kudos*, which Patroclus might gain if he fought in his own interest and which is manifested in the capture of an opponent's arms.[39]

While Achilles suffers a social death through becoming an *atimos* or *atimētos*, the insult to his *timē* causes the actual death of a great number of Greeks.[40] After Brisëis has been taken from his tent, Achilles turns to

38. For discussion see Scheid-Tissinier 1994: 50-54. On the material meaning of bridewealth (*hedna*) see Wagner-Hasel 1988: 41-50; Leduc 1991: 270.
39. See Greindl 1938: 50 on the case of Achilles, with whom Athena promises to collaborate to bring great *kudos* to the ships of the Achaeans (οἴεσθαι μέγα κῦδος Ἀχαιοῖσι προτὶ νῆας, *Il.* 22.217). 'Da das Medium von *pherein* nach Ameis-Hentze oftmals vom Davontragen der Kampfpreise verwendet wird, kann hier bei dem *mega kydos* durchaus an die Rüstung des Hektors gedacht werden, welche sie so als äußeres sichtbares Zeichen gleichsam ihres ruhmvollen Erfolges zu dem Schiffslager der Danaer bringen würden'. Greindl tends to emphasise the visible character of *kudos*, as it also occurs outside battle scenes, in cases where it often suggests external shine (ibid. 38-40). Steinkopf (1937: 24-25) also emphasises the visibility of *kudos* and suggests that it means a form of elevation that results in visibility. In passages where this is the case, we find *kudos* used in combination with *charis*. While *charis* refers to the gleam of clothing, it is worth considering whether *kudos* may in these passages refer to the gleam of armour. Gruber (1963: 73-89) interprets *kudos* as both success in battle and as the precondition for it, valour in battle, as well as the resulting prestige. Benveniste (1969: I, 60-62) points out the divine provenance of *kudos*, which he views as a kind of talisman of superiority.
40. Post-Homeric sources use the term *atimos* in the sense of political exclusion, together with material connotations. With the creation of the right of citizenship (through Solon's reforms, according to Philip Brook Manville (1990: 124-56), or through those of Cleisthenes, according to Raphael Sealey (1983: 97-129), an *atimos* becomes a person lacking citizen's rights, evidenced through the disenfranchisement of *atimia*. Atimia often affected people who had leased land from the *polis* and could not pay their lease (Hansen 1982: 113-20). Robin Osborne (1988: 279-323) shows that these were by no means the poorest of citizens. *Atimia* implied a prohibition against entering the *agora*, or sanctuaries, and against taking part in any of the institutions of the *polis*. (Hansen 1976: 61-63; Manville 1980: 213-21). In epic poetry the term occurs only once, when Zeus argues against dishonouring Poseidon because it would be hard to assail the eldest and the best with *atimia* (χαλεπὸν δέ κεν εἴη | πρεσβύτατον καὶ ἄριστον ἀτιμίῃσιν ἰάλλειν, *Od.* 13.141-42).

his mother to remind her he is owed some *timē* by Zeus in return for the short life span she bore him to (τιμήν πέρ μοι ὄφελλεν [...] ἐγγυαλίξαι, *Il.* 1.353). The reversal of Agamemnon's *timē* and of the Greeks' fortune in battle will restore *timē* for Achilles, as we see in Thetis's appeal to Zeus: 'Give power to the Trojans until the Greeks compensate (τίσωσιν) my son and increase his honour' (ὀφέλλωσιν τέ ἑ τιμῇ, *Il.* 1.509-10). In receipt of such *timē* from the gods (τετιμῆσθαι, *Il.* 9.608), Achilles has no need of the *timē* he would achieve if he were to accept the precious compensatory gifts finally offered by Agamemnon in order to persuade him to return to battle (οὔ τί με ταύτης | χρεὼ τιμῆς, *Il.* 9.607-8).

4.2.2. The economic meaning of honour: Dōtinai, themistes, temenos

The gifts offered by Agamemnon give a good idea of the varied sources of worth and status in the Homeric world, and they also lead us to consider the character of Homeric rulership. Agamemnon offers Achilles ten talents of gold, seven tripods, and twenty cauldrons, twelve horses, seven women skilled in handiwork, and, in the case of victory, twenty Trojan women. In addition, he offers marriage to one of his own daughters upon their return to Greece. This last offer is linked to the promise of further riches, suggested by the terms *dōtinai* and *themistes*:

> τρεῖς δέ μοί εἰσι θύγατρες ἐνὶ μεγάρῳ εὐπήκτῳ [...]
> τάων ἥν κ' ἐθέλῃσι φίλην ἀνάεδνον ἀγέσθω
> πρὸς οἶκον Πηλῆος: ἐγὼ δ' ἐπὶ μείλια δώσω
> πολλὰ μάλ', ὅσσ' οὔ πώ τις ἑῇ ἐπέδωκε θυγατρί:
> ἑπτὰ δέ οἱ δώσω εὖ ναιόμενα πτολίεθρα
> Καρδαμύλην Ἐνόπην τε καὶ Ἱρὴν ποιήεσσαν
> Φηράς τε ζαθέας ἠδ' Ἄνθειαν βαθύλειμον
> καλήν τ' Αἴπειαν καὶ Πήδασον ἀμπελόεσσαν.
> πᾶσαι δ' ἐγγὺς ἁλός, νέαται Πύλου ἠμαθόεντος:
> ἐν δ' ἄνδρες ναίουσι πολύρρηνες πολυβοῦται,
> οἵ κέ ἑ δωτίνῃσι θεὸν ὣς τιμήσουσι
> καί οἱ ὑπὸ σκήπτρῳ λιπαρὰς τελέουσι θέμιστας.

I have three daughters in my strong palace [...]
Of these he shall choose for his own whichever he likes best and take her back to Peleus's house, without the usual bride-gifts (*anahednon*). Indeed, I will give him gifts (*meilia dōsō*), generous ones, more than anyone has ever given with his daughter. Not

only that, but I will give him seven prosperous towns: Cardamyle, Enope and grassy Hire; holy Pherae and Antheia with its deep meadows; beautiful Aepeia and Pedasus rich in vines. They are all near the sea, in the farthest part of sandy Pylos. Their people are rich in flocks and cattle. They will honour him with their gifts (*dōtinai*) as though he were a god and, being under his authority, give him rich dues (*liparas teleousi themistas*) (*Il.* 9.144 and 146-56; similar *Il.* 9.286 and 288-98; tr. adapted from Rieu).

The offer of seven cities has caused scholars some difficulty since land is never handed over by an individual in Homeric epic and is never part of compensatory offers (*apoina*) such as those offered here by Agamemnon (*Il.* 9.180). Some scholars therefore view this passage as a recollection of Mycenaean kingship. Juri V. Andreev argues: 'Only under the conditions of Mycenaean monarchy with its complex hierarchical structure and its comparatively large territories would such an act of generosity be a natural expression of the power and authority of a head of state'.[41] Leaving aside the difficult question of whether Homeric epic has any awareness of the sociopolitical conditions of the Mycenaean era, more recent research on Mycenaean rulership suggests that the structures were far smaller in scale than Andreev presupposes.[42] Even in Mycenaean times giving seven whole cities to one individual would be an unlikely act.[43] Christoph Ulf, who has rejected the principle underlying Andreev's interpretation, proposes that the passage suggests a—somewhat hyperbolic—promise of dowry in the form of *temenos* ('a piece of land cut off, assigned as a domain to kings and chiefs').[44] It should be noted, however, that in most cases dowries are mobile goods (*ktēmata*) rather than land (cf. *Od.* 7.314).

41. Andreev 1979: 365. See also Vlachos 1974: 278. He suspects that the offer points to the existence of a state of Pylos in Mycenaean times. Finsler 1906: 410 views it as the private property of Spartan kings. Nilsson 1927: 32 sees the offer as an allusion to vassal kings installed in conquered territories. Havelock 1978: 92-93 views the offer as pure fantasy based on the idea of oriental tyranny. Beidelman 1989: 236-38 interprets the passage within the framework of gift-exchange and suggests that Agamemnon's intention is to shame Achilles with the offer.
42. See ch. 1.5.
43. Cf. Darcque 1987: 185-205. Darcque argues that the distribution patterns of grave types must throw some doubt on the idea of the unity and the monarchical organisation of Mycenaean society. Cf. also Hooker 1995: ch. 1 and Schmitt 2009. For discussion of female rulership see Rehak 1995; Morris 2003; Maran and Stavrianopoulou 2007.
44. Ulf 1990: 96, 124. Finsler (1906: 410) and Bethe (1931: 224) both view Agamemnon as the embodiment of a Spartan king and the offer as a dowry.

In cases where a *temenos* is given as a form of dowry, this is offered by a collective, rather than by the father of the bride, as happens in Bellerophon's marriage to the daughter of the Lycian *basileus*. The Lycian *dēmos* cuts him off a piece of land to cultivate (*Il*. 6.192–93). His descendants, Sarpedon and Glaucus, also receive such a *temenos* for their efforts in warfare, as we see in Sarpedon's appeal:

> Γλαῦκε τί ἢ δὴ νῶϊ τετιμήμεσθα μάλιστα
> ἕδρῃ τε κρέασίν τε ἰδὲ πλείοις δεπάεσσιν
> ἐν Λυκίῃ, πάντες δὲ θεοὺς ὣς εἰσορόωσι,
> καὶ τέμενος νεμόμεσθα μέγα Ξάνθοιο παρ' ὄχθας
> καλὸν φυταλιῆς καὶ ἀρούρης πυροφόροιο;
> τὼ νῦν χρὴ Λυκίοισι μέτα πρώτοισιν ἐόντας
> ἑστάμεν ἠδὲ μάχης καυστείρης ἀντιβολῆσαι,
> ὄφρά τις ὧδ' εἴπῃ Λυκίων πύκα θωρηκτάων
> οὐ μὰν ἀκλεέες Λυκίην κάτα κοιρανέουσιν
> ἡμέτεροι βασιλῆες, ἔδουσί τε πίονα μῆλα
> οἶνόν τ' ἔξαιτον μελιηδέα· ἀλλ' ἄρα καὶ ἲς
> ἐσθλή, ἐπεὶ Λυκίοισι μέτα πρώτοισι μάχονται.

Glaucus, why are we most of all singled out for honour (*tetimēmestha*) at home in Lycia, with pride of place, the choicest meat and never empty cups? Why do they all look up to us as gods? And why do we cultivate a great estate (*temenos*) on the banks of the River Xanthus, with lovely orchards and splendid fields of wheat? All this now obliges us to take our places in the front ranks of the Lycians and fling ourselves into the flames of battle. Only then will our Lycian men-at-arms say to us: 'Well! These are no dishonourable lords (*basilēes*) of Lycia that rule over us (*koiraneousin*) and eat fat sheep and drink the best sweet wine: they are indomitable and fight in the forefront of the Lycians (*Il*. 12.310–21; tr. Rieu).

We have here a relationship of immediate reciprocity between the Lycian community and the two warriors described as *basilēes*. The use of the verb *timan* for the honours paid at the feast suggests the perception of the two recipients as godlike, which in turn appears to justify the grant of a *temenos*. Service in battle pays for both the honours of the feast and the grant of the *temenos*.

Other heroes distinguishing themselves in battle also receive such cut-off pieces of land. This is true for Meleager (*Il.* 9.576–80) and possibly for Aeneas, whom Achilles taunts by suggesting he is fighting only in expectation of a *temenos* (*Il.* 20.389–92). In all these cases land is granted by an ethnically defined group, such as the Lycians, the Trojans, or the elders of the Aetolians. In the *Odyssey* both Alcinous (*Od.* 6.293) and Odysseus (*Od.* 11.185; 17.299) have charge of a *temenos*, although here a connection seems to be made with the recipient's legislative functions, since in both cases the recipient of the *temenos* is described as *dikaspolos*.[45]

Finsler, Fanta, and more recently Carlier consider *temenos* to be identical with *geras*, as offered by the *dēmos* to *basilēes* such as Alcinous (*Od.* 7.150).[46] In this case, the *geras* is a woman (*Od.* 7.8–10). An identification of the *geras* with a *temenos* can be deduced from the reassurance given to Odysseus by his mother when she tells him that his fair *geras* is safe and that Telemachus is still in charge of the *temenea* (τεμένεα νέμεται) and taking part in banquets, as is proper for a man who deals judgement (δικασπόλον, *Od.* 11.184–86). However, the qualities of leadership implied in the *geras* of the elders (*Il.* 4.323; 9.422) are necessary for looking after the *temenea* and for dealing out justice, and thus should be assumed to underlie Odysseus's *geras* here. It is up for debate whether *temenea* are the property of those honoured with them, or whether they are just to be managed by such individuals. The range of meanings associated with the term *nemeomai* ('to dispense', 'to manage', 'to possess') allows both possibilities (τέμενος νεμόμεσθα, *Il.* 12.313; τέμενος τάμον [...] ὄφρα νέμηαι, 20.184–85).[47]

Even if we must then exclude the father of the bride—and thus Agamemnon—as a sponsor of *temenea*, he does still play an important role. In Bellerophon's case the bride's father apportions the groom half of his kingly honour (τιμῆς βασιληίδος, *Il.* 6.193). It is possible that this is also the

---

45. In the description of Achilles's shield, we find a *temenos basilēion* (*Il.* 18.550). In the *Iliad temenos* mostly denotes divine realms (*Il.* 2.696; 8.48; 23.148; see also *Od.* 8.363).
46. Finsler 1906: 328; Fanta 1882: 50 and 80; Carlier 1984: 160.
47. Laroche 1949: 10 reads *nemeomai* to mean 'posséder'. Carlier 1984: 153–60 also assumes permanent possession, while Fanta (1882: 50; 80), Finsler (1906: 328) and Finley (1967: 99) view the arrangement as temporary. Link 1994: 241–45 suggests that the *temenea* are an anachronism, alluding to Mycenaean practice. Van Wees 1992: 297 differentiates between private lots of land (*klēroi*) and communal *temenea*, which can be seen as a 'gift of the community to an individual'. According to him '(t)he existence of such crown-land confirms that the Homeric monarchy has an institutional character'.

timē Agamemnon is offering to Achilles. Within the context of Sarpedon's testimony, we can take this to include the honours enjoyed by the *basilēes* at the Lycian feast (*Il.* 4.247–64). It is also possible, however, to understand *timē* here as an entitlement to the kind of labour that is necessary to enjoy the usufruct of the apportioned land.[48] Such an interpretation of Agamemnon's offer explains why there is mention of *themistes* and *dōtinai* in the passage but not of *temenea*. Agamemnon is not offering to give Achilles possession of the land as such but instead offers him the benefit of the labour of those who work the lands mentioned, or the right to the fruits of that land and labour.[49]

Homeric scholarship has long viewed the services described by the terms *dōtinai* and *themistes* as formally voluntary and unregulated. The difference between this system and modern taxation or feudal 'dues' has been underlined, although not always with sufficient specificity and detail.[50] In my own analysis of the Polyphemus episode, and of Odysseus's stay with the Phaeacians, I suggested that *dōtinē* offered by Alcinous and putatively promised by Polyphemus is to be understood as the granting of safe conduct.[51] This conclusion can be drawn for the present passage, too, in so far as the coastal location of the places mentioned and the characterisation of the inhabitants as owners of herds suggest that they have at their disposal both ships and pack-animals. The granting of such safe conduct may also involve offers of material goods, which may equally be evoked by the term *dōtinē*. So *dōtinai* may take the form of specific resources such as

---

48. See my arguments in Wagner-Hasel 1988: 44–50 and 57–58.
49. See also Cobet 1981: 31–32.
50. Finsler 1906: 410 saw the cities as the private property of Spartan kings, and the dues paid as private donations. Fanta 1882: 53 sees them as tributes paid to a Spartan ruler by the *perioeci* of the surrounding towns. He assumes that generally such tributes were formally voluntary and irregular, and that they were given as gifts (for guests or towards the equipment of an army) rather than taxes. Andreades (1931: 19) differentiates between regular payments (*themistes*) and extraordinary expenses (*dotinai*) and assumes that a change takes place as tributes initially voluntary become obligatory. Finley (1967: 100–1) speaks of occasional and voluntary gifts, and emphasises reciprocity, underlining the military services provided by leaders in return for the tributes paid by the people. Qviller (1981: 117) and Morris (1986: 4) concur. Qviller assumes that '(m)ost of the king's income came from raiding abroad and his own household production. In addition, he demanded and received occasional "gifts" from his subjects. There were no regular revenues like taxes or feudal dues' (118). Benveniste (1969: I, 69) considers *dotinai* to be gifts that have a binding character. See now Domingo Gygax 2016: 63 who interprets *dotinai* and *themistes* as 'chiefly dues'.
51. See ch. 2.1.

wool, cheese, meat, and wine (one of the places mentioned by Agamemnon is described as rich in vines) but also material goods such as the tripods collected by Alcinous from his fellow Phaeacians once the promise of *dōtinē* has been made.[52] When Achilles rejects the gifts offered by Agamemnon he underlines his rejection by saying that he would not take the gifts even if Agamemnon offered all the treasures of Orchomenus or Thebes where the houses are filled with the greatest treasure (*ktēmata*), thus emphasising the close link between the places and the treasures offered (*Il.* 9.381–84). There is no contradiction between this interpretation and Pierre Carlier's suggestion that Agamemnon's offer implies a migration or move to the territory of the seven cities.[53] Menelaus makes a similar offer to Odysseus (*Od.* 4.174–76). The practice is known to Achilles himself, whose father Peleus had settled Phoenix on the edge of his own territory (the *eschatia*) and had granted him rule over the Dolopians (*Il.* 9.484). In both cases, settling in the new territory goes hand in hand with gaining the benefit of the resources of the local population.

The term used for this type of rule is ἀνάσσειν (*anassein*). Along with the related noun ἄναξ (*anax*), 'master', 'ruler', the word has a strong association with groups. In the *Iliad* ἄναξ ἀνδρῶν (*anax andrōn*) is often used to characterise Agamemnon.[54] The term is also used to denote Idomeneus (*Il.* 13.452), Augias (*Il.* 9.701), Euphetus (*Il.* 15.532), Ortilochus (*Il.* 5.546), Eumelus (*Il.* 24.288), Anchises (*Il.* 5.278), and Aeneas (*Il.* 5.311). Therefore the term is often interpreted as one that denotes personal rule.[55] In

---

52. In the *Odyssey* the guests of Menelaus are also said to bring wine, lambs for slaughter, and bread (*Od.* 4.621–23). See n. 34. In Odysseus's story about the Cretan Aëthon, the *dēmos* provides flour, wine, and cattle for the feast (*Od.* 19.197–98). It is unclear who provides the eight boars, twelve sheep, and two oxen for Alcinous's feast for the young and the old men (*Od.* 8.57–60). For discussion of these *dēmia* see Donlan, 1970: 384; 1982: 164.
53. Carlier 1984: 179–80.
54. Carlier 1984: 216 counts 38 examples.
55. See Descat 1979: 231, who argues that *anax* has no political meaning. According to him, *anax* denotes the personal authority but not the title of the king. For a similar argument see Cobet (1982: 15–16) who interprets *anassein* as personal leadership in the sense of 'Herr sein': 'Herren sind offenbar all die, denen viel zu Gebote steht, als Besitzer von Schätzen, Häusern, Herden, Sklaven' (16). See also Yamagata 1997: 12, who argues: 'ἄναξ stands for patronage formed on a personal basis, while βασιλεύς stands for a social status, objectively defined by birth and wealth.' On the other hand, *anax* is proved as an old Mycenaean title in Linear B tablets. Here, it appears to be associated with dues, a clear reference to the economic side of rulership. See Vlachos 1974: 107, who calls the *anaktes* 'rois souverains'. Similarly, Havelock 1978: 95.

both the *Iliad* and *Odyssey* this rulership is mostly over a group of people characterised either by its ethnic name, or by their male gender.[56] Often this group of people is identical with the group of warriors recruited for service and under obligation to an *anax*.[57] The term used for recruitment of this type is *ageirein* (ἀγείρειν),[58] also a term for the collection of goods in the Odyssey.[59] Another group of people over whom it is possible to rule is formed by herdsmen and house servants form.[60] Animals, such as sheep,

---

56. Thoas rules over the Aetolians (*Il.* 2.643; 13.218); Peleus (*Il.* 24.537) and Achilles (*Il.* 1.180; 21.188) rule over the Myrmidons; Phoenix the Dolopians (*Il.* 2.643; 9.480); Altes over the Lelegans (*Il.* 21.86). Diomedes (*Il.* 23.471), Agamemnon (*Il.* 14.94), and Eurystheus (*Il.* 19.129) rule over the Argives. In the *Odyssey* Mentes (*Od.* 1.181 and 419), Alcinous (*Od.* 7.10-11; 11.349), Laërtes (*Od.* 24.378) and Theoclymenus (*Od.* 15.240) rule over the Taphians, Phaeacians, Cephallenians, and Argives. Andromache's father Eëtion ruled over the Cilicians (*Il.* 6.397), the Phocian Schedius is said to have ruled over many men (*Il.* 17.307). Agamemnon rules over many (*Il.* 1.281; 9.73; *Od.* 24.26). In Nestor's case we hear about the duration of his rule over three generations (*Il.* 1.252; *Od.* 3.245). The good *basileus* rules over many brave men (*Od.* 19.110). Priam rules over his own (*Il.* 24.202), Eurystheus will rule over all of those who dwell in the surrounding areas (*Il.* 19.109).
57. Thrasymelos is described as *therapōn* to his *anax* Sarpedon (*Il.* 16.464). Leaders in battle are often described as *anaktes*: Idomeneus (*Il.* 10.112; 15.301), Sarpedon (*Il.* 12.413-14), Menelaus (*Il.* 24.588), Philoctetes (*Il.* 2.725), Asius (*Il.* 12.139).
58. Collectively these warriors are called *laos*, e.g. when Nestor and Odysseus travel to Phthia to gather the host (*Il.* 11.769: λαὸν ἀγείροντες). Similarly, Polyneices and Tydeus travel to Mycenae to wage war against Thebes (λαὸν ἀγείρων, *Il.* 4.377). Achilles describes the Achaean army as *laon ageiras* (λαὸν ἀγείρας, *Il.* 9.338) and speaks of gathering the *laos* in order to defend the Greek ships (ἐγὼ δέ κε λαὸν ἀγείρω, *Il.* 16.129). Hera claims to have gathered the Greek army before Troy (λαὸν ἀγειρούσῃ, *Il.* 4.28). Nestor gathered the Pylians to go to war against Elis (Πύλον κάτα λαὸν ἄγειρεν, *Il.* 11.715). The verb *ageirein* is also used for the gathering of oarsmen (ἐπιτηδὲς ἀγείρομεν, *Il.* 1.142) and for hunters and their dogs (θηρήτορας ἄνδρας· ἀγείρας | καὶ κύνας, *Il.* 9.544-45).
59. Here *ageirein* occurs in connection with the term *dēmos*, e.g. to collect repayment for the tripods and cauldrons the Phaeacians give to Odysseus (ἀγειρόμενοι κατὰ δῆμον | τεισόμεθ', *Od.* 13.14). Athena suggests that Odysseus should gather loaves of bread from the suitors (πύρνα κατὰ μνηστῆρας ἀγείροι, *Od.* 17.362), while Odysseus claims to have gathered unspecified goods, *chrēmata*, abroad (*Od.* 3.301; 14.285-86).
60. See Telemachus (*Od.* 16.14; 17.186) and Odysseus (*Od.* 1.397-98; 14.8; 40; 60; 63; 139; 170; 366; 376; 395; 398; 438; 450; 15.557; 17.201; 255; 320; 20.216; 21.395) who rule over the herdsmen Eumaeus, Philoetius, and other *dmōes*. Odysseus is also *anax* of the female servants: *dmōiai gynaikes* (*Od.* 18.313; 19.358; 392; 475; 20.111; 21.9). *Anaktes* are principally masters of those who bring labour services, called *ergazesthai* (*Il.* 24.733-34; *Od.* 17.320-21).

horses, and dogs,[61] and material goods may also be ruled over,[62] as may territories such as Mycenae, Pylos, or Troy.[63] In these cases, we are dealing with places which are located on popular shipping routes or crossroads. Controlling access to the Black Sea, Troy especially must have profited from its position, either through toll charges or by charging for navigation services.[64] But Pylos and Mycenae also occupy key geopolitical positions, with Pylos dominating access to the shipping routes to the west, while Mycenae's location allowed it to control access points to and from the Argolid and the mountains of Arcadia.[65] This means that in such cases *anassein* suggests access to resources via the granting of safe conduct, which in turn would mean that *anassein* includes economic aspects of rulership.

The *themistes*, also offered by Agamemnon to Achilles, are similar to the *dōtinai* in their double meaning. Usually in epic poetry, *themis* denotes the customs or traditional norms according to which *basilēes* take their decisions. In our passage, *themistes* may be understood as services offered in return for the exercise of legal authority. This is how the scholiasts interpret the word when they explain it as *phoroi* (tributes/dues).[66] This would

---

61. Polyphemus is *anax* of his sheep (*Od.* 9.440 and 452); Mentor resembles the sons of *anaktes* (*Od.* 13.223). In Libya there is no *anax* and no herdsman who suffers from a lack of milk and cheese (*Od.* 4.87). Horses: *Il.* 13.38; 16.371 and 507; 23.417; 446; 517. Dogs: *Il.* 23.173; *Od.* 10.216; 17.296; 303; 318. Herds: *Od.* 15.397.

62. See *Od.* 1.117: κτήμασιν οἷσιν ἀνάσσοι; 4.93: τοῖσδε κτεάτεσσιν ἀνάσσω. Cf. also *Od.* 1.402: δώμασι ςοῖσἀνάσσοις. A person can also be *anax* of goods like *keimēlia* (*Od.* 21.9), prizes (*Od.* 21.62) or weapons (*Od.* 21.56 = 83).

63. Menelaus rules over plains (*Od.* 4.604), Agamemnon over islands and over Argos (*Il.* 2.118); for seven years Aegisthus ruled over Mycenae rich in gold (*Od.* 3.304). Dmetor ruled over Cyprus with strenght (*Od.* 17.443) and Amphion over Orchomenos (*Od.* 11.284). In Thebes Oedipus ruled over the Cadmeans (*Od.* 11.275-76). Achilles's son rules in the city (*asty*) of the Myrmidons (*Od.* 4.9). Troy is described as *asty* or *polis* and Priam its *anax* (*Il.* 4.18; 7.296). Nestor was *anax* of Pylos (*Il.* 6.173), Lobates *anax* of Lycia (*Il.* 6.173).

64. For the geographical situation and control of access to the Dardanelles see Korfmann 1986: 1-16. For Troy as the end point of trade routes see also Zengel 1991: 30-67, whose argumentation is marked by modernism. For discussion see Wagner-Hasel 2002.

65. Mycenae controlled the pass of Dervenaki and therefore the entrance into the Argolis as well as the path to Corinth and to the Arcadian mountains. Three routes meet at Mycenae, 'the main highway, the Koatoporeia, and the Nemean hill route'. Adshead (1986: 10) argues: 'Mycenae was a foothills state and her early power rested on the control to the mountain passes.' For Pylos, which has a similar function, see Agourides 1997: 13 and 18-20.

66. Scholion A: ὑπ' αὐτοῦ βασιλευόμενοι βιώσονται | ὅσα δεῖ βασιλέα—λαμπροὺς φόρους τελέσουσιν. For discussion see Yamagata 1994: 76, who proposes a meaning

also explain the linking of tributes to places, since court proceedings such as that depicted on the shield of Achilles take place in the central location of the *agora*. On the shield there is payment in gold due to the man who pronounces the most righteous judgement (*Il.* 18.497). This mention of gold may help to explain the use of *liparos* (bright or brilliant, shiny with oil, oily) we find with the *themistes* in our passage. However, it must be borne in mind that *liparos* is normally used of linen clothing, so that our *themistes* in this case may also be tributes of linen, such as those raised in the *Odyssey* by the Phaeacians.[67] The fact that our seven cities are located in Messenia would support this since this is the only region of Greece that is suited to the cultivation of flax.[68]

The many varied meanings associated with the terms *themistes* and *dōtinai* finally suggest that their use is intended to convey the entire spectrum of privileges and offices that contribute to a person's *timē*. These would include honours paid in the form of safe conduct and attendant material and natural goods as well as the exercise of legal authority and the material compensation due for this. Before considering the social or normative aspect of *timē* more closely, I want to reflect on the role of the community.

---

of *themistes* as 'god-given customs'. She translates the phrase οἱ ὑπὸ σκήπτρῳ λιπαρὰς τελέσουσι θέμιστας as follows: 'under his sceptre they will practise their pleasant customs'.

67. The adjective *liparos* is used for the veils of high-ranking women like Penelope (*Od.* 1.334; 18.210) or Hecuba (*Il.* 22.406) and the veil of the goddess Charis (*Il.* 18.382). For men, *liparos* must describe the gleam of the lower hem of a *chitōn* or *pharos*, which were made of linen, as we saw earlier. It is possible that this is meant to describe the effect of a purple border. See *Il.* 2.43-44: περὶ δὲ μέγα βάλλετο φᾶρος ποσσὶ δ' ὑπὸ λιπαροῖσιν ἐδήσατο καλὰ πέδιλα (Agamemnon); *Il.* 10.21-22 and 131-32: ὀρθωθεὶς δ' ἔνδυνε περὶ στήθεσσι χιτῶνα, ποσσὶ δ' ὑπὸ λιπαροῖσιν ἐδήσατο καλὰ πέδιλα (Agamemnon and Nestor). The dative *possi* does not mean 'the feet' as often translated but 'the hem': see Pollux 7.62. For discussion see Stulz 1990: 140-45; Buschor 1912: 24-25. The adjective *liparos* is derived, like the adverb *lipa* ('unctuously, richly with oil'), from the noun *lipos* ('fat'). The oily shine can refer to ointments or oils (Handschur 1970: 78). We know that oils were used in linen production (cf. ch. 3.3. n. 91). The word is also used for the shine of the head or hair (*Il.* 19.126; *Od.* 15.322). In such instances it might refer to the shine of hair, or of gold decorations placed in it (see *Il.* 17.51, where we hear that Euphorbus's hair was braided with gold and silver like the hair of the Graces). We also find *liparos* connected to old age, *gēras* (*Od.* 11.136; 19.368; 23.283) or to aging, *gēraskein* (*Od.* 4.210). In these instances, there is a connection made with the spinning of the thread of life, which will be of interest in our next section (4.2, n. 148).

68. See Robkin 1979: 469-74; Barber 1991: 12-19. In Mycenaean times Messenia was a centre of linen production. See Rougement 2007: 46-49. Cf. also ch. 5.3.

4.2.3. Rulership and social control: Aidōs

The gifts Achilles rejects are not only of material value; they are meant to demonstrate his status visually. A look at Agamemnon's *geras* shows this clearly. Just as Achilles seems himself as *atimos* after the loss of his *geras*, so Agamemnon complains that to return Chrysëis to her father would leave him *agerastos* in the eyes of the Argives. This loss of face is the reason for his demand for compensation after he agrees to give up his prize:

> αὐτὰρ ἐμοὶ γέρας αὐτίχ᾽ ἑτοιμάσατ᾽ ὄφρα μὴ οἶος
> Ἀργείων ἀγέραστος ἔω, ἐπεὶ οὐδὲ ἔοικε
> λεύσσετε γὰρ τό γε πάντες ὅ μοι γέρας ἔρχεται ἄλλῃ.

> But give me another prize (*geras*) at once or I will be the only one of us without one. That cannot be right. You can all see for yourselves that the prize (*geras*) I was given is on its way elsewhere (*Il*. 1.118-20; tr. Rieu).

The main insult is the visibility of Agamemnon's loss, which threatens to diminish his status in the eyes of the community. In this sense, the hero's *geras* is not unlike the female form of *charis* in its concrete and abstract manifestations.[69] Like the gleam of *charis* that shines forth from clothing, *geras* also makes visible the hero's value. Indeed, Chrysëis, Agamemnon's *geras*, is valued by him as equal to his wife, Clytemnestra, as he announces to the assembled Argives: 'for she is not inferior to her, in beauty or stature, or in mind or in handiwork' (*Il*. 1.115). Earlier, Agamemnon had told the girl's father, Chryses, that his daughter was destined to walk to and fro before the loom (ἱστὸν ἐποιχομένην) at Argos and share his bed there (*Il*. 1.31).

---

69. In the *Iliad geras* normally denotes a woman taken captive as booty: *Il*. 1.118; 123; 133; 135; 138; 161-62; 163; 9.344; 367; 16.54; 56; 18.444 (Brisëis and Chrysëis); *Il*. 11.626 (Hekamede of Nestor). In the *Odyssey* Eurymedusa, the *tamiē* in the house of Alcinous, is called a *geras* (*Od*. 7.10). See also *Od*. 11.234, where the booty of Neoptolemus is characterised as *geras*. Besides this, *geras* denotes the honouring portion of the sacrificial meal for the gods (only *Il*. 4.49; 24.70) and for men (only *Od*. 4.66; 20.297). The *geras* of the elderly can be identified as the competence to weave a plan (only *Il*. 4.323; 9.422). Finally, there is also the *geras* of the dead, which is materialised as tears (*Il*. 16.457 and 679; 23.9; *Od*. 4.197; 24.190 and 296). No specific meaning is given to *geras* in *Il*. 20.182; *Od*. 11.175; 184; 534; 15.522.

When Agamemnon and Achilles are finally reconciled, it is important that the return of Brisëis and the presentation of the many other gifts offered in compensation take place in full view of the entire community. So Odysseus demands of Agamemnon: 'As for the gifts, let Agamemnon, the leader of men, bring them to the middle of the assembly place so that all the Achaeans may see them with their own eyes' (ὀφθαλμοῖσιν ἴδωσι, *Il.* 19.172-74).

The 'eyes' of the people provide the proof or evidence of a man's *timē* and *geras*. By taking place in full view of the assembled community, the presentation of the gifts offers a visible measure of the *timē* of Achilles.[70] In watching the presentation, the assembled community also watches over the maintenance of established norms of behaviour. Status and norms are maintained by being enacted and also by being *seen* to be enacted.

The central words connected to this public visibility are αἰδεῖσθαι (*aideisthai*) and αἰδώς (*aidōs*), most often rendered in terms of shame or shaming.[71] Their opposite is ἀναιδείη (*anaideiē*), the word used by Achilles to describe Agamemnon's behaviour and often translated as 'shameless'. It expresses a demonstration or spectacle of wrong behaviour resulting from the inability to see what would be the correct or normative choice. Metaphorically, Achilles describes Agamemnon as 'clothed' or 'wrapped' in *anaideiē* (ἀναιδείην ἐπιειμένε, *Il.* 1.149). In a different metaphor, the slave girls in the *Odyssey* who disobey Penelope and Eurycleia and sleep with the suitors are said to 'walk on' *anaideiē* (ἀναιδείης ἐπέβησαν, *Od.* 22.424-25). It is a matter then of seeing and of proceeding, that is of insight into what is right, and of observing the appropriate behaviour. There is no question or doubt over the correct path or the proper insight. It is assumed that these are recognisable, so that any divergence from the proper code of conduct is viewed as blindness or a state of being blinded.[72]

Such blindness or delusion, ἄτη (*atē*), is the cause of the conflict between Agamemnon and Achilles. Agamemnon's explanation for taking away Achilles's *geras* is that Zeus, Moira, and Erinys cast *atē* onto his mind, *phrēn*

---

70. Cf. Linden 1992: 111, who assumes a regular procedure. For the public character of *timē* see Ulf 1990: 41-49.
71. See Erffa 1937: 4-43; Verdenius 1944: 47-60. Hooker 1987b: 121-25 assumes an original religious meaning.
72. See Erffa 1937: 8-9. For the metaphor of social blindness in tragedy see Flaig's analysis of *OT* (Flaig 1998). Here, correct behaviour is hidden rather than visible, as it is in epic.

(*Il.* 19.88).⁷³ Achilles, too, is subjected to this form of blinding. In his case *atē* is connected with the Litae, the goddesses of supplication, described as daughters of Zeus. When Achilles refuses to accept Agamemnon's compensatory gifts, Phoenix warns him of the Litae's power to invoke *atē* in pursuit of those who do not pay due respect to them (αἰδέσεται, *Il.* 9.507-12). Phoenix exhorts Achilles: 'You too must give to the daughters of Zeus, so that *timē* may attend you'.⁷⁴ Achilles's *timē* depends on his preparedness to supplicate the Litae. They represent Agamemnon's plea for Achilles's return and thus the correct behaviour that is under the control of public opinion.

The terms *aideisthai* and *aidōs* express the moral force that enables and governs Homeric society. *Aidōs* is found alongside *dikē* in Plato's *Protagoras* as an ordering principle of the society of the *polis* (Pl. *Prt.* 320c-323a). Understood as a public form of conscience,⁷⁵ *aidōs* also has a distinctly

73. Cf. *Il.* 9.115. Agamemnon admits that Nestor has laid bare his 'blind folly'. All the major conflicts in the epics are considered to be the results of *atē*. The Trojan war itself is blamed on the blindness of Paris in *Il.* 6.356 and 24.28, and on the blindness of Helen in *Od.* 4.261 and 23.223. I do not agree with Richard E. Doyle (1984: 14-16) who suggests that in this case *atē* must be interpreted as 'infatuation' rather than one of the other three meanings he gives for the word (blindness, folly, ruin). Even where *atē* takes effect between men and women, it still evokes the impossibility of perceiving the proper course of action—thus a state of blindness. See also Gruber 1963: 57-61 who shows how in all its different effects on people, *atē* is always a state of being blinded.
74. *Il.* 9.513-14: πόρε καὶ σὺ Διὸς κούρῃσιν ἕπεσθαι | τιμήν. It is debatable whether *timē* in this passage belongs to Achilles. I follow Andersen's rejection (1982: 7-13) of the widespread translation 'you also give, so the *timē* may attend the daughters of Zeus'. Anderson takes the accusative τιμήν to refer to the subject addressed with ϛὺ, which fits the context of the scene better. Also see Doyle (1984: 9-12) for whom the decisive contrast is between ἄτην [...] ἕπεσθαι (9.512) and ἕπεσθαι τιμήν (9.513-14).
75. Dihle (1985: 35) defines *aidōs* as 'kollektives, prospektives Gewissen'. Similarly, Erffa 1937: 36; Verdenius 1944: 50. Verdenius argues against a metaphysical meaning of *aidōs* as religious behaviour or metaphysical order and timeless possibility of the cosmos, proposed by Karl Kerenyi (1942: 88-99). For a different view see Cairns 1993: 139-46 who argues that it is not right to call *aidōs* 'a public form of conscience [...] as it suggests complete reliance on external standards. [...] Even where *aidōs* refers quite straightforwardly to anxiety occasioned by the prospect of others' disapproval, there is not absolute dichotomy between the internal and the external, the personal and the public' (141-42). According to Cairns public standards have to 'become part and parcel of the individual's character' (144). He prefers to understand *aidōs* as 'an internal state of conscience which is based on internal standards and an awareness of the values of society; these standards will have become internal to the individual precisely because of their uniformity and of the power of popular opinion to enforce them, and will have been imparted early in the process of socialization' (144). Cf. also Stahlmann 1997: 103 who argues: '"mit einnehmender Scheu (bzw. Scham) sprechen" heißt die Normen der Gemeinschaft kennen und in öffentlicher Rede für alle einsichtig und konsensfähig ausdrücken'.

visual component, as demonstrated in a proverb cited by Aristotle: 'shame belongs to the eyes' (τὸ ἑω ὀφθαλμοῖς εἶναι αἰδῷ, Arist. *Rhet.* 1384 a 35). By contrast with *anaideiē*, due respect for *aidōs* means avoidance of that which 'must not be seen' (a literal translation of α-ἰδείσθαι). Thus, *aideisthai* is best understood as a fear or shame of the judgement of others.[76] So when Hector says that he 'would be ashamed before the Trojans and their wives' (αἰδέομαι Τρῶας καὶ Τρῳάδας, *Il.* 6.442 and 22.105), this is because he knows that he needs to stand up in battle in order to retain *kleos* for himself and his family (*Il.* 6.446). For Penelope, a sense of shame about her husband's bed and the talk of the *dēmos* (εὐνήν τ' αἰδομένη πόσιος δήμοιό τε φῆμιν) means that she must continue to look after the house of Odysseus rather than accept one of the suitors (*Od.* 16.74-75).[77] The thought of *aidōs* also keeps soldiers in battle when they are ready to take flight (*Il.* 5.787; 8.228; 13.95; 16.422). When Agamemnon spurns on the Greeks by reminding them of the deeds of their ancestors we see Diomedes throw himself into battle (*Il.* 4.402) out of awe (αἰδεσθείς) for the awe-inducing king (βασιλῆος [...] αἰδοίοιο).[78]

In all these situations, *aideisthai*, a sense of awe or shame, is displayed in relation to others and out of a sense of obligations to others—be they the obligation of a warrior to his leader or a wife to her husband. The term *aideisthai* has a bearing on all those relationships contained by the idea of *philotēs*.[79] That sense of shame or awe never involves only the two people in the relationship but always includes the presence of an observing third party in the form of a community.

The conflict between Agamemnon and Achilles is less about achieving equilibrium between two leaders and more about the relationship between the leaders and the Greek army in front of whose eyes the argument is played out. This collective is not only the judge of Achilles's *timē*,[80] it is also said to be the sponsor of his *geras*. Both Achilles and Nestor say that it is the sons of the Achaeans who gave Briseis to Achilles (*Il.* 1.162 and

---

76. *Aidōs* also has a bodily meaning, denoting a person's private parts (χλαῖνάν τ' ἠδὲ χιτῶνα, τά τ' αἰδῶ ἀμφικαλύπτει, *Il.* 2.262; cf. also *Il.* 13.568; 22.75; *Od.* 22.474-77). Erffa (1937: 39) argues that the concrete meaning is derived from a more abstract meaning in the sense of 'awe'. Beil 1961: 51-64 views it as a term suggesting a fear of bodily exposure. On *phēmis* see now Gödde 2011.
77. For the connection between *aidōs* and *phēmis* see Verdenius 1944: 60; Greindl 1938: 82-86.
78. For further evidence see Erffa 1937: 5-43 and Cairns 1993: 68-146.
79. For evidence see Erffa 1937: 12-14.
80. For the relationship between *aidōs* and *timē* see Riedinger 1980: 62-79.

276; 1.278).⁸¹ It would be the same sons of the Achaeans who would have to compensate Agamemnon for the loss of Chryseïs (*Il.* 1.123 and 135). Agamemnon, named once by Achilles as the giver of his *geras* (*Il.* 9.367), is responsible for the distribution of *gera* when he hands them out to the 'best men' (*aristoi*), and to *basilees*, and when he distributes portions at the feast (*Il.* 9.334).⁸²

It has been suggested that granting *temenea* to *basilees* provides them with the wherewithal to hand out honours at feasts. Agamemnon fulfils this function at Troy—although here the origin of the natural resources is unclear:

πλεῖαί τοι οἴνου κλισίαι, τὸν νῆες Ἀχαιῶν
ἠμάτιαι Θρήκηθεν ἐπ' εὐρέα πόντον ἄγουσι
πᾶσά τοί ἐσθ' ὑποδεξίη, πολέεσσι δ' ἀνάσσεις.

Day by day Greeks ships bring wine to you over the broad seas from Thrace. Your huts are full of it; and as a ruler over many people (*polessi d' anasseis*), it is for you to offer hospitality (*Il.* 9.71-73, tr. Rieu).

With these words Nestor asks Agamemnon to offer up a feast for the council of elders so that they may offer advice and discuss the situation (*Il.* 9.69-70). It is not clear whether Agamemnon is in a position to host the feast because he can commandeer wine from the many people he rules over, or if he can use the many people he rules over in order to transport the resources from his *temenea*. The use of *anassein* certainly allows both possibilities. Elsewhere there is mention of a *xeinos*, a friend of Agamemnon's from Lemnos who is named as providing a delivery of wine. This wine, commandeered from abroad, is distributed by Agamemnon to the troops. They have to give some compensation in return (*Il.* 7.467-75), while the select circle of counsellors is honoured with the wine without being required to pay back compensation.

The term used for such honours at the feast is τίειν (*tiein*) or τίμαν (*timan*), denoting a visible distinction through special treatment of a

---

81. Cf. *Il.* 16.56: κούρην ἥν ἄρα μοι γέρας ἔξελον υἷες Ἀχαιῶν.
82. Évelyne Scheid-Tissinier argues—following Louis Gernet and Marcel Detienne—that the 'chef' represents the collective of the warriors (1994: 443-44). According to Bjørn Qviller (1981: 129) the distribution of booty by the leader denotes the beginning of exploitation. For the *dēmos* as sponsor see Carlier 1994: 152-54.

distinguished individual at the feast. Such special attention is usually earned through service in battle; when it is administered by a leader such as Agamemnon or Hector the term *tiein* is used. So Agamemnon is able to motivate the Cretan Idomeneus to fight with a reminder of *tiein* at the feast:

Ἰδομενεῦ περὶ μέν σε τίω Δαναῶν ταχυπώλων
ἠμὲν ἐνὶ πτολέμῳ ἠδ' ἀλλοίῳ ἐπὶ ἔργῳ
ἠδ' ἐν δαίθ', ὅτε πέρ τε γερούσιον αἴθοπα οἶνον
Ἀργείων οἳ ἄριστοι ἐνὶ κρητῆρι κέρωνται.
εἴ περ γάρ τ' ἄλλοι γε κάρη κομόωντες Ἀχαιοὶ
δαιτρὸν πίνωσιν, σὸν δὲ πλεῖον δέπας αἰεὶ
ἕστηχ', ὥς περ ἐμοί, πιέειν ὅτε θυμὸς ἀνώγοι.
ἀλλ' ὄρσευ πόλεμον δ' οἷος πάρος εὔχεαι εἶναι.

Idomeneus, of all my Greeks (*Danaoi*) with their swift horses, there is not one I honour more than you, on the battlefield, on other missions and at feasts for senior advisers when the Greek (*Argeioi*) leaders mix themselves sparkling wine. When the rest of the long-haired Greeks (*Achaioi*) have drunk up their portion, your cup stands full, like mine, to drink from as you wish. Off, then, into battle and be the man you have always said you were! (*Il.* 4.257-64; tr. Rieu).

The means for such special treatments of individuals—in this case the ever-full drinking cup—are provided by a group, not by a single individual. This is clear when Menelaus addresses his fellow warriors and reminds them that their wine comes from the people:

ὦ φίλοι Ἀργείων ἡγήτορες ἠδὲ μέδοντες
οἵ τε παρ' Ἀτρεΐδης Ἀγαμέμνονι καὶ Μενελάῳ
δήμια πίνουσιν καὶ σημαίνουσιν ἕκαστος
λαοῖς· ἐκ δὲ Διὸς τιμὴ καὶ κῦδος ὀπηδεῖ.

Friends (*philoi*), rulers and leaders of the Greeks (*Argeioi*)! All you who drink your wine at the public cost (*dēmia*) by the side of Agamemnon and Menelaus; who share in the command (*sēmainousin*) and derive your honour (*timē*) and glory (*kudos*) from Zeus (*Il.* 17.249-52, tr. Rieu).

Hector similarly refers to the Danaans as the sponsors of honours given to Diomedes in his taunting speech: 'Son of Tydeus, the Danaans with their swift horses would honour you (σε τίον Δαναοί) above all others with a seat of honour and portions of meat, and a full cup' (*Il.* 8.161-62). Defeat in battle will mean a loss of these honours: 'The Danaans will scorn you (σ' ἀτιμήσουσι)!' (*Il.* 8.163).

When Hector treats his fellow fighters with honours (*tiein*), he also has recourse to the means of the *dēmos* (*Il.* 18.300-1). Elsewhere, Hector spurs on his allies by letting them know that he is using up the resources of his own people to provide them with gifts and food (*Il.* 17.225-26). After Hector's death, when Priam denounces his sons as robbers of lambs and kids from their own people (ἐπιδήμιοι), he points to the goods Hector was able to claim from the *dēmos*, the animals available for slaughter at the feast (*Il.* 24.263). The point is that the remaining sons will not be able to repay the goods received from the people, the *dēmia*, with the kind of performance in battle of which Hector or Deïkoon, Aeneas's comrade, were capable. The Trojans honoured him like the sons of Priam because he always fought in the front ranks (τῖον, ἐπεὶ θοὸς ἔσκε μετὰ πρώτοισι μάχεσθαι, *Il.* 5.536).[83]

While *tiein* describes the distribution of public goods, *timan* is used to describe the honours due to a person who takes on the role of distributing these goods, which will range from special 'portions of honour' offered at the feast to pieces of land and its produce.[84] All this is offered in return for service in war as well as for leadership and judicial functions, as we have seen in connection with Agamemnon's offer. Only in the *Odyssey* do we find the portion of honour given at the feast to an individual described as *geras* (*Od.* 4.66)—and in one case the term is used ironically (*Od.* 20.297).

4.2.4. Honouring the basileus and the basileia

In Homeric epic, individuals to whom honours and attention are paid in the form of *timan* are always either of divine descent or in possession of

---

83. Qviller's suggestion (1981: 123) that the passage hints at a development of the reciprocal relationship into one of exploitation is not convincing.
84. This is expressed by the phrase θεὸς δ' ὣς τίετο δήμῳ: *Il.* 5.78 (the Trojan priest Hypsenor); 10.33 (Agamemnon); 11.58 (Aeneas); 13.218 (Thoas in Aetolia); 16.605 (the Trojan priest of Zeus, Laogonos); *Od.* 14.205 (the Cretan Castor). The phrase can be translated as 'he was honoured like a god with fat' (cf. δημός = fat) or 'he was honoured by the people as a god' (cf. δῆμος = people). For the first meaning see Paola Ceccarelli, Françoise Létoublon, and Martin Steinrück (1998: 47-58).

the title of *basileus* or its feminine form *basileia*.[85] This is true of Sarpedon and Glaucus (*Il.* 12.319; 16.660) as much as of Agamemnon, who is most frequently described as *basileus* in the *Iliad*.[86] After Achilles's withdrawal, Agamemnon announces that there will be others prepared to honour him (τιμήσουσι, *Il.* 1.175). In this case *timan* refers to service in battle, which Achilles has refused to give, although as a *basileus* himself he can expect it to be rendered to him by the Myrmidons (*Il.* 1.331; 16.211). Both *timan* and *tiein* are used of Achilles's relationship to his comrades, the Myrmidons. We find Patroclus, for instance, calling on the Myrmidons to honour Achilles (τιμήσομεν) and to fight on his behalf (*Il.* 16.271). Indirectly Odysseus is described as a *basileus*, whom the Phaeacians are expected to honour as though he were a god (θεὸν ὣς τιμήσουσιν, *Od.* 5.36; 23.339). His house is described as that of a godlike *basileus* (δόμον θείου βασιλῆος), and his features as resembling those of a *basileus* (δέμας βασιλῆϊ; *Od.* 16.335; 20.194). Of Arete we hear in the *Odyssey* that she is honoured (τετίμηται) by her children, her husband, and the people. In the case of the people, we are told (as with Sarpedon and Glaucus in the *Iliad*) that they view her as a god (θεὸν ὣς εἰσορόωντες, *Od.* 7.71). She too bears the title *basileia* (*Od.* 7.241; 11.345; 13.59).

In all these cases, the honours described by *timan* are paid by a collective: the group of comrades, the *hetairoi* and *philoi*, in the case of Achilles (*Il.* 16.269-70); unspecified 'others' (*alloi*) who are part of the army in Agamemnon's case (*Il.* 1.174); in Arete's case, the collective is the people, *laoi* (*Od.* 7.71). These *laoi* may denote the Phaeacian community in its entirety, or may refer to those men whose disputes she adjudicates elsewhere in the poem (ἀνδράσι νείκεα λύει, *Od.* 7.74). In that case the honour paid to her is in return for the judicial functions we have discussed in connection

---

85. Where this is not the case, the honoured individuals are backed by gods (e.g. Athena in the case of Deiphobus honoured (τιμήσασθαι, *Il.* 22.235) by Hector) or by *basilees* as in the case of the beggar Odysseus, when Telemachus asks whether Eurycleia has honoured him (ἐτιμήσασθ', *Od.* 20.129) or for the illegitimate son Odysseus pretends to be in his Cretan tale and who is honoured by his father (ἐτίμα, *Il.* 23.649). Nestor is honoured with a prize by Achilles (τετιμῆσθαι, *Il.* 23.649), and he has a particular connection to the gods, whom he can ask for grace on behalf of the sponsor of the prize. It is the gods who actually show honour to the older men (τιμῶσι, *Il.* 23.788). In Eumaeus, honoured like a son by Odysseus's mother, we have a true exception (ἐτίμα, *Il.* 23.788). In the *Iliad* the word *tiein* is used in the context of honouring sons-in-law (*Il.* 9.142), the offspring of concubines (*Il.* 13.176), shepherds (*Il.* 15.551), or suppliants (*Il.* 1.439).

86. For evidence see Carlier 1984: 142; 222-25 and Finsler 1906: 401-7.

with the offer made to Achilles by Agamemnon. This role is also mentioned in the praise of Penelope, when the disguised Odysseus compares her to a good king:

ὦ γύναι, οὐκ ἄν τίς σε βροτῶν ἐπ' ἀπείρονα γαῖαν
νεικέοι· ἦ γάρ σευ κλέος οὐρανὸν εὐρὺν ἱκάνει,
ὥς τέ τευ ἢ βασιλῆος ἀμύμονος, ὅς τε θεουδὴς
[ἀνδράσιν ἐν πολλοῖσι καὶ ἰφθίμοισιν ἀνάσσων]
εὐδικίας ἀνέχῃσι, φέρῃσι δὲ γαῖα μέλαινα
πυροὺς καὶ κριθάς, βρίθῃσι δὲ δένδρεα καρπῷ,
τίκτῃ δ' ἔμπεδα μῆλα, θάλασσα δὲ παρέχῃ ἰχθῦς
ἐξ εὐηγεσίης, ἀρετῶσι δὲ λαοὶ ὑπ' αὐτοῦ.

'My lady', answered the resourceful Odysseus, 'there is not a man in the wide world who could find fault with you. For your fame (*kleos*) has reached broad heaven itself, like that of some illustrious king (*basileus*), ruling (*anassōn*) a populous and mighty country with fear of the gods in his heart, and upholding justice (*eudikia*). As a result of his good leadership (*euēgesiē*), the dark soil yields its wheat and barley, the trees are laden with rope fruit, the sheep never fail to bear their lambs, nor the sea to provide its fish, and his people (*laoi*) prosper under him' (*Od.* 19.107–14; tr. Rieu).

Odysseus speaks here of the king's role in upholding justice (*eudikiai*) as well as of good rulership more generally (*euēgesiē*), both of which contribute to the prosperity of his people.[87] It fits with this model of rulership that Telemachus is also referred to as a *dikaspolos*, a judge, when Odysseus's mother in the underworld responds to her son's enquiry about the fate of his *geras* (*Od.* 11.186). Similarly, the twelve *basilēes* who collect contributions to the gifts for Odysseus from the Phaeacian *dēmos* (*Od.* 13.14) are referred to as counsellors (βουληφόροι).

These roles are also relevant in wartime, as we see when Odysseus refers to the good king's ability to lead and to judge when the army threatens to disband after the withdrawal of Achilles from battle. Inspired by Athena, Odysseus seizes Agamemnon's sceptre and urges the troops to return to

---

87. According to Christoph Ulf (1990: 100) εὐηγεσίη means the organisation of field work. Cobet (1981: 20) views the term more generally as collective responsibility and the king's role as helping to bring communities together.

the assembly and listen to Agamemnon, rather than incur his wrath, because 'the heart of god-reared kings is great, their honour is from Zeus (τιμὴ δ' ἐκ Διός ἐστι), and Zeus, who is wise in counsel, loves them (φιλεῖ δέ ἑ μητίετα Ζεύς)' (*Il.* 2.196-97). Having argued for subordination on the grounds of the power of Zeus and *timē*, Odysseus then moves on to invoke Agamemnon's position as *basileus* (*Il.* 2.203-6): 'We cannot all be leaders here (οὐ μέν πως πάντες βασιλεύσομεν), we Greeks, and a multitude of leaders is not a good thing (οὐκ ἀγαθὸν πολυκοιρανίη), let there be one *koiranos* only, one *basileus* to whom the son of crooked-counselled Cronos has given the sceptre and *themistes* so that he may rule (βασιλεύῃ).' While a *koiranos* is primarily a military leader, the terms *basileus* and *basileuein* refer to political leadership. When an individual is described as a *basileus*, this is frequently found in the context of political counselling.[88] Similarly, the verb *basileuein* is found in connection with assemblies (*Il.* 2.203 and 206) or linked to particular places.[89] It is at such named locations that decisions are taken, be that in the context of political assembly, by counsellors, or in the form of judgements in legal proceedings.[90] The exercise of such decision-making must be guaranteed by the gods. As we see in the passage just cited, *timē* is represented as having been granted by Zeus. Minos, for instance, who ruled (βασίλευε) in Knossos is said to confer with Zeus every nine years (*Od.* 19.178-79). The decision over who will rule at Ithaca also lies with Zeus, that is, in the lap of the gods (ταῦτα θεῶν ἐν γούνασι κεῖται, [...] Ἰθάκῃ βασιλεύσει, *Od.* 1.400-1).[91] In conclusion, then, I view *basileuein* as an act of decision-making that expresses the nonmaterial aspect of *timē*.

88. Cf. *Il.* 2.196 and 205 (Agamemnon); 2.54 (Nestor). Descat 1979: 232 and Cobet 1981: 13 interpret *basileus* as a term of political leadership, not as a term of personal rule. According to Drews (1982: 104-5) the term is linked with leadership. Carlier (1984: 143) translates the verb *basileuein* as 'régner'. According to him the *basilēes* were 'chefs héréditaires d'une communauté'. The term for military leadership is *koiranos*. See Finsler 1906: 331-32; Carlier 1984: 202; Ulf 1990: 88-89. According to Cobet (1981: 16-17) *koiranos* denotes the high-ranking position of the *basileus*.
89. *Il.* 6.425 (Plakos); 2.572 (Sikyon); *Od.* 1.401; 22.52-53 (Ithaca); 11.285 (Pylos); 19.179 (Knossos).
90. According to Telemachus it is not bad to 'rule' because goods come in and one becomes more honoured (οὐ μὲν γάρ τι κακὸν βασιλευέμεν αἶψά τέ οἱ δῶ | ἀφνειὸν πέλεται καὶ τιμηέστερος αὐτός, *Od.* 1.392-93). He remembers how his father Odysseus used to rule (ὅς ποτ' ἐν ὑμῖν | τοίσδεσσιν βασίλευε, *Od.* 2.46-47).
91. Telemachus would happily accept from Zeus the position of *basileus* at Ithaca, for which he is qualified by heredity and by his rhetorical ability (*Od.* 1.383-86; 390). The suitor Antinous strives to reign himself at Ithaca (βασιλεύοι αὐτός, *Od.* 22.52-53). For the symbolic meaning of the knees see ch. 4.3.

4.2.5. Themistes and the sceptre

The power to make decisions is symbolised by the sceptre, given by Zeus, and by the grant of *themistes*, perhaps best translated as 'customary rules'.[92] The sceptre conveys the right to speak, and it is also the means by which to say the correct or appropriate thing, in accordance with the *themistes*. Predominantly, sceptres are carried by *basilēes* and lawgivers (*Il.* 2.206; 9.99), but we also see this with priests such as Chryses or the prophet Teiresias, who speak on behalf of the gods (*Il.* 1.15; 28; 374; *Od.* 11.91), and indeed with any speaker in the assembly, such as a herald (*Il.* 10.328; 23.567) or Telemachus at Ithaca (*Od.* 2.37). In the situation discussed above, the significance of the decision is emphasised through a detailed account of the sceptre's provenance which, just like a hero's family tree, leads back to the gods:

> [...] ἀνὰ δὲ κρείων Ἀγαμέμνων
> ἔστη σκῆπτρον ἔχων τὸ μὲν Ἥφαιστος κάμε τεύχων.
> Ἥφαιστος μὲν δῶκε Διὶ Κρονίωνι ἄνακτι,
> αὐτὰρ ἄρα Ζεὺς δῶκε διακτόρῳ ἀργεϊφόντῃ
> Ἑρμείας δὲ ἄναξ δῶκεν Πέλοπι πληξίππῳ,
> αὐτὰρ ὃ αὖτε Πέλοψ δῶκ' Ἀτρέϊ ποιμένι λαῶν,
> Ἀτρεὺς δὲ θνῄσκων ἔλιπεν πολύαρνι Θυέστῃ,
> αὐτὰρ ὃ αὖτε Θυέστ' Ἀγαμέμνονι λεῖπε φορῆναι,
> πολλῇσιν νήσοισι καὶ Ἄργεϊ παντὶ ἀνάσσειν.

> [...] Lord Agamemnon rose holding his sceptre (*skēptron*), which Hephaestus himself had made. Hephaestus gave it to lord (*anax*) Zeus son of Cronos, and Zeus to Hermes, the guide (*diaktoros*) and slayer of Argus. Lord Hermes presented it to Pelops the great charioteer, and Pelops passed it on to Atreus, shepherd of the people (*laoi*). When Atreus died, he left it to Thyestes rich in flocks; and he in turn left it to Agamemnon to carry, to be a token of his lordship (*anassein*) over many islands and all Argos (*Il.* 2.100-8, tr. Rieu).

The human possessors of the sceptre are distinguished in this account through excellence in charioteering, wealth in flocks, and rulership over

---

92. Cf. *Il.* 9.97-99: πολλῶν | λαῶν ἐσσι ἄναξ καί τοι Ζεὺς ἐγγυάλιξε | ϛκῆπτρόν τ' ἠδὲ θέμιστας, ἵνά σφισι βουλεύῃσθα.

people and places—all of which are captured in the phrase 'shepherd of the people' and the term '*anassein*'. The transition from the human to the divine sphere is effected by the figure of Hermes, the guide of men and herds (*diaktoros*).[93]

The history of the sceptre's provenance suggests a world in which winning prestige in competitions and accumulating wealth and resources are key.[94] The *themistes*, on the other hand, stand for societal coherence. Responsibility for the latter lies with Themis, the personification of divine law or, as Rudolf Hirzel put it, of 'good counsel'.[95] Themis opens and closes the assemblies of gods and men (*Il.* 20.4; *Od.* 2.68-69), and she welcomes participants with a full cup (*Il.* 15.87). She ensures that there is balance between antagonists in the assembly and between strangers as well as between the living and the dead. It is *themis* to welcome a stranger and to grant him *xeinia* in the form of a meal or of gifts and *dōtinē*.[96] When someone dies, it is *themis* for women to shed tears (*Od.* 14.129-30), while it is also *themis* for men not to wash the dirt from their head until the dead have been cremated and the grave monument erected (*Il.* 23.44).[97] It is also *themis* that a son recognises and welcomes his father (*Od.* 11.451). In the warriors' assembly it is *themis* to persuade with words and to speak out in opposition (*Il.* 2.73; 9.33). Fundamentally, *themis* is connected with the coming together of men, hence *agora* and *themis* belong together (*Il.* 11.807). Ares, the god of war, does not therefore know what *themis* is (ὃς οὔ τινα οἶδε θέμιστα, *Il.* 5.761). Since *themis* affects many areas, there are

---

93. Eumaeus (*Od.* 15.319) calls him a guide (*diaktoros*), Priam, guided safely by Hermes to the camp of Achilles, refers to him as *hodoiporos* (traveller) (*Il.* 24.374). For more detail see ch. 5.1, n. 63.
94. The sceptre was interpreted as a sign of primitive sacral kingship. Cf. e.g. Mondi 1980 (following the tradition of J. G. Frazer) and Vernant 1962. Fanta 1882: 46-49 and Köstler 1950: 9 understood the sceptre as symbol of a divinely sanctioned kingship and as a sign of state power. This tradition is taken up again by Carlier 1984: 191, who characterises the sceptre as a sign of monarchic authority. According to Finsler 1906: 405-8 and Nilsson 1927: 27 the sceptre denotes military leadership or hereditary kingship. More convincingly is Bethe 1931: 22. He hints at the practical use of the sceptre as the sign of the speaker in the assembly, which accounts for its frequent use by the *basilēes*, who are qualified by their rhetorical ability. For a similar argument see Qviller 1981: 119 and Easterling 1989: 115.
95. Hirzel 1907: 17-21. Cf. also Köstler 1950: 9-13. According to Yamagata 1994: 76, 'θέμις is always a public matter'.
96. *Xeinia*: *Il.* 11.779; *Od.* 24.286; *dotinē*: *Od.* 9.268; 24.286. See also *Od.* 14.56.
97. Cf. *Il.* 16.796. Here *themis* means the recognition of the moment of dying, associated with the loss of gleam from the head or hair.

a range of *themistes* which lawgivers must be aware of, but which they may also at times pervert (*Il.* 1.238; 16.387). On the shield of Achilles, we find a visual component of the process. In the court scene, the term used to describe the wise man who adjudicates between the two quarrelling parties is ἵστωρ (*istōr*)—that is, translated literally, one who is able to see, ἰδεῖν (*idein*) or recognise what is right, or *themis* (*Il.* 18.501).[98]

As divine law, as social norms, or as mere 'décisions politiques', the *themistes* do not represent an abstract legal system.[99] In my opinion, the *themistes* offer a view of human society as it could actually be seen on decorated objects. This is not, however, to be understood in a figurative sense. Given my reflections on the charisma of images in the previous chapter, we may assume that such decorated objects helped to remember social norms and rules. The shine-adjective *liparos*, associated with Themis in Hesiod's *Theogony*, suggests this too. In the *Theogony* (135 and 901), Themis is the mother of the Moirae and of the personifications of Order (Eunomia), Justice (Dike), and Peace (Eirene). The notion that the future of Ithaca's rule lies in the lap of the gods (literally, 'on the knees of the gods') suggests a connection to wool, the raw material from which the textile images we have already discussed are created, because wool is laid out on the knees for carding before it is spun into the thread of life by the Moirae, the daughters of Zeus and Themis.[100]

In the *Iliad* we find the order of the cosmos represented in metalwork on the shield of Achilles. In later literature, we find descriptions of the representation of such symbolic worlds on textile objects. The images on Jason's cloak in Apollonius's *Argonautica* are a good Hellenistic example.[101] Later still, an epigram from the Greek Anthology speaks of a tapestry that represents the Roman Empire given to the emperor Caligula by the wife

---

98. For this interpretation of ἵστωρ see Köstler 1950: 68. For the relationship between the verbs of seeing and recognition see Bechert 1964: 22.
99. See Carlier 1984: 193-94 who argues against the meaning of *themistes* as divine laws. According to him the decisions of the *basilēes* can be interpreted as inspired by the gods, but they cannot be understood as divine laws because the *basilēes* did not see themselves as gods. He interprets the *themistes* as political and legal decisions as well as social customs ('les règles de la vie en société'). For a similar argument see Hirzel (1907: 21), who interpreted the *themistes* as decrees or counsels but not as laws. His view is that Agamemnon's power over the *themistes* suggests the fact that he has foresight such as befits a leader, which inspires him to know what must be done.
100. Cf. *Il.* 17.514; 20.535; *Od.* 1.267; 16.129. For the meaning of this phrase see Onians 1989: 303. See also ch. 4.2, n. 150.
101. Levin 1970: 21-32; Shapiro 1980: 287.

of king Herod (*Anthologia Graeca* IX 778). We know of similar tapestries from other cultures: Tibetan temples are decorated to this day with Thangkas, paintings on silk, which depict scenes from the life of the Buddha.[102] Medieval and Early Modern Europe prized tapestries depicting historical and religious motifs often created by groups of women in convents.[103] Garments given as offerings to the dead and to the gods must have had similar functions. Athens is a particularly important example of the significance attached to the images depicted on such garments, since in classical Athens it was the council's business to approve the pattern for the robe offered to Athena.[104]

4.2.6. The distribution of *timē* and the character of Homeric kingship

The symbolic meaning of the *themistes* may also offer an explanation for the differentiation in the distribution of *timē* amongst the Homeric *basilēes*. We see Nestor, for example, call on Agamemnon to leave Brisëis to Achilles but at the same time also place some limitations on Achilles:

> μήτε σὺ Πηλείδη 'θελ' ἐριζέμεναι βασιλῆϊ
> ἀντιβίην, ἐπεὶ οὔ ποθ' ὁμοίης ἔμμορε τιμῆς
> σκηπτοῦχος βασιλεύς, ᾧ τε Ζεὺς κῦδος ἔδωκεν.
> εἰ δὲ σὺ καρτερός ἐσσι θεὰ δέ σε γείνατο μήτηρ,
> ἀλλ' ὅ γε φέρτερός ἐστιν ἐπεὶ πλεόνεσσιν ἀνάσσει.

> And you, Achilles, give up your desire to cross swords with your leader (*basileus*). Through the success (*kudos*) he derives from Zeus, a leader (*basileus*) who holds the sceptre of power has more claim to our respect (*timē*) than anyone else. Even if you, with a goddess for mother, are the better fighter (*karteros*), yet Agamemnon is your superior since he rules (*anassei*) more people (*Il.* 1.277-81, tr. adapted from Rieu).

According to Nestor, there are three different ways to gain *timē*: through service in war as indicated by the description of Achilles as *karteros* (strong), through divine ancestry, and through the number of

---

102. Lavizzari-Raeuber 1989: 142.
103. Wunder 1994: 324-54.
104. [Arist.] *Ath. Pol.* 49 and 60; Eur. *Hec.* 466-474; Eur. *IT* 218-24. For offering the robe to the gods see Barber 1992: 103-17 and now Brøns 2017.

people under one's command—for which the word *anassein* is used here. Nestor is here measuring Achilles's *timē* against Agamemnon's and pointing out the two leaders' different circumstances. This has led some scholars to assume that there are competing ways to gain *timē* when in fact these are merely three aspects of the same rationale. While it is true that service in battle is an essential precondition for gaining the material side of *timē*, it is also true that the number of those under a leader's command can enhance the potential for success in battle—the *kudos* mentioned by Nestor. This means that Agamemnon's *timē* must be greater. The mention of the sceptre, on the other hand, points to the nonmaterial side of *timē*, the possession of divine wisdom that enables good judgement. This is needed in wartime too. Menelaus, called *basileuteros*, addresses this when he calls upon his fellow warlords to join in battle, reminding them of the contributions made by their people, and of their power to command (σημαίνουσιν) their people, and also emphasising that their *timē* and their *kudos* stem from Zeus (*Il.* 10.239; 17.249–51). In the midst of battle, divine wisdom is needed in order to succeed. This is the point made by Sthenelus in his rebuttal of Agamemnon's attempt to inspire him and Diomedes to fight by citing the example of their ancestors: 'Do not say our fathers were equal to us in *timē*' (τῶ μή μοι πατέρας ποθ' ὁμοίη ἔνθεο τιμῇ, *Il.* 4.410). Sthenelus sees himself as a better fighter than those of his father's generation and also as better guided by the support of Zeus and signs sent by the gods (*Il.* 4.404–8).

The mention of the divinity of Achilles's mother as the third aspect of his *timē* need not necessarily suggest that *timē* is hereditary, especially as there is no instance of direct transfer of *timē* from a father to a son. We do find it in the hands of sons whose fathers are also in possession of *timē*.[105] But when it is handed from one generation to the next, then this takes place—as we have seen in the case of Bellerophon—only through marriage.[106] For Christoph Ulf, this is a reason to doubt the hereditary character of *timē* and to assume that in the case of the dispute over the *timē* of Achilles, there is a failure of rational arguments.[107] Pierre Carlier, on the other hand, suspects that 'dignité royale' (which he links to *geras* rather than *timē*) was

---

105. Peleus, the father of Achilles, is still in possession of the *timē*, as the shadow of Achilles considers in the underworld. *Od.* 11.495 and 503. In the *Iliad* Achilles offers half of his *timē* to his teacher Phoenix (*Il.* 9.616).
106. See Bellerophon, the ancestor of the Lycian *basilēes* Glaucus and Sarpedon. *Il.* 6.192–195.
107. Ulf 1990: 10–11, 80.

'le privilège collectif de la maison royale'.[108] This is not altogether wrong, except that the royal house is constituted by the bond between the couple and by the different groups that support them and are responsible for the production of the goods and services connected to them. The word *tiein* describes not only the relationship between a leader and his troops or a master and his servants but also that between a mistress, called a *basileia*, and her serving women.[109]

In the *Odyssey*, the title *basileia* is given to Arete and Penelope, and to Tyro, the mother of Neleus (*Od.* 11.258). Arete is seen as *basileia* from the point of view of Nausicaa, Odysseus, and the *basilēes* (*Od.* 6.115; 7.241; 11.345; 13.59), while Penelope is seen as *basileia* by the suitors, by Eumaeus, and by Medon, the herald (*Od.* 4.770 and 697; 16.332 and 337; 17.370 and 583; 18.314 and 351; 21.275; 23.149). In the *Iliad*, high-ranking women are always called *potnia*, never *basileia*.[110] Usually, this is from the point of view of their children, or with respect to their children, in the context of mourning or lamentation (Hecuba: *Il.* 22.341 and 352; 24.70; Thetis: 18.35 and 70; 24.126; mother of Socus: 11.452; mother of Deiphobus: 22.239; Andromache: 6.471; Althaea: 9.591 and 584).[111] Some women are, however, said to rule (*basileuein*). In the *Iliad*, the mother of Andromache is said to have ruled in Plakos (ἣ βασίλευεν ὑπὸ Πλάκῳ ὑληέσσῃ, *Il.* 6.425). In the *Odyssey*, Chloris, the mother of Nestor, is said to rule in Pylos (ἡ δὲ Πύλου βασίλευε, *Od.* 11.285).[112] There are six more individuals who are also

---

108. Carlier 1984: 190. He argues that birth qualifies to rule (*basileuein*) everywhere. The heroes lost their kingdom and gained a new one through marriage.
109. Together with Telemachus, Odysseus wants to prove which of his *dmōes andrōn* had esteemed or dishonoured him: καί κέ τεο δμώων ἀνδρῶν ἔτι πειρηθεῖμεν, | ἠμὲν ὅ πού τις νῶϊ τίει καὶ δείδιε θυμῷ, | ἠδ' ὅτις οὐκ ἀλέγει, σὲ δ' ἀτιμᾷ τοῖον ἐόντα (*Od.* 16.305–307). While still disguised as the beggar, Odysseus orders the handmaids, the *dmōiai gynaikes*, to follow their honoured *basileia* (αἰδοίη βασίλεια) to her rooms and see to their work (*Od.* 18.314). Eurycleia reports that in all there were twelve women, taught to work by herself and Penelope, who did not honour either her or Penelope: οὔτ' ἐμὲ τίουσαι οὔτ' αὐτὴν Πηνελόπειαν (*Od.* 22.425). For discussion of this passage see Wagner-Hasel 1988.
110. Mothers in the *Odyssey* are also called *potnia*: *Od.* 6.30 and 154 (Arete); 15.385 (mother of Eumaeus); 18.5 (mother of Arneus); 19.462; 11.180 and 215; 24.333 (Penelope). Elsewhere *potnia* refers to goddesses: Athena (*Il.* 6.305), Circe and Calypso (*Od.* 8.448; 1.14), especially Hera (*Il.* 8.472; *Od.* 4.513, etc.).
111. Hiller 1987: 350 thinks it an old Mycenaean title. According to Rehak (1995) the *potnia* ruled at Pylos; Maran and Stavrianopoulou (2007) assume that the *potnia* shared the throne with a *potnios anēr*. Havelock 1978: 95 n. 12 only sees *potniai* as housewives.
112. Later commentators derive *basileuein* from the position of Neleus (Eustath. p. 1685.61; Paus. 9.36.8).

said to *basileuein*: Agamemnon, Adrastus in Sikyon, Odysseus, Minos, and Eurymedon, an ancestor of Alcinous and Arete who is said to have been king over the giants (*Od.* 7.59), and finally, Achilles.

This participation in rulership and honour would suggest that *timē* was distributed between the genders, and that the female part of the *timē* of men, required for their proper exercise of rulership, was provided by their wives or their mothers.

We find such a gender-specific distribution of *timē* in the household of Alcinous and Arete, where it corresponds to the symbolism of the sceptre and *themistes* discussed above. We have already seen that Arete is seen as a god by the people.[113] The Phaeacian *dēmos* listen (*akouen*) to Alcinous like a god (θεοῦ δ' ὣς δῆμος ἄκουεν, *Od.* 7.11). This gender-specific differentiation also applies to the distribution of *timē* in Phaeacia. When Odysseus has completed his tale, Arete is the first to speak, and she judges the stranger's inner and outer appearance, his *eidos* and his *phrēn*:

> Φαίηκες, πῶς ὔμμιν ἀνὴρ ὅδε φαίνεται εἶναι
> εἶδός τε μέγεθός τε ἰδὲ φρένας ἔνδον ἐΐσας;
> ξεῖνος δ' αὖτ' ἐμός ἐστιν, ἕκαστος δ' ἔμμορε τιμῆς.

> Phaeacians! How does this man seem to you in his appearance (*eidos*), his stature, and the inner workings of his mind (*phrēn*)? He is my guest, but each of you has a share of *timē* (*Od.* 11.336–38).[114]

After this, the queen calls on the collected *basilēes* not to send Odysseus off without gifts:

> τῶ μὴ ἐπειγόμενοι ἀποπέμπετε μηδὲ τὰ δῶρα
> οὕτω χρηΐζοντι κολούετε· πολλὰ γὰρ ὑμῖν
> κτήματ' ἐνὶ μεγάροισι θεῶν ἰότητι κέονται,

---

113. *Od.* 7.71-2: [...] οἵ μίν ῥα θεὸν ὣς εἰσορόωντες | δειδέχαται μύθοισιν, ὅτε στείχῃσ' ἀνὰ ἄστυ. Besides this, the phrase is also used in the context of military (Sarpedon und Glaukos: *Il.* 12.312;) or rhetorical ability (*Od.* 8.167-83). See also *Od.* 15.520 (Eurymachos). Cf. Bechert 1964, vol. 2: 414-16.
114. Ulf 1990: 4 misses the point when he argues that everybody, even a stranger or a beggar, is in the possession of *timē*.

So do not send him on his way with undue haste, nor stint your generosity to one who stands in such need. For the gods have filled your homes with riches (*Od.* 11.339-41, tr. Rieu).

The final judgment is then spoken by the aged Echeneus, who confirms:

οὐ μὰν ἥμιν ἀπὸ σκοποῦ οὐδ' ἀπὸ δόξης μυθεῖται βασίλεια περίφρων,

The wise queen has not spoken against our own views (*Od.* 11.344-45).

He asks the other *basilēes* to go along with the queen's request (ἀλλὰ πίθεσθε, *Od.* 11.345), but he also immediately gives the power of both word (*epos*) and deed (*ergon*) to Alcinous (Ἀλκινόου δ' ἐκ τοῦδ' ἔχεται ἔργον τε ἔπος τε, *Od.* 11.346). Amongst the Phaeacians, who listen to Alcinous as to a god, the king's word is command. And so it is Alcinous who sees to Odysseus's safe passage—a task which he sees as exclusively male:

πομπὴ δ' ἄνδρεσσι μελήσει
πᾶσι, μάλιστα δ' ἐμοί· τοῦ γὰρ κράτος ἔστ' ἐνὶ δήμῳ.

The passage shall be men's business, all men's, but most of all mine, since mine is the *kratos* in the *dēmos* (*Od.* 11.352-53).

The interplay between *basileia*, *basileus*, and the assembled *basilēes* in this situation clarifies the different aspects on which the possession of *timē* is based.[115] Judgement through sight is the *basileia*'s business, while the implementation of the judgement is up to the *basileus*, who is in charge of directing through speech (*epos*). Both need to be affirmed by the other *basilēes* represented by Echeneus.[116] On a different occasion we find the

---

115. See *Od.* 6.289-315; 7.139-71. Here Nausicaa first refers Odysseus to Arete, whom he should ask for hospitality. Eventually it is Alcinous who leads the stranger from the hearth to his seat, after Echeneus asks for the king's counsel.
116. See Ruzé 1989: 216 and 222-23 who stresses the importance of the agreement of the Phaeacian *basilēes*. The consensual manner of the king's decision-making is discussed by Flaig 1994: 13-31 and Schulz 2011: 73 who neglect the role of the queen. Most scholars interpret the action of Alcinous as an attempt to put Arete back in her place (see e.g. Clark 2001: 346) and do not see the interaction

inclusion of the *dēmos* and the *laoi*, the Phaeacian community (*Od.* 8.1-44). Here too the sceptre, carried by all the Phaeacian *basilēes*, symbolises their power to give direction, as we see when Alcinous addresses them as 'sceptre-bearing *basilēes*' (σκηπτοῦχοι βασιλῆες, *Od.* 8.40-41).

In the description of the provenance of Agamemnon's sceptre, we saw a clear indication of the fields of influence and authority connected with it: rule over individuals (contained in the metaphor of the shepherd of people), ownership of herds and flocks, and possession of land and its resources, islands, and named places. In Alcinous's case, his authority is over the granting of safe passage across the sea, the sphere granted as *timē* to Poseidon (*Il.* 15.189-90). Arete's evaluation by sight suggests to me an authority over the social aspects of 'safe passage'. She is able to recognise a stranger's background and social network by evaluating the clothing that lends him his outward appearance (*eidos*). She also has knowledge of the correct patterns of gift-giving for guests, as it is she who calls on the Phaeacians to offer gifts.

A second hospitality scene helps to confirm the gender-specific distribution of competencies between evaluation by sight and directive speech. When Telemachus arrives at Sparta, it is once again the female partner in the hosting couple, Helen, who identifies the guest and recognises Telemachus as the son of Odysseus (*Od.* 4.138-46). Penelope displays a similar ability to judge by sight when she welcomes the disguised Odysseus, although at Ithaca there is no one to grant safe passage and gifts, as Penelope points out in answer to the stranger's prophecy:

αἲ γὰρ τοῦτο, ξεῖνε, ἔπος τετελεσμένον εἴη
τῷ κε τάχα γνοίης φιλότητά τε πολλά τε δῶρα
ἐξ ἐμεῦ, ὡς ἄν τίς σε συναντόμενος μακαρίζοι.
ἀλλά μοι ὧδ' ἀνὰ θυμὸν ὀΐεται, ὡς ἔσεταί περ·
οὔτ' Ὀδυσεὺς ἔτι οἶκον ἐλεύσεται, οὔτε σὺ πομπῆς
τεύξῃ, ἐπεὶ οὐ τοῖοι σημάντορές εἰσ' ἐνὶ οἴκῳ,
οἷος Ὀδυσσεὺς ἔσκε μετ' ἀνδράσιν, εἴ ποτ' ἔην γε,
ξείνους αἰδοίους ἀποπεμπέμεν ἠδὲ δέχεσθαι.

---

between the couple, as I have argued in Wagner-Hasel 1997. See now Canevaro (2018: 58) who has taken up the argument in her study on *Women of Substance. Homeric Epos, Objects, Gender, Agency*: 'Arete and Alcinous are working together towards the same goal, Arete coming up with the idea and Alcinous using his way to validate it.'

Friend (*xeinos*), may what you say (*epos*) prove true! If it does, you will soon receive from me such friendship (*philotēs*) and generosity (*polla te dōra*) that anyone who meets you will call you a fortunate man. But what my heart forebodes is this, and this is how it will be. Odysseus will not come home nor will you secure your passage (*pompē*) from here; for we have no leaders (*sēmantores*) of men like Odysseus (if ever there was such a man), to receive strangers (*xeinoi*) with proper respect and send them on their way (*Od.* 19.309–16, tr. Rieu).

Here, too, safe passage or convoy (*pompē*) is men's business, and it requires the presence of those who can give orders, σημάντορες (*sēmantores*). The absence of masters does not stop Penelope giving her guest such goods, as she is in charge of blankets for his bed and the promise of clothing (*Od.* 19.317–22).[117] Her granting of these is described with the same words used of the honours paid to warriors at the feast: *tiein* and *timan*.[118]

This literary presentation of the female power of decision-making does not appear to be an exception. A Corinthian *kratēr* of around 560 BCE depicts the Greek envoys to Troy wanting to negotiate the return of Helen. Their counterpart in these negotiations is not Priam, or one of the elders, but the Trojan priestess Theano with two of her companions. According to

---

117. The role of the *sēmantores* is discussed by Cobet 1981: 18 and Winkler 1990: 152. On Penelope's authority in this scene see Chaston 2002: 13: 'She cannot provide an escort to her guest as Odysseus would [...] but she can bestow the hospitality of bed, bath, and meal [...]'.
118. See Telemachus, who asks the old Eurycleia, whether the guest was treated well (*etimēsasth'*) with bed and food in the house (μαῖα φίλη, πῶς ξεῖνον ἐτιμήσασθ' ἐνὶ οἴκῳ | εὐνῇ καὶ σίτῳ, *Od.* 20.129), for he is afraid that Penelope would honour (*tiei*) a person of lower status and dishonour a high-ranking person (*atimēsaso*). Eurycleia gives a list of the food and clothing which she had wanted to give to the guest but which were refused by him (*Od.* 20.142–44). On the other side the beggar's poor clothing could be the reason for dishonouring the guest, as Odysseus argues (νῦν δέ μ' ἀτιμάζουσι κακὰ χροΐ εἵματ' ἔχοντα, *Od.* 14.506; κακὰ δὲ χροΐ εἵματα εἶμαι, | τοὔνεκ' ἀτιμάζει με καὶ οὔ πώ φησι τὸν εἶναι, 23.115–16). In fact, his worry is unfounded: Penelope promises him beautiful clothing, *heimata kala*, a *chlaina*, and a *chitōn* (*Od.* 17.550) in the event that his prediction should come true. Dressed in these, he would be able to ask for bread in the *dēmos* (*Od.* 17.557–59). Penelope also wants to reward his victory in the contest with clothing as well as arms and an escort (*Od.* 21.338–42). Similarly, Telemachus asks his companion Peraeus to honour (*tiemen*) the seer Theoclymenus (*Od.* 15.543 = 17.56). Bellerophon is honoured (*tiein*) by the Lycian king with a nine-day long feast (*Il.* 6.173).

Sarah Morris, this representation corresponds to the cultic origin of positions of rank in early Greece.[119]

While the women in the *Odyssey* are in charge of welcoming strangers and providing them with textile gifts, the *Iliad*'s high-ranking women are in charge of funeral arrangements. Such arrangements are always made by mothers, *potniai mētēres*, whose own status is decisive for the degree of *timē* owed to their dead sons. In the conflict over the proper burial of Hector, we find Achilles's divine mother once again to be a key factor in the measuring of *timē*. According to Hera, it is not right that Achilles, the son of a goddess raised by Hera herself, should be considered by Zeus as equal with Hector in *timē*. Hector, she argues, was fed at only a mortal woman's breast (*Il.* 24.57–60). She will not therefore permit the gods to take Hector's corpse away and protect it from further abuse by Achilles. Zeus confirms that indeed Hector and Achilles are not equals in *timē* (οὐ μὲν γὰρ τιμή γε μί' ἔσσεται, *Il.* 24.66), but he nonetheless arranges the ransoming of the body on the grounds that Hector always paid the due *geras* to the gods at sacrificial feasts (*Il.* 24.70). Zeus negotiates this with Thetis, whose *philotēs* and *aidōs* he wishes to preserve (*Il.* 24.111). When Thetis persuades her son to accept the compensatory gifts, these consist partly of textile goods (*peploi, chlainai, tapētes, pharea,* and *chitōnes*) and partly of metal objects such as tripods, cauldrons, a drinking cup, and gold (*Il.* 24.229–35). Textile goods, which touch upon the *timē* of women, thus make up half of Achilles's greater *timē* in this exchange.[120]

The epics present us with a plurality of uses of the term *basileus*, corresponding to a range of different spheres of influence and areas of responsibility; this variation has supported the idea that Homeric epic presents a shift from monarchy to forms of aristocratic rule.[121] However, this is not an adequate interpretation. The title of *basileus* denotes persons assembling in order to take decisions; only in wartime does it become necessary to decide who amongst the *basilēes* is the most powerful, that is, *basileutatos*.[122] In both conflict situations in the assembly in the Greek camp outside

---

119. Morris 2003: 15.
120. Achilles has a trunk full of textiles, which Thetis has given him. He takes the pieces needed for making up his guests' beds from this. *Il.* 16.221–24; 24.643–46.
121. See Barceló 1993: 72–74, for whom the *basilēes* of the *Odyssey* are simply landed gentry, and Ruzé 1989: 211–23, who attempts to place them into a hierarchy between *archontes* and tyrants.
122. See Ulf 1990: 85–98. The special situation is also stressed by Ruzé 1989: 215 and Carlier 1984: 144. Carlier supposes that Agamemnon is seen as the *plus noble* because of his wealth and the number of ships and at last because of the origin of his sceptre.

Troy, that person is Agamemnon to whom the warriors are all bound by oath.¹²³ As Erich Bethe argued back in 1931, when he rejected contemporary ideas about feudal kingship, Agamemnon's superior power in these instances need not imply a form of *Großkönigtum*.¹²⁴ In effect, Agamemnon only temporarily holds the high command that would ordinarily be shared between the *basilēes* who make up the council. Similarly, when the seer Theoclymenus refers to the *genos* of Odysseus as *basileuteron* (*Od.* 15.533), this is not a reminiscence of a past *Großkönigtum* but instead suggests the restoration of the former position of Odysseus's house—or possibly anticipates the Peisistratid tyranny and its alleged sponsorship of the edition of the Homeric epics.¹²⁵

The divine provenance of *timē* and of the symbols of the power or the *basileus*, the sceptre and *themistes*, just like the divine provenance of *charis*, appear to suggest that positions of power are transcendent and eternal. However, the presence of a community in charge of the distribution and evaluation of *timē* implies that positions of power encompassed by *timai* remain connected to social controls.

Yet the *Iliad* tells us that divine *timē* must always be greater than human (*Il.* 9.469). This makes sense, since divine *timē* represents the principle according to which *timē* is distributed among humans.¹²⁶ Thus the distribution of *timē* amongst the Phaeacians, as spoken of by Arete, follows the model suggested by Poseidon in *Iliad* 15 when he speaks of the distribution of *timē* between the three sons of Cronos: 'Each has his portion of *timē*' (ἕκαστος δ' ἔμμορε τιμῆς, *Il.* 15.189). This *timē* consists of control over the three domains:

---

123. *Il.* 2.206; 9.69. Cf. the use of the comparative *basileuteros* for Agamemnon (*Il.* 9.160). Besides this the comparative is only used for his brother Menelaus (*Il.* 10.239) and for the future son-in-law of Agamemnon (*Il.* 9.392).
124. Bethe 1931: 223.
125. Carlier 1984: 214 sees aspects of an *idéologie tyrannique*. On this argument see Svenbro 1984: 49–63. For the imitation of Odysseus by Peisistratus see Blok 2000. Cf. also note 44 in my introductory remarks.
126. There is no scholarly consensus on the role of the gods in epic narrative. There are those who view the gods as mere poetic devices whose actions serve as a foil to human action (see Bremmer 1987: 31–46), and those who argue that epic needs the gods because humans were not thought to have free will (see Kullmann 1956 and Erbse 1986). Graf (1991: 331–64) offers a good survey of the scholarly field. My position here is based only on examination of the text itself, and my focus is on the role of the gods with respect to gifts and giving. In the tradition of Weber, Durkheim and Geertz, I do see the gods in epic as embodying human principles and central social values rather than confining them to the sphere of the irrational and the unreal. See Kippenberg 1971: 54–82, esp. 59–63; 1997.

ἤτοι ἐγὼν ἔλαχον πολιὴν ἅλα ναιέμεν αἰεὶ
παλλομένων, Ἀΐδης δ' ἔλαχε ζόφον ἠερόεντα,
Ζεὺς δ' ἔλαχ' οὐρανὸν εὐρὺν ἐν αἰθέρι καὶ νεφέλῃσι
γαῖα δ' ἔτι ξυνὴ πάντων καὶ μακρὸς Ὄλυμπος.

We cast lots, and I received the grey sea as my inalienable realm, Hades drew the darkness below and Zeus was allotted the broad sky in the upper air among the clouds. But the earth was left common to all of us, and high Olympus too (*Il.* 15.190-93, tr. Rieu).

Poseidon's point here is to reject Zeus's claim to sole rulership and to demand to be equal in honour (ὁμότιμον, *Il.* 15.186). This separation of the domains is seen by some as a borrowing from Akkadian epic and, therefore, as belonging to a comparatively younger version of the *Iliad*, since it appears to contradict the usual separation of the cosmos into heaven, earth, and underworld.[127] The fact that the passage addresses the distribution of divine *timē* distinguishes it from other passages involving the cosmic domains, which are usually connected to sacrifice; thus it is possible that the variation is due to the context, although this does not exclude Ancient Near Eastern influence.[128] Taken against the background of the distribution of *timē* amongst men within the poem, the divine distribution of *timē* certainly seems coherent.

The presentation of the cosmos as divided into separate domains corresponds to the way in which *timē* amongst humans is distributed into different spheres and areas of responsibility. In Poseidon's account we find that the unmovable elements, earth and Mount Olympus, belong to all. The waters of the sea, and the light and darkness of the sky, however, are subject to individual deities, so that the three gods are not in charge of specific territories but of permeable spaces. This may be understood in cosmological as well as in topographical terms. The darkness allotted as the *timē* of Hades suggests the loss of light associated with death in Greek thought,[129] while

---

127. See Burkert 1984: 87-88.
128. *Il.* 3.277-279 (Helios, Gaia, rivers, shadow of the dead); *Il.* 15.36-40 (water of the Styx, Gaia, Ouranos); *Il.* 18.483 (Gaia, Ouranos, Thalassa, Helios, Selene); *Od.* 5.184 (Gaia, Ouranos, water of the Styx). Cf. also Hes. *Theog.* 736 (Ge, Tartaros, Thalassa, Ouranos); similar: 839-49.
129. This may be a possible explanation for the name 'Hades' = *a-ides*. See Griffin 1984: 90, n. 25; Vermeule, 1979: 29. Death itself is imagined as a dark cloud in the epics: *melan nephos* (*Il.* 5.68; 16.350 and 502; *Od.* 4.180).

Zeus's rule over the sky contains his responsibility for the light of life.[130] The grey colour of the sea represents an intermediate stage inhabited by the nymph Leucothea. She gives Odysseus the veil which enables his passage from the world of the immortals to that of mortals (*Od.* 5.367). As we shall see, the *potniai mētēres* with their shrouds enable the reverse version of this transition during the burial rituals. As we already know, responsibility for safe passage across land and sea is the responsibility of *basilēes* in Homeric epic. Our examination has also shown that the granting of safe passage, both spatial and social, is a nonmaterial part of *timē*, shared between *basileus* and *basileia* at Phaeacia. The divine distribution of *timai* as outlined by Poseidon reflects the two aspects of safe passage, which correspond to two key spheres of power: social or generative and spatial power.

To encapsulate Homeric rulership in one term, I want to propose the word *Geleitherrschaft*, that is, rule over safe passage or convoy ('Geleit'). My investigation so far has shown that control over safe passage is the defining element of Homeric rulership, which subsumes all the aspects of *timē* we have determined without supposing any hierarchy between them. This *timē* is not the honour of kings, nor is it the respect shared by all, be they beggars or high-status individuals. This *timē* belongs only to those who have control over safe passage in space and those who mediate between the human and the divine sphere: *basilēes* in charge of taking decisions according to divine wisdom and collecting goods in return; the *basileia* who welcomes strangers and makes goods available to them; the *potnia mētēr* who—as we shall see—conducts the dead safely towards immortality; the elders who receive prizes from Achilles as *timē* and in return pray for divine favour (*Il.* 23.648); and finally, the bards who also have a share in *timē* since they sing in keeping with divine wisdom (*Od.* 8.480).

4.3. Penelope's trick and the geras of Odysseus: Weaving as a symbol of power

While the *Iliad* is concerned with the refusal of service in war, the *Odyssey* tells of what happens when the service of women is disrupted.[131] This is

---

130. On the meaning of light as life see Griffin 1984: 90.
131. See Linden 1992: 110–114, who argues that the main theme of the *Iliad* was the restitution of honour (*timē*), whereas the *Odyssey* deals with the restitution of marriage. According to Papadopoulou-Belmehdi (1994: 169) the *Odyssey* is about memory (mémoire) through *mētis*. She argues that the shroud of Penelope functions as 'Leitmotiv' and interprets Penelope as incorporating both cunning (*mētis*) and memory.

when *timē* and *geras* cannot be accessed, and a man's goods are consumed without compensation: *atimos*.

At the beginning of the *Odyssey* we find Telemachus complaining to Mentes, his father's guest-friend, and to the assembled Ithacans about the conduct of the *aristoi* of Ithaca and its surrounding islands who are wooing his mother and consuming his economic resources, his *oikos*: each day they slaughter cattle, sheep, and goats and drink sparkling wine, showing no sense of shame in the face of local public opinion (*Od.* 1.245-51; 2.55-66). The suitors reject the accusation: 'It is not the Achaean suitors who are the cause of this', Antinous objects, 'it is your own mother, who is looking to your profit' (*Od.* 2.87-88). He then proceeds to tell of Penelope's trick, which had linked her remarriage to the completion of a shroud for Laërtes, Odysseus's elderly father:

ἡ δὲ δόλον τόνδ' ἄλλον ἐνὶ φρεσὶ μερμήριξε
στησαμένη μέγαν ἱστὸν ἐνὶ μεγάροισιν ὕφαινε,
λεπτὸν καὶ περίμετρον· ἄφαρ δ' ἡμῖν μετέειπε
κοῦροι, ἐμοὶ μνηστῆρες, ἐπεὶ θάνε δῖος Ὀδυσσεύς,
μίμνετ' ἐπειγόμενοι τὸν ἐμὸν γάμον, εἰς ὅ κε φᾶρος
ἐκτελέσω, μή μοι μεταμώνια νήματ' ὄληται,
Λαέρτῃ ἥρωϊ ταφήϊον, εἰς ὅτε κέν μιν
μοῖρ' ὀλοὴ καθέλῃσι τανηλεγέος θανάτοιο,
μή τίς μοι κατὰ δῆμον Ἀχαιϊάδων νεμεσήσῃ,
αἴ κεν ἄτερ σπείρου κεῖται πολλὰ κτεατίσσας.
ὣς ἔφαθ', ἡμῖν δ' αὖτ' ἐπεπείθετο θυμὸς ἀγήνωρ.
ἔνθα καὶ ἡματίη μὲν ὑφαίνεσκεν μέγαν ἱστόν,
νύκτας δ' ἀλλύεσκεν, ἐπὴν δαΐδας παραθεῖτο.

And here's another example of her duplicity (*dolos*). On her loom in her house (*megaron*) she set up a great web (*histon*) and began weaving a large and delicate piece of work. She said to us: 'My lords (*kouroi*), my Suitors, now the noble Odysseus is dead, restrain your ardour, do not urge on this marriage till I have done this work (*pharos*), so that the threads I have spun may not be altogether wasted. It is a shroud (*taphēion*) for Lord Laërtes. When he succumbs to the dread hand of remorseless Death that stretches all men out at last, I must not risk the scandal there would be among my countrywomen here if one who had amassed such wealth were laid to rest without shroud (*speiron*)'. That's what she said; and we magnanimously consented. So by day she used to weave at the great web (*histon*), but every night had torches set beside it and undid the work (*Od.* 2.93-105 = 24.128-40, tr. Rieu).

By undoing at night what she has woven during the day, Penelope effectively halts the passage of time and makes it impossible for the suitors to obtain Odysseus's *geras*, which they hope to gain through marriage to her.[132] Unlike Clytemnestra, whose marriage to a new husband, Aegisthus, results in the loss of Agamemnon's *timē* (*Od.* 3.304; 24.30),[133] Penelope stays on the side of her husband, who returns home just as she has been forced to complete the shroud. Indirectly, her delay enables the restitution of Odysseus to his rightful position and the killing of the suitors. The final book of the *Odyssey* begins with a reprise of the complaint about Penelope's trick and its consequences, told to Agamemnon in Hades by Amphimedon, one of the recently dispatched suitors:

ὣς τρίετες μὲν ἔληθε δόλῳ καὶ ἔπειθεν Ἀχαιούς
ἀλλ' ὅτε τέτρατον ἦλθεν ἔτος καὶ ἐπήλυθον ὧραι,
[μηνῶν φθινόντων, περὶ δ' ἤματα πόλλ' ἐτελέσθη,]
καὶ τότε δή τις ἔειπε γυναικῶν, ἣ σάφα ᾔδη,
καὶ τήν γ' ἀλλύουσαν ἐφεύρομεν ἀγλαὸν ἱστόν.
ὣς τὸ μὲν ἐξετέλεσσε καὶ οὐκ ἐθέλουσ', ὑπ' ἀνάγκης.
εὖθ' ἡ φᾶρος ἔδειξεν, ὑφήνασα μέγαν ἱστόν,
πλύνασ', ἠελίῳ ἐναλίγκιον ἠὲ σελήνῃ,
καὶ τότε δή ῥ' Ὀδυσῆα κακός ποθεν ἤγαγε δαίμων
ἀγροῦ ἐπ' ἐσχατιήν, ὅθι δώματα ναῖε συβώτης.
ἔνθ' ἦλθεν φίλος υἱὸς Ὀδυσσῆος θείοιο,
ἐκ Πύλου ἠμαθόεντος ἰὼν σὺν νηΐ μελαίνῃ·
τὼ δὲ μνηστῆρσιν θάνατον κακὸν ἀρτύναντε
ἵκοντο προτὶ ἄστυ περικλυτόν [...].

---

132. The connection between wooing and gaining access on the *geras* is stressed by Telemachus talking with the seer Theoclymenus: *Od.* 15.521-22. Cf. Wagner-Hasel 1988: 54-55. Foley (1978: 11) speaks of Penelope's power 'to stop change'. Similar Papadopoulou-Belmehdi 1994: 46. See also Heubeck 1990: 136-37.
133. Penelope contrasts herself with Helen, who was affected by *atē* and followed a stranger (*Od.* 23.218-24). See Morgan 1991: 1-3. For comparison between Clytemnestra and Penelope see Katz 1991: 6-7; 48-53.

For three years she took us in by this stratagem (*dolos*). A fourth began, and the seasons were slipping by, when one of her women, who knew all about it, gave her mistress away. We caught her unravelling her beautiful work (*aglaon histon*), and she was forced reluctantly to complete it. But no sooner had she woven the great web (*pharos*), laundered the robe and shown it to us gleaming like the sun (*Helios*) and the moon (*Selene*), than some evil god landed Odysseus out of the blue in a distant corner (*eschatia*) of his estate (*agros*) where the swineherd had his hut. Noble Odysseus's son, just back from sandy Pylos in his black ship, made for the same place. The two of them plotted our assassination, and made their way to the famous city of Ithaca [...] (*Od.* 24.141-54, tr. Rieu).

Agamemnon responds to Amphimedon's account of the suitors' demise by praising Odysseus for Penelope's great virtue (μεγάλη ἀρετῇ) and good sense (ἀγαθαὶ φρένες), and by prophesying that the gods would create songs of *charis* in praise of Penelope (*Od.* 24.191-98). The *Odyssey* ends with the reinstating of Odysseus's rights as the son of Laërtes (*Od.* 24.336-46) and his right to always rule at Ithaca: βασιλευέτω αἰεί (*Od.* 24.483). This end is preceded by Penelope's recognition of her husband and thus the restitution of his *geras*—which Odysseus had asked about when he met his mother in the Underworld (*Od.* 11.175 and 184).

Unlike the *geras* fought over by Agamemnon and Achilles, the *geras* of Odysseus does not consist of a share of booty such as a captured woman. Nor is it a portion of meat such as that received by Telemachus and Peisistratus at Sparta as *geras* at the feast (*Od.* 4.66). In the *Odyssey geras* takes a more abstract form and should be understood as a collective term to capture the status and rank of Odysseus. In speaking to Arete, Odysseus expresses the idea that such *geras* should be maintained and passed on through the generations:

Ἀρήτη, θύγατερ Ῥηξήνορος ἀντιθέοιο,
σόν τε πόσιν σά τε γούναθ' ἱκάνω πολλὰ μογήσας,
τούσδε τε δαιτυμόνας, τοῖσιν θεοὶ ὄλβια δοῖεν,
ζωέμεναι, καὶ παισὶν ἐπιτρέψειεν ἕκαστος
κτήματ' ἐνὶ μεγάροισι γέρας θ', ὅ τι δῆμος ἔδωκεν.

> Arete, daughter of godlike Rhexenor, I come to your husband and to your knees after much suffering and to these banqueters, to whom the gods may grant happiness (*olbia*) in life, and may each of them hand down to his children the wealth in his halls and the *geras* that the *dēmos* have given him (*Od.* 7.147-50).

Pointing out the futility of striving for the *timē* and the *geras* of Priam, Achilles reminds his opponent, Aeneas, of Priam's heirs who stand to receive what he has: 'Priam shall not hand you the *geras*, for he has his own children and he is strong and sound of mind' (*Il.* 20.182-83). Ulf sees in this remark an anticipation of the institutionalisation of rank, while Justus Cobet takes Hector to be the obvious heir to Priam and considers *geras* to be attendant on the office, expressed through the word *timē*.[134] Penelope's role in the securing of *geras* in the sense of a position of privilege has caused some consternation in scholarship but not, as yet, a satisfactory explanation. Neither Bachofen's search for the lost original matriarchy[135] nor Finley's (and more lately Carlier's or van Wees's) total rejection of any form of power held by Penelope[136] do justice to the question. It is indeed the *basilēes* who are in control of *geras*; but mothers and wives are aware of *geras* and they seek to preserve it. In the case of Odysseus, this attempt at preservation is done by means of Penelope's shroud weaving, and we shall see that this involves precisely the generative power that enables the transferral of Odysseus's position of honour, his *geras*. In order to understand this, it is important to conceive of the temporal dimension incorporated in the shroud.

As she works on the shroud, Penelope causes time to stand still; the shroud embodies this time. Epic does not conceive of the passing of time in a linear fashion; indeed, within the poems time is represented merely as duration, or as an allotted fate. The narrative itself circles around fateful days (αἴσιμον ἦμαρ) and around events which fulfil the heroes'

---

134. Ulf 1990: 11 and 106-17; Cobet 1981: 25.
135. See Thomson [1949] 1978: 416-20.
136. Finley 1967: 91: 'There was nothing about the woman Penelope, either in beauty or wisdom or spirit, that could have won her this unprecedented and unwanted right of decision as a purely personal triumph.' Carlier 1984: 207, n. 340: 'Il est arbitraire d'interpréter le rôle de Pénélope comme un vestige de matriarcat primitif.' Van Wees 1992: 288: 'The traditional notion that they [the suitors] court Penelope because whomever she chooses to wed will be the new monarch, is mistaken. This view would give her a surprising amount of power, and in any case is not borne out by evidence'.

fate.[137] These lie ready on Zeus's scales, like wool ready for weighing and working. In a warning to Achilles, who refuses a meal before going to battle, Odysseus compares Zeus to a housekeeper, a *tamiē*, who allocates the household's provisions (*Il.* 19.223-24). In Book 8 Zeus places the lots of the Greeks and the Trojans onto his scales:[138]

> καὶ τότε δὴ χρύσεια πατὴρ ἐτίταινε τάλαντα
> ἐν δ' ἐτίθει δύο κῆρε τανηλεγέος θανάτοιο
> Τρώων θ' ἱπποδάμων καὶ Ἀχαιῶν χαλκοχιτώνων,
> ἕλκε δὲ μέσσα λαβών· ῥέπε δ' αἴσιμον ἦμαρ Ἀχαιῶν.

But when the sun was high in the sky, the Father held out (*epitaine*) his golden scales (*chryseia* [...] *talanta*), and putting death that lays men low in their pan, on one side for the horse-taming Trojans, on the other for the bronze-armoured Greeks (*Achaioi*), raised the balance by the middle of the beam. The beam came down on the Greek's side, spelling doom for them (*Il.* 8.69-72, tr. Rieu).

The metaphor of weighing alludes to the weighing of wool. This is clarified by the simile of the wool-worker used in Book 12 to illustrate the precarious balance of the battle:[139]

> ἀλλ' οὐδ' ὣς ἐδύναντο φόβον ποιῆσαι Ἀχαιῶν,
> ἀλλ' ἔχον ὥς τε τάλαντα γυνὴ χερνῆτις ἀληθής,
> ἥ τε σταθμὸν ἔχουσα καὶ εἴριον ἀμφὶς ἀνέλκει
> ἰσάζουσ', ἵνα παισὶν ἀεικέα μισθὸν ἄρηται
> ὣς μὲν τῶν ἐπὶ ἶσα μάχη τέτατο πτόλεμός τε,

---

137. Onians 1989: 411-15; Fränkel 1955: 1; Patzek 1992: 179-80; Garcia 2013: 232. This symbolic meaning of the web makes it possible to interpret the *pharos* of Penelope as Odysseus's wedding robe, and in doing so she reconfirms his identity as her husband: see Yamagata 2005: 544.
138. The image is also used in advance of the final duel between Hector and Achilles (*Il.* 22.209-12). Hector is not to be sent to Hades against fate (*aisa*), but no one escapes fate (*moira*) (*Il.* 6.487-88). There is a little room for manoeuvre. When Hector recognises the sacred scales of Zeus (*hiera talanta*), he turns to flight (*Il.* 16.656-58).
139. This amount of wool is mentioned again in a subsequent simile when Hector picks up a heavy rock that is as light to him as the wool shorn from a ram is to a shepherd (*Il.* 12.451).

πρίν γ' ὅτε δὴ Ζεὺς κῦδος ὑπέρτερον Ἕκτορι δῶκε
Πριαμίδῃ, ὃς πρῶτος ἐσήλατο τεῖχος Ἀχαιῶν.

The Greeks held on, like a careful wool-worker who holds up her scale (*talanta*) to balance the wool against the weights and check the accuracy of the meagre pittance she is earning for her children. The struggle was as tight and even as that, till the moment when Zeus gave the upper hand (*kudos*) to Hector son of Priam, who was the first to leap inside the Greek wall (*Il.* 12.432-37, tr. Rieu).

A person's life is determined by what Zeus takes for them from his storage jars—these contain good as well as bad gifts (*Il.* 24.527-29). The thread of life is spun from these gifts as Achilles tells Priam: 'This is how the gods have spun the thread (ἐπεκλώσαντο) for us wretched mortals so that we may live in grief' (*Il.* 24.525-26). The necessary amount of these gifts is described by the word *olbos*; Peleus is distinguished by this alongside his wealth, *ploutos* (*Il.* 24.535-36). It is allotted twice, once at birth and again upon marriage: Menelaus says to Nestor's son Peisistratus that Zeus had 'spun the thread of happiness (ὄλβον ἐπικλώσῃ)' for Nestor when he married (γαμέοντί), and when he was born (γεινομένῳ) (*Od.* 4.208).

Most frequently the thread of life is said to be spun by the Fates, Moira, Aisa, and Clotho. So Hecuba says that it was Moira who spun for Hector, at his birth, the thread (ἐπένησε λίνῳ) that he should remain unburied (*Il.* 24.209-10). The use of the past tense here is typical and expresses the notion of fate as already complete, merely waiting to be fulfilled. According to Hera, Achilles will also suffer the fate (αἶσα) that was spun for him at birth (γιγνομένῳ ἐπένησε λίνῳ, *Il.* 20.127). Alcinous speaks in similar terms of the fate of his guest as the Phaeacians prepare to send him off:

[...] ἔπειτα δὲ καὶ περὶ πομπῆς
μνησόμεθ', ὥς χ' ὁ ξεῖνος ἄνευθε πόνου καὶ ἀνίης
πομπῇ ὑφ' ἡμετέρῃ ἣν πατρίδα γαῖαν ἵκηται
χαίρων καρπαλίμως, εἰ καὶ μάλα τηλόθεν ἐστί,
μηδέ τι μεσσηγύς γε κακὸν καὶ πῆμα πάθῃσι
πρίν γε τὸν ἧς γαίης ἐπιβήμεναι. ἔνθα δ' ἔπειτα
πείσεται, ἅσσα οἱ αἶσα κατὰ Κλῶθές τε βαρεῖαι
γεινομένῳ νήσαντο λίνῳ, ὅτε μιν τέκε μήτηρ.

We will then take up the matter of his passage (*pompē*) so as to ensure him without trouble or anxiety the happiness of a speedy return to his country under our escort (*pompē*), however far away it is. We will safeguard him on the way from any further hardship or accident till he sets foot on his own land. After which he must suffer whatever Destiny (Aisa) and the restless Fate (Clotho) spun for him with the first thread of life when he came from his mother's womb (*Od.* 7.190–98, tr. Rieu).

The image for the conflict between Zeus and Poseidon over the outcome of the war also refers to the processes of weaving, as the mighty struggle is described as a thread (ἔριδος κρατερῆς καὶ ὁμοιίου πτολέμοιο | πεῖραρ), which the gods take it in turn (ἐπαλλάξαντες) to stretch out over the Greeks and the Trojans (ἐπ' ἀμφοτέροισι τάνυσσαν) and which is unbreakable (ἄρρηκτόν) and unsolvable (ἄλυτόν) (*Il.* 13.358–60). The *polemoio peirar* could be understood as a rope, such as one might use to tie up a person.[140] But it may also be understood to mean the woof thread (or weft thread), which is drawn through or crosses the stationary warp thread in both directions on the loom.[141] This process would be alluded to by the participle ἐπαλλάξαντες (*epallaxantes*), which I translated above as 'taking it in turns' but which actually suggests the crossing of warp and weft.[142] The verb *tanyein*, used elsewhere for the stringing of a lyre and for the stretching of the weft thread across the loom, here must refer to the drawing of the weft thread through the 'shed' created by the heddle-rod.[143] A tightly stretched weft thread will result in a strong woven fabric, which will, as in the simile above, be unsolvable.[144] Of course,

---

140. This is the meaning of *peirar* in *Od.* 12.51; 162; 179.
141. Cf. Onians 1989: 338; Bergren 1975: 8–11; 177. The later term for the weft thread is *krokē*. See Blümner 1912: 128; 142.
142. See Onians 1989: 311–14; 318. Bergren (1975: 172) translates: 'having crossed over'.
143. Onians 1989: 320, 339: 'τείνειν or τανυεῖν, used by Homer for the analogous processes of stringing a lyre or bow, naturally describes the stretching or drawing of the woof thread across the warp'. See also Bergren 1975: 177. *Tanyein* has a special meaning in *Il.* 23.760–63, tr. Rieu: '[...] like the rod (*kanōn*) near the breast of a girdled weaving-woman: she carefully draws (*tanyssei*) it along with her hands to get the spool (*pēnion*) out past the warp (*miton*) and brings it right up to her breast [...]'. For the meaning of the weaving terminology used here see Blümner 1912: 148–49; Barber 1991: 270. *Mitos* is also the heddle.
144. A further meaning of *peirar* is the cosmological border, Oceanus. Onians 1989: 316; Bergren 1975: 22–28. This meaning as border fits with the textile meaning of *peirar*. According to Ellen Harlizius-Klück, *peirar* denotes the starting-border of the fabric ('Gewebeanfangskante') that is produced separately before being fixed at the loom (Harlizius-Klück and Fanfani 2016).

patterns are created with the weft thread, so that it makes sense to qualify the thread with a reference to the kinds of patterns seen on woven fabrics, which include battle-scenes.[145] Thus it is the *polemoio peirar*, which 'loosens the knees', that is, brings death, for many men (*Il.* 13.359-60). If we stay within the weaving image, it is clear that death occurs when the weft thread has been used up and the fabric is completed, like Penelope's shroud, anticipating death and completed under duress. Elsewhere in the *Iliad*, when heroes' knees are loosened in death, we also hear of *telos thanatoio*, the completion of death. That *telos* covers the eyes and nose of the dying heroes like a shroud: τέλος θανάτοιο κάλυψεν | ὀφθαλμοὺς ῥῖνάς θ'.[146]

These similes make reference to various stages in the preparation and working of wool into a fabric. A portion (*moira*) of unspun wool is weighed on the scales (*talanta*).[147] This amount or weight (*aisa*) determines fate, which is called either *moira* or *aisa*. The Fates, Moira or Clotho (later Lachesis), personify fate.[148] Fate, which men cannot predict, lies on the knees of the gods,[149] just like wool placed on the spinners' knees for carding before it is spun.[150] The process of carding is described as *neein*, *epineein*, and *nethein*, while the word for the spinning of a thread (*linon*) or a weft thread (*peirar*) is *klothein*.[151] The to-and-fro of the weft on the loom ultimately makes up the fabric of life, the fulfilment of fate, the τέλος (*telos*). Fate is weighed with the help of the *kēres*. In the singular, *Kēr* (Κήρ) is a

145. See my discussion in ch. 3.2.
146. *Il.* 16.502 (Sarpedon); 5.553 (Krethon and Orsilochus); 16.855 (Patroclus); 22.361 (Hector).
147. Plato (*Resp.* 620e) uses *moira* for wool. See Onians 1989: 404.
148. Plato (*Resp.* 617c) differentiates between several phases of time. Clotho, the spinner, represents the present (*ta onta*), Lachesis, first seen in the *Theogony* (219; 905) as the personification of destiny, sings of what has happened already, the past, (*ta gegonota*) and Atropos, who turns the spindle, knows what will happen, the future (*ta mellonta*). They all sing like the Sirens, the daemons of death. In Theocritus (*Id.* 24.51-59) the *moirai* are spinning the thread of fate. See also Seneca (*Apocol.* 3.1-5.2), where the spindle represents fate and the span of life. Here, the wool is handed out by Lachesis. For the Homeric belief in fate see Dietrich 1957: 289-94; Erbse 1986: 276-78; Yamagata 1994: 105-20.
149. *Il.* 17.514; 20.535; *Od.* 1.267; 16.129. Vernant (1982: 140) defines the knee as a symbol of male power (*puissance virile*).
150. See e.g. Theocr. *Id.* 24.76-78: 'Many an Achaean woman will sing your name, Alkmene, as they card the soft wool over their knee (μαλακὸν περὶ γούνατι νῆμα χειρὶ καταρίψουσιν)'. In Archaic and Classical times, the *epinētron* was used for carding. For evidence see Lissarrague 1991: 179, fig. 10; 230, fig. 48; 247, fig. 61. Barber 1991: 77-78 hints at Mycenaean traditions.
151. For the terms of spinning and weaving see Blümner 1912: 98-170.

goddess of doom who brings death for the warrior; used in the plural they are weights (κῆρες).[152]

In his analysis of Greek notions of the body and death, Richard Onians interprets *telos* as a band which encloses and binds a completed whole.[153] Given how concrete and technical the similes are, I think it more likely that *telos*, like the other terms we have considered, refers to a specific phase in the weaving process, namely, to the completion of the fabric which contains the shape of a life. It is striking that the word *telos*, which may mean an ending as much as goal or completion, is frequently used in situations involving transformation and in which textiles are used to effect or to visualize that process. Primarily this applies to death, which will be addressed in chapter 5.[154] We do, however, have one example where the transformation in question is marriage, when Aphrodite prays for the *telos* of marriage for the daughters of Pandareus (*Od.* 20.74). Generally, we find *telos* and the verb τέλεω (*teleō*) associated with periods of time, to do with days (*Od.* 5.390; 10.470), nights (*Il.* 7.282), years (*Il.* 19.32), and age (*Od.* 23.286), but also with passage through space, such as homecoming (*Od.* 22.323), journeys (*Od.* 2.256), horse-racing (*Il.* 23.373), the return of booty to the homeland (*Il.* 12.222), and seafaring. Time spent in careful toiling (*kamnein*) leads to *telos* in seafaring,[155] as in battle (τέλος πολέμου/πολέμοιο: *Il.* 16.630; 20.101; 3.291). Time spent working in another's service may also lead to *telos* in the form of remuneration, the *misthoio telos*. The Horae, who are in charge of the passage from day to night, bring this *misthos* to Poseidon and Apollo in payment for their

---

152. For the *daimon* of death see Neumer-Pfau 1987: 21-23; Vernant 1982: 140; Erbse 1986: 280.
153. Onians 1989: 463.
154. Odysseus escapes the *telos* of death (*Od.* 5.356: *telos thanatou*) with the help of the veil (*krēdemnon*) of Leucothea. The suitors experience the evil *telos* of death (*Od.* 24.124: *thanatoio kakon telos*). Zeus knows for whom the *telos* of death is prepared (*Il.* 3.309). Achilles knows from Thetis about the *telos* of death that awaits him (*Il.* 9.411), and he knows that that *telos* will not come so swiftly if he returns home (*Il.* 9.416; 13.602). Odysseus warns Socus that the *telos* of death is upon him (*Il.* 11.451), although he also recognises that the *telos* has not pierced the *kairos* (*Il.* 11.439), that is, the row of thrums in a loom, through which the threads of the warp are attached. So Onians 1989: 346; Blümner 1912: 145-46, who also gives alternative interpretations.
155. The Cyclopes do not have *tektones* able to build ships (κάμοιεν) and to accomplish (τελέοιεν) everything (*Od.* 9.127). The Phaeacians accomplish shipping without tribulation for Rhadamanthys within one day (καὶ ἄτερ καμάτοιο τέλεσσαν, *Od.* 7.325-26).

service to the Trojan ruler Laomedon (μισθοῖο τέλος πολυγηθέες ὧραι | ἐξέφερον, *Il.* 21.450-51).

Finally, there is the *telos* of words, *mythoi*, which may not achieve their goal, however finely spoken, as Nestor tells Diomedes (*Il.* 9.56), or words which will not be fulfilled, as is the case for Achilles (*Il.* 19.107; 20.369). Words may be either completed or cut off midway (*Il.* 20.370). Words may be good or bad, but Agamemnon accuses Calchas that he has 'never spoken a good word nor fulfilled one' (ἐσθλὸν δ' οὔτέ τί πω εἶπας ἔπος οὔτ' ἐτέλεσσας, *Il.* 1.108). *Mythos* is powerful (*karteros*) when given as a leader's command to be fulfilled (*Il.* 16.199; 1.25; 326; 379). The fulfilment of such words lies in the hands of the gods, as for instance in the case of the suitors' plan to kill Telemachus (*Od.* 4.699).[156] Occasionally their fulfilment may be predicted by prophets or by individual leaders (*Il.* 2.330; 14.48). A plan, such as that of the suitors who seek to murder Telemachus (*Od.* 4.774-76), may be woven like a web. Odysseus and Menelaus weave words (*mythoi*) and thoughts (*mēdea*) in their embassy at Troy (ἀλλ' ὅτε δὴ μύθους καὶ μήδεα πᾶσιν ὕφαινον, *Il.* 3.212). It is especially common for ominous or fatal plots or plans (*dolos* or *mētis*) to be described as woven, as is the case for the plot woven against Bellerophon (πυκινὸν δόλον ἄλλον ὕφαινε, *Il.* 6.187). When Odysseus is shipwrecked, he fears that the immortals may have woven a *dolos* against him (μή τίς μοι ὑφαίνῃσιν δόλον αὖτε | ἀθανάτων, *Od.* 5.356-57), and he himself is said to weave a plot as he fears for his life in the cave of Polyphemus (πάντας δὲ δόλους καὶ μῆτιν ὕφαινον, *Od.* 9.422).

Whenever a plan (*mētis*) or plot (*dolos*) is woven, the object is the death and destruction of the person for whom it is woven. This is true of the *mētis* the suitors weave for Telemachus (μῆτιν ὕφαινον, *Od.* 4.678) and of the *mētis* woven by Athena and Odysseus for the suitors (*Od.* 13.303; 13.386). All these plans bring the *telos* of death—like the *doloi* Penelope winds for the suitors by unravelling her weaving each night (δόλους τολυπεύω, *Od.* 19.137). The physical place of this metaphorical weaving is the *phrēn*, the spirit or wit located in the lungs or in the diaphragm, and of which women who are valued for their weaving skills are especially possessed.[157] Penelope

---

156. Cf. *Od.* 2.34: Zeus fulfils (*teleseien*) the good, Aegyptius says in the Ithacan assembly. See also *Il.* 1.5.

157. It is Penelope who is especially characterised as *periphrōn* (e.g. *Od.* 21.321). Chryseis, whom Agamemnon is unwilling to give up, is also equipped with a good mind *phrēn* (*Il.* 1.115). Whereas the adjective *periphrōn* is used only for women, *echephrōn* denotes both sexes. For evidence see Papadopoulou-Belmehdi 1994: 185-89; Ceccarelli 1995: 186-91.

hopes to discover if Laërtes has woven some *mētis* in his *phrēn* when she asks the shepherd Dolius to take a seat next to Odysseus's aged father (ἐνὶ φρεσὶ μῆτιν ὑφήνας, *Od.* 4.739). She also tells the disguised Odysseus that she herself was unable to come up with further *mētis* after the suitors discovered her trick at the loom (οὔτε τιν' ἄλλην | μῆτιν ἔθ' εὑρίσκω, *Od.* 19.157–58). In Penelope's weaving trick the concrete and the metaphorical come together.[158] Her *mētis* and her *dolos*, which, together with the *mētis* of Odysseus, bring about the demise of the suitors, are a concrete version of the metaphorical fabrics woven (*hyphainein*) by gods for men, and by cunning men for their enemies. The gods and Odysseus weave their *mētis* and their *dolos*; the word used for what Penelope does with her *dolos* is *tolypeuein*, which means to wind or wind off a skein of wool. Only her *mētis* is metaphorically woven. The difference is significant, as in reality she unravels her weaving and winds the threads off again.[159] This action is also suggested by the ancient etymology of Penelope's name: the loosener of threads (from πήνη, thread, and λέπω, to peel, to thrash, and/or λώπη, robe, mantle).[160]

In the *Iliad* the ability to weave a plan metaphorically for another is a *geras* which belongs to the elders. Thus we hear that in the council of the elders it is Nestor who first begins to weave a plan: τοῖς ὁ γέρων πάμπρωτος ὑφαίνειν ἤρχετο μῆτιν (*Il.* 7.324). Elsewhere we find this activity described as *geras*, when Nestor draws the difference between the elders' functions and the young men's prowess in battle: 'I guide with counsel and words, for that is the *geras* of the elders', κελεύσω βουλῇ καὶ μύθοισι· τὸ γὰρ γέρας ἐστὶ γερόντων (*Il.* 4.323).[161] Nestor's power to give counsel rests on the same preconditions as those which enable the *basilēes* to take proper and wise decisions, that is, knowledge of social norms and conventions. Through his advanced age, Nestor practically embodies a store of divine wisdom, or *themistes*. The metaphor of weaving makes all the more sense then since woven cloths are also seen as stores of memory and wisdom, as discussed earlier. Thus, the adjective *liparos*,

---

158. Papadopoulou-Belmehdi 1994: 83 draws attention to the fact that metaphorical weaving of a plan is attributed only to men. Besides this, Penelope is also sending written messages to the suitors. See Marquardt 1993: 153.
159. The deceiving character of weaving is often stressed. See e.g. Murnaghan 1987: 110; Papadopoulou-Belmehdi 1994: 57–58; 155–58.
160. Kretschmer 1945: 80–93; Papadopoulou-Belmehdi 1994: 81.
161. See *Il.* 9.422-23: τὸ γὰρ γέρας ἐστὶ γερόντων | ὄφρ' ἄλλην φράζωνται ἐνὶ φρεσὶ μῆτιν ἀμείνω, Achilles argues against the envoy of Agamemnon.

which suggests the visual power of these stores of memory, is used for old age, for illustrated weaving, and for the *themistes*.[162]

Building on this interpretation, we can add further concrete meaning to *geras*, which will explain both the parallelism of the terms *timē* and *geras*, and the role played by Penelope in securing the *geras* of Odysseus. Just like *timē*, *geras* also has both a material and an intangible meaning. On the one hand, *geras* denotes the concrete privileges of a high-status leader, a woman skilled in weaving, and a portion at the feast, which give visible expression to his status. On the other hand, *geras* can be understood as the ability to store or memorise social norms and knowledge and to use these stores of wisdom in counsel and decision-making. In this way *geras* is the precondition for the achievement of *timē*, which distinguishes *basileus* and *basileia*: the right to offer safe conduct in social and geographic space and to recruit goods and services for this. Carrying out this function requires knowledge of social norms such as we saw in our analysis of the distribution of *timē* between high-ranking men and women.

The female contribution to this is not only to help the *basileus* enjoy his privilege, his *geras*. Women's weaving of winding sheets, of the fabric of fate, whose completion (*telos*) signifies the completion of life, and so death, is a parallel to the elders' weaving of plans in speech. And this too can be understood as *geras*, since providing a corpse with such fabric is a part of the gift of honour, the *geras*, given to the dead.[163] We know from our examination of *charis* that such winding sheets have important transformatory powers, since they bear the dead man's posthumous fame and thus contribute to the transformation of the mortal body into an immortal one. This is the reason why it is not only Penelope who preserves the *geras* of Odysseus but his mother, too, is able to pass on information about his beautiful *geras* (*Od.* 11.175 and 184). Indeed, his mother tells Odysseus to pass this knowledge on to Penelope (ταῦτα δὲ πάντα | ἴσθ', ἵνα καὶ μετόπισθε τεῇ εἴπῃσθα γυναικί, *Od.* 11.223–24). In Phaeacia, Odysseus turns to Arete rather than Alcinous when asking to be taken in and expresses his good wishes to the other *basilēes* for the preservation of their *geras* (*Od.* 7.147–50). It is mothers and wives who have the power,

---

162. For γῆρας in the sense of a long life surrounded by blessed people (*laoi olbioi*) see *Od.* 11.136; 23.293; in connection with raising a son see *Od.* 19.368 and 4.210 (linked to the verb aging: *gēraskein*). Nestor's shining old age (*liparōs gēraskemen*) is a consequence of the plenty (*olbos*) spun out for him by Zeus at his birth and wedding (4.208).
163. See the following chapter.

made manifest in their weaving, to bridge the discontinuity of experience and memory and to ensure the handing on of status and rank to the next generation.[164]

This state of affairs also explains the use of the term *tiein*, which usually refers to material gifts given as tokens of respect in guest-friendships or between spouses. In Phaeacia, where the position of the *basileus* is safe, Arete is honoured (τίεται) by Alcinous (*Od.* 7.67). When a female *geras*, an enslaved woman who must weave for another and share the master's bed, is brought home, a couple's relationship is shaken, as happened when Phoenix's father 'dishonoured his wife' (ἀτιμάζεσκε δ' ἄκοιτιν) by taking a concubine (*Il.* 9.450). In contrast, Laërtes honoured Eurycleia as much as his wife but never went to bed with her for fear of his wife's wrath (ἶσα δέ μιν κεδνῇ ἀλόχῳ τίεν ἐν μεγάροισιν, *Od.* 1.432-33).[165] Such wrath, χόλος (*cholos*), like that of Achilles, has dire consequences for the sons in these circumstances: Phoenix must flee the country after taking his mother's side, since he does not wish to commit patricide (*Il.* 9.458-83). We find Orestes praised at the beginning of the *Odyssey*, his fame resting on the fact that he slew his mother's new husband (*Il.* 1.29-30; 196-98; 298-300; 305-10). In the *Oresteia* Clytemnestra's plot (*dolos*) against her returning husband is also manifested as a concrete woven textile, the πετάσματα (*petasmata*) or εἶμα (*heima*) which is spread on the ground before him and forms the purple path (πορφυρόστρωτος πόρος) upon which Agamemnon will be led into the house and to his death (Aesch. *Ag.* 908-10).[166] In the *Odyssey* as in the *Oresteia*, the poets side with sons and fathers whose relationships are seen as endangered by the woman's taking a new spouse, rather than by any of the fathers' own actions. There is repeated mention of the misfortune that befalls husbands when their wives receive gifts from strangers (*Od.* 11.326-27; 11.251). To view this as the beginning of a tradition of misogyny, as Sheila Murnaghan has proposed, is to give the problem a moral dimension that the text does not justify.[167] The problem is the fragility of the relationship of *philotēs* between the sexes, which is of interest not only to male audiences, as Lilian Doherty has shown.[168]

---

164. See also Papadopoulou-Belmehdi 1994: 183 and 199-203 who emphasises the relationship between memory and power.
165. According to Scheid-Tissinier (2015) Eurycleia was a high-ranking woman originally chosen as second wife by Laërtes to secure transmission of the *oikos*.
166. See Seaford 1984; Wagner-Hasel 2006.
167. Murnaghan 1987: 108-10.

This is why Agamemnon may claim in the final book of the *Odyssey* that the *kleos* of Penelope, who was faithful to her husband and preserved the *geras*, will be the subject of songs. He is referring, of course, to the *Odyssey* itself (*Od.* 24.196).[169]

4.4. The geras of the dead and the process of renewal in the death ritual

The death of warriors in battle and their burial are central events in the epic narrative. There are two important burials depicted in the *Iliad*: Patroclus's and Hector's. The burial of Patroclus is the catalyst for the reintegration of Achilles into the Greek army and initiates a turn of events that ultimately concludes with the death and burial of Hector. In the final book of the *Odyssey*, the burial of Achilles is recalled. The honours paid to the deceased warrior during burial rituals are denoted with the same term as the privileges of the *basilēes* and kings: once again, we are dealing with *geras*, a gift of honour. Once again both key communities, the domestic and the military, partake in the presentation of the gift.

The lament for the dead, for which the terms *goaein* (γοάειν), *klaiein* (κλαίειν), and *kōkyein* (κωκύειν) as well as *goos* (γόος) and *thrēnos* (θρῆνος) are used, is a prominent part of the *geras* of the dead, performed during the laying-out (*prothesis*). When Penelope's suitors arrive in Hades, they complain that their relatives (*philoi*) are not aware of their misfortune. If they knew, the relatives would have 'wash[ed] the black blood off our wounds, and laid out our bodies and lamented (γοάοιεν)'. For that is the *geras* of the dead (ὃ γὰρ γέρας ἐστὶ θανόντων', *Od.* 24.189-90). Similarly, Laërtes fears for Odysseus that he may have died without his parents' weeping (κλαῦσε) for him, or his wife wailing for him (κώκυσ'), nor closing his eyes when he is laid out for burial as is proper. He too concludes: 'For such is the *geras* of the dead (τὸ γὰρ γέρας ἐστὶ θανόντων', *Od.* 24.292-96). Using the same

---

168. Doherty 1992: 161-77. While Doherty does not assume that women were present as audiences, she considers them none the less as implied or external audiences. She runs into difficulties explaining the presence of Arete at Demodocus's performance. It seems to me to make more sense to consider that different occasions allowed for different audiences. Cf. also McIntosh Snyder 1989 and Chaston 2002: 6. Chaston stresses Penelope's authority to speak to a male audience and to be heard by them.
169. For the *kleos* of Penelope see Katz 1991: 25 (she 'becomes the celebrator of her own *kleos*' by her weaving trick). Pantelia 1993; Papadopoulou-Belmehdi 1994: 185-91; Felson-Rubin 1994: 125-44, 178-85; Chaston 2002: 7.

phrase, Achilles begins the lament, the *goos*, (ἐξῆρχε γόοιο) for Patroclus at the start of the funeral: 'Let us weep (κλαίωμεν) for Patroclus, for that is the *geras* of the dead (ὃ γὰρ γέρας ἐστὶ θανόντων', *Il.* 23.9 and 17).

Such *gooi* are performed only by the deceased's close relatives, and they contain the value system of Homeric society. In Patroclus's case the lament is led by Achilles and Brisëis. Achilles's theme is the fulfilment of vengeance for his beloved friend:

χαῖρέ μοι ὦ Πάτροκλε καὶ εἰν Ἀΐδαο δόμοισι
πάντα γὰρ ἤδη τοι τελέω τὰ πάροιθεν ὑπέστην
Ἕκτορα δεῦρ' ἐρύσας δώσειν κυσὶν ὠμὰ δάσασθαι,
δώδεκα δὲ προπάροιθε πυρῆς ἀποδειροτομήσειν
Τρώων ἀγλαὰ τέκνα σέθεν κταμένοιο χολωθείς.

Farewell and rejoice, Patroclus, even in the halls of Hades. I am now keeping all the promises I made you: I have dragged Hector's body here for the dogs to eat raw; and at your pyre I am going to cut the throats of a dozen splendid sons of Troy to vent my anger at your death (*Il.* 23.19–23; tr. Rieu).

Achilles's revenge fantasies attach to the obligations which attend the bond between warriors; Brisëis, however, laments the loss of the protection she received from Patroclus:

Πάτροκλέ μοι δειλῇ πλεῖστον κεχαρισμένε θυμῷ
ζωὸν μέν σε ἔλειπον ἐγὼ κλισίηθεν ἰοῦσα,
νῦν δέ σε τεθνηῶτα κιχάνομαι ὄρχαμε λαῶν
ἂψ ἀνιοῦσ'· ὥς μοι δέχεται κακὸν ἐκ κακοῦ αἰεί.
ἄνδρα μὲν ᾧ ἔδοσάν με πατὴρ καὶ πότνια μήτηρ
εἶδον πρὸ πτόλιος δεδαϊγμένον ὀξέϊ χαλκῷ,
τρεῖς τε κασιγνήτους, τούς μοι μία γείνατο μήτηρ,
κηδείους, οἳ πάντες ὀλέθριον ἦμαρ ἐπέσπον.
οὐδὲ μὲν οὐδέ μ' ἔασκες, ὅτ' ἄνδρ' ἐμὸν ὠκὺς Ἀχιλλεὺς
ἔκτεινεν, πέρσεν δὲ πόλιν θείοιο Μύνητος,
κλαίειν, ἀλλά μ' ἔφασκες Ἀχιλλῆος θείοιο
κουριδίην ἄλοχον θήσειν, ἄξειν τ' ἐνὶ νηυσὶν
ἐς Φθίην, δαίσειν δὲ γάμον μετὰ Μυρμιδόνεσσι.
τώ σ' ἄμοτον κλαίω τεθνηότα μείλιχον αἰεί.

> Oh Patroclus, my heart's delight! Oh, my misery! I left you in this hut alive when I went away; and now I have come back, commander of men, to find you dead. Such is my life, an endless chain of disaster. I saw the husband to whom my father and my lady mother (*potnia mētēr*) gave me mangled in front of his town by the cruel spear; and I saw my three brothers, my dear brothers, borne by the same mother as myself, all meet their doom. But you, when swift-footed Achilles killed my husband and sacked lord Mynes' town, you would not even let me weep (*klaiein*); you said you would make me Achilles' lawful wife (*kouridiē alochos*) and take me in your ships to your home in Phthia and give me a wedding-feast among the Myrmidons. You were always so gentle (*meilichos*) with me. So in death I mourn (*klaiō*) you inconsolably (*Il.* 19.286-300; tr. Rieu).

The other women in the Myrmidon camp join in with this lament, as we understand from the narrator's comments after the conclusion of the speech:

> Ὣς ἔφατο κλαίουσ', ἐπὶ δὲ στενάχοντο γυναῖκες
> Πάτροκλον πρόφασιν, σφῶν δ' αὐτῶν κήδε' ἑκάστη.

> So she spoke in tears (*klaiousa*), and the other women took up the cry (*stenachonto*), each one recalling through Patroclus her own misfortunes (*Il.* 19.301-2; tr. Rieu).

The lament of Brisëis has been considered as atypical by some scholars,[170] not least because of the narrator's comment that follows it. But the qualities ascribed to Patroclus by Brisëis, the taking on the role of a parent, and his mild personality (*meilichos*), are not unique to this lament.

Andromache, Hecuba, and Helen all perform *gooi* for Hector. When his body is returned, Cassandra's lament resounds throughout the city:

> ὄψεσθε Τρῶες καὶ Τρῳάδες Ἕκτορ' ἰόντες,
> εἴ ποτε καὶ ζώοντι μάχης ἐκνοστήσαντι
> χαίρετ', ἐπεὶ μέγα χάρμα πόλει τ' ἦν παντί τε δήμῳ.

---

170. See Andronikos 1968: 11; Heiden 1991: 7-8.

THE GERAS OF THE DEAD

Trojans and women of Troy, if ever in the past you welcomed
Hector back when he came home safe from battle—a moment
for everyone in the town to rejoice—come out and see him now!
(Il. 24.705-7, tr. Rieu).

Andromache and Hecuba, the wife and the mother, are the first to rush to the procession, while the women bystanders are weeping (κλαίων, Il. 24.710-12). The body is then laid out in Priam's house, with singers standing by its side and sounding the songs of lamentation, called *thrēnoi* (Il. 24.720-22). The content of these songs is not specified. But the laments of the relatives, the *gooi*, are cited in detail. Here, too, the problem of vengeance is addressed, albeit from the perspective of the relative threatened by revenge. But the more harmonising or equalising aspect of the hero's personality that we saw mentioned in the lament of Brisëis is a factor in the laments for Hector as well.

Andromache's goos is the first:

Ἕκτορος ἀνδροφόνοιο κάρη μετὰ χερσὶν ἔχουσα
ἆνερ ἀπ᾽ αἰῶνος νέος ὤλεο, κὰδ δέ με χήρην
λείπεις ἐν μεγάροισι· πάϊς δ᾽ ἔτι νήπιος αὔτως
ὃν τέκομεν σύ τ᾽ ἐγώ τε δυσάμμοροι, οὐδέ μιν οἴω
ἥβην ἵξεσθαι· πρὶν γὰρ πόλις ἥδε κατ᾽ ἄκρης
πέρσεται· ἦ γὰρ ὄλωλας ἐπίσκοπος, ὅς τέ μιν αὐτὴν
ῥύσκευ, ἔχες δ᾽ ἀλόχους κεδνὰς καὶ νήπια τέκνα,
αἳ δή τοι τάχα νηυσὶν ὀχήσονται γλαφυρῇσι,
καὶ μὲν ἐγὼ μετὰ τῇσι σὺ δ᾽ αὖ τέκος ἢ ἐμοὶ αὐτῇ
ἕψεαι, ἔνθά κεν ἔργα ἀεικέα ἐργάζοιο
ἀθλεύων πρὸ ἄνακτος ἀμειλίχου, ἤ τις Ἀχαιῶν
ῥίψει χειρὸς ἑλὼν ἀπὸ πύργου λυγρὸν ὄλεθρον
χωόμενος, ᾧ δή που ἀδελφεὸν ἔκτανεν Ἕκτωρ
ἢ πατέρ᾽ ἠὲ καὶ υἱόν, ἐπεὶ μάλα πολλοὶ Ἀχαιῶν
Ἕκτορος ἐν παλάμῃσιν ὀδὰξ ἕλον ἄσπετον οὖδας.
οὐ γὰρ μείλιχος ἔσκε πατὴρ τεὸς ἐν δαῒ λυγρῇ·
τῶ καί μιν λαοὶ μὲν ὀδύρονται κατὰ ἄστυ,
ἀρητὸν δὲ τοκεῦσι γόον καὶ πένθος ἔθηκας
Ἕκτορ ἐμοὶ δὲ μάλιστα λελείψεται ἄλγεα λυγρά.
οὐ γάρ μοι θνῄσκων λεχέων ἐκ χεῖρας ὄρεξας,
οὐδέ τί μοι εἶπες πυκινὸν ἔπος, οὔ τέ κεν αἰεὶ
μεμνῄμην νύκτάς τε καὶ ἤματα δάκρυ χέουσα.

Husband, you were too young to die and leave me widowed in our home. Your son, the boy we luckless parents brought into the world, is but a little baby. And I have no hope that he will grow to manhood: Ilium will come tumbling to the ground before that can ever be. For you, her guardian (*episkopos*), have perished, you that watched over her, you that kept her cherished wives and little babies safe. They will be carried off soon in the hollow ships, and I with them.

And you, my child, will go with me to labour somewhere at degrading tasks under the eye of a merciless master (*anax ameilichos*); or some Greek will seize you by the arm and hurl you from the walls to an ugly death, venting his fury on you because Hector perhaps killed a brother of his, maybe, or else a father, or a son. Yes, at Hector's hands many a Greek bit the dust of the broad earth; for your father was no gentle soul in the cruelty of battle.

And that is why everyone in Ilium now laments him. Ah, Hector, you have brought untold tears and misery to your parents. But my grief is cruellest of all because you did not die reaching out from our bed to me with your arms, or utter some memorable word I might have treasured night and day through my tears (*Il.* 24.724–45; tr. Rieu).

Next is the *potnia mētēr*, Hecuba:

Ἕκτορ ἐμῷ θυμῷ πάντων πολὺ φίλτατε παίδων,
ἦ μέν μοι ζωός περ ἐὼν φίλος ἦσθα θεοῖσιν
οἳ δ' ἄρα σεῦ κήδοντο καὶ ἐν θανάτοιό περ αἴσῃ.
ἄλλους μὲν γὰρ παῖδας ἐμοὺς πόδας ὠκὺς Ἀχιλλεὺς
πέρνασχ' ὅν τιν' ἕλεσκε πέρην ἁλὸς ἀτρυγέτοιο,
ἐς Σάμον ἔς τ' Ἴμβρον καὶ Λῆμνον ἀμιχθαλόεσσαν
σεῦ δ' ἐπεὶ ἐξέλετο ψυχὴν ταναήκεϊ χαλκῷ,
πολλὰ ῥυστάζεσκεν ἑοῦ περὶ σῆμ' ἑτάροιο
Πατρόκλου, τὸν ἔπεφνες· ἀνέστησεν δέ μιν οὐδ' ὥς.
νῦν δέ μοι ἑρσήεις καὶ πρόσφατος ἐν μεγάροισι
κεῖσαι, τῷ ἴκελος ὅν τ' ἀργυρότοξος Ἀπόλλων
οἷς ἀγανοῖσι βέλεσσιν ἐποιχόμενος κατέπεφνεν.

Hector, dearest (*philtate*) to me of all my sons, you were dear (*philos*) to the gods too while you were with me in the world;

and even now you have met your destiny and died, it turns out that they still care for you. Swift-footed Achilles took other sons of mine and sent them over the murmuring seas for sale in Samothrace or in Imbros or in misty Lemnos. And he took your life with his long spear; but though he dragged you many times round the grave-mound of Patroclus, the companion of his you killed, that did not bring Patroclus back to life. But you have come home to me fresh as the dew and lie in the palace (*megaron*) like one whom Apollon lord of the silver bow has visited and put to death with his gentle shafts (*Il.* 24.748–59; tr. Rieu).

The final *goos* is that of Helen:

Ἕκτορ ἐμῷ θυμῷ δαέρων πολὺ φίλτατε πάντων,
ἦ μέν μοι πόσις ἐστὶν Ἀλέξανδρος θεοειδής,
ὅς μ' ἄγαγε Τροίηνδ'· ὡς πρὶν ὤφελλον ὀλέσθαι.
ἤδη γὰρ νῦν μοι τόδε ἐικοστὸν ἔτος ἐστὶν
ἐξ οὗ κεῖθεν ἔβην καὶ ἐμῆς ἀπελήλυθα πάτρης
ἀλλ' οὔ πω σεῦ ἄκουσα κακὸν ἔπος οὐδ' ἀσύφηλον
ἀλλ' εἴ τίς με καὶ ἄλλος ἐνὶ μεγάροισιν ἐνίπτοι
δαέρων ἢ γαλόων ἢ εἰνατέρων εὐπέπλων,
ἢ ἑκυρή, ἑκυρὸς δὲ πατὴρ ὣς ἤπιος αἰεί,
ἀλλὰ σὺ τὸν ἐπέεσσι παραιφάμενος κατέρυκες
σῇ τ' ἀγανοφροσύνῃ καὶ σοῖς ἀγανοῖς ἐπέεσσι.
τὼ σέ θ' ἅμα κλαίω καὶ ἔμ' ἄμμορον ἀχνυμένη κῆρ
οὐ γάρ τίς μοι ἔτ' ἄλλος ἐνὶ Τροίῃ εὐρείῃ
ἤπιος οὐδὲ φίλος, πάντες δέ με πεφρίκασιν.

Hector, dearest to me of all my Trojan brothers, godlike Paris brought me here to Troy and married me—I wish I had perished first—but in all the nineteen years since I came away and left the land of my fathers, I never heard a single harsh or spiteful word from you. Others in the Palace insulted me—your brothers, your sisters, your brother's well-robed wives, and your mother, though your father was the soul of kindness. But you calmed them down every time and stopped them out of the gentleness of your heart (*aganophrosynē*), with your gentle words (*agana epea*). So these tears of sorrow I shed (*klaiō*) are both for you and for my luckless self. No one else is left in the wide realm of Troy to treat me kindly (*ēpios*) and befriend (*philos*) me. They all shudder at me (*Il.* 24.762–75; tr. Rieu).

The three women's laments are accompanied by the groaning and lamentation of the other women assembled around the body (στενάχοντο γυναῖκες, *Il.* 24.722 and 746), and at the end the lament involves the entire *dēmos* (ὣς ἔφατο κλαίουσ', ἐπὶ δ' ἔστενε δῆμος ἀπείρων, *Il.* 24.776).

In lamenting the loss of a husband, a son, and a brother-in-law, the three women also bewail their own fate, just as Brisëis had done. For Andromache and her son, this loss means the threat of enslavement, possibly death; for Helen it is the loss of protection from insults. Hecuba weaves her sorrow over the loss of her other dead sons into her lament. But the *gooi* reveal more than just personal grief. They address three social functions of the deceased: Hector's role as warrior and as the protector of the city, as darling of the gods, and as solver of conflict. His toughness in battle and the worry about resulting acts of vengeance are at the centre of his wife's lament as she grieves that the city has lost its protector, its *episkopos* (*Il.* 24.729). In Helen's speech the key point is Hector's gentleness, his *aganophrosynē*, that is, his ability to make use of gentle words (*agana epea*) to make peace between people.[171] This is the gentleness of which Brisëis speaks in her lament for Patroclus (*Il.* 19.300). Hector's role as *philos* of the gods is the concern of his mother, whose own status, as we know, is decisive for proximity to the gods. Such proximity to the gods is necessary for the Homeric hero since only those who are 'loved' by the gods are successful in battle and gain lasting fame amongst the living when they are dead and buried.[172]

The laments, therefore, address three qualities of a Homeric leader and *basileus*. These we have already seen, in part, as a precondition for and measure of *timē*: bravery in battle, the power to resolve conflicts through speech, and the favour of the gods.[173] Despite the individual esteem expressed in each lament, each one also refers to the community. Military prowess serves to protect both the immediate family and the community or *polis*; the ability to solve conflict through speech ensures peace within a wide network of relations. Burial guarantees the lasting memory of the dead and ensures lasting bonds among the living. The laments performed by the three women not only announce the deceased's identity for all to see and hear, they also set out the social values of the community to whom the deceased belongs. Although at first it appears as though the laying out and

---

171. For the term *aganos* see Scott 1981: 1–15.
172. See ch. 2.4 and 3.1. Thucydides (1.10) argues in a similar way when he stresses the responsibility of the gods for gaining booty.
173. For the meaning of the mediating speech see Cobet 1981: 22–23; Qviller 1981: 119.

the laments take place in the privacy of Priam's home, it becomes apparent during the course of the laments that the entire *dēmos* forms the audience for them. Indeed, later scholiasts assume that the *prothesis* took place in front of the house rather than inside.[174]

There is no basis for the contrast often drawn in earlier scholarship between the three women's laments, taken solely as expressions of their personal grief, and the *thrēnoi* performed by hired singers.[175] Formally, the *goos* most resembles a well-composed, balanced funeral eulogy, such as the public funeral orations held in honour of fallen soldiers in the fifth century.[176] The primary focus of the public funeral oration was to praise the excellence of the *polis* and the warrior as a member of that community,[177] while the Homeric *goos* revolves around praising the individual warrior's glory. This need not constitute a contrast, however, since the *goos* directly addresses the warrior's contributions to the community. He is praised as a member of the city (*asty* and *dēmos*), the community of Trojans whom he protects, and as a husband and member of the wider family which constitutes the domestic community at Troy.[178] The two groups, the local community (*dēmos*) and the family, come together to mourn the dead communally—with the women's actions being markedly emphasised in the narrative.

Despite its formal and public character, it is important not to underestimate the emotional impact the lament for the dead has on its audiences. In Troy the women of the city accompany the lament with their groans, and the entire *dēmos* ends up joining in the lamentation (*Il.* 24.722; 746; 776). During the lament for Patroclus, his comrades wet their armour and the ground with their tears (*Il.* 23.15-16). When the Muses sing the

---

174. Photios s.v. πρόθεσις [...] προετίθεσαν δὲ πρὸ τῶν θυρῶν [...]. Siurla (1989: 61-62) supposes that the *prothesis* took place indoors (*Il.* 24.719); Boardman 1955: 55-66 and Seaford 1994: 90 argue that the *prothesis* was carried out in public places.
175. See e.g. Andronikos 1968: 13-14; Vermeule 1979: 15; Siurla 1989: 93-94. The separation between poetic *thrēnoi* and emotional *gooi* goes back to Nilsson, who interpreted the *goos* as relic of primitive lament. Similarly, Reiner 1938: 8-18. In the absence of contemporary evidence such notions may only be speculative. The earliest evidence for elaborate *thrēnoi* are those of Simonides in the fifth century. Past scholarship erroneously interprets the fact of payment offered to the singer of the *thrēnoi* as a pointing to greater professionalisation.
176. See the judgment of Weber 1935: 28. Cf. also Holst-Warhaft 1992: 118; Monsacré 1984: 57-75. Easterling 1991: 149 stresses the 'unexpected authority to what women say and create'.
177. Loraux 1981: 56-75; Wagner-Hasel 2000b.
178. Cf. the description of the household of Priam in *Il.* 6.243-50.

lament for Achilles, called a *thrēnos* here, there is not a man left dry-eyed (ἀδάκρυτόν), 'so deeply did the clear song of the Muse move them' (*Od.* 24.62). This emotional effect—the production of tears—must have been an essential purpose of the lament. The shedding of tears (*dakryein*, or once *kamnein*) forms a part of the relationship of obligation between the family of the dead and the community of mourners, who receive a place at the feast in return (*Il.* 24.613).[179] Communal weeping and communal feasting both strengthen solidarity among the survivors, which is manifested in concrete actions. Revenge, such as Achilles promises and fantasises in his lament for Patroclus (*Il.* 23.17-24), is the most important of these actions and forms the obligation of male friends and family. Hecuba too is preoccupied with thoughts of vengeance and indeed imagines eating Achilles's innards in order to take revenge for her son (*Il.* 24.212-14).[180]

Another part of the *geras* of the dead is the erecting of the grave monument or funeral mound, which is the responsibility of male family members and comrades: the cousins, brothers, and comrades (ἔται κασίγνητοι and ἕταιροι). Hera suggests to the council of the gods that the brothers and comrades of Sarpedon should bury their leader underneath a grave-stone (στήλη) and a mound (τύμβος): 'For that is the *geras* of the dead' (τὸ γὰρ γέρας ἐστὶ θανόντων, *Il.* 16.456-57). Zeus passes the instruction on to Apollo when he sends him to wash and clothe Sarpedon's body (ταρχύσουσι κασίγνητοί τε ἔται τε | τύμβῳ τε στήλῃ τε: τὸ γὰρ γέρας ἐστὶ θανόντων, *Il.* 16.474-75). The brothers and comrades of Hector similarly build a grave mound for him, as do the Achaeans for the dead Achilles.[181] These men also then come together for the feast in honour of the dead (*Il.* 24.802).

Another word used for the graves of the heroes is σῆμα (*sēma*), a 'sign'. These are not just memorials, μνῆμα (*mnēma*), like later gravestones, but also spatial signals.[182] Unlike the lament, which addresses only the deceased's immediate community, the *sēma* sends its message to strangers

---

179. Achilles remembers the fate of Niobe, who lost her twelve children but did not forget to eat after the lament for the dead. For further detail see ch. 3.2.
180. In tragedy, swearing revenge is a feature of *gooi* performed by the chorus. See Holst-Warhaft 1992: 128-33; 147-49. For the obligation to avenge the dead in classical times see Plato, *Nomoi* 866b; Dem. 43.57; *IG* I³ 104, 20-23.
181. *Il.* 24.792-800 (Hector); *Od.* 24.80 (Achilles). *Stēlē* and *tymbos* are built by Odysseus for his *hetairos* Elpenor (*Od.* 12.14). At Troy, the Dardanids' ancestor Ilos has such a *tymbos* (*Il.* 11.371). Cf. 17.434.
182. See the grave of Hector: *Il.* 24.801. For further evidence see Andronikos 1968: 32-34; Grethlein 2008: 30-32 stresses the connection between poetry and tombs. Both functioned as 'commemorative media'. Cf. also Garcia 2013: 131-57.

THE GERAS OF THE DEAD

and passers-by into future generations. This is apparent from the account given in the *Odyssey* of the funeral mound erected for Achilles and Patroclus:

ἀμφ' αὐτοῖσι δ' ἔπειτα μέγαν καὶ ἀμύμονα τύμβον
χεύαμεν Ἀργείων ἱερὸς στρατὸς αἰχμητάων
ἀκτῇ ἔπι προὐχούσῃ, ἐπὶ πλατεῖ Ἑλλησπόντῳ,
ὥς κεν τηλεφανὴς ἐκ ποντόφιν ἀνδράσιν εἴη.

Over their bones we soldiers of the mighty Argive force built up a great and glorious mound (*tymbos*), on a foreland jutting out over the broad waters of the Hellespont, so that it might be seen far out at sea by the men of today and future ages (*Od.* 24.80–84; tr. Rieu).

Archaic funerary epitaphs confirm this, although here the word *mnēma* is more commonly used for the memorial. These inscriptions address a passing stranger, asking for remembrance of the dead.[183]

The grave of Achilles on the Hellespont serves as a signpost for seafarers, while the *sēma* of the Dardanid ancestor Ilus in the Trojan plain serves both as signpost (*Il.* 11.166 and 371; 24.349) and as a political monument where Hector assembles the council (*Il.* 10.414–15).[184] Erected by male relatives and comrades-in-arms, the monument forms a fixed point for their communal activity, and as such it serves to preserve the warrior's *kleos*. Menelaus erects such a monument in Egypt for his brother Agamemnon so that his fame (*kleos*) might never be extinguished (χεῦ' Ἀγαμέμνονι τύμβον, ἵν' ἄσβεστον κλέος εἴη, *Od.* 4.584). This *kleos* is not only the fame of the deceased but also that of the man who caused his death. In case he is victorious in the duel, Hector promises to deliver his opponent back to his comrades so that they may build him a *sēma* on the Hellespont; he anticipates that this will be a memorial also to his own glory:

καί ποτέ τις εἴπῃσι καὶ ὀψιγόνων ἀνθρώπων
νηΐ πολυκληΐδι πλέων ἐπὶ οἴνοπα πόντον·
ἀνδρὸς μὲν τόδε σῆμα πάλαι κατατεθνηῶτος,

---

183. For evidence of grave inscriptions see Humphreys 1983: 91–95. See also Garcia 2013: 151: '[...] the σῆμα can only function as a "sign" which conveys meaning as long as it is connected to a living memory or tradition of memory'.
184. See Bérard 1982: 92.

ὅν ποτ' ἀριστεύοντα κατέκτανε φαίδιμος Ἕκτωρ.
ὥς ποτέ τις ἐρέει· τὸ δ' ἐμὸν κλέος οὔ ποτ' ὀλεῖται.

Then one day some future traveller, sailing by in his many-oared ship across the wine-dark sea, will say: 'This is the monument (*sēma*) of some great warrior of an earlier day who was killed in action by glorious Hector'. That is what he will say, and my fame (*kleos*) will never die (*Il.* 7.87–91; tr. Rieu).

Like the *sēma*, the prizes awarded at funeral games also contribute to the posthumous fame of the fallen warrior. At the funeral of Achilles, the prizes are sponsored by his divine mother, Thetis, as we hear from Agamemnon in Hades:[185]

μήτηρ δ' αἰτήσασα θεοὺς περικαλλέ' ἄεθλα
θῆκε μέσῳ ἐν ἀγῶνι ἀριστήεσσιν Ἀχαιῶν.
ἤδη μὲν πολέων τάφῳ ἀνδρῶν ἀντεβόλησας
ἡρώων, ὅτε κέν ποτ' ἀποφθιμένου βασιλῆος
ζώννυνταί τε νέοι καὶ ἐπεντύνωνται ἄεθλα·
ἀλλά κε κεῖνα μάλιστα ἰδὼν θηήσαο θυμῷ,
οἷ' ἐπὶ σοὶ κατέθηκε θεὰ περικαλλέ' ἄεθλα,
ἀργυρόπεζα Θέτις· μάλα γὰρ φίλος ἦσθα θεοῖσιν.
ὣς σὺ μὲν οὐδὲ θανὼν ὄνομ' ὤλεσας, ἀλλά τοι αἰεὶ
πάντας ἐπ' ἀνθρώπους κλέος ἔσσεται ἐσθλόν, Ἀχιλλεῦ

Then, in the middle of the arena where the Achaean champions were to test their skill, your mother placed the magnificent prizes (*aethla*) she had asked the gods to give. You have attended the funeral of many heroes, when young men strip and make ready for the games in honour of their dead king, but if you had seen the splendid prizes offered in your honour by the divine silver-footed Thetis you would have marvelled at them as the most wonderful you had ever seen. For the gods loved you very dearly. So even death, Achilles, did not destroy your name, and your great glory (*kleos*) will last forever among all mankind (*Od.* 24.85–94; tr. Rieu).

---

185. According to Bacchylides (fr. 5.65–67; fr. 13.63–66 Maehler) immortal (*athanaton*) *kleos* is created by the games. Morris 1989: 308.

Like the *kleos* proclaimed by the gravestone, the fame connected to the prizes becomes known to a very wide circle: in this case, to all mortals.

At Patroclus's funeral games, we find as prizes all those objects we have already encountered in the context of guest-friendship: tripods, cauldrons, and mixing bowls as well as goblets of silver and gold, armour, and horses and mules.[186] In addition, there is an ox, an iron disc, and a two-handled urn[187] as well as captured women. A woman, 'skilled in flawless work', is the first prize in the chariot race and in the wrestling match. Alongside tripods, such skilled women come top in the hierarchy of prizes (*Il.* 23.263–65; 704–5). Achilles proffers all of them from his own and Patroclus's property. This property in turn consists of guest-gifts, booty, and items inherited from his father. The iron disc was looted from Eëtion, Andromache's father (*Il.* 23.827), while the horses, which are the second prize in the chariot race, are inherited from his own father Peleus (*Il.* 23.276–78). A Sidonian silver mixing bowl, the prize for the fastest runner, used to belong to Thoas and ended up in Achilles's possession when it was used as ransom, or *ōnos*, for Lycaon, a son of Priam (*Il.* 23.740–47).[188] The armour looted by Patroclus after his victory over Sarpedon is the first prize in the sword duel (*Il.* 23.798–804). These gifts, sponsored from the estate of the fallen man and his comrade, serve to confirm and strengthen the bond between the warriors and the hierarchy which underpins it.[189] The distribution of gifts in the form of prizes, or *aethla*, at the games is perhaps best described as a process of collective inheritance, as it enables the circulation of gifts to transcend death and carry on into the following generation.

Although textiles also circulate as guest-gifts and are used during the burial ritual, there are none amongst the prizes distributed at the games. Nonetheless, they emanate *kleos* comparable to that associated with *aethla* and the *sēma*. Before the return of Hector's body to Troy, Andromache laments his nakedness and speaks bitterly of the fine and lustrous garments in her house: 'I will burn all of them in a blazing fire, not to benefit you, since you are not laid out in them, but as honour (*kleos*) before the men and women of Troy (ἀλλὰ πρὸς Τρώων καὶ Τρωϊάδων κλέος εἶναι,

---

186. *Il.* 23.263; 702 (tripods); 267–68; 885 (cauldron); 656; 740; 751 (mixing bowls and cups); 809; 851; 885 (weapons); 265; 654 (horses and mules).
187. *Il.* 23.750 (cattle); 826 (iron); 270 (*phialē*).
188. For the meaning of *ōnos* see the following chapter.
189. Sourvinou-Inwood 1995: 42 also emphasises the notion that the competitive games increase solidarity within the group. See also Siurla 1989: 142 and Ulf 2011.

Il. 22.513–15). The ancient scholiasts regard it as typically female that Andromache believes the clothes could be of use if Hector lay in them.[190] Modern authors are less sceptical and assume that the garments were intended to provide clothing for the dead in Hades and/or to represent his wealth and status.[191] Textiles have symbolic as well as practical functions—this is true of the burial ritual as much as it is true of the rituals of guest-friendship. During burial they serve to conduct the deceased to a new stage, and they thus function as the bearers of a new—immortal—identity.

After washing and embalming, the corpse is wrapped in sheets. After his comrades have covered him with a fine linen robe (*heanos*), Patroclus's body is covered in a sheet, described as a gleaming (*leukos*) *pharos*, such as those handed to guests on other occasions. After cremation the bones are placed in a golden bowl (*phialē*) and once again wrapped in a linen *heanos* (*Il.* 18.346–53; 23.254).[192] In Hector's case, a *pharos* is placed over the body once the serving women of Achilles have washed him and dressed him in a *chitōn* (*Il.* 24.587–88).[193] After the lament and the cremation of the body male relatives collect the bones and store them in a golden casket (*larnax*) which is wrapped in soft purple *peploi* (πορφυρέοις πέπλοισι καλύψαντες μαλακοῖσιν) and then placed into a grave over which the comrades erect a gravestone (*Il.* 24.796). In the case of Achilles, the Nereids dress him in 'immortal garments' (ἄμβροτα εἵματα, *Od.* 24.59) and carry out the lament. He is then cremated wearing the 'clothes of the gods' (ἐσθῆτι θεῶν', *Od.* 24.67).[194]

190. See the bt-Scholia: *Il.* 22.513. Cf. de Jong 1991: 19. For a different argument see Papadopoulou-Belmehdi 1994: 119, where Andromache's declaration refers to the breaking of the bond between the couple, and the uselessness of the clothing laments the fact that Hector and Andromache will not be reunited.
191. See Helbig 1901: 237–53; Marwitz 1961: 8; Andronikos 1968: 27; Griffin 1984: 3. See now Mueller 2010: 13 who stresses the function of the cloth to contribute to the making of Hector's *kleos*.
192. Helbig (1901: 218) suspected that the *heanoi* were used for the purposes of mummification, although there is no evidence for such forms of post-mortem conservation in Greece (Andronikos 1968: 3–7). There are some suggestions, however, that measures were taken to preserve bodies for the duration of the *prothesis*. For instance, the ambrosian oil used on Hector's corpse is presumed to have been a mixture of oil and myrrh that is used for embalming in other cultures (Berg, Rolle and Seemann 1981: 100). Similarly, 'nectar', which was probably honey, has antibacterial and dehydrating effects. Honey was also used as a preservative when dyeing textiles, so that the symbolic use of nectar may also allude to clothing. Cf. Kardara 1961: 265.
193. Priam had kept back two such *pharea* and a *chitōn* when he set out to ransom Hector's body with textiles and other valuables. *Il.* 24.228–35; 580.
194. Odysseus's companion Elpenor wants to be cremated wearing his armour. *Od.* 11.74.

THE GERAS OF THE DEAD

The washing, embalming, and clothing of the dead is equivalent to the treatment of guests as a ritual of integration during which a new identity is formed. In the rituals of guest-friendship, a stranger (*xeinos*) is transformed into an insider (*philos*), while the rituals for the dead effect their transition into immortality, and thus the transformation of a lifespan into eternity.[195] Shrouds and winding sheets, carriers of that lifespan, accompany the deceased on the journey and are burnt along with them.[196] Cremation accelerates the process of transformation. It was common in parts of Greece from late Mycenaean times and practised in Attica during the seventh century BCE, and it is not considered an act of destruction but of preservation.[197] During cremation the body is liberated from its perishable parts (Richard Onians calls this 'drying'),[198] and the remaining bones have an improved consistency.[199] In Homer, the *psychē*, that intangible part of life often translated as 'soul', can leave the perishable body only once the process of cremation is completed. Such *psychai* then wander as shadow images, called *eidola kamontōn*, in Hades (εἴδωλα καμόντων, *Il.* 23.72-74; *Od.* 24.14).[200] In seventh-century clay tablets, these images, which in Homer are able to fly, are depicted as birds or Sphinges.[201] Such

---

195. See Humphreys 1981: 269: '[...] allowing the bones of the dead to become separated from the flesh which once encased them is only one of a number of ways representing the separation of a part of the person which is capable of achieving immortality from the parts which are subject to destruction by time'. See Sourvinou-Inwood (1981: 38), who interprets the ritual as change of status expressed by cloth.
196. The burning of cloth at death is known until Hellenistic and even Roman times. Cf. e.g. Xen. *Eph.* 3.7.4; Suet. *Iul.* 84.
197. Cremation is common in Attica between 1100 and 900, and again from 700. Homeric funerals appear to resemble most closely the practices seen in Cyprus during the middle of the eighth century BCE. Finds from Lefkandi from the eleventh and tenth centuries BCE also correspond closely to Homeric descriptions. Cf. Andronikos 1968: 21-32; 51-69; Coldstream 1977: 34; Blome 1984: 18-19; Hägg 1987: 207-11; Morris 1987: 32-35.
198. Onians [1951] 1989: 254-70.
199. Burnt bones are more resistant than unburnt skeletons. Cf. Hägg 1987: 208-9.
200. On the *eidolon* see Bremmer 1987: 73; Sourvinou-Inwood 1995: 89-92. On images of Hades, compare Garland 1985: 48-76.
201. Vermeule 1979: 7-11, 23-24; Peifer 1987: 15-16; Niemeyer 1996: 72. For Homeric evidence see *Od.* 11.218-22 (tr. Rieu): the mother of Odysseus knows: 'It is the law of our mortal nature, when we come to die. We no longer have sinews keeping the bones and flesh together; once life has departed from our white bones, all is consumed by the fierce heat of the blazing fire, and the soul (*psychē*) slips away like a dream and goes fluttering on its way'. In the *Iliad* (23.71; 76, tr. Rieu) Patroclus asks Achilles: 'Bury me as quickly as possible and let me pass the gates of Hades. [...] for once you have passed me through the flames, I shall never come back again from Hades'.

Figure 7: The mourning Penelope. Red-figure *skyphos* of the Penelope painter, ca 440 BCE. Chiusi, Museo Nazionale Archaeologico Inv. 1831. After Boardman 1989: Fig. 247 (= J. D. Beazley, *Attic Red-figure Vase-paintings* 1963: 1300, 2 = A. Furtwängler and K. Reichhold, *Griechische Vasenmalerei*, 1904-32).

Sphinges, assumed to be Eastern borrowings,[202] decorate Penelope's shroud on an early fifth-century vase painting (Figure 4 and 7).[203] These winged *eidola* can also be weighed (Figure 8)—just like the fate of heroes, which we have seen can be measured according to the wool required to make one shroud.[204] Just as clothing established the appearance (*eidos*) of the living, so these shrouds seem to lend the shades of the dead their own postmortal appearance. Indeed, the widely used ancient metaphor of the 'garment of the soul' appears to confirm this function of the shroud.[205]

Leucothea's 'immortal veil' conducts Odysseus, clothed in Calypso's 'fragrant garments', along a reversal of this journey—from the threat of death

202. See Vermeule 1979: 17-19, 56, 69, 212, who stresses Egyptian influence, and Neumer-Pfau 1987: 19-20.
203. Boardman 1989, fig. 247.
204. Vermeule 1979: 161, fig. 14 and 15. According to Peifer (1987: 33-43), who interprets the *eidola* as lots of death (Todeslose) and identifies the Keres with the *psychai*, the motive of the *kerostasia* starts in the last quarter of the sixth century BCE in black-figure vase painting.
205. For evidence see Kehl 1978: 945-1025, who interprets the phrase as just a manner of speaking, without any deeper meaning (1023).

Figure 8: Hermes weighing *eidola*. Attic black-figure *lekythos*, 5th century BCE. London, British Museum B 639. https://research.britishmuseum.org/research/collection_online/collection_object_details/collection_image_gallery.aspx?partid=1&assetid=1305668001&objectid=459047

by drowning back to life (*Od.* 5.367).[206] The veil does not dress Odysseus; it merely conducts him safely to shore, where he receives his new garments from Nausicaa and Arete. While the welcoming and dressing of the

---

206. I do not agree with Mueller 2010: 6 who (mis)understands the veil as a gift of hospitality: 'Ino's gift extends hospitality to Odysseus for as long as he remains in her dominion'.

stranger is part of Arete's *timē*, the *timē* of safe conduct across the threshold of death belongs to Ino Leucothea. Leucothea had received a portion of the *timē* of the gods when she herself died by drowning (νῦν δ' ἁλὸς ἐν πελάγεσσι θεῶν ἒξ ἔμμορε τιμῆς, *Od.* 5.335).²⁰⁷ Helen's brothers, Castor and Polydeuces, have the *timē* of conducting the journey both ways, since they receive *timē* from Zeus even beneath the earth, that is, after death (οἳ καὶ νέρθεν γῆς τιμὴν πρὸς Ζηνὸς ἔχοντες). They spend alternate days amongst the living and the dead. Their ability to complete the transition between life and death in both directions means that their *timē* is equal to that of the gods (τιμὴν δὲ λελόγχασιν ἶσα θεοῖσι, *Od.* 11.302-4). They are able to walk along the path of the gods and partake in the transformation of a human lifespan into immortality.

Immortality should not be understood as a state of being but as a lasting act of visualization and memorialisation of the dead by the living, which in turn ensures the order of the living. That is why it requires memorials and why the *kleos* of the dead is attached to objects such as the prizes at the funeral games, the grave-markers, and textiles.²⁰⁸ Just as the communal activity at the funeral games and the erection of a grave-stone renew the bond among the warrior community, so the work on the clothing for the dead strengthens bonds within the domestic community and amongst the women who collaborate within it. The production of these clothes requires lasting cooperation and the expense of time and energy over years, while by contrast the erection of the tomb-stone and the transformation of the deceased's goods into *aethla* requires only temporary cooperation amongst the men. Despite this, a moment of permanence attaches itself to the materiality of both the metal *aethla* and the stone *sēma*, while the textile memorials, which are burnt with the body, require periodic renewal. It would be interesting to determine whether the annual offering of garments in memory of the battle of Plataea, recorded by Thucydides, was an example of a more widely spread practice connected with perpetuating the *kleos* of the dead through textile memorials.²⁰⁹ Homeric epic does not inform us about this.

---

207. Indonesian textiles from southern Sumatra decorated with a pattern of ships have functions similar to those attributed to shrouds in the epics. See Kahn Majlis 1984: 47-53.
208. Cf. Murray 1991: 27-30.
209. Thuc. 3.58. It is possible this is a reference to the classical practice of winding patterned ribbons around grave *stēlai*. Cf. Mitchell and Havelock 1981: 103-18, fig. 93; 96.

The *geras* for the dead reflects the social structures of Homeric epic. Both military and household communities need to work together in order to provide the *geras* that is due to the dead. We can see images of both types of cooperative labour on the large funerary amphorae and kraters used as grave-markers in Attica and other parts of Greece during the eighth and seventh centuries. The bottom half of the vases shows warriors with chariots and horses, while the top part depicts the *prothesis* and lament for the dead. At the centre of the *prothesis* image we can see the shroud raised for all to see and distinguished by its pattern (Figure 5).[210] Scholarship has long suspected that geometric vases imitate textile patterns, and Elizabeth W. Barber has now produced plausible arguments for this theory.[211] If it is true, then it is also the case that the shrouds, like the laments of female relatives, depict communities working together and therefore thematise not individual glory but social cohesion.[212] This need not contradict the fact that clothing for the dead is also a way to demonstrate status, as we have seen in Penelope's intention to ensure that Laërtes, who possessed so much in life, should not lie naked in death. The following chapter will show the degree to which the status of *basilēes* was based on access to foreign resources. Indeed, the use of purple dye for the garments of the dead, as in Hector's case, suggests access to precious goods.

In current scholarship Homeric burial practices have come to be seen in the context of hero-cults developed during the course of the eighth and seventh centuries around Mycenaean grave sites.[213] The heroes' tombs, and the temple structures that develop alongside them, are taken as signs of the demarcation of territories that accompanies the emerging process of *polis*-formation.[214] Scholars posit that the hero-cult served to create local

---

210. Kurtz and Boardman 1971, fig. 4 and 5; Andronikos 1968, fig. 2; Marwitz 1961: 7–18; Huber 2001: 61–86.
211. Barber 1991: 365–72. See now Harlizius-Klück 2019. For further discussion see ch. 3.2.
212. Whitley (1991: 45–53) reads such geometric vase painting as social code. Despite referring to a striking anthropological parallel, the geometric patterning of clothing in Nuristan which is controlled by the older women in family groups, he does not connect geometric vase painting to the art of weaving. See now Harlizius-Klück 2019.
213. This is the case in Mycenae (Peloponnese), in Menidi (Attica), in Prosymna near the Argive Heraion, in Eretria (Euboea) and in Messenia. For evidence see Coldstream 1977: 341–57; Patzek 1992: 162–85; Whitley 1988: 173–82.
214. See esp. Snodgrass 1982: 107–17, who stresses a change from pastoral to farming economy, which went ahead with the internal colonisation of Attica. Cf. de Polignac 1984: 47–48, whose research underlines the symbolic meaning of the spatial order of this process. For more detail see ch. 5.4.

group identities and to consolidate power.[215] Such power can be thought of as being concentrated in the hands of aristocratic families and local elites who used the hero-cult as ideological justification for their own influence.[216] On the other hand, the power associated with hero-cults is identified with the emergence of the *polis* as a new type of community.[217]

My observations on Homeric death rituals confirm and modify these categories. The supraregional orientation of the permanent memorials, prizes, and tomb-markers points towards peaceful communication and military cooperation that transcend regional and local boundaries rather than towards the protection of territories. In Homeric epic, the tombs of heroes do not mark boundaries but signpost places and pathways of communication. This corresponds to the practice of the eighth to the sixth centuries in so far as they can be discerned from the position of excavated tombs such as the Heroon at Eretria, or Attic hero tombs situated by the city gates, as well as from the grave epitaphs mentioned earlier.[218] This supraregional orientation supports the process of *polis*-formation, but it does not express it. A reference to the *polis* in the sense of a community that reaches beyond the household is found more clearly in the women's rituals, the lament, and the presentation of the shroud, which address a local community, a *dēmos*, as a whole.[219] There is no evidence for the idea of a claim to power made by individual groups of descendants, such as Ulf connects to Homeric cults of the dead.[220] It is true that it is female relatives

---

215. Cf. Antonaccio 1994: 103. According to her, hero-cult symbolises the authority of the *polis* and a collective identity. See also Bérard 1982; Snodgrass 1982.
216. This is assumed for Attica. See Snodgrass 1980: 23; Morris 1977: 133-37.
217. According to Whitley (1988: 181) this was the case in the Argolid. A conflict between 'Dark Age aristocratic structures and the emergence of the *polis*' is expressed by the cult of the hero (Morris 1988: 768).
218. Patzek 1992: 168; Whitley 1991: 41-45; Hölscher 1998: 70-72 suspects they may serve to protect the *polis*. See ch. 5.4.
219. There is a debate over the existence of the *polis* as a political community in the epics. Cf. e.g. Scully 1990 [1994]: 6 and Seaford 1994: 1-10, neither of whom considers the Homeric *polis* as a political community. Raaflaub 1991: 246, on the other hand, is correct to draw attention to the political roles played by the council and assembly. In my view the decisive differences between the Homeric *polis* and the *polis* of archaic and classical times are: the subordination of the domestic or household community to a larger civic community, and—from the point of view of the geography of settlements—the spatial integration of different communities. See Wagner-Hasel 2017: 52-60, 100-1.
220. Ulf 1990: 245-50. Compare Humphreys 1983 for a critique of the interpretation of grave cults as ancestor cults. See now Humphreys 2018. Cf. also ch. 2, n. 89.

who cooperate in the lament for the dead, and that the textile offerings at the funeral display the wealth of a household. But the lamented deceased is never in Homeric epic the head of a greater family. Here, the lamented is an idealised young warrior who earns his *kleos* through dying for the community and who embodies the central values of Homeric society. The contrast between community and household we see in the fifth century after the Persian wars is not present in Homeric epic.

CHAPTER 5

The Benefits of Travel and Supraregional Exchange in the Archaic Age

Many of the objects and persons circulating as gifts in the epics are not locally sourced but stem from abroad. This is true of the enslaved women offered as prizes at the games and as *gera* to leaders in war as much as it is for raw materials which these women, working at the spindle and the loom, make into gifts for guests, for the dead, and for the gods. Dyes, especially purple, as well as flax, which is required for the production of linen fabrics, are available only in particular regions, as we can see in a late fifth-century description of Egypt that tells us of a place 'where flax is plentiful, the land is flat and lacking in timber' (Ps. Xen. *Ath. Pol.* 2.12). The production of metal objects also requires the addition of 'imported' components such as tin to be added to copper. Nor is the cultivation of grain and vines equally possible everywhere, and the drought-prone regions of Eastern Greece lack sufficient pasture for livestock farming.

Homeric epic contains numerous indications of supraregional exchange of resources, especially in the *Odyssey*, which can be viewed, by contrast with the *Iliad*, as a poem marked by the ethics of trade rather than battle.[1] The question of who carried out such trade, whether it was handled by aristocrats themselves or, out of necessity, by lower and poorer strata of the population, is up for debate. In a series of studies on trade in archaic times from the 1970s and 1980s, Benedetto Bravo assumed two types of trader: the aristocrat, trading through an agent and aiming to purchase grain with a view to creating bonds with clients, and the nonaristocrat, driven by poverty and exemplified, for instance, by the father of the poet Hesiod. An example of an aristocratic trader is seen by Bravo in Euneos

---

1. See e.g. von Reden 1995: 58–76. She argues that *kleos* is associated with property in the *Odyssey* and with honour in the *Iliad*.

of Samos, who provides wine for Agamemnon to give to his army.² Paul Cartledge has objected that Bravo's model is altogether too modernist and excludes political aspects of archaic trade while also taking a 'too minute and not always relevant philological approach', and neglecting archaeological evidence.³ Like Anthony Snodgrass, Cartledge recognises evidence of transport by sea for the archaic period but not for extensive trading by sea. Both deny the need for a typology of traders, and, in so far as they accept the existence of trade, they define it as import rather than export trade.⁴

Against this antimodernizing view in the tradition of Karl Bücher, Johannes Hasebroek, and Karl Polanyi,⁵ Robin Osborne took the view in the 1990s that archaic Greece did have a complex exchange network comparable to a modern system of interdependent markets.⁶ By contrast, Lin Foxhall does not see any tangible evidence in the archaeological sources for the existence of supraregional markets allowing for profitable trade. She considers trade not as a matter of supply and demand but takes instead as her starting point the notion of desire, asking why goods that were in fact available locally, such as grain, wine, or clothing, were imported at all. Foxhall argues that these are 'semi-luxuries' which were often consumed especially in ritual contexts and contributed to the development of a set of values that transcended regional boundaries.⁷

Building on these reflections, I want to place less emphasis on the issue of status but consider more closely the traded goods themselves and their uses and ask further questions regarding the character and the necessities of exchange. The terms at the centre of my analysis are πρῆξις (*prēxis*), χρεῖος (*chreios*), and ἀμοιβή (*amoibē*), partly translated as 'trade', 'debt', and 'exchange', as well as the terms ὦνος (*ōnos*) and κέρδος (*kerdos*), which are sometimes rendered as 'price' and 'profit'. Most of these terms, or their derivatives, appear in the famous diatribe in *Odyssey* 8, launched by the Phaeacian Euryalus because he suspects Odysseus of foul play:

οὐ γάρ σ' οὐδέ, ξεῖνε, δαήμονι φωτὶ ἐΐσκω
ἄθλων, οἷά τε πολλὰ μετ' ἀνθρώποισι πέλονται,

---

2. Bravo 1983: 17; 1977: 3–4. Cf. also Kopcke 1990: 123–24; Mele 1979; Reed 1984: 31–44.
3. Cartledge 1983: 8 and 12.
4. Cartledge 1983: 12; Snodgrass 1983: 16–28 and 182f.
5. Cf. Wagner-Hasel 2011: 315–40; Morley 2007: 2–16.
6. Osborne 1996: 31–44.
7. Foxhall 1998: 295–309. Cf. also Morley 2007: 36–39.

ἀλλὰ τῷ, ὅς θ' ἅμα νηΐ πολυκλήϊδι θαμίζων,
ἀρχὸς ναυτάων, οἵ τε πρηκτῆρες ἔασι,
φόρτου τε μνήμων καὶ ἐπίσκοπος ᾖσιν ὁδαίων
κερδέων θ' ἁρπαλέων· οὐδ' ἀθλητῆρι ἔοικας."

You are quite right, sir (*xeinos*). I should never have taken you for an athlete, good at any of the games men play. You are more like a skipper of a merchant crew (*archos nautaōn [...] prēktēres*), who spends his life on a hulking tramp, worrying about his outward freight (*phortos*), or keeping a sharp eye on the cargo when he comes home with his extortionate profits (*kerdos hodaiōn*). No: one can see you are no athlete (*Od.* 8.159–64; tr. Rieu).

We find in this passage almost all those terms that have been taken as evidence for the existence of trade in the poem: πρηκτήρ (*prēktēr*), the alleged trader, φόρτος (*phortos*), the freight, and κέρδος ὁδαίων (*kerdos hodaiōn*), home-bound cargo or profit.[8] None of these terms, however, are exclusively applied to trade. To anticipate one result of my examination: *kerdos* is a general term for advantage, found in a number of contexts, but predominantly connected to journeys, both metaphorical and literal. There is a difference between this and the ὦνος ὁδαίων (*ōnos hodaiōn*), which can be understood as the proceeds or profit made on a journey, and with one exception represents the value of a captured person, such as a shepherd or a skilled weaver. In this, *ōnos* resembles the *apoina*, the goods handed over as ransom by families in return for a captured relative. In the case of *ōnos*, the ransom is paid by strangers in order to purchase the right to the captured person's slave-labour. Such traffic in humans, goods, or animals is contrasted in the epic to *prēxis*, which is practised with a view to personal or communal requirements such as the reclaiming of a debt, a *chreios*. This may at times demand the undertaking of a journey by

---

8. For the terminology of trade see Bravo 1984: 129–36 (*prēktēr, phorton agein, phortizesthai, hode/hodaia, empolē/empolon/emporo/emporiē*). He assumes that *prēktēres* were *kakoi*, working for the aristocrats (ibid. 138), whereas Reed (1984: 34) sees them as 'independent maritime traders' called *emporoi* (Semonides), *phortēgoi* (Theognis), or *nauklēroi* (epigraphic evidence of the fifth century BCE) and who had become increasingly specialised since the seventh century. For a different view see Humphreys 1978: 167. According to her a class of traders cannot be identified terminologically or socially in the archaic period. See also Reed 2003: 70–71 who argues that the transformation of the Greek aristocracy 'from a warrior elite to one preoccupied with international games [...] was hardly compatible with regular maritime trading'.

sea, which is the business of a *prēktēr*.⁹ A *prēktēr* may also be one who accomplishes military deeds.¹⁰ There is a difference between the two types of *prēktēr*—but it is not one of status. Furthermore, the contrast in Euryalus's speech is not one between traders and fighters as most translations suggest; what matters is the contrast between intended plunder and peaceful undertakings, such as athletes travelling to contests. This must be what Euryalus has in mind when he claims that Odysseus does not look like an athlete. Despite the insult, Odysseus does in fact distinguish himself as an athlete, excelling at the discus and in wrestling (*Od.* 8.186–94).¹¹

The combination of mobility and plunder is distinctive of the character of exchange as represented in epic and elsewhere. This chapter therefore begins with an examination of the terms *prēxis*, *chreios*, and *amoibē* in the context of the pastoral economy. The exchange of grazing lands plays a key role in the supraregional exchange of resources, and yet its political and economic significance has hitherto received little attention. When it comes to the creation of networks across regional boundaries, such as we observe in the context of gift-exchange, grazing land is probably of much greater significance than the frequently overestimated sea-trade. Following on from this discussion we will consider the terms *ōnos* and *kerdos* as two forms of yields connected to mobility of herdsmen and pirates. In connection to the pastoral economy, *kerdos* represents the yield gained by the owners of herds and flocks and their shepherds and herdsmen working under supervision. Indeed, as will become clear, it is mainly the lone shepherds or herdsmen who are at risk of being kidnapped and exchanged for *ōnos*. The final part of this chapter is concerned with the exchange of resources beyond Greece and especially where it relates to livelihood, βίοτος (*biotos*), and necessary goods, χρήματα (*chrēmata*). These terms do not so much refer to the supply of grain needed by *basilēes* to feed their people, as to goods required for the production of signs of status and memorials: alum, the secretion of the murex snail for dying textiles, linen fabrics, and metals. These are goods that feature in ritual contexts and they provide evidence for the emergence of a set of values which transcends regional

---

9. See Descat 1986: 282–85.
10. Phoenix teaches Achilles to be a *prēktēr* in war and in rhetoric. *Il.* 9.443. The goal-directedness of *prēxis* is understood in a remark made by Achilles to Priam: οὐ γάρ τις πρῆξις πέλεται κρυεροῖο γόοιο, 'for there is no gain from this chill lament' (*Il.* 24.524).
11. The Phaeacians themselves are praised as good dancers, singers, and players of the *kithara*; in addition, they were excellent runners and oarsmen (*Od.* 8.246–48).

boundaries.¹² The implementation of this form of exchange confirms the necessity of ritual communication, to which we will turn in the final chapter. We will draw on post-Homeric sources more frequently for this part of the discussion than in the previous chapters.

5.1. Paying debts of cattle and exchanging pasture lands: Prēxis, chreios, and amoibē

During Odysseus's stay in Phaeacia, his son Telemachus goes in search of his missing father. Before his departure he asks the Ithacan assembly for a ship and twenty men to accomplish his journey for him: διαπρήσσωσι κέλευθον (*diarēssosi keleuthon*). These men are to provide the service we saw provided by the *prēktēres* in our initial passage: they are to do the rowing (*Od.* 2.213). In return Telemachus is obliged to supply food and wine, which he asks to be brought from the *thalamos* where they are stored (*Od.* 2.290; 349–55). Upon Telemachus's arrival at Pylos, Nestor asks the young man the same question posed by Polyphemus to Odysseus:

> ὦ ξεῖνοι, τίνες ἐστέ; πόθεν πλεῖθ' ὑγρὰ κέλευθα;
> ἤ τι κατὰ πρῆξιν ἢ μαψιδίως ἀλάλησθε
> οἷά τε ληϊστῆρες ὑπεὶρ ἅλα, τοί τ' ἀλόωνται
> ψυχὰς παρθέμενοι, κακὸν ἀλλοδαποῖσι φέροντες;

> Who are you, friends (*xeinoi*)? From what port have you sailed over the highways of the sea? Is yours a trading adventure (*kata prēxin*); or are you sailing the seas recklessly, like roving pirates, who risk their lives to ruin other people? (*Od.* 3.71–74 = *Od.* 9.252–55 = *Hom. Hymn Ap.* 452–55, tr. Rieu).

The translation of *prēxis* as 'trading adventure' does not adequately capture the full meaning. It seems that *chreios* (perhaps an unresolved debt or an emergency) can often be substituted. Both terms describe matters undertaken in one's own interest or that of the community. For example, in his answer to Nestor's question Telemachus differentiates between his own *prēxis* and a communal one: 'It is my own *prēxis* I speak of, not that of the *dēmos*' (πρῆξις δ' ἥδ' ἰδίη, οὐ δήμιος, ἣν ἀγορεύω, *Od.* 3.82). The same distinction is also drawn by Menelaus when he, like Nestor, enquires

---

12. See Foxhall 1998: 306.

after the purpose of Telemachus's journey, albeit using the word *chreios* rather than *prēxis*:

τίπτε δέ σε χρειὼ δεῦρ' ἤγαγε, Τηλέμαχ' ἥρως,
ἐς Λακεδαίμονα δῖαν ἐπ' εὐρέα νῶτα θαλάσσης;
δήμιον ἦ ἴδιον; τόδε μοι νημερτὲς ἐνίσπες.

Telemachus, what kind of *chreios* brought you here over the wide seas to our pleasant land of Lacedaemon? Was it public business (*dēmion*) or private affairs (*idion*)? Tell me the truth (*Od.* 4.312–14; tr. Rieu with modification).

Telemachus, too, uses the word *chreios* when he calls an assembly at Ithaca to discuss an emergency of his own:

ὃς λαὸν ἤγειρα· μάλιστα δέ μ' ἄλγος ἱκάνει.
οὔτε τιν' ἀγγελίην στρατοῦ ἔκλυον ἐρχομένοιο,
ἥν χ' ὑμῖν σάφα εἴπω, ὅτε πρότερός γε πυθοίμην,
οὔτε τι δήμιον ἄλλο πιφαύσκομαι οὐδ' ἀγορεύω,
ἀλλ' ἐμὸν αὐτοῦ χρεῖος, ὅ μοι κακὰ ἔμπεσεν οἴκῳ,

The man who summoned this gathering is not far to seek. It was I—I am in great distress. Of an army's approach I have heard nothing to tell you. Nor is it some other question of public concern (*dēmion*) that I propose to bring forward, but my own business (*emon autou chreios*), the affliction, the double affliction, that has fallen on my house (*oikos*) (*Od.* 2.41–46, tr. Rieu).

As in the *chreios* Menelaus enquires after, this *chreios* concerns his search for his missing father, but above all it refers to the damage done to Telemachus's estate by the suitors' consumption of his cattle (*Od.* 2.51; 4.316–31). *Prēxis* is, then, a more general term that expresses an action with a specific goal,[13] while *chreios* is more concrete and can often be understood as a loss of livestock ('Viehschuld'), as in Telemachus's situation. After dinner at Pylos, Telemachus's friend Mentor takes off to visit the Cauconians, where there is a *chreios* owing to him (χρεῖός μοι ὀφέλλεται,

---

13. Descat 1986: 282–85 sees *prēxis* as a deed achieved rather than a vain effort. Bravo 1984: 105 similarly understands *prēxis* as involving more than just trade, while Mele 1979: 58–60 takes *prēxis* as the term for aristocratic trade.

Od. 3.367). We can assume this kind of *chreios* to be a debt of cattle, on account of the literal meaning of the verb *ophellein* as 'grow' or 'increase'.[14]

The use of the same turn of phrase refers to a conflict over cattle in two other instances. One is the dispute between the Ithacans and Messenians, the other between the inhabitants of Pylos and those of Elis. A digression in *Odyssey* 21 gives an account of the provenance of Odysseus's famous bow. It was a gift from Iphitos, a guest-friend whom Odysseus met at Messene at the home of Ortilochus. Odysseus had gone there for a *chreios* (μετὰ χρεῖος) that was owed him by the entire *dēmos* of Messene: τό ῥά οἱ πᾶς δῆμος ὄφελλε (*Od.* 21.17). In this account Odysseus is called a παῖς (*pais*), a word which can mean a child but also a shepherd boy or shepherd, and it is this sense that is evidently the case here (*Od.* 21.21). The context tells us once again that the debt in question is flocks, namely three hundred sheep that had been taken from Ithaca, along with their shepherds, by men from Messene travelling on ships (*Od.* 21.18-19). Iphitos had come to Messene on similar business, following the loss of some mules and horses. He meets his death on this expedition, being slain by his *xeinos* Heracles who intends to keep the livestock for himself, regardless of the convention of hospitality symbolised by the loaded table the hero offered his guest-friend (ξεῖνον ἐόντα κατέκτανεν ᾧ ἐνὶ οἴκῳ, [...] αἰδέσατ᾽ οὐδὲ τράπεζαν, τὴν ἥν οἱ παρέθηκεν, *Od.* 21.26-28).

A similar debt of livestock is referred to as *chreios* in the conflict between Pylos and Elis recounted by Nestor in *Iliad* 11. According to Nestor, the military conflict between the two peoples breaks out over a row about some stolen cattle—although it is unclear who were the perpetrators and who were the victims:

> εἴθ᾽ ὣς ἡβώοιμι βίη δέ μοι ἔμπεδος εἴη
> ὡς ὁπότ᾽ Ἠλείοισι καὶ ἡμῖν νεῖκος ἐτύχθη
> ἀμφὶ βοηλασίῃ, ὅτ᾽ ἐγὼ κτάνον Ἰτυμονῆα
> ἐσθλὸν Ὑπειροχίδην, ὃς ἐν Ἤλιδι ναιετάασκε,
> ῥύσι᾽ ἐλαυνόμενος ὃ δ᾽ ἀμύνων ᾗσι βόεσσιν
> ἔβλητ᾽ ἐν πρώτοισιν ἐμῆς ἀπὸ χειρὸς ἄκοντι,
> κὰδ δ᾽ ἔπεσεν, λαοὶ δὲ περίτρεσαν ἀγροιῶται.
> ληΐδα δ᾽ ἐκ πεδίου συνελάσσαμεν ἤλιθα πολλὴν
> πεντήκοντα βοῶν ἀγέλας, τόσα πώεα οἰῶν,
> τόσσα συῶν συβόσια, τόσ᾽ αἰπόλια πλατέ᾽ αἰγῶν,

---

14. LSJ s.v. ὀφέλλω.

Ah, if only I were still as young and with all my powers intact, as I was when we and the Eleans came to blows over some cattle-raids, and I killed strong Itymoneus who lived in Elis. I was raiding his herds by way of reprisal (*rhysion*) for what the ruler Augias lord of the Eleans had done to us, and while Itymoneus was defending them I hit him with a spear and killed him, and his rustic followers scattered in panic. We drove off a vast quantity of booty from the plain—fifty herds of cattle, and as many flocks of sheep, droves of pigs and scattered herds of goats (*Il.* 11.670–79, tr. Rieu).

Nestor describes himself as raiding the herds of the Eleans in reprisal, but *rhysion* can mean both 'that which is dragged away' and that which is seized as pledge or surety, that is, in lieu of that which was dragged away.[15] It is unclear, therefore, whether Nestor is recovering his own stolen cattle, or whether he is seizing Elean property in lieu.[16] In any case, the assault on Itymoneus's cattle develops into a full-blown raid, as Nestor describes how the Pylians drove a great quantity of booty from the plain of Elis to the Pylian citadel: fifty herds of cattle and as many flocks of sheep, herds of goats and swine, as well as horses (*Il.* 11.677–83). The livestock is distributed amongst all those owed a debt at Elis: (οἷσι χρεῖος ὀφείλετ' ἐν Ἤλιδι δίῃ, *Il.* 11.686; 11.688). Nestor's father, Neleus, takes a herd of cattle along with three hundred sheep and their shepherd, since 'a great *chreios* was owed to him at sacred Elis' (*Il.* 11.698). This *chreios* was a four-horse chariot that had been sent to race at Elis to compete for a tripod but had been kept instead by Augeas, the ruler of the Eleans (*Il.* 11.699–702). It is not clear whether this chariot was the rhysion originally fought over by Nestor, nor is there any further information that would explain how the other Pylians' *chreios* came about. The only background given in Nestor's account is the weakened state of Pylos resulting from attacks by Heracles which had emboldened the Eleans to plunder and insult the Pylians (*Il.* 11.695).[17]

A possible hint at the cause of the conflict may be given by the location of events at sacred Elis. The livestock represented as *chreios* is located in the plain of Elis and driven to the citadel of Pylos. According to Stefan

---

15. LSJ s.v. ῥύσιον. See Jackson 1993: 73 hinting at a similar wording in Polyb. 22.4.
16. See now McInerney (2010: 99) who examines the background of Nestor's tale and reconstructs several attacks and counter-raids.
17. On cattle-raiding as *rite de passage* see now Newton 2015: 266.

Hiller's examination of the geography of Pylos in Mycenaean and Homeric texts, Homeric Pylos is not the Mycenaean excavation site of Ano Englianos but Pylos in Triphylia.[18] The area of Triphylia stretches out to the south of the river Alpheus and is both more mountainous than Elis and less rich in water.[19]

With Peneus in the north and Alpheus in the south, Elis has two rivers that are abundant in water year-round. In this western part of the Peloponnese, average annual precipitation today is 1000 mm, while in the east, in the region of Attica, it is only 400 mm. Thus Olympia, at present located in the flood zone of the Alpheus, but two metres lower in antiquity, is green even in summer, while the eastern and southern Peloponnese are very dry during the summer months.[20] Geographic and climatic conditions make the plain around Olympia ideal for year-round pasture, which must have been very attractive for inhabitants of dryer regions. Ancient authors from Homer to Strabo repeatedly emphasize the significance of Elis as an area for pasture (Homer, *Od.* 21.347).[21] There is a detailed description in Theocritus of herds and flocks pasturing all over the area at the river-banks and being driven back at the end of the day for milking, with the noise of the animals resounding throughout the entire plain and all the paths (Theoc. *Id.* 26.96). All this points to a dispute over the use of Elean pasture for Pylian herds as the root cause of the conflict in Nestor's story. On his visit to Messene, Pausanias suspected this much:

> ἐνέμοντο δὲ ἐμοὶ δοκεῖν αἱ τοῦ Νηλέως βοῦς ἐν τῇ ὑπερορίᾳ τὰ πολλά· ὑπόψαμμός τε γάρ ἐστιν ὡς ἐπίπαν ἡ τῶν Πυλίων χώρα καὶ πόαν βουσὶν οὐχ ἱκανὴ τοσαύτην παρασχέσθαι. μαρτυρεῖ δέ μοι καὶ Ὅμηρος ἐν μνήμῃ Νέστορος ἐπιλέγων ἀεὶ βασιλέα αὐτὸν ἠμαθόεντος εἶναι Πύλου.

> But the cattle of Neleus were pastured for the most part across the border, I think. For the country of the Pylians in general is sandy and unable to provide much grazing. Homer testifies to this, when he mentions Nestor, always adding that he was king of sandy Pylos (Paus. 4.36.5; tr. Jones).[22]

18. Hiller 1972: 214–16.
19. For the geology of Elis see Lienau 1989: 93.
20. Lienau 1989: 250–51, 264; Gehrke 1986: 103–4.
21. For further evidence see Semple 1922: 26. According to Semple, Elis has the best pastures in the Peloponnese.
22. By Pylos Pausanias means the foothills of Koryoasia (4.36.1).

Around the time of Polybius Messenian flocks and herds were grazing around the area of Phigalia, which had been claimed by the Aetolians during the second century BCE (Polyb. 4.3). Today Sarakatsani shepherds from the Pindus mountains settle in the hills of northern Elis for the winter, while the local population graze their livestock around their villages all year long.[23]

The movement of herds and flocks for pasture is well documented for classical and Hellenistic times and is mentioned in Homeric epic too.[24] Eumaeus, for instance, states that Odysseus's herds graze both on the mainland and on Ithaca, and that they are tended by local as well as foreign shepherds. Indeed, Eumaeus lists a dozen each of cattle, sheep, goat, and swineherds (*Od.* 14.96-104). The shepherd Philoetius brings a regular delivery of cattle and sheep from the mainland to the suitors feasting at Odysseus's house (*Od.* 20.185-88). He tells the disguised Odysseus how he was sent as a young boy to herd cattle at the *dēmos* of the Cephallenians (*Od.* 20.209-10), and that out of loyalty to Telemachus, he is not now moving away with the herds. It would be dishonourable in his view to depart to foreign lands with the cattle, while his old master's son is still alive (*Od.* 20.218-20). Noëmon, who lets Telemachus use his ship, also has horses and mules grazing at Elis (*Od.* 4.635-37). Close ties to the mainland are found too in the catalogue of ships in the *Iliad*, which has Odysseus leading soldiers from the mainland facing the islands of Ithaca, Samos, and Zakynthos (*Il.* 2.631-37). Pylos and Elis are mentioned as potential places of refuge for Odysseus (*Od.* 24.430-32).

The use of pasture in alien lands gives rise to conflict, not only in Homeric epic. Pausanias for instance gives the unlawful taking of livestock grazing in Lacedaemonian territory as one of the causes for the outbreak of the Messenian War that is dated around the time of the fourth Olympiad (c. 764 BCE). According to Pausanias the Messenian Polychares, lacking his own grazing land, gave his cattle to the Spartan Euaephnus for grazing on his land, promising a share (*moira*) of the produce or offspring (μοῖραν εἶναι [...] τοῦ καρποῦ τῶν βοῶν) in return. Euaephnus places unjust profit (κέρδη τε ἄδικα) over loyalty and sells the cattle to some traders (*emporoi*), pretending to Polychares that he had been robbed by pirates. The fraud is uncovered by one of the herdsmen who has managed to escape from the

---

23. Lienau 1989: 217 and 149. Büdel 1976: 18-40 describes the varied history of the use of Elis.
24. Cf. Georgoudi 1974; Petropoulou 1985: 54; Chaniotis 1995: 39-89. Chandezon 2003.

merchants, and Euaephnus promises to repay the price (*timē*) he received for the cattle (τιμὴν δὲ ἥντινα εἰλήφει τῶν βοῶν). He then proceeds to commit an even greater crime by killing the son of Polychares when he comes to collect the *timē*. Polychares now takes his complaint to the Lacedaemonian *basilēes* and *ephors*, lamenting and recounting the wrong done to him by one who he had made his friend and trusted above all Lacedaemonians (ὃν αὐτὸς ξένον ἐποιήσατο καὶ πρὸ πάντων Λακεδαιμονίων ἐπίστευσεν). Since he is unable to gain redress, war eventually breaks out between Messene and Sparta (Paus. 4.4.5-8).

Against this background it is possible to get a clearer sense of the meaning of *chreios*. Quite apart from the question of whether the story is a true account of the outbreak of the Messenian War, it does explain why we hear in Homer that a debt of livestock 'grows'. This must refer to the increase in the size of the herd, of which Euaephnus in Pausanias's story is promised a portion. It seems likely then that Mentor, himself described as a shepherd (*Od*. 13.222), intends to collect just such a portion, described by Pausanias as *moira* and *kerdos*, on his trip to the Cauconians. In Pausanias we see the exchange based on a guest-friendship. Just such a guest-friendship (*xeinosynē*) is initiated by the exchange of weapons between Odysseus and Iphitos when they meet, both searching for their livestock (*Od*. 21.35).[25] Since this is the only instance in Homeric epic of the institution of guest-friendship encapsulated in one term, I suspect that we are not here dealing with a military cooperation but that this guest-friendship enables a peaceful exchange of pasture and the safe migration of livestock and herdsmen.

The term for such mutual exchange is ἀμοιβή (*amoibē*), with its verb ἀμείβω/ἀμείβομαι (*ameibō/ameibomai*). Both in Homer and in later sources *amoibē* describes the compensation people may expect for services rendered to guest-friends and for sacrifices made to gods as well as divine retribution for wicked deeds. Frequently the context is the pastoral economy or a sacrificial feast. So we find Athena asking Poseidon for a 'pleasing recompense' (χαρίεσσαν ἀμοιβήν) for sacrifice (*Od*. 3.58-59).[26] In the episode about the cattle of Helios, the word *amoibē* is used to mean the compensation for his stolen cattle in the threats made by Helios to Zeus (*Od*.

25. For more detail see ch. 2.2.
26. Manticlus asks Apollo for a counter-gift, called *chariessan amoiban*, for his offer of a bronze statue. *Lexikon Iconographicum Mythologiae Classicae* 11, Zürich 1984, s.v. Apollon No. 40. See Plato, *Symp*. 202 E. For further evidence see Laum 1924: 31; Jeffrey 1961: 94, n.1.

12.382).[27] In the context of guest-friendship *amoibē* and the verb *ameibō/ameibomai* appear in situations in which reciprocity has failed. Mentes, whose father Anchialus once provided goods from his resources (*pharmaka*) to Odysseus because he loved him (φιλέεσκε, *Od.* 1.260-64), can now expect from Telemachus a gift that is worthy (*axion*) of *amoibē*, that is, of compensation (*Od.* 1.318).[28] This exchange is not ultimately realised because of the problematic situation at Ithaca, but it is based on an existing bond, as is made clear by the use of *philein* to characterise Anchialus's relationship with Odysseus.[29] Guest-friendship is also the background when Laërtes assures the supposed Cretan Aëthon that if he were at Ithaca Odysseus would compensate him amply with gifts (εὖ δώροισιν ἀμειψάμενος) for the many presents and hospitality he received (*Od.* 24.273 and 285). Telemachus's plea to the suitors not to consume the property of just one man but to take turns in different houses (ἀμειβόμενοι κατὰ οἴκους) goes unheeded (*Od.* 1.375). The verb *ameibomai* and *ameibō* is otherwise often used for the exchange of words and song, either in council, in hospitality situations, or during burial rituals.[30] Here its metaphorical use depends especially on the idea of endangered grazing livestock. Visually *ameibō* carries the meaning of a concrete change of location, or the crossing of a boundary, as in the much-used formula 'to cross the barrier (*herkos*) of the teeth'. Achilles makes use of this turn of phrase when he wants to emphasise that not even all the treasures of Delphi will be sufficient to weigh up his life (ἀνδρὸς δὲ ψυχὴ πάλιν ἐλθεῖν οὔτε λεϊστὴ | οὔθ' ἑλετή, ἐπεὶ ἄρ κεν ἀμείψεται ἕρκος ὀδόντων, *Il.* 9.408-9).[31] In these cases, passing through the *herkos*, the fence or boundary, means death, just as would be suffered by livestock if they left their enclosures. In other instances, the passing (*ameibein*) into an enclosure may equally be imagined as transformation into livestock. Such a transformation takes place when Circe's potions (*pharmaka*) turn men into swine when they cross 'the barrier of the teeth' (φάρμακ' [...] ἀμείψεται ἕρκος ὀδόντων, *Od.* 10.328).

27. For a stronger meaning in the sense of revenge (*tisis*) see *amoibē* in Hes. *Op.* 327-34 or Pind. *Pyth.* 2.24.
28. Scheid-Tissinier 1994: 37-40 underlines the reciprocal aspect.
29. See ch. 2.3.
30. For evidence see Scheid-Tissinier 1994: 38.
31. *Herkos* is the fence around the yard (*Il.* 9.472; 976; *Od.* 24.442 and 449) and the yard itself (*Il.* 16.231; 24.306), where Eumaeus's pigs are held (*Od.* 20.164). The fence encloses fields (*Il.* 5.90; *Od.* 21.191; 240) and orchards (*Il.* 18.564). In Linear B *herkos* (we-re-ke) is a fold for animals. See Hiller and Panagl 1976: 135-37. For a linguistic connection between *herkos* and *horkos*, 'oath', see Hiersche 1993: 30-31 and Hirzel 1912: 153.

We can therefore say that *ameibē* and *ameibō/ameibomai* occur in epic in connection with the crossing of boundaries, albeit metaphorically as in rituals, in speech, and in the exchange of weapons and gifts. Etymologically, an idea of movement is inherent in the term, which would suggest an ultimate derivation from the Indogermanic root **mei = migrare*.³² The fact that in Homer *ameibō* also has this concrete meaning of movement in the context of pastoral farming allows for the possibility that the migration of livestock is the core from which the term's various uses have developed.³³ The fact that the only exchange of weapons in Homeric epic that results in the creation of a bond between people is occasioned by the practice of moving livestock for pasture fits well with this. The exchange of grazing lands may also have helped with the exchange of other resources, usually subsumed under the term of trade, as well as with pacts and agreements, and the exchange of oaths.

Such a connection between the pastoral economy and the exchange of resources and oaths is encompassed in the term ἐπαμοίβιμα ἔργα (*epamoibima erga*), which refers to the responsibilities of Hermes. According to the Homeric Hymn, deeds of mutual exchange, or barter (ἐπαμοίβιμα ἔργα) are conducted under the supervision of Hermes, who also rules over grazing livestock (ἐπὶ προβάτοισιν).³⁴ In keeping with the meaning

32. See Prellwitz 1905: 32; Bosacq 1916: 51–52; Hofmann 1950 s.v. ἀμείβω; Frisk 1960: 90; Benveniste 1969: I, 96–98; Chantraine s.v. ἀμείβω.
33. Alongside *Il.* 9.408–9 compare also *Il.* 11.547, describing the retreat of Ajax as that of a wild beast, 'a little changing knee by knee', i.e. step by step (ὀλίγον γόνυ γουνὸς ἀμείβων). The composite *parameibō* is used for changes of location, as Nausicaa suggests that Odysseus might walk past Alcinous (τὸν παραμειψάμενος) and clasp her mother's knee instead (*Od.* 6.310). A similar sense occurs in the Homeric Hymn to Apollo where *parameibō* describes the circumnavigation of Maleia (*Hom. Hymn Ap.* 409: παρημείβοντο Μάλειαν). Tragedians and historians of the fifth century begin to use *ameibō*, e.g. for crossing the threshold (Eur. *El.* 750: δέσποιν', ἄμειψον δώματ', Ἠλέκτρα, τάδε; Aeschyl. *Choe.* 571: εἰ δ' οὖν ἀμείψω βαλὸν ἑρκείων πυλῶν; Hdt. 5.72: τὰς θυρὰς ἀμεῖψαι), or for passing through maritime straits and paths (Aesch. *Pers.* 69: πορθμὸν ἀμείψας; Eur. *Or.* 1295: ἀμείβω κέλευθον).
34. *Hom. Hymn Herm.* 516. In archaic art Hermes is usually a messenger, or companion to heroes. His role as messenger from Hades only begins in fifth-century Attic art. The name *psychopompos* occurs only in Roman times. See Zanker 1965: 56–59; 104–6; Simon 1985: 302; Kahn 1979: 201–11. Strauss Clay 1989: 98 views Hermes as embodying the principle of movement. For *hermai* serving as road markers at crossings and boundaries see Osborne 1985a: 48–73; Athanassakis 1989: 33–49. Simon (1985: 301) suggests that these *stēlai*, or heaps of stones, may have served to mark boundaries between different pasture regions but assumes that they were originally used as memorials for the dead. Athanassakis argues for the reverse.

of *probata*, these animals tend to wander (προβαίβειν).³⁵ In both literature and iconography, Hermes is predominantly pictured as a shepherd, which suggest that *probata* are usually sheep.³⁶ Yet Hermes is also the herdsman who promises to take the cattle of his master Apollo to graze in pastures on mountains and in the plains and who will receive a portion of Apollo's treasure in return (*Hom. Hymn Herm.* 491-92; 529).³⁷ According to the myth of Hermes dated to the sixth century BCE he achieves this through a trick. As a child Hermes steals Apollo's cattle as they graze in the untouched pastures in the mountains of Pieria. Swapping their hooves around so that their traces appear to go in the opposite direction, Hermes leads the cattle over Mt Onchestos into the plain and all the way to the shore at Pylos (*Hom. Hymn Herm.* 70-96). The journey he makes is of course that of the transhumant shepherd who leads animals from mountain to plain and vice versa.³⁸ On the banks of the river Alpheus, he lets the animals graze and drink. In the evening he drives them into an enclosure and slaughters two of them as a feast for the gods, during which, in keeping with his role in presiding over the gods' banquets, he gives to each his portion or *geras* (*Hom. Hymn Herm.* 104-29).³⁹ Hermes intends to put himself in charge of the finest art of cattle farming through his theft (*Hom. Hymn Herm.* 166-67; 172-73). The hymn ends once Hermes and Apollo come to

35. On the derivation of *probata* from *probainō* see Shipp 1979: 474; Orth 1921: 382.
36. Post-Homeric sources use *probata* as well as *mēla* for sheep (see e.g. Dem. 47.52; Arist. *Pr.* 893a17; Polyb. 9.17; Athenaeus 5.219a; 9.402d-e). According to the ancient commentators Homer includes sheep, goats, and pigs in the term *probata* (see Schmidt 1979: 174-82). On Hermes as shepherd see Brendel 1934, fig. VII 1; XXX 1 and 2; XLVI-XLIX; Simon 1985: 300, fig. 287; Orth 1924: 602 and 609; Athanassakis 1989: 33-49. There are numerous references to the many flocks found in Hermes's birthplace Arcadia (*Hom. Hymn Herm.* 1-9), e.g.: Hom. *Il.* 2.605; Pind. *Ol.* 1.669; Theocr. *Id.* 22.157; Apoll. Rhod. *Argon.* 1.575. See also Pausanias (2.3.4) on a Hermes statue in Corinth: 'Proceeding on the direct road to Lechaeum we see a bronze image of a seated Hermes. By him stands a ram, for Hermes is the god who is thought most to care for and to increase flocks, as Homer puts it in the *Iliad*', (tr. Loeb). The passage cited from the *Iliad* by Pausanias associates Hermes with the adjective *polymēlos* (wealthy of flocks), lent to him by Eudoros (the good gift), the son of Polymele and Hermes: *Il.* 14.490; 16.174-92.
37. The terms for this treasure are *ploutos* or *olbos*, most likely alluding to wealth amassed at Delphi. Apollo also profits from the shepherd's labour in that he has a share in income from the livestock (*Hom. Hymn Herm.* 493-95).
38. For a similar argumentation see Hodkinson 1988: 51, although he denies the importance of transhumance for ancient Greece. See ch. 5.4.
39. See Clay 1989: 117-25: she sees this as staging the typical human feast such as that prepared by Eumaeus for Odysseus (*Od.* 15.319) from which the gods (in the case of Eumaeus it is Hermes and the Muses) receive a portion.

an agreement, expressed through the exchange of the lyre for the whip, and the swearing of oaths, and finally through Zeus granting the charge of *epamoibima erga* as the *timē* of Hermes (*Hom. Hymn Herm.* 514-20).

There is no reason to assume that the term 'deeds of exchange' applies exclusively to bartering, as the dictionaries suggest.[40] Just like the underlying verb *ameibō* the term has a wider meaning that corresponds to the spheres associated with Hermes and encompasses the exchange of livestock and pasture as well as oaths exchanged between people and the reciprocal relations between gods and men. Jenny Strauss Clay sees in 'movement and passage' the theme that unifies the various manifestations of *epamoibima erga* (theft, exchange, verbal communication in the form of lies, oaths, and treaties).[41] Viewed against the Homeric uses of the verb *ameibō*, this is not merely an abstract point. With his *epamoibima erga* Hermes is responsible for the concrete movement of livestock and commodities across boundaries, which in turn necessitates agreements in the form of oaths and rituals (such as the exchange of arms) in order to avoid the ever-present dangers of robbery, deceit, and lies so familiar to Hermes and to the Homeric heroes.

Before moving on to illustrate the connection between transhumance and exchange, it is first necessary to consider the profits resulting from exchange across boundaries.

5.2. Kerdos and ōnos hodaiōn: Pastoral yields and profits from kidnapping

5.2.1. Kerdos, kerdea, kerdios, kerdaleos

The distinction made in the *Odyssey* between the athlete and the man who has an interest in the *kerdea hodaiōn* is not a social one between a class of traders and a class of aristocrats distinguished by their participation in athletic and musical competitions. The warriors competing at the funeral games for Patroclus certainly have an interest in *kerdea*. The term κέρδος (*kerdos*) tends to apply to profit or gain made without battle and in secret. Since there are a number of instances of deliberation around the potential

---

40. LSJ s.v. ἐπαμοίβιμα ἔργα = barter. For the meaning of *epamoibima erga* in the hymn see Clay (1989: 145), who interprets the *epamoibima erga* of Hermes as 'theft' and 'exchange', whereas Viechnicki (1994: 113-32) underlines a connection with 'gift-exchange'.
41. Clay 1989: 146.

kerdos to be made through a particular course of action, it makes sense also to translate *kerdos* as 'advantage', and its related adjective κερδίων/ κέρδιον (*kerdion*) as 'more advantageous'. Although scholarship suggests that *kerdos* is a term for trading profits, we will see that this is only indirectly the case.[42] The advantage expressed by *kerdos* is achieved through cunning and depends on intellectual power or perception, referred to as νόος (*noos*) and associated with mobility.[43] Since *kerdos* is used especially in the context of taking a metaphorical or physical journey or path, we may also take *kerdos* to mean the advantage or profit gained by choosing the correct path, which includes journeying by sea. A person described as *kerdaleos* is one who has the wisdom to choose the right path. By contrast, someone described as *kerdaleophrōn* is entirely and exclusively directed at achieving *kerdea* and thus lacking in wisdom. Hesiod's treatment of reciprocal ethics between neighbours clarifies the differences between good and bad *kerdea* alluded to in the *Odyssey*.

I will begin by examining the warriors' quest for *kerdea* and what in the *Iliad* is considered *kerdion*, and will then move to the *kerdea* sought in the *Odyssey* by Penelope and Odysseus. The key contexts for the quest for *kerdea* are to be found in competitions, the reconnaissance of the Trojan camp, in the provision of goods from shepherds, and in the weaving trick. In Hesiod's *Works and Days* we find *kerdea* connected to a sea journey, although here, as in Euryalus's speech in the *Odyssey*, a connection is made to athletic and musical competitions.

In the *Iliad*, an understanding of *kerdea* is primarily necessary during competitions, as Nestor suggests when he states that success in the chariot race depends not merely on the speed of the horses but also on knowledge about *kerdea* (κέρδεα εἰδῇ). What he means is that his son Antilochus's skilful driving will compensate for the fact that Antilochus's horses are slower than those of Menelaus (*Il.* 23.322; 515). Odysseus, too, is said to have knowledge of *kerdea* (κέρδεα εἰδώς) when he competes in the wrestling at the funeral games and resorts to cunning in order to defeat his opponent Ajax, whom he cannot match in strength (*Il.* 23.709; 725-26).

---

42. See de Jong 1987: 79-81 for the difference between *kerdos* as advantage for oneself, by contrast with *ophelos* as 'advantage for another'. Bamberger 1976: 1-32 differentiates between three aspects of *kerdos*: profit (*Od.* 8.164), advantage (*Il.* 10.225; *Od.* 16.311) and cunning plan. Descat (1986: 286-88) differentiates between the spheres of trade and exchange, in which *kerdos* is respectively 'profit' and 'use' (*besoin*).
43. Onians (1989: 82-3) interprets νόος (from νέομαι, 'I go', and νέω, 'I move in a liquid, swim') as dynamic and movable power.

In battle, too, *kerdos* is not gained through the use of physical power, as we see when Menelaus and Agamemnon are in need of counsel described as *kerdaleos* (βουλῆς [...] κερδαλέης) after they have fallen behind in battle against the Trojans (*Il.* 10.44). The plan is to send a scout into the Trojan camp for reconnaissance. Diomedes volunteers as the scout, asking for a companion to go with him since 'when two go together, one will notice (ἐνόησεν) before the other where there is advantage to be had' (κέρδος ἔῃ', *Il.* 10.224–25). The ability to discern advantage, *kerdos*, depends on agility of *noos*, the intellectual power of perception. It also depends on strength in cunning (*mētis*), as we see in Diomedes's subsequent remarks: 'If one is alone he may notice it, but his mind is slower (βράσσων τε νόος) and his cunning weak: λεπτὴ δέ τε μῆτισ' (*Il.* 10.225–26). The adjective *leptos* used here to describe *mētis* is more commonly used to describe the fine and transparent texture of woven fabrics such as those worn by Calypso (αὐτὴ δ' ἀργύφεον φᾶρος μέγα ἕννυτο νύμφη, | λεπτὸν καὶ χαρίεν, περὶ δὲ ζώνην βάλετ' ἰξυῖ | καλὴν χρυσείην, κεφαλῇ δ' ἐφύπερθε καλύπτρην, *Od.* 5.230–31). Diomedes, of course, decides on Odysseus as his companion, as the most skilled when it comes to the kind of perception described with the verb *noein* (ἐπεὶ περίοιδε νοῆσαι, *Il.* 10.247). It is indeed Odysseus who then discovers the Trojan spy Dolon as they make their way to the enemy camp. The two companions manage to outrun Dolon, who is then persuaded by *polymētis* Odysseus to provide information about the situation in the Trojan camp (*Il.* 10.339–445).

In all three cases *kerdos/kerdea* may be rendered as advantage(s), resulting from the mastery of routes or paths taken at the chariot race or on the reconnaissance expedition. The advantages are seized for the sake of a gain or profit consisting in the prize at the competition (*aethlon*) and in glory or fame (*kleos*). The material gift promised in return to the scout is a black ewe with her lamb as well as a standing invitation to the feasts to be given by each of the leaders in charge of ships (*Il.* 10.213–17). This places the capacity to gain *kerdos* and the compensation given for gaining it into a close semantic relationship with each other. The common denominator is movement in space and in spirit.

Predominantly in the *Iliad* we are dealing with deliberation about which is the 'more advantageous' or 'more profitable' (κέρδιον) path to take. Here, the more advantageous path is retreat. The gods themselves consider it so, as when Zeus states that it would have been much more advantageous (*poly kerdion*) for himself as well as for Poseidon if Poseidon had thrown himself in the sea instead of supporting the Greeks (*Il.* 15.226). This is also true for Athena, to whom Zeus indicates that withdrawing from battle would be *poly kerdion* (*Il.* 7.28). In the mortal sphere a preference for retreat as the *kerdion* option is similarly expressed by Deiphobus when he opts to withdraw and seek reinforcement through Aeneas in the face of the Greeks' superior power (*Il.* 13.458).[44] The advantage does not only adhere to those who retreat. According to Achilles his own withdrawal from battle was *kerdion* for Hector and the Trojans because during that time victory was on the side of the Trojans (*Il.* 19.63).

It may, however, also be *kerdion* to stand up and fight—although a negative outcome is implied in such cases. So, Hector considers it *kerdion* to go into combat against Achilles and die; equally the Achaeans risk their lives to recover the body of Patroclus because it is *kerdion*. The warrior's *kleos* or *kudos* are key in such deliberations over what is *kerdion* (κέρδιον εἴη, *Il.* 22.103-110: Hector; 17.417-19: Achaeans). When Paris reveals his cowardice in combat, Hector claims it would have been better (*poly kerdion*) if Paris had never been born, or had died unmarried (*Il.* 3.41). The weighing up of the more advantageous option does not take place without a normal system of social values—even if the means by which advantages, *kerdea*, are gained may at times lead one to suspect this. Thus, Antenor's sense of what is the more advantageous option takes into account the obligations between Trojans and Greeks, the *horkia pista*. He proposes to the Trojan council that Helen and her goods should be returned because otherwise no advantage would issue to the Trojans (οὔ [...] τι κέρδιον [...] ἐκτελέεσθαι, *Il.* 7.351-53).

Andromache, too, has a negative definition of what is *kerdion*, when she fears for Hector's life and calls it *kerdion* if she were to sink into the earth after his death since she has no father or mother (*Il.* 6.410). While in this example it is the loss of protection that leads to the consideration of what is *kerdion*, a lack of military equipment can provoke similar thoughts. Pandarus reflects in *Iliad* 5 that it would have been more advantageous, *poly kerdion*, if he had not left his horses at home in order to spare them. Without them he is afraid he is not properly armed and may not see his home and his wife again (*Il.* 5.201; 213).

The accusation of being κερδαλεόφρων (*kerdaleophrōn*) made by Achilles against Agamemnon and again by Agamemnon against Odysseus is one of the rare instances of a negative judgement made of the consideration of

---

44. The return home is described as *poly kerdion* in *Od.* 11.358-59.

kerdion (*Il.* 1.149; 4.339).⁴⁵ In both cases the accusation refers to a neglect of reciprocal obligation: in the case of Agamemnon the taking of Achilles's prize, and in the case of Odysseus the apparent reluctance to fight despite having received honours at the feast. The attitude described as *kerdaleophrōn* suggests deception—a skill that of course particularly distinguishes Odysseus.

Penelope and Odysseus are the experts on *kerdea* in the *Odyssey*. There is one case of *kerdea* achieved by taking paths physically—in this case profits made from trading in livestock. In Book 19, when Odysseus in his guise as the Cretan Aëthon promises the imminent return of Odysseus, he also tells Penelope that her husband has chosen to gather wealth (*chrēmata*) by roaming widely because he considers it *kerdion* to do so (ἀλλ' ἄρα οἱ τό γε κέρδιον εἴσατο θυμῷ, | χρήματ' ἀγυρτάζειν πολλὴν ἐπὶ γαῖαν ἰόντι, *Od.* 19.283-84). The Cretan then adds, by way of explanation, that 'Odysseus knows more than any mortal about gainful ways (κέρδεα πολλὰ [...] οἶδ'), nor could any other mortal compete with him there' (*Od.* 19.285-86).⁴⁶ Since Aëthon alleges that Odysseus takes the decision to travel farther after leaving the Phaeacians, we might assume that the *chrēmata* he mentions are different in type from the *keimēlia* Odysseus has received in Phaeacia, unless they refer back to the previous mention of Odysseus asking around the *dēmos* for many rich *keimēlia* (*Od.* 19.272-73). Some specificity may be found in Telemachus's explanation that there is no *kerdos* to be gained (οὔ τοι τόδε κέρδος ἐγὼν ἔσσεσθαι) from questioning the shepherds on whether they honoured (τίει) their master during his absence or dishonoured him (ἀτιμᾷ), as Odysseus proposes they should do (*Od.* 16.305-7; 311). Here too we find a mention of the path that needs to be taken in order to achieve *kerdos*: Telemachus points out that they would waste a lot of time walking around in search of each man at his pasture while the suitors would continue to feast on the household goods. Telemachus suggests that they should postpone checking up on the men at their shepherds' stations until a later time (*Od.* 16.313-15; 318-19). Given that these considerations have demonstrated that the honour (*tiein*) and dishonour (*atimazein*) in question always involve material benefits, we must assume that the *kerdos* Telemachus temporarily rejects must be whatever profit the shepherds have made from their journeys to different pastures on behalf of Odysseus. When father and son eventually travel to the countryside after the punishment of the suitors, and Odysseus wonders what *kerdos* the

---

45. See the superlative *kerdistos* used for Sisyphus in *Il.* 6.153.
46. Kopcke 1990: 126 assumes a reference to economic profit.

Olympian will now pay out to him (ὅττι κε κέρδος Ὀλύμπιος ἐγγυαλίξῃ), this too is connected with profit made from livestock trading. We know that Odysseus is concerned to recover the flocks consumed by the suitors without payment, νήποινον (nēpoinon), and without compensation, ἄτιμον (atimon) (Od. 23.140; 356-58).

In the *Homeric Hymn to Hermes* the term κερδαλέος (kerdaleos) explicitly refers to profit made from trading in livestock. The adjective is used of Apollo who here appears in his role as the owner of herds, which he leaves Hermes to tend. The latter will lead the animals to graze on mountains and in plains and will guarantee the herds' growth for Apollo: 'We will graze the pastures of the hill and of the horse-feeding plain with the cattle penned in the *agros*. There cows covered by bulls shall bring forth male and female progeny abundantly. There is no need for you, who are *kerdaleos*, to be furiously angry'.[47] The term *kerdaleos* here describes an attitude specifically interested in the profit to be made from cattle which, like that of Odysseus, grazes in a variety of pastures.

In the *Odyssey* a lot of *kerdea* are gained through thinking and through weaving. Like Odysseus in the *Iliad*, Penelope has a reputation, attested by Antinous, for knowing about *kerdea*. She too achieves her goal through the cunning trick (*dolos*), which enables her to postpone remarriage (*Od.* 2.88; 105). Penelope's knowledge of *kerdea*, just like the good sense which she needs for her weaving work, and her ability to fashion fabrics of outstanding beauty, stem from Athena (*Od.* 2.116-18). The goddess is praised amongst all the gods for her cunning intelligence (*mētis*) and for her *kerdos* (ἐν πᾶσι θεοῖσι μήτι τε κλέομαι καὶ κέρδεσιν, *Od.* 13.298-99). Penelope's *kerdos* too can be understood as a concealed form of thought which, along with cunning intelligence, leads to advantage.

While Penelope's wisdom about *kerdea* refers to her weaving work, Odysseus's knowledge of *kerdea* involves the use of thought and words. Athena confirms that they both know about *kerdea* (εἰδότες ἄμφω κέρδε', *Od.* 13.296-97). Penelope is famed for this amongst the immortals, while Odysseus is renowned amongst the mortals when it comes to counsel and speech (βουλῇ καὶ μύθοισιν). The goddess tells him this while at the same time gently mocking him for attempting to deceive her without recognising her divine status behind her disguise as a shepherd (*Od.* 13.222). These

---

47. Hom. *Hymn Herm.* 491-95: ἡμεῖς δ' αὖτ' ὄρεός τε καὶ ἱπποβότου πεδίοιο | βουσὶ νομοὺς Ἑκάεργε νομεύσομεν ἀγραύλοισιν. | ἔνθεν ἅλις τέξουσι βόες ταύροισι μιγεῖσαι | μίγδην θηλείας τε καὶ ἄρσενας· οὐδέ τί σε χρὴ | κερδαλέον περ ἐόντα περιζαμενῶς κεχολῶσθαι.

qualities earn him the description of being like a *kerdaleos*, that is, according to Athena, one who exceeded Odysseus in all manner of cunning (ἐν πάντεσσι δόλοισι, *Od.* 13.291–92).

Counsel, words (*mythoi*), and thoughts (*noēmata*) are also described with the adjective *kerdaleos*. Thus, the speech (*mythos*) addressed by Odysseus to Nausicaa to gain her support is *kerdaleos* (*Od.* 6.148), as is the thought which Odysseus must not conceal when asked by Alcinous for his background and the purpose of his journey (τῷ νῦν μηδὲ σὺ κεῦθε νοήμασι κερδαλέοισιν | ὅττι κέ σ' εἴρωμαι, *Od.* 8.548–49). The word suggests concealed interests and deception, such as are associated with Odysseus and his guile and cunning. With *kerdalea noēmata*, Odysseus could easily deceive Alcinous. When meeting Nausicaa, Odysseus considers it *kerdion* not to take the customary position of a supplicant by grasping the girl's knees but instead to address her with words alone in order not to unsettle her. He also addresses her as (*w*)*anassa*, a term used predominantly for goddesses and alluding to the notion of human fate lying on the knees of the gods; thus in his address, characterised as *kerdaleos*, he is able to mention her knees, without touching them: 'By your knees, I beg, mistress' (γουνοῦμαί σε, ἄνασσα, *Od.* 6.149).[48]

The ability to conceal personal interest is described with the term κερδοσύνη (*kerdosynē*), also rendered as 'cunning' or 'craft'. Helen tells Telemachus at Sparta how Odysseus used *kerdosynē* to avoid meeting her and being discovered at Troy (*Od.* 4.251). In his own home Odysseus has to act with *kerdosynē* in order to stop the dogs from uncovering his disguise in their joyful recognition of their master (*Od.* 14.31). Athena leads Hector into the duel against Achilles and thus to his destruction with *kerdosynē* (*Il.* 22.247).

Penelope demonstrates her knowledge of the deception and cunning involved in the achievement of *kerdea*, which she refers to as *kaka*, wicked, when she explains to Odysseus her hesitation and reticence in finally recognising him as her lost husband. She was afraid because there are many who are intent on wicked *kerdea* (πολλοὶ γὰρ κακὰ κέρδεα βουλεύουσιν, *Od.* 23.217). Her fear was that she might be taken in by lies and made to believe that Odysseus had returned. Mostly the perception of *kerdea* is positively valued. Thus, Penelope chides her son that he had better sense (*phrēn*) for perceiving *kerdea* as a child and that he would not have allowed the mistreatment of a guest (μᾶλλον ἐνὶ φρεσὶ κέρδε' ἐνώμας, *Od.* 18.216).

---

48. For the symbolic meaning of the knees see Onians [1951] 1989: 174–86.

Her remark suggests that here too advantage, *kerdea*, has its place in the proper order of things in which respect for a guest is valued.

In Hesiod's *Works and Days*, we find explicit condemnation of wicked *kerdea*. The issue is that a breakdown in neighbourly reciprocity results in endangering the safety of livestock:

πῆμα κακὸς γείτων, ὅσσον τ' ἀγαθὸς μέγ' ὄνειαρ
ἔμμορέ τοι τιμῆς ὅς τ' ἔμμορε γείτονος ἐσθλοῦ
οὐδ' ἂν βοῦς ἀπόλοιτ', εἰ μὴ γείτων κακὸς εἴη.
εὖ μὲν μετρεῖσθαι παρὰ γείτονος, εὖ δ' ἀποδοῦναι,
αὐτῷ τῷ μέτρῳ, καὶ λώιον αἴ κε δύνηαι,
ὡς ἂν χρηίζων καὶ ἐς ὕστερον ἄρκιον εὕρῃς.
μὴ κακὰ κερδαίνειν· κακὰ κέρδεα ἶσ' ἄτῃσι.

A bad neighbour is as big a bane as a good one is a boon: he has got good value who has got a good neighbour. Get good measure from your neighbour, and give good measure back, with the measure itself and better if you can, so that when in need another time you may find something to rely on. Seek no evil gains (*kaka kerdainein*): evil gains (*kaka kerdea*) are no better than losses (*atai*) (Hes. *Op.* 346-52, tr. West).

Base *kerdea* are similar to the *atai* which cause states of blindness in the epic that then lead to insults of individuals' *timē*. Possession of *timē* in turn justifies a claim on goods and services. Here the balance of *timē* ('respect') between neighbours forms the point of reference for judging *kerdea* as wicked or devious (*kaka*). *Timē* is materially represented here in the form of agricultural goods, especially cattle, that neighbours give to one another. These goods must also be the substance of the *kerdea*, which are better rendered as 'benefits' rather than 'profits' since the context is not one of trade and selling, but of neighbourly exchange.[49]

The *kerdos* that Hesiod recommends can be made through seafaring,[50] is understood as profit made from trade:

---

49. According to Descat 1986: 291 we have here a hint at a change in reciprocal relations towards measurability and contractual obligation, but the use of the term *timē* in epic contradicts this. Hesiod simply considers the problem with respect to different groups from those the epics are concerned with. For the morality of reciprocity in Hesiod's poems see Millett 1984: 84-115 and Schmitz 2004: 63-82.
50. Solon (*fr.* 1 D 41-46) and Alcaeus (*fr.* 45 D) also gain *kerdos* from sea journeys.

καὶ τότε νῆα θοὴν ἅλαδ' ἑλκέμεν, ἐν δέ τε φόρτον
ἄρμενον ἐντύνασθαι, ἵν' οἴκαδε κέρδος ἄρηαι,
ὥς περ ἐμός τε πατὴρ καὶ σός, μέγα νήπιε Πέρση,
πλωΐζεσκ' ἐν νηυσί, βίου κεχρημένος ἐσθλοῦ
ὅς ποτε καὶ τεῖδ' ἦλθε πολὺν διὰ πόντον ἀνύσσας,
Κύμην Αἰολίδα προλιπὼν ἐν νηὶ μελαίνῃ,
οὐκ ἄφενος φεύγων οὐδὲ πλοῦτόν τε καὶ ὄλβον,
ἀλλὰ κακὴν πενίην, τὴν Ζεὺς ἄνδρεσσι δίδωσιν.

Then drag the swift ship to the sea, and in it arrange your cargo (*phorton*) fittingly so that you may win profit (*kerdos*) for your return: just as my father and yours, foolish Perses, used to sail in ships in want of fair livelihood. And one day he came here, making the long crossing from Aeolian Cyme in his dark ship, not running from riches (*aphenos*), nor from wealth (*plouton*) and prosperity (*olbon*), but from evil poverty, which Zeus dispenses to men (Hes. *Op.* 631–38, tr. West).

The need for *kerdos* arises from *peniē*, a lack of goods outlined with the terms *aphenos*, *ploutos*, and *olbos*, which ultimately suggest agricultural commodities such as cattle, grain, and wool. Hesiod follows this with further reasons for seafaring, which are *chrea*, need, and *limos*, hunger:

τύνη δ', ὦ Πέρση, ἔργων μεμνημένος εἶναι
ὡραίων πάντων, περὶ ναυτιλίης δὲ μάλιστα.
νῆ' ὀλίγην αἰνεῖν, μεγάλῃ δ' ἐνὶ φορτία θέσθαι
μείζων μὲν φόρτος, μεῖζον δ' ἐπὶ κέρδεϊ κέρδος
ἔσσεται, εἴ κ' ἄνεμοί γε κακὰς ἀπέχωσιν ἀήτας.
Εὖτ' ἂν ἐπ' ἐμπορίην τρέψας ἀεσίφρονα θυμὸν
βούληαι [δὲ] χρέα τε προφυγεῖν καὶ λιμὸν ἀτερπέα,
δείξω δή τοι μέτρα πολυφλοίσβοιο θαλάσσης,
οὔτε τι ναυτιλίης σεσοφισμένος οὔτε τι νηῶν.

But you, Perses, must attend to all tasks in season, and in the matter of seafaring above all. Compliment a small ship, but put your cargo (*phortia*) in a big one: bigger will be the cargo (*phortos*), bigger the extra gain (*kerdos*), provided that the winds withhold their ill blasts. When you want to escape debt (*chrea*) and joyless hunger (*limon*) by turning your blight-witted heart to trade (*emporiē*), I will show you the measure of the resounding sea—quite without instruction as I am either in seafaring or in ships (Hes. *Op.* 641-69, tr. West).

The cargo of a ship, *phortos*, and the *kerdos* to be obtained through the journey are proportional to one another and also interchangeable: the bigger the *phortos*,[51] the greater the *kerdos* that will be obtained. Scholars assume that Hesiod here refers to the sale of agricultural surplus, so that his *kerdos* includes the profit made on those sales.[52] Generally, this is thought to apply to grain,[53] although Hesiod also mentions wool weighing down the sheep (εἰροπόκοι δ' ὄιες μαλλοῖς καταβεβρίθασι, *Op.* 234), which contributes, together with the gifts of Demeter, to save good men from hunger (*Op.* 230). Wool can only keep hunger away if it is traded for consumable goods. This is not true of the livestock itself which can be slaughtered or kept alive in store for times of hunger.[54] Thus I suspect that Hesiod's *kerdos* alludes to animal products such as wool, or the breeding of animals, which are more likely than grain to yield surplus quantities for trade.[55]

The only concrete destinations mentioned for the sea journeys in Hesiod are the supraregional festivals; these must therefore be the locations for the exchange of freights (*phortia*) into gain (*kerdea*). One such occasion is the poetry festival at Chalkis at which Hesiod claims to have won a tripod (*Op.* 650-57). In the *Homeric Hymn to Hermes*, the divine herdsman is also a skilled singer and credited with the invention of the lyre, which he ultimately hands over to Apollo, the owner of the herd, who then, of course, becomes known as the god of the lyre (*Hom. Hymn Herm.* 47-54, 475-90).[56] It seems therefore that the singer who travels to a poetry

---

51. Hesiod does not differentiate between *phortos* (see *Op.* 672) and *phortia* (see *Op.* 693) and gives no information about the content. Hesiod's advice is to minimize potential losses by not taking the entirety of one's possessions along: 'do not put all your substance (*bios*) in ships' holds, but leave the greater part and ship the lesser; for it is a fearful thing to meet with disaster' (Hes. *Op.* 689-90, tr. West).
52. Perysinakis 1986: 116; Reed 1984: 33-43.
53. Bravo supposes the sale of grain (1983: 31). According to him Hesiod was the dependent agent of an aristocratic trader, 'qui envoie des cargoisons de marchandises' (Bravo 1984: 135). Jameson (1983: 8) and Garnsey ([1988]1993: 75) assume the sale of the surplus of the harvest.
54. See Halstead 1980: 307-9.
55. All calculations of surplus (e.g. Garnsey [1988] 1993: 53-58; 89-106) are based on speculation. See the critique by Isager and Skydsgaard 1992: 108-14. On the difficulty of calculating the productivity of ancient agriculture see also Osborne 1987: 44-47.
56. For the meaning of the lyre see now Scheid and Svenbro 2014.

competition may also be a herdsman or an owner of livestock, out to make some profit or gain, *kerdos*, from his herds and flocks. This is especially likely given that animals were required for the hecatombs at festivals and that the earliest written evidence for trade in livestock is found in the context of sacrifice.[57]

In summary, *kerdos* is best defined as a term for concealed interest, aimed at a gain or benefit. Especially in the context of a pastoral economy *kerdos* may be understood as a benefit earned by moving herds to pastures and market places. This benefit comes closer to being a form of trading profit when it is transported over unspecified distances, primarily by sea, without, however, any evidence for the existence of professional traders. Such benefits, *kerdea*, can be sought by any agent in epic: warriors and athletes, counsellors and weaving women, herd-owners and farmers. But the term also points to the existence of another field of activity, namely robbery and piracy. As we will see, robbers and warriors are not necessarily different in status.

5.2.2. Ōnos and apoina

In the epic poems, the proper term for the benefit earned on a journey, or by transport, is ὦνος (*ōnos*). The term is frequently rendered as 'price' or 'purchase' but also as 'transaction'.[58] Such transactions are mainly handled by warriors but also by the Phoenicians, who, in antiquity, were thought of as prototypical traders.[59] They differ in no way from the Greeks.

In *Odyssey* 20 the suitors complain to Telemachus about the quality of his guests and tell him it would be more advantageous (*poly kerdion*) to send the strangers to the Sicilians where they would 'fetch you a fitting price' (ὅθεν κέ τοι ἄξιον ἄλφοι', *Od.* 20.383). The 'fitting price' fetched by

---

57. For epigraphic and archaeological evidence see Jameson 1988: 87–119 and now Jim 2014.
58. According to Bravo (1977: 7) *ōnos* belongs to the commercial terms and means 'achat'. More convincing is Edouard Will (1957: 5) who argues that *ōnos* never means 'achat' but only 'transaction'. See also Gallagher 1988: 85–106 who discusses the Mycenaean roots of the term. According to him, the term goes back to *o-no*, that means 'ass-load' (91).
59. See von Jhering 1884: 373–82, who also attributes the development of guest-friendship to the Phoenicians. Hasebroek [1928] 1966: 18 has a more negative reading. Reed 1984: 32–35 argues against the notion of the Phoenicians as traders, assuming rather that gift-exchange was a part of Phoenician culture. See also Aubet 1993: 103–11.

transporting a person abroad is here called *axios*, a word we have encountered before in the context of weighing up a person's value, their *timē*, and which properly means 'that which is weighed up'. What is meant is the quantity of goods that weighs up a person's value, which in this case is determined through the use of force and through transportation. The verb ἄγειν (*agein*) connected to *axios*, which means 'to lead' and 'to weigh', is frequently found linked to the term *ōnos*. Alongside *apoina*, *ōnos* is the proper technical term for the value of a person who has been taken by force. Where *apoina* are the goods collected by the relatives of a kidnapped or conquered person in return for their recovery, *ōnos* is realised only once the person has been transported abroad.

The ransom paid to Achilles for Lycaon, the son of Priam and Laothoë, is an instance of *ōnos*. The story of this *ōnos* is remembered when Lycaon meets Achilles in combat: Achilles had caught Lycaon cutting branches off a fig tree in his father's garden and had taken him off to Lemnos by boat (ἐπέρασσε νηυσὶν ἄγων). There he handed him over to the son of Jason, who gave him an *ōnos* (ὦνον ἔδωκε). A guest-friend then ransomed (ξεῖνός μιν ἐλύσατο) Lycaon for a great price and sent him to Arisbe, presumably selling him on, since Lycaon escapes back to his father's land only to fall back into the hands of Achilles some days later (*Il.* 21.35-48).[60] Despite being offered three times the previous ransom, Achilles kills the Trojan (*Il.* 21.80). The value of the *ōnos* Lycaon had fetched before is given as one hundred oxen, as Lycaon reminds his enemy Achilles (καί μ' ἐπέρασσας ἄνευθεν ἄγων πατρός τε φίλων τε | Λῆμνον ἐς ἠγαθέην, ἑκατόμβοιον δέ τοι ἦλφον, *Il.* 21.78-79). Another part of the same *ōnos* reappears during the funeral games: a silver mixing bowl offered as the prize for the winner in the footrace had been given by Euneos, the son of Jason, as *ōnos* for Lycaon (ὦνον ἔδωκε, *Il.* 23.740-41). Like other objects circulating as guest-gifts or souvenirs, this silver bowl too has a provenance: it had been handed down by the grandfather, Thoas, who had received it as a gift from the Sidonians (*Il.* 23.741-47).

The ransom, ἄποινα (*apoina*), Achilles would receive from Priam if his sons Lycaon and Polydorus were still alive also includes bronze and gold items from their mother's property (*Il.* 22.49-51). Where such ransoms are actually paid by relatives—as for the release of Hector's body—the objects handed over are textiles and gold, as well as tripods and bowls (*Il.* 24.229-37). Thus, the only difference between *ōnos* and *apoina* is that the former is paid by strangers, the latter by the family.

---

60. Garlan (1984: 45) assumes an 'achat'.

This difference also explains the phrase ἀνάποινον ἀπριάτην (*an-apoinon apriatēn*) used in the context of the negotiations for the release of Chrysëis. After Agamemnon's refusal to accept *apoina* for the daughter of Chryses (*Il.* 1.20),[61] and following the outbreak of the plague, the seer Calchas determines (*Il.* 1.99) that Chrysëis must now be returned without *apoina* (ἀνάποινον) and *apriatēn* (ἀπριάτην). This suggests the waiving of payments from relatives in the form of *apoina* and the payment of *ōnos* from strangers. The adverb *apriatēn* is derived from the deponent verb πρίασθαι (*priasthai*) whose aorist form ἐπριάμην (*epriamēn*) is integrated into the conjugation of the verb ὠνέομαι (*ōneomai*). While the verb *ōneomai* does not occur in Homer, the aorist *epriamēn* is used to describe the actions of someone paying an *ōnos* for a person who thus gains possession of that person (*Od.* 1.430; 14.115; 452; 15.483). The action of the person who hands over another person in return for *ōnos* is described with the verb πέρνημι (*pernēmi*), the basic meaning of which is 'to lead away'.[62] So Achilles boasts to Lycaon that he has caught many men and 'led them away' (πολλοὺς [...] πέρασσα, *Il.* 21.102). The mere mention of transportation abroad is enough to express the circumstances of the receipt of *ōnos* and thus the 'sale' of the person abroad. Such is the fate envisaged for Apollo and Poseidon when Laomedon threatens to lead them off to far-away islands (περάαν νήσων ἔπι τηλεδαπάων) instead of paying them their wages (*Il.* 21.454). A similar understanding of transportation as enslavement can still be found in the Hunza valley in Pakistan, where 'to drag over the river' means 'to enslave'.[63]

In the *Odyssey* those transported over the sea and exchanged for *ōnos* are Euameus and his Sidonian nurse, Odysseus's nurse Eurycleia, and allegedly Odysseus himself. The perpetrators are not warriors, however, but Phoenicians of uncertain status.

During his conversation with Eumaeus, Odysseus claims that a Phoenician had pretended to want to transport a cargo to Libya with him, when in reality he had wanted only to take Odysseus himself over there (περάσειε) in order to achieve a vast *ōnos* (ἄσπετον ὦνον ἕλοιτο, *Od.* 14.296-97). According to Odysseus they are shipwrecked, but he himself is rescued by Pheidon, the king of the Threspotians, who does not make a profit from

---

61. See also *Il.* 1.13: λυσόμενός τε θύγατρα φέρων τ᾽ ἀπερείσι᾽ ἄποινα.
62. Chantraine 1940: 12-15. In post-Homeric sources περάω (*peraō*), to cross, occurs more frequently, denoting specifically transportation by sea. The derivative πόρνη (*pornē*, a prostitute) remains.
63. Jettmar 1993: 42.

Odysseus (ἐκομίσσατο Φείδων | ἥρως ἀπριάτην, *Od.* 14.316–17).[64] Following from my earlier remarks, the use of the adverb *apriatēn* suggests that transport abroad and the receipt of *ōnos* are here renounced.

When Odysseus goes on to ask after Eumaeus's own fate, we have a clear indication of the kinds of situation in which a person might be carried off to be exchanged for *ōnos*:

ἀλλ' ἄγε μοι τόδε εἰπὲ καὶ ἀτρεκέως κατάλεξον,
ἠὲ διεπράθετο πτόλις ἀνδρῶν εὐρυάγυια,
ᾗ ἔνι ναιετάασκε πατὴρ καὶ πότνια μήτηρ,
ἦ σέ γε μουνωθέντα παρ' οἴεσιν ἢ παρὰ βουσὶν
ἄνδρες δυσμενέες νηυσὶν λάβον ἠδ' ἐπέρασσαν
τοῦδ' ἀνδρὸς πρὸς δώμαθ', ὁ δ' ἄξιον ὦνον ἔδωκε.

Won't you tell me what happened? Was it sacked, the city of broad streets where your mother and father lived; or did some band of raiders capture you as you tended your sheep and cattle alone and bring you by ship to the palace here and get a good price (*axion ōnon*) from your master? (*Od.* 15.383–88, tr. Rieu).

The payment of *ōnos* can hardly be a guarantee of survival, as Garlan believes;[65] it is clear that the achievement of *ōnos* is the purpose of such abductions.

The Sidonian woman, whose story is closely linked to that of Eumaeus, is taken by Taphians on her way from the *agros*, which may mean either field or pasture (*Od.* 15.428: ἀγρόθεν ἐρχομένην, πέρασαν δέ με δεῦρ' ἀγαγόντες). She too is 'led away' (πέρασαν) and brought (ἀγαγόντες) to the house of a man, Eumaeus's father, who had given an appropriate *ōnos*, as she explains to Eumaeus's Phoenician kidnappers (ὁ δ' ἄξιον ὦνον ἔδωκε, *Od.* 15.428–29). In return for taking her back home to Sidon, the woman promises to take with her the child of Eumaeus: 'I would lead him (ἄγοιμ') on board, and he would fetch you a countless *ōnos* when you lead him off (περάσητε) to men of strange speech' (*Od.* 15.452–53). The Sidonian woman dies on the journey, but Eumaeus is 'acquired' by Laërtes (*Od.* 15.483), just as he had previously 'acquired' Eurycleia (πρίατο κτεάτεσσιν ἑοῖσιν, *Od.* 1.430–31). We hear nothing of the precise

---

64. According to Heubeck (1989: 215) the term ἀπριάτην does not make sense here; he therefore assumes a misunderstanding.
65. Garlan 1984: 45.

value of the vast *ōnos* the child Eumaeus was expected to fetch; of Eurycleia we know that the wealth (*ktear*) Laërtes gave to acquire her had been the value of twenty oxen.[66]

In these cases, *ōnos* is realised only through transport abroad. Thus, *ōnos* is a form of ransom, but one paid by strangers rather than relatives. There is one case in which *ōnos* is proposed to be paid for objects: the Phoenicians offer jewellery to Eumaeus's mother (*Od.* 15.463), who in turn promises to give an *ōnos* for it (ὦνον ὑπισχόμεναι). Given, however, that the real *ōnos* the men will take with them is the child Eumaeus, it is not unlikely that the word is used here as a form of foreshadowing of subsequent events. This is also true of the phrase *ōnos hodaiōn* used by the Sidonian woman as she gives them their instructions after they have sworn an oath to her:

ἀλλ' ἔχετ' ἐν φρεσὶ μῦθον, ἐπείγετε δ' ὦνον ὁδαίων.
ἀλλ' ὅτε κεν δὴ νηῦς πλείη βιότοιο γένηται,
ἀγγελίη μοι ἔπειτα θοῶς πρὸς δώμαθ' ἱκέσθω.

No; keep the idea to yourselves, and collect your homeward cargo (*ōnon hodaiōn*) as fast as you can. When all the stores (*biotos*) are on board the ship, quickly send word to me up at the house (*Od.* 15.445-47, tr. Rieu).

This *ōnos hodaiōn*, often rendered as 'homeward cargo', will of course turn out to be the child Eumaeus, so that the phrase *epeigete d'ōnon hodaiōn* may also refer to the future profit that Eumaeus will fetch. In other words, and differing from Rieu's translation, what the woman may also be saying to the Phoenicians is: 'Keep my words in mind and seek the proceeds of your cargo!'[67] Once more we would then have an example of *ōnos* realised through transportation.

The term *ōnos* alludes to rudimentary origins of the slave-trade, and it is in this context we find the verb *ōneomai* in classical written sources.[68] This

---

66. Cf. *Od.* 14.115, where Odysseus asks Eumaeus: ὦ φίλε, τίς γάρ σε πρίατο κτεάτεσσιν ἑοῖσιν. This is the case of Mesaulius, whom Eumaeus had acquired with his own revenues (*Od.* 14.452), which must have been yields of his livestock. The mobile character of possessions named *ktear* is stressed by Scheid-Tissinier 1994: 46.
67. LSJ s.v. ἐπείγω.
68. See the argumentation of Finley 1955: 173, and Rihll 1993: 77-107, who associates the founding of colonies with slave trade. For the slave trade in archaic and classical Greece see Garlan 1984: 51-54.

form of trade is structurally connected to kidnap and robbery, since *ōnos* is acquired through the transportation of a kidnapped person. *Ōnos* may consist of metal objects, such as those circulating as gifts (e.g. the silver mixing bowl offered as *ōnos* for Lycaon) as well as unspecified *kteata*; it may also be said to consist of *biotos*, the means of living, often rendered as 'wealth' or 'substance'. So, the goatherd Melanthius threatens to take Eumaeus away from Ithaca by boat in order that he might fetch him much wealth (ἵνα μοι βίοτον πολὺν ἄλφοι, *Od.* 17.250). The quest for a *biotos* is the catalyst for many journeys in Homer, and it will be the focus of the final section.

5.3. The quest for the means of living (biotos) and other necessary goods: Alum, purple, linen, and metals

Within the Homeric poems a series of journeys is undertaken for the purpose of earning both the means of living, βίοτος (*biotos*) and necessary goods such as χρήματα (*chrēmata*) or κτήματα (*ktēmata*). The Phoenicians who carry off Eumaeus spend a year on the island of Syria, where Eumaeus's father rules, and fill their ship with *biotos* (ἐν νηῒ γλαφυρῇ βίοτον πολὺν ἐμπολόωντο, *Od.* 15.456).

Egypt is frequently named as a place where there is plenty of such 'means of living' to be found. Nestor tells Telemachus of Menelaus's exploits there, where he collected (*ageirein*) much *biotos* and gold, taking these goods (also described as *ktēmata*) back home on ships.[69] Achilles alludes to the plentiful *ktēmata* to be found in the houses of Egyptian Thebes when he rejects Agamemnon's gifts of compensation (*Il.* 9.382). Telemachus learns during his visit at Sparta that Helen and Menelaus had been staying for some time at Thebes, where there were so many *ktēmata* (ὅθι πλεῖστα δόμοισ' ἐν κτήματα κεῖται, *Od.* 4.127). The goods they brought back from Egypt are specified and the names of the donors given: there are two silver baths, a tripod, and ten talents of gold that Menelaus claims to have received from Polybus of Thebes. His wife Alkandre gave Helen the golden spindle and the silver basket she uses during Telemachus's visit (*Od.* 4.125-35). In addition, there are the φάρμακα (*pharmaka*) Helen uses to induce Telemachus to forget his grief over his father. These *pharmaka* also come from Egypt where many harmful as well as many beneficial

---

[69]. *Od.* 3.301: πολὺν βίοτον καὶ χρυσὸν ἀγείρων; *Od.* 3.312: πολλὰ κτήματ' ἄγων, ὅσα οἱ νέες ἄχθος ἄειραν.

pharmaka are said to grow (*Od.* 4.228-30). We hear from Mentes that Odysseus had tried to obtain such *pharmaka* from Ilus, at Ephyra, to use as poison to smear on the tips of his arrows. When Ilus refused to provide the poison, Mentes's father gave it to Odysseus instead (*Od.* 1.259-64).

In the Cretan tale, Odysseus also alleges a stay in Egypt, where he claims to have collected many goods, described here with the term *chrēmata*. He emphasises that everyone gave goods, without going into any further detail about the circumstances (πολλὰ δ' ἄγειρα | χρήματ' ἀν' Αἰγυπτίους ἄνδρας· δίδοσαν γὰρ ἅπαντες, *Od.* 14.285-86). He also claims to have spent seven years in Egypt, just like Menelaus in the story told by Nestor at Pylos (*Od.* 3.305-12: Menelaus and Helen; 14.287: Odysseus). In his story Odysseus paints himself as a leader of companions-in-arms who go to Egypt in order to rampage and plunder. This suggests that the *chrēmata* obtained by Odysseus are most likely booty, sometimes including human booty. He claims that his companions had taken women and children off and killed their men. Whereas his companions are destroyed in battle with Egyptian fighters, he claims that he himself was spared by the king and taken in as a guest-friend (*Od.* 14.276-84). This may mean that he is taken on as a mercenary, in keeping with a similar tale in Herodotus about some Ionian and Carian pirates who are taken on as mercenaries by Psammetichus I (Hdt. 2.152).[70] According to Sarah Humphreys, such exchanges of manpower are more important in archaic times than the exchange of goods.[71] But equally, this type of traffic in mercenaries cannot be imagined without an attendant exchange of goods.

The list of objects brought back from Egypt to Menelaus's home in Sparta suggests that some of the goods are gifts of remembrance, such as we have already met in the context of our treatment of guest-friendships. But we have also noted that such gifts, brought home from abroad, are always also differentiated according to their material value as metal and textile goods. The terms *biotos* (means of living, from βιόω—I live), *ktēma* (acquired good, from κτάομαι, I acquire), and *chrēma* (a thing one needs, from χράομαι, I need) do not suggest anything about the materiality of the goods encompassed by the terms. This must mean that there is no fixed material content attached to these terms. What they all have in common is

---

70. Herodotus also uses the term *chrēmata*, when he enumerates booty taken from the Persians after the battle of Plataea, including women, horses, camels, talents and other goods (*talla chrēmata*) which are then specified as silver and gold and patterned garments (Hdt. 9.81-82).

71. Humphreys 1978: 169.

mobility. *Chrēmata*, only mentioned in the *Odyssey*, are collected during a journey, or consumed by the suitors, so that it can be assumed that these tend to be natural goods, mostly the products of livestock farming.[72] The possibility should not be excluded, however, that they may also include human booty, acquired during a journey and exchanged for other commodities, as we saw in our discussion of *kerdos* and *ōnos*. These other goods are what *ktēmata* tends to stand for: the treasures found in homes, the *keimēlia* brought from abroad, and which can also be carried off again; these may be metal or textile goods, depending on the given context.[73] *Biotos* appears often to be used as a synonym for agricultural goods or raw materials. The suitors make a distinction between *biotos* and *ktēmata* in their plans for dividing among themselves Telemachus's property, which consists of livestock and of material objects.[74] It seems likely that in this instance *biotos* refers to the herds and flocks and their products, such as meat and wool.[75]

As for the *biotos* brought over from Egypt by Menelaus, it can be assumed that the term is meant to point to linen fabrics, or flax. Scholarship tends to assume a Greek interest in Egyptian grain, linen, papyrus, fayence, gold, and medicinal plants.[76] The Egyptians in turn are thought to have imported oil, wine, woollen fabrics, and silver from Greece. There can be no doubt that gold was a key interest, since Egypt was the main purveyor of gold throughout antiquity, and Homeric epic explicitly

---

72. The word is also used for the goods consumed by the suitors (*Od.* 16.389) and the goods Telemachus would have to seek from the city (χρήματ' ἀπαιτίζοντες, *Od.* 2.78), once the suitors had consumed all the treasure and livestock (κειμήλιά τε πρόβασίν, *Od.* 2.75). This suggests that *chrēmata* mostly refers to agricultural but also material goods.
73. Such *ktēmata* are found in the *megaron* or the house (*oikos*) itself (*Od.* 7.150; 11.341; 17.532; 23.354), like the *keimēlia* of bronze, gold, and iron that Odysseus claims to have brought and stored in the house of the king of the Thesprotians (*Od.* 14.323-6). They are often enumerated alongside captured women (*Od.* 9.41). Shepherds are also given *ktēmata* (*Od.* 3.154; 21.214). In the *Iliad* the fighting is for the sake of Helen and the *ktēmata* (*Il.* 3.70; 72; 91; 93; 255; 285; 458; 7.35; 363; 389; 400; 13.626).
74. *Od.* 16.384-85: ἴστον δ' αὐτοὶ καὶ κτήματ' ἔχωμεν | δασσάμενοι κατὰ μοῖραν ἐφ' ἡμέας.
75. *Od.* 1.160: βίοτον νήποινον ἔδουσιν; cf. also 14.377: βίοτον νήποινον ἔδοντες; 14.417: κάματον νήποινον ἔδουσιν.
76. Austin 1970: 35-40; Bravo 1983: 18-19; Reed 1984: 36; Boardman 1981: 151-52. Contacts between Egypt and Greece can be traced back to Minoan and (post-)Mycenaean times. See Kelder 2009 and Kramer-Hajos 2016. On the social use of Egyptian exotica in Mycenaean Greece see Burns 2010.

describes gold as an Egyptian commodity.[77] Egyptian imports of grain are, however, more doubtful. There is a mention of grain shipments from Egypt in a Bacchylides fragment,[78] which leads Benedetto Bravo to suspect that the *biotos* brought from Egypt by Menelaus is grain.[79] However, there is no evidence in the epics to substantiate this.[80] Peter Garnsey's research shows that grain imports only became a significant factor during the Peloponnesian war. According to Plutarch, the Egyptian pharaoh sent 40,000 *medimnoi* of wheat as a gift (*dōron*) to the Athenians when there was a shortage of grain.[81] Lin Foxhall has pointed out that in any case it was not barley, which was cultivated in Attica, but finer grain species, such as wheat, that were imported.[82] It is therefore more likely that Menelaus's Egyptian *biotos* consists of special commodities which were not available at home but which were not immediate necessities. As well as wheat, these might include fabrics such as linen and raw materials such as flax. There is solid written evidence from early on for the cultivation of flax and the production of linen in Egypt, with only isolated examples for Greece.[83] Egyptian votive offerings made from linen, such as the decorated linen breastplate offered by Amasis to Athena at Lindos, attracted the attention of ancient authors like Herodotus who gave detailed descriptions (Hdt. 2.182; 3.47).[84] The assumption that *biotos* refers to textiles is also in keeping with Homeric usage, since *biotos* is used to describe wealth possessed by those who are in a position to take in guests.[85] The word *biotos* is also used for life at the point when it is about to end in death

---

77. See Edzard 1960: 18–40; Liverani 1987: 66–73 assumes that the Egyptian monopoly on gold was broken at the end of the second millennium by Syria and Palestine. For gold resources in Egypt see Helck and Otto 1977, s.v. Gold, Goldgewinnung, Goldminen. For further resources of gold in the Aegean (Siphnos, Thasos, Sardis) see Treister 1996: 25–27, 140–41.
78. Bacchylides fr. 20 D: πορυφόροι δὲ κατ' αἰγλάεντα πόντον | νᾶες ἄγοθσιν ἀπ'Αἰγύπτοῦ μέγιστον | πλοῦτον.
79. Bravo 1983: 17–19.
80. Odysseus's allusion to the Thesprotians' journeys to wheat-rich Dulichium may well suggest an interest in grain deliveries (τύχησε γὰρ ἐρχομένη νηῦς | ἀνδρῶν Θεσπρωτῶν ἐς Δουλίχιον πολύπυρον, *Od.* 14.335).
81. Plut. *Per.* 37; cf. Philochoros FGrHist 328 F 119; Schol. Ar. *Vesp.* 718 a–b. See Garnsey 1985: 62–75; [1988] 1993: 110–13. Jameson 1983: 6–13 believes that precautions taken against potential famines were generally poor.
82. Foxhall 1998: 300–6.
83. Cf. Robkin 1979: 469–74; Rougement 2007: 46–49.
84. In 2.105 Herodotus compares Egyptian linen with linen from Colchis.
85. Axylos, a *philos* of men (*Il.* 6.14), and Diocles (*Od.* 3.490) are called rich in goods, *aphneios biotoio*. Both have houses at main routes and are able to host guests.

(*Il.* 4.170; 7.104; 13.563; 16.787). Thus, it may also mean the material through which human fate is materialised, and which is necessary for the accommodation of guests: wool and woven cloths. Of course, the gift of the silver wool basket and the golden spindle also indirectly point to this interest in textiles from Egypt.

We have already made the assumption that depictions of the use of oil during weaving suggest knowledge of linen weaving. The dancing girls on the shield of Achilles in their fine linen dresses (λέπτας ὀθόνας) are a concrete example of linen clothing (*Il.* 18.595). Pliny lists *othoninum* as one of the most common types of Egyptian linen (Plin. *HN* 19.2.15). Elsewhere adjectives such as σιγαλόεις (*sigaloeis*), shimmering, ἀργύφεος (*argypheos*), silver, and λιπαρός (*liparos*), gleaming, point to the use of linen fabrics.[86] We have seen already that the garments mostly characterised with these adjectives are *chitōnes* and *pharea*, which may therefore be assumed to be made from linen. To these we may add *peploi* and *rhēgea*. Thus, we find *sigaloeis* attributed to the *chitōnes* worn by Odysseus and Telemachus (*Od.* 19.232; 15.60–61), and the garments (*heimata*) laundered by the Trojan women in basins (*Il.* 22.154) and by Nausicaa and her friends in the river (*Od.* 6.26). The latter are specified as *peploi* and *rhēgea*, which are also described elsewhere as *sigaloeis* (*Od.* 6.38; 11.189). Circe and Calypso both wear *pharea* described with the adjective *argypheos* (*Od.* 5.230: Calypso; 10.543: Circe). For the veils worn by Penelope (*Od.* 1.334; 18.210), Charis (*Il.* 18.381), and Hecuba (*Il.* 22.406) the adjective used is *liparos*. According to Herodotus and Thucydides the long linen *chitōn* was worn in the cities of Asia Minor up until the fifth century (Thuc. 1.6; Hdt. 5.87–88). In classical times we find linen fabrics listed in the inventories of Hera's sanctuary at Samos but not at any Attic sanctuaries.[87] The assumption, already made by Ernst Buschor, is that linen clothing was a result of relations with Egypt, relations that were particularly cultivated in the cities of Asia Minor.[88] A memory of the importation of such linen fabrics would not then be unsurprising in an Ionian epic such as the *Odyssey*.

Helen's Egyptian *pharmaka* are also connected with a potential interest in textiles. Scholarship in the field of Graeco-Egyptian relations tends to assume that the plants in question are medicinal or poisonous. But Pollux

---

86. See Blümner 1912: 191–99; Bieber 1967: 25. The word *lita* for textiles draped over chariots (*Il.* 8.441) and over chairs in the *megaron* (*Od.* 1.130; 10.352) and used as shrouds (*Il.* 18.352) suggests the use of linen fabrics. See also ch. 2.3, n. 116.
87. Betalli 1982: 266. Cf. now Brøns 2017.
88. Buschor 1912: 44. For confirmation see also Pliny (*HN* 19.1) and Pollux (6.71).

and Hesychius show that *pharmakon* was also used for dyes.⁸⁹ The *pharmaka* Helen uses to cause Telemachus to forget his grief over his father may well have a double use too. They are described as 'banishing sorrow, lacking gall, and eliminating painful memories':

ἔνθ' αὖτ' ἄλλ' ἐνόησ' Ἑλένη Διὸς ἐκγεγαυῖα
αὐτίκ' ἄρ' εἰς οἶνον βάλε φάρμακον, ἔνθεν ἔπινον,
νηπενθές τ' ἄχολόν τε, κακῶν ἐπίληθον ἁπάντων.
ὃς τὸ καταβρόξειεν, ἐπὴν κρητῆρι μιγείη,
οὔ κεν ἐφημέριός γε βάλοι κατὰ δάκρυ παρειῶν,
οὐδ' εἴ οἱ κατατεθναίη μήτηρ τε πατήρ τε,
οὐδ' εἴ οἱ προπάροιθεν ἀδελφεὸν ἢ φίλον υἱὸν
χαλκῷ δηϊόῳεν, ὁ δ' ὀφθαλμοῖσιν ὁρῷτο.

Helen, meanwhile, the child of Zeus, had had an idea. Into the bowl in which their wine was mixed, she slipped a drug (*pharmakon*) that had the power of robbing grief and anger of their sting and banished all painful memories. No one that swallowed this, dissolved in wine, could shed a single tear that day, even for death of his mother and father, or if they put his brother or his own son to the sword and he were there to see it done (*Od.* 4.219-26, tr. Rieu).

Pliny the Elder ascribes just such a function of calming the flow of tears to alum, which he otherwise describes in term of its uses for the dying of wool (Plin. *HN* 35.183-88). Before the invention of synthetic dyes, alum was an important fixing agent, used for dying as well as tanning.⁹⁰ According to Pliny it occurs in different varieties in a number of regions in the Mediterranean and Asia Minor. The most prized variety is from Egypt, followed by that from Melos (*laudatissimum in Aegypto, proximum in Melo*, Plin. *HN* 35.184). Herodotus provides evidence that the Greeks obtained alum from Egypt when he has Amasis send a thousand talents of alum to the Delphians to help with rebuilding the temple of Apollo (Hdt. 2.180). It is possible then that Helen's Egyptian *pharmaka* are an allusion to alum, which has the power to stop tears flowing, and is also used for the dyeing of wool and fabrics.⁹¹

89. Pollux 7.169; Hesychius s.v. *pharmakon*. Empedocles (fr. 31 B 23 Diels-Kranz) uses *pharmaka* for colours used by painters of votive tablets. See Stulz 1990: 30-32.
90. Blümner 1912: 228-32; Faber 1937: 698-711. See now Grand-Clément 2011.
91. The symbolic dimension of Helena's gift as medium of memorializing and forgetting is discussed in ch. 3.2.

Dye itself, and purple especially, is among the raw materials that must have been at least partly obtained from abroad. There is evidence for purple sea snails both on the Greek and the Phoenician coasts. According to Pausanias, the best sea snails for the manufacture of purple dye—after those of Phoenicia—were found on the coast of Laconia (Paus. 3.21.6). According to Pliny the best purple in Asia is from Tyre, in Europe from Laconia; he adds to these the North-African coast of Gaetulia, which was a source of purple during the first century CE (Plin. *HN* 9.127). Meliboean purple from Thessaly was also known in Roman antiquity.[92] Remains of the purple sea snail or its shell have been found at Cythera on the southern Laconian coast, at a number of locations on Crete, at Akrotiri on Thera, at Troy, and at Rachi by the Isthmus of Corinth. Recent finds at Rachi indicate dying as an activity conducted here on a large scale.[93] According to Plutarch the five thousand talents of purple Alexander took possession of at Susa came from Hermione, a coastal town in the Argolid not far from Rachi. In his opinion, the addition of honey to the purple dyes resulted in the special brilliance and longevity of the colour (Plut. *Alex.* 36).

This interest in purple dyeing in the Western Peloponnese may be alluded to in Odysseus's search for *pharmaka*, as related by Mentes. His search brings him first to Ephyra before he arrives at Taphos. Ephyre is an old name for Corinth, which of course is close to the dyeing-works at Rachi.[94] The names of the Cypselid family, who ruled at Corinth during the seventh century are revealing in this context: Labda, the mother of the dynasty's founder, is said to have hidden her son in a beehive, a κυψέλη (*kypselē*), in order to keep him safe from assassination attempts by rivals (Hdt. 5.92). The son of Cypselus, Periandrus, called his wife Melissa, bee (Hdt. 5.92; Diog. Laert. 1.94). According to Pollux the weirs in which murex snails were caught were also called *kypselai* (Poll. 1.47). Thus, the name of Cypselus himself may allude either to the significance of honey for the preservation of purple dyes, or to the catching of the murex snails.[95]

---

92. Lucretius 2.499–500; Vergil, *Aen.* 5.250–51. Cf. also Pind. *Pyth.* 4.80. For Thessalian purple see Silver 1991: 249.
93. For an overview of purple-dyeing see Alfaro 2004 and Marín-Aquilera, Iacona and Gleba 2018: 132–35, 138. On Rachi see Kardara 1960: 261–66; 1970: 94–97; Anderson-Stojanovic 1988: 268–69; 1991: 303–4.
94. See the scholiast on *Il.* 6.152. Compare also Pausanias (2.1.1) on the foundation history of Corinth (Ephyra). Thucydides (1.46.4) and Apollodorus (Strab. 7.7.10) think of Ephyra as a place in Thesprotia.
95. This is assumed by Kardara 1960.

There is some degree of overlap between the regions associated with murex and with purple dyeing and the characters who wear purple in Homer. The adjectives πορφύρεος (*porphyreos*) and φοινικόεις (*phoinikoeis*) especially point to the use of purple dye, and both are used in connection with the clothing worn by high-status individuals such as Agamemnon, Achilles, Nestor, Thoas, Odysseus, or Telemachus. Achilles, who is said to bring with him purple-coloured textiles referred to as *rhēgea* and *tapētes*, comes from Thessaly. Helen, weaving a purple *diplax*, is of course from Laconia.[96] A purple mantle, *pharos*, is worn by Agamemnon (*Il.* 8.221), who is from the Argolid, as well as by Odysseus (*Od.* 8.84). The cloths and blankets used at Odysseus's house to cover the chairs and to make beds for strangers are also described as *porphyreos* and *phoinokeis*.[97] The Trojans also possess purple-coloured fabrics, as do the inhabitants of mythical locations such as Phaeacia, and mythical figures such as the nymphs at Ithaca. Andromache weaves a purple *diplax* (*Il.* 22.441); Arete spins sea-purple threads (ἠλάκατα στρωφῶσ' ἁλιπόρφυρα, *Od.* 6.53; 306); the nymphs weave sea-purple cloths (φάρε' ὑφαίνουσιν ἁλιπόρφυρα) in their grotto at Ithaca. Nearby in the cave there are mixing bowls and jars in which bees store up honey (*Il.* 4.141–42). Chrysoula Kardara reads the Ithacan cave of the nymphs as a description of a purple dye-works, not least since the location is characterised as rich in water, as well as windy, both necessary conditions for dye-works.[98] The only explicit instance of purple dyeing in Homer are the Carian and Maeonian women mentioned in the *Iliad*.[99] It has frequently been assumed that the purple called *phoinix* must stem

---

96. *Il.* 24.644–45; 9.200 (Achilles); *Od.* 4.297–8 (Helen). According to scholia on Il. 9.661 and Od. 13.13 the term *rhēgea* (ῥήγεα, from ῥῆξαι = βάψαι, 'dyed') suggests that the fabric is dyed. Stulz 1990: 116, n. 37.
97. *Od.* 4.115; 154 (woollen *chlainai*); 20.250–51 (*rhēgea, pharea,* and *tapētes*), described with the adjective *porphyreos*. Those worn by Nestor at Pylos (*Il.* 10.133), Telemachus (*Od.* 21.118), and Thoas of Lemnos (*Od.* 14.500) are described as *phoinikoeis*. The adjective *porphyreos* is also used for the *peploi* used to wrap Hector's remains (*Il.* 24.796). According to Marinatos (1967: 3) the two terms refer to different shades of red. He also suggests that cherry-red and dark violet tones were achieved through the use of the orchil-producing lichen dyes (made from *Roccella tinctoria*) rather than murex. Cf. also Barber 1994: 113 and Grand-Clément 2011: 168–69, who assume madder, a plant (*Rubia tinctorum*, see Baumann 1982: 156, fig. 317 and 320), and *kermes*, a type of insect living on oaks (see Baumann 1982: 156–58, fig. 38 and 318), as sources of red colours.
98. Kardera 1960: 261–66. See also Silver 1991: 267.
99. *Il.* 4.141–42. The women in the simile are dyeing ivory ornaments for a horse's bridle. Murex snails have been found also at Troy. Silver 1991: 260.

from Phoenicia.[100] There is, however, no clear evidence for this in Homeric epic. When products from Phoenicia appear, these are silver vessels and patterned textiles, which probably included purple colouring—but purple itself is never mentioned.[101]

Given the huge number of murex snails that were required (12,000 creatures to make just two and half kilos of dye),[102] it is likely that Phoenicians as well as Greeks were interested in exploring new sources. This may account for the foundation of Cyrene by Therans (around 630 BCE) and Carthage by Phoenicians (eighth/seventh century).[103] We have already seen that Pliny speaks of the Gaetulian coast, which stretches from modern Libya to Morocco, as being rich in murex snails. In Herodotus's account of the foundation of Cyrene, a key role is played by a Cretan murex-fisher who guides the Therans, in search of Libya, to the island of Plataea where they leave him behind. Herodotus gives no explanation for this strange stay on what is described as a deserted island.[104] The story makes more sense if one assumes that the murex-fisher was exploiting local resources. In Herodotus's account the Therans, in fact, settled in Cyrene, after an interlude at Plataea, because of a famine caused by years of drought.[105] But the outcome of the move is that the new settlers have access to resources beyond just grain. A Laconian bowl from around 560 BCE shows Arcesilaus, the Cyrenaean ruler, weighing goods usually

---

100. Blümner 1912: 233; Reinhold 1970: 9–16; Stulz 1990: 97. According to Muhly (1970: 32–34) *phoinix* is the original Greek word for purple, which was known in Mycenaean times and used by the Sidonians later on.
101. The silver mixing vessel received by Menelaus from the king of the Sidonians and handed on to Telemachus (*Od.* 4.616–19) provides an example, as does the silver *kratēr* given as a prize by Achilles from Patroclus's estate and which had been presented to Thoas by Phoenicians (*Il.* 23.740–47). The decorated *peploi* dedicated to Hera by Hecuba are said to be the work of Sidonian women (*Il.* 6.289–91).
102. Blümner 1912: 240; Marín-Aquilera, Iacona and Gleba 2018: 136.
103. For the founding of Cyrene see Boardman 1981: 183–89; Niemeyer 1990: 57–58; Aubet 1993: 202–17 underlines the interest of the Phoenicians to gain purple and iron.
104. Hdt. 4.151. Purple-dyeing is attested on Crete since Minoan times. See Reese 1987: 201–6.
105. Hdt. 4.151. On famines and over-population as explanations for the development of colonisation see e.g. Camp 1979: 397–411; Cawkwell 1992: 289–303. For a critique see Osborne 1998: 251–69. Modern research on migration has demonstrated the deficiencies of such models (which can be traced to Thomas Robert Malthus's *Essay on the Principle of Population* (1798). See for instance Ehmer 1998: 5–29, who shows that modern migration processes are frequently caused by the coalescing of a variety of political, social, and economic factors.

Figure 9: Arcesilaus weighing silphium or wool. Laconian *kylix*, ca 560 BCE. Bibliothèque Nationale, Cabinet des Médailles 1899. http://medaillesetantiques.bnf.fr/ark:/12148/c33gbhc8h

assumed to be silphium, a plant attested as native to the region in ancient sources,[106] or perhaps wool, for which the region is also known.[107] On the lowest part of the image, however, we observe what appear to be nets, which may be devices used to catch murex snails (Figure 9).[108] In Pindar's fourth *Pythian Ode* we find Arcesilaus celebrated because of his victory in a chariot race as a descendant of the Argonauts who flourishes 'as at the peak of purple-flowered spring' (ὥστε φοινικανθέμου ἦρος ἀκμᾷ [...] θάλλει, Pyth. 4.64-65). The phrase *phoinikanthemou ēros akmai* is not just a poetic image—it very specifically evokes the season during which

---

106. Hdt. 4.169; Theophr. *Caus. pl.* 6.3; Plin. *HN* 20.100. Hopper 1982: 46 and Murray 1980: 118 assume silphium. See also Crielaard 2011: 103 who stresses the connection between weighing and authority. The king is considered the guarantee of justice.
107. Hdt. 4.155; 157. Boardman [1964] 1999 assumes wool.
108. Simon 1976, table XV.

the murex harvest, which runs from the hottest days of summer until spring, reaches its peak.[109]

Certainly, the search for metals, including Egyptian gold but also iron, copper, and silver as well as alloys needed for the production of bronze, was of great significance. Homeric epic clearly indicates this. The ostensible Taphian Mentes claims to be transporting iron on his ship and to be planning to obtain copper at Temesa (ἄγω δ' αἴθωνα σίδηρον, *Od.* 1.183–84), a city in Magna Graecia according to the scholia.[110] The search for metal only comes into focus properly, however, in later historians' accounts. Tartessous, the Spanish silver mine discovered by the Samian Colaeus when he is blown off course on his way to Egypt, is modern Huelva.[111] Upon his return to Samos, Colaeus dedicates a tenth of his profits to the sanctuary of Hera. He is said to be the first Greek to have taken a ship to Tartessus (Hdt. 4.151–52).[112] According to the Old Testament, the Phoenicians of Tyre also went to Tartessus for silver, iron, tin, and lead.[113] In the epics, the search for such resources usually goes hand in hand with the forging of guest-friendships, which are remembered through special objects such as mixing bowls, drinking vessels, or spinning apparatus. This is not only true of the Egyptian contacts made by Menelaus and Helen when they enjoyed the hospitality of Polybus and Alkandre at Thebes. Menelaus also has networks at Sidon in Phoenicia; the mixing bowl received by Telemachus at Sparta was originally given to Menelaus by a guest-friend, the *basileus* of the Sidonians (*Od.* 4.615–19). A mixing bowl from Lemnos that fell into the hands of Patroclus as booty was also a Sidonian guest-gift. Based on Herodotus's account, Latacz suspects that Lemnos was an important staging post for Phoenicians on the way to the silver mines of Thasos, and that the Phoenicians therefore cultivated guest-friendships with the local elite at

---

109. Blümner 1912: 237. On Pindar's metaphorical language see Krummen 1990: 48–50, 58–59. She shows that Pindar's metaphors are not just decorative, they have paradigmatic power to affect the listener or reader since 'he already knows the images'. This becomes especially clear in references to ritual and cult at Cyrene (98-151). Silver 1991: 241–81 connects the myth of the Argonauts to the quest for purple.
110. Schol. *Od.* 1.184.
111. Chamorro 1987: 197–232.
112. For dating the journey of Colaeus in the seventh century (638 BCE) see Coldstream 1983: 203.
113. Ezechiel 27.12–13. Cf. Aubet 1993: 98–102; Treister 1996: 30–31; 148–81.
114. Latacz 1990: 11–13. Cf. also Muhly 1970: 42–43 and Stanley 1986: 4–9. Stanley interprets the gift for Thoas as an 'opening gift' to start trading activities. Archaeological evidence is not attested before the second half of the seventh century BCE yet. See Treister 1996: 25–26. Aubet (1993: 117–18) understands the gifts as 'payment in advance'.

Lemnos.¹¹⁴ We must also assume that the guest-friendship between Mentes and Odysseus is based on reciprocal exchange of commodities, even though we only explicitly hear of the *pharmaka* received by Odysseus.

The combination of two kinds of goods—commemorative and prestige gifts on the one hand, and agricultural and similar resources on the other— is known to us from other cultures. Michael Rowlands has pointed out that wherever 'prestige objects' are in circulation they are seen as rights, and that this circulation is followed by different, subordinate, systems of exchange.¹¹⁵ It is not surprising that this leads to the foundation of settlements or colonies only reported by the historians of the fifth century, although the process had already begun by 750–700 BCE. The difficulties surrounding transport and preparation of provisions for journeys made lengthy stays necessary in places where materials needed to be gathered or mined, as is the case with murex and with metals. It makes sense that this then leads to agricultural activity designed to meet the settlers' own needs.¹¹⁶

For John Nicholas Coldstream this also provides an explanation for the distribution of Attic geometric pottery around the Mediterranean. Finds of such geometric ware in graves at Salamis on Cyprus, at Knossos, in Israel, at Tyre, and in Huelva in Spain are not, as John Boardman believes, evidence of widespread trade in ceramics but an indication of the existence of guest-friendships forged for the purpose of procuring metals. Coldstream interprets vessels that sometimes serve as grave markers in Athens as guest-gifts for local leaders who had control over metal-routes to Syria, Mesopotamia, or Spain. He does not envisage direct contact between the inhabitants of ninth and eighth century Athens and the population of the sites where the items have been found. Especially in the case of Huelva, Coldstream supposes that ceramics made their way via Tyre to Spain.¹¹⁷ Tyre itself lies at the end of a tin-route that led via Syria to Iran during

---

115. Rowlands 1987: 8.
116. This must have been the case for mining in Etruria. Mining was a seasonal activity until the sixth century BCE. See e.g. the rich metal finds and remains indicating metal smelting processes at the eighth-century Euboean settlement of Pithekussai. See Kopcke 1992: 101–8; Treister 1996: 30–37, 146–81, with warning against overly close connections between colonisation and metal processing. Snodgrass 1980: 335 and Morris 1992: 141 emphasise the link between colonisation and the search for metals. According to Ridgway 2006: 300 the 'Italian connection' goes back to Mycenaean times.
117. Coldstream 1983: 201–7; 1994: 47–59. Ridgway 1992 also argues with the concept of gift-exchange. Osborne 1996: 31–44 assumes a complex network of exchange similar to the modern system of interdependent markets. On earlier Phoenician contacts with the West see Niemeyer 1990: 45–64; Treister 1996: 157–58.

THE QUEST FOR THE MEANS OF LIVING (BIOTOS)

the second millennium; Michael Heltzer has proposed that this is where the Minoans and Cypriots obtained the tin they required for their bronze production.[118] Copper and iron can be mined in Greece itself, but tin needed to be imported from Asia Minor, the Taurus mountains, and Afghanistan, or from Spain or England.[119] The rare find of a seventh-century Greek mixing bowl in the famous Vix-grave in Burgundy is also assumed to be connected to an interest in the western tin-route which led to Cornwall.[120] While *apoikiai* with ethnically unified populations grew in the west from the eighth and seventh centuries onwards, the endpoints of the eastern metal-routes became *emporia*, inhabited by ethnically varied populations. Judging from ceramic finds, one such place, Al Mina, was inhabited by Phoenicians, Cypriots, and Greeks and formed a trading centre for commodities from Asia Minor and the Near East.[121] Naucratis was another such *emporion*, founded around 638 BCE by Greeks of Eastern Ionian origin.

Nestor's tale of Odysseus's stay in Egypt fits well into the context of the foundation of Naucratis, according to Michel Austin who also sees in the journey of Helen and Menelaus to Egyptian Thebes a memory of contacts between Egypt and the Minoans.[122] This distinction may not be particularly important since archaeological finds point to continuity of contacts from the second to the first millennium in almost all locations where archaic and classical written sources attest to exchange between Greeks and other Mediterranean peoples.[123] This would suggest that there is no reason in the poems to distinguish between tradition and contemporary practice. In Herodotus's account the pharaoh Amasis hands over the city of Naucratis as a privilege, which is presented as a novel act, although the circumstances

---

118. According to the texts from the archives of Mari examined by Heltzer, this was the form of gift-exchange conducted amongst rulers. The rulers of Mari gave tin from Elam to Ugarit and Crete as gifts, while sending gold and silver back to Elam. In return they received textiles, arms, and ceramics from Crete. Heltzer 1989: 7–27.
119. The origin of tin is highly contested. Muhly 1985: 275–291 argues that tin came from Afghanistan. For discussion see Treister 1996: 28–29, 152–57.
120. Graham 1984: 5–6. The Phocaeans were especially engaged here, through the founding of Massilia and contacts with Tartessos. Cf. Hdt. 1.163. For the Greek engagement in Tartessos see Treister 1996: 148–50.
121. Kearsley 1999; Villing 2005. For oriental influences see Burkert 1984: 1992. On the meaning of the *emporion* see Demetriou 2011: 272: 'Emporia were nodes along trade networks that connected the Mediterranean on the local level, as redistribution centers that had contacts with their immediate surroundings, the regional level, as stopping points on regional trade networks, and the Mediterranean level, as export and import centers'.
122. Austin 1970: 12–33.
123. See e.g. Smith 1987 for the Italian evidence. Cf. also de Polignac 1994: 11.

are not clear. Herodotus also says that ships arriving at any other mouth of the Nile had to sail or bring their cargo to Naucratis, in 'such honour was it held' (ἐτετίμητο, Hdt. 2.178–80). There is some argument over the exact nature of this honour, once again featuring the word *timan*, which we explored earlier in the context of the examination of the privileges of the Homeric *basileus*. Polanyi considered Naucratis a 'port of trade' supposing that trade there was politically regulated and goods bought and sold at set prices.[124] Others assume that Egypt feared the free market and reject the idea of trading with set prices. Figueira proposes that the Pharaoh received a 10 per cent tax on all traded goods, as is shown by a Stele of Nektunebo I (380–363 BCE).[125]

There is no contradiction between the two proposals. As we can see, there are very recent examples of privileges granted to individuals and families residing at key points on trade-routes. These would include the right to set the price for certain goods: for example, salt. In return for this right, the individuals would make payments, equivalent to a tax, to an administrative centre.[126] We might also think of the customs duties that are found in many regions during antiquity, such as the duties levied at the gates of Palmyra for each camel load.[127] Cypselid Corinth was also a profitable *emporion* that benefited from toll charges given as the reason for its wealth in *chrēmata*, by Thucydides (Thuc. 1.13). Hasebroek supposes that the *chrēmata* are toll charges which Corinth was able to levy because of its strategic location, especially as Thucydides says that the Corinthians fought the pirates and made the roads safe.[128] According to Heraclides the tyrant Periandrus levied similar charges when he built the port of Lechaion in the Corinthian gulf (Heraclides fr.5 = FGH Müller 2.212). Strabo tells us that having control over two harbours, one on each side of the Isthmus, made Corinth wealthy, since one allowed access to Italy and the other to Asia, and this made it easy to exchange cargoes between the two (ἀμοιβὰς τῶν φορτίων πρὸς ἀλλήλους, Strabo 8.6.20). For Aristophanes the Isthmus as a point of transfer becomes a source of comedy: 'You have

---

124. Polanyi [1963] 1968: 238–60. See now Möller 2000, who works with the concept of Polanyi.
125. Figueira 1984: 25.
126. Scholars could observe such practices in the Nepalese kingdom during the last century. See Graafen and Seeber 1993: 675; Fürer-Haimendorf 1975: 132–222.
127. See Drexhage 1988: 120–25; Ruffing 2019.
128. Hasebroek 1928: 48; 56. For another view see Hopper (1982: 43), who explains the wealth of Corinth as result of transit trading activities. According to Salmon (1984: 133) the role of trade has been overestimated.

an Isthmus there man! You glide that cock of yours back and forth faster than the Corinthians' (Ar. *Thesm.* 647–48). The reference is to the practice of dragging ships travelling in from the Aegean Sea from the Saronic gulf through the Isthmus into the gulf of Corinth to save the journey around the entire Peloponnese. In Aristophanes's *Birds* we find further reference to such tolls, when Peithetairos schemes to raise a toll, called a *phoros*, for the passage of the scent from sacrifices from earth to heaven. This is compared to the fee demanded by the Boeotians to let the Athenians travel to Delphi (Ar. *Av.* 190). Catherine Morgan argues that Corinth was the starting point for two metal-routes, one of which led via Ithaca to Italy, and the other via Delphi to Thessaly and Macedonia.[129] Although David K. Pettegrew denies the importance of trade in his recent study *The Isthmus of Corinth*, he underlines the role of the site of Isthmia as the meeting point of maritime and terrestrial roads and stresses its function as 'a gateway for controlling traffic flows'.[130] In any case, such *emporia*, which were much frequented by travellers, were clearly a source of wealth for those in charge of them. The importance of clinging on to such advantage is well illustrated in Herodotus's account of the Chians' refusal to sell the Oenussae islands to the Phocaeans: the reason given is that they feared the islands would become an *emporion* and that this would cut Chios itself off from the market (Hdt. 1.165).

In chapter four I argued that Homeric rulership should be seen as rule over safe conduct. In this chapter so far we have seen the material basis on which such rulership rested. The ability to organise resources, be they pastures and livestock, be they human beings or commodities, must be seen as an essential basis for the power of the *basilēes*. In order to be able to organise such resources, the safe passage of goods, people, and animals through various regions needed to be guaranteed. The raising of road tolls (*dōtinai* have also been interpreted as such) was a part of this system.

The social status of travellers—whether they were aristocrats themselves, or agents acting on their behalf—is not important here. There is no activity in the Homeric poems that does not involve the recruitment of labour: from the service of soldiers in battle, compensated through gifts

---

129. Morgan 1988: 330–38.
130. Pettegrew 2016: 45–46 and 47. He claims that the site of Isthmia 'was explicitly valued not for its facility of long-distance trade or trans-shipment but for its particular associations with congregating traffic and contest. Greek writers were concerned especially with the sanctuary of Poseidon, the historic centre of Hellenic assembly, as well as with the strategic value of the region for the defense of Corinth and the broader Peloponnese' (31).

and portions of booty, to labour needed for weaving or shepherding, which may be obtained by force. The sea-journeys undertaken by *basilēes* or the sons of *basilēes* also require the recruitment of labour. The work of the rowers, such as those recruited by Telemachus, is rewarded in advance by the provision of a banquet. There is no differentiation in status between the different activities; the only difference made is between those who lead and grant safe passage and those who were obligated through gifts or compelled through force to follow.

The acquisition of goods is governed by an ambivalence between gift-giving and plundering. The same ambivalence can be seen in the acquisition of labour forces. The same circle of people who take part in a system of reciprocity and provide each other with war-service in return for gifts, also undertake the kidnapping of other human beings. Instead of gifts of honour (*gera*) and honour paid at the feast, the return sought for such kidnapping is the ransom (*apoina*) raised by the victim's relatives, or the price paid by a stranger (*ōnos*) to acquire the victim for themselves. There are some scholars who think that the colonizing activities of the early Greeks were essentially motivated by such kidnappings. According to Old Testament sources, the Phoenicians at Tyre obtained their human cargo from Greece.[131] The idea that trade is somehow incompatible with the Greek aristocratic ethos, though it occurs repeatedly in scholarship, is clearly not borne out by evidence.[132] This is especially true of the one area that our examination has determined is closest to the notion of trade in the sense of the sale of a 'commodity': the trafficking of abducted persons in return for a price, an *ōnos*.

Apart from this human trafficking, there is no mention of any interest in the export of goods in Homeric epic, although there are plenty of goods that are imported. Mostly, these are acquired while establishing guest-friendships, as we saw in our examination of the term *xeinion*. This is true of the majority of goods described with the terms *chrēmata*, *ktēmata*, and *biotos*, which, as discussed earlier, are likely to have comprised livestock, wool, linen, alum, purple, and metals. Where there is a relationship described as *philotēs* this implies, according to the argument of chapter 2, a mutual exchange of resources and goods. The exchange of arms plays a special part and must be understood as forming a bond between warriors, equivalent to the sharing of grazing lands, which forms a similar bond

---

131. Ezechiel 27.12-13. Cf. Jackson 1993: 64-76; Rihll 1993: 77-107.
132. See Aubet 1993: 103.

between herd-owners. In both contexts, reciprocity is suggested through the use of the terms of mutual exchange (*amoibē, ameibō/ameibomai*) and of reciprocity (*charis, charizomai*). Both genders take part in supraregional exchange, which goes hand in hand with the forging of guest-friendships, and in the giving of memorial gifts. The representation of the supraregional exchange of goods also reflects the structures of Homeric society and its organisation in terms of the bond between a married couple and the bond between warriors.

While warriors, seafarers, shepherds and herd-owners, and robbers tend to have a lot in common, this is true also for seafarers and athletes, although they were contrasted in Euryalus's speech cited at the beginning of this chapter. Classical sources indicate that from the seventh and sixth centuries onwards both successful athletes and successful seafarers dedicated a portion of their profits to the gods.[133] Archaeological finds and post-Homeric sources suggest that this practice was an innovation following the establishment of central sanctuaries where increasing quantities of dedications were made. There is little evidence of this practice in the Homeric poems, however, where the normal endpoint of the circulation of gifts is the ritual for the dead. Excavations suggest that the sanctuaries of the gods increasingly came to be the final destination of the objects in question, as we shall see.[134]

5.4. Transhumance, supraregional exchange, and the emergence of extra-urban sanctuaries

5.4.1. The golden tripod of the Seven Sages

I return here to my initial example of the circuit of the golden tripod among the Seven Sages: According to ancient tradition, the golden tripod, handed around by the Seven Sages, 'with glorious good will' (μετ' εὐμενείας φιλοτίμου), arrived finally in the hands of Apollo and thus in the divine sphere (Plut. *Sol.* 4).[135]

Antiquity knew a number of variations of this myth, some of which speak of the origin of the tripod, others of the object itself. In a version related by Diogenes Laërtius, Hephaestus gives the tripod as a wedding gift to Pelops, who hands it over to Menelaus, who in turn loses it to Paris

133. See Jim 2014.
134. See note 142.
135. See my introductory remarks.

(Diog. Laert. 1.32 and 82). Elsewhere the tripod's journey is as recounted in Plutarch's *Life of Solon*, in which Helen, recalling an oracle, is said to have thrown it into the sea on her return from Troy. The tripod is recovered by Coan fishermen, who had sold (*priamenon*) their catch unseen to strangers (*xeinoi*) from Miletus prior to their departure. A dispute over the tripod results in military conflict between Coans and Milesians, which is resolved by an oracular decree from Delphi determining that the tripod must be given to the wisest man. Thales of Miletus receives it first but sends it on to Bias at Priene, whom he considers to be wiser. Bias also knows of a wiser man, and thus the circuit of the tripod amongst the wise gets underway, resulting in the eventual return of the tripod to Thales, or, in another version known to Plutarch, to Bias. Finally, the tripod is dedicated to Ismenian Apollo (Plut. *Sol.* 4). In Diogenes's version the circuit of the tripod ends at the temple of Apollo at Didyma (Diog. Laert. 1.32).[136] In another version told by Diogenes the tripod is dispatched to Bias, who had restored a group of girls captured in war to their parents in Messenia, having furnished them with dowries himself. In this version, Bias declares that Apollo is wise and refuses to accept the tripod. Diogenes also refers to a variant in which Bias dedicates the tripod to Heracles at Thebes (Diog. Laert. 1.82).

A further two variants occur in Plutarch. According to these, the circulated gift was not a tripod but a *phialē*, originally a gift from Croesus, or a cup, an heirloom of Bathycles (Plut. *Sol.* 4). This beaker is mentioned in a Callimachean fragment (191.32–77, Pfeiffer) that gives the most detailed description of its journey: the cup travels from Thales to Bias at Priene, from there to Periandrus at Corinth, and onwards to Solon at Athens. The remaining recipients are Chilon of Sparta, Pittacus of Mytilene, and Cleobulus of Lindos. The cup is then finally displayed in the temple of Apollo at Didyma.[137]

The tripod's circuit touches upon every sphere of exchange we have seen in the epic poems: marriage, trade, war, transregional guest-friendships, and relations with the divine. Only its endpoint is different: dedication in a sanctuary rather than at a funeral ritual. In every variation of the myth, the object (be it the tripod or the *phialē*), whatever its original function, completes its circuit by being transformed into a votive offering to the gods, most often to Apollo. In a number of cases, conflicts

---

136. Similar: Sch. Ar. *Pl.* 9 = Or. 247 Parke-Wormell. The sources are collected by Snell [1938] ⁴1971.
137. Fehling 1985: 23–24 suspects that Callimachus is the original author of the story of the circulating tripod.

surrounding the ownership of the objects are resolved either by decree from the Delphic oracle or by voting in the assembly. The conduct of the seven wise men also has a regulatory function. Only they are in possession of the quality described by Plutarch as *eumeneia philotimon*. This can be translated as 'generosity' and stands in contrast to the self-interest of the fishermen and their employers. In this episode the object itself is an emblem of knowledge,[138] as it is assigned to the wisest. Finally, it must be Apollo, the divinity who is closest to the epic seer and singer, who is distinguished as the wisest.

The dating of the tradition can be traced back to the fourth (or at a push, the late fifth) century,[139] and in form it probably mirrors the practice of Hellenistic benefactors.[140] But there is much literary, historical, and epigraphic evidence of tripods given as votive offerings to gods, and material remains dating back to the ninth and eighth centuries that can be found at central sites such as Delphi and Olympia as well as at Ithaca and other locations.[141] Louis Gernet, who was the first to consider the Seven Sages' tripod with reference to gift-exchange, interpreted the tripod as an object with magical-religious significance and connected it to an originally magical notion of kingship.[142] Based on the uses of tripods as winners' prizes and as guest-gifts in the Homeric poems, contemporary scholarship tends to view

138. According to Diodorus (9.13.2) the tripod given to Bias because of the testimony of the Messenian maidens was inscribed with the words 'for the wisest'. See also Phanodikos ap. Diog. Laert. 1.82.
139. Plutarch refers to Theophrastus (372–287 BCE). See Fehling 1985: 12–19, who assumes the fifth and fourth centuries BCE as its origin, although Rösler 1991: 357–65 argues against this, connecting the emergence of the idea of the sage with the development of the Delphic oracle. Martin 1993: 108–28 takes a similar position to Rösler and emphasises the significance of secularization and internationalizing as distinctive to early Greek notions of wisdom. See now Papalexandrou 2005; Wagner-Hasel 2015.
140. See the *philotimoi euergetai* and honorific statues which are materialized honour (*doxa*). Cf. Bolkestein 1939: 154–55. On Plutarch specifically see Frazier 1988: 109–27, claiming that for Plutarch generosity is a concrete manifestation of a striving for honour. The characterisation of the Seven Sages as free from self-interest fits better with Solon's interest in the communal good. Cf. Rösler 1991: 360–61. On the continuity of euergetism from archaic to hellenistic times see now Herman 2006 and Domingo Gygax 2016:58–79.
141. Olympia: Willemsen 1957; Maaß 1978; Delphi: Willemsen 1955; Rolley 1977: 105–49; Armandry 1987; Morgan 1990: 138–40; Ithaca: Benton 1934–35: 45–73. For an overview see Reisch 1905: 1669–96; Schwendemann 1921: 155; Coldstream 1977: 332–39; Magou, Philippakis and Rolley 1986: 121–36; Snodgrass 1990: 287–94; de Polignac 1996: 59–66; Papalexandrou 2005.
142. Gernet 1948: 415–62.

them as evidence of aristocratic exchanges of prestige goods, and thus to connect them to the processes of *polis*-formation, a consequence of which the possession of land had become the only significant form of wealth. The transfer of objects of aristocratic exchange to the gods forges a reciprocal relationship between gods and humans, as Susan Langdon, for example, argues: 'What these men of wealth received in turn was status, legitimacy, and proof of class and claims to land'.[143] Removed from circulation among humans, tripods would now be purely symbolic objects, representing the power of those who organised religious cults in their own interests. Langdon also suggests a change from pastoral to agricultural society which took place in post-Homeric times and in which land replaced cattle as the main source of wealth.[144] Catherine Morgan, whose work focusses specifically on the rise of supraregional sanctuaries such as Olympia and Delphi, views the tripod as a symbol of *xenia* that comes to be used to forge interstate ties.[145] François de Polignac takes a similar view in interpreting tripods as prestige goods representing memorials in honour of the sponsor, or of elite interstate alliances, at locations of supra- or intra-regional significance such as Olympia or Ithaca, or the Isthmus and the Heraion at Argos.[146] A more recent study by Nassos Papalexandrou also underlines such territorial symbolism while emphasising the significance (especially for Delphi) of the idea of wisdom in association with the tripod. Papalexandrou views tripods as 'symbols of truthful discourse', and considers the ability to tell stories and remember the heroic past as the essential basis for legitimizing positions of power in early Greece.[147]

However, evidence from Homeric epic does not suggest ways to connect the tripod to magical kingship or to aristocratic land rule. Whether used for bathing guests and washing the dead, or as a tribute or prize, the tripod always invokes a supraregional context of widespread networks of

---

143. Langdon 1987: 113. Similarly, Linders 1987: 115–22. Cf. also Morris 1986: 12–13, who interprets the tripod as a symbol of an ever-widening circle of aristocratic contest which ends with the display of the tripod in a temple instead of its use as a grave gift. Ulf 1997: 42 thinks that the tripods are dedicated by larger groups, who are able to express their economic power through such dedications.
144. Langdon 1987: 110.
145. Morgan 1990: 218.
146. De Polignac 1996: 63.
147. Papalexandrou 2005: 19: '[...] nothing less than the indispensable tokens of the legitimate right to leadership'. Similar Papadopoulos 2012: 285: 'Such emblems [tripods, animal statuettes, etc.] served as a conscious link between past and present, and in their everyday use they helped define the future'.

guest-friendships or military alliances. Found as votive offerings in supraregional cult centres tripods remain bound to the realm of supraregional communication. If there is any link between the tripod and claims on land, then this must be land used interregionally, such as pasture, or road networks, passage through which is guaranteed, as demonstrated earlier, by *basilēes*.

The view that tripods are emblems of wisdom, as underlined by Papalexandrou, does not apply to the epic practice but only to Delphi, and only in connection with the goddess Themis as the embodiment of *themistes*. The placing of Themis on the tripod at Delphi presents the unification of two types of conflict resolution: one agonistic, within which the tripod functions as a prize at the funeral games, the other verbal, connected to *themistes*. At Delphi both forms are connected to supraregional communication and to the regulation of transhumance.[148]

5.4.2 Transhumance and exchange

Recent years have seen much controversy regarding the spread of transhumance in antiquity. Anthropogeography defines transhumance as the seasonal migration of livestock belonging to fixed agricultural or pastoral settlements between high pastures in summer and lower valley pastures in winter.[149] The climatic and geographical conditions of Greece (mild, damp winters in the valleys and moderately warm summers in mountainous regions) suggested to older scholarship the widespread existence of a transhumant economy, in the sense of the migration of herds from winter pastures in the valleys to summer pastures in the mountains.[150] Recent scholarship assumes more regional and historical differentiations and so questions the extent of the spread of transhumance.

The most recent debate originates in prehistorical research, focussed especially on Minoan society, and the assumption here is that transhumance does not begin to develop before the first half of the second millennium. The Minoan peak sanctuaries erected in summer pasture regions are thought of as early evidence of this.[151] One example is the sanctuary of Kato Symi on the southern slopes of Mount Dicte, excavated in 1972; this

---

148. Wagner-Hasel 2002b; 2015; 2019.
149. Zöbl 1982: 1.
150. Cf. Semple 1922: 3–38; 1931: 100 and 317–24; Beuermann 1967: 34 and 80–82; Michell 1963: 59; Brendel 1934.
151. Halstead 1980: 331; 1987: 77; Cherry 1988: 6–34.

was in use from the middle of the second millenium up until the third century CE, with Hellenistic inscriptions suggesting it was dedicated to Hermes and Aphrodite.[152] Transhumance, for which there are also written sources from the second half of the second millennium, accompanies the development of textile production, which was centrally organised according to evidence from the Linear B tablets.[153] For Mycenaean Pylos seasonal migration of herds from the valleys into the mountains is assumed, based on evidence from the Cn Texts in the Linear B archive that list flocks of sheep in connection with place names and personal names. The L-series at Knossos shows a similar picture.[154]

Stella Georgoudi was the first scholar to undertake a systematic investigation of the evidence for transhumance from archaic and classical times, and to consider written evidence for agreements between *poleis* regarding the use of grazing lands in this capacity.[155] A study by Angelos Chaniotis considers post-Minoan Crete.[156] Although the written sources presented in these two studies do provide evidence for forms of transhumance in a range of areas, more recent research—based on climatic, political, and economic factors—suggests that the practice played only a small role in archaic and classical times. Stephen Hodkinson points to the Kopais basin in Boeotia and the Mantinean plain in Arcadia as examples where the summer heat does not prevent the year-round use of lowland regions.[157] Paul Halstead assumes that denser forestation of mountainous regions in antiquity would mean less intensive use of those regions as pasture lands.[158] Hodkinson uses allusions to the cultivation of feed crops, such as clover in Pliny and Theophrastus, and new evidence regarding settlement structures, to argue that, even in regions where the climate is less amenable, livestock was kept near to farms all year round.[159] Regional studies in Boeotia, for

---

152. Lebessi 1976: 2–13.
153. Killen 1964: 1–15; 1985: 241–305; Nosch 2000.
154. Hiller 1976: 126–41 and 190–91; Rougement 2004.
155. For epigraphic evidence see Georgoudi 1974: 155–85 and now Chandezon 2003, who discusses all the epigraphic evidence for stock-rearing in the Mediterranean from the late fifth century BCE to the late first century CE.
156. Chaniotis 1995: 39–89.
157. Hodkinson 1988: 47–48.
158. Halstead 1987: 80 and Garnsey 1988: 206. Geomorphological research casts doubt on the dating of this assumption, however, placing it back during the Weichsel Ice Age. See Hempel 1993a: 161–79.
159. Cf. Plin. *HN* 13.130 for dried clover used to feed pigs at Athens: *Frutux est et cytisus, ab Amphilocho Atheniense miris laudimus praedictus pabulo omnium, aribus vero etiam suum*. The cultivation of fodder crops presupposes crop

instance, show that settlements were not always concentrated around villages or *poleis* but scattered over the land, and that therefore pasture lands must have been available close to farmsteads.[160]

Jens Erik Skydsgaard, whose research focusses on transhumance in ancient Italy, has argued that feed crops were cultivated only for specific animals such as horses, and that sheep farming was conducted without the cultivation of fodder crops.[161] He also points out that animals kept for the purpose of dairy farming would need to be kept close to the farmstead, while the location of animals bred for wool was less important.[162]

A fundamental problem for current scholarship is the lack of clarity when it comes to defining transhumance. Hodkinson, for example, tends to view transhumance as a form of nomadism in contrast to agriculture; he also does not count migration within a radius of 100 km as transhumance. In his view, the preconditions for the development of transhumance include a lack of strong agriculture, a high market demand for wool, and the existence of a central organisation of the movement of flocks comparable to the Spanish sheep ranchers' association, the 'Mesta'.[163] Using a modern phenomenon as a criterion for the evaluation of ancient evidence, however, means that forms of transhumance on a smaller scale, or those not geared towards market production, fall out of the picture. Skydsgaard, on the other hand, distinguishes between 'long-distance transhumance', with ranges between 200 and 800 km, and 'short-distance transhumance', with ranges between 20 and 100 km. He regards the latter as typical for ancient Greece, while supposing the development of a system of 'long-distance transhumance' for ancient Italy.[164] Michael H. Jameson assumes long-distance transhumance for Western Greece, and 'small-scale transhumance' for the regions around the *poleis* of central and Eastern Greece.[165]

---

rotation, assumed by Hodkinson against earlier scholarship. Hodkinson 1988: 43. Similarly Halstead 1987: 82; Garnsey 1988: 207. By contrast see Isager and Skydsgaard 1992: 110–14. More generally on cultivation of fodder crops see Khazanov 1984: 72.

160. Hodkinson 1988: 39–46. For settlement archaeology see for example: Snodgrass 1991: 1–23; Osborne 1985b: 37–42; Bintliff 1994: 212–27; Lohmann 1993; 1997.
161. Skydsgaard 1974: 7–36.
162. Skydsgaard 1988: 78–82.
163. Hodkinson 1988: 50–56. Given the lack of central political authority Hodkinson declines to speak of Homeric evidence for transhumance. Hodkinson 1990: 144.
164. Skydsgaard 1974: 7–36; 1988: 80; Isager and Skydsgaard 1992: 99–104 (with further references). For Italy see now Santillo-Frizell 2004 and 2009.
165. Jameson 1989: 9–11. Similarly, Osborne 1987: 47–52.

Differentiations in range, such as are made by Skydsgaard and Jameson, seem to me to be crucial when it comes to evaluating the ancient evidence. In Dorothea Zöbl's study of the spread of transhumance in the Mediterranean during the medieval and early modern eras, there are not just two but four different forms of transhumance, each with a different spatial range. On the one hand, she identifies intra- and inter-local transhumance based on the common or reciprocal use of grazing lands by several villages. On the other hand, she identifies intra- and inter-regional transhumance, in which pastures are located in alien territories necessitating arrangements for rights of passage. In the latter cases, transhumance is no longer organised by villages but by larger units such as monasteries or state-like institutions.[166] The Mesta, which Hodkinson also refers to, is the most well-known example of such inter-regional transhumance. This association enabled the organisation of a frictionless migration of herds across a widespread network of pathways and in close cooperation with the crown. The Spanish crown's fiscal interest in taxing herds and in the use of the network built up through transhumance in turn led to the intensification of transhumance, which then began to come into conflict with agriculture.[167] Zöbl's study shows that it is not, as Hodkinson suggests, the existence of centralised power that enables the development of transhumance. She shows instead that transhumance brings about spatial integration and thus furthers the development of bigger political units.[168]

In prehistorical scholarship the argument that the practice of transhumance is a 'unifying mechanism' has long been recognised, and it is assumed that networks of communication, which become evident in the spread of pottery styles or funeral practices, are created through transhumant relationships.[169] For the geometric and archaic periods the location of the early sanctuaries suggests that the supraregional use of pasture lands effected such a density of communication. New insights into the development of the *polis* also support this by replacing old hypotheses of

166. Zöbl 1982: 56–58. Cleary and Delano Smith 1990: 21–38 and Waldherr 2001 also work with the concept developed by Zöbl.
167. See Klein 1964.
168. Zöbl 1982.
169. Bintliff 1977: 116–17; Cherry 1988: 11–12; Papadopoulos 1987: 137–42 interprets the distribution of grave mounds (*tumuli*) as evidence of the presence of transhumant shepherds in Ephyra. For the Neolithic era see Jacobsen 1984: 27–43 using ceramic evidence to suggest that the entire northeastern Peloponnese was a unified region of transhumance. For the classical period see Jameson 1989: 13: 'long-distance transhumance acted as intermediaries between mountains and coastal regions'.

autarchy with a model of much greater mobility. Nicholas Purcell describes this as a 'flexible ecological response' in which resources from different locations are redistributed strategically in order to manage crises.[170] Although Purcell focusses predominantly on seafaring and on the sea as the space of communication, pointing to the example of Anthedon on the eastern coast of the Aegean, whose inhabitants worked as 'waterborne distributors' of salt and purple dye, and as boat builders and ferrymen, he also mentions the transhumant shepherd 'who engages with a whole range of ecologies and participates in the annual interplay of sedentary and pastoral existence'. He equates this shepherd to the 'coastwise caboteur' who 'exchanges the surpluses of his ports of call.'[171] This suggests that the land routes taken by shepherds must have been no less important than the better-known sea routes.[172]

In Sophocles's *Oedipus Tyrannus* we have a very good illustration of the encounter between two shepherds on Cithaeron, the mountain range that forms the border between Boeotia, Megara, and Attica. It is in this border region between two *poleis* that a shepherd employed by Polybus in Corinth received the cursed child from a Theban shepherd, a slave who had grown up in the house of Laius (Soph. *OT* 1025-29, 1040-44). Polybus's shepherd reports when questioned by Oedipus: 'I am certain he knows well of the time we both stayed in the region of Cithaeron, he with two flocks and I with one. I was close enough to this man for three entire six-month periods from spring to Arcturus. In winter I would drive my flock to my own fold, and he took his to Laius's fold' (1133-39).[173] According to this statement the two shepherds both stayed in the mountains with their flocks from the rise of the Pleiades (between 22 April and 10 May) up until the rise of Arcturus in October.[174] The statement about the duration of their stay in the mountains serves to emphasise the shepherd's truthfulness. The shepherds know each other well because of the length of time they have spent together. This

---

170. Purcell 1990: 42. Cf. also Morgan 1990: 202.
171. Purcell 1990: 52.
172. Jameson 1989: 13 criticises a tendency to underestimate the significance of land routes.
173. This is the main evidence for the practice of transhumance in ancient Greece. Cf. Semple 1922: 28; Beuermann 1967: 80; Georgoudi 1974: 147; Skydsgaard 1988: 75; McInerney 2006: 45.
174. Further sources provide evidence of the use of grazing land in the mountains. See Eur. *IT* 260-325; Theocr. *Id.* 13.25-26. The Vlachs begin their herd migrations on St George's day, 23 April, and complete them by St Demetrius's day on 26 October: Ivanka 1950: 352. Cf. also Koster 1976: 19-28, who joined shepherds in such a migration from Epidaurus to Mt. Cyllene in Arcadia in the spring of 1972.

also emphasises that the mountains are not empty space but are perceived as a meeting place for shepherds from different regions.[175] Epigraphic and literary evidence of agreements regarding such common use of pasture lands confirms that the case of the Theban and Corinthian shepherds in Sophocles corresponds to actual practices. Thucydides, for instance, mentions the sworn treatises (*horkoi*) between Boeotians and Athenians which set down that the area of Panakton was to be used only as common grazing land rather than for settlement.[176] The change to the economy of the *polis* is not then a change from a pastoral to an agricultural economy but rather a process of spatial integration and concentration which epic poetry alludes to through the use of pasture lands in alien territories.

5.4.3. Sanctuaries at the periphery

The very first temples, emerging in the final third of the eighth century BCE, indicate connections to a pastoral economy rather than supraregional trade. These are mostly temples dedicated to Apollo, such as that at Eretria dated to around 725 BCE. Based on the presence of circular houses and apsidal buildings, archaeologists assume that Eretria was originally a seasonally used shepherds' station that gradually developed into a permanent settlement over the course of the eighth century.[177] Other early sanctuaries were located entirely outside settlements and used by several different communities: the Heraion at the northern edge of the Argive plain, which was used by both Argos and Mycenae (Strabo 8.6.10),[178] the Heraion of

---

175. This is confirmed by observations in other mountain regions. In the Himalayas the high summer pastures are meeting places for friends and relatives and the location of numerous festivities: Snoy 1993: 52-53. For the use of border regions in ancient Greece see now Daverio Rocchi 2016: 70-76.
176. Thuc. 5.42.1: ὅρκοι παλαιοὶ μηδετέρους οἰκεῖν τὸ χωρίον, ἀλλὰ κοινῇ νέμειν. For interpretation see Osborne 1987: 37; Skydsgaard 1988: 80. For further evidence see Georgoudi 1974: 178-80; Chaniotis 1995; Waldherr 2001; Howe 2008: 95-106 argues that the outbreak of the Peloponnesian War can be explained with a struggle for pastures between Megara and Athens. See also Daverio Rocchi 2016: 75.
177. Summarising: Snodgrass 1987: 203-4; Coldstream 1977: 317-27; Blome 1991: 51. For the Euboean trading connection with Italy see Crielaard 2006: 291-92. He denotes the *basileis* as leading figures in all kinds of external affairs. Cf. Crielaard 2012: 147.
178. Morgan 1990: 11 doubts Strabo's notion that both cities used the sanctuary, suspecting instead that Argos used the foundation of the Heraion after the victory over Asine as manifestation of its sole claim over the plain. By contrast de Polignac 1984: 59 assumes that Mycenae and Argos used the sanctuary jointly, at least during the archaic period, since Argos only achieved hegemony over the entire Argolid by 460 BCE, at which point it began to make use of the Heraion for political purposes.

SANCTUARIES AT THE PERIPHERY 321

Perachora located in the foothills of the Geraneia mountains, and the Apollo sanctuary located in the Geraneia mountains, the latter two being both under the control of Corinth and Megara (Paus. 1.3.8).[179] A similar situation obtained at the sanctuary of Poseidon at Onchestos in Boeotia, today the location of the Mazaraki monastery, which was used jointly by Thebes and Orchomenus, two communities located in the same region.[180] The sanctuary of Artemis Limnatis, located on the border between Laconia and Messenia served as a meeting point for communities from different regions, as did the Heraion of Perachora and the Apollo temple in the Geraneia mountains. The joint use of the Artemis sanctuary by the Spartans and the Messenians is associated with the outbreak of the Messenian War which we have discussed already in connection with the conflict around the use of pasture lands in foreign territories. The Messenian explanation for the outbreak of the war involves provocation caused by the theft of cattle,[181] while in the Spartan version the conflict involves women. Pausanias reports that the First Messenian War broke out following the rape of Spartan maidens by Messenians.[182] Such stories suggest that liminal territories can be defined as 'ritual space', as Daverio Rocchi has proposed.[183]

Many of these 'boundary temples' are associated with wars of the archaic period.[184] The building of the Apollo temple and the Heroon at Eretria are connected to the dispute between Chalkis and Eretria over the Lelantine plain,[185] reported by Thucydides as the occasion for one of the first pan-Hellenic coalitions (Thuc. 1.15).[186] De Polignac assumes that the background for the establishment of the Heraion of Perachora must be a dispute between Megara and Corinth over the use of the Isthmian plain,[187] the gateway to the winter pastures around Epidaurus. The Poseidon sanctuary

179. For discussion see de Polignac 1984: 40–41; Gehrke 1986: 131; Morgan 2003.
180. The Poseidon sanctuary is mentioned at *Il.* 2.506. Pausanias (9.26.5-37.1) describes the remains at the site which was abandoned by his time. On the history of the location see de Polignac 1984: 58.
181. Cf. ch. 5.1.
182. Paus. 4.4.2–3. Cf. also Strab. 6.257 and 8.362. The temple of Artemis at Caryae built by Spartans on the border with Arcadia had a function similar to the Artemis Limnatis sanctuary according to Pausanias (3.10.7). Cf. also Howe 2008: 81–82.
183. Daverio Rocchi 2016: 76.
184. See van Wees 2004: 28–30 who argues that the struggle for land has been underestimated.
185. De Polignac 1984: 61; Sartre 1979: 220; Raaflaub 1988: 520; Parker 1996.
186. Cf. Howe 2008: 83–84.
187. De Polignac 1984: 60 (with further evidence); 1994: 5. Cf. Morgan and Whitelaw 1991: 79–108; Antonaccio 1992: 85–105.

at Onchestos is linked to the joint use of the Copais basin by Thebes and Orchomenus.[188] The origin of the temple of Apollo Horaios, or Apollo of the border, at Argos is suggested by Pausanias as a dispute over the borders, won by the Argives (Paus. 2.35.2).

These peripheral sanctuaries, to use my preferred term for the sanctuaries found on the borders of emerging *poleis*, have been viewed since the 1980s as serving to define the territorial boundaries of *poleis* and, together with hero-cult sites, as means of establishing 'a beneficial relationship to a usable ideological past'.[189] In de Polignac's considerations of this spatial dimension to the emergence of sanctuaries, peripheral temples appear to enact a symbolic separation between wilderness and civilisation, which he claims was necessitated by the shift from pastoral to agricultural society.[190] He suggests that these contrasts were performed and mediated in initiation rituals and rural festivals, and he finds that this symbolic function of peripheral sanctuaries also explains the concentration on Hera and Apollo. Both are interpreted as protectors of civilisation in the form of marriage and in the form of the social order of the *polis*. By contrast he suggests that the gods of the wild such as Artemis tended to be worshipped within the city itself.[191]

The discussion above on the character of transhumant economy shows that the fundamental contrast between pastoral and agricultural economy posited by de Polignac's interpretation cannot be assumed. He identifies the life of the *polis* with a supposed basis in agriculture and associates the world of Homeric epic with a pastoral way of life. In this schema a new definition of space is necessitated by the change from pastoral to

---

188. De Polignac 1984: 46, 58.
189. Whitley 1988: 181. Cf. also Osborne 1987: 189 and de Polignac 1984: 29, 132–40. Coldstream 1985: 66–97 argues for a multiplicity of explanations. Burkert 1988: 43 argues that sanctuaries were important for the creation of communal identity through the display of votive gifts. Ulf 1997: 48–53 emphasises the political and communicative role played by the temples. More recent research on sanctuaries in southern Italy show that these were also used as locations for the processing of wool. See García Morcillo 2013; Meo 2019.
190. De Polignac 1984: 44 calls such temples 'le sanctuaire extra-urbain' to distinguish them from sanctuaries within the settlement ('sanctuaire urbain') and from those on the margins of the city ('sanctuaire sub-urbain'). He considers them as symbolic protection walls ('rempart symbolique') against the area of disorder and lack of organisation 'et de l'éphémère, où dominent les conjonctions anormales placées sous le signe de la ruse et de la violence non institutionalisée: entre hommes et dieux [...] entre les êtres humains eux-mêmes [...] entre hommes et animaux'.
191. De Polignac 1984: 35–39, 49–84.

agricultural ways of living: territorial boundaries do not feature in pastoral economies, while agricultural societies depend on the recognition of land ownership and territorial relations.[192]

The supposition that Homeric society was pastoral is as doubtful as the contrast between agricultural and pastoral economies. My analysis of the myth of Polyphemus showed that a key moment of poetic tension is caused precisely by the disruption of a regular exchange of goods between the world of the shepherd and the household of the livestock owner. Epic evidence shows that shepherds and livestock owners act in different production units but within a regulated system of exchange such as is characteristic of transhumant economies.[193] In addition to this, studies of pastoral societies show that the boundaries of pasture lands are defined with precision and that the concept of boundaries is very much present.[194] And the mountainous regions in which rural sanctuaries were located were not areas of wilderness but, as Michael Jameson correctly points out, cultural spaces which were used for cattle farming.[195] Since inhabitants of different regions and *poleis* were often frequenting mountain areas simultaneously, it makes more sense to view the sanctuaries established in such border territories as meeting places rather than as structures intended as protection from the wild. In a later work, de Polignac admits to this problem and pays more attention to the role of the sanctuaries as places of supraregional exchange.[196]

The sanctuary of Apollo at Delphi, the final recipient of the tripod of the Seven Sages, is surrounded by grazing land, just like Olympia.[197] Unlike Olympia, which served as a seasonal meeting point for Arcadians, Eleans, and Messenians but remained under the control of Elis,[198] Delphi came under the control of a supraregional power, the Amphictyonic League. According to the historians the amphictyony included the Thessalians,

---

192. De Polignac 1984: 19–20, 46–57. Similarly, Qviller 1981: 137. De Polignac leans on the work of Anthony Snodgrass (1987: 199–209), who sees evidence for this transformation in the frequent abandonment of settlements in the geometric era. Snodgrass speaks of transhumance in this context. According to Irad Malkin (1993: 231), the 'only clear evidence both for the institution of heroic cults and their territorial implications is in the world of Greek colonies'.
193. Cf. ch. 2.1.
194. Cf. von Fürer-Haimendorf 1975: 177; Khazanov 1984: 75.
195. Jameson 1989: 7–12. Cf. also Daveri Rocchi 1990: 95–110.
196. De Polignac 1994: 5–11. See now McInerney 2006: 34; García Morcillo 2013.
197. Jameson 1988: 97; Sourvinou-Inwood 1993: 11.
198. Morgan 1990: 192.

Dolopians, Perrhoebians, Magnesians, Boeotians from the northeast, the Dorians, Ionians from Euboea, Locrians, Oeteans, Phthiotae, Malians, and Phocians until 346 BCE.[199] The League is linked to the first 'Sacred War', which resulted in the transformation of the Krisean plain into grazing land. What was at issue was not so much the securing of pasture land to cater to the high demand for sacrificial animals, as argued recently by Timothy Howe and Jeremy McInerney,[200] but more likely the integration of Delphi into a supraregional transhumant network, which necessitated the use of the plain as winter grazing land.[201] Morgan does not exclude the possibility of a transhumance background for this interregional integration of Delphi, which can be dated to as early as the ninth century, on the basis of ceramic evidence. But in Morgan's view the importance of Delphi is above all as a base along the trading route to Thessaly and as a sea route to Italy.[202] De Polignac now attributes a similar gateway function to Olympia and Ithaca, along the lines of the argument made for the southern Italian settlements of the second millennium BCE by Thyrza Smith.[203] There is no contradiction between these different functions, since the movement of flocks mostly goes hand in hand with trading relations. The wool trade is of course also closely connected with pasture farming.[204]

The dedications at the Heraion at Perachora offer a further point of interest, since a large portion (74 per cent) of the finds there are of Phoenician artefacts. Contrary to earlier assumptions, these cannot be attributed to visits from Phoenician travellers, since a substantial part of the finds are ointment jars, pearls, scarabs, and faience objects that are also found at women's burial sites. On this basis, Imma Kilian-Dirlmeier suspects

199. On the membership of the league cf. Walek 1911: 13–25; Tausend 1992: 35–43; Sanchez 2000.
200. Howe (2003; 2008: 85–93) as well as McInerney (2006: 34) argue that 'large-scale animal husbandry designed to serve the needs of sanctuaries and the pilgrims who consulted them'. Emile Bourguet (1905: 26–31 with note 1) argues that the office of the *poleteres* suggests that pasture lands were leased.
201. See my arguments in Wagner-Hasel 2000a; 2002b and forthcoming.
202. According to Morgan, Delphi was part of a northeastern (Euboean and Thessalian) network of exchange relations during the ninth century. At the end of the eighth century the previously dominant southeastern connection was reoriented towards Thessaly, with the addition of ceramics from Attica, Boeotia, the Argolid, and Corinth. Morgan 1990: 112–37, 199; 1988: 319.
203. Smith 1987; de Polignac 1994: 11. Cf. also Eder 2006.
204. This was my argument in Wagner-Hasel 2000: 295; 2002b; 2016. See now Chandezon 2003, who argues that sanctuaries kept cattle not only for sacrifice but also as a source for revenues when their offspring or wool were sold.

that the artefacts were gifts or dedications made by local women who had been married abroad.[205] There is evidence, for instance, that a woman living on Cyprus dedicated a *peplos* at the sanctuary of Athena Alea at Tegea (Paus. 8.5.3).[206] Exogamy, which must have also influenced the transfer of techniques and styles, is a feature of the majority of marriages mentioned in Homer, and it was also practised by the tyrants.[207] The tendency to marry out of the community is contrary to the advice and practice found in Hesiod and in the Attic orators of the fourth century, where it is considered best to marry within the neighbourhood or the extended family (Hes. *Op.* 695–700).[208] Although Louis Gernet's initial research into exogamy proposed that such bonds were a way of forging political alliances, it is not the case that politics is the only reason for such marriages. Just like guest-friendships, marriages could also be a way of securing supraregional exchange networks, as the example of the Cypselids shows. Melissa, the wife of the tyrant Periandrus, was a daughter of the tyrant of Epidaurus, who in turn was married to a woman from Arcadia (Hdt. 5.92; Diog. Laert. 1.94; Heraclides *fr.* 144–151 Wehrli). These marriages establish a link between Corinth and two other regions: Arcadia, known for its wealth in sheep, and the coastal region of Epidaurus, from where even today farmers send their flocks into the mountains of Arcadia for summer pasture.[209] Contemporary coin imagery depicts beehives, Hermes, and a ram. This suggests the Cypselids' interest in wool products, and later sources attest to the high quality of Corinthian wool products.[210] The degree to which such marriage practices were peculiar to the tyrants may be indicated by Theognis's scorn for the practice when he accuses the Cypselids of departing from the earlier endogamous marriage conventions of the Bacchiads (Thgn. 183–92; 891–94).[211] In Homer the abduction of women and female fidelity are key themes, and the stability of marriage bonds plays

---

205. Kilian-Dirlmeier 1985: 228–32.
206. See Buschor 1912: 45.
207. Wagner-Hasel 1988; Gernet 1968. Coldstream 1993: 80–107 argues that the practice of mixed marriage in Al Mina and other *emporia* was the reason for the adoption of Eastern cultural elements.
208. See Cox 1998: ch. 2.
209. See Koster 1976. Howe 2008: 87.
210. Corinthian *strōmata* are mentioned by Athenaeus 1.27d; 12.525d; 13.582d. Orth 1924: 609 and Salmon 1984: 136 suggest that the wool products mentioned by Athenaeus stem from Arcadia. Morgan 1988: 338 does not say what Corinth exchanged for metals.
211. On the addressee of Theognis's critique of tyranny, see van der Lahr 1992: 134–51.

a prominent role at strategic moments in the narrative so that it appears that the poetic world may reflect the interests of the tyrants of the archaic period. The competition for superiority between these tyrants and other aristocrats led to extravagant spending on purple clothing and jewellery as status symbols which can still to be observed in accounts of the fifth and fourth centuries.[212]

It appears that the early tyrants were especially instrumental in furthering supraregional exchange and that their wide-ranging guest-friendships and marriage alliances helped to forge a dense network of communications.[213] This is not only true of the Cypselids at Corinth or for Samos, where a new type of ship, the Samaina, was developed under the tyrant Polycrates for the transport of large freights.[214] Herodotus and Aristotle link the Athenian tyrant Peisistratus to the exploitation of Thracian silver mines.[215] Theognis complains that under the tyrants the *phortēgoi*, the 'porters' or carriers of freight, are in charge. He accuses the tyrants of giving people hope of *kerdoi*, the advantages and profits we have seen linked to the undertaking of journeys in the epics.[216] The administration of this form of trading during the archaic age, best described as exchange of resources, provided individual local leaders with substantial powers. This exchange of resources appears to be much more important than land ownership as the basis for positions of power such as we see crystallised during the age of the tyrants.

Above all, the exchange of resources is a precondition for the processes of networking and centralisation observed in the archaic period. To understand the political aspect of the role of the tyrants and the development of the *polis*, one should not underestimate the economic factors that played a leading role in the development of an increasingly dense network of communication. Often interpreted as the result of 'peer-polity interaction' and

---

212. For evidence see Alföldi 1955: 15–55; Geddes 1987: 317–21; Stein-Hölkeskamp 1989: 104–10; Stulz 1990: 121–53. Presumably the critique was a projection of the fifth century, since Theognis 53–68 directs his critique at the nonurban dress of the tyrants. But in any case, it is clear that dress has political significance.
213. Cf. Gernet 1968; Stahl 1987: 93–96; Sancisi-Weerdenburg 2000; Morris 2003: 14.
214. Presumably he had access to the gold and silver of Siphnos. Hdt. 3.57. Treister 1996: 24, 135–36. Cf. also Kurke 1999.
215. Hdt. 1.64; [Arist.] *Ath. Pol.*15. See Boardman 1981: 271; Treister 1996: 136–38; Lavelle 1995; 2005.
216. Thgn. 667–682 and 823–24. According to Plato (*Resp.* 579d–e) tyranny is *philochrēmatia*. See Domingo Gygax 2002 and 2016: 106, who regards the tyrant as a big-man like the Homeric *basileus* and stresses their generous behaviour.

rivalry between different political elites,[217] rivalry and emulation should be considered within a framework of economic relationships. This increase in supraregional exchange forms the economic background that may help us to understand the evolution of extra-urban sanctuaries.[218]

---

217. Peer-polity-interaction: Renfrew 1986: 1–18; Snodgrass 1986: 47–58. Elite competition: Duplouy 2002; 2006; Ulf 2011; Fisher and van Wees 2011; 2015.
218. This is assumed by Graham (1984: 9) for southern Italy, where Greek objects are found especially in extra-urban sanctuaries. For the economic role of sanctuaries in Italy see now García Morcillo 2013 and Kistler 2015.

Conclusion

The Sensory World of Gifts: Weaving, Signs, and Communication

'Next to agriculture, the arts of making clothing are without dispute the most necessary and useful. There are few inventions which have displayed such sagacity, and done so much honour to the human understanding.'[1] So we are told in *The Origin of Laws, Arts, and Sciences and Their Progress among the Most Ancient of Nations*, first published in French in 1758. Although he praises the art of textile work itself, the book's author, Antoine-Yves Goguet, shows no appreciation of the products of this 'sagacity', that is, of ancient clothing itself. He is, in fact, harsh in judging the apparel of the ancient Greeks: 'But it must be agreed, that the dress of the Greeks, as well for the men as for the women, was very imperfect. Is it not astonishing, for example, that these people never knew neither breeches, nor stockings, nor drawers, nor pins, nor buckles, nor buttons, nor pockets?'[2] Bronze tripods are singled out for praise in Goguet's otherwise negative judgement of Greek artistry: 'Their moveables for luxury at that time consisted in beautiful tripods designed only to ornament the apartment; for they made no other use of them'.[3]

Goguet himself wrote during an era in which dress was, alongside home-furnishings, the key means of signalling social rank and distinction. Regulated by numerous rules and laws, dress was a key way of defining and displaying social status, gender, and age during the Middle Ages and especially during the Early Modern Period.[4] In the upper echelons of society, this way of visibly displaying distinctions in rank and status was sharpened

---

1. Goguet, vol. 1, 1775: 121.
2. Goguet, vol. 2, 1775: 385.
3. Goguet, vol. 2, 1775: 386.
4. Bulst 1988; Medick 1996: ch. 6; Slanicka 2002.

by elite competition and rapidly changing fashions.[5] It is not surprising then that in a work of this period we find special attention given to the appearance of clothing and that its manufacture is especially praised as a sign of reason—the highest praise during this era. It is equally unsurprising that the author uses dress as a means of distinguishing between cultures as well as between the civilised peoples of his own age and the 'savages', amongst whom Goguet counts the Greeks.[6]

With the arrival of the industrial revolution, and the invention of the Spinning Mule in 1775, the notion that textile work was a product of reason and intellect—found not only in Goguet but in other works of the period too—disappeared.[7] For a long time, histories of technology and economics tended largely to ignore textile work in favour of metallurgy.[8] This seems to follow nineteenth-century patterns of thought: the age of industrialisation conceived of progress according to the metals that would come to govern the age of the machine rather than the steps that led to Crompton's Spinning Mule—the spindle, the loom, and the spinning wheel. The three-ages system that orders events and artefacts of prehistory and history into the Stone Age, Bronze Age, and Iron Age—and is still in use today—was developed during this period, in 1819, by the Danish prehistorian Christian Jörgensen Thomsen.[9] If we were to complement this schema, which accounts only for developments in metallurgy, with a similar one that accounts for developments in textile work, this would take the form (for Europe) of: flax and hemp, wool, cotton, and silk. Taking into account

---

5. Dinges 1992.
6. Goguet, vol. 2, 1775: 387.
7. Lenz [1790] 1976: 38-39: 'So wenig wir auch bestimmen können, wie vollkommen oder unvollkommen die kunst zu sticken damals seyn mußte, die doch einige regeln des zeichnens, genie, gebildeten geschmack u.s.w. voraussetzt, so wenig läßt uns die allgemeine bewunderung dieser weiblichen werke im alterthum zweifeln, daß man es wenigstens für jene Zeiten sehr weit darin gebracht habe'.
8. Cf. e.g. Roebuk 1969; Burford 1972; Landels 1978. A few remarks on textile technology can be found in Hopper 1978 and Schneider 1989. By contrast, Hugo Blümner's four-volume history of the technology and terminology of the arts and crafts in Greece and Rome published in 1912 contains much technical information on ancient textile production. Nineteenth-century histories of ancient private lives ('Privataltertümer') also contain extended reflections on the fabrication of textiles. Publications on ancient economy show a similar picture. See e.g. Finley 1973. The situation has changed during the last decade. See e.g. Bresson 2008, I: 196-99 ('Le cas de l'artinasat textile'); Harris, Lewis and Woolmer 2016. Their book *The Ancient Greek Economy* contains several articles dealing with textiles. For discussion of the development see Wagner-Hasel and Nosch 2019: 13-15.
9. See Childe 1947.

tools as well as materials, we would have: spindle and needle, followed by loom and spinning wheel. Neither schema, however, fits well with the traditional three-ages system. Flax processing can be traced back to the Palaeolithic; weaving on looms with wool and flax begins in the Neolithic and is older than the melting of metals; the distaff first occurs in the archaic period, during the Iron Age, while the spinning wheel was invented only in medieval times.[10]

It is not my intention here to redraw current systems of periodisation. The key question is not to reevaluate the sequence of the technological developments of the premodern era. The real problem is the the change from the premodern to the modern age and the way in which this change is determined by the process of industrialisation. This has transformed our perception of the sensory world to a significant degree. For this reason, I think it is worth looking back to the perspective taken by an eighteenth-century scholar contemplating ancient material culture in order to focus on the ways in which we might profit today from taking a cultural-historical view of ancient gift objects.[11] Let us start by sketching out the state of contemporary scholarship in cultural history.

During Goguet's time, the definition of culture was firmly anchored in the worlds of farming, forestry, and botany from which the term is derived. Eighteenth-century bureaucratic language defines culture according to the ancient *cultura* (derived from *colere*, to inhabit, till, cultivate, worship) as the cultivation of soil, crops, and woodlands. Although the major semantic shift that established culture as a social rather than as an agricultural term did not occur completely until the mid-nineteenth century (sometime between 1830 and 1860), we can already detect a sense of civilisation and refinement in Goguet's cultural-historical observations.[12] In this sense, culture and civilisation are closely connected concepts, perhaps especially so in the French-speaking world.[13] Understood as a whole, culture suggests the *mores*, attitudes and practices of a society or era but also refinement, or a refined way of life, precisely that use of buckles and buttons suggested in the earlier quotation. In this way, culture, in Goguet's work, is inextricably bound to the progress of civilisation.

10. For an overview see Barber 1991: 249–59. For a discussion of the criteria of technical periodisation see Paulinyi 1990. He stresses the factor of 'Mechanisierung der Stofformungstechnik' that means the use of machines.
11. For such an approach see now Schmitt Pantel 2009: 12.
12. Sobrevilla 1971: 2–3.
13. Cf. Bausinger 1980; Rehberg 1986.

Since then, the concept of culture has undergone a number of shifts in meaning and has changed from a concept defining agricultural practice and a refined way of life to a way of interpreting practice as such. The academic disciplines that shape our understanding of culture include those that specialise in present, past, and alien cultures (sociologists, historians, and ethnologists) along with those whose expertise is the material and literary remains of the past (archaeologists, art historians, and philologists). The concept of culture used in these disciplines can be roughly divided into two areas. Archaeologists and anthropologists tend to make use of an instrumental and substantial concept of culture, in the sense of civilisation, in order to interpret material remains and lived practices. Here, culture is viewed from the perspective of social processes, as by Gordon Childe, and understood as 'the durable material expression of an adaptation to an environment [...] that enabled a society to survive and develop'.[14] Sometimes culture is seen, as by Marvin Harris, from the perspective of the individual adapting to the environment and defined as the entirety of technologies suitable for ensuring survival.[15] Functionalists such as Malinowski, critical of progress and keen to stress the intrinsic value of culture, also espouse a similar understanding of culture as being linked to civilisation when they observe the functional connections between *mores* and customs, and technologies and ideas, as well as institutions and practices.[16] Such an understanding of culture also underlies sociological research into the process and development of patterns and standards of behavioural practices undergone by the individual during the transition from the premodern to the modern age.[17] With the 'cultural turn' in historical studies, as the discipline shifted from structural and social history to a history of culture and *mentalité*, we see by contrast the formation of a semiotic concept of culture that builds on a different tradition and emphasises inner values and individual creativity rather than social structures, technological developments, and supra-individual patterns of behaviour.[18] This semiotic concept of culture looks to research in the field of semantic anthropology to understand culture as the world of symbolic practice.[19] In this view, culture

---

14. Childe 1947: 16.
15. Harris 1985. Cf. also Hansen 1995: 195, 204.
16. Malinowski 1944.
17. See e.g. Elias [8]1981.
18. See e.g. Jacob Burckhardt's *Griechische Kulturgeschichte*. For the background to Burckhardt's approach see Gossman 2000: ch. 12.
19. The key reference must always be Clifford Geertz, *The Interpretations of Cultures* 1973. On semantic anthropology compare Hastrup 1986: 54–67.

comprises all the thoughts, actions, and perceptions that together are seen as constituting reality.[20] The concept transcends its tradition, which also contains an antimodern impetus, directed precisely against the notion of progress in the 'process of civilisation', and at times criticised for elitism.[21]

In anthropology reflecting on culture as a system of meanings, culture must be understood as a way to counteract the objective status of anthropological knowledge and more generally as a part of a process of reflection on the status of ostensibly objective data. In historical studies, the search for a new definition of the concept of culture should be seen in the context of the reevaluation of the role of the subject, as societal structures are seen to dominate. A similar shift of perspective from the study of social structures to the study of the construction of meaning is debated in sociology[22] and should be understood as a reaction (similar in character to the cultural historical debates that emerged around 1900) to the absence of sense in an increasingly complex and incomprehensible environment.[23] My aim in choosing a cultural-historical perspective is to bridge the gap between social structures and the semiotic concept of culture.[24]

Classical studies have for some time been especially dominated by the idea of universal values inherent in humanist cultural history, so that the shift to semiotic readings of culture has been especially important here.[25] This is true for art-historical and archaeological research[26] as much as for philological and ancient historical studies of thought, behaviour, and imagination in the ancient world,[27] and for research into the political and ritual practices of ancient communities.[28] When forms of cultural expression such as artefacts and literary texts, but also practices and forms of behaviour such as the *symposium*, are interpreted from a sociopolitical perspective, we find that the subjects of the universal histories of the eighteenth century (e.g. marriage and funeral rituals, dress, and food culture)

---

20. See the overview of Daniel 1993: 72; 1997: 195–218 and 259–278.
21. Rehberg 1986: 92–95; vom Bruch, Graf and Hübinger 1989; Bausinger 1980: 62.
22. Cf. Neidhardt 1986: 10.
23. Vom Bruch 1989: 9–17.
24. For a critique of the neglect of the social dimension of culture see Kaschuba 1995: 27–46; Canning 2002.
25. 'Third Humanism' is a case in point, see Jaeger 1925; Schadewaldt 1931.
26. Cf. e.g. Hölscher 1989; Zanker 1987; Bérard and Vernant 1984; Giuliani 1986.
27. Cf. e.g. Winkler 1990; Meyer-Zwiffelhoffer 1995; Barghop 1995; Rohweder 1998; Hartmann 2016; Chaniotis 2011; 2017.
28. Cf. e.g. Murray 1990; Schmitt Pantel 1992, reprint 2011; Hunter 1994; Davidson 1997; Dunbabin 2003; Vössing 2004; Stein-Hölkeskamp 2005; Stavrianopoulou 2009; Tietz 2013.

can be reintegrated into political history. During the course of the increasing professionalisation of historical studies, and their concentration on political events and institutions, those subjects were seen to be relevant only to the lives of individuals and had been marginalised.[29]

The purpose of this study on the materiality of the terms and objects connected to gift-giving was not to determine a new cultural code or symbolic system. My purpose was to find ways to use the material world as we see it in the depiction of exchange in the Homeric epics in order to find new ways to analyse and to read ancient society. In the course of my enquiry it has become clear that the economic value of gifts was far greater than had been recognised in research focussed only on political and social functions. Taking symbolic value into account suggested that gift-exchange had a hitherto little-recognised economic function even in the political sphere, be that Homeric kingship or the formation of the *polis*. The focus on determining the sensory content of the objects and terms involved, rather than on reconstructing systems for their interpretation, led to this recognition. The exchange relationships and areas of conflict belonging to the world of the eighth to sixth centuries BCE were brought into focus by paying close attention to that sensory, material content. And the very things Goguet singled out particularly in his negative assessment of Greek civilisation—tripods and clothing—prove to be of central significance.

In antiquity, tripods and textiles were never merely utilitarian or decorative objects. Both types of objects represented symbolic action, such as when they were presented as gifts or donations on particular occasions, or when they served to visualize status or service as well as bonds and identity. The three-legged cauldron may be an exceptionally and universally useful object, not least because it has the advantage of being very stable on uneven ground; but the tripod also signifies Greek culture particularly.[30] Contrary to Goguet's assumption, it did have utilitarian functions both for cooking and for bathing, but it was also and above all a guest-gift, a prize, and a votive offering. At Delphi the tripod came to symbolise Apollo's prophecy and, therefore, to be connected to the transmission of wisdom.[31]

29. Schmitt Pantel [1992] 2011: 493–94; Nippel 1990: 78; Wagner-Hasel 1998: 25–35. See also Schmitt Pantel 2009: 11; 2012.
30. Around 1900 the Vlachs were using tripods to cook their national dish. See Wace and Thompson 1914: 51. Tibetan shepherds were exchanging sheep for iron tripods even at the end of the twentieth century: Goldstein and Beall 1991: 22. In 1970s Euboea, farmers still used iron tripods as du Boulay (1974: 25) could observe.
31. The symbolic meaning of the Delphic tripod is discussed by Papalexandrou 2005.

We have found that Homeric epic suggests a correspondence on the symbolic level between metal and textile gifts. Even if Greek dress could be criticised for its lack of buttons, buckles, and pockets (the eighteenth-century critique would eventually be reversed when this lack of elaboration was seen as the virtue of timeless and utilitarian beauty once the dress reforms of the 1920s took hold[32]), it was clearly as impressive and distinctive in its use of colour and patterns as any courtly fashion. Recent years have seen a new interest in textile production[33] and in the symbolic value of clothes.[34] When we do see studies into the symbolic value of textiles as gifts, structuralist approaches dominate over investigations into historical functional contexts. This is true for instance of the work of Ian D. Jenkins on the destructive effects of textile gifts in tragedy. Without paying any attention to the social and political contexts within which textiles are offered as gifts, Jenkins places textiles within the domain of the basic ambiguity of the feminine that can be both a gift and an evil.[35] But ignoring contexts means that the messages carried by gifts are concealed. Even in a new study titled *Body, Dress, and Identity in Ancient Greece* (2015), which deals with the visual, haptic, and olfactory appearance of the clothed body, we find such binary patterns of interpretation with the result that the cultural importance of textiles gets lost. Its author, Mireille M. Lee, assumes an *a priori*, general idealisation of the naked male body and a contempt in principle for the dressed female body,[36] an assumption that archaeological research has long since proved wrong.[37] Deborah Lyons, on the other hand, in her *Dangerous Gifts* of 2012, emphasises the importance of female gifts in the epics and in tragedy, while ruling out the possibility of genuine reciprocity between husbands and wives. In her view, women were strangers within the household (the *oikos*), and within the *polis* they did not have the status of citizens.[38] Josine Blok and other historians have proved that

32. Bieber [1928] 1977: 1–2.
33. Cf. Pekridou-Gorecki 1989; Barber 1991; Reuthner 2006; Gillis and Nosch 2003; Bundrick 2008; Spantidaki 2016.
34. Bergren 1983; 2008; Jenkins 1985; Koch-Harnack 1989; Scheid and Svenbro 1994; Papadopoulou-Belmehdi 1994; Llewellyn-Jones 2003; Gherchanoc and Huét 2012; Lee 2015; Cifarelli and Gawlinski 2017.
35. Jenkins 1985; cf. also Keuls 1983: 209.
36. Lee 2015; cf. also Lyons 2012.
37. Cf. e.g. research on female nudity (Kreilinger 2007) or on the symbolic meaning of female dress in funeral rites (Sojc 2005).
38. Lyons 2012. Like Jenkins, Lyons also argues that tales of the perils emanating from women's gifts in tragedy reflect fears of female agency, while also suggesting the dependence of men on women with respect to household economy.

the concept of the citizen, the *politēs*, existed alongside the *politis*, i.e. its female form, and that female Athenians were considered as citizens.[39] The significance of textiles is increasingly recognised in philological research based on discourse-analysis. In such work we find a concentration of interest in the narrative function of objects such as Penelope's shroud or the ritual background of textile metaphors.[40] In social anthropology, research into technologies of dyeing and into the production of patterns led to extremely illuminating results concerning questions about the messages conveyed by gift-objects.[41] Research on technologies of patterned weaving yielded insight into poetic techniques[42] and into the basic structures of communication within which textiles functioned as symbolic capital.

I wish to stress five points to summarise some of the findings of this study. They concern (1) the sensory content of gifts, which can be traced to the terminology used for them and provide insight into (2) the structures of exchange found in the Homeric world, and into (3) the economic dimension of Homeric kingship and centre formation. Two further factors are critical to understanding such gifts: (4) the ritual context of the reception of Homeric epic and (5) the tension between remembrance and forgetting that affects both the epics themselves and the modern processes of the appropriation of the ancient material world.

1. The sensory content of the gift and its meaning.

We have pursued gift-objects mentioned in the Homeric epics in their various functions as they circulate as gifts and counter-gifts. In the ritual of guest-friendship tripods are used for bathing, while textiles serve to prepare the stranger's bed and to clothe him. Bathing and clothing effect a change in status, and the establishment of a new identity, as the stranger

---

39. Blok 2004. The idea of female citizenship through participation in cultic activity is argued for by Waldner 2000b in her examination of the Attic Brauronia.
40. Pantelia 1993: 493–501; Papadopoulou-Belmehdi 1994; Felson-Rubin 1994. The ritual practice is considered by Scheid and Svenbro [1994] 2001. See now Harich-Schwarzbauer 2016; Harlizius-Klück and Fanfani 2016.
41. Cf. Weiner and Schneider 1989: 1: '[...] cloth has furthered the organization of social and political life [...] cloth helps social groups to reproduce themselves [...] possibilities of color and patterning give cloth an almost limitless potential for communication.'
42. Cf. Nagy 2002 who considers technological aspects of weaving metaphors, and Harlizius-Klück (2004; 2016; 2019) whose interpretation of weaving metaphors is based on a close knowledge of textile technology. See also Adeline Grand-Clément's (2011) research on colours and Florence Gherchanoc's (2019) research on the symbolic meaning of patterned cloth in rituals of initiation.

(*xeinos*) is transformed into a friend (*philos*). Epic shows how textiles and metal gifts, such as golden beakers and silver mixing bowls given as commemorative gifts to guest-friends, guarantee permanent attachments and two different types of bonds. Textile gifts used as wedding presents integrate the guest into the domestic community and into the host couple's own marriage ties. In addition, the metal gifts, objects associated with the aristocratic symposium, symbolise the guest's ties to a male community of peers.

Both textiles and tripods develop their own symbolism within the context of the funeral ritual. During the washing and clothing of the dead they play a transforming role, as in the guest rituals. They contribute to the body's change in status and serve to grant safe passage (this is especially true of the shroud). They travel with the dead, whose post-mortem appearance they affect, and they are cremated along with the body. The posthumous fame and glory of the dead adhere to the textiles worn by them, as they do to the tripods presented as prizes at funeral games. The prizes remain in circulation among the living, for whom the ritual ensures the renewal of their hierarchies of achievement; the textiles used during the funeral ritual on the other hand are objects of generative power serving to secure the bond between the dead and the living.

Whenever textiles are attributed such important functions, reference is made to their colour and to the effects of their colour and patterning. The assumption that emerged from the debate on gift-exchange had been that objects circulating as gifts bear significant messages inherent in their materiality and that this refers back to their social function. On this, the evidence from the Homeric epics is clearer than that provided by Weiner's classical sites of gift-exchange in the Southern Pacific. In Homer gifts are presented as bearing messages in their decoration, and objects are used purposefully as signs of memory and identity in guest-friendship and in funeral rituals as signs of attachment in social relationships and finally as normative signs in situations requiring decision-making.

In decision-making contexts in the epics two objects are significant: one is the golden sceptre which is connected with guiding both herds and humans and is used to convey the right to speak; the second are the *themistes*. These *themistes* have a material and a nonmaterial meaning, as I have argued: they represent customary rules visualized and preserved in woven textures.

Scholarship has often pointed out the lack of clear rules of heredity in the distribution of positions of power, explaining this either as the result of a transition from monarchy to aristocracy or as part of the relatively low level of institutionalisation in early Greek kingship. Viewed against the background of the textile aspect of kingship, however, and especially through the analysis of the mythical world of the Phaeacians, we see a different explanation for this lack. Power is based on economic and symbolic capital, on access to stores of knowledge and tradition, and on the ability to recruit services and tributes from others. In the world of the Homeric epics we are not dealing with a monolithic system of government in which functions are fixed but with a range of spheres of power which are divided between the male and female members of high-ranking households, and between male representatives of different households. The world of the Phaeacians presents us with an idealised example of this system.

The symbolism of the material worlds as a whole shows a dual structure with respect to both space and time: messages emanating from the prizes and shrouds used during funeral rituals address both, the supraregional community of warriors and the local community. Both types of gifts, metal and textile objects, are able to symbolise time in different ways: as duration and as a process of renewal. The production and presentation of objects requires communal action by different groups, the supraregional warrior community and the domestic or local community. The cohesion of these communities is established by their collaboration and commemorated in the objects themselves.

2. Terminology and social structure.

Our enquiry into the symbolic content of gift-objects led us to an analysis of the terminology used in connection with gifts. Among the terms for guest-gifts, honorific offerings, and gifts of thanks investigated here, the word *charis* stood out as central, as it offered insight into the symbolic as well as the material processes that reproduced the social body. On the one hand, the term *charis* belongs in the realm of symbolic production, as it is used to describe the effect of images, be they woven, literary, or worked in metal. At the same time, *charis* also describes the making of such images undertaken as a service or as thanks for services given, and it therefore must be understood as a term of material production and social practice.

The use of the term affords insight into structures of cooperation we find in the epics. One such structure is the bond between husband and wife, underpinned by the collaborative community of weaving women, which in turn has its divine equivalent in the Graces. Another bond is the supraregional community of warriors, bound into a relationship of reciprocity with the gods through the sacrificial banquet. In the context of the bond between the married couple, *charis* can be interpreted as the thanks given by the wife in the form of her work on the loom and the products of that work. These are offered in recompense for bridal gifts given by the husband in the form of cattle and jewellery, and which emanate *charis* in the sense of a visual effect. In a military context, *charis* is the service given to a leader in battle, and the thanks expected for this. Divine *charis* often takes the form of the granting of success in battle given by the gods in return for sacrifice made to them.

If there is one term among those here examined that embodies reciprocity, that term is *charis* because it describes both service given and service returned. If we wanted to determine different types of reciprocity, as Donlan attempts with reference to Sahlin's ethnological studies, it would make sense to determine classifications by differentiating between the different relationships characterised by the term *philotēs*, which include both collaborative communities and relationships of exchange. The use of the term *charis*, however, also demonstrates that exchange is not merely a twofold act of giving and returning but that individual acts of exchange form part of a greater circulation. The epics show us that the funeral ritual is at the very heart of that circulation.

Another term with a similar double perspective is *amoibē*. This word describes the necessary return offered after gifts have been given, be it as sacrificial offerings or guest-gifts. While *charis* emphasises reciprocity and community, *amoibē* has a more individualistic character and refers specifically to the reciprocity of exchange between individuals. Unlike previous scholars, I see the function of such reciprocal exchange between guest-friends to be less connected to the formation of political bonds and more to the organisation of an exchange of resources, albeit within the framework of existing guest-friendships. This includes the sharing of pasture lands but above all focusses on moveable goods. Guest-gifts share a material content with these goods and thus form an important reminder of the relationship that underpins the exchange of resources such as textiles, especially linen, dyes, and metals.

Materials imported from abroad are only very rarely referred to as guest-gifts or *xeinia*. When the term is used, it appears to suggest tribute provided by foreign shepherds or foreign masters. This is true of some of the natural *xeinia* which, as we have established, form part of a relationship of exchange between a shepherd's station and the homestead. When gifts of armour are described as *xeinia* they are substitutes for personal military service. When textile and metal *xeinia* are given to strangers, contributions in kind are collected by high-ranking sponsors from the people. Such objects can therefore not properly be counted as tokens of a reciprocal relationship of obligation between strangers but should instead be interpreted as tributes offered to a *basileus*.

This relationship of exchange, or tribute, between a *basileus* and his people is best understood through *dōtinai* and *themistes* rather than *xeinia*. These are offerings, probably consisting of textiles, animal products, and metal objects, which are given in return for judgements or perhaps also for the granting of safe passage. It remains the case that there appears to be no system of regular taxation in antiquity, as our investigation shows that the tributes given to kings are always tied to specific benefits or services received. But we have somewhat modified the current image of Homeric kingship. While previous scholarship emphasised the rituals of generosity a *basileus* needed to perform in order to maintain his power, my examination of the services described by *dōtinai* and *themistes* has highlighted the functional aspect of the position of the *basileus*. Apart from their military leadership, Homeric kings owe their privileged position to the granting of spatial passage and the fulfilment of judgement, which can be interpreted as social guidance.

3. The economics of centre-formation.

Advancing a functional interpretation of Homeric kingship, which I defined as 'Geleitherrschaft', enabled us to consider the spatial dimension of rulership and thus to review established ideas of pre-state structures based exclusively on personal ties. It is true that personal ties established through guest-friendships and marriages do play a role in the creation of a widespread net of relationships. However, rulership is also connected with fixed places or clearly identified settlements where leadership and decision-making are exercised (*basileuein*) and where tributes and gifts are collected. This means that the Greek tyrants of the sixth century, whose positions of power depended on far-reaching networks based on marriages and guest-friendships, and on the organisation of imported resources,[43] were able to relate to the Homeric world, notwithstanding the influence of Eastern culture on the design of the works.[44] Previous research on the spatial aspects of *polis* formation assumed a transition from a pastoral (Homeric) to an agricultural society, in which land became the only significant form of wealth. However, it is clear that Homeric society in no way corresponds to a pastoral model. Instead, the use of shared pasture lands we find in the epic poems suggests an economy of transhumance which goes hand in hand with agriculture. My observations lead to the conclusion, therefore, that the processes of centralisation and *polis* formation are a result of this transhumant economy as well as of an intensification of the exchange of resources. Research on Homeric gift-exchange has tended to interpret conflicts in terms of oppression and exploitation and to deduce from this a development of increasing social inequality, which in turn is assumed to have led by necessity to new, institutional ways of regulating conflict.[45] Our spatial perspective demonstrates the extent to which centre formation, driven by the need for supraregional communication, perpetuated and updated Homeric traditions for regulating conflict and organising spatial movement and social conduct.

4. Text and ritual, event and discourse.

The manifold practices and singular objects of giving and exchanging do not display only patterns of behaviour, attitudes, and social values. Investigation of the semantics and the circulation of gifts allows us also to reconstruct a model of social structure whose historical location is a ritual rather than a specific city or region. Epic songs were recited at festival days, such as the Panathenaic Games instituted in 566/5 BCE.[46] Through

---

43. Stahl 1987: 201–26.
44. Burkert 1991: 155–81.
45. Qviller 1981; Morris 1986: 4. Cf. also Rose 2012.
46. Peisistratus and his sons were also responsible for the so-called edition of the Homeric epics. This is the argument of Seaford 1994: 144–50 and Stanley 1993: 280–82. For a discussion of the iconographic evidence see Shapiro 1989: 43–48. Cf. also Blok 2000.

the two key elements of the ritual of the Great Panathenaia represented on the Parthenon frieze, the sacrificial procession and the presentation of the *peplos* to Athena, the city presents itself as a sacrificial community and, at the same time, places itself under divine protection through the dedication of the *peplos*.[47] Thus the Panathenaic ritual suggests two types of bond, both of which we have seen in the epics: ties between warriors and ties between the women of a domestic community. While the sacrifice is supported by a community of young men, the dedication of the *peplos* (just like the presentation of the shroud at the funeral ritual and the handing over of textile commemorative gifts to guests) is a communal task undertaken by the women weavers. These women are represented in Athenian ritual by the two *arrhēphoroi* who, on the Acropolis, lead the weaving of the *peplos* directed by the priestess of Athena.[48] The two *arrhēphoroi* suggest the pairs of Homeric *amphipoloi*, who in turn represent the Charites, the divine weavers, and in classical times were the guardians of festivals. They belong to the group of multiple divinities understood by Nicole Loraux as part of a strategy of deindividualising the feminine.[49] Loraux's interpretation, however, misreads the social practice embodied by these multiple divinities, which are manifested in the *Theogony*. They all represent aspects of the symbolic function of woven textiles.[50] Alongside the Charites, who here grant pleasure at festivities, there are the daughters of Themis, the Horae and the Moirae, who represent law and order in the form of Eunomia (good order) and Dike (righteousness), and the thread of life. While the Graces represent the effects that emanate from woven or poetic images, the Horae embody social values and norms which, in epic poetry, are represented by the (textile) *themistes* and which we see described in literature and philosophy through the image of the political or communal garment.[51] Finally, Hesiod also names the Muses, the divine singers who inspire poets, the daughters of Mnemosyne, or memory. Images from the classical period show couples as well as groups of men and groups of women wrapped in a common cloak or mantle, in pairs, or in groups of three or nine (Figure

47. The dedication of the *peplos* in *Iliad* 6 is often thought of as a late, Attic addition. See Stanley 1993: 282.
48. See Mansfield 1985; Barber 1992 and now Brøns 2017.
49. Loraux 1991: 45.
50. Hes. *Theog.* 901–11; 915–17. On the Charites see Wagner-Hasel 2002.
51. Aristoph. *Lys.* 568–86; Plato, *Politikos* 31a–c; Scheid and Svenbro [1994] 2001: 9–34; Wagner-Hasel 2005.

Figure 10: Nine women wrapped in a common cloak. Black-figure *kylix*, 5th century BCE. Berlin, Antikenmuseum F 3993. After Koch-Harnack 1989: 111, Fig. 1.

Figure 11: A group of women on Sumba wrapped in an Indian cotton textile performing a dance prior to the burial of King Umbu Nai Wolang of Kapunduk. After Kahn-Majlis 1991: Fig. 2.

10).[52] Gundel Koch-Harnack suggests these images carry erotic symbolism. It is, however, equally possible that the common mantle is a symbol of community resulting from communal action and communal performance in ritual. This is confirmed by a glance at an ethnographic parallel from Indonesia; here a group of women at a funeral ceremony are wrapped in a large mantle in a manner evoking the image on our ancient *kylix* (Figure 11).[53] The bonding, or community-building, function of woven garments could suggest that Mauss's supposition that there was a social purpose adhering to the giving, receiving, and returning of gifts might, after all, be true for ancient Greece. However, the integration of objects into concrete rituals of orchestrated communal action makes it quite clear that the social groups behind those objects are tied together through their collaboration rather than by the objects themselves. The objects merely represent this social integration.

While ritual focusses on basic social values and serves to create an idealised or simplified image of reality and to create a sense of social cohesion,[54] narrative performances can thematise social conflict instead. It has been common in scholarship on the practice of gift-giving to look for depictions of the realities of giving, often without reference to the narrative logic of the epics. But epic narrative depicts ideal practice only selectively, as it is mostly concerned with what occurs when the processes of gift-giving are disturbed. This potential for conflict only becomes comprehensible when we tie it to social structures, not by considering events but by considering the semantics of things and of terms. This means that we have to read on two levels: (1) the narrative level on which events are related and (2) the level of social code or unconscious discourse that underlies the narrative, even when the subject is also the addressee of the narrative and when the narrative revolves around transmitting values and attitudes through poetic images that replicate the world as it is perceived in day-to-day reality, which are always socially determined. Thus, social structures are tacitly inscribed into the text.

---

52. Koch-Harnack 1989: 111 (fig. 1) and 117 and 143–63.
53. Kahn-Majlis 1991: 16 (fig. 2): 'An Indian cotton textile unites and protects a group of women on Sumba, who are performing a dance prior to the burial of King Umbu Nai Wolang of Kapunduk. They are wearing ceremonial sarongs which indicate that they are members of an aristocratic family'.
54. Bell 1992: 98–99. For ancient evidence see Seaford 1994: XI–XVI; Waldner 2000: 21–28.

Even when its social structures did not entirely correspond with those represented in epic poetry, Athenian society of the classical period could recognise itself in the rituals and practices depicted in the poems. Once new literary forms such as tragedy came into play, with a public status comparable to that of the epics, it would appear that epic worldviews became increasingly incompatible with contemporary circumstances, so that the role of the Homeric epics in the formation of civic identity also diminished. With Theagenes of Rhegium in the sixth century we see the rise of allegorical interpretations of Homeric epic and the increasing presence of competing versions of poetic 'truths'.[55] This uncertainty also determines the depiction of epic subject matter, and its continuation, on the tragic stage of the fifth century. So, tragedy treats the contradiction or tension between domestic ties and military alliances between citizens, which were absent from the epics but present in Athenian concerns after the Persian wars. The new dominance of the ties of citizenship over the ties of the couple and the domestic community forms the subject of the fifth-century funeral oration[56] and of Aeschylean tragedy;[57] it can also be seen in woven images, such as the pattern on Athena's *peplos* which depicted the gigantomachy.[58]

5. Remembering and forgetting.

Ancient tradition makes the singer Simonides of Ceos (556–468 BCE) the inventor of the art of memory, which consisted of the ability to link images (*imagines*) with places (*loci*). The well-known story of the invention of this technique takes place after a banquet hosted by the Thessalian Scopas, who tried to deduct half of the fee promised to the poet for his recital because he had included a lengthy passage in praise of Castor and Pollux in his song for Scopas. The Dioscuri take their revenge on Scopas by causing his house to collapse but save Simonides. The poet is able to identify the victims, crushed beyond recognition by the collapse of the house, according to the places where they had been sitting at the banquet.[59]

In this myth of the origin of memory the banquet is transformed into a funeral feast, a place of memorialising the dead. Pauline Schmitt Pantel's

---

55. Svenbro 1976: 16–17; Rösler 1980: 301; Feeney 1991: 5–56; Boyd 1995: 2–6.
56. Loraux 1981.
57. Wagner-Hasel 2007 (an English version is in preparation).
58. Wagner-Hasel 2005; Geddes 1987.
59. For evidence and discussion see Blum 1969: 41–46.

investigation of the history of the banquet highlights the role communal meals play in Greek memorial cult.[60] In Homeric funerary ritual, the key bearers of the posthumous glory of the dead are the funerary garments and the prizes awarded at funeral games. Mnemonic technique alludes to the manufacture of those objects: the ability of the weaver and the smith to place images in specific places and thus to award a spatial dimension to memory. But in the myth of memory, the singer's art predominates and erases the role of the place and the material media we see so clearly in Homer. And yet, the singer's art itself consisted of the ability to create images that inscribed themselves into the memory of the living.

Instead of Homer's woven garments and tripods, it is the written word of the poet that is anchored in the collective memory of modernity, although a late antique scholiast did suggest that Homer's depiction of the Trojan war was indebted to Helen's tapestry.[61] It is not necessary to assume an actual priority of the woven image over the poetic one in order to understand Uvo Hölscher's suggestion that Homeric epic 'emerg[ed] at a time that is not illuminated by even a glimmer of history', and is 'as though created from nothing during the first rise of the Hellenic spirit, as a product of a narrative imagination and at the same time of a perfection that must appear as a marvel'.[62] 'A marvel to behold' (*thauma idesthai*) is of course how Homer describes the purple threads and garments that are woven and spun by high-ranking women in the epics. In order to trace their role within the circulation of gifts and to inscribe it into our collective memory, it is necessary to define the contexts within which we ask questions about historical circumstances, and to gain some distance from our own cultural values. One way of achieving this is through looking back at the history of scholarship in our field, and through ethnological comparison. Another way was a historical investigation of terminology, which allowed a systematic approach unencumbered by any ready-made conceptual model. To undertake this journey into the past and into alien territories, and reconsider ancient culture based on the new insights gained, is a time-consuming task. When he came face to face with the Persian king, the aptly named Themistocles ('glory of Themis') asked for 'time' (*chronos*), to be

---

60. Schmitt Pantel 1992: 418–20, 490: Cf. also Scheid-Tissinier 1994: 267–84.
61. Sch. Hom. *Il.* 3.125. Barber 1991: 373. On the technical similarities see Bergren 1980: 22.
62. Hölscher 1990: 16.

used to gain a greater understanding of Greece from abroad and to give a good account of it. I will end my own journey into the faraway past with his words and a final invocation of patterned textiles:

ὁ δὲ Θεμιστοκλῆς ἀπεκρίνατο,) τὸν λόγον ἐοικέναι τοῦ ἀνθρώπου τοῖς ποικίλοις στρώμασιν· ὡς γὰρ ἐκεῖνα καὶ τοῦτον ἐκτεινόμενον μὲν ἐπιδεικνύναι τὰ εἴδη, συστελλόμενον δὲ κρύπτειν καὶ διαφθείρειν· ὅθεν αὐτῷ χρόνου δεῖν.

Themistocles answered that the word of man was similar to multicoloured tapestries (*poikiloi strōmata*). Like them, it needed to be spread out in order to display its figures, but when it was rolled up it concealed and destroyed them. For that reason, he was in need of time. (Plut. Them. 29.4–5).[63]

---

63. For the meaning of the simile see Gera 2007: 452. The reference point is not the spoken word but the translated speech. According to her, 'Themistocles compares translated speech, words that are conveyed by interpreters, to a rolled-up tapestry. Interpreters compress one's words and consequently the patterns, the subtleties and intricacies of one's thought, are lost'.

BIBLIOGRAPHY

Adkins, Arthur W. H. (1960) "'Friendship' and 'Self Sufficiency' in Homer and Aristotle," *Classical Quarterly* n.s. 12: 30–45.

——. (1971) "Homeric Values and Homeric Society," *The Journal of Hellenic Studies* 91: 1–14.

Adloff, Frank and Steffen Mau (eds.) (2005) *Vom Geben und Nehmen: Zur Soziologie der Reziprozität*. Francfort.

Adorno, Theodor W. (1985) "Einleitung" to Emile Durkheim, *Soziologie und Philosophie*, trans. Eva Moldenhauer. 2nd edn. Francfort: 7–44 (orig. 1924).

——. (1971) *Minima Moralia*. Francfort.

Adshead, K. (1986) *Politics and Archaic Peloponnese: The Transition from Archaic to Classical Politics*. Amersham.

Agourides, Christos (1997) "Searoutes and Navigation in the Third Millenium Aegean," *Oxford Journal of Archaeology* 61/1: 1–24.

Alcock, Susan E. (1991) "Tomb Cult and the Post Classical Polis," *American Journal of Archaeology* 95: 441–67.

Alcock, Susan E. and Robin Osborne (eds.) (1994/1996) *Placing the Gods: Sanctuaries and Sacred Space in Ancient Greece*. Oxford.

Alexiou, Margaret (1974) *The Ritual Lament in Greek Tradition*. Cambridge.

Alfaro, Carmen, John Peter Wild, and B. Costa (eds.) (2004) *Purpureae Vestes: Textiles y tintes del Mediterráneo en epoca romana*. Valencia.

Alföldi, Andreas (1955) "Gewaltherrscher und Theaterkönig," in *Late Classical and Medieval Studies in Honor of Albert Mathias Friend Jr.* ed. Kurt Weitzmann. Princeton: 15–55.

Algazi, Gadi, Valentin Groebner, and Bernhard Jussen (eds.) (2003) *Negotiating the Gift: Pre-Modern Figurations of Exchange*. Göttingen.

Allgemeines Landrecht für die Preußischen Staaten von 1794: Textausgabe (1970). With an introduction by Hans Hattenhauer. Francfort and Berlin.

Alram-Stern, Eva and Georg Nightingale (eds.) (2007) *Keimelion: Elitenbildung und elitärer Konsum von der mykenischen Palastzeit zur homerischen Epoche; Akten des internationalen Kongresses vom 3. bis zum 5. Februar 2005 in Salzburg*. Vienna.

Althoff, Gerd (1990) *Freunde und Getreue: Zum politischen Stellenwert von Gruppenbindungen im frühen Mittelalter*. Darmstadt.

Amira, Karl von (1882–1885) *Nordgermanisches Obligationenrecht*. 2 vols. Leipzig.

Ammerman, A. J. (1985) "Anthropology and the Study of Neolithic Exchange Systems in Calabria," *Dialoghi di Archeologia* 3/1: 11–33.

Ampolo, Carmine (1986) "Storia antica ed antropologia. Un rapporto difficile?" *Dialoghi di Archeologia* 4/1: 127–31.

Anderson, Eva and Marie-Louise Nosch (2003) "With a Little Help from My Friends: Investigating Mycenaean Textiles with Help from Scandinavian Experimental Archaeology," in *Metron: Measuring the Aegean Bronze Age; Proceedings of the 9th International Aegean Conference*, ed. Karen P. Foster and Robert Laffineur. Liège and Austin: 197-203.

Anderson, Øivind (1982) "Litai und Ehre: Zu Ilias 9, 513f." *Glotta* 60: 7-13.

Anderson, Øivind and Matthew Dickie (eds.) (1995) *Homer's World: Fiction, Tradition, Reality*. Bergen.

Anderson-Stojanovic, V. R. (1988) "Cult and Industry of Isthmia," *American Journal of Archaeology* 92: 268-69.

——. (1991) "The Rachi Settlement at Isthmia: Report on the 1989 Excavations," *American Journal of Archaeology* 95: 303-4.

Andreades, Andreas M. (1931 [Greek version 1926/27]) *Geschichte der griechischen Staatswirtschaft. I: Von der Heroenzeit bis zur Schlacht bei Chaironeia*. Munich.

Andreau, Jean (1995): "Vingt ans après *L'économie antique* de M. I. Finley. Présentation du dossier 'L'économie antique'", *Annales H.S.S.* 50: 947-960 = "Twenty years after Moses I. Finley's 'The Ancient Economy'", in: Walter Scheidel and Sitta von Reden (eds.) *The Ancient Economy*. Edinburgh 2002: 33-49.

Andreau, Jean and Etienne, Roland (1984): "Vingt ans de recherches sur l'archaïsme et la modernité des sociétés antiques," *Revue des Études Anciennes* 86,1-4: 55-83.

Andreev, Juri V. (1979) "Könige und Königsherrschaft in den Epen Homers," trans. Eberhard Dressler, *Klio* 61: 361-84.

Andronikos, Manilos (1968) *Totenkult*. Archaeologia Homerica III/W 1. Göttingen.

——. (1980) *The Royal Graves at Vergina*. Athen.

——. (1984) *Vergina: The Royal Tombs and the Ancient City*. Athen.

Antonaccio, Carla M. (1992) "Terraces, Tombs and the Early Argive Heraion," *Hesperia* 61: 85-105.

——. (1994) "Placing the Past: The Bronze Age in the Cultic Topography of Early Greece," in Alcock and Osborne 1994: 79-104.

——. (2001) "Ethnicity and Colonization," in her *Ancient Perceptions of Greek Ethnicity*, Cambridge, MA: 113-57.

Appadurai, Arjun (ed.) (1986) *The Social Life of Things: Commodities in Cultural Perspective*. Cambridge.

Armandry, Pierre (1987) "Trépieds de Delphes et du Péleponnèse," *Bulletin de Correspondance Héllenique* 91: 79-131.

Arru, Angiolina (1998) "Schenken heißt nicht verlieren. Schenkungen und Vorteile der Gegenseitigkeit in Rom im 18. und 19. Jahrhundert," *L'Homme* 9/2: 232-251.

Assmann, Jan (1990) *Ma'at—Gerechtigkeit und Unsterblichkeit im Alten Ägypten*. Munich.

Åström, Paul and Elsa Gullberg (1970) *The Thread of Ariadne: A Study in Ancient Greek Dress*. Studies in the Mediterranean Archaeology 21. Göteborg.

Athanassakis, Apostolos (1989) "From the Phallic Cairn to Shepherd God and Divine Herald," *Eranos* 87: 33-63.

Aubet, Maria Eugenia (1993) *The Phoenicians and the West: Politics, Colonies and Trade*, trans. Mary Turton. Cambridge.

Audinet, Eugène (1914) "Les traces du droit international dans l'Iliade et dans l'Odyssée," *Revue générale du droit international public* 21–22: 29–63.

Audring, Gert (1981) "Zur sozialen Stellung der Hirten in archaischer Zeit: Thesen," *Antike Abhängigkeitsformen in den griechischen Gebieten ohne Polisstruktur und den römischen Provinzen. Actes du colloque sur l'ésclavage, Jena 29 septembre–2 octobre 1981*, ed. Heinz Kreissig and F. Kühnert. Berlin: 12–19.

——— . (1989) *Zur Struktur des Territoriums griechischer Poleis in archaischer Zeit (nach den schriftlichen Quellen)*. Berlin.

Austin, Michel M. (1970) *Greece and Egypt in the Archaic Age*. Cambridge.

Austin, Michel M. and Pierre Vidal-Naquet (1977) *Economy and Social History of Ancient Greece*. London.

Azoulay, Vincent (2004) *Xénophon et les grâces du pouvoir: De la cháris au charisme*. Paris.

——— . (2012) "Du paradigme du don à une anthropologie pragmatique de la valeur," in *Anthropologie de l'Antiquité: Anciens objects, nouvelles approches*, ed. Pascal Payen and Evelyne Scheid-Tissinier. Turnhout: 17–42.

Bakchylides. *Die Lieder des Bakchylides. I: Die Siegeslieder; II: Die Dithyramben und Fragmente; Text, Übersetzung und Kommentar* (1997), ed. with an introduction and commentary by Herwig Maehler. Leiden.

Bakker, Egbert J. (2013) *The Meaning of Meat and the Structure of the Odyssey*. Cambridge.

Bakker, Egbert J. and Ahuvia Kahane (eds.) (1997) *Written Voices, Spoken Signs: Tradition, Performance, and the Epic Text*. Cambridge.

Baltrusch, Ernst (1994) *Symmachie und Spondai: Untersuchungen zum griechischen Völkerrecht der Archaischen und Klassischen Zeit (8.–5. Jh. v. Chr.)*. Berlin and New York.

Bamberger, F. (1976) "κέρδος et sa famille (emplois homériques): Contribution aux recherches sur le vocabulaire de la 'richesse' en grec," *Centre de recherches comparatives sur les langues de la Méditerranée ancienne* 3: 1–32.

Barber, Elizabeth Wayland J. (1991) *Prehistoric Textiles: The Development of Cloth in the Neolithic and Bronze Ages with Special References to the Aegean*. Princeton.

——— . (1992) "The Peplos of Athena," in Neils 1992: 103–17.

——— . (1994) *Women's Work: The First 20,000 Years: Women, Cloth, and Society in Early Times*. New York and London.

Barceló, Pedro (1993) *Basileia, Monarchia, Tyrannis: Untersuchungen zur Entwicklung und Beurteilung der Alleinherrschaft im vorhellenistischen Griechenland*. Historia Einzelschriften 79. Stuttgart.

Barghop, Dirk (1994) *Forum der Angst: Eine historisch-anthropologische Studie zu Verhaltensmustern von Senatoren im Römischen Kaiserreich*. Francfort and New York.

Barkai, Avraham (1988) *Das Wirtschaftssystem des Nationalsozialismus: Ideologie, Theorie, Politik 1933–1945*. Francfort.

Barnes, Ruth and Joanne Eicher (eds.) (1992) *Dress and Gender: Making and Meaning in Cultural Contexts*. New York and Oxford.

Bartoloni, Gilda, Giovanni Colonna, and Christiano Grottanelli (eds.) (1989/90) *Anathema: Regime delle offerte e vita dei sanctuari nel mediterraneo antico*. Scienze dell' antiquità. Storia archeologia antropologia 3/4. Rome.

Battegazzore, Antonio E. (1987) "La donna e la tessitura nei poemi omerici," *Cultura e scuola* 26 (104): 30–40.

Bausinger, Hermann (1980) "Zur Problematik des Kulturbegriffs," in *Fremdsprache Deutsch I*, ed. Alois Wierlacher. Paderborn: 57–69.

Bazant, Jan (1981) *Studies in the Use and Decoration of Athenean Vases*. Prag.

Bazelmans, J., P. Kehne, and W. Ogris (1998) "Geschenke," in *Reallexikon der Germanischen Altertumskunde* 11: 466–77.

Bechert, Johannes (1964) *Die Diathesen von ἰδεῖν und Ὁρᾶν bei Homer*. 2 vols. Munich.

Becker, Andrew S. (ed.) (1995) *The Shield of Achilles and the Poetics of Ekphrasis*. Lanham, MD.

Behrends, Okko (1992) "Rudolf von Jhering, der Rechtsdenker der offenen Gesellschaft: Ein Wort zur Bedeutung seiner Rechtstheorie und zu den geschichtlichen Gründen ihrer Mißdeutung," in his *Rudolf von Jhering: Beiträge und Zeugnisse aus Anlaß der einhundertsten Wiederkehr seines Todestages am 17.9.1992*. Göttingen: 8–10.

——. (1991) "Rudolf von Jhering und die Evolutionstheorie des Rechts," in *Der Evolutionsgedanke in den Wissenschaften: Kolloquium der Akademie der Wissenschaften zu Göttingen am 9. Februar 1990*, ed. Günther Patzig. Göttingen: 290–310.

——. (2002) "Der ungleiche Tausch zwischen Glaukos und Diomedes und die Kauf-Tausch-Kontroverse der römischen Rechtsschule," *Historische Anthropologie* 10/2: 245–66.

Beidelman, Thomas O. (1989) "Agonistic Exchange: Homeric Reciprocity and the Heritage of Simmel and Mauss," *Cultural Anthropology* 4/3: 227–50.

Beil, A. (1961) "Αἰδώς bei Homer," *Der Altsprachliche Unterricht* 5/1: 51–64.

Bell, Catherine (1992) *Ritual Theory, Ritual Practice*. New York and Oxford.

Bennett, Ian (1977) *Rugs and Carpets of the World*. London.

Benton, Sylvia (1934/35) "The Evolution of the Tripod-Lebes," *The Annual of the British School of Athens* 35: 74–130.

Benveniste, Emile ([1951] 1966) "Don et échange dans le vocabulaire indoeuropéenne," *L'année sociologique* 3rd sér. 2: 7–20. Rpt. in *Problèmes de linguistique génerale I*. 1966: 313–26.

——. (1969) *Le vocabulaire des institutions indo-européennes. I: Economie, parenté, société*. Paris.

Bérard, Claude (1982) "Récuperer la mort du prince: héroïsation et formation de la cité," in Gnoli and Vernant 1982: 89–105.

Bérard, Claude and Jean-Pierre Vernant et al. (1984) *La cité des images*. Lausanne.

Berg, Steffen, Renate Rolle, and Henning Seemann (1981) *Der Archäologe und der Tod: Archäologie und Gerichtsmedizin*. Munich and Luzern.

Bergier, Jean-François (ed.) (1989) *Montagnes, Fleuves, Forêts dans l'Histoire: Barrières ou lignes de convergence?* St. Katharinen.

Bergren, Ann L. (1975) *The Etymology and Usage of* ΠΕΙΡΑΡ *in Early Greek Poetry: The Study in the Interrelationship of Metrics, Lingustics and Poetics.* New York.

——. (1980) "Helen's Web: Time and Tableau in the Iliad," *Helios* 7: 19–34.

——. (1983) "Language and the Female in Early Greek Thought," *Arethusa* 16: 69–95.

——. (2008) *Weaving the Truth: Essays on Language and the Female in Greek Thought.* Cambridge, MA and London.

Beringer, Walter (1985) "Freedom, Family, and Citizenship in Early Greece," in *The Craft of the Ancient Historian: Essays in Honor of Chester G. Starr*, ed. John W. Eadie and Josiah Ober. London and New York: 41–56.

Berking, Helmuth (1996) *Schenken: Zur Anthropologie des Gebens.* Francfort and New York.

Bernhardt, Rainer (2003) *Luxuskritik und Aufwandsbeschränkungen in der griechischen Welt.* Stuttgart.

Berolzheimer, Fritz (1907) *System der Rechts- und Wirtschaftsphilosophie. IV: Philosophie des Vermögens einschliesslich des Handelsverkehrs.* Munich.

Bertelli, Lucio (2014) "The Ratio of Gift-Giving in Homeric Poems," in Carlà and Gori 2014: 103–34.

Berthoud, Gerald (1991) "Le marché comme simulacre du don," *La Revue du Mauss* 11: 72–89.

Beßlich, Barbara (2000) *Wege in den „Kulturkrieg": Zivilisationskritik in Deutschland 1890-1914.* Darmstadt.

Betalli, Marco (1982) "Note sulla produzione tessile ad Atene in età classica," *Opus* 1: 261–78.

Bethe, Erich (1931a): "Der homerische Apollonhymnos und das Proiomion," *Berichte über die Verhandlungen der Sächsischen Akademie der Wissenschaften zu Leipzig, Philologisch-Historische Klasse* 83/2: 1–40.

——. (1931b) "Troia, Mykene, Agamemnon und sein Großkönigtum," *Rheinisches Museum* 80: 218–36.

Beuermann, Arnold (1967) *Fernweidewirtschaft in Südosteuropa: Ein Beitrag zur Kulturgeographie des östlichen Mittelmeergebietes.* Braunschweig.

Beyeler, Markus (2011) *Geschenke des Kaisers. Studien zur Chroologie, zu den Empfängern und zu den Gegenständen der kaiserlichen Vergabungen im 4. Jahrhundert n. Chr.* Berlin.

Bieber, Margarete (1928) *Griechische Kleidung.* Berlin and Leipzig (rpt. 1977).

——. (1934) *Entwicklungsgeschichte der griechischen Tracht von der vorgriechischen Zeit bis zum Ausgang der Antike.* Berlin (rpt. 1967).

Bintliff, John L. (1977) *Natural Environment and Human Settlement in Prehistoric Greece.* British Archaeological Reports 28/1. Oxford.

——. (1994) "Territorial Behaviour and the Natural History of the Polis," in *Stuttgarter Kolloquium zur Historischen Geographie des Altertums IV, 1990*, ed. Eckart Olshausen and Holger Sonnabend. Amsterdam: 207–49.

Bloch, Françoise and Monique Boisson (1991) "Du don a la dette: La construction du lien social familial," *La Revue du Mauss: Mouvement Anti-Utilitariste dans les Sciences Sociales* 11: 54–71.

Bloch, Maurice and Jonathan Parry (eds.) (1989) *Money and the Morality of Exchange*. Cambridge.

Block, Elizabeth (1985) "Clothing Makes the Man: A Pattern in the Odyssey," *Transactions of the American Philological Association* 115: 1–11.

Blok, Josine (2000) "Phye's Procession. Culture, Politics and Peistratid Rule", in Sancisi-Weerdenburg 2000: 17–48.

——. (2004), "Recht und Ritus in der Polis. Zu Bürgerstatus und Geschlechterverhältnissen im klassischen Athen," *Historische Zeitschrift* 278/1: 1–26.

Blome, Peter (1984) "Lefkandi und Homer," *Würzburger Jahrbücher für Altertumswissenschaft* 10: 9–21.

Blösel, Wolfgang et al. (2014) *Grenzen politischer Partizipation im klassischen Griechenland*. Stuttgart.

Blum, Hartmut (1998) *Purpur als Statussymbol in der griechischen Welt*. Bonn.

Blum, Herwig (1969) *Die antike Mnemotechnik*. Spudasmata 15. Hildesheim and New York.

Blümner, Hugo (1912) *Technologie und Terminologie der Gewerbe und Künste bei Griechen und Römern*. 2nd edn. 4 vols. Berlin.

Boardman, John (1955) "Painted Funery Plaques and Some Remarks on Prothesis," *Annual of the British School of Athens* 50: 55–66.

——. (1974) *Athenian Black Figure Vases: The Classical Period*. 4th edn. London.

——. (1988) "Trade in Greek Decorated Pottery," *Oxford Journal of Archaeology* 7: 27–33

——. (1989) *Athenian Red Figure Vases: The Classical Period*. London.

——. (1999) *The Greeks Overseas: Their Early Colonies and Trade*. 4th edn. London (1st edn. 1964).

——. (ed.) (2006) *The World of Ancient Art*. London (1st edn. 1993).

Bodei Giglioni, Gabriella (1989/90) "Economia e religiosità tra Aristotle e Teofrasto. Gratitudine e scambio," *Scienze dell' Antichità* 3/4: 55–64.

Bohannan, Paul (1955) "Some Principles of Exchange and Investment among the Tiv," *American Anthropologist* 57: 60–70.

Bohannan, Paul und Laura (1968) *Tiv Economy*. Evanston.

Bohringer, F. (1979) *Cultes et actes des fondateurs de la cité grecque: 8ème-7ème siècles*. Paris.

Bol, Peter C. (1985) *Antike Bronzetechnik: Kunst und Handwerk antiker Erzbildner*. Munich.

Bolchazy, Ladislaus J. (1978) "From Xenophobia to Altruism: Homeric and Roman Hospitality," *Ancient World* 1: 45–64.

Bolkestein, Hendrik (1939) *Wohltätigkeit und Armenpflege im vorchristlichen Altertum*. Utrecht.

——. (1958) *Economic Life in Greece's Golden Age*. Leiden.

Bonnefoy, Yves (ed.) (1992) *Greek and Egyptian Mythologies*, trans. Gerald Honigsblum. Chicago and London.

Borgeaud, Willy Alfred and Bonnie MacLachlan (1985) "Les Kharites et la lumière," *Revue Belge de Philologie d'Histoire* 63: 5–14.

Borlandi, Massimo (1998) "Durkheim, Les Durkheimiens et la sociologie générale: de la première section de L'Année à la reconstruction d'une problématique perdue," *L'Année sociologique* 48 : 27–65.

Bosacq, Émile (1916) *Dictionnaire étymologique de la langue grecque*. Heidelberg and Paris.

Bothmer, Dietrich von (1985) *The Amasis Painter and His World: Vase-Painting in Sixth-Century B.C. Athens*. Malibu, CA: New York and London.

Bourdieu, Pierre (1977) *Outline of a Theory of Practice*. Cambridge (= *Esquisse d'une Théorie de la Pratique*. Genf 1972).

Bourguet, Emile (1905) *L'administration financière du sanctuaire pythique au IV siècle avant J.C*. Paris.

Bourriot, Felix (1976) *Recherches sur la nature du génos*. Lille and Paris.

Boyd, Timothy W. (1995) "Libri confusi," *The Classical Journal* 91/1: 35–45.

Bradley, Mark (ed.) (2015) *Smell and the Ancient Senses*. London and New York.

Bradley, Richard (1982) "The Destruction of Wealth in Later Prehistory," *Man* n.s. 17: 108–22.

———. (1985) "Exchange and Social Distance: The Structure of Bronze Artefact Distributions," *Man* n.s. 20: 692–704.

Bravo, Benedetto (1977) "Remarques sur les assises sociales, les formes d'organisation et la terminologie du commerce maritime grec à l'époque archaïque," *Dialogues d'Histoire Ancienne* 3: 1–59.

———. (1983) "Le commerce des céréales chez les Grecs de l'époque archaïque," in Garnsey and Whittaker 1983: 17–29.

———. (1984) "Commerce et noblesse en Grèce archaïque: À propos d'un livre d'Alfonso Mele," *Dialogues d'Histoire Ancienne* 10: 99–160.

Bréhier, Louis (1904) "La royauté homérique et les origines de l'état en Grèce," *Revue historique* 84 : 1–34.

Bremmer, Jan (1987a) *The Early Greek Concept of the Soul*. Princeton.

———. (1987b) "The So-Called 'Götterapparat' in Iliad XX–XXII," in his *Homer: Beyond Oral Poetry: Recent Trends in Homeric Interpretation*, ed. Irene J. F. de Jong and J. Kalff. Amsterdam: 31–46.

Brendel, Otto (1934) *Die Schafzucht im alten Griechenland*. Würzburg.

Brentano, Lujo (1923) "Ethik und Volkswirtschaft in der Geschichte," in his *Der wirtschaftende Mensch in der Geschichte: Gesammelte Reden und Aufsätze*. Leipzig: 34–76.

Bresson, Alain (2008) *L'économie de la Grèce des cites. I: Les structures et la production; II: Les espaces de lèchange*. Paris.

Breuer, Stefan (1990) *Der archaische Staat. Zur Soziologie charismatischer Herrschaft*. Berlin.

Brice, Philip (1989/90) "Archaische Bronzevotive aus dem Heraion von Samos," in Bartoloni 1990: 317–326.

Brice, W. C. (1988) "Notes on Linear A," *Kadmos* 27: 155–65.

Brommer, Frank (1942) "Gefäßformen bei Homer," *Hermes* 77: 356–73.

Brøns, Cecilie (2017) *Gods and Garments: Textiles in Greek Sanctuaries in the 7th–1st Centuries BC*. Oxford and Philadelphia.

Brown, Norman O. (1947) *Hermes, the Thief: The Evolution of a Myth*. Madison, WI.

Bruch, Rüdiger vom (1988) "Gustav Schmoller," in Hammerstein 1988: 219–38.

Bruch, Rüdiger vom, Friedrich Wilhelm Graf, and Gangolf Hübinger (eds.) (1989) *Kultur und Kulturwissenschaft um 1900*. Stuttgart.

Bruck, Eberhard Friedrich (1926) *Totenteil und Seelgerät im griechischen Recht*. Munich.

Brulé, Pierre (1987) *La fille d'Athènes: La religion des filles à Athènes à l'époque classique: Mythes, cultes et société*. Paris.

Brun, Waclaw von (1912) *Die Wirtschaftsorganisation der Maori auf Neuseeland*. Leipzig.

Brunner, Otto (1943) *Land und Herrschaft: Grundfragen der territorialen Verfassungsgeschichte Südwestdeutschlands im Mittelalter*, 3rd rev. edn. Brünn.

Bruns, Gerda (1970) *Küchenwesen und Mahlzeiten*. Archaeologia Homerica II Q. Göttingen.

Bücher, Karl (1893) *Die Entstehung der Volkswirtschaft*. Vol I. Tübingen.

——. (1901) *Industrial Evolution*. Translated from the third German edition by S. Morley Wickett. London.

——. (1918) "Schenkung, Leihe und Bittarbeit," in his *Die Entstehung der Volkswirtschaft*. Vol II. Tübingen: 3–24.

——. (1922) *Beiträge zur Wirtschaftsgeschichte*. Tübingen.

Buchholz, Eduard (1871) *Homerische Kosmographie und Geographie*. Leipzig.

Buchholz, Hans-Georg (1987) "Das Symbol des gemeinsamen Mantels," *Jahrbuch des Deutschen Archäologischen Instituts* 102: 1–55.

——. (1988) "Der Metallhandel des zweiten Jahrtausends im Mittelmeerraum," in *Society and Economy in the Eastern Mediterranean c. 1500–1000 B.C.: Proceedings of the International Symposium held at the University of Haifa from the 28th of April to the 2nd of May 1985*, ed. Mikha'el Heltzer and Edward Lipiński. Leuven: 187–228.

Büdel, Ernst (1976) "Bevölkerungsabwanderung, demographische Struktur und Landwirtschaftsformen im West-Peloponnes," *Gießener Geographische Schriften* 37: 18–40.

Bulst, Neithard (1988) "Zum Problem städtischer und territorialer Kleider-, Aufwands- und Luxusgesetzgebung in Deutschland (13.–Mitte 16. Jahrhundert)," in *Renaissance du pouvoir legislatif et genèse de l'état*, ed. André Gouron and Albert Rigaudière. Montpellier: 29–57.

Bunsdorff, Hans (1992) *Zur Rolle des Aussehens des homerischen Menschenbildes*. Göttingen and Zürich.

Burckhard, Hugo (1891) *Die Stellung der Schenkung im Rechtssystem*. Erlangen.

——. (1899) *Zum Begriff der Schenkung*. Erlangen.

Burford, Alison (1972) *Craftsmen in Greek and Roman Society*. London.

Bürgin, Alfred (1996) *Zur Soziogenese der politischen Ökonomie*. 2nd rev. edn. Marburg.

Burke, Brendan (2007) "The Kingdom of Midas and Royal Cloth Production," in Gillis and Nosch 2007: 64–70.

——. (2010) *From Minos to Midas. Ancient Cloth Production in the Aegean and in Anatolia.* Oxford.

Burkert, Walter (1976) "Das hunderttorige Theben und die Datierung der Ilias," *Wiener Studien* 89: 5–21.

——. (1977) *Griechische Religion der archaischen und klassischen Epoche.* Stuttgart.

——. (1984a) *Anthropologie des religiösen Opfers: Die Sakralisierung der Gewalt.* Veröffentlichung der Carl Friedrich von Siemens-Stiftung. Munich.

——. (1984b) *Die orientalisierende Epoche in der griechischen Religion und Literatur.* Heidelberg = *The Orientalizing Revolution: Near Eastern Influence on Greek Culture in the Early Archaic Age.* Cambridge, MA 1992.

——. (1987) "Offerings in Perspective: Surrender, Distribution, Exchange," in Linders and Nordquist 1987: 43–50.

——. (1988) "The Meaning and Function of the Temple in Classical Greece," in *Temple in Society*, ed. Michael V. Fox. Winona Lake: 27–47.

——. (1991) "Homerstudien und Orient," in Latacz 1991: 155–81.

Burns, Bryan E. (2010) *Mycenaean Greece, Mediterranean Commerce, and the Formation of Identity.* New York.

Buschor, Ernst (1912) *Beiträge zur Geschichte der griechischen Textilkunst: Die Anfänge und der orientalische Import.* Diss. Munich.

Cahill, Nicholas (1985) "The Treasury at Persepolis: Gift-Giving at the City of the Persians," *American Journal of Archaeology* 89: 373–89.

Caillé, Alain (2008) *Anthropologie der Gabe.* Francfort and New York.

Caillé, Alain and Jacques T. Godbout (1991) "Le don existe-t-il (encore)?" *La Revue du Mauss* 11: 11–32.

Cairns, Douglas L. (1993) ΑΙΔΩΣ: *The Psychology and Ethics of Honour and Shame in Ancient Greek Literature.* Oxford.

Calame, Claude (1976) "Mythe grec et structures narratives: Le mythe des Cyclopes dans l'Odyssée," *Ziva Antika* 26: 311–28.

Calder, William M. III (1984) "Gold for Bronze: Iliad 6, 232–236," in *Studies Presented to Sterling Dow on his Eightieth Birthday.* Durham, NC: 31–35.

Campagner, Roberto (1988) "Reciprocità economica in Pindaro," *Quaderni Urbinati d Cultura Classica* 29: 787–93.

Canciani, Fulvio (1984) *Bildkunst.* II: *Homer und die Denkmäler.* Archaeologia Homerica N/2. Göttingen.

Canevaro, Lilah Grace (2018) *Women of Substance in Homeric Epic: Objects, Gender, Agency.* Oxford.

Canning, Cathleen (2002) "Problematische Dichotomien: Erfahrung zwischen Narrativität und Materialität," *Historische Anthropologie* 10/2: 163–82.

Carlà, Filippo and Maja Gori (eds.) (2014) *Gift Giving and the 'Embedded' Economy in the Ancient World.* Heidelberg.

Carlier, Pierre (1984) *La Royauté en Grèce avant Aléxandre.* Strasbourg.

Cartledge, Paul A. (1983) "Trade and Politics Revisited: Archaic Greece," in Garnsey, Hopkins and Whittaker 1983: 1–15.

Cartledge, Paul A. and F. David Harvey (eds.) (1985) *Crux: Essays in Greek History Presented to G. E. M. de Ste. Croix on his 75th Birthday.* London.

Carroll, Diane Lee (1965) *Pattern Textiles in Greek Art*. Los Angeles.

——. (1983) "Warping the Greek Loom: A Second Method," *American Journal of Archaeology* 87: 96–98.

Cathercole, P. (1978) "Hau, mauri and utu: A Reexamination," in *Trade and Exchange in Oceania and Australia*, ed. Jim Specht and John P. White. Sydney: 324–40.

Cavanagh, William H. (1991) "Surveys, Cities and Synoicism," in Rich and Wallace-Hadrill 1991: 197–332.

Ceccarelli, Paola (1995) "Le tissage, la mémoire et la nymphe: Une recénte lecture de l'Odyssée," *Dialogues d'Histoire Anciennes* 21/1: 181–91.

Ceccarelli, Paola, Françoise Létoublon und Martin Steinrück (1998) "L'individu, le territoire, la graisse; du public et du privé chez Homère," *Ktema* 23: 47–58.

Cefaï, Daniel and Alain Mahé (1998) "Échanges rituels de dons, obligation et contrat : Mauss, Davy, Maunier. Trois perspectives de sociologie juridique," *L'Année sociologique* 48: 209–28.

Chamorro, J. G. (1987) "Survey of Archaeological Research on Tartessos," *American Journal of Archaeology* 91: 197–232.

Chandezon, Christophe (2003) *L'élevage en Grèce (fin Ve–fin Ier s. a. C.): L'apport des sources epigraphiques*. Bordeaux.

Chaniotis, Angelos (1995) "Problems of 'Pastoralism' and 'Transhumance' in Classical and Hellenistic Crete," *Orbis Terrarum* 1: 39–89.

——. (2011) "Emotional Community through Ritual: Initiates, Citizens, and Pilgrims as Emotional Communities in the Greek World," in his *Ritual Dynamics in the Ancient Mediterranean: Agency, Emotion, Gender, Representation*. Stuttgart: 263–90.

Chaniotis, Angelos, Nikolaos Kaltsas and Ioannis Mylonopopoulos (2017) (eds.) *A World of Emotions: Ancient Greece, 700 BC–200 AD*. New York.

Chantraine, Pierre (1940) "Conjugation et histoire des verbes signifiant 'vendre'," *Revue philologique* 14: 11–24.

——. (1977) *Dictionnaire étymologique de la langue grecque*. 3 vols. Paris.

Charle, Christophe and Eva Teklès (1988) *Les professeurs du Collège de France: Dictionnaire biographique 1901–1939*. Paris.

Chaston, Colleen (2002) "Three Models of Authority in the 'Odyssey'," *The Classical World* 96/1: 3–19.

Cheal, David (1988) *The Gift Economy*. London and New York.

Cherry, John F. (1984) "The Emergence of the State in the Prehistoric Aegean," *Proceedings of the Cambridge Philological Society* n.s. 30: 18–48.

——. (1988) "Pastoralism and the Role of Animals in the Pre- and Protohistoric Economies of the Aegean," in Whittaker 1988: 6–34.

Childe, V. Gordon (1951) *Social Evolution*. London.

Chiozzi, Paoli (1983) "Marcel Mauss: Eine anthropologische Interpretation des Sozialismus," *Kölner Zeitschrift für Soziologie und Sozialpsychologie* 35: 655–79.

Christ, Matthew R. (2012) *The Limits of Altruism in Democratic Athens*. Cambridge.

Christien, Jacqueline (1989) "Les liaisons entre Sparte et son territoire malgré l'encadrement montagneux," in Bergier 1989: 18–44.

Cifarelli, Megan and Laura Gawlinski (eds.) (2017) *What Shall I Say of Clothes? Theoretical and Methodological Approaches to the Study of Dress in Antiquity.* Boston.

Clark, Louise (1983) "Notes on Small Textile Frames Pictured on Greek Vases," *American Journal of Archaeology* 87: 91–96.

Clark, Matthew (2001) "Was Telemachus Rude to His Mother? Odyssey 1.356–59," *Classical Philology* 96/4: 335–54.

Clavero, Bartolomé (1996) *La grâce du don. Anthropologie catholique de l'économie modern.* Paris.

Clay, Jenny Strauss (1989) *The Politics of Olympus: Form and Meaning in the Major Homeric Hymns.* Princeton.

Clayton, Barbara (2004) *A Penelopean Poetics: Reweaving the feminine in Homer's Odyssey.* Lanham, MD.

Cleary, Mark C. and Catherine Delano Smith (1990) "Transhumance Reviewed: Past and Present Practices in France and Italy," *Rivista di Studi Liguri* 56/1–4: 21–38.

Cobet, Justus (1981) "König, Anführer, Herr, Monarch, Tyrann," in Welskopf 1981: 11–66.

——. (1983) "Synoikismos als Konzept für die politischen Anfänge Athens und Roms," in *Concilium Eirene XVI: Proceedings of the 16. International Eirene Conference, Prague, 31.8.–4.9.1982*, ed. Pavel Oliva. Prague: 21–26.

Codere, Helen (1950) *Fighting with Property: A Study of Kwakiutl Potlatching and Warefare (1872–1936).* New York.

——. (1976) "Exchange and Display," *International Encyclopedia of the Social Sciences* 5: 239–45.

Coffee, Neil (2017) *Gift and Gain: How Money Transformed Ancient Rome.* New York.

Cohen, Beth (1995) *The Distaff Side: Representing the Female in Homer's Odyssey.* New York and Oxford.

Cohen, David (1980) "'Horkia' und 'horkos' in der Ilias," *Revue internationale des droits de l'antiquité* 27: 49–68.

——. (1991) *Law, Sexuality and Society: The Enforcement of Morals in Classical Athens.* Cambridge.

Coldstream, John Nicholas (1979) *Geometric Greece.* 2nd edn. London.

——. (1983) "Gift Exchange in the Eighth Century B.C.," in Hägg 1983: 201–7.

——. (1985) "Greek Temples: Why and Where?" in *Greek Religion and Society*, ed. Patricia E. Easterling and J. V. Muir. Cambridge: 67–97.

——. (1993) "Mixed Marriages at the Frontiers of the Early Greek World," *Oxford Journal of Archaeology* 12/1: 80–107.

Cole, Susan Guettel (2004) *Landscapes, Gender and Ritual Space: The Ancient Greek Experience.* Berkeley, CA.

Constable, Olivia Remie (2003) *Housing the Stranger in the Mediterranean World: Lodging, Trade, and Travel in Late Antiquity and the Middle Ages.* Cambridge.

Conze, Alexander (1870) *Zur Geschichte der Anfänge griechischer Kunst.* Vienna.

Cox, Cheryl Anne (1998) *Household Interests: Property, Marriage Strategies, and Family Dynamics in Ancient Athens.* Princeton.

Cozzo, Andrea (1991) κέρδος: *Le passione economiche nella grecia antica*. Palermo.

Craig, J. D. (1967) "ΧΡΥΣΕΑ ΧΑΛΚΕΙωΝ," *Classical Review* n.s. 17: 243–45.

Crane, Gregory (1988) *Calypso: Backgrounds and Conventions of the Odyssey*. Francfort.

——. (1993) "Politics of Consumption and Generosity in the Carpet Scene of the Agamemnon," *Classical Philology* 88/2: 117–36.

Crielaard, Jan P. (1992/93) "How the West Was Won, Euboeans vs. Phoenicians," *Hamburger Beiträge zur Archäologie* 19/20: 234–59.

——. (2002) "Past or Present? Epic Poetry, Aristocratic Self-Reprentation and the Concept of Time in the Eighth and Seventh Centuries BC," in Franco Montanari (ed.), *Omero tremille anni dopo*. Roma: 239–295.

——. (2006) "*Basileis* at Sea: Elites and External Contacts in the Euboean Gulf Region from the End of the Bronze Age to the Beginning of the Iron Age," in *Ancient Greece: From the Mycenaean Palaces to the Age of Homer*, ed. Sigrid Deger-Jalkotzy and Irene S. Lemos. Edinburgh: 271–97.

——. (2011) "The 'Wanax to Basileus Model' Reconsidered: Authority and Ideology after the Collapse of the Mycenaean Palaces," in *The 'Dark Ages' Revisited: Acts of an International Symposium in Memory of William D. E. Coulson; University of Thessaly, Volos, 14–17 June 2007*, ed. Alexandros Mazarakis-Ainian. Volos: 83–111.

——. (2010) "*Hygra Keleútha*: Maritime Matters and the Ideology of Seafaring in the Greek Epic Tradition," in *Alle origini della Magna Grecia mobilità migrazioni fondazioni. Atti del cinquantesimo convegno di studi sulla Magna Grecia, Taranto 1–4 Ottobre 2010*. Taranto: 135–157.

Cristofani, Mauro (1975) "Il dono nell' Etruria arcaica," *Parola del Passato* 161: 132–52.

Culham, Phyllis (1986) "Again, What Meaning Lies in Colour?" *Zeitschrift für Papyrologie and Epigraphik* 64: 235–45.

Curtius, Ernst (1892) "Die Gastfreundschaft," in his *Alterthum und Gegenwart: Gesammelte Reden und Vorträge I*. 4th edn. Berlin: 203–18.

Dabney, Mary K. and James C. Wright (1990) "Mortuary Customs, Palatial Society and State Formation in the Aegean Area: A Comparative Study," in Hägg and Nordquist 1990: 45–53.

Dahme, Heinz Jürgen (1988) "Der Verlust des Fortschrittsglaubens und die Verwissenschaftlichung der Soziologie: Ein Vergleich von Georg Simmel, Ferdinand Tönnies und Max Weber," in *Simmel und die frühen Soziologen: Nähe und Distanz zu Durkheim, Tönnies und Max Weber*, ed. Otthein Rammstedt. Francfort: 222–74.

Dalby, Andrew (1996) *Siren Feast: A History of Food and Gastronomy in Greece*. London.

Dalton, George (1961) "Economic Theory and Primitive Society," *American Anthropologist New Series* 63: 1–25.

——. (1967) *Tribal and Peasant Economies: Readings in Economic Anthropology*. Austin and London.

Damon, Frederick H. (1980) "The Kula and Generalized Exchange: Considering Some Unconsidered Aspects of the Elementary Structures of Kinship," *Man* n.s. 15: 267–92.

Daniel, Ute (1993) "'Kultur' und 'Gesellschaft': Überlegungen zum Gegenstandsbereich der Sozialgeschichte," *Geschichte und Gesellschaft* 19: 69–99.

——. (1997) "Clio unter Kulturschock," *Geschichte in Wissenschaft und Unterricht* 48: 195–218 and 259–278.

Darcque, Pascal (1987) "Les Tholoi et l'organisation socio-politique du monde mycénien," in Laffineur 1987: 185–205

Dargun, Lothar von (1885) *Soziologische Studien I: Egoismus und Altruismus in der Nationalökonomie*. Leipzig.

Daverio Rocchi, Giovanna (1993) "Politische, wirtschaftliche und militärische Grenze im alten Griechenland," in Eckart Olshausen and Holger Sonnabend (eds.) *Gebirgsland als Lebensraum. Stuttgarter Kolloquium zur Historischen Geographie des Altertums 4, 1990*, Amsterdam 1993: 95–110.

——. (1996) "Kulturmodelle und Gerichtserfahrungen bei Hirtengemeinschaften der Gebirgsländer Nordgriechenlands," in Eckart Olshausen, Holger Sonnabend (eds.) *Gebirgsland als Lebensraum. Stuttgarter Kolloquium zur Historischen Geographie des Altertums 5, 1993*. Amsterdam 1996: 335–42.

——. (2016) "Systems of Borders in Ancient Greece," in *Brill's Companion to Ancient Geography: The Inhabited World in Greek and Roman Tradition*, ed. Serena Bianchetti et al. Leiden: 58–77.

Davidson, James N. (1997) *Courtisans and Fishcakes: The Consuming Passions of Classical Athens*. London.

Davis, Natalie Zemon (2000) *The Gift in Sixteenth-Century France*. Madison.

Davy, Georges (1922) *La foi jurée : La formation du lien social*. Paris.

Day, Joseph W. (1989) "Rituals in Stone: Early Greek Grave Epigrams and Monuments," *The Journal of Hellenistic Studies* 109: 16–28.

Deger, Sigrid (1970) *Herrschaftsformen bei Homer*. Vienna.

Deger-Jalkotzy, Sigrid (1979) "Homer und der Orient: Das Königtum des Priamos," *Würzburger Jahrbücher für die Altertumswissenschaft* N.F. 5: 25–31.

Deger-Jalkotzy, Sigrid and Irene S. Lemos (eds.) (2006) *Ancient Greece from Mycenaean Palaces to the Age of Homer*. Edinburgh.

Deichgräber, Karl (1971) *Charis und die Chariten, Grazie und Grazien*. Munich.

Demand, Nancy (1996) "*Poleis* on Cyprus and Oriental Despotism," in *More Studies in the Ancient Greek Polis*, ed. Mogens Herman Hansen and Kurt Raaflaub. Stuttgart: 7–15.

Demetriou, Denise (2011) "What is an Emporion? A Reassessment," *Historia* 60/3: 255–72.

Denis, Jacques François (1856) *Histoire des théories et des idées morales dans l'antiquité II*. Paris and Straßbourg.

Deroy, Louis (1987) "La tablette mycénienne PY FR 1338 et l'hospitalité au 'Palais de Nestor'," *Ziva Antica* 37: 5–10.

Descat, Raymond (1979) "L'idéologie homérique du pouvoir," *Revue des Etudes Anciennes* 81: 229–40.

——. (1986) *L'acte et l'effort: Une idéologie du travail en Grèce ancienne (8ème–5ème siècle av. J.-C.)*. Besançon and Lille.

Detienne, Marcel (1963) *Crise agraire et attitude religieuse chez Hésiode*. Brussels.

——. (1967) *Les maîtres de la verité dans la Grèce archaïque*. Paris.
——. (1998) *Apollon le couteau à la main*. Paris.
Dietrich, Bernard C. (1957) *Death, Fate and the Gods: The Development of a Religious Idea in Greek Popular Belief and in Homer*. 2nd edn. London.
Dihle, Albrecht (1985) *Die Vorstellung vom Willen in der Antike*. Göttingen.
Dinges, Martin (1992) "Der ‚feine Unterschied': Die soziale Funktion von Kleidung in der höfischen Gesellschaft," *Zeitschrift für Historische Forschung* 19/1: 49–76.
Dirlmeier, Franz (1931) ΦΙΛΟΣ *und* ΦΙΛΙΑ *im vorhellenistischen Griechentum*. Dissertation. Munich.
Dmitriev, Sviatoslav (2018) *The Birth of Athenian Community: From Solon to Cleisthenes*. London and New York.
Dodds, Eric R. (1951) *The Greeks and the Irrational*. Berkeley and Los Angeles.
——. (1973) *The Ancient Concept of Progress and other Essays on Greek Literature and Belief*. Oxford.
Doherty, Lillian Eileen (1992) "Gender and Internal Audiences in the Odyssey," *American Journal of Philology* 113: 161–77.
——. (1993) "Tyro in Odyssey 11: Closed and Open Readings," *Helios* 20: 3–17.
——. (1995) *Siren Songs: Gender, Audiences and Narrators in the Odyssey*. Ann Arbor, MI.
Domingo Gygax, Marc (2002) "Peisistratos und Kimon. Anmerkungen zu einem Vergleich bei Athenaios", *Hermes* 130/2: 245–49.
——. (2003) "Euergetismus und Gabentausch," *Mètis* N.S. 1: 181–200.
——. (2016) *Benefaction and Rewards in the Ancient Greek City: The Origins of Euergetism*. Cambridge.
Domingo Gygax, Marc and Arjan Zuiderhoek (eds.) (forthcoming) *Benefactors and the Polis*. Cambridge.
Donlan, Walter (1970) "Changes and Shifts in the Meaning of Demos in the Literature of the Archaic Period," *Parola del Passato* 25: 381–95.
——. (1981) "Scale, Value, and Their Function in the Homeric Economy," *American Journal of Ancient History* 12: 101–17.
——. (1982a) "Reciprocities in Homer," *Classical World* 75: 137–75.
——. (1982b) "The Politics of Generosity in Homer," *Helios* 9: 1–15.
——. (1989a) "Pre-State-Community in Greece," *Symbolae Osloenses* 64: 5–29.
——. (1989b) "The Unequal Exchange between Glaucus and Diomedes in the Light of Homeric Gift-Economy," *Phoenix* 43: 1–15.
Dougherty, Carol (1993) *The Poetics of Colonization: From City to Text in Archaic Greece*. New York and Oxford.
Douglas, Mary (^{2}1973) *Natural Symbols. Explorations in Cosmology*. London.
Doyle, Richard (1984) *ἌΤΗ, Its Use and Meaning: A Study in the Greek Poetic Tradition from Homer to Euripides*. New York.
Drews, Robert (1983) *Basileus: The Evidence for Kingship in Geometric Greece*. New Haven and London.
Drexhage, Hans-Joachim, Heinrich Konen and Kai Ruffing (2002) *Die Wirtschaft des Römischen Reiches (1.-3. Jahrhundert). Eine Einführung*. Berlin.

Drexhage, Raphaela (1988) *Untersuchungen zum römischen Osthandel*. Bonn.

Droß-Krüpe, Kerstin and Marie-Louise Nosch (2016) *Textiles, Trade, and Theories: From the Ancient Near East to the Mediterranean*. Münster.

Drucker, Peter (1967) "The Potlach," in Dalton 1967: 481–493.

Dumont, Louis (1972) "Une Science en devenir," *L'Arc: Marcel Mauss* 48: 8–21.

Dunbabin, Katherine M. D. (2003) *The Roman Banquet: Images of Conviviality*. Cambridge.

Dunbar, Henry (1962) *A Complete Concordance to the Odyssey of Homer*. Rev. and enlarged by Benedetto Marzullo. Hildesheim.

Duplouy, Alain (2002) "L'aristocratie et la circulation des richesses, " *Revue belge de philologie et d'histoire* 80/1: 5–24.

——. (2006) *Les prestige des élites: Recherches sur le modes de reconnaissance sociale en Grèce entre les Xe et Ve sièces avant J.-C*. Paris.

——. (2015) "Genealogical and Dynastic Behaviour in Archaic and Classical Greece: Two Gentilician Strategies," in Fisher and van Wees 2015: 59–84.

——. (2016) "'Crises' au sein des élites grecques: utilité et ambiguité d'un concept," in *Elite und Krise in antiken Gesellschaften*, ed. Lennart Gilhaus et al. Stuttgart: 33–46.

Dürbeck, Helmut (1967) *Zur Charakteristik der griechischen Farbenbezeichnungen*. Bonn.

Durkheim, Émile (1964) *The Division of Labor in Society*. Trans. George Simpson. New York.

Easterling, Patricia E. (1989) "Agamemnon's σκέπτρον in the Iliad," in *Images of Authority: Papers Presented to Joyce Reynolds on the Occasion of Her Seventieth Birthday*, ed. Mary Margaret Mackenzie and Charlotte Roueché. Cambridge: 104–21.

——. (1991) "Men's κλέος and Women's γόος: Female Voices in the *Iliad*," *Journal of Modern Greek Studies* 9/2: 145–51.

Easterling, Patricia E. and E. J. Kenney (eds.) (1985) *The Cambridge History of Classical Literature. I: Greek Literature*. Cambridge.

Easterling, Patricia E. and J. V. Muir (eds.) (1985) *Greek Religion and Society*. Cambridge.

Ebert, Joachim (1984) *Die Arbeitswelt der Antike*. Cologne and Vienna.

Eckstein, Felix (1974) *Handwerk. I: Die Aussagen des frühgriechischen Epos*. Archaeologia Homerica L/1. Göttingen.

Edelman, Murray J. (1970) *The Symbolic Uses of Politics*. 4th edn. Urbana.

Eder, Birgitta (2006) "The World of Telemachus: Western Greece 1200–700 BC, in Deger-Jalkotzy and Lemos 2006: 549–80.

Edmonds, J. M. (1931) *Theognis, Elegy and Iambus*. With an English translation. Cambridge and London.

Edwards, Mark W. (1975) "Type-Scenes and Homeric Hospitality," *Transactions of the American Philological Association* 105: 51–72.

Edzard, D. O. (1960) "Die Beziehungen Babyloniens und Ägyptens in der mittelbabylonischen Zeit und das Gold," *Journal of the Economic and Social History of the Orient* 3: 38–55.

Ehmer, Josef (1998) "Migration und Bevölkerung: Zur Kritik eines Erklärungsmodells," *Tel Aviver Jahrbuch für deutsche Geschichte* 27: 5–29.

Eich, Armin (2006) *Die politische Ökonomie des antiken Griechenland (6.–3. Jahrhundert v. Chr.).* Cologne, Weimar and Vienna.

Eichler, F. (1914) "ΣΗΜΑ and ΜΝΗΜΑ in älteren griechischen Grabinschriften," *Mitteilungen des Kaiserlich Deutschen Archäologischen Instituts, Athenische Abteilung* 39: 138–43.

Eideneier, Hans (ed.) (1991) *Ptochoprodromus. Einführung, kritische Ausgabe, deutsche Übersetzung.* Cologne.

Eisler, Robert (1910) *Weltenmantel und Himmelszelt: Religionsgeschichtliche Untersuchungen zur Urgeschichte des antiken Weltbildes.* 2 vols. Munich.

Elias, Norbert (1981) *Über den Prozeß der Zivilisation: Soziogenetische und psychogenetische Untersuchungen.* 8th edn. 2 vols. Francfort.

Ella, Rev. Samuel (1899) "Polynesian Native Clothing," *The Journal of the Polynesian Society* 8: 165–70.

Elmer, David (2013) *The Poetics of Consent: Collective Decision Making and the Iliad.* Baltimore.

Elwert, Georg (1985) "Märkte, Käuflichkeit und Moralökonomie," in *Soziologie undgesellschaftliche Entwicklung: Verhandlungen des 22. Soziologentages in Dortmund 1984*, ed. Burkart Lutz. Francfort and New York: 509–13.

———. (1991) "Gabe, Reziprozität und Warentausch: Überlegungen zu einigen Ausdrücken und Begriffen," in *Ethnologie im Widerstreit: Kontroversen über Macht, Geschäft, Geschlecht in fremden Kulturen; Festschrift Lorenz G. Löffler*, ed. Eberhard Berg, Jutta Lauth, and Andreas Wimmer. Munich: 159–77.

Endrödi, Julia (1991) "'Figurative Discourse' and Communication in the Emerging State of Egypt," *Göttinger Miszellen* 125: 21–36.

Engemann, Josef (2005) "Diplomatische ‚Geschenke': Objekte aus der Spätantike?" *Mitteilungen zur Spätantiken Archäologie und Byzantinischen Kunstgeschichte* 4: 39–64.

Erbse, Hartmut (1986) *Untersuchungen zur Funktion der Götter im homerischen Epos.* Berlin and New York.

Erffa, Carl E. Freiherr von (1937) ΑΙΔΩΣ *und verwandte Begriffe in ihrer Entwicklung von Homer bis Demokrit.* Philologus Supplement 30/2. Leipzig.

Eustathius, *Commentarii ad Homeri Iliadem et Odysseam*, ed. G. Stalbaum. 6 vols. Leipzig (1825–1839, rpt. 1960).

Evjen, Harold D. (1986) "Competitive Athletics in Ancient Greece: The Search for Origins and Influences," *Opuscula Atheniensia* 16: 51–56.

Faber, G. A. (1947) "Färberei und Gerberei im klassischen Altertum," *Ciba-Rundschau* 1/20: 698–711.

Fanta, Adolf (1882) *Der Staat in Ilias und Odyssee: Ein Beitrag zur Beurtheilung der homerischen Verfassung.* Innsbruck.

Fardon, Richard (1990) "Malinowskis Precedent: The Imagination of Equality," *Man* n.s. 25: 569–87.

Fatheuer, Thomas (1988) *Ehre und Gerechtigkeit: Studien zur Entwicklung der gesellschaftlichen Ordnung im frühen Griechenland.* Münster.

Faure, Paul (1987) *Parfums et aromates de l'Antiquité*. Paris.

Feeney, Denis C. (1993) *The Gods in Epic: Poets and Critics of the Classical Tradition*. London.

Fehling, Detlev (1985) *Die sieben Weisen und die frühgriechische Chronologie: Eine traditionsgeschichtliche Studie*. Bern.

Fehr, Burkhard (1979) "Zur religionspolitischen Funktion der Athena Parthenos im Rahmen des Delisch-Attischen Seebundes I," *Hephaistos* 1: 71–91.

Felson-Rubin, Nancy (1994) *Regarding Penelope: From Character to Poetics*. Princeton.

Ferguson, Adam (1986) "Essay on the History of Civil Society (1767)," in *Versuch über die Geschichte der bürgerlichen Gesellschaft*, ed. and introduced by Zwi Batscha and Hans Medick. Francfort.

Ferrari, Gloria (2002) *Figures of Speech: Men and Maidens in Ancient Greece*. Chicago.

Fidio, Pia di (1979) "La donna e il lavoro nella Grecia arcaica," *Nuova DWF, DonnaWomanFemme* 12/13: 188–217.

Figueira, Thomas J. (1984) "Karl Polanyi and the Ancient Greek Trade: The Port of Trade," *Ancient World* 10: 15–30.

Figueira, Thomas J. and Gregory Nagy (eds.) (1985) *Theognis of Megara: Poetry and the Polis*. Baltimore and London.

Finley, John H. Jr. (1978) *Homer's Odyssey*. Cambridge.

Finley, Moses I. (1954) *The World of Odysseus*. New York.

——. (1967) *The World of Odysseus*. Rev. edn. 1965. New York.

——. (1978) "The World of Odysseus revisited", in his *The World of Odysseus*. Rev. edn. New York.

——. (2001) *The World of Odysseus*. New York.

——. (1955) "Marriage, Sale and Gift in the Homeric World," *Revue internationale des droits de l'antiquité* 3rd sér. 2: 167–94.

——. (1970) "Aristotle and the Economic Analysis," *Past and Present* 47: 4–25 = *Jahrbuch für Wirtschaftsgeschichte* 2 (1971): 87–105.

——. (1970) "Metals in the Ancient World," *Journal of the Royal Society of Arts* 118: 597–607.

——. (1973) *The Ancient Economy*. Berkeley

——. (1975) *The Use and Abuse of History*. London.

——. (1981) *Economy and Society in Ancient Greece*, edn. with an introduction by Brent D. Shaw and Richard Saller. London.

——. (1983) *Politics in the Ancient World*. Cambridge.

——. (1985) *Ancient History: Evidence and Models*. London.

Finsler, Georg (1906) "Das Homerische Königtum," *Neue Jahrbücher für das Klassische Altertum* 17: 313–36 and 395–412.

Firebaugh, W. C. (1928) *The Inns of Greece and Rome and a History of Hospitality from Dawn of Time to the Middle Ages*. Chicago.

Firth, Raymond (1963) "The Place of Malinowski in the History of Economic Anthropology," in his *Man and Culture: An Evaluation of the World of Bronislaw Malinowski*. 4th edn. London: 209-27.

———. (1972) "Methodological Issues in Economic Anthropology," *Man* n.s. 7/3: 465-75.

Fisher, Nick (2010) "*Kharis, Kharites*, Festivals, and Social Peace in the Classical Greek City," in *Valuing Others in Classical Antiquity*, ed. Ineke Sluiter and Ralph M. Rosen. Leiden: 71-112.

Fisher, Nick and Hans van Wees (eds.) (1998) *Archaic Greece: New Approaches and New Evidence*. London.

———. (2011) *Ancient Competition*. Swansea.

———. (2015) *'Aristocracy' in Antiquity: Redefining Greek and Roman Elites*. Swansea.

Fittchen, Klaus (1964) *Untersuchungen zu den Sagendarstellungen bei den Griechen*. Dissertation. Tübingen.

Flaig, Egon (1993) "Loyalität ist keine Gefälligkeit: Zum Majestätsprozeß gegen C. Silius 24 n. Chr.," *Klio* 75: 289-305.

———. (1994) "Das Konsensprinzip im Homerischen Olymp. Überlegungen zum Göttlichen Entscheidungsprozeß Ilias 4, 172," *Hermes* 122: 13-31.

———. (1998) *Ödipus: Tragischer Vatermord im klassischen Athen*. Munich.

———. (2007) "Mit Kapitalismus keine Stadtkultur," in Reinhard and Stagl 2007: 133-57.

Flinthoff, Everard (1987) "The Treading of the Cloth," *Quaderi Urbinati di Cultura Classica* n.s. 25: 119-30.

Flückinger-Guggenheim, Daniela (1984) *Göttliche Gäste: Die Einkehr von Göttern und Heroen in der griechischen Mythologie*. Bern.

Flügel, Peter (1985) *Zum Begriff 'Tausch' in der Ethnologie*. Master thesis. Mainz.

Foley, Helen P. (1978) "'Reverse Similes' and Sex Roles in the Odyssey," *Arethusa* 11: 7-26.

Fornaro, Sotera (1992) *Glauco e Diomede: Lettura di Iliade VI 119-236*. Venosa.

Forrester, Viviane (1997 [French version 1996]) *Der Terror der Ökonomie*. Francfort.

Forstenpointner, Gerhard et al. (2007) "Saitenspiel und Purpurschimmer: archäozoologische Ehrengaben aus dem späthelladischen Ägina Kolonna," in Alram-Stern and Nightingale 2007: 141-49.

Forster, Ellen D. (1981) "The Flax Impost at Pylos and Mycenaean Landholding," *Minos* 17: 67-121.

Fortes, Meyer (1975) "Strangers," in Meyer Fortes and Sheila Patterson (eds.) *Studies in African Social Anthropology*. London et al.: 229-53.

Fournier, Marcel (2006) *Marcel Mauss. A Biography*. Trans. Jane Marie Todd. Princeton and Oxford (= Paris 1994).

Fowler, Robert (ed.) (2004) *The Cambridge Companion to Homer*. Cambridge.

Foxhall, Lin (1998) "Cargoes of the Heart's Desire: The Character of Trade in the Archaic Mediterranean World," in Fisher and van Wees 1998: 295-309.

———. (2007) *Olive Cultivation in Ancient Greece: Seeking the Ancient Economy*. Oxford.

Foxhall, Lin and Karen Stears (2000) "Redressing the Balance: Dedications of Clothing to Artemis and the Order of Life Stages," in Moira Donald and Linda Hurcombe (eds.) *Gender and Material Culture in Historical Perspective*. New York and London: 3–16.

Fränkel, Hermann (1955) "Die Zeitauffassung in der frühgriechischen Literatur," in his *Wege und Formen des frühgriechischen Denkens*. Munich: 1–22.

——. (1977) *Die Homerischen Gleichnisse*. 2nd edn. Göttingen (orig. 1921).

Frankenstein, Susan (1979) "The Phoinicians in the Far West: A Function of Neo-Assyrian Imperialism," in *Power and Propaganda: A Symposium on Ancient Empires*, ed. Mogens Trolle Larsen. Copenhagen: 263–94.

Fraß, Stefan (2014) *Egalität, Gemeinsinn und Staatlichkeit im archaischen Griechenland*. Munich.

Frayn, Joan M. (1984) *Sheep-Rearing and the Wool-Trade in Italy during the Roman Period*. Liverpool.

Frazier, Françoise (1988) "À propos de la 'philotimia' dans les 'Vies'," *Revue de Philologie de littérature et d'histoire anciennes* 62: 109–27.

Frei, Norbert (1993) "Wie modern war der Nationalsozialismus?" *Geschichte und Gesellschaft* 19/3: 363–87.

Frevert, Ute (2019) *Kapitalismus, Märkte und Moral*. Salzburg.

Fried, Morton H. (1967) *The Evolution of Political Society: An Essay in Political Anthropology*. New York.

Friedman, Jonathan (1975) "Tribes, States and Transformation," in *Marxist Analyses and Social Anthropology*, ed. Maurice Bloch. London: 161–202.

Frisk, Hjalmar (1960/1972) *Griechisches etymologisches Wörterbuch*. 3 vols. Heidelberg.

Frontisi-Ducroux, Françoise (1975) *Dédale: Mythologie de l'artisan en Grèce ancienne*. Paris.

Fürer-Haimendorf, Christoph von (1975) *Himalayan Traders: Life in Highland Nepal*. London.

Gage, John (1993) *Colour and Culture: Practice and Meaning from Antiquity to Abstraction*. London.

Gale, Noel H. and Zofia Stos-Gale (1981) "Blei und Silber in der ägäischen Kultur," *Spektrum der Wissenschaft* 8: 92–105.

Gallagher, William R. (1988) "A Reconsideration of o-no in Mycenaean Greek," *Minos* 23: 85–106.

Gallant, Tom W. (1988) "Agricultural Systems, Land Tenure, and the Reforms of Solon," *Annual of the British School of Athens* 77: 111–24.

Gane, Mike (ed.) (1992) *The Radical Sociology of Durkheim and Mauss*. London and New York.

Ganzer, Burkhard (1981) "Altruismus, Egoismus, Interaktion: Bemerkungen zu M. D. Sahlins Reziprozitätskontinuum," *Zeitschrift für Ethnologie* 106: 23–41.

Garcia, Lorenzo F., Jr. (2013) *Homeric Durability: Telling Time in the Iliad*. Cambridge, MA and London.

García Morcillo, Marta (2013) "Trade and Sacred Places: Fairs, Markets and Exchange in Ancient Italy Sanctuaries," in *Religiöse Vielfalt und Soziale Integration*, eds. Martin Jehne, Bernhard Linke and Jörg Rüpke. Heidelberg: 236-274.

——. (2014): "Limiting Generosity: Conditions and Restrictions on Roman Donations," in Carlà and Gori 2014: 241-266.

Garlan, Yvon (1984) *Les esclaves en Grèce ancienne*. Paris.

——. (1989) *Guerre et économie en Grèce ancienne*. Paris.

Garland, Robert (1985) *The Greek Way of Death*. London.

——. (2014) *Wandering Greeks: The Ancient Greek Diaspora from the Age of Homer to the Death of Alexander the Great*. Princeton.

Garnsey, Peter (1985) "Grain for Athens," in Cartledge and Harvey 1985: 62-65.

——. (1986) "Mountain Economies in Southern Europe or: Thoughts on the Early History; Continuity and Individuality of the Mediterranean Upland Pastoralism," in *Wirtschaft und Gesellschaft in Berggebieten*, ed. Markus Mattmüller. Basel: 7-29 = Whittaker 1988: 196-209.

——. (1988) *Famine and Food Supply in the Graeco-Roman World: Responses to Risk and Crisis*. Cambridge (rpt. 1993).

Garnsey, Peter and C. R. Whittaker (eds.) (1983) *Trade and Famine in the Classical Antiquity*. Cambridge.

Garnsey, Peter, Keith Hopkins, and C. R. Whittaker (eds.) (1983) *Trade in the Ancient Economy*. London.

Gauer, Werner (1984) "Was geschieht mit dem Peplos?" in *Parthenon-Kongress: Referate und Berichte 4.-8. April 1982 I*, ed. Ernst Berger. 2 vols. Mainz: 220-29.

Gaul, Wilhelm (1914) "Das Geschenk nach Form und Inhalt im Besonderen untersucht an afrikanischen Völkern," *Archiv für Anthropologie* 13/3: 223-79.

Gauthier, Philippe (1972) "Notes sur l'étranger et hospitalité en Grèce et à Rome," *Ancient Society* 3: 1-21.

——. (1992) *Symbola : Les étrangers at la justice dans les cités grecques*. Nancy.

Geary, Patrick (2003) "Gift Exchange and Social Science Modelling: The Limitations of a Construct," in Algazi, Groebner and Jussen 2003: 129-40.

Geddes, Ann G. (1984) "Who's Who in Homeric Society," *Classical Quarterly* 34: 17-36.

——. (1989) "Rags and Riches: The Costume of Athenian Men in the Fifth Century," *Classical Quarterly* 37: 307-31.

Geertz, Clifford (1973) "Thick Description: Towards an Interpretative Theory of Culture", in his *The Interpretations of Cultures. Selected Essays*. New York: 3-30.

Gehrig, Ulrich (1990) "Die Phönizier in Griechenland," in his *Die Phönizier im Zeitalter Homers*, ed. Hans-Georg Niemeyer. Mainz: 23-31.

Gehrke, Hans-Joachim (1986) *Jenseits von Athen und Sparta: Das dritte Griechenland und seine Staatenwelt*. Munich.

——. (1987) "Die Griechen und die Rache: Ein Versuch in historischer Psychologie," *Saeculum* 38: 121-49.

Gellner, Ernest (1985) "Malinowski Go Home. Reflections on the Malinowski Centenary Conference," *Anthropology Today* 1/5: 5-7.

Georgoudi, Stella (1974) "Quelques Problèmes de la transhumance dans la Grèce ancienne," *Revue des Études Grecques* 87: 155–85.

Gernet, Louis (1948) "La notion mythique de la valeur en Grèce," *Journal de Psychologie normale et pathologique* 41: 415–462.

——. (1951) "Droit et prédroit en Grèce ancienne," *L'Année sociologique* 3rd sér. 2: 21–119 = *Droit et institutions en Grèce antique*. 2nd edn. Paris 1982: 7–119.

Gernet, Louis (1968) "Mariages de tyrans" (1954) in *Anthropologie de la Grèce antique*, Paris: 344-359.

Gherchanoc, Florence (2009) "Des cadeaux pour *nymphai*: *dôra, anakalyptêria* et *epaula*," in *La religion des femmes en Grèce ancienne: Mythes, cultes et société*, ed. Lydie Bodiou and Véronique Mehl. Rennes: 207–23.

——. (2019) "Poikilia: Zur Symbolik gemusterter Stoffgeschenke in Übergangsriten im antiken Griechenland," in Wagner-Hasel and Nosch 2019: 375–94.

Gherchanoc, Florence and Huét, Valerie (eds.) (2012) *Vêtements antiques: s'habiller, se déshabiller dans les mondes anciens*. Paris.

Giddens, Anthony (1976) "Classical Social Theory and the Origin of Modern Sociology," *American Journal of Sociology* 81(4): 703–729.

Gierke, Otto F. von (1917) *Deutsches Privatrecht. II: Schuldrecht*. Munich and Leipzig.

——. ([1902] 1962) *Vom Wesen der menschlichen Verbände*. Darmstadt.

Gilbert, Felix (1990) *History: Politics or culture? Reflections on Ranke and Burckhardt*. Princeton.

Gill, Christopher, Norman Postlethwaite, and Richard Seaford (eds.) (1998) *Reciprocity in Ancient Greece*. Oxford.

Gill, David W. J. (1991) "Pots and Trade: Space-fillers or Objects d'Art," *Journal of Hellenic Studies* 111: 29–47.

Gillis, Carole and Marie-Louise Nosch (eds.) (2007) *Ancient Textiles: Production, Craft and Society*. Oxford.

Giuffrida, Margherita (1985) "Cipro nei poemi omerici," *Seia* 2: 15–39.

Giuliani, Luca (1986) *Bildnis und Botschaft*. Francfort.

Gleba, Margarita (2018) "Textile Culture in Europe 1200–500 BC: A View from Greece," in *Arachne* 5: 14–23.

Gleba, Margarita, Beatrix Marín-Aquilera and Francesco Iacona (2018) "Couloring the Mediterranean: Production and Consumption of Purple-dyed Textiles in Pre-Roman Times," *Journal of Mediterranean Archaeology* 31(2): 127–154.

Gnoli, Gherardo and Jean-Pierre Vernant (eds.) (1982) *La mort, les morts dans les sociétés anciennes*. Cambridge.

Godart, M. Louis (1970) "The Grouping of Place-Names in the Cn Tablets," *Bulletin of the Institute of Classical Studies of the University of London* 17: 159–61.

Godbout, Jacques T. and Alain Caillé (1991) "Le don existe-t-il (encore)?" *Revue du Mauss* 11: 11–32.

Godbout, Jacques T. and Alain Caillé (1992) *L'esprit du don*. Paris.

Gödde, Susanne (2011) *Euphêmia: Die gute rede in Kult und Literatur in der griechischen Antike*. Heidelberg.

Godelier, Maurice (1966) *Rationalité et irrationalité en économie*. Paris.

———. (1969) "La monnaie de sel des Barayu de Nouvelle Guinée," *L'Homme* 9/2: 5–37.
———. (1980) "L'État: les processus de sa formation, la diversité de ses forms et de ses bases," *Revue internationale des sciences sociales* 37/4: 18–35.
———. (1984) *L'Idéel et le Matériel*. Paris.
———. (1996) *L'énigme du don*. Paris.
Godley, A. D. (2004) *Herodotus*. With an English translation. Cambridge and London.
Goguet, Antoine Yves (1775 [French version 1758]) *The Origin of laws, arts, and sciences: and their progress amongst the most ancient of nations I*, trans. Robert Henry; II, trans. D. Dunn. Edinburgh.
Golden, Mark (1992) "The Uses of Cross-Cultural Comparison in Ancient Social History," *Echos du monde classique* 36: 309–31.
Goldstein, Melwyn C. and Cynthia M. Beall (1991) *Die Nomaden Westtibets*. Nürnberg.
Gossman, Lionel (2000) *Basel in the Age of Burckhardt. A Sudy in Unseasonable Ideas*. Chicago, Illinois.
Gottesman, Alex (2010) "The Beggar and the Clod: The Mythic Notion of Property in Ancient Greece," *Transactions of the American Philological Association* 140/2: 287–322.
———. (2014) "The Authority of Telemachus," *Classical Antiquity* 33/1: 31–60.
Gould, John P. (1991) *Give and Take in Herodotus: Myres Memorial Lecture*. Oxford: 5–19.
Graafen, Rainer and Christian Seeber (1993) "Alte Handelsrouten im Himalaya," *Geographische Rundschau* 45/11: 674–79.
Graf, Fritz (1991) "Religion und Mythologie im Zusammenhang mit Homer: Forschung und Ausblick," in Latacz 1991: 331–64.
Graham, A. J. (1984) "Commercial Interchanges Between Greeks and Natives," *Ancient World* 10: 3–10.
———. (2001) *Collected Papers on Greek Colonization*. Leiden.
Grand-Clément, Adeline (2011) *La fabrique des couleurs: Histoire du paysage sensible des Grecs anciens (VIIIe s.—début du Ve s. av. N. è.)*. Paris.
Grand-Clément, Adeline et al. (eds.) (2017) *Les traces du sensible: pour une histoire des sens dans les sociétés anciennes*. Trivium: revue franco-allemande de sciences humaines et sociales 27. Paris.
Grant, Adam (2014) *Give and Take. A Revolutionary Approach to Success*. London.
Gras, Michel (1986) "La coupe et l'échange dans la Méditerranée archaïque," in *Hommages à F. Daumas*. Montpellier: 351–59.
Grassl, Herbert (1985) "Hirtenkultur in Griechenland," in *Bericht über den 16. österreichischen Historikertag in Krems/Donau in der Zeit vom 3. bis 7. September 1984*, ed. vom Verband österreichischer Historiker und Geschichtsvereine. Vienna: 77–85.
———. (1990) "Zur Rolle der Frau in antiken Hirtenkulturen," *Laverna* 1: 13–17.
Gregory, Chris A. (1980) "Gifts to Men and Gifts to God: Gift Exchange and Capital Accumulation in Contemporary Papua," *Man* n.s. 15: 626–52.
———. (1982) *Gifts and Commodities*. London.

Greenewalt, Crawford H. and Lawrence J. Majewski (1980) "Lydian Textiles," in de Vries 1980: 133–47.

Greindl, Max (1938) ΚΛΕΟΣ, ΚΥΔΟΣ, ΕΥΧΟΣ, ΤΙΜΗ, ΦΑΤΙΣ, ΔΟΧΑ: Eine bedeutungsgeschichtliche Untersuchung des epischen und lyrischen Sprachgebrauchs. Diss. Munich.

Grethlein, Jonas (2008) "Memory and Material Objects in the Iliad and the Odyssey," The Journal of Hellenic Studies 128: 27–51.

——. (2017) Homer und die Kunst des Erzählens. Munich.

Griffin, Jesper (1984) Homer on Life and Death. Oxford.

——. (1995) "Homer, Pastoral, and the Near East," Studi italiani di filologia classica 85, 3rd sér 10: 552–76.

Griffin, Miriam (2003) "De Beneficiis and Roman Society," The Journal of Roman Studies 93: 92–113.

Grimm, Jacob (1865) "Ueber Schenken und Geben (1848)," in his Kleinere Schriften. II: Abhandlungen zur Mythologie und Sittenkunde. Berlin: 173–210.

Groebner, Valentin (2000) Gefährliche Geschenke. Korruption und politische Sprache am Beginn der Neuzeit. Konstanz (Postdoctoral thesis. Basel 1998).

Groh, Dieter (1988) "Strategien, Zeit und Ressourcen," in Ökonomie und Zeit, ed. Eberhard K. Seifert. Francfort: 131–88.

Grothe, Hermann (1866) "Die Geschichte der Wolle und Wollmanufaktur im Alterthum," Deutsche Vierteljahrs-Schrift 29: 259–304.

Grottanelli, Cristiano (1976/77) "Notes on Mediterranean Hospitality," Dialoghi di Archeologia 9–10: 186–94.

——. (1989/90) "Do ut des?" in Bartoloni 1990: 45–54.

Gruber, Joachim (1963) Über einige abstrakte Begriffe des frühen Griechischen. Beiträge zur klassischen Philologie 9. Meisenheim am Glan.

Grünbart, Michael (ed.) (2011) Geschenke erhalten die Freundschaft: Gabentausch und Netzwerkpflege im europäischen Mittelalter I. Berlin.

Grüner, Andreas (2007) "Gabe und Geschenk in der römischen Staatskunst," in Geschenke und Steuern, Zölle und Tribute: Antike Abgabenformen in Anspruch und Wirklichkeit, ed. Hilmar Klinkott, Sabine Kubisch, and Renate Müller-Wollermann. Leiden and Boston: 431–84.

Guery, Alain (1976) Studien zur Terminologie der Sklaverei. II: Untersuchungen zur älteren insbesondere homerischen Sklaventerminologie. Wiesbaden.

——. (1984) "Le roi dépensier: Le don, la contrainte, et l'origine du système financier de la monarchie française d'Ancien Régime," Annales E. S. C. 6: 1241–69.

——. (1991) "Zur homerischen Staats- und Gesellschaftsordnung: Grundcharakter und geschichtliche Stellung," in Latacz 1991: 182–204.

——. (1992) "Volk, Nation: Altertum," in Geschichtliche Grundbegriffe VII, ed. Otto Brunner, Werner Conze, and Reinhart Koselleck. Stuttgart: 151–71.

——. (1997) Gschnitzer, Fritz (1965) "ΒΑΣΙΛΕΥΣ: Ein terminologischer Beitrag zur Frühgeschichte des Königtums bei den Griechen," Innsbrucker Beiträge zur Kulturwissenschaft 11: 99–112.

Hägg, Robin (ed.) (1983) The Greek Renaissance of the Eighth Century B.C.: Tradition and Innovation; Proceedings of the Second International Symposium at the Swedish Institute in Athens, 1–5 June, 1981. Stockholm.

———. (1987a) "Gifts to the Heroes in Geometric and Archaic Greece," in Linders and Nordquist 1987: 93–99.

———. (1987b) "Submycenaean Cremation Burials in the Argolid," in Laffineur 1987: 207–11.

———. (ed.) (2002) *Peloponnesian Sanctuaries and Cults: 11–13 June 1994*. Proceedings of the International Symposium at the Swedish Institute in Athens 48. Stockholm.

Hägg, Robin and Gullög C. Nordquist (eds.) (1990) *Celebrations of Death and Divinity in the Bronze Age Argolid: Proceedings of the Sixth International Symposium at the Swedish Institute at Athens, 11.–13. June 1988*. Stockholm.

Hagner, Michael (1987) *Zur Geschichte vom Licht im Auge und der Physiologie des Druckphosphens im Verhältnis zu den jeweils zeitgenössischen Sehtheorien*. Diss. Berlin.

Hall, Jonathan (2004) "How Greek Were the Early Western Greeks," in *Greek Identity in the Western Mediterranean: Papers in honour of Brian Shefton*, ed. Kathryn Lomas. Leiden: 35–54.

Halstead, Paul (1981) "Counting Sheep in Neolithic and Bronze Age Greece," in Hodder, Isaac and Hammond 1981: 307–39.

———. (1987a) "Man and Other Animals in Later Greek Prehistory," *Annual of the British School at Athens* 82: 71–83.

———. (1987b) "Traditional and Ancient Rural Economy in Mediterranean Europe: Plus ça Change," *The Journal of Hellenic Studies* 107: 77–87.

Halverson, John (1985) "Social Order in the 'Odyssey'," *Hermes* 113: 129–45.

———. (1986) "The Succession Issue in the 'Odyssey'," *Greece & Rome* 33/2: 119–28.

Hamilakis, Yannis (ed.) (2014) *Archaeology of the Senses: Human Experience, Memory, and Affect*. New York.

Hammerstein, Notker (ed.) (1988) *Deutsche Geschichtswissenschaft um 1900*. Stuttgart.

Hammond, Nicholas (1983) "Migration and Assimilation in Greece," in *Greece Old and New*, ed. Tom Winnifrith and Penelope Murray. London and Basingstoke: 39–64.

Hamp, Eric P. (1982) "ΦΙΛΟΣ," *Bulletin de la Société de Linguistique* 77/1: 251–62.

Hampe, Roland and Erika Simon (1985) *Griechisches Leben im Spiegel der Kunst*. Mainz.

Hands, Arthur R. (1968) *Charities and Social Aid in Greece and Rome*. London.

Handschur, Erna (1970) *Die Farb- und Glanzwörter bei Homer und Hesiod*. Diss. Vienna.

Hannig, Jürgen (1988) "Ars donandi: Zur Ökonomie des Schenkens im frühen Mittelalter," in *Armut, Liebe, Ehre: Studien zur historischen Kulturforschung*, ed. Richard van Dülmen. Francfort: 11–37.

Hansen, Klaus P. (1995) *Kultur und Kulturwissenschaft*. Tübingen and Basel.

Hansen, Mogens Herman (1976) *Agagoge, Endeixis und Ephegesis against Kakourgoi, Atimoi, and Pheugontes. A Study in the Athenian Administration of Justice in 4th Century B.C.* Odense.

BIBLIOGRAPHY

——. (1982) "*Atimia* in Consequence of Private Debts," in *Symposion 1977. Vorträge zur griechischen und hellenistischen Rechtsgeschichte*, ed. Joseph Modrzejewski and Detlef Liebs. Cologne: 113–20.

——. (1998) *Polis and City-State: An Ancient Concept and Its Modern Equivalent; Acts of the Copenhagen Polis Centre*. Copenhagen.

Hanson, Victor D. (1983) *Warfare and Agriculture in Classical Greece*. Cambridge.

Harbsmeier, Michael (1994) *Wilde Völkerkunde*. Francfort and New York.

Harding, Anthony F. (1987) "Fernhandel in der Bronzezeit: Analyse und Interpretation," *Saeculum* 38/4: 297–311.

Harich-Schwarzbauer, Henriette (2011) "Gewebte Bilder. Textilekphrasis in Claudians Raub der Proserpina (*rapt.* I, 246-275)," *Bild und Text im Mittelalter*, ed. Karin Krause and Barbara Schellewald. Cologne, Weimar and Vienna: 29–39.

——. (ed.) (2016) *Weben und Gewebe in der Antike: Materialität—Repräsentation—Episteme—Metapoetik*. Oxford and Philadelphia.

Harlizius-Klück, Ellen (2004) *Weberei als episteme und die Genese der deduktiven Mathematik*. Berlin.

——. (2006) "Nur nicht von einer Frau geboren werden …'. Genealogisches zu Mathematik und Weberei in der Antike," in Ingeborg Kader (ed.) *Penelope rekonstruiert: Geschichte und Deutung einer Frauenfigur*. Munich: 121–133.

——. (2016) "Denkmuster in der antiken Weberei: Eine Spurensuche," in Harich-Schwarzbauer 2016: 87–107.

——. (2019) "Der Stoff und die Ordnung des Kosmos: Zur Bedeutsamkeit des textilen Mustertransfers im frühen Griechenland," in Wagner-Hasel and Nosch 2019: 397–430.

Harlizius-Klück, Ellen and Giovanni Fanfani (2016) "(B)orders in Ancient Weaving and Archaic Greek Poetry," in *Spinning Fates and Song of the Loom: The Use of Textiles, Clothing and Cloth Production as Metaphor, Symbol and Narrative Device in Greek and Latin Literature*, ed. Giovanni Fanfani, Mary Harlow, and Marie-Louise Nosch. Oxford: 61–99.

Harris, Edward M., David M. Lewis and Mark Woolmer (eds.) (2016) *The Ancient Greek Economy: Markets, Households and City-States*. Cambridge.

Harris, Marvin (1968) *The Rise of Anthropological Theory*. New York.

Hartmann, Elke (2016) *Ordnung in Unordnung. Kommunikation, Konsum und Konkurrenz in der frühen Kaiserzeit*. Stuttgart.

Harvey, F. David (1985) "Dona Ferentes: Some Aspects of Bribery in Greek Politics," in Cartledge and Harvey 1985: 76–117.

Hasebroek, Johannes (1928) *Staat und Handel im Alten Griechenland: Untersuchungen zur antiken Wirtschaftsgeschichte*. Tübingen (rpt. 1966).

Hastrup, Kirsten (1986) "Ethnologie und Kultur: Ein Überblick über neuere Forschungen," in *Vom Umschreiben der Geschichte*, ed. Ulrich Raulff. Berlin: 54–67.

Hattenauer, Hans (1992) *Europäische Rechtsgeschichte*. Heidelberg.

Hauck, Gerhard (1984) *Geschichte der soziologischen Theorie: Eine ideologiekritische Einführung*. Reinbek bei Hamburg.

Havelock, Christine Mitchell (1981) "Mourners on Greek Vases," in Hyatt 1981: 103–18.
Havelock, Eric A. (1963) *Preface to Plato*. Oxford.
——. (1978) *The Greek Concept of Justice: From Its Shadow in Homer to Its Substance in Plato*. Cambridge, MA and London.
——. (1986) *The Muse Learns to Write: Reflections on Orality and Literacy from Antiquity to the Present*. New Haven, MA.
Haverkamp, Anselm (ed.) (1996) *Theorie der Metapher*. 2nd edn. Darmstadt.
Hawke, Jason (2011) *Writing Authority. Elite Competition and Written Law in Early Greece*. Illinois.
Hecht, Ann (1989) *The Art of the Loom: Weaving, Spinning & Dyeing Across the World*. London.
Heiden, Bruce (1991) "Shifting Contexts in the Iliad," *Eranos* 89: 1–12.
Heitsch, Ernst (1992) "Die epische Schicksalswaage," *Philologus* 136/2: 143–57.
Helbig, Wolfgang (1901) "Zu den homerischen Bestattungsgebräuchen," in *Sitzungsberichte der philosophisch-philologischen Classe der königlich bayrischen Akademie der Wissenschaften Jahrgang 1900*. Munich: 199–279.
Helck, Wolfgang and E. Otto (eds.) (1977) *Lexikon der Ägyptologie* II. Wiesbaden: s.v. "Gold, Goldgewinnung, Goldminen."
Helfer, Christian (1970) "Jherings Gesellschaftsanalyse im Urteil der heutigen Sozialwissenschaft," in Wieacker and Wollschläger 1970: 79–88.
Heltzer, Michael (1989) "The Trade of Crete and Cyprus with Syria and Mesopotamia and Their Eastern Tin-Sources in the XVIII–XVII Centuries B.C.," *Minos* 24: 7–27.
Hempel, Ludwig (1993a) "Jungquartäre Klimaveränderungen im ostmediterranen Raum. Auswirkungen auf Reliefgestalt und Pflanzendecke," in *Rundgespräche der Kommission für Ökologie: Probleme der Umweltforschung in historischer Sicht*. Munich: 161–79.
——. (1993b) "Natürliche Höhenstufen und Siedelplätze in griechischen Hochgebirgen," *Hellenika*: 77–91.
Hénaff, Marcel (2002) *Le prix de la verité: Le don, l'argent, la philosophie*. Paris.
Herman, Gabriel (1987) *Ritualised Friendship in the Greek City*. Cambridge.
——. (1998) "Reciprocity, Altruism and the Prisoner's Dilemma: The Special Case of Classical Athens," in Gill 1998: 199–226.
——. (2006) *Morality and Behaviour in Democratic Athens: A Social History*. Cambridge.
Hesiod (1984) *Theogonia, Opera et dies, Scutum*, ed. Friedrich Solmsen. Oxford Classical Texts. Oxford.
Hettne, Björn (1990) The Contemporary Crisis: The Rise of Reciprocity, in Polanyi-Levitt 1990: 208–20.
Heubeck, Alfred (1974) *Die homerische Frage: Ein Bericht über die Forschung der letzten Jahrzehnte*. Darmstadt.
Heubeck, Alfred et al. (eds.) (1988–1992) *A Commentary on Homer's Odyssey*. 3 vols. Oxford.
Hicks, R. D. (1950) *Diogenes Laertius. Lives of Eminent Philosophers*. With an English translation. Vol I. London and Cambridge.

Hiersche, Rolf (1993) "Zu griech. πολιορκέω belagere'," *Glotta* 61: 30–31.

Hildebrandt, Berit (2007) *Damos und Basileus. Überlegungen zu Sozialstrukturen in den Dunklen Jahrhunderten Griechenlands*. Munich.

———. (2019) "Von der Gabe zur Entlohnung: Kleidung als kaiserliches Geschenk in Rom," in Wagner-Hasel and Nosch 2019: 117–36.

Hildebrandt, Berit and Caroline Veit (eds.) (2009) *Der Wert der Dinge: Güter im Prestigediskurs*. Munich.

Hilger, Dietrich (1982) "Der Herrschaftsbegriff im Zeitalter der Revolutionen: Grundzüge seiner Geschichte," in *Geschichtliche Grundbegriffe III*, ed. Otto Brunner, Werner Conze and Reinhart Koselleck. Stuttgart: 64–102.

Hiller, Stefan (1972) *Studien zur Geographie des Reiches um Pylos nach den Mykenischen und Homerischen Texten*. Vienna.

———. (1987) "A-PI-QO-RO Amphipoloi," *Minos* 2: 239–55.

Hiller, Stefan and Oswald Panagl (1976) *Die frühgriechischen Texte aus mykenischer Zeit*. Darmstadt.

Hiltbrunner, Otto (1972) "Gastfreundschaft," in *Reallexikon für Antike und Christentum* 8: 1061–123.

———. (1983) "Gastfreundschaft und Gasthaus in der Antike," in *Gastfreundschaft, Taverne und Gasthaus im Mittelalter*, ed. Hans Conrad Peyer in collaboration with Elisabeth Müller-Luckner. Munich and Vienna: 1–20.

———. (2005) *Gastfreundschaft in der Antike und im frühen Christentum*. Darmstadt.

Hilzheimer, Max (1936) "Sheep," *Antiquity* 10: 195–206.

Hirzel, Rudolf (1902) *Der Eid: Ein Beitrag zu seiner Geschichte*. Leipzig.

———. (1907) *Themis, Dike und Verwandtes: Ein Beitrag zur Geschichte der Rechtsidee bei den Griechen*. Leipzig.

Hitch, Sarah (2009) *King of Sacrifice: Ritual and Royal Authority in the Iliad*. Cambridge, MA and London.

Hodder, Ian (1989) *The Meaning of Things: Material Culture and Symbolic Expression*. London.

Hodder, Ian, Glynn Isaac, and Norman Hammond (eds.) (1981) *Patterns of the Past: Studies in Honour of David Clarke*. Cambridge.

Hodkinson, Stephen (1988) "Animal Husbandry in the Greek Polis," in Whittaker 1988: 35–74.

———. (1990) "Politics as a Determinant of Pastoralism: The Case of Southern Greece, ca. 800–300 B.C.," *Rivista di studi Liguri* 56: 139–63.

Hoëg, Carsten (1925) *Les Saracatsans, un tribu nomade grecque*. Paris and Copenhagen.

Hoffmann, Marta (1964) *The Warp-Weighted Loom: Studies in the History of Technology in an Ancient Implement*. Oslo.

Hofmann, Inge (1973) *Bürgerliches Denken: Zur Soziologie Emile Durkheims*. Francfort.

Hofmann, J. B. (1950) *Etymologisches Wörterbuch des Griechischen*. Munich, s.v. ἀμείβω.

Holenstein, Andre (1991) *Die Huldigung der Untertanen: Rechtskultur und Herrschaftsordnung 800–1800*. Stuttgart.

Hölkeskamp, Karl-Joachim (1992) "Written Law in Archaic Greece," *Proceedings of the Cambridge Philological Society* 38: 87–117.

———. (1999) *Schiedsrichter, Gesetzgeber und Gesetzgebung im archaischen Griechenland*. Stuttgart.

———. (2002) "Ptolis and Agore. Homer and the Archaeology of the City-State," in *Omero tremila anni dopo*, ed. Franco Montanari. Storia e letteratura 210. Roma: 297–342.

———. (2004) "The Polis and its Spaces—The Politics of Spatiality. Tendencies in Recent Research," *Ordia Prima* 3: 25–40.

Hollander, Anne (1980) *Seeing through Clothes*. New York.

Hollier, Denis (1972) "Malaise dans la Sociologie," *L'Arc. Marcel Mauss* 48: 55–61.

Hölscher, Lucian (1979) *Öffentlichkeit und Geheimnis: Eine begriffsgeschichtliche Untersuchung zur Entstehung von Öffentlichkeit in der frühen Neuzeit*. Stuttgart.

Hölscher, Tonio (1989) *Die unheimliche Klassik der Griechen*. Bamberg.

Hölscher, Uvo (1983) "Die Odyssee—Epos zwischen Märchen und Literatur," in *Schrift und Gedächtnis Beiträge zur Archäologie der literarischen Kommunikation*, ed. Aleida and Jan Assman, and Christof Hardmeier. Munich: 94–108.

———. (1990) *Die Odyssee zwischen Märchen und Roman*. Munich.

Holst-Warhaft, Gail (1992) *Dangerous Voices: Women's Laments and Greek Literature*. London.

Homeri Opera, 4 vols. (1979) Ed. Thomas W. Allen. Oxford Classical Texts. Oxford.

Hooker, James T. (1987a) "Homeric φίλος," *Glotta* 65: 44–65.

———. (1987b) "Homeric Society. A Shame-Culture?" *Greece & Rome* 34: 121–25.

———. (1989) "Gifts in Homer," *Bulletin of the Institute of Classical Studies* 36: 79–90.

———. (1995) "Linear B as a Source for Social History," in *The Greek World*, ed. Anton Powell. London: 7–26.

Hopper, Robert J. (1979) *Trade and Industry in Classical Greece*. London.

Howe, Timothy (2003) "Pastoralism, the Delphic Amphictiony and the First Sacred War: The Creation of Apollo's Sacred Pastures," *Historia* 52/2: 129–46.

———. (2008) *Pastoral Politics, Animals, Agriculture and Society in Ancient Greece*. Claremont.

Huber, Ingeborg (2001) *Die Ikonographie der Trauer in der griechischen Kunst*. Peleus: Studien zur Geschichte Griechenlands und Zyperns 10. Mannheim and Möhnesee.

Humphreys, Sarah C. (1981) "Death and Time," in Humphreys and King 1981: 261–83 = Humphreys 1983a: 144–64.

———. (1983a) *The Family, Women and Death: Comparative Studies*. London.

———. (1983b) "Family Tombs and Tomb-Cult in Classical Athens: Tradition or Traditionalism?" in Humphreys 1983a: 79–129.

———. (1983c) *Anthropology and the Greeks*. 2nd edn. London.

———. (1983d) "History, Economics and Anthropology: The Work of Karl Polanyi," in Humphreys 1983c: 31–75.

———. (1983e) "Homo politicus and homo oeconomicus: War and Trade in the Economy of Archaic and Classical Greece," in Humphreys 1983c: 159–74.

——. (1983f) "The Work of Louis Gernet," Humphreys 1983c: 283–88.
——. (2018) *Kinship in Ancient Athens*. Oxford.
Humphreys, Sarah C. and Helen King (eds.) (1981) *Mortality and Immortality. The Anthropology and Archaeology of Death*. London.
Hunter, Virginia J. (1981) "Classics and Anthropology," *Phoenix* 35: 144–55.
——. (1994) *Policing Athens: Social Control in the Attic Lawsuits, 420–320 B.C.* Princeton.
Hyatt, Stephen L. (ed.) (1981) *The Greek Vase*. Latham, N.Y.
Hyde, Lewis (1983) *The Gift: Imagination and Erotic Life of Property*. 3rd edn. New York.
Isler, Hans Peter (1994) "ΓΕΡΡΑΙ: Ein neuer inschriftlicher Beleg aus Sizilien," *Zeitschrift für Papyrologie und Epigraphik* 101: 104–6.
Issing, Otmar (ed.) (1988) *Geschichte der Nationalökonomie*. 2nd rev. edn. Munich.
Ivánka, Endre von (1950) "Berghirtentum und Staatenbildung im antiken und mittelalterlichen Balkan," *Saeculum* 1: 349–61.
Jachmann, Günther (1953) "Das homerische Königtum," *Maia* 6: 241–56.
Jackson, Alastar (1993) "War and Raids for Booty in the World of Odysseus," in Rich and Shipley 1993: 64–76.
Jacobsen, Thomas W. (1984) "Seasonal Pastoralism in Southern Greece: A Consideration of the Ecology of Neolithic Urfirnis Pottery," in *Pots and Potters: Current Approaches in Ceramic Archaeology*, ed. Prudence M. Rice. Los Angeles: 27–43.
Jacoby, Felix (1933) "Der homerische Apollonhymnos," in *Sitzungsberichte der Preußischen Akademie der Wissenschaften, Philosophisch-Historische Klasse*. Berlin: 682–751.
Jaeger, Friedrich (1994) *Bürgerliche Modernisierungskrise und historische Sinnbildung: Kulturgeschichte bei Droysen, Burckhardt und Max Weber*. Göttingen.
Jameson, Michael (1983) "Famine in the Greek World," in Garnsey and Whittaker 1983: 6–16.
——. (1988) "Sacrifice and Animal Husbandry," in Whittaker 1988: 87–119.
——. (1989) "Mountains and the Greek City States," in Bergier 1989: 7–17.
Janko, Richard (1982) *Homer, Hesiod and the Homeric Hymns*. Cambridge.
Janssen, Jac J. (1982) "Gift-Giving in Ancient Egypt as an Economic Feature," *Journal of the Egyptian Archaeology* 68: 253–58.
Jeffrey, Lilian H. (1961) *The Local Scripts of Archaic Greece*. Oxford.
Jenkins, Ian D. (1985) "The Ambiguity of Greek Textiles," *Arethusa* 18: 109–32.
Jensen, Minna Skafte (1980) *The Homeric Question and the Oral-Formulaic Theory*. Copenhagen.
Jettmar, Karl (1993) "Voraussetzungen, Verlauf und Erfolg menschlicher Anpassung im nordwestlichen Himalaya mit Karakorum," in Schweinfuhrt 1993: 31–47.
Jhering, Rudolf von (1887) "Die Gastfreundschaft im Alterthum," *Deutsche Rundschau* 51: 357–97.
——. (1970) *Der Zweck im Recht I (1877) and II (1883)*, ed. with a foreword by Christian Helfer and two yet unpublished additions of Jhering's inheritance. Hildesheim and New York (rpt. of the 4th edn. 1904/05).

Jim, Theodora Suk Fong (2014) *Sharing with the Gods, Aparchai and Dekatai in Ancient Greece*. Oxford.

Johnson, Marie (ed.) (1964) *Ancient Greek Dress: A New Illustrated Edition Combining Greek Dress by Ethel Beatrice Abrahams; Chapters of Greek Dress by Lady Maria Midington Evans*. Chicago.

Jones, W. H. S. and Litt, D. (1964) *Pausanias' Description of Greece*. Vol. I. Cambridge and London.

Jong, Irene J. F. de (1987) "Homeric κέρδος and ὄφελος," *Museum Helveticum* 44: 79–81.

——— . (1991) "Gynaikeion ethos: Misogyny in the Homeric Scholia," *Eranos* 89: 13–24.

Kabadias, G. B. (1965) *Pasteurs-Nomads Méditerrannées: Les Saracatsans de Grèce*. Paris.

Kahn, Maurice (1979) "La frontière et l'identité ambigue," *Ktema* 4: 201–11.

Kahn-Majlis, Brigitte (1984) *Indonesische Textilien: Wege zu Göttern und Ahnen*. Cologne.

——— . (1991) *Woven Messages. Indonesian Textile Tradition in Course of Time. Gewebte Botschaften: Indonesische Traditionen im Wandel*. Hildesheim.

Kahrstedt, Ulrich (1953) "Delphoi und das Heilige Land des Apollon," in Mylonas and Raymond 1953: 749–57.

Kakridis, Hélène J. (1963) *La notion de l'amitié et de l'hospitalité chez Homère*. Thessaloniki.

Kan, Sergei (1986) "The XIXth Century Tlingit Potlatch: A New Perspective," *American Anthropologist* 13/2: 191–212.

Karali, Llilian and F. Megaloudi (2008) "Purple Dyes in the Environment and History of the Aegean: A Short Review," in *Vestidos, Textiles Y Tintes. Estudios sobre la producción de bienes de consumo en la Antigüedad*, ed. Carmen Alfaro and Llilian Karali, Valencia: 181–84.

Karanastassi, Pavlina (1997) "Themis," in *Lexicon Iconographicum Mythologiae Classicae* 8/1: 1199–205.

Karanika, Andromache (2014) *Voices at Work: Women, Performance, and Labor in Ancient Greece*. Baltimore.

Karavites, Peter Panayiotis (1986) "Philotes, Homer and the Near East," *Athenaeum* 3/4: 474–81.

Karavites, Peter Panayiotis in collaboration with Thomas Wren (1992) *Promise-Giving and Treaty-Making: Homer and the Near East*. Leiden.

Kardera, Chrysoula (1960) "Dyeing and Weaving Works at Isthmia," *American Journal of Archaeology* 65: 261–66.

——— . (1970) "Athena Phoinika," *Athens Annals of Archaeology* 3: 94–97.

Kaschuba, Wolfgang (1995) "Kulturalismus: Vom Verschwinden des Sozialen im gesellschaftlichen Diskurs," *Zeitschrift für Volkskunde* 91: 27–46.

Kaser, Max (1971) *Das römische Privatrecht*. 2nd edn. Munich.

Katluhn, Carl (1914) ΓΕΡΑΣ. Diss. Königsberg.

Katz, Marylin A. (1991) *Penelope's Renown: Meaning and Indeterminacy in the Odyssey*. Princeton.

Kearsley, R. (1999) "Greeks Overseas in the 8th Century B.C. Euboeans, Al Mina and Assyrian Imperialism," in *Ancient Greeks West and East*, ed. Gocha R. Tsetskhladze. Leiden: 109–34.

Kehl, Alois (1978) "Gewand (der Seele)," in *Reallexikon für Antike und Christentum* 10: 945–1025.

Kelder, Jorrit M. (2009) "Royal Gift Exchange between Mycenae and Egypt: Olives as 'Greeting Gifts' in the Late Bronze Age Eastern Mediterranean," *American Journal of Archaeology* 113/3: 339–52.

Kelsen, Hans (1982) *Vergeltung und Kausalität: Mit einer Einleitung von Ernst Topitsch*. Vienna (rpt. of 1941 edn.).

Kemper, Peter (1988) *"Postmoderne" oder der Kampf um die Zukunft*. Francfort.

Kerenyi, Karl (1942) *Die antike Religion*. Amsterdam.

Keuls, Eva C. (1983) "Attic Vase-Painting and Home Textile Industry," in *Ancient Greek Art and Iconography*, ed. Warren G. Moon. Madison, WI: 209–29.

Khazanov, Anatoly M. (1984 [Russian version 1983]) *Nomads of the Outside World*. Cambridge.

Kiekebusch, Joachim (1928) "Schenkung," in *Handwörterbuch der Rechtswissenschaft* V, ed. Fritz Stier-Somlo and Alexander Elster. Berlin and Leipzig: 282–88.

Kiesel, Helmuth (1989) "Aufklärung und neuer Irrationalismus in der Weimarer Republik," in *Aufklärung und Gegenaufklärung in der europäischen Literatur, Philosophie und Politik von der Antike bis zur Gegenwart*, ed. Jochen Schmidt. Darmstadt: 497–521.

Kilian-Dirlmeier, Imma (1985) "Fremde Weihungen in griechischen Heiligtümern vom 8. bis zum Beginn des 7. Jahrhunderts v. Chr.," *Jahrbücher des Römisch-Germanischen Zentralmuseums* 32: 215–54.

Killen, John T. (1964) "The Wool Industry of Crete in Late Bronze Age," *Annual of the British School at Athens* 59: 1–15.

——. (1966) "The Knossos Lc(Cloth)Tablets," *Bulletin of the Institute of Classical Studies* 13: 105–9.

——. (1985) "The Linear B Tablets and the Mycenaean Economy," in *Linear B: A 1984 Survey*, ed. Anna M. Davies and Y. Duhoux. Louvain-la-Neuve: 241–305.

——. (2007) "Cloth Production in Late Bronze Age Greece: The Documentary Evidence," in Gillis and Nosch 2007: 50–58.

King, Helen (1983) "Bound to Bleed: Artemis and the Greek Women," in *Images of Women in Antiquity*, ed. Averil Cameron and Amélie Kuhrt. London: 109–27.

Kippenberg, Hans Gerhard (1971) "Wege zu einer historischen Religionssoziologie," *Verkündigung und Forschung: Beiheft zur Evangelischen Theologie* 16: 54–82.

——. (1997) *Die Entdeckung der Religionsgeschichte: Religionswissenschaft und Moderne*. Munich.

Kirk, Geoffrey S. (1971) *Myth: Ist Meaning and Function*. Cambridge.

——. (1985) "The Homeric Hymns," in Easterling and Kenney 1985: 114–15.

Kirk, Geoffrey S. et al. (eds.) (1985–1993) *The Iliad: A Commentary*. 6 vols. Cambridge.

Kirsten, Ernst (1956) *Die griechische Polis als historisch-geographisches Problem des Mittelmeerraumes*. Colloquium Geographicum 5. Bonn.

Kistler, Erich et al. (eds.) (2015) *Sanctuaries and the Power of Consumption. Networking and the Formation of Elites in the Archaic Western Mediterranean World.* Proceedings of the International Conference in Innsbruck, 20th to 23rd March 2012 (= Philippika 92). Wiesbaden.

Kitts, Margo (2005) *Sanctified Violence in Homeric Society: Oath-Making Rituals and Narratives in the Iliad.* Cambridge.

Klein, Julius (1964) *The Mesta: A Study in Spanish Economic History 1273-1836.* Port Washington, NY.

Klinkott, Hilmar, S. Kubisch, and Renate Müller-Wollermann (eds.) (2007) *Geschenke und Steuern, Zölle und Tribute: Antike Abgabenformen in Anspruch und Wirklichkeit.* Leiden and Boston.

Knigge, Ursula (1988) *Der Kerameikos von Athen.* Athen.

Knox, Mary O. (1970) "'House' and 'Palace' in Homer," *The Journal of Hellenic Studies* 90: 117-20.

Koch-Harnack, Gundel (1983) *Knabenliebe und Tiergeschenke: Ihre Bedeutung im päderastischen Erziehungssystem Athens.* Berlin.

——. (1989) *Erotische Symbole: Lotosblüte und gemeinsamer Mantel auf antiken Vasen.* Berlin.

Köcke, Jasper (1979) "Some Early German Contributions to Economic Anthropology," *Research in Economic Anthropology* 2: 119-67.

Kolb, Frank (1973) "Römische Mäntel: *paenula, lacerna,* μανδύη," *Mitteilungen des Deutschen Archäologischen Instituts, Römische Abteilung* 80: 69-165.

Komornicka, A. M. (1984) "Poésie et poète: Termes et notions dans la littérature grecque," *Giornale filologica ferrarese* 7: 3-17.

König, René (1972) "Marcel Mauss (1872-1950)," *Kölner Zeitschrift für Soziologie und Sozialpsychologie* 24: 633-57.

Konstan, David (1997) *Friendship in the Classical World.* Cambridge.

Kopcke, Günter (1990) *Handel.* Archaeologia Homerica M. Göttingen.

Koppers, Wilhelm (1915/16) "Die ethnologische Wirtschaftsforschung," *Anthropos* 10-11: 611-51, 971-1097.

Korfmann, Manfred (1986) "Troy: Topography and Navigation," in *Troy and the Troyan War: A Symposium held at Bryn Mawr College October 1984,* ed. Machteld J. Mellink. Bryn Mawr: 1-16.

Koster, Harold A. (1976) "The Thousand Year Road," *Expedition* 19/1: 19-28.

Koster, Harold A. and Joan Bouza (1976) "From Spindle to Loom: Weaving in the Southern Argolid," *Expedition* 19/1: 20-39.

Köstler, Rudolf (1950) *Homerisches Recht.* Vienna.

Krämer, Augustin (1902) *Die Samoa-Inseln: Entwurf einer Monographie mit besonderer Berücksichtigung Deutsch-Samoas.* 2 vols. Stuttgart.

Kramer, Fritz (1979) "Nachwort," in Bronislaw Malinowski, *Argonauten des Westlichen Pazifik.* Translation Heinrich Ludwig Herdt, ed. Fritz Kramer. Francfort 1979: 548-70.

——. (1981) *Verkehrte Welten: Zur imaginären Ethnographie des 19. Jahrhunderts.* 2nd edn. Francfort.

Kramer-Hajos, Margaretha (2016) *Mycenaean Greece and the Aegean World: Palace and Provinces in the Late Bronze Age*. Cambridge.

Kreilinger, Ulla (2007) *Anständige Nacktheit. Körperpflege, Reinigungsriten und das Phänomen weiblicher Nacktheit im archaisch-klassischen Athen*. Rahden.

Kretschmer, Paul (1945) "Penelope," in *Anzeiger der Akademie der Wissenschaften, Philosophisch-Historische Klasse*. Vienna: 80–93.

Krischer, Tilman (1989) "Aretes Frage: Zur Phäakenepisode der Odyssee," *Mnemosyne* 42: 12–23.

Kromer, Karl (1982) "Gift Exchange and the Hallstatt Courts," *Bulletin of the Institut of Archaeology* 19: 21–30.

Krug, Antje (1968) *Binden in der griechischen Kunst: Untersuchungen zur Typologie, 6.–1. Jh. v. Chr.* (Diss. Mainz 1967) Hösel.

Krummen, Eveline (1990) *Pyrsos Hymnon: Festliche Gegenwart und mythisch-rituelle Tradition als Voraussetzung einer Pindartradition (Isthmie 4, Pythie 5, Olympie 1 und 3)*. Berlin and New York.

Kullmann, Wolfgang (1956) *Das Wirken der Götter in der Ilias: Untersuchungen zur Frage der Entstehung des Homerischen „Götterapparats"*. Berlin.

——. (1988) "'Oral Tradition/Oral History' und die frühgriechische Epik," in Ungern-Sternberg and Reinau 1988: 184–96.

Kullmann, Wolfgang and Michael Reichel (eds.) (1990) *Der Übergang von der Mündlichkeit zur Literatur bei den Griechen*. Tübingen.

Kurke, Leslie (1999) *Coins, Bodies, Games, and Gold. The Politics of Meaning in Archaic Greece*. Princeton.

Kurtz, Donna Carol and John Boardman (1971) *Greek Burial Customs. Aspects of Greek and Roman Life*. London.

Laffineur, Robert (ed.) (1987) *Thanatos: Les coutumes funéraires en Égée à l'âge du bronze. Actes du colloque de Liège (21–23 avril 1986)*. Liège.

Lahr, Stefan van der (1992) *Dichter und Tyrannen im archaischen Griechenland: Das Corpus Theognideum als zeitgenössische Quelle politischer Wertvorstellungen archaisch-griechischer Aristokraten*. Munich.

Lamberterie, Charles de (1992) "Le problème de l'homonymie: Les trois verbes *ophello* en grec ancien," in *La langue et les textes en grec ancien. Actes du colloque Pierre Chantraine, Grenoble 5–8 Septembre 1989*, ed. Françoise Létoublen. Amsterdam: 201–17.

Landels, John Gray (1978) *Engineering in the Ancient World*. London.

Landercy, Mathilde (1933) "La destination de la κερκίς dans le tissage en Grèce au IVe siècle," *L'Antiquité Classique* 2: 357–362.

Landfester, Manfred (1966) *Das griechische Nomen φίλος und seine Ableitungen*. Spudasmata 11. Hildesheim.

Langdon, Susan (1987) "Gift Exchange in the Geometric Sanctuaries," in Linders and Nordquist 1987: 107–13.

Laroche, Emmanuel (1949) *Histoire de la racine nem- en grec ancienne*. Paris.

Latacz, Joachim (1966) *Zum Wortfeld 'Freude' in der Sprache Homers*. Heidelberg.

——. (ed.) (1979) *Homer: Tradition und Neuerung*. Darmstadt.

——. (1988) "Zu Umfang und Art der Vergangenheitsbewahrung in der mündlichen Überlieferungsphase des griechischen Heldenepos," in Ungern-Sternberg and Reinau 1988: 153–83.

——. (1989) *Homer: Der erste Dichter des Abendlandes*. 2nd edn. Munich and Zurich.

——. (ed.) (1991) *Zweihundert Jahre Homer-Forschung: Rückblick und Ausblick*. Colloquium Rauricum 2. Leipzig and Stuttgart.

——. (2001) *Homer: His Art and His World*, trans. James P. Holoka. Ann Arbor (1st edn. 1996).

——. (2004) *Troy and Homer: Towards a Solution of an Old Mystery*, trans. Kevin Windle and Rosh Ireland. Oxford.

Laughlin, C. D. Jr. (1986) "On the Spirit of the Gift," *Journal of the Indian Anthropological Society* 21/2: 156–76.

Laum, Bernhard (1924) *Heiliges Geld: Eine historische Untersuchung über den sakralen Ursprung des Geldes*. Tübingen.

——. (1933) *Die geschlossene Wirtschaft: Soziologische Grundlegung des Autarkieproblems*. Tübingen.

——. (1960) *Schenkende Wirtschaft: Nicht marktmäßiger Güterverkehr und seine soziale Funktion*. Francfort.

Lavelle, Brian M. (1980/81) "Archilochos Fr. 6 West and ΧΕΙΝΙΑ," *Classical Journal* 76: 197–99.

——. (1995) "The Pisistratids and the Mines of Thrace", *Athenaeum* 83: 45–66.

——. (2005) *Fame, Money, and Power: The Rise of Peisistratos and 'Democratic' Tyranny at Athens*. Ann Arbor.

Lavizzari-Raeuber, Alexandra (1989) *Thangkas: Rollbilder aus dem Himalaya; Kunst und mythische Bedeutung*. 3rd edn. Cologne.

Lay, Rupert (1990) *Die Macht der Moral: Unternehmenserfolg durch ethisches Managment*. Düsseldorf.

——. (1991) *Ethik für Wirtschaft und Politik*. Francfort.

Leacock, Eleanor (1978) "Women's Status in Egalitarian Society: Implications for Social Evolution," *Current Anthropology* 19/2: 247–75.

——. (1981) *Myths of Male Dominance: Collected Articles on Women Cross-culturally*. New York.

Leacock, Seth (1954) "The Ethnological Theory of Marcel Mauss," *American Anthropologist* 56: 58–73.

Lebessi, Angeliki (1976) "A Sanctuary of Hermes and Aphrodite on Crete," *Expedition* 18/3: 2–13.

Leduc, Claudine (1991) "Comment la donner en mariage? La mariée en pays grec (Ixe–IVe siècle av. J.-C.)," in Schmitt-Pantel 1990 : 259–316.

Lee, Mireille M. (2015) *Body, Dress, and Identity in Ancient Greece*. New York.

Leeuw, Gerardus van der (1920/21) "Die do-ut-des Formel in der Opfertheorie," *Archiv für Religionswissenschaft* 20: 241–53.

Lemos, Irene (2007) "'... ἐπεὶ πόρε μύρια ἔδνα ...' *Iliade* 22, 472: Homeric Reflections in Early Iron Age Elite Burials," in Alram-Stern and Nightingale 2007: 275–83.

Lenz, Carl Gotthold (1790) *Geschichte der Weiber im heroischen Zeitalter.* Hannover (rpt. 1976).

Lenz, Ilse and Ute Luig (eds.) (1990) *Frauenmacht ohne Herrschaft: Geschlechterverhältnisse in nichtpatriarchalen Gesellschaften.* Berlin.

Lepenies, Wolf (ed.) (1981) *Geschichte der Soziologie: Studien zur kognitiven, sozialen und historischen Identität einer Disziplin.* 4 vols. Francfort.

Lesky, Albin (1971) *Geschichte der griechischen Literatur.* 3rd edn. Bern and Munich.

Letourneau, Charles (1897) *L'évolution du commerce.* Paris.

Levin, Donald N. (1970) "ΔΙΠΛΑΧ ΠΟΡΦΥΡΕΗ," *Rivista di Filologia* 98: 17–36.

Lévi-Strauss, Claude (1967) *The Elementary Structures of Kinship,* tr. Harle Bell, v. Sturmer, Needham. Boston.

Lévy, Edmond (1985) "Lien personel et titre royal: anax et basileus dans l'Iliade," in his *Le système palatial en Orient, en Grèce et à Rome: Actes du Colloque de Strasbourg, 19–22 juin 1985.* Leiden: 291–314.

Lévy, Harry L. (1963) "The Odyssean Suitors and the Host-Guest Relationship," *Transactions of the American Philosophical Society* 94: 145–53.

Lévy-Bruhl, Henri (1948/49) "In memoriam Marcel Mauss," *L'Année Sociologique,* 3rd sér. 2: 1–4.

Lewis, Thomas S. W. (1981) "Homeric Epic and the Greek Vase," in Hyatt 1981: 81–102.

Lexicon Iconographicum Mythologiae Classicae 2/1. (1984) Ed. Fondation pour LIMC. Zürich.

Liddel, Peter (2007) *Civic Obligation and Individual Liberty in Ancient Athens.* Oxford.

Liddell, Henry George and Robert Scott (1968) *A Greek-English Lexicon: With a Supplement 1968,* rev. and augmented by Sir Henry Stuart James and Roderick McKenzie. Oxford (orig. 1940).

Lienau, Cay (1989) *Griechenland: Geographie eines Staates der europäischen Südperipherie.* Darmstadt.

Ligt, Luuk de and Pieter W. de Neeve (1988) "Ancient Periodic Markets: Festivals and Fairs," *Athenaeum* n.s. 66: 391–416.

Linden, David (1992) "Ehre und Ehe: Handlung und Gerechtigkeit in Ilias und Odyssee," *Hermes* 120: 110–14.

Linders, Tullia (1987) "Gods, Gifts, Society," in Linders and Nordquist 1987: 115–22.

——. (1989/90) "The Melting Down of Discarded Metal Offerings in Greek Sanctuaries," in Bartoloni 1990: 281–85.

Linders, Tullia and Brita Alroth (eds.) (1992) *Economics of Cult in the Ancient World: Proceedings of the Uppsala Symposium 1990.* Uppsala.

Link, Stefan (1994) "Temenos und ager publicus bei Homer?" *Historia* 43/2: 241–45.

Lissarrague, François (1987) *Un flot d'images : Une esthétique du banquet grec.* Paris.

——. (1991) "Femmes au figuré," in Schmitt-Pantel 1991: 159–251.

Liverani, Mario (1987) "The Collapse of the Near Eastern Regional System at the End of the Bronze Age: The Case of Syria," in Rowlands, Larsen and Kristiansen 1987: 66–73.

Llewellyn-Jones, Lloyd (2003) *Aphrodite's Tortoise. The Veiled Woman of Ancient Greece,* Swansea.

Loew, Otto (1908) ΧΑΡΙΣ. Marburg.

Lohmann, Hans (1985) "Landleben im klassischen Attika: Ergebnisse und Probleme einer archäologischen Landesaufnahme des Demos Atene," in *Jahrbuch der Ruhruniversität Bochum*. Bochum: 71–96.

——. (1992) "Agriculture and Country Life in Classical Attica," in *Agriculture in Ancient Greece. Proceedings of the Seventh International Symposium at the Swedish Institute at Athens, 16–17 May 1990*, ed. B. Wells. Stockholm: 29–60.

——. (1993) *Atene: Forschungen zur Siedlungs- und Wirtschaftsstruktur des klassischen Attika*. Cologne.

——. (1997) "Antike Hirten in Westkleinasien und der Megaris: Zur Archäologie der mediterranen Weidewirtschaft," in *Volk und Verfassung im vorhellenistischen Griechenland: Beiträge auf dem Symposium zu Ehren von Karl-Wilhelm Welwei in Bochum, 1.-2. März 1996*, ed. Walter Eder and Karl-Joachim Hölkeskamp. Stuttgart: 63–89.

Lonsdale, H. Steven (1990) *Creatures of Speech: Lion, Herding, and Hunting Similes in the Iliad*. Stuttgart.

Loraux, Nicole (1981) *L'invention d'Athènes: Histoire de l'oraison funèbre dans la cité classique*. Paris.

——. (1991) "Qu'est-ce qu'une déesse," in Pauline Schmitt-Pantel 1991: 31–62 = (1992) 'What is a goddess?' in *History of Women in the West. I: From Ancient Goddesses to Christian Saints*, ed. Georges Duby and Michelle Perrot. Cambridge, MA: 11–44.

Lordkipanidze, Otar (ed.) (1985) *Das alte Kolchis und seine Beziehungen zur griechischen Welt vom 6. bis zum 4. Jahrhundert v. Chr.* Konstanz.

Low, Poly (2007) *Interstate Relations in Classical Greece: Morality and Power*. Cambridge.

Loycke, Almut (ed.) (1992) *Der Gast, der bleibt: Dimensionen von Georg Simmels Analyse des Fremdseins*. Francfort and New York.

Luhmann, Niklas (1988) *Die Wirtschaft der Gesellschaft*. Francfort.

Luke, Joanna (1994) "The Krater, *Kratos*, and the *Polis*," *Greece & Rome* 41: 23–32.

Lullies, Reinhard and Wolfgang Schiering (ed.) (1988) *Archäologenbildnisse*. Mainz.

Lundgreen, Christoph (ed.) (2014) *Staatlichkeit in Rom? Diskurse und Praxis (in) der römischen Republik*. Stuttgart.

——. "Schlüsselmonopole oder Governance-Funktionen? Alternative Annäherungen an Staatlichkeit in der griechischen Archaik," in Meister 2020: 157–92.

Lupi, Elisabetta (2016) "Milesische Wolle in Sybaris: Neuentdeckung eines Fragments von Timaios (FGrH 566 F 50) und die Frage nach dem Textilhandel," in Droß-Krüpe and Nosch 2016: 169–91.

Lyons, Deborah (2003) "Dangerous Gifts. Ideologies of Marriage and Exchange in Ancient Greece," *Classical Antiquity* 22/1: 93–134.

——. (2012) *Dangerous Gifts: Gender and Exchange in Ancient Greece*. Austin.

Maaß, Michael (1978) *Die geometrischen Dreifüße von Olympia*. Olympische Forschungen X. Berlin.

MacCamp, J. II (1979) "A Draught in the Late Eighth Century B.C.," *Hesperia* 48: 397–411.

Macfie, Lawrence (1985) "Adam Smith's Theorie der Ethischen Gefühle als Grundlage für seinen ‚Wohlstand der Nationen' (1957)," in *Ethik, Wirtschaft und Staat: Adam Smiths Politische Ökonomie heute*, ed. Horst Claus Recktenwald. Darmstadt: 131–57.

Maehle, Ingvar B. (2018) "The Economy of Gratitude in Democratic Athens," *The Journal of the American School of Classical Studies at Athens* 87/1: 55–90.

Maffi, Alberto (1979) "Rilevanza delle 'regole di scambio' omeriche per la storia e la metodologia del diritto," in *Symposion 1974: Vorträge zur griechischen und hellenistischen Rechtsgeschichte*, ed. Arnaldo Biscardi. Cologne and Vienna: 33–62.

Maftei, Marta (1976) *Antike Diskussionen über die Episode von Glaukos und Diomedes im VI. Buch der Ilias*. Meisenheim am Glan.

Magou, E., S. Philippakis, and Cl. Rolley (1986) "Trépieds géométriques de bronze," *Bulletin de correspondance hellénique* 110: 121–36.

Maine, Henry S. (1894) *Ancient Law*. 15th edn. London.

Malinowski, Bronislaw ([1922] 1999) *Argonauts of the Western Pacific: An Account of Native Enterprise and Adventure in the Archipelagoes of Melanesian New Guinea*. Preface by Sir James G Frazer. London.

——. ([1926] 1952) *Crime and Custom in Savage Society*. New York.

——. (1944) *A Scientific Theory of Culture*. Chapel Hill.

Malkin, Irad (1989) "Delphoi and the Founding of Social Order in Archaic Greece," *Métis* 4/1: 129–53.

——. (1993) "Land Ownership, Territorial Possesion, Hero Cults and Scholarly Theory," in *Nomodeiktes: Greek Studies in Honor of Martin Ostwald*, ed. Ralph M. Rosen and Joseph Farrell. Ann Arbor: 225–34.

——. (2011) *A Small Greek World: Networks in the Ancient Mediterranean*. Oxford.

Mann, Christian (2007) *Die Demagogen und das Volk. Zur politischen Kommunikation im Athen des 5. Jahrhunderts v. Chr*. Berlin.

Mann, Michael (1986) *The Sources of Social Power. I: A History of Power from the Beginning to A.D. 1760*. Cambridge.

Mannsprenger, Dietrich (1992) "Das Gold Troias und die griechische Goldprägung im Bereich der Meerengen," in *Troia: Brücke zwischen Orient und Okzident*, ed. Ingrid Gamer-Wallert. Tübingen: 124–51.

Mansfield, John (1985) *The Robe of Athena and the Panathenaic 'Peplos'*. Dissertation. Berkeley, CA.

Manville, Philip Brook (1980) "Solon's Law of Statis and ATIMIA in Archaic Athens," *Transactions of the American Philological Association* 10: 213–21.

——. (1990) *The Origins of Citizenship in Ancient Athens*. Princeton.

Maran, Joseph and Eftychia Stavrianopoulou (2007) "Πότνιος Ἀνήρ—Reflections on the Ideology of Mycenaean Kingship," in Alram-Stern and Nightingale 2007: 285–98.

Marek, Christian (1984) *Die Proxenie*. Francfort.

Marg, Walter (1970) *Hesiod, Sämtliche Gedichte: Theogonie, Erga, Frauenkataloge*. Zürich and Munich.

Marinatos, Spyridon N. (1967) *Kleidung, Haar- und Barttracht*. Archaeologia Homerica A. Göttingen.

Marinatos, Nanno and Robin Hägg (eds.) (1993) *Greek Sanctuaries: New Approaches.* London and New York.

Marquardt, Penelope A. (1993) "Penelope as Weaver of Words," in *Woman's Power, Man's Game: Essays on Classical Antiquity in Honor of Joy K. King*, ed. Mary De Forest. Illinois: 149–58.

Martin, Jochen (1990) "Aspekte antiker Staatlichkeit," in *Staat und Staatlichkeit in der frühen Römischen Republik: Akten eines Symposiums 12.–15. Juli 1988*, ed. Walter Eder. Stuttgart: 220–32.

——. (1994) "Der Verlust der Stadt," in Meier 1994: 95–114.

Martin, Richard P. (1993) "The Seven Sages as Performers of Wisdom," in *Cultural Poetics in Archaic Greece: Cult, Performance, Politics*, ed. Carol Dougherty and Leslie Kurke. Cambridge: 108–28.

Marwitz, Herbert (1961) "Das Bahrtuch," *Antike und Abendland* 10: 7–18.

Mattingly, David J. and Salmon, John (ed.) (2001): *Economies Beyond Agriculture in the Classical World.* London and New York.

Maucourant, Jérôme (2008) "Figures du néomodernisme: le 'marché' est-il un 'signifiant vide'?" in *L'économie antique, une économie de marché?*, ed. Yves Roman and Julie Dalaison. Paris: 17–47.

Mauss, Marcel (1921) "Une forme ancienne de contract chez les Thraces," *Revue des Etudes Grecques* 34: 388–97.

——. (1923/24) "Essai sur le don: Forme et raison de l'échange dans les sociétés archaiques," *L'Année sociologique* n.s. 1: 30–196 (rpt. 1950/1975).

——. (1990) *The Gift: The Form and Reason for Exchange in Archaic Societies*, trans. W. D Halls, with a foreword by Mary Douglas. London and New York = (1923/42) "Essai sur le don: Forme et raison de l'échange dans les sociétés archaïques." *L'Année sociologique* n.s. 1: 30–196.

——. (2011) *The Gift: Forms and Functions of Exchange in Archaic Societies*, trans. Ian Cunnison. Mansfield Centre, CT.

——. (2016) *The Gift*. Expanded edn. Selected, annotated, and translated by Jane I. Guyer. Foreword by Bill Maurer. Chicago.

Mauzé, Marie (1986) "Boas, les kwagul et le potlatch : Eléments pour une réévaluation," *L'Homme* 26/4: 21–63.

Maxwell-Stuart, P. G. (1981) *Studies in Greek Colour Terminology*. 2 vols. Mnemosyne Supplement 65. Leiden.

McCall, Grant (1982) "Association and Power in Reciprocity and Requital: More on Mauss and the Maori," *Oceania* 52/4: 303–19.

McCartney, Eugene S. (1953) "Undoing by Night Work Done by Day: A Folklore Motif," in Mylonas and Raymond 1953: 1249–53.

McCormack, Geoffrey (1976) "Reciprocity," *Man* n.s. 11: 89–103.

——. (1982) "Mauss and the 'Spirit' of the Gift," *Oceania* 52/4: 286–93.

McInerney, Jeremy (2006) "On the Border: Sacred Land and the Margins of the Community," in *City, Countryside, and the Spatial Organization of Value in Classical Antiquity*, ed. Ralph M. Rosen and Ineke Sluiter. Leiden and Boston: 33–59.

——. (2010) *The Cattle of the Sun: Cows and Culture in the World of the Ancient Greeks.* Princeton, NJ.

McLachlan, Bonnie (1993) *The Age of Grace: Charis in Early Greek Poetry*. Princeton.

McNeil, Linda (2005) "Bridal Cloths, Cover-Ups, and *kharis*: The 'Carpet Scene' in Aeschylus' Agamemnon," *Greece & Rome* 52/1: 1–17.

Medick, Hans (1973) *Naturzustand und Naturgeschichte der bürgerlichen Gesellschaft: Die Ursprünge der bürgerlichen Sozialtheorie als Geschichtsphilosophie und Sozialwissenschaften bei Samuel Pufendorf, John Locke und Adam Smith*. Göttingen.

——. (1984) "'Missionare im Ruderboot'? Ethnologische Erkenntnisweise als Herausforderung an die Sozialgeschichte," *Geschichte und Gesellschaft* 10: 295–319.

——. (1996) *Weben und Überleben in Laichingen 1650–1900: Lokalgeschichte als allgemeine Geschichte*. Göttingen.

Meier, Christian (1985) *Politik und Anmut*. Berlin.

——. (1989) *Die Welt der Geschichte und die Provinz des Historikers: Drei Überlegungen*. Berlin.

——. (ed.) (1994) *Die okzidentale Stadt nach Max Weber: Zum Problem der Zugehörigkeit in Antike und Mittelalter*. Historische Zeitschrift Beiheft 17. Munich 1994.

Meister, Jan (forthcoming) *"Adel" und gesellschaftliche Differenzierung im archaischen und frühklassischen Griechenland*. Stuttgart.

Meister, Jan and Gunnar Seelentag (eds.) (2020) *Konkurrenz und Institutionalisierung in der griechischen Archaik*. Stuttgart.

Mele, Alfonso (1979) *Il commercio greco arcaico*. Naples.

Melena, José L. (1975) *Studies on Some Mycenaean Inscriptions from Knossos Dealing with Textiles*. Minos Supplement 5. Salamanca.

Merkelbach, Reinhold (1952) "Die pisistratische Redaktion der homerischen Gedichte," *Rheinisches Museum* N. F. 95: 23–47.

Meyer, Eduard (1910) *Geschichte des Altertums. I: Elemente der Anthropologie*. 3rd edn. Stuttgart and Berlin.

Meyer, Richard (1898) "Zur Geschichte des Schenkens," *Zeitschrift für Kulturgeschichte* 5: 18–29.

Meyerfeld, Franz Wilhelm Ludwig von (1835) *Die Lehre von den Schenkungen nach Römischem Recht I*. Marburg.

Meyers, Gretchen E. (2013) "Women and the Production of Ceremonial Textiles: A Reevaluation of Ceramic Textile Tools in Etrusco-Italic Sanctuaries," *American Journal of Archaeology* 117/2: 247–74.

Meyer-Zwiffelhoffer, Eckhard (1995) *Im Zeichen des Phallus: Die Ordnung des Geschlechtslebens im antiken Rom*. Francfort and New York.

Michel, Cécile and Marie-Louise Nosch (eds.) (2010) *Textile Terminologies in the Ancient Near East and Mediterranean from the Third to the First Millenia BC*, Oxford and Oakville.

Michel, Jacques (1962) *Gratuité en droit Romain : Etudes d'histoire et d'ethnologie juridique*. Bruxelles.

Michell, Humfrey (1963) *The Economics of Ancient Greece*. 2nd edn. Cambridge.

Militello, Pietro (2007) "Textile Industry and Minoan Palaces," in Gillis and Nosch 2007: 36–45.

Millett, Paul (1984) "Hesiod and his World," *Proceedings of the Cambridge Philological Society* 30: 84–115.
——. (1991) *Lending and Borrowing in Classical Athens*. Cambridge.
Mills, Harriane (1984) "Greek Clothing Regulations: Sacred or Profane?" *Zeitschrift für Papyrologie und Epigraphik* 55: 255–65.
Missfelder, Jan-Friedrich (2014) "Ganzkörpergeschichte: Sinne, Sinn und Sinnlichkeit für eine Historische Anthropologie," *Internationales Archiv für Sozialgeschichte der deutschen Literatur* 39/2: 457–75.
Mitchell, Lynette G. (1997) *Greeks Bearing Gifts: The Public Use of Private Relationship in the Greek World 435–323 B.C.* Cambridge.
Möller, Astrid (2000) *Naukratis: Trade in Archaic Greece*. Cambridge.
Mommsen, Theodor (1864) "Römisches Gastrecht," in his *Römische Forschungen I*. Berlin (rpt. 1962).
Mondi, Robert (1980) "ΣΚΗΠΤΟΥΧΟΙ ΒΑΣΙΛΕΙΣ: An Argument for Divine Kingship," *Arethusa* 13/2: 203–16.
Monsacré, Hélène (1984) *Les larmes d'Achille : Le héros, la femme et la souffrance dans la poésie d'Homère*. Paris.
——. (1984) "Weeping Heroes in the Iliad," *History and Anthropology* 1: 57–75.
Moonwoman, Birch (1994) "Color Categorization in Early Greek," *Early Journal of Indo-European Studies* 22/1–2: 37–65.
Moravia, Sergio (1989) *Beobachtende Vernunft. Philosophie und Vernunft in der Aufklärung*. Trans. Elisabeth Piras. Francfort (= *La scienza dell' uomo nel settecento*. Bari 1970).
Morgan, Catherine (1988) "Corinth, the Corinthian Gulf and Western Greece During the Eighth Century B.C.," *Annual of the British School at Athens* 88: 313–38.
——. (1990) *Athletes and Oracles: The Transformation of Olympia und Delphi in the Eighth Century B.C.* Cambridge.
——. (1993) "The Origins of Pan-Hellenism," in Marinatos and Hägg 1993: 18–44.
——. (2003) *Early Greek States Beyond the Polis*. London and New York.
Morgan, Catherine and Todd Whitelaw (1991) "Pots and Politics: Ceramic Evidence for the Rise of the Argive State," *American Journal of Archaeology* 95: 79–108.
Morgan, Kathleen (1991) "Odyssey 23, 218–24: Adultery, Shame, and Marriage," *American Journal of Philology* 112: 1–3.
Morley, Neville (2007) *Trade in Classical Antiquity*. Cambridge.
Morris, Ian (1986a) "Gift and Commodity in Archaic Greece," *Man* n.s. 21: 1–17.
——. (1986b) "Use and Abuse of Homer," *Classical Antiquity* 5: 81–129.
——. (1987) *Burial and Ancient Society: The Rise of the Greek City State*. Cambridge.
——. (1988) "Tomb Cult and the 'Greek Renaissance': The Past and the Present in the 8th Century B.C.," *Antiquity* 62: 750–61.
——. (1989) "Attitudes Toward Death in Archaic Greece," *Classical Antiquity* 8/2: 268–320.
——. (1991) "The Early Polis as City and State," in Rich and Wallace-Hadrill 1991: 25–57.

——. (1996) *Death-Ritual and Social Structure in Classical Antiquity*. Cambridge.

Morris, Sarah (2003) "Imaginary Kings: Alternatives to Monarchy in Early Greece," in *Popular Tyranny: Sovereignty and Its Discontents in Ancient Greece*, ed. Kathryn A. Morgan. Austin: 1–24.

Morris, Sarah P. (1992) *Daidalos and the Origins of Greek Art*. Princeton.

Mosley, D. J. (1971) "Greeks, Barbarians, Language and Contact," *Ancient Society* 2: 1–6.

Moszkowski, Max (1911) *Vom Wirtschaftsleben der primitiven Völker*. Jena.

Mueller, Melissa (2001) "The Language of Reciprocity in Euripides 'Medea'," *American Journal of Philology* 122/4: 471–504.

——. (2007) "Penelope and the Poetics of Remembering," *Arethusa* 40: 337–62.

——. (2010) "Helen's Hands: Weaving for *Kleos* in the Odyssey," *Helios* 37: 1–21.

Muhly, James D. (1970) "Homer and the Phoinicians," *Berytus* 19: 19–64.

——. (1985) "Sources of Tin and the Beginnings of Bronze Metallurgy," *American Journal of Archaeology* 89: 272–91.

Müller, Dietram (1974) *Handwerk und Sprache: Die sprachlichen Bilder aus dem Bereich des Handwerks in der griechischen Literatur bis 400 v. Chr.* Meisenheim am Glan.

Müller, Ernst W. (1981) *Der Begriff „Verwandtschaft" in der modernen Ethnosoziologie*. Mainzer Ethnologica 2. Berlin.

Müller, Rudolf Wolfgang ($2$1981) *Geld und Geist*. Francfort and New York.

Münch, Richard (1984) *Die Struktur der Moderne: Grundmuster und differenzielle Gestaltung des institutionellen Aufbaus der modernen Gesellschaften*. Francfort.

Münkler, Marina, Antje Sablotny, and Matthias Standke (eds.) (2015) *Freundschaftszeichen: Gesten, Gaben und Symbole von Freundschaft im Mittelalter*. Heidelberg.

Murnaghan, Sheila (1987) "Penelope's Agnoia: Knowledge and Gender in the Odyssey," in *Rescuing Creusa: New Methodological Approaches to Women in Antiquity*, ed. Marylin Skinner. Lubbock, Tex.: 103–15.

——. (1992) "Maternity and Mortality in Homeric Poetry," *Classical Antiquity* 11/2: 242–64.

Murra, John V. (1962) "Cloth and Its Function in the Inca State," *American Anthropologist* 65: 710–25.

Murray, A. T. and G. E. Dimock (1998) *Homer, Odyssey*. With an English translation. Cambridge and London.

Murray, A. T. and W. F. Wyatt (1999) *Homer, Iliad*. With an English translation. Cambridge and London.

Murray, Caroline and Peter Warren (1976) "Po-ni-ki-jo Among the Dye Plants of Minoan Crete," *Kadmos* 15: 40–60.

Murray, Oswyn (1980) *Early Greece*. Brighton (2nd edn., London 1993).

——. (ed.) (1990) *Sympotica: A Symposium on the Symposium*. Oxford.

——. (1991) "The Social Function of Art in Early Greece," in *New Perspectives in Early Greek Art*, ed. Diana Buitron-Oliver. Hanover and London: 23–30.

Murray, Oswyn and Simon Price (eds.) (1990) *The Greek City from Homer to Alexander*. Oxford.

Mylonas, George E. and Doris Raymond (eds.) (1953) *Studies Presented to David Moore Robinson on his Seventieth Birthday II*. St. Louis, MO.

Nafissi, Mohamed (2005) *Ancient Athens and Modern Ideology. Value, Theory and Evidence in Historical Sciences: Max Weber, Karl Polanyi & Moses I. Finley*. London.

Nagy, Gregory (2002) *Plato's Rhapsody and Homer's Music*. Cambridge, MA and London.

——. (2003) *Homeric Responses*. Austin.

Nagy, Joseph F. (1981) "The Deceptive Gift in Greek Mythology," *Arethusa* 14: 191–204.

Nash, Manning (1968) "Economic Anthropology," *International Encyclopedia of the Social Sciences* 4: 359–65.

Neils, Jenifer (ed.) (1992) *Goddess and Polis: The Panathenaic Festival in Ancient Athens*. Princeton.

Nestle, Wilhelm (1942) "Odysseus: Interpretationen I," *Hermes* 77: 46–139.

Neumann, Manu (1950) *Homerische Wörter*. Basel.

Neumer-Pfau, Wiltrud (1987) "Töten, Trauern, Sterben: Weiblichkeitsbilder in der antiken griechischen Kultur," in *Weiblichkeit und Tod in der Literatur*, ed. Renate Berger and Inge Stephan. Cologne and Vienna: 12–34.

Newton, Rick M. (2015) "Eumaeus Rustles up Dinner," *Classical Journal* 110/3: 257–78.

Niemeyer, Hans Georg (ed.) (1982) *Phönizier im Westen*. Mainz.

——. (1990) "Die phönizischen Niederlassungen im Mittelmeerraum," in his *Die Phönizier im Zeitalter Homers*, ed. Ulrich Gehrig. Mainz: 45–64.

——. (1996) *Semata: Über den Sinn griechischer Standbilder*. Hamburg.

Niethammer, Lutz in collaboration with Dirk van Laak (1989) *Posthistoire: Ist die Geschichte zu Ende?* Reinbek bei Hamburg.

Nilsson, Martin P. (1927) "Das homerische Königtum," in *Sitzungsberichte der preußischen Akademie der Wissenschaften, Philosophisch-Historische Klasse* 7: 25–40.

——. (1967) *Geschichte der griechischen Religion*. 3rd edn. 2 vols. Munich.

Nippel, Wilfried (1982) "Die Heimkehr der Argonauten aus der Südsee: Ökonomische Anthropologie und die Theorie der griechischen Gesellschaft in klassischer Zeit," *Chiron* 12: 1–39.

——. (1988) "Sozialanthropologie und Alte Geschichte," in *Historische Methode*, ed. Christian Meier and Jörn Rüsen. Munich: 300–18.

——. (1990a) *Griechen, Barbaren und ,Wilde': Alte Geschichte und Sozialanthropologie*. Francfort.

——. (1990b) "Prolegomena zu Eduard Meyers *Anthropologie*," in *Leben und Leistung eines Universalhistorikers*, ed. William M. Calder III and Alexander Demandt. Leiden: 311–28.

——. (1991) "Finley und Weber: some Comments and Theses," *Opus* VI–VII: 43–50.

———. (1993) *Max Weber und die Althistorie seiner Zeit: Antrittsvorlesung 30. Juni 1992.* Berlin.

Noonan, John T. Jr. (1984) *Bribes.* New York.

Nosch, Marie-Louise (2000) "Schafherden unter dem Namenspatronat von Potnia und Hermes in Knossos," in *Österreichische Forschungen zur ägäischen Bronzezeit 1998: Akten der Tagung am Institut für Klassische Archäologie der Universität Vienna 2.-3. Mai 1998*, ed. Fritz Blakolmer. Wiener Forschungen zur Archäologie 3. Vienna: 211–15.

———. (2003) "The Women at Work in the Linear B tablets," in *Gender, Cult, and Culture in the Ancient World from Mycenae to Byzantium*, eds. Lena Larsson-Lovèn and Agneta Strömberg. Sävedalen: 12–26.

———. (2006) "More Thoughts on the Mycenaean ta-ra-si-ja System," in *Fiscality in Mycenaean and Near Eastern Archives*, ed. Massimo Perna. Naples: 161–82.

———. (2007) *The Knossos Od Series: An Epigraphical Study.* Vienna.

Nosch, Marie-Louise et al. (2008) "New Research on Bronze Age Textile Production," *Bulletin of the Institute of Classical Studies* 51: 171–74.

Nosch, Marie-Louise, Henriette Koefoed and Eva Andersson Strand (eds.) (2013) *Textile Production and Consumption in the Ancient Near East: Archaeology, Epigraphy, Iconography.* Oxford.

Nybakken, Oscar E. (1945/46) "The Moral Basis of Hospitium Privatum," *Classical Journal* 41: 248–53.

Oakley, John H. and Rebecca Sinos (1993) *The Wedding in Ancient Greece.* Madison.

Oates, Joan (ed.) (1993) *Ancient Trade: New Perspectives.* London.

Oexle, Otto Gerhard (1984) "Memoria und Memorialbild," in *Memoria: Der geschichtliche Zeugniswert des liturgischen Gedenkens im Mittelalter*, ed. Karl Schmid and Joachim Wollasch. Munich: 384–440.

———. (1988) "Otto Gierkes 'Rechtsgeschichte der Deutschen Genossenschaft': Ein Versuch wissenschaftsgeschichtlicher Rekapitulation," in Hammerstein 1988: 193–217.

———. (1994) "Kulturwissenschaftliche Reflexionen über soziale Gruppen in der mittelalterlichen Gesellschaft: Tönnies, Simmel, Durkheim und Max Weber," in Meier 1994: 115–59.

———. (ed.) (1995) *Memoria als Kultur.* Göttingen.

Ogris, W. (1990) "Schenkung," in *Handwörterbuch zur Deutschen Rechtsgeschichte* IV, ed. Adalbert Erler and Ekkehard Kaufmann in collaboration with Ruth Schmidt-Wiegand. Berlin: 1382–84.

Olson, S. D. (2010) *Athenaeus, the Learned Banqueters.* Cambridge and London.

Onians, Richard B. (1989) *The Origins of European Thought about the Body, the Mind, the Soul, the World, Time and Fate.* 3rd edn. Cambridge (1st edn. 1951).

Osborne, Robin (1985a) "The Erection and Mutilation of the *hermai*," *Proceedings of the Cambridge Philological Society* n.s. 31: 47–73.

———. (1985b) *Demos: The Discovery of Classical Attica.* Cambridge.

———. (1987) *Classical Landscape with Figures: The Ancient Greek City and Its Countryside.* London.

——. (1988) "Social and Economic Implications of Leasing of Land and Property in Classical and Hellenistic Greece," *Chiron* 18: 279–323.

——. (1991) "Pride and Prejudice, Sense and Subsistence: Exchange and Society in the Greek City," in Rich and Wallace-Hadrill 1991: 7–17.

——. (1994) "Archaeology, the Salaminioi, and the Politics of Sacred Space in Archaic Attica," in Alcock and Osborne 1994: 143–60.

——. (1998) "Early Greek Colonization? The Nature of Greek Settlement in the West," in Fisher and van Wees 1998: 251–269.

——. (2004) "Homer's Society," in Fowler 2004: 206–19.

O'Sullivan, James N. (1990) "Nature and Culture in Odyssey 9?" *Symbolae Osloenses* 65: 7–17.

Page, Denys L. (1955) *The Homeric Odyssey*. Oxford.

Pallas, Peter S. (1776) *Sammlungen historischer Nachrichten über die Mongolischen Völkerschaften*. St. Petersburg (rpt. 1980).

Panagl, Otto (1970) "Apollons Pythonkampf und die delphische Orakelgründung im Spiegel antiker Mythenkritik," *Kairos* 12: 31–41.

Pantelia, Maria C. (1993) "Spinning and Weaving: Ideas of Domestic Order in Homer," *American Journal of Philology* 114: 493–501.

Papadopoulos, John K. and Gary Urton (eds.) (2012) *The Construction of Value in the Ancient World*. Los Angeles.

Papadopoulos, Thanasis J. (1987) "Tombs and Burial Customs in Late Age Epirus," in Laffineur 1987: 137–42.

Papadopoulou-Belmehdi, Ioanna (1994) *Le chant de Pénélope: Poétique du tissage féminin dans l'Odyssée*. Paris.

Papalexandrou, Nassos (2005) *The Visual Poetics of Power: Warriors, Youth, and Tripods in Early Greece*. Lanham.

Pappenheim, Max (1933) "Über die Rechtsnatur der altgermanischen Schenkung," *Zeitschrift der Savigny-Stiftung für Rechtsgeschichte, Germanistische Abteilung* 53: 35–88.

Parke, Herbert W. and Donald E. W. Wormell (1956) *The Delphic Oracle. I: The History*. Oxford.

Parker, Victor (1996) *Untersuchungen zum Lelantischen Krieg und verwandten Problemen der frühgriechischen Geschichte*. Stuttgart.

Patzek, Barbara (1990) "Mündliche Dichtung als historisches Zeugnis: Die 'homerische Frage' in heutiger Sicht," *Historische Zeitschrift* 250: 529–48.

——. (1992) *Homer und Mykene: Mündliche Dichtung und Geschichtsschreibung*. Munich.

Paulinyi, Akos (1990) "Die Entwicklung der Stoffformungstechnik als Periodisierungskriterium der Technikgeschichte," *Technikgeschichte* 57: 299–314.

Payen, Pascal and Évelyne Scheid-Tissinier (eds.) (2012) *Anthropologie de l'Antiquité: Anciens objects, nouvelles approaches*. Turnhout.

Pedrick, Victoria (1988) "The Hospitality of Noble Women in the Odyssey," *Helios* n.s. 15: 85–101.

Peifer, Egon (1987) *Eidola und andere mit dem Sterben verbundene Flügelwesen in der attischen Vasenmalerei in spätarchaischer und klassischer Zeit*. Bern.

Pekridou-Gorecki, Anastasia (1989) *Mode im antiken Griechenland: Textile Fertigung und Kleidung.* Munich.

Pernice, Herbert (1882) *Zur Lehre von der Insinuation der Schenkungen.* Diss. Greifswald.

Perysinakis, Ioannis (1986) "Hesiod's Treatment of Wealth," *Métis* 1/1: 97-119.

Petropoulou, Angeliki (1985) *Beiträge zur Wirtschafts- und Gesellschaftsgeschichte Kretas in hellenistischer Zeit.* Francfort.

Petruso, Karl M. (1986) "Wool-Evaluation at Knossos and Nuzi," *Kadmos* 25: 26-37.

Pettegrew, David K. (2016) *The Isthmus of Corinth: Crossroads of the Mediterranean World.* Ann Arbor.

Peukert, Detlev J. K. (1989) *Max Webers Diagnose der Moderne.* Göttingen.

Pflüger, H. H. (1942) "Die Gerichtsszene auf dem Schilde des Achilleus," *Hermes* 77: 140-48.

Philippson, Alfred (1951) *Die griechischen Landschaften: Eine Landeskunde* 1/2, edn. in collaboration with Herbert Lehmann, with an appendix by Ernst Kirsten: "Beiträge zur historischen Landeskunde des östlichen Mittelgriechenlands und Euboeas," Francfort.

Phillipson, Coleman (1911) *International Law and Customs of Ancient Greece and Rome I and II.* London.

Pielhoff, Stephen (2007) "Stifter und Anstifter: Vermittler zwischen ‚Zivilgesellschaft' Kommune und Staat im Kaiserreich," *Geschichte und Gesellschaft* 33/1: 20-45.

Pindar 1992 (Greek and German) *Siegeslieder,* ed. and trans. with an introduction by Dieter Bremer. Munich.

Pirenne-Delforge, Vinciane (1996) "Les Charites à Athènes et dans l'île de Cos," *Kernos* 9: 195-214.

Pitt-Rivers, Julian A. (1977) *The Fate of Shechem or the Politics of Sex: Essays in the Anthropology of the Mediterranean.* Cambridge.

Plumpe, Werner (2007) "Die Geburt des 'Homo oeconomicus': Historische Überlegungen zur Entstehung und Bedeutung des Handlungsmodells der modernen Wirtschaft," in Reinhard and Stagl 2007: 319-52.

——. (2009) "Ökonomisches Denken und wirtschaftliche Entwicklung: Zum Zusammenhang von Wirtschaftsgeschichte und historischer Semantik der Ökonomie," *Jahrbuch für Wirtschaftsgeschichte/Economic History Yearbook* 1: 27-52.

Plutarchus 1959. *Lives.* I: *Theseus and Romulus; Lycurgus and Numa; Solon and Publicola,* trans. Bernadotte Perrin. London.

Podlecki, A. J. (1961) "Guest-Gifts and Nobodies in the Odyssey 9," *Phoenix* 15: 125-33.

Pöhlmann, Egbert (1990) "Zur Überlieferung griechischer Literatur vom 8. zum 4. Jh.," in Kullmann and Reichel 1990: 11-30.

Polanyi, Karl (1935) "The Essence of Fascism," *Christianity and the Social Revolution,* eds. John D. Lewis, Karl Polanyi and Donald Kitchin. London 1935.

——. ([1944] 2001) *The Great Transformation: The Political and Economic Origins of Our Time.* Foreword by Joseph E. Stiglitz. With a new introduction by Fred Block. Boston.

———. ([1947] 1968), "Our Obsolete Market Mentality," in Polanyi and Dalton 1968: 59–77.

———. (1957a) "The Economy as Instituted Process," in Polanyi et al. 1957: 243–70 = Polanyi and Dalton 1968: 139–74.

———. (1957b) "Aristotle Discovers the Economy," in Polanyi et al. 1957: 64–94.

———. ([1963] 1968), "Ports of Trade in Early Societies," in Polanyi and Dalton 1968: 238–60.

———. (1968) *Primitive, Archaic and Modern Economies: Essays of Karl Polanyi*, ed. George Dalton. Garden City, NY. 1968.

Polanyi, Karl, Conrad M. Arensberg and Harry W. Pearson (eds.) (1957) *Trade and Market in the Early Empires: Economies in History and Theory*. Glencoe/Illinois.

Polanyi-Levitt, Kari (ed.) (1990) *The Life and Work of Karl Polanyi: A Celebration*. Montréal and New York.

Polignac, François de (1984) *La naissance de la cité grecque: Cultes, espace et sociétés VIIIe–VIIe siècles avant J.-C.* Paris = de Polignac 1995.

———. (1994) "Mediation, Competition, and Sovereignty: The Evolution of Rural Sanctuaries in Geometric Greece," in Alcock and Osborne 1994: 3–18.

———. (1995) *Cults, Territory, and the Origins of the Greek City-State*, trans. Janet Lloyd. Chicago.

———. (1996) "Offrandes, mémoire et compétition ritualisée dans les sanctuaires grecs à l'époque géometrique," in *Religion and Power in the Ancient Greek World*, ed. Pontus Hellström. Boreas 24. Uppsala: 59–66.

Post, Albert Hermann (1895) *Grundriss der ethnologischen Jurisprudenz II*. Oldenburg and Leipzig.

Pötscher, Walter (1960) "Moira, Themis und *time* im homerischen Denken," *Wiener Studien* 73: 5–39.

Prellwitz, Walther (1905) *Etymologisches Wörterbuch der griechischen Sprache*. 2nd edn. Göttingen.

Prendergast, Guy L. (1962) *A Complete Concordance to the Iliad of Homer*. Rev. and enlarged by Benedetto Marzullo. Hildesheim.

Price, Simon (1986) "Delphi and Divination," in Easterling and Muir 1986: 128–54.

Pritchett, William K. (1985) *Studies in Greek Topography V.* Berkeley.

Prodi, Paolo (1997) *Das Sakrament der Herrschaft: Der politische Eid in der Verfassungsgeschichte des Okzidents*. Schriften des Italienisch-Deutschen Historischen Instituts in Trient 11. Berlin.

Puhvel, Jan (1958) "Helladic Kingship and the Gods," in *Minoica: Festschrift für Johannes Sundvall*, ed. Ernst Grumach. Berlin: 327–33.

Pullen, Daniel J. (2013) "Crafts, Specialists, and Markets in Mycenaean Greece: Exchanging the Myenaean Economy," *American Journal of Archaeology* 117/3: 437–45.

Purcell, Nicholas (1990) "Mobility and the Polis," in Murray and Price 1990: 29–58.

Purves, Alex (ed.) (2018) *Touch and the Ancient Senses*. London and New York.

Quijano, Anibal (1993) "Modernity, Identity and Utopia in Latin America," *Boundary 2*. Vol 20/3: 140–55.

Qviller, Bjørn (1981) "The Dynamics of the Homeric Society," *Symbolae Osloenses* 56: 109–55.

Raaflaub, Kurt (1991) "Homer und die Geschichte des 8. Jhs. v. Chr." in Latacz 1991: 205–56.

———. (ed.) (1993) *Die Anfänge des politischen Denkens in der Antike: Die nahöstlichen Kulturen und die Griechen*. Munich.

———. (1997) "Politics and Interstate Relations in the World of Early Greek *Poleis*: Homer and Beyond," *Antichthon* 31: 1–27.

———. (1998) "A Historian's Headache: How to Read 'Homeric Society'?" in Fisher and van Wees 1998: 169–93.

Raaflaub, Kurt and Hans van Wees (eds.) (2009) *A Companion to Archaic Greece*. Malden, MA and Oxford.

Racine, Luc (1987) "Les formes élémentaires de la reciprocité," *L'Homme* 99: 97–118.

Rackham, H. (1952) *Aristotle, The Athenean Constitution*. With an English translation. London and Cambridge, MA.

———. ([1934] 1990) *Aristotle, The Nicomachean Ethics*. With an English translation. London and Cambridge, MA.

Rackham, Oliver (1990) "Ancient Landscapes," in Murray and Price 1990: 85–111.

Ready, Jonathan L. (2011) *Character, Narrator, and Simile in the Iliad*. Cambridge.

Rebenich, Stefan (2012) "Monarchie," *Reallexikon für Antike und Christentum* 24: 1112–1196.

Recktenwald, Horst C. (1985) *Ethik, Wirtschaft und Staat: Adam Smiths Politische Ökonomie heute*. Darmstadt.

Reden, Sitta von (1995) *Exchange in Ancient Greece*. London.

Redfield, James E. (1983) "The Economic Man," in *Approaches to Homer*, ed. Cynthia W. Shelmerdine. Austin: 218–47.

Reece, Steve (1993) *The Stranger's Welcome: Oral Theory and the Aesthetics of the Homeric Hospitality Scenes*. Ann Arbor.

Reed, C. M. (1984) "Maritime Traders in the Archaic Greek World," *Ancient World* 10: 31–44.

———. (2003) *Maritime Traders in the Ancient Greek World*. Cambridge.

Reese, David S. (1987) "Palaikastro Shells and Bronze Age Purple-Dye Production in the Mediterranean Basin," *The Annual of the British School at Athens* 82: 201–6.

Rehak, Paul (ed.) (1995) *The Role of the Ruler in the Prehistoric Aegean*, Aegaeum II, Lüttich.

Rehberg, Karl-Siegbert (1986) "Kultur versus Gesellschaft: Anmerkungen zu einer Streitfrage in der deutschen Soziologie," in *Kultur und Gesellschaft: René König, dem Begründer der Sonderhefte, zum 80. Geburtstag gewidmet*, ed. Friedhelm Neidhardt, Mario Rainer Lepsius, and Johannes Weiss. Opladen: 92–117.

Rehbinder, Manfred (ed.) (2012) *Vom homo oeconomicus zum homo reciprocans? Auf der Suche nach einem neuen Menschenbild als Erklärungsmuster für Recht, Wirtschaft und Kultur*. Bern.

Reiner, Eugen (1938) *Die rituelle Totenklage der Griechen*. Tübinger Beiträge zur Altertumswissenschaft 30. Stuttgart and Berlin.

Reinhard, Wolfgang (1999) *Geschichte der Staatsgewalt. Eine vergleichende Verfassungsgeschichte Europas von den Anfängen bis zur Gegenwart*. Munich.

Reinhard, Wolfgang and Justin Stagl (eds.) (2007) *Menschen und Märkte: Studien zur historischen Wirtschaftsanthropologie*. Vienna.

Reinhold, Meyer (1970) *History of Purple as a Status Symbol in Antiquity*. Collection Latomus 116. Brüssel.

Reisch, R. (1905) "Dreifuß," in *Realencyclopädie der classischen Altertumswissenschaften* 5/2: 1669–96.

Renfrew, Colin (1975) "Trade as Action at a Distance: Questions of Integration and Communication," in *Ancient Civilization and Trade*, ed. Jeremy A. Sabloff and C.C. Lamberg-Karlovsky. Albuquerque: 3–59.

——. (1986) "Introduction: Peer-Polity Interaction and Socio-Political Change," Renfrew and Cherry 1986: 1–18.

Renfrew, Colin and Stephen Shennan (eds.) (1982) *Ranking, Resource and Exchange: Aspects of the Archaeology of Early European Society*. Cambridge.

Renfrew, Colin and John F. Cherry (eds.) (1986) *Peer Polity Interaction and Socio-Political Change*. Cambridge.

Rengakos, Antonios and Bernhard Zimmermann (eds.) (2011) *Homer Handbuch: Leben—Werk—Wirkung*. Stuttgart and Weimar: 257–78.

Reuthner, Rosa (2006) *Wer webte Athenes Gewänder? Die Arbeit von Frauen im antiken Griechenland*. Francfort and New York.

Rhodes, Peter J. (1984) *Aristotle, the Athenean Constitution*. Translated with introduction and notes. Harmondsworth.

Rich, John and Andrew Wallace-Hadrill (eds.) (1991) *The City and the Country in the Ancient World*. London.

Rich, John and Graham Shipley (eds.) (1993) *War and Society in the Greek World*. London and New York.

Richter, Gisela M. A. (1966) *The Furniture of the Greeks, Etruscans, and Romans*. London.

Richter, Will (1968) *Die Landwirtschaft im Homerischen Zeitalter*. Archaeologia Homerica II/H. Göttingen.

Ridgway, David (1990) "The First Western Greeks and Their Neighbours, 1935–1985," in *Greek Colonists and Native Populations: Proceedings of the First Australian Congress of Classical Archaeology held in honour of Emeritus Professor A. D. Trendall*, ed. Jean-Paul Descoeudres. Canberra: 61–72.

——. (1992) *The First Western Greeks*. Cambridge.

——. (2000) "The First Western Greeks Revisited," in his *Ancient Italy in Its Mediterranean Setting: Studies in Honour of Ellen MacNamara*. London: 179–91.

——. (2006) "Aspects of the Italian Connection," Deger-Jalkotzy and Lemos 2006: 299–313.

Riedinger, Jean-Claude (1976) "Remarques sur la TIMH chez Homère," *Revue des études grecques* 89: 244–64.

——. (1980) "Les deux αἰδώς chez Homère," *Revue de Philologie* 54: 62–79.

Riegl, Alois (1893) *Stilfragen: Grundlagen zu einer Geschichte der Ornamentik*. Berlin.

Rieu, E. V. (ed.) (2003) *Homerus, The Iliad*, trans. E. V. Rieu. With an introduction and notes by Peter Jones. London.

Rieu, E. V. (ed.) (2003) *Homerus, The Odyssey*, trans. E. V. Rieu, rev. trans. D. C. H. Rieu with an introduction by Peter Jones. London.

Rihll, Tracey (1993) "War, Slavery, and Settlement in Early Greece," in Rich and Shipley 1993: 77-107.

Rihll, Tracey H. and Andrew G. Wilson (1991) "Modelling Settlement Structures in Ancient Greece: New Approaches to the Polis," in Rich and Wallace-Hadrill 1991: 59-95.

Robkin, Ann L. H. (1979) "The Agricultural Year, the Commodity SA and the Linen Industry of Mycenaean Pylos," *American Journal of Archaeology* 85: 469-74.

Roebuk, Carl (ed.) (1969) *The Muses at Work: Art, Crafts and Professions in Ancient Greece and Rome*. Cambridge and London.

Rohweder, Christine (1998) *Macht und Gedeihen: Eine politische Interpretation der Hiketiden des Aischylos*. Francfort.

Rolley, Claude (1977) *Les trépieds à cuve clouée*. Fouilles de Delphes V/3. Paris.

Römisches Recht (1987). On basis of the work of Paul Jörs, Wolfgang Kunkel, and Leopold Wenger. 4th edn. rev. Heinrich Hionsell, Theo Meyer-Maly, and Walter Selb. Berlin.

Röpke, Jochen (1969) "Nationalökonomie und Ethnologie: Die ökonomische Theorie primitiver Gesellschaften in kritischer Betrachtung," *Sociologus* N.F. 19: 101-34.

Rose, A. (1985) "Clothing Imagery in Apollonius' Argonautica," *Quaderni Urbinati di Cultura Classica* 50: 29-44.

Rose, Peter (2012) *Class in Archaic Greece*. Cambridge.

Rosen, Ralph M. (1989) "Poetry and Sailing in Hesiod's *Works and Days*," *Classical Antiquity* 8: 99-113.

Rösler, Wolfgang (1980) "Die Entdeckung der Fiktionalität in der Antike," *Poetica* 12: 293-319.

——. (1991) "Die Sieben Weisen," in *Weisheit: Archäologie der literarischen Kommunikation III*, ed. Aleida Assmann. Munich: 357-65.

Rougement, Françoise (2004) "The administration of Mycenaean sheep-rearing (flocks, shepherds, "collectors")," in Santillo-Frizell 2004: 24-34.

——. (2007) "Flax and Linen Textiles in the Mycenaean Palatial Economy," in Gillis and Nosch 2007: 46-63.

——. (2009) *Contrôle économique et administration à l'époque des palais mycéniens (fin du IIe milléniaire av. J.-C.)*. Bibliothèque des Écoles françaises d'Athènes et de Rome 332. Athènes.

Rouillard, Pierre (ed.) (2005) *Autour de Polanyi. Vocabulaires, théories et modalités des échanges. Nanterre, 12-14 juin 2004*. Colloques de la Maison René-Ginouvès. Paris.

Rowlands, Michael (1987) "Centre and Periphery: A Review of a Concept," in Rowlands, Larsen, and Kristiansen 1987: 1-11.

Rowlands, Michael, Mogens Larsen and Kristian Kristiansen (eds.) (1987) *Centre and Periphery in the Ancient World*. Cambridge.

Rudolph, Kelli C. (ed.) (2018) *Taste and the Ancient Senses*. London and New York.

Ruffing, Kai (2019) "Nach Westen und dann immer geradeaus ... Zum Seidenhandel üer Palmyra in das Imperium Romanum," in Wagner-Hasel and Nosch 2019: 317–30.

Runciman, W. G. (1982) "Origins of the States: The Case of Archaic Greece," *Comparative Studies in Society and History* 24: 351–77.

Runnels, Curtis and Tjeerd van Andel (1988) "Trade and the Origins of Agriculture in the Eastern Mediterranean," *Journal of the Mediterranean Archaeology* 1/1: 83–109.

Rüstow, Alexander (1952) *Ortsbestimmung und Gegenwart: Eine universalhistorische Kulturkritik.* II: *Weg der Freiheit.* Zürich.

Ruzé, Françoise (1989) "Basileis, Tyrans et Magistrats," *Métis* 4/2: 211–23.

Ryder, Michael L. (1982) "Sheep: Hilzheimer 45 Years On," *Antiquity* 56: 15–23.

——. (1983) *Sheep and Men.* London.

——. (1991) "The Last Word on the Golden Fleece Legend," *Oxford Journal of Archaeology* 10/1: 57–60.

Sahlins, Marshall (1974) "On the Sociology of Primitive Exchange," in his *Stone Age Economics.* London: 185–275.

——. (1984) "The Spirit of the Gift," in his *Stone Age Economics.* 3rd edn. London: 149–83.

Sakellariou, Michael B. (1989) *The Polis-State: Definition and Origin.* Athen.

Sakowski, Anja (1997) *Darstellungen von Dreifußkesseln in der griechischen Kunst bis zum Beginn der Klassischen Zeit.* Francfort.

Sallares, Robert (1998) "Getreide", in *Der Neue Pauly* 4: column 1029–38.

Salmen, Walter (1980) "Musizierende Sirenen," in Krinzinger et al. 1980: 293–400.

Salmon, J. B. (1984) *Wealthy Corinth: A History of the City to 338 B.C.* Oxford.

Salomon, Max (1937) *Der Begriff der Gerechtigkeit bei Aristoteles: Nebst einem Anhang über den Begriff des Tauschgeschäftes.* Leiden.

Samter, Ernst (1911) *Geburt, Hochzeit und Tod: Beiträge zur vergleichenden Volkskunde.* Leipzig and Berlin.

Sanchez, Pierre (2001) *L'Amphictionie des Pyles et de Delphes: recherches sur son rôle historique, des origines au IIe siècle de notre ère.* Historia Einzelschriften 148. Stuttgart.

Sancisi-Weerdenburg, Helen (ed.) (2000) *Peisistratos and the Tyranny: A Reappraisal of Evidence.* Amsterdam.

——. (2000) "The Tyranny of Peisistratos," in Sancisi-Weerdenburg 2000: 1–15.

Sandel, Michael (2012) *What Money Can't Buy: The Moral Limits of Markets.* London.

Santillo-Frizell, Barbro (ed.) (2004) *Pecus: Man and Animal in Antiquity.* Proceedings of a Conference at the Swedish Institute in Rome, September 9–12. Rome.

——. (2009) *Arkadien: Mythos und Wirklichkeit,* trans. Ylva Eriksson-Kuchenbuch. Cologne.

Sarasin, Philipp (1990) *Die Stadt der Bürger: Struktureller Wandel und bürgerliche Lebenswelt, Basel 1870–1890.* Basel and Francfort.

Sartre, Maurice (1979) "Aspects économique et aspects religieux de la frontière dans les cités grecques," *Ktema* 4: 313–24.

Satlow, Michael L. (ed.) (2013) *The Gift in Antiquity*. Oxford.

Schadewaldt, Wolfgang (1931) "Begriff und Wesen der antiken Klassik," in *Das Problem des Klassischen und die Antike: Acht Vorträge gehalten auf der Fachtagung der Klassischen Altertumswissenschaft zu Naumburg 1930*, ed. Werner Jaeger. Leipzig and Berlin: 15-32.

——. (1959) "Kleiderdinge: Zur Analyse der Odyssee," *Hermes* 87: 13-26. Rpt. in his *Hellas und Hesperien: Gesammelte Schriften zur Antike und zur Neueren Literatur*. 1970: 79-93.

Schäfer, G. (1944) "Zur Geschichte des Flachsanbaues," *Ciba-Rundschau* 62: 2262-64.

Schefold, Bertram (1988) "Karl Bücher und der Historismus in der Deutschen Nationalökonomie," Hammerstein 1988: 239-68.

Scheid, Evelyne (1979) "Il matrimonio omerico," *Dialoghi di Archeologia* n.s. 1: 60-73.

Scheid, John and Jesper Svenbro (1994 [English version 2001]) *Le métier de Zeus: Mythe du tissage et du tissu dans le monde gréco-romain*. Paris.

——. (2014) *La tortue de la lyre. Dans l'átelier du mythe antique*. Paris.

Scheid-Tissinier, Evelyne (1994) *Les usages du don chez Homère: Vocabulaire et pratiques*. Nancy.

——. (2005) "'Le monde d'Ulysse' de M. I. Finley. Le vocabulaire et les pratiques," in Rouillard 2005: 217-28.

——. (2015) "Eurykléia, une vie, un nom," *Pallas* 99: 21-29.

Schein, Seth L. (1970) "Odysseus and Polyphemus in the Odyssey," *Greek, Roman and Byzantine Studies* 11: 73-83.

Schlesier, Renate (1994) *Kulte, Mythen und Gelehrte: Anthropologie der Antike seit 1800*. Francfort.

Schlicht, Ekkehart (1976) *Einführung in die Verteilungstheorie*. Hamburg.

Schmidt, Leopold (1882) *Ethik der Alten Griechen II*. Berlin.

Schmidt, Manfred (1979) "Hom. μῆλα und die antiken Erklärungen," *Glotta* 57: 174-82.

——. (1982) "ἀγέραστος, γεραίρω, γεραρός, γεράσμιος, γέρας," in *Lexikon des Frühgriechischen Epos* 10: 133-36.

Schmidt-Colinet, Andreas (ed.) (1995) *Palmyra: Kulturbegegnung im Grenzbereich*. Mainz.

——. (2019) "Bauornamentik und Textilmuster in Palmyra," in Wagner-Hasel and Nosch 2019: 477-85.

Schmitt, Tassilo (2009) "Kein König im Palast: Heterodoxe Überlegungen zur politischen und sozialen Ordnung in der mykenischen Zeit," *Historische Zeitschrift* 288: 281-346.

Schmitt-Pantel, Pauline (1990) *Marcel Mauss et les historiens de l'antiquité: Beitrag zur Konferenz 'The Gift and Its Transformations'; National Humanities Center, Research Triangle Park, North Carolina, November 1-3*. Unpublished manuscript.

——. (ed.) (1991) *Histoire des femmes en occident. I: L'Antiquité*. Rome.

——. (1992) *La cité au banquet : Histoire des repas publics dans les cités grecques*. Paris and Rome (rpt. 2011).

——. (2019) "Der Gürtel. Körperschmuck, Statussymbol und Geschlechtsmerkmal," in Wagner-Hasel and Nosch 2019: 333–55.

Schmölders, Günter (1988) "Historische Schule," in *Geschichte der Nationalökonomie*, ed. Otmar Issing. 2nd edn. Munich: 109–21.

Schmoller, Gustav von (1900) *Grundriss der Allgemeinen Theorie der Volkswirtschaftslehre* I. Leipzig.

Schneider, Helmuth (1989) *Das griechische Technikverständnis: Von den Epen Homers bis zu den Anfängen der technologischen Fachliteratur*. Darmstadt.

——. (1990) "Die Bücher-Meyer Kontroverse," in Calder III and Demandt 1990: 417–45.

——. (1992) *Einführung in die antike Technikgeschichte*. Darmstadt.

Schortman, E. M. (1989) "Interregional Interaction in Prehistory: The Need of a New Perspective," *American Antiquity* 54/1: 52–65.

Schulz, Fabian (2011) *Die homerischen Räte und die spartanische Gerusie*. Düsseldorf.

Schurtz, Heinrich (1898) *Grundriss der Entstehungsgeschichte des Geldes*. Weimar.

Schwabl, Hans (1982) "Traditionelle Gestaltung, Motivwiederholung und Mimesis im homerischen Epos," *Wiener Studien* 16: 13–33.

Schwarzenberg, Erkinger (1966) *Die Grazien*. Bonn.

Schwendemann, K. (1921) "Der Dreifuß," *Jahrbuch des Archäologischen Instituts* 36: 98–185.

Scott, John A. (1938/39) "Odysseus and the Gifts from the Phaeacians," *Classical Journal* 34: 102–93.

Scott, Mary (1981) "Some Greek Terms in Homer Suggesting Non-Competitive Attitudes," *Acta Classica* 24: 1–15.

——. (1982) "Philos, Philotes and Xenia," *Acta Classica* 25: 1–19.

——. (1983) "Charis in Homer and the Homeric Hymns," *Acta Classica* 26: 1–13.

——. (2014) *Delphi and Olympia: The Spatial Politic of Panhellenism in Archaic and Classical Greece*. 2nd edn. Cambridge.

Scully, Stephen (1990/1994) *Homer and the Sacred City*. Ithaca and London.

Seaford, Richard A. S. (1994) *Reciprocity and Ritual: Homer and Tragedy in the Developing City State*. London and Oxford.

——. (2004) *Money and the Early Greek Mind: Homer, Philosophy, Tragedy*. Cambridge.

Sealey, Raphael (1983) "How Citizenship and the City Began in Athens," *American Journal of Ancient History* 8: 97–129.

Seelentag, Gunnar (2015) *Das archaische Kreta. Institutionalisierung im frühen Griechenland*. Berlin.

Semper, Gottfried (1878) *Die Textilkunst*. 2nd edn. Munich.

Semple, Ellen C. (1922) "The Influence of Geographic Conditions upon Ancient Mediterranean Stock-Raising," *Annuals of the Association of American Geographers* 12: 3–38.

——. (1931) *The Geography of the Mediterranean Region: Its Relation to Ancient History*. New York.

Sergent, B. (1978) "Sur les frontières de l'Élide aux hautes époques," *Revue des Etudes Anciennes* 80: 16–36.

Service, Elman R. (1975) *Origins of the State and Civilization: The Process of Cultural Evolution*. New York.

Settis, Salvatore (2005) *Die Zukunft des Klassischen. Eine Idee im Wandel der Zeiten*. Trans. Friederike Hausmann. Berlin.

Seybold, Klaus and Jürgen von Ungern-Sternberg (1993) "Amos und Hesiod: Aspekte eines Vergleichs," in Raaflaub 1993: 215–39.

Shapiro, H. Alan (1980) "Jason's Cloak," *Transactions of the American Philological Association* 110: 263–86.

——. (1989) *Art and Cult under the Tyrants in Athens*. London.

Shaw, Brent D. and Richard Saller (1981) 'Editor's introduction', in Finley 1981: ix–xxvi.

Shaw, Maria C. and Anne P. Chapin (eds.) (2016) *Woven Threads: Patterned Textiles of the Aegean Bronze Age*. Oxford and Philadelphia.

Shipp, George P. (1979) *Modern Greek Evidence for the Ancient Greek Vocabulary*. Sydney.

Siebert, Wolfgang (1938) "Schenkung," in *Rechtsvergleichendes Handwörterbuch für das Zivil- und Handelsrecht des In- und Auslandes VI*, ed. Franz Schlegelberger. Berlin: 144–59.

Siemons, Mark (1993) *Schöne Neue Gegenwelt: Über Kultur, Moral und andere Marketingstrategien*. Francfort and New York.

Siewert, Peter (1982) *Die Trittyen Attikas und die Heeresreform des Kleisthenes*. Munich.

Silber, Ilana F. (2002) "Echoes of sacrifice? Repertoires of Giving in the Great Religions," in *Sacrifice in Religious Experience*, ed. Albert I. Baumgarten. Leiden, Boston and Cologne: 291–312.

Silver, Morris (1991) "The Commodity Composition of Trade in the Argonautic Myth," in his *Ancient Economy in Mythology: East and West*. Savage, MD: 241–81.

Simmel, Georg (1897) "Comment les formes sociales se maintiennent," *L'Année sociologique* 1: 71–109.

——. (1898) "Die Selbsterhaltung der socialen Gruppe. Sociologische Studie," *Schmollers Jahrbuch für Gesetzgebung, Verwaltung und Volkswirtschaft im Deutschen Reich* 22/1: 235–86.

——. (1911) "Soziologie der Geselligkeit," in his *Verhandlungen des Ersten Deutschen Soziologentages vom 19.-22. Oktober 1910 in Frankfurt a. M.: Reden und Vorträge*. Tübingen.

——. (1989) *Philosophie des Geldes*. Francfort (rpt. 1901).

Simon, Erika (1985) *Die Götter der Griechen*. Darmstadt.

Simon, Erika and Max Hirmer (1976, ²1981) *Die griechischen Vasen*. Munich.

Singer, Peter (2015) *The Most Good You Can Do: How Effective Altruism Is Changing Ideas about Living Ethically*. New Haven et al.

Siurla-Theodoridou, Vasiliki (1989) *Die Familie in der griechischen Kunst und Literatur des 8. bis 6. Jahrhunderts v. Chr.* Munich.

Skydsgaard, Jens Erik (1974) "Transhumance in Ancient Italy," *Analecta Romana Instituti Danici* 7: 7–36.

——. (1988) "Transhumance in Ancient Greece," in Whittaker 1988: 75–86.

Skydsgaard, Jens Erik and Signe Isager (1992) *Ancient Greek Agriculture*. London and New York.

Slanicka, Simona (2002) *Krieg der Zeichen: Die visuelle Politik Johanns ohne Furcht und der armagnakisch-burgundische Bürgerkrieg*. Göttingen.

Slawisch, Anja (ed.) (2013) *Handels- und Finanzgebaren in der Ägäis im 5. Jh. v. Chr.* Istanbul.

Smith, C. F. (1977) *Thucydides, History of the Peloponnesian War*. With an English translation. Vol. III. London and Cambridge.

Smith, Jonathan (1982) *Imagining Religion*. Chicago.

Smith, Thyrza (1987) *Mycenaean Trade and Interaction in the West Central Mediterranean 1600-1000 B.C.* Oxford.

Snell, Bruno ([1938] 41971) *Leben und Meinungen der Sieben Weisen*. Munich.

Snodgrass, Anthony M. (1974) "An Historical Homeric Society?" *Journal of Hellenic Society* 94: 114-25.

———. (1982) "Les origines du culte des Heros dans la Grèce antique," in Gnoli and Vernant 1982: 107-19.

———. (1983) "Heavy Freight in Archaic Greece," in Garnsey, Hopkins and Whittaker 1983: 16-26.

———. (1986) "Interaction by Design: The Greek City State," in Renfrew and Cherry 1986: 47-58.

———. (1987) *An Archaeology of Greece: The Present State and Future Scope of a Discipline*. Berkeley.

———. (1989/90) "The Economics of Dedication," in Bartoloni 1990: 287-94.

———. (1991) "Archaeology and the Greek City," in Rich and Wallace-Hadrill 1991: 1-23.

Snoy, Peter (1993) "Alpwirtschaft im Hindukusch und Karakorum," in *Neue Forschungen im Himalaya*, ed. Ulrich Schweinfuhrt. Stuttgart: 49-73.

Snyder, Jane M. (1980/81) "The Web of Song: Weaving Imagery in Homer and the Lyrik Poets," *Classical Journal* 76: 193-96.

———. (1989) *Women and the Lyre: Women Writers in Classical Greece and Rome*. Illinois.

Sobrevilla, David (1971) *Der Ursprung des Kulturbegriffs, der Kulturphilosophie und der Kulturkritik: Eine Studie über deren Entstehung und deren Voraussetzung*. Dissertation. Tübingen.

Solmsen, Friedrich (1954) "The 'Gift' of Speech in Homer and Hesiod," *Transactions of the American Philological Association* 85: 1-15.

Sojc, Natascha (2005) *Trauer auf attischen Grabreliefs: Frauendarstellungen zwischen Ideal und Wirklichkeit*. Berlin.

Somló, Felix (1909) *Der Güterverkehr in der Urgesellschaft*. Brüssel and Leipzig.

Sommer, Michael (2004) "Die Peripherie als Zentrum: Die Phöniker und der interkontinentale Fernhandel," in *Commerce and Monetary Systems in the Ancient World: Means of Transmission and Cultural Interaction; Proceedings of the Fifth Annual Symposium of the Assyrian and Babylonian Intellectual Heritage Project Held in Innsbruck, Austria, October 3rd-8th 2002*, ed. Robert Rollinger and Christoph Ulf. Melammu Symposia V. Stuttgart: 233-41.

Sommerstein, Alan H. and Isabelle C. Torrance (2014) *Oaths and Swearing in Ancient Greece*. Berlin et al.

Sontheimer, Kurt (1978) *Antidemokratisches Denken in der Weimarer Republik*. Munich.

Sorge, Christoph (2012) "Die Schenkung im Bürgerlichen Recht: Gabe oder Vergeltung? Eine rechtshistorische Untersuchung über den Einfluss von Reziprozitätsbeziehungen auf das Schenkungsrecht des BGB," in *Vom homo oeconomicus zum homo reciprocans: Auf der Suche nach einem neuen Menschenbild als Erklärungsmuster für Recht, Wirtschaft und Kultur*, ed. Manfred Rehbinder. Bern: 145–82.

——. (2016) "Die rechtshistorischen Wurzeln des Wirtschaftsmenschen: Grabungen in der Ideengeschichte von Descartes bis Bentham," in *Der homo oeconomcus in der Rechtsanwendung*, ed. Andreas Dieckmann and Christoph Sorge. Tübingen: 39–122.

Sourvinou-Inwood, Christiane (1983) "A Trauma in Flux: Death in the 8th Century and After," in Hägg 1983: 33–48.

——. (1991) *'Reading' Greek Culture: Texts and Images, Rituals and Myths*. London.

——. (1993) "Early Sanctuaries: The Eighth Century and Rituals Space: Fragments of a Discourse," in Marinatos and Hägg 1993: 1–17.

——. (1995) *Reading Greek Death: To the End of the Classical Period*. Oxford.

Spahn, Peter (1998) 'Die Steuer der Peisistratiden—*idion, koinon* oder *hieron?*' in François de Polignac and Pauline Schmitt Pantel (eds.) *Public et privé en Grèce ancienne: lieux, conduites, pratiques. Ktèma* 23: 197–206.

Spantidaki, Stella (2016), *Textile Production in Classical Athens*. Oxford and Philadelphia.

Späth, Späth and Beate Wagner-Hasel (eds.) (2000) *Frauenwelten in der Antike*. Stuttgart and Weimar.

Speyer, W. (1983) "Gürtel," in *Reallexikon für Antike und Christentum* 12/96: column 1232–66.

Spisak, Arthur L. (1998) "Gift-giving in Martial," in *Toto Notus in Orbe: Perspektiven der Martial-Interpretation*, ed. Farouk Grewing. Stuttgart: 243–55.

Spittler, Gerd (2008) *Founders of the Anthropology of Work. German Social Scientists of the 19th and Early 20th Centuries and the First Ethnographers*. Münster.

Squire, Michael (ed.) (2016) *Sight and the Ancient Senses*. London and New York.

Stagl, Justin (1974) *Die Morphologie segmentärer Gesellschaften: Dargestellt am Beispiel des Hochlandes von Neuguinea*. Meisenheim am Glan.

——. (1991) "Malinowskis Paradigma," *Geschichte und Gegenwart* 2: 91–105.

——. (1998) "Geschenk und Gabe," *Ethik und Sozialwissenschften* 9/3: 414–16.

Stahl, Michael (1987) *Aristokraten und Tyrannen im archaischen Athen: Untersuchungen zur Überlieferung, zur Sozialstruktur und zur Entstehung des Staates*. Stuttgart.

——. (2003) *Gesellschaft und Staat bei den Griechen: Archaische Zeit; Klassische Zeit*. 2 vols. Paderborn et al.

Stählin, G. (1987) "Ξένος, ξενία, ξενίζω, ξενοδοχέω, φιλοξενία, φιλόξενος," in *Theologisches Wörterbuch zum Neuen Testament V*, ed. Gerhard Friedrich. Stuttgart.

Stahlmann, Ines (1998) "Scham. Zu einem Verhaltensregulativ der homerischen Gesellschaft," in *Psychologie und Geschichte* 8/1: 85-111.

Stanfield, J. Ron (1990) "Karl Polanyi and the Contemporary Economic Thought," in Polanyi-Levitt 1990: 195-207.

Stanley, Keith (1993) *The Shield of Homer: Narrative Structure in the Iliad*. Princeton.

Stanley, Philip V. (1986) "The Function of Trade in Homeric Society," *Münstersche Beiträge zur antiken Handelsgeschichte* 5/2: 5-15.

Starbatty, Joachim (ed.) (1989) *Klassiker des ökonomischen Denkens II*. Munich.

Starr, Chester G. (1961) "The Decline of the Early Greek Kings," *Historia* 10: 129-38.

——. (1986) *Individual and Community: The Rise of the Polis. 800-500 B.C.* New York and Oxford.

Stavrianopoulou, Eftychia (2009) "Die Bewirtung des Volkes: Öffentiche Speisungen in der römischen Kaiserzeit," in *Ritual Dynamics and Religious Change in Roman Empire*, ed. Oliver Hekster, Sebastian Schmidt-Hofner, and Christian Witschel. Leiden and Boston: 159-80.

Stein-Hölkeskamp, Elke (1989) *Adelskultur und Polisgesellschaft: Studien zum griechischen Adel in archaischer und klassischer Zeit*. Stuttgart.

——. (2005) *Das römische Gastmahl: Eine Kulturgeschichte*. Munich.

Steinkopf, Gerhard (1937) *Untersuchungen zur Geschichte des Ruhms bei den Griechen*. Diss. Halle.

Stengel, Paul (1910) *Opferbräuche der Griechen*. Leipzig and Berlin.

Stocking, G. W. (1978) "Die Geschichtlichkeit der Wilden und die Geschichte der Ethnologie," *Geschichte und Gesellschaft* 4: 520-35.

Straten, Folkert T. van (1981) "Gifts for the Gods," in *Faith, Hope and Worship: Aspects of Religious Mentality in the Ancient World*, ed. Hendrik S. Versnel. Leiden: 65-151.

Streissler, Erich (1989) "Carl Menger (1840-1921)," in *Klassiker des ökonomischen Denkens II*, ed. Joachim Starbatty. Munich: 119-34.

Stulz, Heinke (1990) *Die Farbe Purpur im frühen Griechentum: Beobachtet in der Literatur und in der bildenden Kunst*. Beiträge zur Altertumskunde 6. Stuttgart.

Stupperich, Reinhard (1977) *Staatsbegräbnis und Privatgrabmal im klassischen Athen*. Diss. Münster.

Sussman, Linda S. (1978) "Workers and Drones: Labor, Idleness and Gender Definition in Hesiod's Beehive," *Arethusa* 11: 27-41.

Svenbro, Jesper (1976) *La parole et le marbre: Aux origines de la poétique grecque*. Lund and Paris.

——. (1984) "Vengeance et société en Grèce archaïque: A propos de la fin de l'Odyssée," in *Vengeance: pouvoirs et idéologies dans quelques civilisations de l'Antiquité*, ed. Raymond Verdier and Jean-Pierre Poly. Paris: 49-63.

Swoboda, Heinrich (1905) "Beiträge zur griechischen Rechtsgeschichte," *Zeitschrift der Savigny-Stiftung für Rechtsgeschichte, Romanistische Abteilung* 26: 149-284.

Taillardat, Jean (1982) "ΦΙΛΟΤΕΣ, ΠΙΣΤΙΣ et *FOEDUS*," in Revue des Etudes Grecques 95: 1-14.

Takabatake, Sumio (1988) "The Idea of *xenos* in Classical Athens: Its Structure and Peculiarities," in *Forms of Control and Subordination in Antiquity*, ed. Toru Yuge and Masaoki Doi. Leiden and New York: 449–55.

Tausend, Klaus (1992) *Amphiktyonie und Symmachie: Formen zwischenstaatlicher Beziehungen im archaischen Griechenland*. Stuttgart.

Theognis, Mimnermos, Phokylides (2005). *Frühe griechische Elegien*. Greek and German. Introduction and translation by Dirk Uwe Hansen. Darmstadt.

Theokrit 1999. *Gedichte*. Greek and German. Ed. and trans. by Bernd Effe. Darmstadt

Thesaurus Linguae Graecae (ed.) (1982–1991) *Lexikon des Frühgriechischen Epos*, founded by Bruno Snell, im Auftrag der Akademie der Wissenschaften in Göttingen. 2 vols. Göttingen.

Thomas, Carol C. (1966) "The Roots of Homeric Kingship," *Historia* 15: 387–407.

——. (1978) "From Wanax to Basileus," *Hispania Antiqua* 6: 187–204.

Thomas, Rosalind (1992) *Literacy and Orality in Ancient Greece*. Cambridge.

Thommen, Lukas (1996) "Nacktheit und Zivilisationsprozeß in Griechenland," *Historische Anthropologie* 4: 435–50.

Thompson, Edward P. (1977) "Folklore, Anthropology and Social History," *The Indian Historical Review* 3: 247–366.

Thompson, Wesley (1982) "Weaving: A Man's Work," *Classical World* 75: 217–22.

Thomson, George D. (1941) *Aischylus and Athens: A Study in the Social Origin of the Drama*. London.

——. (1978) *Prehistoric Aegean*. 4th edn. London.

Thornton, Robert J. (1985) "'Imagine yourself set down ...': Mach, Frazer, Conrad, Malinowski and the Role of Imagination in Ethnography," *Anthropology Today* 1/5: 7–14.

Thurnwald, Richard (1911) "Stufen der Staatsbildung bei den Urvölkern," *Zeitschrift für vergleichende Rechtswissenschaft* 25: 417–32.

——. (1912) *Forschungen auf den Salomon-Inseln und dem Bismarck-Archipel*. Berlin.

——. (1921) *Die Gemeinde der Bánaro*. Stuttgart.

——. (1932) *Werden, Wandel und Gestaltung der Wirtschaft im Lichte der Völkerforschung*. Berlin.

——. (1936) "Gegenseitigkeit im Aufbau und Funktionieren der Gesellungen und deren Institutionen," in *Reine und angewandte Soziologie: Eine Festgabe für Ferdinand Tönnies zu seinem achtzigsten Geburtstag am 26. Juli 1935*. Leipzig: 275–97.

Tietz, Werner (2013) *Dilectus ciborum: Essen im Diskurs der römischen Antike*. Göttingen.

——. (2015) *Hirten–Bauern–Götter: eine Geschichte der römischen Landwirtschaft*. Munich.

Tölle-Kastenbein, Renate (1994) *Wasserleitungsnetz für Athen*. Mainz.

Tomasello, Michel (2010) *Warum wir kooperieren*. Berlin.

Tönnies, Ferdinand (1991) *Gemeinschaft und Gesellschaft: Grundbegriffe der reinen Soziologie*. Darmstadt (orig. 1887; rpt. of 8th edn. 1935).

Tracy, Catherine (2014) "The Host's Dilemma: Game Theory and Homeric Hospitality," *Classical Studies* 39: 1–16.
Treister, Michail Y. (1976) *The Role of Metals in Ancient Greek History*. Leiden.
Tsetskhladze, Gocha R. (ed.) (2006/2008) *Greek Colonsation: An Account of Greek Colonies and Other Settlements Overseas*. 2 vols. Leiden.
Tuck, Anthony (2006), "Singing the Rug: Patterned Textiles and the Origins of Indo-European Metrical Poetry," *American Journal of Archaeology* 110: 539–50.
Uchitel, Alexander (1984) "Women at Work: Pylos and Knossos, Lagash and Ur," *Historia* 33/3: 257–82.
Uhlig, Harald (1973) "Wanderhirten im westlichen Himalaya," in *Vergleichende Kulturgeographie der Hochgebirge des südlichen Asiens*, ed. Carl Rathjens, Carl Troll, and Harald Uhlig. Erdkundliche Forschungen 5. Wiesbaden.
Ulf, Christoph (1990) *Die homerische Gesellschaft: Materialien zur analytischen Beschreibung und historischen Lokalisierung*. Vestigia 43. Munich.
——. (1997) "Überlegungen zur Funktion überregionaler Feste im archaischen Griechenland," in *Volk und Verfassung im vorhellenistischen Griechenland. Beiträge auf dem Symposium zu Ehren von Karl-Wilhelm Welwei in Bochum, 1.–2. März 1996*, ed. Walter Eder and Karl-Joachim Hölkeskamp. Stuttgart: 37–61.
——. (2001): "Gemeinschaftsbezug, soziale Stratifizierung, polis—drei Bedingungen für das Entstehen aristokratischer und demokratischer Mentalität im archaischen Griechenland," in *Gab es das griechische Wunder? Griechenland zwischen dem Ende des 6. Und der Mitte des 5. Jahrhunderts v. Chr.*, eds. Dietrich Papenfuß and Volker Michael Strocka. Mainz: 153–86.
——. (2002): "Herkunft und Charakter der grundlegenden Prämissen für die Debatte über die historische Auswertung der homerischen Epen," *Klio* 84/2: 319–54.
——. (2011) "Zur ‚Vorgeschichte der Polis': Die Wettbewerbskultur als Indikator für die Art des griechischen Bewusstseins," *Hermes* 139/3: 291–315.
Ungern-Sternberg, Jürgen von (1998) "Innovation in Early Greece: The Political Sphere," in *Political Competition, Innovation and Growth: A Historical Analysis*, ed. Peter Bernholz, Manfred E. Streit, and Roland Vaubel. Berlin and Heidelberg: 85–107.
Ungern-Sternberg, Jürgen von and Hansjörg Reinau (eds.) (1988) *Vergangenheit in mündlicher Überlieferung*. Colloquium Rauricum 1. Stuttgart.
Urry, James (1992) "Would the Real Malinowski Please Stand up?" *Man* 27/1: 181–82.
Vasilescu, Michael (1989) "Hellènes et barbares dans l'épopées homeriques," *Klio* 71: 70–77.
Vatin, Claude (1982) "Poinè, Timè, Thoiè dans le droit homérique," *Ktema* 7: 275–80.
Varto, Emily (2017): "The Idea of Descent in Early Greek Kinship," in *Mediterranean Families in Antiquity: Households, Extended Families, and Domestic Space*, eds. Sabine R. Huebner and Geoffrey Nathan. Malden, Oxford and Chichester: 44–64.
Venturi, Franco (1963) "Despotism," *Journal of the History of Ideas* 24: 133–42.
Verboven, Koenraad (2002) *The Economy of Friends: Economic Aspects of amicitia and Patronage in the Late Republic*. Bruxelles.
Verdenius, W. J. (1944) "AIDOS bei Homer," *Mnemosyne* 3rd sér. 12: 47–60.

Vermeule, Emily (1979) *Aspects of Death in Early Greek Art and Poetry*. Berkeley.

Vernant, Jean-Pierre (1962) *Les origines de la pensée grécque*. Paris.

——. (1975) "Hestia—Hermès: Sur l'expression religieuse de l'espace et du mouvement chez les Grecs," in his *Mythe et pensée chez les Grecs Paris*. Paris: 97–143.

——. (1986) "Corps obscur, corps éclant," in his *Corps des dieux*, ed. Charle Malmoud. Paris : 19–46.

——. (1989) "Figures féminines et la mort en Grèce," in his *L'individue, la mort, l'amour*. Paris : 131–52 = (1985) "La douceur amère de la condition humaine" *Lettre international* 6: 45–48.

Veyne, Paul (1976) *Le pain et le cirque: Sociologie historique d'un pluralisme politique*. Paris (= *Bread and Circuses: Historical Sociology and Political Pluralism*. Trans. B. Pearce. London 1990).

Vidal-Naquet, Pierre (1968) "Fonction de la monnaie dans la Grèce archaïque," *Annales* 23: 206–8.

——. (1983) *The chasseur noir. Formes de pensées et formes de société dans le monde grec*. Ed rev. et corr. Paris (= *The Black Hunter: Forms of Thought and Forms of Society in the Greek World*. Trans. Andrew Szegedy-Maszak. Baltimore 1986).

Viechnicki, P. (1994) "Ἀμείβω: An Interdisciplinary Etymology," *Journal of Indo-European Studies* 22/1–2: 113–32.

Viehweg, Theodor (1970) "Rechtsdogmatik und Rechtszetetik bei Jhering," in Wieacker and Wollschläger 1970: 211–16.

Villing, Alexandra (ed.) (2005) *The Greeks in the East: British Museum Research Publication* 157. London.

Vlachos, Georges C. (1974) *Les sociétés politiques homériques*. Paris.

Vlemick, Serge (1982) "L'aspect institutionel de la τιμή homérique à la lumière de l'étymologie," *Ziva antiqua* 32/2: 151–64.

Vogt, Wolfgang P. (1981) "Über den Nutzen des Studiums primitiver Gesellschaften: Eine Anmerkung zur Durkheim-Schule 1890–1940," in *Geschichte und Soziologie III*, ed. Wolf Lepenies. Francfort: 276–97.

Vössing, Konrad (2004) *Mensa Regia: Das Bankett beim hellenistischen König und römischen Kaiser*. Munich.

Vries, Keith de (1980) "Greeks and Phrygians in the Early Iron Age," in his *From Athens to Gordion: Papers of a Memorial Symposium for Rodneys S. Young*, Philadelphia, PA: 41–42.

Wace, Alan J. B. (1934) "The Veil of Despoina," *American Journal of Archaeology* 38: 107–11.

——. (1948) "Weaving or Embroidery," *American Journal of Archaeology* 52: 51–55.

Wace, Alan J. B. and Maurice S. Thompson (1914) *The Nomads of the Balkans*. London (rpt. 1972).

Wagner, Adolph (1876) *Allgemeine und theoretische Volkswirthschaftslehre: Mit Benutzung von Rau's Grundsätzen der Volkswirthschaftslehre*. Rau'schen Volkswirthschaftslehre. 9th edn. Leipzig and Heidelberg.

Wagner, Günther A., Gerd Weisgärber, and Werner Kroker (eds.) (1985) *Silber, Blei und Gold auf Sifnos: Prähistorische und antike Metallproduktion*. Veröffentlichungen aus dem Deutschen Bergbau-Museum Bochum 31. Bochum.

Wagner-Hasel, Beate (1988) "Geschlecht und Gabe: Zum Brautgütersystem bei Homer," *Zeitschrift der Savigny Stiftung für Rechtsgeschichte, Romanistische Abteilung* 105: 32–73.

——. (ed.) (1992) *Matriarchatstheorien der Altertumswissenschaft*. Darmstadt.

——. (1997) "Die Macht der Penelope: Zur Politik des Gewebes im homerischen Epos." in *Kybele—Prophetin—Hexe: Religiöse Frauenbilder und Weiblichkeitskonzeptionen*, ed. Richard Faber and Susanne Lanwerd. Würzburg: 127–46.

——. (1998a) "Wissenschaftsmythen und Antike: Zur Funktion von Gegenbildern der Moderne am Beispiel der Gabentauschdebatte," in *MythenMächte—Mythen als Argument*, ed. Wolfgang Schmale and Annette Völker-Rasor. Berlin: 33–63.

——. (1998b) "Le privé n'éxiste pas: Quelques remarques sur la construction du privé par l'Altertumswissenschaft au 19ième siècle," *Ktema* 23: 25–35.

——. (1998c) "Herakles und Omphale im Rollentausch: Mythologie und Politik in der Antike," in *Geschlechterperspektiven: Forschungen zur Frühen Neuzeit*, ed. Gisela Engel and Heide Wunder. Königstein: 205–28.

——. (1998d) "Gastfreundschaft," in *Der Neue Pauly* 4: column 794–97.

——. (1998e) "Geschenke, Griechenland," in *Der Neue Pauly* 4: column 984–88.

——. (2000a) "Zentrumsbildung und überregionale Kommunikation: Delphi und der Dreifuß des Apollon," in Beate Wagner-Hasel, *Der Stoff der Gaben: Kultur und Politik des Schenkens und Tauschens im archaischen Griechenland*. Francfort and New York 2000: 261–305 and 422–38.

——. (2000b) "Die Reglementierung von Traueraufwand und der Nachruhm der Toten," in Späth and Wagner-Hasel 2000: 81–102.

——. (2002a) "The Graces and Colour-Weaving," in *Women's Dress in the Ancient Greek World*, ed. Lloyd Llewellyn-Jones. London: 17–32.

——. (2002b) "Kommunikationswege und die Entstehung überregionaler Heiligtümer: Das Fallbeispiel Delphi,"in Eckart Olshausen and Holger Sonnabend (eds.) *Zu Wasser und zu Land: Verkehrswege in der antiken Welt*. 7. Kolloquium zur Historischen Geographie des Altertums. Stuttgart: 160–80.

——. (2003a) "Egoistical Exchange and Altruistic Gift," in Algazi, Groebner, and Jussen 2003: 141–71.

——. (2003b) "Streit um Troia. Eine wirtschaftsanthropologische Sicht," *Historische Anthropologie* 11/2: 263–77.

——. (2006a) "Gift-Exchange: Ancient Attitudes and Modern Theories," in Deger-Jalkotzy and Lemos 2006: 257–69.

——. (2006b [French version 2017]) "Duftende Kleider—Gesalbte Körper," in *Duftnoten: was Griechen und Römern in die Nase stieg; Ausstellungskatalog Kestner-Museum Hannover*, ed. Angelika Dierichs and Anne Viola Siebert. Hannover: 20–25.

——. (2007) "Der Stoff der Macht—Kleideraufwand, elitärer Konsum und homerisches Königtum," in Alram-Stern and Nightingale 2007: 325–37.

——. (2009a) "Brautgut oder Mitgift? Das textile Heiratsgut in den Solonischen Aufwandbestimmungen," in Hildebrandt and Veit 2009: 143–81.

——. (2009b) "Hundert Jahre Gelehrtenstreit über den Charakter der antiken Wirtschaft: Zur Aktualität von Karl Büchers Wirtschaftsanthropologie," *Historische Anthropologie* I 7/2: 178–201.

——. (2011) *Die Arbeit des Gelehrten: Der Nationalökonom Karl Bücher (1847–1930)*, Francfort and New York.

——. (2012a) "*Tria himátia*: Vêtement et mariage en Grèce ancienne," in Gherchanoc and Huét 2012: 39–46.

——. (2012b) "L'étoffe du pouvoir: La royauté homérique et le genre," in *Le banquet de Pauline Schmitt Pantel: Genre, mœurs et politique dans l'antiquité grecque et romaine*. Paris: 207–23.

——. (2013) "Marriage Gifts in Ancient Greece," in Satlow 2013: 158–72.

——. (2014) "Karl Bücher and the Birth of the Theory of Gift-Giving," in Carlà and Gori 2014: 51–69.

——. (2015) "Dreifußkessel und der Stoff der Gaben: Plädoyer für einen materiellen Kulturbegriff," *Historische Anthropologie* 23/3: 326–52.

——. (2018a) "Hektemoroi—Kontraktbauern, Schuldknechte oder abgabenpflichtige Bauern?" in E*mas non quod opus est, sed quos necesse est: Beiträge zur Wirtschafts-, Sozial-, Rezeptions- und Wissenschaftsgeschichte der Antike; Festschrift für Hans-Joachim Drexhage zum 70. Geburtstag*, ed. Kai Ruffing and Kerstin Droß-Krüpe. Philippika 125. Wiesbaden: 295–308.

——. (2018b) "Penelopes Wohnzimmer: Polemische Anmerkungen zu Mary Beards Streitschrift ‚Frauen & Macht'," *Historische Anthropologie* 26/3: 414–21.

——. (forthcoming) "The Garden of Pisistratus: Benefactions and Dues in Archaic Athens," *Benefactors and the Polis*, ed. Marc Domingo Gygax and Arjan Zuiderhoek. Cambridge.

Wagner-Hasel, Beate and Marie-Louise Nosch (eds.) (2019) *Gaben, Waren und Tribute: Stoffkreisläufe und antike Textilökonomie*. Stuttgart.

——. (forthcoming) "Herakles und Dreifußraub von Delphi. Überlegungen zu den Hintergründen eines Mythos," in Balbina Bäbler and Günther Nesselrath (forthcoming) *Delphi: Apollons Orakel in der Welt*. Stuttgart.

Waibl, Elmar (1992) *Ökonomie und Ethik. I: Die Kapitalismusdebatte in der Philosophie der Neuzeit*. 3rd edn. Stuttgart.

Walcot, Peter (1970) *Greek Peasants, Ancient and Modern: A Comparison of Social and Moral Values*. Manchester.

Waldherr, Gerhard (2001) "Antike Transhumanz im Mediterran: Ein Überblick," in his *Landwirtschaft im Imperium Romanum*, ed. Peter Herz. St. Katharinen: 331–57.

Waldner, Katharina (2000a) *Geburt und Hochzeit des Kriegers: Geschlechterdifferenz und Initiation in Mythos und Ritual der griechischen Polis*. Religionsgeschichtliche Versuche und Vorarbeiten 46. Berlin and New York.

——. (2000b) "Kulträume von Frauen in Athen: Das Beispiel der Artemis Brauronia," in Späth and Wagner-Hasel 2000: 53–81.

Walek, Tadeusz B. (1911) *Die delphische Amphiktyonie in der Zeit der aitolischen Herrschaft*. Dissertation. Berlin.

Walter, Uwe (1993) *An der Polis teilhaben: Bürgerstaat und Zugehörigkeit im archaischen Griechenland.* Stuttgart.

——. (2004) "Paradigmen für fast alle Typen: Migration in der Antike," *Geschichte, Politik und ihre Didaktik* 32: 62–73.

Weber, Leo (1935) *Solon und die Schöpfung der Attischen Grabrede.* Francfort.

Weber, Martha (1971) "Die geometrischen Dreifußkessel: Fragen zur Chronologie der Gattungen und deren Herstellungszentren," *Mitteilungen des Deutschen Archäologischen Instituts* 86: 15–30.

Weber, Max (1980) *Wirtschaft und Gesellschaft: Grundriss der verstehenden Soziologie*, edn. with a foreword by Johannes Winckelmann. 5th edn. Tübingen.

Wees, Hans van (1992) *Status Warriors, War, Violence and Society in Homer and History.* Amsterdam.

——. (1998) "The Law of Gratitude: Reciprocity in Archaeological Theory," in Gill et al. 1998: 13–49.

——. (2002) "Greed, Generosity and Gift-Exchange in Early Greece and the Western Pacific," in *After the Past: Essays in Ancient History in Honour of H. W. Pleket*, ed. Willem Jongman and Marc Kleijwegt. Leiden: 341–378.

——. (2004) *Greek Warfare: Myths and Realities.* London.

——. (2005) "Trailing Tunics and Sheepskin Coats: Dress and Status in Early Greece," in *The Clothed Body in the Ancient World*, ed. Liza Cleland, Mary Harlow, and Lloyd Llewellyn-Jones. Oxford: 44–51.

——. (2013) "Farmers and Hoplites: Models of Historical Development," in *Men of Bronze: Hoplite Warfare in Ancient Greece*, ed. Donald Kagan and Gregory F. Viggiano. Princeton and Oxford: 222–55.

Wehler, Hans-Ulrich (1987) *Deutsche Gesellschaftsgeschichte. II: Von der Reformära bis zur industriellen und politischen 'Deutschen Doppelrevolution' 1815–1845/9.* Munich.

Weigand, Gustav (1894/95) *Die Aromunen.* 2 vols. Leipzig.

Weiher, Anton (ed.) (^{5}1986) *Homerische Hymnen.* Greek and German. Darmstadt.

Weiner, Annette B. (1976) *Women of Value, Men of Renown: New Perspectives in Trobriand Exchange.* Austin.

——. (1980) "'Reproduction': A Replacement for Reciprocity," *American Ethnologist* 7/1: 71–85.

——. (1983) "'A World of Men is not a World of Born': Doing Kula in Kiriwana," in *The Kula: New Perspectives on Massim Exchange*, ed. Jerry W. and Edmund Leach. Cambridge: 147–70.

——. (1989) "Why Cloth? Wealth, Gender, and Power on Oceania," in her *Cloth and Human Experience*, ed. Jane Schneider. Washington: 33–72.

Welskopf, Charlotte (ed.) (1981) *Soziale Typenbegriffe im alten Griechenland und ihr Fortleben in den Sprachen der Welt. III: Untersuchungen ausgewählter altgriechischer sozialer Typenbegriffe.* Berlin.

Welwei, Karl-Wilhelm (1992) *Athen: Vom neolithischen Siedlungsplatz zur archaischen Großsiedlung.* Darmstadt.

Wenzel, Horst (1988) "Partizipation und Mimesis: Die Lesbarkeit der Körper am Hof und in der höfischen Literatur," in *Materialität und Kommunikation*, ed. Hans Ulrich Gumbrecht and K. Ludwig Pfeiffer. Francfort: 178–202.

——. (1991) "Imaginatio und Memoria: Medien der Erinnerung im höfischen Mittelalter," in *Mnemosyne: Formen und Funktionen der kulturellen Erinnerung*, ed. Aleida Assmann and Dietrich Hardt. Francfort: 57-82.

——. (1995) *Hören und Sehen, Schrift und Bild: Kultur und Gedächtnis im Mittelalter*. Munich.

Wesel, Uwe (1988) *Juristische Weltkunde*. 4th edn. Francfort.

West, Martin L. (1990) "Archaische Heldendichtung: Singen und Schreiben," in Kullmann and Reichel 1990: 33-50.

West, M. L. (2008) *Hesiod, Theogony and Works and Days*. A new translation. Oxford and New York.

Wéry, Louise-Marie (1967) "Le fonctionnement de la diplomatie à l'époque homérique," *Revue Internationale des droits de l'antiquité* 3rd sér. 14: 169-205.

White, Kenneth D. (1977) *Country Life in Classical Times*. London.

Whitley, James (1988) "Early States and Hero-Cults: A Re-appraisal," *The Journal of Hellenic Studies* 108: 173-82.

——. (1991) *Style and Society in Dark Age Greece: The Changing Face of a Pre-literate Society 1100-700 B.C.* Cambridge.

Whittaker, C. R. (ed.) (1988) *Pastoral Economies in Classical Antiquity*. Cambridge.

Wickert-Micknat, Gisela (1982) *Die Frau*. Archaeologia Homerica Q. Göttingen.

Widzisz, Marcel (2012) "Timing Reciprocity in the Iliad," *Arethusa* 45/2: 153-76.

Wieacker, Franz (1942) *Rudolf von Jhering: Eine Erinnerung zu seinem 50. Todestag*. Leipzig.

——. (1973) "Jhering und der ‚Darwinismus'," in *Festschrift für Karl Larenz zum 70. Geburtstag*, ed. Gotthard Paulus, Uwe Diederichsen, and Claus-Wilhelm Canaris. Munich: 63-92.

Wieacker, Franz and Christian Wollschläger (eds.) (1970) *Jherings Erbe: Göttinger Symposium zur 150. Wiederkehr des Geburtstages von Rudolf von Jhering*. Abhandlungen der Akademie der Wissenschaften zu Göttingen, Philologisch-Historische Klasse 3/75. Göttingen.

Wild, John Peter (2008) "Textile Production," in *The Oxford Handbook of Engineering and Technology in the Classical World*, ed. John P. Oleson. Oxford: 465-82.

Will, Eduard (1954a) *Korinthiaka*. Paris.

——. (1954b) "Trois quarts de siècle de recherches sur l'économie grecque antique," *Annales* 9: 7-22.

——. (1954c) "De l'aspect éthique des origines grecques de la monnaie," *Revue historique* 212/2: 209-31.

——. (1955) "Reflections et hypothèses sur l'origine du moyannage," *Revue numismatique* 5th sér. 17: 5-23.

——. (1957) "Aux origines du régime foncier grec: Homère, Hésiode et l'arrière-plan mycénien," *Revue des Etudes Anciennes* 59: 5-50.

Willemsen, Franz (1955) "Der delphische Dreifuß," *Jahrbuch des Deutschen Archäologischen Instituts* 70: 85-104.

——. (1957) *Dreifußkessel von Olympia*. Berlin.

Willenbrock, Harro (1944) *Die poetische Bedeutung der Gegenstände in Homers Ilias*. Diss. Marburg (rpt. 1969).

Wilson, J.-P. (1997) "The Nature of Greek Overseas Settlements in the Archaic Period: Emporion or apoikia?" in *The Development of the "Polis" in Archaic Greece*, ed. Lynette G. Mitchell and P. J. Rhodes. London: 199–207.

Winkel, Harald (1977) *Die deutsche Nationalökonomie im 19. Jahrhundert*. Darmstadt.

——. (1989) "Gustav von Schmoller (1838–1917)," in *Klassiker des ökonomischen Denkens II*, ed. Joachim Starbatty. Munich: 97–118.

Winkler, John J. (1990) *The Constraints of Desire: The Anthropology of Sex and Gender in Ancient Greece*. New York and London.

Winterling, Aloys (1999) *Aula Caesaris*. Munich.

Wittenburg, Andreas (1995) "Bernhard Laum und der sakrale Ursprung des Geldes," in *Altertumswissenschaft in den 20er Jahren: Neue Fragen und Impulse*, ed. Helmut Flashar. Stuttgart: 259–74.

——. (2012) "Antiquité et anthropologie en Allemagne: Eduard Meyer et après," in Payen and Scheid-Tissinier 2012: 323–42.

Wöhrle, Georg (1999) *Telemachs Reise: Väter und Söhne in Ilias und Odyssee oder ein Beitrag zur Erforschung der Männlichkeitsideologie in der homerischen Welt*. Göttingen.

Wolf, Eric R. (1982) *Europa and the People Without History*. Berkeley, Los Angeles and London.

Wood, Ellen Meiksins (1989) *Peasant-Citizen and Slave: The Foundations of Athenian Democracy*. London and New York.

Wright, James C. (1987) "Death and Power at Mycenae: Changing Symbols in Mortuary Practice," in Laffineur 1987: 171–84.

Wunder, Heide (1994) "'Gewirkte Geschichte': Gedenken und ‚Handarbeit': Überlegungen zum Tradieren von Geschichte am Beginn der Neuzeit," in *Modernes Mittelalter: Neue Bilder einer populären Epoche*, ed. Joachim Heinzle. Francfort and Leipzig: 324–54.

Yamagata, Naoko (1993) *Homeric Morality*. Leiden, New York and Cologne.

——. (1997) "ἄναξ and βασιλεύς in Homer," *Classical Quarterly* 47: 1–14.

——. (2005) "Clothing and Identity in Homer: The Case of Penelope's Web," *Mnemosyne* 58: 539–546.

Young, Michael (1984) "The Intensive Study of a Restricted Area, Or, Why Did Malinowski Go to the Trobriand Island?" *Oceania* 55/1: 1–26.

Zaccagnini, C. (1987) "Aspects of Ceremonial Exchange in the Near East During the Late Second Millenium B.C.," in Rowlands, Larsen, and Kristiansen 1987: 57–65.

——. (1989/90) "Dono e tributo come modelli istituzionali di scambio: Echi e persistenze nella documentazione administrativa vicino-orientale del Tardo bronze," in Bartoloni 1989/90: 105–10.

Zanker, Paul (1965) *Wandel der Hermesgestalt in der attischen Vasenmalerei*. Bonn.

Zeisel, Hans (1968) "Karl Polanyi," *International Encyclopedia of the Social Sciences* 12: 172–74.

Zengel, Eva (1991) "Troia," in *Troia: Katalog*, ed. Ruhrland Museum der Stadt Essen. Essen: 30–67.

Zielinski, Tadeusz (1924) "Charis und die Chariten," *Classical Quarterly* 18: 158–63.

Zöbl, Dorothea (1982) *Die Transhumanz (Wanderschafhaltung) der europäischen Mittelmeerländer im Mittelalter in historischer, geographischer und volkskundlicher Sicht*. Berliner Geographische Studien 10. Berlin.

Zschietzmann, Willy (1928) "Die Darstellungen der Prothesis in der griechischen Kunst," *Mitteilungen des Deutschen Archäologischen Instituts, Athenische Abteilung* 53: 17–47.

Zuiderhoek, Arjan (2009) *The Politics of Munificence in the Roman Empire: Citizens, Elites and Benefactors in Asia Minor*. Cambridge.

——. (forthcoming) "Benefactors and the Poleis in the Roman Empire: Civic Munificence in the Roman East in the Context of the *longue durée*," in Domingo Gygax and Zuiderhoek (forthcoming).

Zweigert, Konrad (1970) "Jherings Bedeutung für die Entwicklung der rechtsvergleichenden Methode," in Wieacker and Wollschläger 1970: 240–51.

Index
including Glossary of Greek Terms

Achaeans, 96, 100-101, 107-108, 110, 134, 154, 163, 199, 210, 212-213, 254, 283
Achilles, 15, 78, 84, 92-93, 98, 101-102, 106, 109-110, 126, 131, 133-134, 141-143, 147-148, 150, 153-154, 162, 167-168, 174, 177-178, 185, 189, 191-199, 201, 203-213, 216-217, 220-225, 229, 232, 235-238, 241-243, 245-248, 251, 254-259, 269, 277, 283-284, 286, 291-292, 295, 299, 302-303
Adrastus, 150, 225
advantage s. κέρδος (*kerdos*)
Aegisthus (Aigisthos), 94, 143, 207, 234
Aegyptius, 242
Aeneas (Aineias), 102-103, 153, 156, 161, 203, 215, 236, 283
Aeolus (Aiolos), 103, 131, 136
Aepeia, 201
Aeschylus (Aischylos), 10, 89, 278, 344
Aëthe, 147
aethla (ἄεθλα): prizes of contest, 61, 100, 119, 153, 182, 191, 199, 207, 216, 232, 256-257, 262, 264, 266, 282, 291, 303, 313-315, 333, 336-337, 345
Aëthon, 119, 128, 147, 205, 277, 284
Aetolians, 203, 206, 275
Afghanistan, 307
Agamemnon, 16, 69, 91-92, 94, 98, 101, 105-106, 108, 133-135, 138, 147-150, 153, 176, 179, 185, 189, 191-196, 198, 200-219, 221-230, 234-235, 242-246, 255-256, 267, 282-284, 292, 295, 302
aganophrosynē (ἀγανοφροσύνη): gentleness, kindliness, 251-252
aganos (ἀγανός): mild, gentle, 251-252
ageirō (ἀγείρω): gather together, 119, 206, 295-296
aglaos (ἀγλαός): splendid, shining, bright, 115, 150, 175-176, 178, 234, 247
agnythes (ἀγνῦθες): loom weights, 164 (Figure)
Agesilaus (Agesilaos), 111-112
Agis, 105
Aglaia, 157

agora, 199, 208, 220
aidōs (αἰδώς): awe, shame, respect, 175, 188, 209-211, 216, 229, 404
aidoios (αἰδοῖος): having a claim to regard, shamefaced 212, 224, 227
aideomai (αἰδέομαι): to be ashamed, stand in awe of 210-212, 272
anaideiē, anaideia (ἀναιδείη, ἀναίδεια): shamelessness 210-212
Aigae, 152
Aisa, 237, 238-239, 240
Ajax, 103, 107, 160, 162, 193, 278, 281
Akrotiri, 301
Alcaeus (Alkaios), 287
Alcinous (Alkinoos), 93, 105, 109, 113, 115-117, 120-121, 126, 128, 132, 141, 149, 154, 179, 203-206, 209, 225-227, 238, 244-245, 278, 286
Alcmaeonids (Alkmeonidai), 112
Alkandre, 119, 295, 305
Alkiphron, 105
alliance, 20, 45, 54, 56, 60-62, 67-70, 73-74, 79, 81-83, 93, 96, 105, 107, 110-112, 149, 314-315, 325-326, 344
Al Mina, 307, 325
alochos (ἄλοχος): partner of one's bed, bedfellow, wife, 103, 141, 245, 248
Alpheus (Alpheios), 274, 279
Althaea (Althaia), 224
altruism, 21, 24, 30-35, 50, 64, 80, 84, 132
alum, 269, 295, 300, 310
amoibē (ἀμοιβή): requital, recompense, counter-gift, 15, 79, 120, 267, 269, 270, 276-277, 311, 338
ameibō, ameibomai (ἀμείβω, ἀμείβομαι): requite, answer, give in exchange, cross, 97, 101, 276-278, 280, 311; *epamoibima erga* (ἐπαμοίβιμα ἔργα): mutual exchange, barter, 278, 280
amphipoloi (ἀμφίπολοι): handmaids, 123-126, 145, 155, 157-161, 169, 171, 341
Amasis, 158, 298, 300, 307
ambrosia, 84-85, 159, 171, 258

412

INDEX & GLOSSARY OF GREEK TERMS

Amira, Karl von, 29
Amphictyonic League, 323
Amphidamas, 106
Amphimedon, 234-235
Amphion, 207
Amyntor, 106
Amythaon, 181
anassō (ἀνάσσω): to be master, 190, 205, 207, 213, 217, 219; *anax* (ἄναξ): master, lord, 85-86, 116, 151, 186, 189-191, 205-207, 219, 250; *anassa* (ἄνασσα): mistress, lady, 286
Anchialus, 277
Anchises, 102, 156, 173, 205
Andromache, 160-161, 163, 165, 176-177, 206, 224, 248-249, 252, 257-258, 283, 302
antapodosis (ἀνταπόδοσις): rendering, requiting, 144
Antenor, 105, 129, 283
Anthedon, 319
Antheia, 201
anthropology, 9-11, 13, 18, 21, 35-36, 53-54, 331-332, 335
anti-individualism, 43-44
Antinous, 218, 233, 285
Antilochus, 281
antion (ἀντίον): cloth beam, 164 (Figure)
aphenos (ἄφενος): revenue, wealth, riches, abundance, 194-195, 288
Aphrodite, 102-103, 134-135, 137-139, 145, 156-157, 159-161, 169, 171, 173-174, 183, 241, 316
apoina (ἄποινα): ransom, compensation, 55, 91, 143, 150, 193, 201, 268, 290-293, 310
anapoinos (ἀνάποινος): without compensation, 292
Apollo, 91, 94, 103, 151-153, 177, 180, 193, 241, 251, 254, 276, 278-279, 285, 289, 292, 300, 311-313, 320-323, 333
Apollodorus, 301
Apollonius Rhodius, 139, 163, 166, 221
Apollophanes, 111
Arcadia, Arcadians, 207, 279, 316, 319, 321, 323, 325
archē, 191
Arcesilaus, 304
Ares, 103, 138-139, 142, 151, 202
Arete, 63, 114-116, 121, 124, 126, 141, 159-161, 173, 216, 224-227, 230, 235-236, 244-246, 261, 302
Argolid, Argolis, 75, 207, 264, 301-302, 320, 324
Argonauts, 9, 12, 19, 26, 40, 55, 304-305, 325

Argos, 97, 104-105, 118, 131, 207, 209, 219, 314, 320, 322
argypheos (ἀργύφεος): silver-shining, silver-white, 114, 282, 299
Ariadne, 139
Arisbe, 131, 291
Aristophanes, 173, 308-309
aristeia, 98, 101, 104
aristocracy, 7, 190, 268, 337
Aristotle, 39, 51, 99, 144, 174, 212, 326
arms-exchange, 98-99, 100-101, 104-105, 107, 109, 128
Arneus, 224
Artemis, Artemis Limnatis, 103, 138, 321-322
Asia Minor, 299-300, 307
Asine, 320
atē (ἄτη): blindness, infatuation, 210-211, 287
Athenaeus, 101, 279, 325
Athena, 103, 109, 120, 133, 137, 141, 145, 148, 151-152, 154, 158-162, 169-175, 177-178, 197, 199, 206, 216-217, 222, 224, 242, 276, 283, 285-286, 298, 325, 341, 344
Athens, 8, 10, 71-72, 111-112, 144, 152, 158, 181, 222, 306, 312, 316, 320
atimia, 199
Atreus, 147, 194, 219
Atropos, 240
Attica, 75, 105, 165, 259, 263-264, 274, 298, 319, 324
Augias, 205, 273
autarchy, 319
authority, 37-38, 58, 60, 188, 190, 201, 205, 207, 208, 220, 227-228, 246, 253, 264), 304, 317
Autolycus (Autolykos), 106, 153
Automedon, 101
Axius (Axios), 102
Axylos, 89, 298

Bacchiads (Bakchiadai), 325
Bacchylides, 113, 146, 181, 256, 298
banquet, 117, 122, 128, 133, 151, 179, 192, 310, 338, 344-345
barley, 217, 298
barter, bartering, 26, 28, 278, 280
basileuō (βασιλεύω): decide, rule, reign, 122, 137, 190, 218, 224-225, 340
basileus, basilēes, basileis (βασιλεύς, βασιλῆες, βασιλεῖς): king, chief, ruler, 83-84, 88, 116, 121-122, 137, 152, 186, 188-192, 198, 202, 206, 215-218, 222, 226, 229, 232, 244-245, 252, 305, 308, 326, 339

basileia (βασίλεια): mistress, queen, female ruler, 186, 189-190, 224-226, 229-230
basileuteros (βασιλεύτερος): more royal, more able to decide, 223
Bathycles, 312
Bellerophon, 97, 99-100, 103, 128, 202-203, 223, 228, 242
benefactor, 313
Bias, 100, 312-313
big-man system, big-men system, 189-190
biotos (βίοτος): livelihood, means of living, 92, 269, 294-298, 310
Bloch, Maurice, 11, 45, 51, 54, 56
Boeotians, 309, 320, 324
Bohannan, Paul, 11, 53, 55
boon, 287
boon-work, 23-24, 36, 40
booty, 100, 119, 149-150, 169, 192, 197, 209, 213, 235, 241, 252, 257, 273, 296-297, 305, 310
bridewealth, 148, 155, 168, 199 s. also hedna
Brisëis, 16, 148, 150, 185, 195-196, 199, 209-210, 212, 222, 247-249, 252
bronze, 69, 97, 102, 104, 116, 118-119, 150, 162, 197, 199, 237, 276, 279, 291, 297, 305, 307, 328
Bücher, Karl, 23-26, 30, 36, 40, 42, 48-49, 61-62, 71, 74, 176, 267
Burckhard, Hugo, 27, 30-31, 37
Burgundy, 307

Cadmeans, 207
Calchas (Kalchas), 193, 242, 292
Caligula, 221
Callimachus (Kallimachos), 312
Calypso (Kalypso), 85, 87-88, 91-92, 109, 121, 125, 130, 138, 157, 176, 224, 260, 282, 299
Cardamyle (Kardamyle), 201
Carthage, 303
Cassandra (Kassandra), 248
Castor, 215, 262, 344
cattle, 89, 91, 94, 119, 133, 155, 195, 197, 199, 201, 205, 233, 257, 270-276, 279, 285, 287-288, 293, 314, 321, 323-324, 338
Cauconians, 271, 276
cauldron, 68, 115-116, 118-119, 122, 154, 200, 206, 229, 257, 333
centralisation, 191, 326, 340
Cephallenians, 206
Chalkis, 289, 321
Charis, wife of Hephaestus, 84, 109, 157, 174, 208, 299

charis (χάρις): service, grace, favour, thankfulness, gratitude, gratification, beauty, 15, 16, 79, 106, 111, 144-146, 149-157, 167-184; χαρίζομαι (*charizomai*): show a favour or kindness, gratify, oblige, 144-146, 148, 150-154, 159, 167-168, 172; χαρίεις (*charieis*): graceful, beautiful, 152-154, 177-179, 182; ἄχαρις (*acharis*): without grace, ungracious, thankless, 151
Charites, 8, 144-146, 155-157, 159, 161, 169, 170-177, 179-181, 341
Charon, 179
cheese, 86, 91, 93, 205, 207
chiefdom, chieftain, 46, 65-67, 113, 116, 189
Chios, 309
chitōn (χιτών): garment worn next to the skin, tunic, 89, 114, 116, 119-120, 122-127, 130-131, 174, 183, 208, 212, 228, 229, 258, 299
chlaina (χλαῖνα): upper-garment, cloak, blanket, 89, 119-120, 122-127, 130-131, 133, 136, 138-139, 212, 228-229, 302
Chloris, 224
chreios (χρεῖος): need, want, use, debt, 15, 55, 79, 267-273, 276
chrēmata (χρήματα): need, wealth, property, 206, 269, 284, 295-297, 308, 310
Chrysēis, 153, 171, 193, 195, 209, 213, 242, 292
Chryses, 91, 152-153, 193, 209, 219, 292
Cilicians, 205
Circe (Kirke), 109, 124-126, 138, 176, 224, 277, 299
Cithaeron (Kithairon), 319
citizenship, 199, 335, 344
class-struggle, 60, 64-65
Cleisthenes (Kleisthenes), 199
Cleitus, 147
Cleobulos, 312
cloth beam s. *antion,* 164 (Figure)
Clotho (Klotho), 238-240
Clytemnestra (Klytaimestra), 171, 209, 234, 245
Coans, 312
coinage, 42, 51
Colaeus (Kolaios) 305
Colchis (Kolchis), 298
colonisation, 263, 303, 306
commodity-exchange, 54
competition, 7, 22-23, 46, 66, 100, 105, 133, 189, 220, 280-282, 290, 326-327, 329
concubine, 216, 245
consensus, 52, 60, 63, 111, 190-191, 230

INDEX & GLOSSARY OF GREEK TERMS

copper, 266, 305, 307
Corinth, 147, 207, 228, 279, 301, 308-309, 312, 319-321, 324-326
Cornwall, 307
cosmos, 78, 211, 221, 231
council, councillor, 66, 69, 186, 190, 213, 222, 230, 243, 254-255, 264, 277, 283
counsellor, 213, 217-218, 290
counter-gift, 15, 23, 28, 29-30, 48-49, 55, 63, 120, 156, 276, 335
couple, married, 8, 27, 121, 139, 140 (Figure), 168, 187, 224, 227, 245, 258, 311, 336, 338, 344
coverlet, 114, 119, 122-124, 126, 138-140 (Figure)
Cranaë, 137
cremation, 258-259
Croesus (Kroisos), 62, 112, 312
Cronos (Kronos), 86, 97, 218-219, 230
Ctesippus, 87
Curetes, 153
cultura, 330
cultural relativism, cultural relativists, 14, 40
cultural turn, 331
currency, 56-57
Cyclops, Cyclopes, 61, 86-92, 94-96, 241
Cyme (Kyme), 288
Cyprus (Kypros), 106, 119, 147, 207, 259, 306, 325
Cypselids (Kyselidai), 325-326
Cypselus (Kypselos), 301
Cyrene (Kyrene), 119, 303, 305
Cythera (Kythera), 106, 301

daidaleos (δαιδάλεος): cunningly or curiously wrought, 161-162, 172-173
Dardanelles, 207
Dargun, Lothar von, 31, 40, 44
debt, 51, 55, 69, 267-268, 270, 272-273, 276, 288
debt-economy, 54
decision-making, 67, 110, 190, 218, 226, 228, 244, 336, 340
Deïkoon, 215
Deinias, 181
Deiphobus, 216, 224, 283
Delphi, Delphians, 8, 17, 105, 112, 180, 277, 279, 300, 309, 312-315, 323-324, 333
Demeter, 175, 289
Democritus (Demokritos), 178
Demodocus (Demodokos), 132, 138, 149, 179, 186, 246

dēmos (δῆμος): people, 79, 97, 115-116, 118-119, 121-122, 152, 154, 180, 186-188, 193, 202-203, 205-206, 212-213, 215, 217, 225-228, 233-236, 248, 252-253, 264, 270, 272, 275, 284
dēmia (δήμια), 205, 214-215
dēmios (δήμιος): belonging to the people, 187, 270-271
dēmosia (δήμοσια), 105
dēmos (δημός): fat, 215
despoina (δέσποινα): mistress, 90-91, 278
diasma (δίασμα): starting-border, 164 (Figure), s. also *exastis*
Didyma, 312
dikaspolos (δικασπόλος): one who gives law, judge, arbiter, 217, 203
dikē (δίκη): custom, usage, order, righteousness, 211
dikaios (δίκαιος) righteous, 89: *eudikia* (εὐδικία) righteous dealing, 217: *adikos* (ἄδικος) wrongdoing, 275
Dike: Goddess of righteousness, justice, 221, 341
Diocles (Diokles), 85, 89, 298
Diodorus (Diodoros), 313
Diogenes Laërtius, 311
Diomedes, 16, 62, 96-99, 101-105, 107-109, 112, 128, 133, 148, 162, 206, 212, 215, 223, 242, 282
Dionysos, 139
Dioscuri (Dioskouroi), 113, 344
diplax (δίπλαξ): double-folded mantle, 120, 163, 302
dishonour(ed), 16, 160, 185-187, 199, 202, 224, 228, 245, 275, 284
distaff, 119, 330
distribution, 11, 17, 32, 44, 50, 57-59, 66, 68-69, 74, 100, 190, 201, 213, 215, 222, 225, 227, 230-232, 244, 257, 306, 318, 337, s. also redistribution
Dmetor, 204
dmōiai gynaikes (δμωαί γυναῖκες): serving women, 123, 159, 169, 206, 224
dmōs, dmōes (δμώς, δμῶες): serving man, 90-91, 160, 206, 224
Dolius, 243
Dolon, 94, 150, 282
Dolopians, 131, 205-206, 324
dolos, doloi (δόλος, δόλοι): trick, wiles, 183, 233, 235, 242-243, 245, 285-286
dōma (δῶμα), 89, 180
Donlan, Walter, 10-11, 16, 55, 63, 65-67, 74, 81, 96, 99-101, 107, 110, 189), 205

dosis (δόσις): giving, gift, 54, 79, 126, 142
dōron, dōra (δῶρον, δῶρα): gift, present, offering, 42, 55, 79, 82, 106-107, 113-120, 132-133, 135-136, 142, 150, 152-157, 225, 227-228, 277, 298
dōtinē (δωτίνη): gift (of the people), due, 55, 79, 83, 86, 92-93, 115-16, 121, 200, 204-205, 220
dowry, 8, 201-202
dues s. *dōtinē*
Dulichium, 298
Durkheim, Émile, 20-21, 36, 41-42, 50, 63, 230
dye-work, 301-302
Dymas, 158

Echeneus (Echeneos), 226
Echepolus (Echepolos), 147
Eëtion, 207, 257
egoism, 21, 31-32, 34, 49, 53, 80
Egypt, 152, 157, 255, 266, 295-300, 305, 307-308
eidōlon, eidōla (εἴδωλον, εἴδωλα): shade of the dead, 256, 259-261
eidos (εἶδος): appearance of a person, form, shape, 183, 225, 227, 260
Eirene, 221, 341
Elam, 307
Electra (Elektra), 166
Elis, 206, 272-275, 323
elite, 7, 55, 72, 264, 268, 305, 314, 327, 329
Elpenor, 254, 258
Empedocles (Empedokles), 300
emporion, 307-308
Enope, 201
Ephyra, 301, 318
Epidaurus (Epidauros), 319, 321, 325
epikouroi, 102, 105-106
epinētron (ἐπίνητρον): a ceramic covering to protect the knee and thigh and to protect a hard surface for working wool, 240
episkopos, 250, 252
ergazomai (ἐργάζομαι): work, labour, make, earn by working, 159-161, 206, 249
Eretria, 263-265, 320-321
Erinys, 210
Eriphyle, 197
esthēs, esthētes (ἐσθής, ἐσθῆτες): clothing, 115-116, 126, 118, 156, 258
eschatia (ἐσχατιά): edge, border, farthest part, 94, 205, 235
Eteoneus, 85, 131

Etruria, 306
Euaephnus (Euaiphnos), 275-276
Euëlthon, 119
Eumaeus (Eumaios), 83, 85-86, 88-92, 94-95, 109, 120, 123, 130-133, 136, 138, 142, 152, 160, 168, 206, 216, 220, 224, 275, 277, 279, 292-295
Eumelus (Eumelos), 205
Euneos, 266, 291
eunomia, 221, 341
Euphetus (Euphetos), 205
Euphorbus (Euphorbos), 177, 208
Euphrosyne, 180
Euripides, 10
Euryalus (Euryalos), 179, 267, 269, 281, 311
Eurycleia (Eurykleia), 159, 210, 216, 224, 228, 245, 292-294
Eurymedon, 225
Eurymedusa, 209
Eurynome, 170
Eurystheus, 206
Eurytos, 107
evolutionism, evolutionary theory, 14, 34, 40, 64, 65
exogamy, 325
exastis (ἔξαστις): starting-border, threading band, 164 (Figure)
Ezechiel, 305, 310

fame, 9, 217, 244-245, 252, 255-257, 282, 285, 336
fate, 147, 159, 169, 217, 236-240, 244, 252, 254, 260, 286, 292-293, 299
favour, 15, 29, 33, 35, 42, 45, 65, 87, 106, 109, 111, 133, 136, 142-148, 150-154, 167, 181-182, 232, 252, 329
Finley, Moses I., 10-12, 14, 16, 49, 61-68, 70, 72, 74, 80, 96, 98-99, 101, 104, 149, 161, 189, 203-204, 236, 294, 329
flax, 208, 266, 297-298, 329-330
footbath, 126
friendship, 25, 35, 68, 105, 107, 109-113, 119, 127, 133-134, 139, 144, 149, 228
funeral, 56-58, 154, 168, 182, 191, 229, 247, 253-256, 259, 265, 312, 318, 332, 334, 336-338f, 341, 343-345
funeral games, 100, 153, 156, 191, 199, 256-257, 262, 280-281, 291, 315, 336, 345

Gaetulia, 301, 303
Gaia, Ge, 108, 231
Gaul, Wilhelm, 34-35, 37

INDEX & GLOSSARY OF GREEK TERMS

Geleitherrschaft, 232, 339
generosity, 8, 10, 28, 31, 33-35, 55, 66, 67, 201, 226, 228, 313, 339
genos, 230
Geraneia mountains, 321
geras (γέρας): gift of honour, reward, 15-16, 79, 142, 150, 168, 185-189, 191-195, 198-199, 203, 209-210, 212-13, 215, 217, 223, 229, 232-236, 243-247, 254, 263, 266, 279, 310; *geraiō* (γεραίω): honour, reward with a gift, 86; *agerastos* (ἀγέραστος): without a gift of honour, unrecompensed, 192, 209
gēras (γῆρας): old age, 208, 244
Gernet, Louis, 10, 62-63, 65, 213, 313, 325-326
Gierke, Otto, 27-30
gift-exchange, 9-25, 27-30, 32-43, 45-55, 60-63, 65, 67-70, 72, 74, 76, 98-100, 109, 201, 269, 280, 290, 306, 307, 313, 333, 336, 340
gift-giving, 9-11, 13-14, 23-25, 27-31, 35, 38-39, 46-47, 49-52, 61-65, 67-68, 71, 76, 83, 98-99, 115, 118, 144, 227, 310, 333, 343
gigantomachy, 344
girdle, 138-139, 156, 239
goblets, 112-113, 257
godlike, 116, 121, 153-154, 202, 216, 236, 251
Glaucus (Glaukos), 16, 62, 96-103, 105, 107-109, 111-112, 128, 150, 202, 216
gold, 94, 97, 99-104, 106, 112, 114-121, 150, 170, 172, 175, 177, 197-198, 200, 207-208, 229, 257, 291, 295-298, 305, 307, 326
golden, 9, 97, 112-114, 118-122, 124-125, 135, 139, 154, 156-157, 172, 175, 237, 258, 295, 299, 311, 336
goods-exchange, 9, 11
goos (γόος): lament, complaint, 246-254, 269 s. also lament
Gorgon, 166
Graces s. Charites
grain, 90, 93-94, 119, 153, 266-267, 269, 288-289, 297-298, 303
gratitude, 29, 34, 182
graves, 114, 119, 165, 254, 306
Grimm, Jacob, 28, 76
guest-friendship, 11, 42, 54, 62, 67, 69-70, 80-83, 86, 88, 91-92, 96, 98-99, 101, 104-105, 107, 109-113, 117, 121-122, 135, 139, 156, 245, 257-259, 276-277, 290, 296, 305-306, 310-312, 315, 325-326, 335-336, 338-340
guest-gift, 15, 29, 35, 42, 54-55, 68, 72, 73, 79, 80, 96-97, 107, 113-114, 119-120, 182, 191, 257, 291, 305-306, 313, 333, 337-339

Hades, 92, 179, 192, 231, 234, 237, 246, 247, 256, 258-259, 278
hair, 109, 130, 169, 177, 183, 208, 214, 220
hairband, 172
Halbwachs, Maurice, 41, 141
Halitherses, 148
Harpalion, 106
Hasebroek, Johannes, 267, 290, 308
heanos (ἑανός): fine robe, 162, 258
Hebe, 176
Hector (Hektor), 94, 101-104, 106-108, 134, 141-143, 147, 149, 154, 160-163, 169, 174, 177-178, 183, 191, 196, 212, 214-216, 229, 236-238, 240, 246-252, 254-258, 263, 283, 286, 291, 302
Hecuba (Hekabe), 88, 174, 208, 224, 238, 248-250, 252, 254, 299, 303
Heddle, s. *mitos*
heddle bar, heddle rod s. *kanōn*, 164 (Figure)
hedna (ἕδνα): bridewealth, wedding-gifts, 55, 155, 199
hēgemonia, 191
heimata (εἵματα): garment, 89, 94, 115-116, 123, 126, 130-133, 170, 173, 176-179, 195, 228, 245, 258, 299
heirloom, 58, 107, 312
Hekamede, 209
Helen, Helena, 85, 113, 117-120, 128-129, 131, 134, 137, 139, 141, 159-163, 166, 173-174, 176, 192, 196-197, 211, 227-228, 234, 248, 251-252, 262, 283, 286, 295-297, 299-300, 302, 305, 307, 312, 345
Helice (Helike), 152
Helios, 152, 91, 108, 135, 138, 231, 235, 276
Hellespont, 112, 255
Hephaestus (Hephaistos), 84, 103, 114, 157, 160-162, 167, 170, 174, 197, 219, 311
Hera 103, 109, 133, 138, 142, 152, 156, 162, 172, 206, 224, 229, 238, 254, 299, 303, 305, 322
Heracles (Herakles), 272-273, 312
Heraclides, 308, 325
Heraion, 263, 314, 320-321, 324
herdsmen, 83-84, 86, 88-95, 120, 206-207, 269, 275-276, 279, 289, 290
herkos (ἕρκος): fence, enclosure, 277
hermai, 278
Hermes, 85, 87-88, 91, 103, 133, 143, 152-153, 176, 179, 180, 219-220, 261 (Figure), 278-280, 285, 289, 316, 325
Hermione, 301
Herod, 222

Herodotus, 10, 84-85, 93, 111-112, 119, 296, 298-300, 303, 305, 307-309, 326
hero-cult, 17, 74-75, 192, 263-264, 322
hero-worship, 14
Hesiod (Hesiodos), 23, 139, 172, 180-183, 221, 266, 281, 287-289, 325, 341
Hestia, 180
Hesychius, 300
hetairoi, 159, 187, 216
Himalaya, 320
Hippolochus, 150
Hippomachus, 147
Hire, 201
histopodes (ἱστόποδες): loom upright, 164 (Figure)
histos (ἱστός): loom, beam of the loom, 162, 169, 173, 176, 178, 209, 233-235
Historical School of national economy, 13-14, 20-26, 42
Historical Legal School, 30-32, 34
homo oeconomicus, 21, 24, 37, 71
honey, 258, 301-302
honour s. *timē*
Horae (Horai), 241, 341
horkia (ὅρκια) oaths, swearing solemnly at a sacrifice, 70, 108-110, 134, 137, 383
horkos (ὅρκος): oath, 109, 277, 320
hospitality, 32-34, 37, 39, 61, 69-71, 80-87, 89, 92-93, 95-96, 106-107, 109, 112-113, 118, 120-121, 123-123, 126-131, 133-136, 139, 144, 151, 213, 226-228, 261, 272, 277, 305
household-economy, 40
Huelva, 305
hyphainō (ὑφαίνω): weave, 116, 162, 169, 181, 233, 242-243, 302
hyphasma (ὕφασμα): woven robe, web, 143, 166
Hypnos, 156
Hypsenor, 215

Idaeus, 135, 196
idion (ἴδιον): one's own, 144, 187, 270-271
Idomeneus, 129, 160, 205-206, 214
Ilus, 255, 296
Imbros, 251
immortality, 177, 179, 232, 259, 262
individualism, 20, 30-31, 37, 40, 43, 48
Indonesia, 164, 343
Ino Leucothea s. Leucothea
international law, 32, 110
Ion, 166

Iphidamas, 155
Iphigenia, 166
Iphitos, 107, 111-112, 272, 276
Iran, 306
iron, 150, 257, 297, 303, 305, 307, 330, 333
Iron Age, 74, 329-330
Isthmia, 309, 321
Isthmus, 301, 308-309, 314
istōr (ἵστωρ): one who knows law and right, judge, 221
Italy, 317, 320, 322, 324, 327
Ithaca, 87, 90, 94-95, 109, 116-122, 131, 135, 160, 170-171, 173-174, 189, 196, 218-219, 227, 233, 235, 271-272, 275, 277, 295, 302, 309, 313-314, 324

Jason, 166, 221, 291
Jhering, Rudolf von, 31-34, 36-37, 39, 72, 73, 80-82, 88, 290
judge, 225, 227, s. also *dikaspolos*

kairos (καῖρος): shed bar, 164 (Figure)
kalyptrē (καλύπτρη): veil, 162, 173, 208, 282
kamnō (κάμνω): toil, labour for someone, 161-162, 166-168, 195, 241, 254; kamatos (κάματος): the product of toil, 94, 168
kanōn (κανών): heddle bar, heddle rod, 164 (Figure), 239
keimēlia (κειμήλια): treasure, 112, 117, 207, 297
keleuō (κελεύω): order one to do, command, 160-161, 243
kerdos (κέρδος): gain, advantage, 15, 79, 94, 267-269, 275-276, 280-290, 297, 326; kerdiōn, kerdion (κερδίων, κέρδιον): more profitable, more advantageously, 280-286, 290; kerdaleos (κερδαλέος): crafty, cunning, 280-282, 285-286; kerdaleophrōn (κερδαλεόφρων): greedy of gain, 193, 283; kerdosynē (κερδοσύνη): craft, cunning, 286
kerkis (κερκίς): weavers's shuttle, 164 (Figure)
kēr, kēres (κήρ, κῆρες): doom, weights in scales of Zeus, 240-241, 260
kerostasia, 260
kidnapping, 280, 310
kinship, 64-66, 68, 104, 107, 149
Kinyras, 106, 147
kleos (κλέος): rumour, good report, fame, 101, 177-118, 212, 217, 246, 255-258, 262, 265-256, 282-283
klēroi (κλῆροι): lots of land, 203
klōthō (κλώθω): spin, twist by spinning, 240

INDEX & GLOSSARY OF GREEK TERMS 419

kindness s. *aganophrosynē*
kingship s. *basileus*
Knossos, 218, 306, 316
Koatoporeia, 207
koiranos (κοίρανος): military leader, 218
komizō (κομίζω): take care of, provide for, attend, 83, 127-131; *komidē* (κομιδή): attendance, care, 130
Köstler, Rudolf, 48, 61-62, 69, 88, 110, 155, 220-221
kratēr (κρατήρ): mixing bowl, 117, 122, 135, 228, 263
kratos (κράτος): strength, might, power, 115, 191-192, 226
krēdemon, krēdemna (κρήδεμνον): woman's head-dress, veil, 141, 171, 197, 208, 232, 241, 260-261, 299
Krethon, 194, 240
Krisean plain, 324
krokē (κρόκη): weft thread, 164 (Figure), 239
ktēmata (κτήματα): (mobile) possessions, 92, 115, 134, 196, 207, 225, 235, 295-297, 310
kudos (κῦδος): glory resulting from victory in the battle, renown, 101, 104, 152, 192, 198-199, 214, 222-223, 238, 283
Kula, Kula ring, Kula traders, 9, 12, 37, 57

Labda, 301
labour, 23, 40, 65, 74, 94, 145, 160-161, 167-168, 183, 204, 206, 250, 263, 279, 309-310
labour force, 74
Lacedaemonians, 111, 275-276
Lachesis, 240
Laconia, 301-304, 321
Laërtes, 89, 120, 122, 127-129, 157, 160, 178, 206, 233, 235, 243, 245-246, 263, 277, 293-294
Laestrygonians, 87, 94, 96
laiai = agnythes: loom weights, 164 (Figure)
Laius (Laios), 319
lament, 192, 246-249, 252-254, 258, 263-265, 269 s. also *goos, thrēnos*
lampros (λαμπρός): bright, radiant, 174-175, 178
lanolin, 174
Laogonos, 215
Laomedon, 94, 138, 151, 242, 292
Laothoë, 102
Laum, Bernhard, 18, 42-43, 48, 50, 61, 120, 276
laos, laoi (λαός, λαοί), men, people, work-people, 106, 151, 171, 186, 206, 214, 216-217, 219, 227, 244, 249, 271-272

lead, 305
Lechaion, 308
Lefkandi, 114, 259
Leiodes, 150
Lelegans, 206
Lemnos, 213, 251, 291, 302, 305
Leto, 103
Leucothea (Leukothea), 232, 241, 260, 262
Levi-Strauss, Claude, 45-46, 54, 68
leukos (λευκός): light, bright, clear, white, 175, 178, 258
liberal theory, 13, 39
Libya, 207, 292, 303
lifespan, 58, 259, 262
Lindos, 298, 312
Linear B, 124, 157, 189, 205, 277, 316
linen, 114, 122, 125, 126, 174, 208, 258, 266, 269, 295, 297-299, 310
liparos (λιπαρός): shiny (with oil), bright, brilliant, radiant, splendid, 171, 174, 200-201, 208, 221, 243-244, 299
Litae (Litai), 211
liturgies (leitourgiai), 29, 50, 152
livestock, 28, 76, 84, 87, 93, 95, 266, 271-280, 284-287, 289-289, 294, 297, 309-310, 315-316, 323
loan, 22
Lobates, 207
loom, 91-92, 114, 157, 161-165, 168, 176, 182, 184-185, 209, 233, 239-243, 266, 329-330, 338
loom weights: *agnythes* (ἀγνῦθες), 145, 164 (Figure)
Lucretius, 301
Lycaon (Lykaon), 257, 291-292, 295, 297
Lycia, 97, 104, 147, 189, 202, 207

Macedonia, 152, 309
Magna Graecia, 305
Maleia, 278
Malinowski, Bronislaw, 9-12, 14, 19, 25-26, 33, 41, 44-45, 50, 53-57, 62-63, 331
Manticlus, 276
market-exchange, market-economy, 19, 48, 52
Mari, 307
marriage, 54, 58, 61-64, 67, 102, 117, 138-139, 141, 144-145, 148, 155-156, 171-172, 200, 202, 223-224, 232-234, 238, 241, 312, 322, 325-326, 332, 336

Martial, 10
Massilia, 307
materialism, 40
matriarchy, 14, 64, 236
Mauss, Marcel, 9-11, 13-14, 19-20, 27-28, 32-39, 41-45, 47-50, 53-57, 60, 62-63, 65, 67, 70, 76, 98
meat, 50, 86, 91, 95, 124f., 128, 180, 197, 202, 205, 215, 235, 297
Medon, 224
Megara, 319-21
megaron (μέγαρον), 115, 128-129, 162, 233, 235, 251, 297, 299
mēla (μῆλα): sheeps or goats, small cattle, 95, 197, 202, 217, 279
Melanthius, 295
Melantho, 160
Meleager, 153, 203
Melissa, 301, 325
Melos, 106, 300
mementoes, 113, 117-118, 122
memorialisation, 262
memory, 16, 59, 63, 77, 79, 98, 118, 121, 136, 146, 176, 181-182, 232, 243-245, 252, 255, 262, 299, 307, 336, 341, 344-345
Menelaus, 85, 101, 103, 105-108, 117-119, 122, 129, 131, 134-136, 139, 150, 160, 181, 183, 187, 194-199, 205-207, 214, 223, 230, 238, 242, 255, 270-271, 281-282, 295-298, 303, 305, 307, 311
Menidi, 263
Mentes, 62, 120, 126, 197, 206, 233, 277, 296, 301, 305-306
Mentor, 109, 207, 271, 276
mercenary, 296
Meriones, 106
Mesopotamia, 306
Messene, 272, 274, 276
Messenia, 208, 263, 312, 321
Messenian War, 275-276, 321
Mesta, 317-318
metal-routes, 306-307, 309
metalwork, 161-162, 221
Metaneira, 175
mētis (μῆτις): cunning, wisdom, skill, craft, counsel, plan, 100, 218, 232, 242-43, 282, 285
Meyer, Richard M., 29-30, 35-36, 51, 70
migration, 205, 276, 278, 303, 315-319
Miletus, 312
Minos, 218, 225

misogyny, 245
misthos (μισθός): hire, wage, recompense, reward, 94, 144, 152, 237, 241-242
mitos (μίτος): warp, heddle, 239
mixing bowl, 113, 117, 119, 122, 125, 135, 166 (Figure), 257, 391, 295, 302, 305, 307, 336
mnēma (μνῆμα): memorial, memento, remembrance, grave mound, 107, 254-255
Mnemosyne, 341
moira (μοῖρα): one's portion of life, lot, fate, destiny, 237, 240, 275-276, 297
Moirae, Moirai, 210, 221, 238, 240, 341
Mommsen, Theodor, 37, 81
monarchy, 64, 189-190, 201, 203, 229, 337
money, 18, 25, 33, 42-43, 51, 54, 195
moral economy, 46, 47, 53
Morocco, 303
mother-right, 63
murex, 269, 301-306
Muse, Muses, 113, 144, 180, 253-254, 279, 341
mutualism, mutuality, 21, 30-31, 53
Mycenae, Mycenaean, 16, 63-64, 74, 98, 100, 105-106, 124, 139, 157, 159, 165, 188-190, 201, 203, 205-208, 224, 240, 259, 263, 274, 290, 297, 303, 306, 316, 320
Myrmidons, 206-207, 216, 248
mythos, 242, 186
Mytilene, 312

Naucratis, 307-308
Nausicaa, 117, 121, 126, 138, 142, 158-159, 169-171, 176, 224, 226, 261, 278, 286, 299
nectar, 84-85, 258
neighbourhood, 325
Nektunebo I., 308
Neleus, 124, 224, 273-274
Neoptolemus, 209
Nereid, 258
Nestor, 84-85, 101, 106, 109, 122, 124, 128-129, 135, 141, 153, 176, 186-187, 206-209, 211-213, 216, 218, 222-224, 238, 242-243, 270, 272-274, 281, 295-296, 302
Niobe, 168, 254
Noëmon, 275
noos (νόος): mind, sense, wit, 138, 281-282
nymph, 85, 88, 91, 232

oath, 62, 69-70, 98, 107-110, 121, 134-135, 137, 141, 144, 178, 180, 230, 277, 294
Oceanus (Okeanos), 138, 239

INDEX & GLOSSARY OF GREEK TERMS 421

Odysseus, 16, 67, 81, 84-95, 101, 105-107, 109, 111-113, 115-123, 125-133, 136-138, 141-142, 147-154, 160, 162, 168-171, 173-176, 178-179, 185, 193-194, 197-198, 203-206, 210, 212, 216-218, 224-228, 230, 232-237, 241-244, 246, 254, 258-261, 267, 269-270, 272, 275-279, 281-286, 292-294, 296-299, 301-302, 306-307

Oedipus (Oidipous), 207, 319

Oenussae (Oinoussai), 309

Oineus, 97, 99-100, 103, 128

oikos, 72, 123, 128, 141, 189, 228, 233, 245, 271, 297, 334

olbos (ὄλβος): happiness, bliss, wealth, 238, 244, 279, 288

Olympia, 108, 274, 285, 313-314, 323-324

offering, 11, 84, 89, 108, 143, 147-148, 150, 152-154, 159, 162, 177, 204, 222, 262, 265, 298, 312-313, 315, 333, 337-339

office holding, 67

Onchestos, 279, 321-322

ōnos (ὦνος): ransom for a person brought to foreign people, purchase-money, price, 15, 55, 79, 89, 257, 267-269, 280, 290-295, 297, 310

ophelos (ὄφελος): use, benefit, advantage, 150, 178, 281

oral poetry, 16, 77, 100, 161, 181

Orchomenos, 174-175, 205, 207, 321-322

Orestes, 166, 245

Orsilochus, 194, 240

Ortilochus, 205, 272

othoninum, 299

Ouranos, 231

Palmyra, 164, 308

Panakton, 320

Panathenaia, 146, 158, 341

Pandora, 162, 172f., 183f.

Pandareus, 160, 241

Pandarus, 147, 150, 283

Paris, 103, 106-107, 129, 134-135, 137, 141, 173, 183-184, 196, 211, 251, 283, 311

passō (πάσσω): sprinkle, besprinkle, 162-163, 166

pasture, 93, 95, 266, 270, 274-276, 278-280, 284-285, 290, 293, 309, 315-318, 320-325, 338, 340

patricide, 245

Patroclus, 84, 101-102, 134, 141, 148-150, 153, 168, 177-178, 194-195, 198-199, 216, 240, 246-248, 251-255, 257-259, 280, 283, 303, 305

patronage, 68, 72, 205

pattern-weaving s. weaving

Pausanias, 104, 274-276, 279, 301, 321-322

Pedasus, 201

peirar (πεῖραρ): rope, weft, end, completion, 239-240

Peisistratus, 16, 85, 89, 118, 124, 131, 135, 230, 235, 238, 326, 340

Peithetairos, 309

Peitho, 172

Peleus, 84, 88, 102, 131, 200, 205-206, 223, 238, 257

Pelops, 219, 311

pēnē (πήνη) = *krokē*: weft thread, 164 (Figure), 243

Penelope, 16, 63, 78, 89, 91-92, 115, 118-122, 126-131, 136, 138, 141, 148, 150, 159-162, 170-173, 178-179, 185, 189, 196-198, 208, 210, 212, 217, 224, 227-228, 232-237, 240, 242-244, 246, 260, 263, 281, 284-286, 299, 335

pēnion (πηνίον) = *kerkis*: (weft) spool, 164 (Figure), 239

peplos (πέπλος): any woven cloth, upper garment worn by women, robe, 117-120, 122, 126, 139, 141-143, 156, 158, 161-162, 174, 177-178, 181, 229, 258, 299, 302-303, 325, 341, 344

Perachora, 321, 324

Peraeus, 129, 228

Periandrus, 301, 308, 312, 325

Pericles, 105

pernēmi (πέρνημι): transfer, sell, 292

Persephone, 92

Perses, 288

Persia, Persian, 10, 85, 111, 152, 190, 265, 296, 344-345

Phaeacia, Phaeacians, 90, 92-93, 113-116, 118, 120-123, 125-128, 130, 141-142, 154, 159, 161, 170-173, 179, 197-198, 204-206, 208, 216-217, 225-227, 230, 232, 238, 241, 244-245, 267-270, 284, 302, 337

Phaidimus, 122

Phainos, 106

Phanodikos, 313

pharmakon (φάρμακον): drug, medicine, chemical reagent, poison, 176, 277, 295-296, 299-301, 306

Pharnabazus, 111-112

pharos (φᾶρος): cloak, mantle, 114, 116, 119, 122, 124, 126-127, 176, 178, 208, 229, 233-235, 237, 258, 282, 299, 302

Pherae, Pherai, 89, 201
Pheretime, 119
phialē, 257-258, 312
Phigalia, 275
philia (φιλία): friendship, belonging, 110-111, 119
Philochoros, 298
Philoctetes, 206
Philoetius, 94-95, 206, 275
philotēs (φιλότης): friendship, belonging, affection, intercourse, 83, 107-108, 110, 118, 127-129, 133-139, 141, 143-144, 149, 155-156, 171, 212, 227-229, 245, 310, 338; *phileō* (φιλέω): love, regard with affection, 83, 89, 105, 127-133, 137, 159, 186, 218, 227, 277; *philos, philē* (φίλος, φίλη): beloved, dear, one's own, 141-142, 144, 159, 170-171, 250-252, 259, 294, 298, 336
phoinikoeis (φοινικόεις): purple-red, crimson, red, 302
phortos, phortia (φόρτος, φορτία): load, freight, cargo, 268, 288-289, 308
phrēn (φρήν): mind, thought, 97, 99, 137, 169, 171, 173, 179, 181, 210, 225, 235, 242-243, 286
Phocaeans, 307, 309
Phoenix, 126, 131-133, 147, 205-206, 211, 223, 245, 269
Phoenicians, 82, 290, 292, 294-295, 303, 305, 307, 310
phoros, phoroi (φόρος, φόροι): that which is brought in, tribute, 207, 309
Phthia, 106, 131, 194, 206, 248
Pieria, 279
pirates, piracy, 269-270, 275, 296, 308
Pithekussai, 306
Plakos, 218, 224
Plataea, 262, 296, 303
Plato, 84, 99, 211, 240, 254, 276, 326, 341
Pliny (Plinius), 299-301, 303, 316
ploutos (πλοῦτος): wealth, riches, 194-195, 238, 279, 288, 298
Plutarch (Plutarchos), 9, 298, 301, 312-313
Pindar (Pindaros), 10, 146, 174-175, 177, 180-182, 304-305
poikilos (ποικίλος): many-coloured, patterned, 117, 138, 161-163, 181, 346
poinē (ποινή): blood-money, were-gild, fine, penalty, 55, 195-196; *nēpoinos* (νήποινος): without fine, without compensation, 92, 168, 196, 285, 297

Polanyi, Karl, 10-11, 39, 43-44, 52-53, 144, 267, 308
polis, 10, 15, 17, 51, 59, 64-68, 71-74, 79, 100-111, 152, 192, 199, 207, 211, 252-253, 263-264, 271, 277, 284, 295, 297, 314, 318, 320, 322, 326, 333-334, 340
Pollux, 208, 299-301, 344
Polybius, 275
Polybus, 119, 295, 305, 319
Polycaste, 124, 126
Polychares, 275-276
Polycrates, 326
Polydeuces, 262
Polydorus, 102, 291
Polygnotus, 105
Polyneices, 105, 206
Polyphemus, 83, 86-89, 91-96, 116, 121, 204, 207, 242, 270, 323
pompē (πομπή): conduct, escort, procession, 93, 115-16, 122, 132, 226-228, 238-239
porphyreos (πορφύρεος): purple, 112, 120, 124-126, 175-176, 258, 302
Poseidon, 94, 103, 151-152, 198-199, 227, 230-232, 239, 241, 276, 282, 292, 309, 321
potlatch, 20, 35, 37, 46, 50, 62-63, 67, 98-100
potnia (πότνια): title of honour, mistress, female ruler, 141, 157, 224, 229, 232, 247-248, 250, 293
power, 17-18, 22, 37-40, 45, 57-60, 63, 67-68, 70, 72-73, 79, 99, 115, 146, 156, 160, 169, 175, 181-182, 185, 189-192, 196, 200-201, 207, 211, 218-219, 220-223, 226-228, 230, 232, 234, 236, 240, 243-245, 252, 264, 281-283, 300, 305, 309, 314, 318, 323, 326, 336-340
prēktēr (πρηκτήρ): accomplisher, one who does or executes, 268-270
pre-state(hood), 16, 61-62, 65, 68-70, 72-73, 339
prestige goods, 9, 11, 53, 67, 69, 73, 314
prēxis (πρῆξις): doing, transaction, business, 15, 79, 187, 267-271
priasthai (πρίασθαι): acquire, buy, purchase, 292-294; *apriatēn* (ἀπριάτην): without purchase-money (ὄνος), 292-293
Priam (Priamos), 93, 102, 105, 129, 141-143, 168, 196, 206-207, 215, 220, 228, 236, 238, 249, 253, 257-258, 269, 291
price, 15, 44, 108, 154, 267, 276, 290-293, 308, 310
Priene, 312
private, 19, 48, 64, 68, 96, 187-188, 201, 203-204, 212, 271, 329

INDEX & GLOSSARY OF GREEK TERMS

prize s. *aethla*
probata (πρόβατα): four-footed cattle, flocks, herds, sheep and goats, 278-279
profit, 15, 19, 25-26, 41-42, 44, 46, 49-52, 54, 66, 94, 98, 233, 267-268, 275, 279-282, 284-285, 287-290, 292, 294, 305, 311, 326, 330
Proserpina, 166
Prosymna, 263
prothesis (πρόθεσις): ritual of laying out the dead corpse and lament, 166, 246, 253, 258, 263
Psammetichus I., 296
psychē, psychai, 259-260
public, 22, 29, 69, 80, 86, 101, 105, 179, 187-188, 197, 210-211, 214-215, 220, 233, 253, 271, 344
purchase, 26, 28, 42, 266, 268, 290
purple, 99-101, 107, 113, 120, 122, 124-126, 139, 163, 173, 175-176, 178, 208, 245, 258, 263, 266, 295, 301-305, 310, 319, 326, 345
purple-dyeing, 301, 303
Pylos, Pylians, 85, 109, 118, 122, 134-135, 152, 171, 201, 206-207, 218, 224, 235, 270-275, 279, 296, 302, 316

quit-money, 195

Rachi, 301
rag, 126
ramson s. *apoina*
rationalism, 19, 40, 42, 48, 51
reciprocity, 9-12, 21-26, 29-30, 36-37, 43-44, 47-48, 50, 52-59, 62, 67-68, 71, 76, 81, 96, 98, 110, 120, 133, 143-144, 146, 149-151, 153-154, 156, 159, 167-168, 182, 184, 186, 188, 190, 202, 204, 277, 287, 310-311, 334, 338
redistribution, 44, 57, 65, 307
replacement, 52, 57, 59, 66
revenge, 88, 129, 135, 198, 247, 249, 254, 277, 344 s. also *tisis*
Rhadamanthys, 241
rhakos (ῥάκος): ragged, tattered garment, 126
rhēgea (ῥήγεα): blankets, 122-126, 138, 299, 302
Rhexenor, 236
robbery, 36, 39, 280, 290, 295
rod s. *kanōn*, 164, 239
rosette-motif, 163, 166
rulership, 10-11, 54, 63, 67, 70-71, 73, 79, 188-190, 192, 200-201, 205-207, 209, 217, 219, 225, 231-232, 309, 339

sacrifice, 11, 29, 50-51, 88, 108-110, 128, 133, 134, 137, 141-142, 152, 154, 231, 276, 290, 309, 324, 338, 341
Sahlins, Marshall, 11, 38, 50, 53-55, 60
Salamis, 119, 306
salt-money, 54
Samaina, 326
Samoa, 55, 57-59
Samos, 267, 275, 299, 305, 326
Samothrace, 251
sanctuary, 299, 305, 309, 312, 315, 320-321, 323, 325
Sappho, 175, 177, 180
Sarakatsani, 275
Sardis, 298
Sarpedon, 101, 103, 150, 178, 202, 204, 206, 216, 233, 225, 240, 254, 257
sceptre s. *skēptron*
Schedius, 206
Schmoller, Gustav von, 21-22, 44
Schurtz, Heinrich, 35, 54, 56
Scopas, 344
sea-trade, 269
Selene, 231, 235
self-interest, 21, 25, 31, 51, 53, 60, 71, 81-82, 313
sēma (σῆμα): sign, mark, mound, 121, 254-257, 262
sēmainō (σημαίνω): give signs, signify, indicate, point out, 214, 223,
sēmantores (σημάντορες): leader, commander, informer, guide, 227-228
Seneca, 10, 240
Service, Elman, 60, 65
Seven Sages, 9, 17, 311, 313, 323
shame s. *aidōs*
sheep, 88, 93-95, 155, 197, 202, 205, 207, 217, 233, 272-273, 275, 279, 289, 293, 316-317, 325, 333
shepherd, 92, 94, 97, 102, 116, 120, 123-123, 136, 151, 216, 219-220, 227, 237, 243, 268-269, 272-273, 275-276, 279, 281, 284-285, 297, 318-320, 323, 333, 339
shroud, 78, 114, 164, 178, 182, 191, 232-236, 240, 259-260, 262-264, 299, 335-337, 341
sigaloeis (σιγαλόεις): glossy, glittering, 114, 229
Sicily, 145
Sikyon, 147, 218, 225
Sidon, Sidonian, 109, 117, 141, 163, 257, 291-294, 303, 305
sight, 24, 54, 138, 154, 226-227

silphium, 304
silver, 101, 107, 114, 117, 119, 124-125, 172, 175, 177, 197, 208, 251, 256-257, 291, 295-297, 299, 301-303, 305, 307, 326, 336
Simiand, François, 36
Simmel, Georg, 36
Simonides, 253, 344
Siphnos, 298, 326
slave-labour, 268
slave-trade, 294
skēptron (σκῆπτρον): staff, stick, sceptre, 175, 208, 217, 218-223, 225-227, 229-230, 236
Smith, Adam, 21, 39-40
Socus, 224, 241
Solon, 8-9, 65, 199, 287, 312-313
Somló, Felix, 24, 36, 74
Sophocles, 320
Spain, 306-307
Sparta, Spartans, 62, 85, 105, 111-112, 118, 124-125, 128, 159, 161, 171, 187, 201, 204, 227, 235, 275-276, 286, 295-296, 305, 312, 321
Sphinges (sg. Sphinx), 259-260
spindle, 119, 161, 168, 173, 240, 266, 295, 299, 329-330
Spinning Mule, 329
spinning wheel, 329
spoils, 116, 185, 194, 199
spool, 239, s. also *pēnion*
starting-border, 239, s. also *exastis, diasma*
state, statehood, 10, 16-17, 32, 38, 42-43, 48, 52, 60-61, 64-73, 91, 99, 107, 133, 136, 144, 187-188, 201, 207, 210-211, 220, 245, 262, 273, 318, 330
stēmōn, s. warp thread
Stesichorus, 177
Sthenelus, 148, 223
Strabo, 274, 308, 320
structuralism, structuralist, 14, 51, 88, 91, 334
Styx, 231
subsistence, 11, 53
Sumatra, 167, 262
symmachia, 110
symposium, 99, 121, 332, 336
Syria, 295, 298, 306

tamiē (ταμίη): housekeeper, one who distributes, dispenser 85, 124-125, 209, 237
tapestry, tapestries, 221-222, 345-346

tapētes (τάπητες): carpets, rugs spread on seats and beds, 112, 119, 122, 124, 126, 131, 229, 302
Taphians, 62, 206, 293
Taphos, 301
Tartaros, 231
Tartessos, 305, 307
Taurus, 307
tax, taxes, taxation, 23, 31, 35, 61, 66, 70, 204, 308, 318, 339
tears, 132, 168, 209, 220, 248, 250-251, 253-254, 300
technē (τέχνη): skill, art, craft, 161, 169, 173, 181
Tegea, 325
Teiresias, 219
Telemachus, 62, 85, 89, 92, 95, 109, 117-118, 120, 122-126, 129-131, 134-136, 139, 141, 148, 154, 161-161, 170-171, 174, 176, 187, 197-198, 203, 206, 216-219, 224, 227-228, 233-235, 242, 270-271, 275, 277, 284, 286, 290, 295, 297, 299-300, 302-303, 305, 310
telos (τέλος): due, toll, a length of time, end, state of completion, something ordered to be done, 180, 196, 240-242, 244
temenos (τέμενος): a piece of land cut off, 153, 200-204, 213
Temesa, 305
Teucer (Teukros), 101
textiles, 7, 18, 56-58, 70, 78, 82-83, 88-92, 112-114, 116-119, 122-124, 127-128, 133, 138-139, 143, 145, 157-158, 161-166, 173, 176, 181-182, 195, 197, 221, 229, 239, 241, 245, 257-258, 262-263, 265, 269, 291, 296-299, 302-303, 307, 328-329, 333-337, 339, 341-343, 346
thalamos (θάλαμος): chamber, store-room, bedroom, 114, 117, 270
thalassa (θάλασσα): sea, 172, 193, 217, 231
Thales, 312
Thangka, 222
thankfulness, 145
Thasos, 298, 305
thauma (θαῦμα): wonder, marvel, 162, 172-173, 194, 345
Theagenes, 78, 344
Theano, 130, 142, 156, 228
Thebes (Boiotian), 105, 157, 206-207, 312, 321-322
Thebes (Egyptian), 119, 205, 295, 305, 307
Themis (personification of good counsel), 69, 220-221, 315, 341, 345

INDEX & GLOSSARY OF GREEK TERMS

themis (θέμις): that which is laid down, law as established by custom, 84, 87, 96, 175, 207, 220-221; *themistes* (θέμιστες): laws as established by custom, *phoroi*, 93, 200-201, 204, 207-208, 218-222, 225, 230, 243-244, 315, 336, 339, 341; *themisteuō* (θεμιστεύω), ministering law 90; *themistopolos* (θεμιστοπόλος): ministering law and right, 175
Themistocles, 346-347
Theoclymenus, 129, 136, 206, 228, 230, 234
Theognis, 268, 325-326
Theocritus, 119, 240, 274
theomachy, 103-104
Theophrastus, 51, 313, 316
Thera, 301
therapōn (θεράπων): retainer, 85, 206
Thersites, 138
Theseus, 174
Thesprotia, Thesprotians, 130, 297-298, 301
Thessaly, 301-302, 309, 324
thēteuō (θητεύω): be a hireling, 94
Thetis, 84, 102-103, 109, 143, 167, 174, 198, 200, 224, 229, 241, 256
Thetys, 138
Thoas, 160, 206, 215, 257, 291, 302-303, 305
thōē (θωή): penalty, 147-148
thōrax (θώραξ): corslet, armour, 106, 147, 162, 202
Thrace, 62, 213
Thrasyllus, 105
Thrasymelos, 206
thrēnos (θρῆνος): lament, complaint, 246, 249, 253-254
Thucydides, 105, 252, 262, 299, 301, 308, 320-321
Thurnwald, Richard C., 9, 24-25, 36-37, 39, 44
Thyestes, 219
timē (τιμή): honour, esteem, worth, dignity, authority, present of honour, 15, 185-189, 191-200, 203-204, 208, 210-212, 214, 218, 222-223, 225-236, 244, 252, 262, 276, 280, 287, 291; *timaō* (τιμάω): to honour, to revere, 92, 116, 186, 192, 200, 202, 213-216, 228-230, 308; *tiō* (τίω): to honour, to esteem, 83, 186, 192, 213-216, 224, 228, 245, 284; *atimazō* (ἀτιμάζω): to bring dishonour upon, suffer dishonour, treat as unworthy of, 186, 213, 215-216, 224, 228, 245, 284; *timēeis, timēessa* (τιμήεις, τιμήεσσα): honoured 114, 193, 197-199, 218;
timios, eritimos (τίμιος, ἐρίτιμος): valued, 198; *atimos, atimētos* (ἄτιμος, ἀτίμητος): dishonoured, without present of honour, 185, 192-199, 209, 233, 285
tin-route, 306-307
tisis (τίσις): vengeance, 195, 200, 277
Tönnies, Ferdinand, 25
toll, 207, 308-309
tomb-markers, 264 s. also *sēma, mnēma*
trade, 9, 11, 15, 26, 29, 32-33, 35, 37, 39, 42, 46, 49, 53, 63, 68, 73, 80, 96, 100, 207, 266-268, 271, 278, 281, 287, 289-290, 295, 306-310, 312, 320, 324
transhumance, 8, 279, 280, 311, 315-319, 323-324, 340
trephō (τρέφω): bring up, rear, nurse, 93, 130, 172
tribute, 7, 34, 84, 142, 147, 154, 194, 196, 314, 339
Triphylia, 274
tripous (τρίπους) s. tripod
tripod, 9, 17, 68, 79, 113, 115-116, 118-119, 122, 125-126, 154, 199-200, 205-206, 229, 257, 273, 289, 291, 295, 311-315, 323, 328, 333, 335-346, 345
Trobriand Islands, 9, 37, 40, 50, 55-56
Troy (Troia), Trojans, 42, 69, 84, 96, 100-102, 105-108, 110, 116, 129, 131, 134-135, 141-142, 147-152, 155-156, 162-163, 178, 183, 188-189, 192, 194, 196, 200, 2003, 206-207, 212-213, 215, 228, 230, 237, 239, 242, 247, 249, 251, 253-254, 257, 282-283, 286, 301-302, 312
Tychios, 161, 162
Tydeus, 97, 103, 105, 206, 215
tyranny, 67, 188-189, 201, 230, 325-326
tyrants, 10, 16, 229, 308, 325-326, 340
Tyro, 224
Tyre (Tyros), 301, 305-306, 310

Ugarit, 307
utilitarianism, 32, 40-42, 50-51

veil, 141, 162, 171, 173-174, 208, 232, 241, 260-261, 299 s. also *krēdemnon, kalyprē*
vengeance, 247, 249, 252, 254, s. also *tisis*
Vergil, 301
Vergina, 164
Vix-grave, 307
Vlachs, 319, 333

Wagner, Adolph, 22
warp (in the upright loom): stēmōn (στήμων), 163, 239, 241
warp-weighted loom, 163-165 (Figures)
weaving: technique, 16, 92, 95, 114, 120, 145-145, 155-157, 159-162, 167, 169, 176, 185, 233, 236, 246, 281, 285, 290, 299, 302, 310, 328, 330, 338, 341; metaphoric weaving, 78, 118, 176, 181, 232, 239-245, 335; pattern weaving, 146, 162-164,173, 179, 181, 263, 335
Weber, Max, 39, 70, 73, 188, 190, 230
wedding, 27, 29, 33, 58, 138-39, 162, 166, 169, 174, 197, 237, 244, 248, 311, 336
wedding bed, 139
wedding cloth, 174, 237
wedding gifts, 29, 33, 311, 336
weft thread, 239-240, s. also pēnē, krokē
weft spool, 239
Weiner, Annette B., 45, 55-59, 78, 335-336
wheat, 202, 217, 298
wine, 42, 84, 86, 90-93, 95, 108, 113, 116, 119, 122, 124-126, 153, 168, 180, 197, 202, 205, 213-215, 233, 267, 270, 297, 300
wisdom, 171, 223, 232, 236, 243-244, 281, 285, 313-315, 333 s. also mētis
woof thread = weft thread, 239
wool, woollen, 93, 95, 106, 114, 122, 124-126, 157, 159, 174, 197, 205, 221, 237, 238, 240, 243, 260, 288-289, 297, 299-300, 302, 304, 310, 317, 322, 324-325, 329-330
wrath, 147, 156, 218, 245

Xanthus, 202
xeinēion, xeinion (ξεινήιον, ξείνιον): provision made to a guest, 15, 55, 79, 80-89, 92-93, 106-107, 112-122, 220, 310, 339; *xeinizō* (ξεινίζω, ξενίζω): receive or entertain a guest, 83, 123, 127-130; *xeinos, xenos* (ξεῖνος, ξένος): stranger, guest-friend, 51, 82, 85-86, 93, 96-97, 105-106, 114-118, 132, 135, 213, 225, 228, 238, 259, 268, 272, 291, 336
xeinodokos (ξεινοδόκος): host, one who receives strangers, 82, 107, 118, 129, 132
xeinosynē (ξεινοσύνη): hospitality, 83, 107, 112, 276; *xeiniē, xenia* (ξεινίη, ξενία): friendly gifts, guest-friendship, 83, 112
xenophobia, 80, 82, 88, 95
Xenophon, 111, 119
Xenophon of Ephesus, 139
Xenophanes, 175

Zakynthos, 275
Zeus, 83, 86, 96-97, 102-103, 106, 108, 116, 121, 123, 129, 135, 137-138, 142-144, 151-152, 156, 162, 172, 188, 198-200, 210-211, 214-215, 218-219, 221-223, 229, 231-232, 237-239, 241-242, 244, 254, 262, 276, 280, 282-283, 288, 300

Summary

When Agamemnon, the leader of the Greeks in the war against Troy, takes for himself the beautiful woman awarded to Achilles as his spoils of battle, the anger of Achilles is boundless. In his critique of modern capitalism, the former Greek finance minister Yanis Varoufakis chooses this Homeric example to explain the difference between market value and experiential value. Varoufakis of course prizes experiential values, among which he counts the spoils of Achilles – a matter of esteem rather than material value – above those of the market. In this, the economist is part of a long scholarly tradition that regards the practices of gift giving as counter models to market relations.

The present study sets out to re-examine the history of the debate on gift-exchange, beginning with the critique of exchange practices found in 19th century economics, long before the emergence of Marcel Mauss's famous *Essai sur le don* (1923-4). Wagner-Hasel's vision of early Greece contradicts the Maussian assumption that gifts had exclusively social functions and were never linked to profitmaking. She analyses the sensory content of a wide range of gifts, including those given to guests, at sacrificial rituals and at funerals, to brides and to heroes. Through close analysis of the very fabric of these gifts Wagner-Hasel's study unfolds a panorama of social networks and models of rulership embedded in a world of pastoral and textile economy. She shows that there are two types of objects that represent this world: tripods, and textile gifts. It is in the textile gifts that she finds the clearest representation of social cohesion – the key value ascribed to the gift by the earliest theorists of gift-giving.

Beate Wagner-Hasel, Professor of Ancient History at the Leibniz University of Hannover from 2001 until 2018, specialises in Ancient Economic History and Gender Studies. She published a biography of Karl Bücher, the founder of the debate on the character of ancient economy, in 2011 (*Die Arbeit des Gelehrten. Der Nationalökonom Karl Bücher 1847-1930*). Her study on *Old Age in Antiquity* (2012) is focussed on women as well as on men. Her last book, published together with Marie-Louise Nosch, deals with textile economics in antiquity (*Gaben, Waren und Tribute* 2019). *The Fabrics of Gifts* is a revised edition of her study of gifts in Early Greece (*Der Stoff der Gaben*, 2000).

www.ingramcontent.com/pod-product-compliance
Lightning Source LLC
Chambersburg PA
CBHW021827220426
43663CB00005B/153